POSTINDUSTRIAL

1945	1950	1955	1960	1965	1970	1975	1980	1985	1990	1995	2000	2003	2005	2008	2010	2011

1954—Brown v. Board of Education

1965 Watts riot

Rodney King arrest & LA riot

Univ. of Mich. AA cases

Hurricane Katrina

Barack Obama runs for president

2008 Barack Obama elected President

2010 Unemployment exceeds 16% for African Americans

← CIVIL RIGHTS MOVEMENT → ← URBAN UNDERCLASS → ←INCREASING CLASS DIFFERENTIATION→

Termination

RED POWER & PANTRIBALISM

1972—Trail of Broken Treaties

1975—CERT

1975 Self-Determination Act

DEVELOPMENT OF RESERVATIONS AND ASSIMILATION

1988 Federal legislation legalizes reservation gambling

DEVELOPMENT OF RESERVATIONS AND GAMBLING

Number of Indians exceeds 4 million

2004 National Museum of American Indians opens in Washington, DC

2009 Revenue from Gaming on reservations exceeds $25 billion

Zoot Suit Riots

Operation Wetback

Cuban immigration

CHICANISMO

NEW IMMIGRATION POLICY

Marielitos

IMMIGRATION INCREASES, URBAN POVERTY, ETHNIC ENCLAVES, ASSIMILATION

Proposition 187 in California

NAFTA passed

2004 Hispanic Americans become largest minority group

2007 Demonstrations against proposed changes in immigration policy in many cities

2010 Arizona SB 1070 passes

Token immigration from China

1982— Vincent Chin murder

IMMIGRATION INCREASES, URBAN POVERTY, ETHNIC ENCLAVES, ASSIMILATION

2001 Hate crimes against Arab and Asian Americans following 9/11 attacks

2010 Asian Americans are 5% of U.S. population

ETHNIC REVIVAL

ASSIMILATION →

World War II

Recession in the U.S. and in the World Economy

FLUID COMPETITIVE

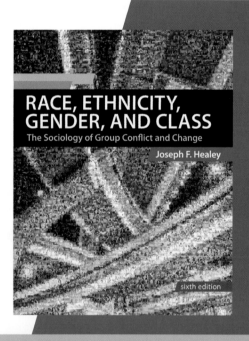

RACE, ETHNICITY, GENDER, AND CLASS

sixth edition

TO PAT

"Grow old along with me, the best is yet to be . . ."

RACE, ETHNICITY, GENDER, AND CLASS

The Sociology of Group Conflict and Change

sixth edition

Joseph F. Healey
Christopher Newport University

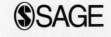

Los Angeles | London | New Delhi
Singapore | Washington DC

Los Angeles | London | New Delhi
Singapore | Washington DC

FOR INFORMATION:

SAGE Publications, Inc.
2455 Teller Road
Thousand Oaks, California 91320
E-mail: order@sagepub.com

SAGE Publications Ltd.
1 Oliver's Yard
55 City Road
London EC1Y 1SP
United Kingdom

SAGE Publications India Pvt. Ltd.
B 1/I 1 Mohan Cooperative Industrial Area
Mathura Road, New Delhi 110 044
India

SAGE Publications Asia-Pacific Pte. Ltd.
33 Pekin Street #02-01
Far East Square
Singapore 048763

Acquisitions Editor: Dave Repetto
Associate Editor: Maggie Stanley
Editorial Assistant: Lydia Balian
Production Editor: Eric Garner
Copy Editor: Megan Granger
Typesetter: C&M Digitals (P) Ltd.
Proofreader: Susan Schon
Indexer: Judy Hunt
Cover Designer: Gail Buschman
Marketing Manager: Erica DeLuca
Permissions Editor: Karen Ehrmann

Printed in Canada

Library of Congress Cataloging-in-Publication Data

Healey, Joseph F.

Race, ethnicity, gender, and class : the sociology of group conflict and change/Joseph F. Healey. — 6th ed.

p. cm.
Includes bibliographical references and index.

ISBN 978-1-4129-8731-8 (pbk. : alk. paper)

1. Minorities—United States. 2. Ethnicity—United States.
3. Group identity—United States. 4. Social conflict—United States.
5. United States—Race relations. 6. United States—Ethnic relations.
7. United States—Social conditions. I. Title.

E184.A1H415 2012
305.800973—dc23   2011039705

This book is printed on acid-free paper.

11 12 13 14 15 10 9 8 7 6 5 4 3 2 1

Only when lions have historians will hunters cease to be heroes.

—African Proverb

Not everything that is faced can be changed, but nothing can be changed until it is faced.

—James Baldwin

BRIEF CONTENTS

Preface   xxi

Acknowledgments   xxiv

About the Author   xxviii

PART I   AN INTRODUCTION TO THE STUDY OF MINORITY GROUPS IN THE UNITED STATES

1. Diversity in the United States: Questions and Concepts   9

2. Assimilation and Pluralism: From Immigrants to White Ethnics   43

3. Prejudice and Discrimination   95

PART II   THE EVOLUTION OF DOMINANT-MINORITY RELATIONS IN THE UNITED STATES

4. The Development of Dominant-Minority Group
   Relations in Preindustrial America: The Origins of Slavery   147

5. Industrialization and Dominant-Minority Relations:
   From Slavery to Segregation and the Coming of Postindustrial Society   179

PART III   UNDERSTANDING DOMINANT-MINORITY RELATIONS IN THE UNITED STATES TODAY

6. African Americans: From Segregation to Modern
   Institutional Discrimination and Modern Racism   231

7. American Indians: From Conquest to Tribal Survival
   in a Postindustrial Society   275

8. Hispanic Americans: Colonization, Immigration, and Ethnic Enclaves   315

9. Asian Americans: "Model Minorities"?   361

PART IV   CHALLENGES FOR THE PRESENT AND THE FUTURE

10. New Americans, Assimilation, and Old Challenges   409

11. Minority Groups and U.S. Society: Themes, Patterns, and the Future   455

Glossary   469

References   475

Index   495

DETAILED CONTENTS

Preface   xxi

Acknowledgments   xxiv

About the Author   xxviii

PART I   AN INTRODUCTION TO THE STUDY OF MINORITY GROUPS IN THE UNITED STATES

What Is Public Sociology?   1

Public Sociology Assignments—Linda M. Waldron   2

Assignment 1: Revealing Diversity in Your Hometown   2

Assignment 2: The Portrayal of Family on Television   4

Assignment 3: Graffiti: Cultural Expression or Discriminatory Act?   5

1. Diversity in the United States: Questions and Concepts   9

Some American Stories   10

The Increasing Variety of American Minority Groups   11

    Trends and Questions   11

    Increasing Diversity   12

    What's in a Name?   13

    Questions About the Future, Sociology, and the Plan of This Book   14

NARRATIVE PORTRAIT: What Does It Mean to Be an American?   15

What Is a Minority Group?   16

The Pattern of Inequality   18

    Theoretical Perspectives   18

    Minority Group Status and Stratification   21

Visible Distinguishing Traits   22

    Race   22

    Gender   25

Key Concepts in Dominant-Minority Relations   28

    Prejudice   28

    Discrimination   29

    Ideological Racism   29

    Institutional Discrimination   30

NARRATIVE PORTRAIT: A White Male Reflects on Privilege   31

A Global Perspective   32

    A Personal Experience With a Global Issue   32

CURRENT DEBATES: Birthright Citizenship:
Who Should Be an American?   37
    Birthright Citizenship Is Too Costly—FAIR   37
    Repealing Birthright Citizenship Will Increase
      the Unauthorized Population—Jennifer Van Hook   38
    The Birthright Citizenship Debate Is Sexist and Racist and
      a Thinly Veiled Attack on Immigrant Mothers—Gebe
      Martinez, Ann Garcia, and Jessica Arons   39
DEBATE QUESTIONS TO CONSIDER   40
MAIN POINTS   40
FOR FURTHER READING   41
QUESTIONS FOR REVIEW AND STUDY   41
INTERNET RESEARCH PROJECT   41

2. **Assimilation and Pluralism: From Immigrants to White Ethnics**   43
Assimilation   44
    Types of Assimilation   44
    The "Traditional" Perspective on Assimilation: Theories
      and Concepts   46
Pluralism   49
    Types of Pluralism   51
Other Group Relationships   53
From Immigrants to White Ethnics   53
    Industrialization and Immigration   55
    European Origins and Conditions of Entry   56
NARRATIVE PORTRAIT: Entering the Promised Land   61
    First Glimpses of American Society—Mary Antin   61
    Chains of Immigration   62
    The Campaign Against Immigration: Prejudice, Racism, and
      Discrimination   62
Patterns of Assimilation   65
    The Importance of Generations   65
    Ethnic Succession   67
NARRATIVE PORTRAIT: Ethnicity, Prejudice, and the
Irish Political Machine   69
    Shadow of the Past—David Gray   69
    Continuing Industrialization and Structural Mobility   72
Variations in Assimilation   73
    Degree of Similarity   73
    Religion   73
    Social Class   74
    Gender   75
    Sojourners   76
The Descendants of the Immigrants Today   76
    Geographical Distribution   76
    Integration and Equality   78

The Evolution of White Ethnicity 79
The Twilight of White Ethnicity? 80
Contemporary Immigrants: Does the
    Traditional Perspective Apply? 82
    Implications for Exploring Dominant-Minority Relations 83
NARRATIVE PORTRAIT: Assimilation, Then and Now 84
    Choosing a Dream: Italians in Hell's Kitchen—Mario Puzo 84
    Always Running: La Vida Loca—Luis Rodriguez 84
COMPARATIVE FOCUS: Immigration, Emigration, and Ireland 85
COMPARATIVE FOCUS: The Political Tension Between 87
Linguistic Assimilation and Pluralism in France—Professor
Kai Heidemann 87
CURRENT DEBATES: English Only? 88
    English Only Will Speed the Assimilation of Immigrants
        —Mauro Mujica 88
    Frequently Asked Questions About Official English
        —James Crawford 89
DEBATE QUESTIONS TO CONSIDER 91
MAIN POINTS 91
FOR FURTHER READING 92
QUESTIONS FOR REVIEW AND STUDY 92
INTERNET RESEARCH PROJECT 93

3. Prejudice and Discrimination 95
Prejudice and Discrimination 96
Prejudice 97
    The Affective Dimension 97
    The Cognitive Dimension: Stereotypes 99
    Cognitive and Affective Dimensions of Stereotypes 103
    Intersections of Race, Gender, and Class 103
Sociological Causes of Prejudice 104
    The Role of Group Competition 104
    Theoretical Perspectives on Group Competition and
        Prejudice: Power/Conflict Models 105
    Summary and Limitations 107
The Persistence of Prejudice 108
    The Vicious Cycle 108
    Prejudice in Children 108
    Social Distance Scales: The Cultural Dimensions of Prejudice 109
NARRATIVE PORTRAIT: The Cultural Sources of Prejudice 112
    The Crazy Ladies of Pearl Street—Trevanian 112
    Situational Influences 113
    Summary and Limitations 113
Recent Trends: Traditional Prejudice and Modern Racism 114
    Traditional Prejudice: Changing Attitudes? 114
    Explaining the Decline of Traditional Prejudice 1:
        The Role of Education 115

Explaining the Decline of Traditional Prejudice 2: The Contact Hypothesis	117
COMPARATIVE FOCUS: The Contact Hypothesis and European Prejudice	121
Modern Racism: The New Face of Prejudice?	122
Limitations	124
Has Sexism Modernized?	124
Hate Crimes	126
NARRATIVE PORTRAIT: The Dynamics of Racial Hatred	132
The Making (and Unmaking) of a Skinhead—Interview by Robert Steinback	132
The Sociology of Prejudice	134
CURRENT DEBATES: A Postracial America?	135
The End of Racism?—John McWhorter	135
A Postracial United States?—Adia Wingfield and Joe Feagin	136
DEBATE QUESTIONS TO CONSIDER	137
MAIN POINTS	137
FOR FURTHER READING	138
QUESTIONS FOR REVIEW AND STUDY	138
INTERNET RESEARCH PROJECT: Implicit Prejudice	139

PART II THE EVOLUTION OF DOMINANT-MINORITY RELATIONS IN THE UNITED STATES

A Note on the Morality and the History of Minority Relations in America: Guilt, Blame, Understanding, and Communication	141
About the Public Sociology Assignments	142
Public Sociology Assignments—Linda M. Waldron	143
Assignment 1: Race and Gender in Children's Books	143
Assignment 2: The Local Diner	144
4. The Development of Dominant-Minority Group Relations in Preindustrial America: The Origins of Slavery	147
The Origins of Slavery in America	148
The Labor Supply Problem	151
The Contact Situation	151
The Creation of Slavery in the United States	154
Paternalistic Relations	155
The Dimensions of Minority Group Status	157
NARRATIVE PORTRAIT: A Slave's Life	159
Narrative of the Life and Adventures of Henry Bibb—Henry Bibb	159
Life as a Slave Girl—Harriet Jacobs	159
The Creation of Minority Status for American Indians and Mexican Americans	162
American Indians	162

COMPARATIVE FOCUS: Hawaii   165

    Mexican Americans   167
Comparing Minority Groups   170
COMPARATIVE FOCUS: Mexico, Canada, and the United States   171
CURRENT DEBATES: How Did Slavery Affect the
Origins of African American Culture?   172

    Slavery Created African American Culture—Stanley Elkins   173
    African American Culture Was Created by an Interplay of
        Elements From Africa and America—William D. Piersen   173
    The Experiences of Female Slaves Have Been Under-Researched
        and Under-Reported—Deborah Gray White   174
DEBATE QUESTIONS TO CONSIDER   175
MAIN POINTS   175
FOR FURTHER READING   176
QUESTIONS FOR REVIEW AND STUDY   176
INTERNET RESEARCH PROJECT: Modern Slavery   177

5. **Industrialization and Dominant-Minority Relations: From**
Slavery to Segregation and the Coming of Postindustrial Society   179
Industrialization and the Shift From Paternalistic to
    Rigid Competitive Group Relations   181
The Impact of Industrialization on the Racial Stratification
    of African Americans: From Slavery to Segregation   181
    Reconstruction   182
    De Jure Segregation   182
    The "Great Migration"   186
    Life in the North   187
    Competition With White Ethnic Groups   187
NARRATIVE PORTRAIT: The Kitchenette   189

    Death on the City Pavement—Richard Wright   189
The Origins of Black Protest   189
Applying Concepts   191
    Acculturation and Integration   191
    Gender and Race   191
COMPARATIVE FOCUS: South African Apartheid   193
Industrialization, the Shift to Postindustrial Society, and
    Dominant-Minority Group Relations: General Trends   196
    Urbanization   196
    Occupational Specialization   196
    Bureaucracy and Rationality   197
    Growth of White-Collar Jobs and the Service Sector   197
    The Growing Importance of Education   199
    A Dual Labor Market   200
    Globalization   200
    Postindustrial Society and the Shift From Rigid to
        Fluid Competitive Relationships   201

Gender Inequality in a Globalizing, Postindustrial World   202
   Trends in the United States   202
   Global Trends   206
Modern Institutional Discrimination   207
   The Continuing Power of the Past   207
   Affirmative Action   209
Social Change and Minority Group Activism   211
CURRENT DEBATES: Reparations   211
   Reparations for African Americans in Historical
      Context—Joe Feagin and Eileen O'Brien   212
   Ten Reasons Why Reparations for Slavery Is a Bad
      Idea for Blacks—and Racist Too—David Horowitz   213
   Ten Reasons: A Response to David Horowitz—
      Ernest Allen and Robert Chrisman   214
DEBATE QUESTIONS TO CONSIDER   216
MAIN POINTS   216
FOR FURTHER READING   217
QUESTIONS FOR REVIEW AND STUDY   217
INTERNET RESEARCH PROJECT   217

PART III   UNDERSTANDING DOMINANT-MINORITY RELATIONS IN THE UNITED STATES TODAY

Understanding Dominant-Minority Relations in the
   United States Today   221
Public Sociology Assignments—Linda M. Waldron   222
Assignment 1: School Cafeterias and Race Relations   222
Assignment 2: Educational Testing Gaps   224
Assignment 3: Literacy Volunteer   226
Assignment 4: Survival and Promotion of Endangered Languages   228

6. **African Americans: From Segregation to Modern Institutional**
Discrimination and Modern Racism   231
The End of De Jure Segregation   232
   Wartime Developments   233
   The Civil Rights Movement   233
Developments Outside the South   237
   De Facto Segregation   237
   Urban Unrest   237
   The Black Power Movement   237
Protest, Power, and Pluralism   238
   The Black Power Movement in Perspective   238
   Gender and Black Protest   239
NARRATIVE PORTRAIT: Growing Up Black and Female
in the Jim Crow South   241
   Bone Black—bell hooks   241

COMPARATIVE FOCUS: Race in Another America   242

Black-White Relations Since the 1960s: Issues and Trends   243

    Continuing Separation   244

    The Criminal Justice System and African Americans   244

    Increasing Class Inequality   247

    Modern Institutional Discrimination   250

    The Family Institution and the Culture of Poverty   252

    Mixed Race and New Racial Identities   255

    Prejudice and Discrimination   256

    Assimilation and Pluralism   257

    Is the Glass Half Empty or Half Full?   267

CURRENT DEBATES: Should the United States Be Colorblind?   268

    Creating Equal: The Importance of Being
       Colorblind—Ward Connerly interview   268

    Colorblindness Will Perpetuate Racial
       Inequality—Ian F. Haney Lopez   269

DEBATE QUESTIONS TO CONSIDER   271

MAIN POINTS   271

FOR FURTHER READING   272

QUESTIONS FOR REVIEW AND STUDY   272

INTERNET RESEARCH PROJECT   273

**7. American Indians: From Conquest to Tribal Survival
in a Postindustrial Society**   275

Size of the Group   276

American Indian Cultures   278

Relations With the Federal Government After the 1890s   279

    Reservation Life   279

NARRATIVE PORTRAIT: Civilize Them With a Stick   281

    Lakota Woman—Mary Crow Dog   281

Protest and Resistance   285

    Early Efforts   285

    Red Power   286

The Continuing Struggle for Development in
    Contemporary American Indian–White Relations   288

    Natural Resources   288

    Attracting Industry to the Reservation   289

    Broken Treaties   291

    Gaming and Other Development Possibilities   291

Contemporary American Indian–White Relations   293

    Prejudice and Discrimination   293

    Assimilation and Pluralism   294

NARRATIVE PORTRAIT: An Indian View of White Civilization   297

    Listening to the Air—John Lame Deer   297

Comparing Minority Groups   304

Progress and Challenges   304

COMPARATIVE FOCUS: Australian Aborigines and American Indians   306

CURRENT DEBATES: Are Indian Sports Team Mascots Offensive?   307

    Indian Symbols and Mascots Are Not Offensive—
      S. L. Price and Andrea Woo   307
    Mascots Are Offensive—C. Richard King, Ellen J. Staurowsky,
      Lawrence Baca, Laurel R. Davis, and Cornel Pewewardy   308

DEBATE QUESTIONS TO CONSIDER   310
MAIN POINTS   310
FOR FURTHER READING   311
QUESTIONS FOR REVIEW AND STUDY   312
INTERNET RESEARCH PROJECT   312

8. Hispanic Americans: Colonization, Immigration, and Ethnic Enclaves   315
Mexican Americans   318
    Cultural Patterns   319

NARRATIVE PORTRAIT: The Meaning of Macho   320

    Americanization Is Tough on "Macho"—
      Rose Del Castillo Guilbault   320
    Immigration   321

NARRATIVE PORTRAIT: An Immigrant's Tale   322

    Developments in the United States   328
    Mexican Americans and Other Minority Groups   331
Puerto Ricans   332
    Migration (Push and Pull) and Employment   332
    Transitions   333
    Puerto Ricans and Other Minority Groups   334

NARRATIVE PORTRAIT: Gender Images of Latinas   335

    The Island Travels With You—Judith Ortiz Cofer   335
Cuban Americans   336
    Immigration (Push and Pull)   336
    Regional Concentrations   336
    Socioeconomic Characteristics   337
    The Ethnic Enclave   337
    Cuban Americans and Other Minority Groups   339

COMPARATIVE FOCUS: Immigration in Europe
Versus Immigration to the United States   340

Contemporary Hispanic–White Relations   341
Prejudice and Discrimination   341
Assimilation and Pluralism   342
Assimilation and Hispanic Americans   352

CURRENT DEBATES: Is the United States
Threatened by "Hispanization"?   353

    Who Are We?—John O'Sullivan   353
    Why We Shouldn't Worry About the "Hispanization"
    of the United States—Francis Fukuyama   354

DEBATE QUESTIONS TO CONSIDER   356
MAIN POINTS   356
FOR FURTHER READING   357
QUESTIONS FOR REVIEW AND STUDY   357
INTERNET RESEARCH PROJECT   358

9. Asian Americans: "Model Minorities"?   **361**
Origins and Cultures   363
Contact Situations and the Development of the Chinese
   American and Japanese American Communities   366
      Chinese Americans   366
NARRATIVE PORTRAIT: Growing Up in Chinatown   370
      Negotiating Chinese and American Cultures—Ben Fong-Torres 370
      Japanese Americans   372
NARRATIVE PORTRAIT: The Relocation   375
      We Were Just Japs—Joseph Kurihara   375
Comparing Minority Groups   377
Contemporary Immigration From Asia   377
Contemporary Relations   379
      Prejudice and Discrimination   379
      Assimilation and Pluralism   380
Comparing Minority Groups: Explaining Asian American Success   392
      Asian Americans and White Ethnics   393
      Asian Americans and Colonized Racial Minority Groups   394
COMPARATIVE FOCUS: Japan's "Invisible" Minority   396
CURRENT DEBATES: Asian American "Success":
What Are the Dimensions, Causes, and Implications for
Other Minority Groups?   397
      The Success of Japanese Americans Is Cultural—Harry Kitano 397
      The "Success" of Chinese Americans Is Structural—Alejandro
         Portes and Min Zhou   398
      A Critique of the Model Minority Thesis—Pyong Gap Min   399
DEBATE QUESTIONS TO CONSIDER   401
MAIN POINTS   401
FOR FURTHER READING   402
QUESTIONS FOR REVIEW AND STUDY   402
INTERNET RESEARCH PROJECT   403

PART IV   CHALLENGES FOR THE PRESENT AND THE FUTURE

Public Sociology Assignments—Linda M. Waldron   405
Assignment 1: Social Change in Your Neighborhood   405
Assignment 2: Working With Refugee Communities   407

10. New Americans, Assimilation, and Old Challenges   409

Current Immigration   410

New Hispanic Groups: Immigrants From the Dominican
Republic, El Salvador, and Colombia   412

Three Case Studies   412

Non-Hispanic Immigrants From the Caribbean   415

Two Case Studies   416

Contemporary Immigration From Asia   417

Four Case Studies   417

NARRATIVE PORTRAIT: Refugees   421

From Saigon to Suburbia—C. N. Le   421

Middle Eastern and Arab Americans   422

9/11 and Arab Americans   425

PHOTO ESSAY: The Arab American Community
in Detroit, Michigan—Steve Gold   426

NARRATIVE PORTRAIT: 9/11 and Middle Eastern Americans   427

Middle Eastern Americans and the American Dream—
Amir Marvasti and Karyn McKinney   427

Immigrants From Africa   428

Summary: Modes of Incorporation   430

Immigrants and the Primary Labor Market   430

Immigrants and the Secondary Labor Market   431

Immigrants and Ethnic Enclaves   431

COMPARATIVE FOCUS: The Roma: Europe's "True
Minority"—Andria D. Timmer   432

Immigration: Issues and Controversies   433

The Attitudes of Americans   433

The Immigrants   435

Costs and Benefits   436

Undocumented Immigrants   437

Is Contemporary Assimilation Segmented?   440

The Case for Segmented Assimilation   440

The Case for "Traditional" Assimilation Theory   444

Summary   445

Recent Immigration in Historical and Global Context   446

New Immigrants and Old Issues   447

CURRENT DEBATES: Is Immigration Harmful or
Helpful to the United States?   448

Immigration Is Hurting the U.S. Worker—Steven A. Camarota   448

Myths and Facts About Immigration—The Anti-Defamation League   449

DEBATE QUESTIONS TO CONSIDER   451

MAIN POINTS   451

FOR FURTHER READING   452

QUESTIONS FOR REVIEW AND STUDY   452

INTERNET RESEARCH PROJECT   453

11. Minority Groups and U.S. Society: Themes, Patterns,
and the Future   455
Some Americans Revisited   455
The Importance of Subsistence Technology   456
The Importance of the Contact Situation, Group
    Competition, and Power   459
Diversity Within Minority Groups   461
Assimilation and Pluralism   462
Minority Group Progress and the Ideology of American Individualism 466
A Final Word   467

Glossary   469

References   475

Index   495

PREFACE

O f all the challenges confronting the United States today, those relating to minority groups continue to be among the most urgent and the most daunting. Discrimination and racial inequality are part of our national heritage and—along with equality, freedom, and justice—prejudice and racism are among our oldest values. Minority group issues penetrate every aspect of society, and virtually every item on the national agenda—welfare and health care reform, crime and punishment, safety in the streets, the future of the family, even defense spending, foreign policy, and terrorism—has some connection with dominant-minority relations.

These issues will not be resolved easily or quickly. Feelings are intense, and controversy and bitter debate often swamp dispassionate analysis and calm reason. As a society, we have little hope of resolving these dilemmas unless we confront them openly and honestly; they will not disappear, and they will not resolve themselves.

This textbook contributes to the ongoing discussion by presenting information, raising questions, and probing issues. My intent is to help students increase their knowledge, improve their understanding of the issues, and clarify their thinking regarding matters of race and ethnicity. This text has been written for undergraduate students—sociology majors and non-majors alike. It makes minimal assumptions about students' knowledge of history or sociological concepts, and the material is presented in a way that students will find accessible and coherent.

For example, a unified set of themes and concepts is used throughout the text. The analysis is consistent and continuous, even as multiple perspectives and various points of view are examined. The bulk of the conceptual framework is introduced in the first five chapters. These concepts and analytical themes are then used in a series of case studies of minority groups in contemporary America and also are used to investigate group relations in various societies around the globe. In Part IV, our concepts are used to analyze contemporary immigration and assimilation, some of the most contentious issues facing the United States. Then, in the final chapter, main points and themes are summarized and reviewed, the analysis is brought to a conclusion, and some speculations are made regarding the future.

The analysis in this text is generally macro and comparative: It is focused on groups and larger social structures—institutions and stratification systems, for example—and systematically compares and contrasts the experiences and situations of America's many minorities. The text is in the tradition of conflict theory, but it is not a comprehensive statement of that tradition. Other perspectives are introduced and applied, but no attempt is made to give equal attention to all current sociological paradigms. The text does not try to explain everything, nor does it attempt to include all possible analytical points of view. Rather, the goals are (a) to present the sociology of minority group relations in a way that students will find understandable as well as intellectually challenging and (b) to deal with the issues and tell the stories behind the issues in a textbook that is both highly readable and a demonstration of the power and importance of thinking sociologically.

Although the text maintains a unified analytical perspective, students also are exposed to a wide variety of perspectives on a number of different levels. For example, clashing points of view are presented in the "Current Debates" at the end of every chapter (except the last).

The debates focus on an issue taken from the chapter but present the views of scholars and analysts from a variety of disciplines and viewpoints. Without detracting from the continuity of the main analysis, these debates reinforce the idea that no one has all the answers (or for that matter, all the questions). The debates can be used to stimulate discussion, bring additional perspectives to the classroom, and suggest topics for further research.

In addition, every chapter (except the last) includes at least one "Narrative Portrait" recounting the personal experiences and thoughts of a wide variety of people: immigrants, minority group members, journalists, sociologists, racists, and slaves, among others. These excerpts reinforce the analysis dramatically, memorably, and personally and are integrated into the flow of the chapters. Also, the experiences of minority groups and the realities of prejudice, racism, and discrimination are documented with photo essays throughout the text.

This text also explores the diversity of experiences within each minority group, particularly gender differences. Too often, minority groups (and the dominant group, for that matter) are seen by nonmembers as single, undifferentiated entities. The text acknowledges the variety of experiences within each group and, in particular, explores differences in the experiences of minority group males and females. The analysis explores the ways in which gender differences cut across ethnic and racial differences and stresses that these sources of inequality and injustice are independent of one another. Solving one set of problems (e.g., prejudice and racial discrimination) will not automatically or directly solve the other (e.g., sexism and gender inequalities).

This text focuses on the experiences of minority groups in the United States, but a considerable amount of comparative, cross-national material also has been included. A series of boxed inserts called "Comparative Focus" explores group relations in other societies.

Finally, this text stresses the ways in which American minority groups are inseparable from the American experience—from the early days of colonial settlements to tomorrow's headlines. The relative success of this society is due no less to the contributions of minority groups than to those of the dominant group. The nature of the minority group experience has changed as the larger society has changed, and to understand America's minority groups is to understand some elemental truths about America. To raise the issues of race and ethnicity is to ask what it means, and what it has meant, to be an American.

Changes in This Edition

Many changes have been made in this edition, most designed to make the material as current as possible and to respond to the ever-changing landscape of minority issues.

- Research findings and data have been updated. In particular, this edition relies on the latest information from the U.S. Bureau of the Census, particularly the *2009 American Community Survey*.
- There is an increased emphasis on immigration, particularly in Chapter 1 and Chapters 8 through 10.
- Opening quotations have been added to each chapter to highlight the theme of the chapter or to emphasize a major point. The quotes were drawn from a wide variety of sources and were selected to be dramatic and memorable.
- A variety of new "Narrative Portraits" have been added to make this feature more current. New "Narrative Portraits" can be found in Chapters 1, 2, 3, 8, 9, and 10.
- The "Current Debates" feature has been updated in Chapters 1, 2, 3, 5, 9, and 10.
- The "Comparative Focus" feature has been updated where necessary, and two new "Comparative Focus" features can be found in Chapters 2 and 10.
- A new set of "Public Sociology Assignments," developed by Professor Linda Waldron, have been included. The new assignments are designed to engage students in their communities and in the larger society and to apply and reinforce the material in the text.

- A new set of "Internet Research Projects" has been included for every chapter. In these assignments, students gather information and data from the Internet and apply concepts and ideas from the chapter. Each project has an "Optional Group Discussion" component.
- The "Applying Concepts" section in Chapter 1 that focused on Hurricane Katrina has been replaced with a section that focuses on undocumented immigrants.
- Chapter 3 has been revised and expanded. New material has been added on the nature of American stereotypes and how they have changed in recent decades, the relationships between group interests and prejudice, diverse conceptions of "modern racism," and hate crimes.
- In Chapter 5, the section on gender inequality has been reorganized into two subsections—one focused on the United States and the other on more global changes. Coverage of the glass ceiling has been expanded. The "Modern Institutional Discrimination" section also has been reorganized into subsections, and the coverage of past-in-present discrimination has been expanded.
- In Chapter 6, the "Black-White Relations Since the 1960s: Issues and Trends" section has been reorganized. A new section on modern institutional discrimination has been added, along with a subsection on the differential effects of the recent recession on blacks and whites. A section on mixed race and new racial identities also has been added.
- In Chapter 8, the sections addressing recent immigration from Mexico have been expanded and updated, and the "New Hispanic Groups" section has been moved to Chapter 10. The material on the Cuban enclave has been updated to include important new research and data.
- In Chapter 9, the case studies in the "Contemporary Immigration From Asia" section have been moved to Chapter 10, but the section now includes mention of several more Asian groups, including the Hmong. There is more material on the diversity of Asian American groups and the inadequacy of the "model minority" label. More material on Asian American intermarriage also has been added.
- Chapter 10 has been expanded to include recent immigrants from Central and South America and from Asia. Information on American attitudes about immigration has been updated, along with the material on costs and benefits and undocumented immigrants. The "Segmented Assimilation" section has been updated to include important new research on the second generation.

ACKNOWLEDGMENTS

All textbooks, even those with a single author's name on the title page, are profoundly collaborative efforts. This book has been shaped by more than 40 years of teaching minority relations and by the thoughts and reactions of hundreds of students. My approach to this subject has grown from years of "field testing" ideas, concepts, theories, and research and constant monitoring of what seemed to help the students make sense of the world they live in. I acknowledge and thank my students for their myriad contributions.

When I was a student, I had the good fortune of learning from faculty members who were both accomplished scholars and exceptionally dedicated teachers. Each of them contributed to my interest in and commitment to sociology, but two stand out in my memory as mentors and intellectual role models: Professors Edwin H. Rhyne and Charles S. Green. Dr. Rhyne encouraged me as a young scholar and quite literally introduced me to the world of ideas and the life of the mind. Later in my career, Dr. Green showed me what it means to be a professional scholar, a sociologist, and a teacher. Their influence on my life was profound, and I thank them deeply.

I am no less indebted to my colleagues, past and present, in the Department of Sociology and Anthropology at Christopher Newport University: Stephanie Byrd, Cheri Chambers, Robert Durel, Marcus Griffin, Mai Lan Gustafsson, Kai Heidemann, Michael Lewis, Marion Manton, Eileen O'Brien, Lea Pellett, Eduardo Perez, Virginia Purtle, Andria Timmer, and Linda Waldron. They have been unflagging in their support of this project, and I thank them for their academic, logistical, and intellectual assistance. I also would like to thank Iris Price, Tracey Rausch, and Ellen Whiting for their indispensable help and support.

I thank Dave Repetto of SAGE Publications for his invaluable assistance in the preparation of this manuscript and Ben Penner and Steve Rutter, formerly of SAGE Publications, for their help in the development of this project.

This text has benefited in innumerable ways from the reactions and criticisms of a group of reviewers who proved remarkably insightful about the subject matter and about the challenges of college teaching. I can no longer even estimate the number of points in the process of writing and research where the reviewers' comments led to significant improvements in scholarship, clarity, and more meaningful treatments of the subject. The shortcomings that remain are, of course, my responsibility, but whatever quality this text has is a direct result of the insights and expertise of these reviewers. I thank the following people:

First Edition Reviewers

A. Seals, Kentucky State University

Timothy Fiedler, Carroll College

Joseph J. Leon, California State Polytechnic University, Pomona

Donna Barnes, University of Wyoming

Ramona Ford, Southwest Texas State University

Seymour Leventman, Boston College

Anne Hastings, University of North Carolina, Chapel Hill

Nicole Grant, Ball State University

Charles Smith, Florida A&M

Min Zhou, University of California, Los Angeles

Raul Fernandez, University of California, Irvine

Audwin Anderson, University of South Alabama

Robert Williams, Jackson State University

Susan Takata, University of Wisconsin, Parkside

Ellen Rosengarten, Sinclair Community College

Wendy Ng, San Jose State University

Joyce Tang, City University of New York, Queens College

Michael Hodge, Georgia State University

Diana Torrez, University of Texas, Arlington

Gerald Rosen, California State University, Fullerton

Norma Burgess, Syracuse University

Maura I. Toro-Morn, Illinois State University

Steven Cornell, University of California, San Diego

Dennis Rome, Indiana University

Ray Hutchison, University of Wisconsin, Green Bay

Gerry R. Cox, Fort Hays State University

Kevin Delaney, Temple University

Carol Poll, Fashion Institute of Technology

Joni Fraser, University of California, Davis

Second Edition Reviewers

Jeremy Hein, University of Wisconsin—Eau Claire

Linda Green, Normandale Community College

David Matsuda, Chabot College

Victor M. Rodriguez, Concordia University

Craig Watkins, University of Texas, Austin

Norma Wilcox, Wright State University

Luis Zanartu, Sacramento City College

JoAnn DeFiore, University of Washington

Min Zhou, University of California, Los Angeles

Third Edition Reviewers

Rick Baldoz, University of Hawaii, Manoa

Jan Fiola, Minnesota State University, Moorhead

David Lopez, California State University, Northridge

Peggy Lovell, University of Pittsburgh

Gonzalo Santos, California State University, Bakersfield

Carol Ward, Brigham Young University

Fourth Edition Reviewers

Samuel Leizear, West Virginia University

Gregory J. Rosenboom, University of Nebraska/Nebraska Wesleyan University

Herman DeBose, California State University, Northridge

Peggy A. Shifflett, Radford University

Debbie Storrs, University of Idaho

Carol Ward, Brigham Young University

Celestino Fernandez, University of Arizona

Abby Ferber, University of Colorado, Colorado Springs

Earl Wright, University of Central Florida

Norma Wilcox, Wright State University

Fifth Edition Reviewers

Sharon Allen, University of South Dakota

Cathy Beighey, Aims Community College

Wendy H. Dishman, Santa Monica College

Bruce K. Friesen, University of Tampa

Susan E. Mannon, Utah State University

David McBride, Pennsylvania State University

Pam Brown Schachter, Marymount College, Palos Verdes

John Stone, Boston University

Merwyn L. Strate, Purdue University

Leigh A. Willis, The University of Georgia

Sixth Edition Reviewers

Janice Kelly, Molloy College

Teri Moran, Jackson Community College

Creaig A. Dunton, Suny College at Plattsburgh

C. Douglas Johnson, Georgia Gwinnett College

Margaret Vaughan, Metropolitan State University

Lisa A. Eargle, Francis Marion University

Tennille Allen, Lewis University

Gerald D. Titchener, Des Moines Area Community College

Elijah G. Ward, Saint Xavier University

Elsa Valdez, California State University, San Bernardino

Kimberly H. Fortin, Cayuga Community College

Deidre Ann Tyler, Salt Lake Community College/The University of Utah

Leslie Baker-Kimmons, Chicago State University

Melanie Deffendall, Delgado Community College

Steven L. Arxer, University of Texas at Dallas

Patricia E. Literte, California State University, Fullerton

Kathy Westman, Waubonsee Community College

Chris Keegan, State University of New York at Oneonta

Margaret A. M. Vaughan, Metropolitan State University

Marci B. Littlefield, Indiana University-Purdue University

Matasha L. Harris, John Jay College of Criminal Justice

Sophia DeMasi, Montgomery County Community College

ABOUT THE AUTHOR

Joseph F. Healey is Professor Emeritus of Sociology at Christopher Newport University in Virginia. He received his PhD in sociology and anthropology from the University of Virginia. An innovative and experienced teacher of numerous race and ethnicity courses, he has written articles on minority groups, the sociology of sport, social movements, and violence, and he is also the author of *Statistics: A Tool for Social Research* (9th ed., 2010).

PART I

AN INTRODUCTION TO THE STUDY OF MINORITY GROUPS IN THE UNITED STATES

Chapter 1 Diversity in the United States: Questions and Concepts

Chapter 2 Assimilation and Pluralism: From Immigrants to White Ethnics

Chapter 3 Prejudice and Discrimination

The United States is a nation of groups as well as individuals. These groups vary along many dimensions, including size, wealth, education, race, culture, religion, and language. Some of these groups have been part of American society since colonial days, and others have formed in the past few years.

How should all these groups relate to one another? Who should be considered American? Should we preserve the multitude of cultural heritages and languages that currently exist and stress our diversity? Should we encourage everyone to adopt Anglo-American culture and strive to become more similar and unified? Should we emphasize our similarities or celebrate our differences? Is it possible to do both?

Questions of unity and diversity are among the most pressing that face the United States today, and we begin to address these and many other issues in Chapters 1 and 2 of this text. Our goal is to develop a broader, more informed understanding of the past and present forces that have created and sustained the groups that compose U.S. society, and we will sustain this focus throughout the text.

Chapter 3 addresses prejudice and discrimination—the feelings, attitudes, and actions that help maintain and reinforce the dividing lines that separate us into groups. How and why do these negative feelings, attitudes, and actions develop? How are prejudice and discrimination related to competition between groups and inequality? Can they be eliminated or at least reduced? This chapter will continue to introduce many of the sociological themes and concepts that will occupy our attention in the remainder of this text.

WHAT IS PUBLIC SOCIOLOGY?

Many sociologists have called for a more "public sociology," a sociology engaged in the community, society, and the world. Although not all sociologists would endorse a call for activism and involvement, the study of American race relations will, for many people, stimulate an impulse to address social problems directly and personally. To facilitate that involvement, we have developed a number of projects for students that will lead them into

IMAGE: Getty/Monica Rodriguez.

1

their communities and the larger society and provide them with the possibility of making a positive difference in the lives of others. The projects will be presented in the introductions to the parts of this book, and each will be keyed to the material covered in the chapters that follow. The assignments, as stated here, should be regarded as outlines and suggestions, and it is quite likely that participants will have to improvise and respond to unanticipated challenges as they arise. Nonetheless, these assignments will allow students to bridge the (sometimes large) gap between the classroom and the community and to develop and practice their own public sociology. Each assignment could be the basis for a semester-long project for individual or teams of students.

The first set of public sociology assignments will lead students to confront diversity in their communities and in the mass media. In Assignment 1, it is very likely that students will discover that diversity is increasing in their communities at a rate that reflects the national trends discussed in Chapter 1 and presented in Exhibit 1.1. The challenges of dealing with diversity are analyzed in various places throughout the text, including the "Current Debates" at the end of Chapters 1 and 2.

Assignment 2 addresses the depiction of diversity in television. The focus is on the family institution, but the concern for the portrayal of difference could be extended into many other areas, including crime and police, poverty and affluence, sexual identity, and politics. Do the media reflect the realities of American diversity accurately? Do they shape or reinforce prejudiced attitudes and stereotypes? To what extent do they reflect American culture? Whose version of culture is validated and sustained in the media?

Assignment 3 draws students into a study of graffiti in their communities. Are these drawings and writings merely vandalism, or do they express values and beliefs, stereotypes, and other representations of culture? What are the connections to local subcultures and lifestyles? Do they reflect local group hierarchies in terms of race, ethnicity, sexuality, or language? Like Assignment 2, the study of graffiti can link students to a variety of cultural and subcultural expressions.

PUBLIC SOCIOLOGY ASSIGNMENTS

Linda M. Waldron

ASSIGNMENT 1: REVEALING DIVERSITY IN YOUR HOMETOWN

People often think they know something about the demographics of their neighborhood but they may not be aware of the actual diversity of their town or city. In this assignment, you will test your knowledge about your hometown by researching both current and historical demographics of the area.

Step 1

Begin by writing down your own assumptions about your hometown. If you moved around a lot, pick the one location where you lived for the longest period of time, or simply pick the location of your current school. What do you expect is the racial and ethnic background of the area? Do you think most people graduated high school? Is there a large military presence in the area? Do you think there is an aging population? What would you expect to find about the status of women in terms of schooling, jobs, and income?

Step 2

Next, visit the U.S. Census Bureau's website to find out some basic demographics of your area (www.census.gov). There are several ways to search this type of information, but an easy way to get some quick facts is to go to the "Area Profile" link and select the state and then city or town where you grew up. (The most recent 2010 data are still not available for most locations, so expect to find older data.) This will give you some basic background information about age, gender, race, ethnicity, and education of the population.

Step 3

Now look into the history of your hometown. The best way to start this is to visit your local library. Most libraries now have a website if you aren't traveling home anytime soon. Libraries often carry historical documents about the local area, including books, photos, and other archival materials. (Many towns also have local museums that you could visit.) Learn what you can about the area. Did it used to be an old farming village before a big corporation came to town? Was it known for its large Irish immigrant population? What year did the first church or synagogue open? When did the schools finally decide to racially integrate?

Step 4

Next, find someone to interview who has lived in the area for a long time. Ideally, you should find someone who has lived in your hometown for more than 40 years. (This won't be as difficult as you might think. Ask your local librarian for a suggestion, visit a senior center, or consider asking a neighbor who you think may have lived in the town for a while.) Tell this person you are researching diversity in your hometown for a class and ask if he/she is willing to be interviewed.

Step 5

Conduct an informal interview with your local participant. Begin your interview by asking some basic questions. When did he/she move to the area? What does he/she like best about the town? Then, use the knowledge you have discovered from your research to develop some additional interview questions about some aspect of diversity you found particularly interesting. What have been his/her experiences with diversity over the years? How does he/she think the area has changed?

Step 6

Compare and contrast the data you found about changing demographics in the area with perceptions about diversity that you and your interviewee had. Were your own assumptions about your hometown accurate? What assumptions did your interviewee have about the area? Did they match what you found? What was the most significant thing you learned about diversity in your hometown?

ASSIGNMENT 2: THE PORTRAYAL OF FAMILY ON TELEVISION

Images of family surround us every day. Advertisements display a family of four eating at McDonald's, news programs depict gay couples lining up to get married in San Francisco, magazine covers happily announce a celebrity's fourth wedding, and signs at every college post the dates for "Parents' Weekend." Images of family are constantly changing, and our notion of family changes along with it. "Family" can be organized in many different ways—for example, "traditional" two-parent families, stay-at-home moms, the increasing visibility of gay families, the changing faces of adopted children, and the growing number of grandparents raising their grandchildren. Your job with this assignment is to examine the representations of family on TV from a sociological point of view.

Step 1

Pick two major television networks and a 1- or 2-hour time slot to view this network for several days. Although prime time is ideal (8 p.m.–11 p.m.), depending on the networks you pick, alternative times or days should be considered.

Step 2

Develop a hypothesis about the depiction of families that relates specifically to race, ethnicity, gender, or sexuality. A hypothesis is essentially just a theory, or logical explanation, that you can actually test—in this case, a theory about what you think might be occurring on these shows. Make sure your hypothesis has an independent and dependent variable. An easy way to do this might be to compare one network with the other or to compare one time frame with another. For example, maybe you think one network may depict more racial diversity than the other, or perhaps you think shows that air earlier in the day might include more traditional representations of family than shows that air later in the evening. In these examples, your independent variables would be *network* and *time of day* and your dependent variables would be *race* and *type of family*.

Step 3

Create a simple tally sheet that allows you to collect some information about the shows that is related to your hypothesis. Although each television show you examine will have its own tally sheet, every tally sheet should be exactly the same. (Essentially, you are conducting a quantitative content analysis.) If you were collecting information about diversity and were interested in racial diversity, you would create a column for every possible race that might be depicted and then just count the race of each family you see. Be sure to include every possible category—for example "biracial" or "multiracial" for families that consist of several races or "don't know" for those incidences when you just can't determine race.

Step 4

Collect your data in a way that makes the most sense for your hypothesis. For example, if you are comparing networks, you may want to pick one of the networks for the first week and watch it during the days and time slot you are examining. Then, during the second week, watch the second network during the same days and time slot.

Step 5

Add up your columns and create some basic frequencies. For example, if 20 total families were represented in the time you collected your data and only 2 of them were African American on the first network but 10 families were African American on the second, it would be safe to conclude that the second network has more (50%) representations of African American families than does the first network (10%).

Step 6

Speculate about what these representations teach us about families in the United States. Do they provide an accurate depiction of diversity? Do they fail to accurately represent certain groups of people? Why do you think this might be?

Step 7

Consider the limitations to your research. What do you think might have happened if you had picked different networks or a different time slot? What if you collected data for months instead of just days, would you expect the same results? Instead of collecting data on *how many* families were depicted, what would you expect to find if you instead focused on *how* the families were represented? Every research endeavor has its limitations, so be sure to consider what you could do better if you were to continue this assignment!

ASSIGNMENT 3: GRAFFITI: CULTURAL EXPRESSION OR DISCRIMINATORY ACT?

Historians note that graffiti dates back to ancient Rome, depicted in sacred messages written inside the catacombs and animal drawings carved inside caves. Today, graffiti can be found spray painted on the sides of buildings or written in marker on the walls of bathrooms. Social scientists continue to debate the merits of graffiti as an "unconventional billboard" (Calvin, 2005). It can be seen as an offensive expression of racist, sexist, and homophobic comments, as well as a symbol of violent gang activity in neighborhoods. On the other hand, it can be used as a tool of social revolution, as was the graffiti placed on the Berlin Wall during the Cold War, or as an act of war, as demonstrated by the slogan "Kilroy Was Here," first used by U.S. servicemen during World War II to mark their presence during combat. In popular culture, the rise of hip hop is said to be intertwined with the "tagging" of subway lines that essentially advertised the work of local rappers throughout New York City. More recently, there has been a commercial growth of video games that feature graffiti as part of the story line. Others consider graffiti high art, as represented in the 1980s when art galleries throughout the world began exhibiting the work of graffiti artists. Also, the Academy Awards gave a nod to *Exit Through the Gift Shop,* a documentary about graffiti artists—in particular, the secretive Banksy, who has gained international notoriety for his satirical and subversive work. This assignment requires you to explore the nature and meaning of graffiti.

Step 1

Use a camera to photograph graffiti in your community. This can include graffiti on public buildings, on street signs, in trains or buses, on school desks, or even inside bathrooms. Gather at least 10 photographs of graffiti and upload the photos to a computer.

Step 2

Begin by attempting to discern what the graffiti is trying to represent. Consider starting off with some general categories, such as offensive, humorous, romantic, political, and artistic. It may take some additional research to uncover the meaning of the drawing. Use an Internet search engine, such as Google Images, to help you decipher certain symbols, or websites such as the Southern Poverty Law Center (www.splcenter.org) to help you uncover gang-related or hate-group graffiti.

Step 3

Next, consider who may have written the graffiti and whether the artist intended to be anonymous or not. For example, a "Debbie loves Bob" inscription on a tree obviously was written by the couple, and a member of a gang clearly did a Bloods or Crips tag—yet, on the other hand, it may be unknown who painted the racial slur outside a local mosque.

Step 4

Use PowerPoint, or a similar computer program, to create a presentation that allows you to represent and organize your results visually. For example, you could create one slide with photos of the gang-related graffiti you found, another slide with graffiti related to sexuality, one for graffiti that you believe use racist comments against a particular minority group, and another of graffiti that appear to be created by the same artist.

Step 5

As you review the themes that start to emerge from your visual representation, try to speculate as to what the intention of the artist might be. Was it an expression of a particular subculture? Was it a statement that directly attacked a person or group of people? Was it a statement that you think was trying to empower a person or group of people? In particular, try to consider how age, race, ethnicity, or gender relates to the graffiti. Do you need to understand something about youth culture to fully comprehend the graffiti? Are gays or lesbians the target of the graffiti? Is the writing in Spanish?

Step 6

As you consider the meaning of individual photos and groups of images in your collection, try to speculate more broadly about what the graffiti might tell us about our culture. This will require you to make some generalizations that connect the graffiti to dominant ideologies in our society. Even if you consider the graffiti humorous, at whose expense is the joke?

Include general statements as part of your presentation. Such statements might look something like this:

- Graffiti in boys' locker rooms condemn certain sexual behavior, in particular homosexuality, which reinforce a hegemonic masculine norm of heterosexuality.
- Gay pride rainbows anonymously drawn on the side of local businesses express a pro-gay sentiment that is not often spoken publicly in this conservative town.
- The word *terrorist* outside an Islamic community center signifies racist hate speech that has been on the rise since 9/11.

Step 7

Finally, take seriously the location of the graffiti in order to think about how context might shift the meaning and power of the message. Several different gang tags outside a school building might signify a growing problem of school violence that officials may need to investigate, whereas similar gang tags under a highway overpass may go unnoticed for years. A derogatory comment in a school bathroom about a female cheerleader carries a particular meaning when placed in the girls' bathroom and perhaps a different meaning when placed in the boys' bathroom.

Step 8

This assignment has hopefully made you more acutely aware of the graffiti in your community. Think about how you reacted to the different types of graffiti you found—were you offended by them, worried by them, impressed by them? Have you started to become more aware of the graffiti that surrounds you? Use your knowledge about graffiti to make a difference in your neighborhood, whether it is to initiate efforts to clean up the graffiti that you consider vandalism or to help raise money for a scholarship fund for a young artist whose work may one day be considered a national treasure.

Resources

Banksy (Director). 2010. *Exit Through the Gift Shop*. London: Paranoid Pictures. (This is a documentary about street graffiti artists, produced and directed by Banksy, which was nominated for a "Best Documentary" Academy Award in 2011.)

Calvin, Lisa. 2005. Graffiti, the Ultimate Realia: Meeting the Standards Through an Unconventional Cultural Lesson. *Hispania* 88(3): 527–530.

1

Diversity in the United States: Questions and Concepts

My great-grandfather didn't come 4,000 miles to America just to see it overrun with immigrants.

—Steven Colbert, comedian and host of *The Colbert Report*

What does it mean to be an American? Does the high rate of recent immigration threaten the traditional values and lifestyles of the Unites States? Does the election of President Barack Obama mean that we have put racism behind us? Should Spanish be recognized as an official second language? How should slavery and the Indian wars be presented to public school children? Is the United States becoming too diverse? How should we think about ourselves as Americans? What traditions and heritages should be included in an American identity? What should it mean to be an American?

Questions such as these are crucial, but they are not new. They have been debated in one form or another over and over in our past, and continuing controversies about race, immigration, ethnicity, and language show that these questions are far from settled. We are a nation of immigrants, and we have been arguing, often passionately, about exclusion and inclusion and unity and diversity since the infancy of American society. Every member of our society is in some sense an immigrant or the descendant of immigrants. Even Native Americans "immigrated" to this continent, albeit thousands of years ago. We are all from someplace else, with roots in another part of the globe. Some came here in chains; others came on ocean liners, on jet planes, or on foot. Some arrived last week, and others have had family here for centuries. Each wave of newcomers has in some way altered the social landscape of the United States. As many have observed, American society is continually becoming, permanently unfinished.

Our immigrant heritage and cultural diversity have made us a nation of both groups and individuals. Some of us feel intensely connected to the groups to which we belong and identify closely with our heritage. For others, the group connection is tenuous and distant. Either way, our groups influence our lives and perceptions. They help shape who we are and how we fit into the larger society.

SOME AMERICAN STORIES

To illustrate the influences of our connections with others who share our heritage, consider the life stories of some members of American society. Each represents millions of others, and each exemplifies a part of what it means to be an American.

Kim Park is a 24-year-old immigrant from Korea. He arrived in New York City about 3 years ago to work in his uncle's grocery store. Kim typically works a 14-hour shift every day, 7 days a week. His duties include stocking and cleaning, and he operates the register when necessary. He is also learning how to do the bookkeeping. Instead of wages, Kim receives room and board and some spending money.

Kim is outgoing and gregarious. His English is improving rapidly, and he practices it whenever possible. He has twice enrolled in English language classes, but the demands of his job prevented him from completing the courses. On a third occasion, he was turned away because the course was already filled and there was no money to hire additional teachers. Eventually, Kim wants to become a U.S. citizen, bring his siblings to America, get married and start a family, and take over the store when his uncle retires. The store is located in a neighborhood that is changing in ethnic composition. Many different minority groups have called this neighborhood home over the years. During the late 1950s, the area was almost exclusively Jewish. The Jewish residents have since died or moved out, and they were followed by a mixture of African Americans and Hispanic and Asian groups.

Not far from Kim's store is the apartment building where Shirley Umphlett, an African American, spent much of her childhood. In search of work, her family moved to New York from Alabama in the l920s. Both her grandfather and father were construction workers, but because most labor unions and employers were white only, they had no access to the better-paying, more stable jobs and were often unemployed. Shirley's mother worked as a housekeeper in a large downtown hotel to help meet family expenses. Shirley did well in school, attended college on scholarship, and is now a successful executive with a multinational corporation. She is in her 40s, is married with two children, and is career oriented and ambitious. At the same time, she is committed to helping other African Americans and poor Americans. She and her spouse volunteer in several community action programs and maintain memberships in three national organizations that serve and represent African Americans.

Shirley's two children attend public school. One of their teachers is Mary Ann O'Brien, a fourth-generation Irish Catholic. Mary Ann's great-grandparents were born in Ireland and came to New York as young adults in the 1880s. Her great-grandfather found work on the docks, and her great-grandmother worked as a housekeeper before her marriage. They had 7 children and 23 grandchildren. Mary Ann keeps in touch with more than 50 of her cousins, most of whom live within an hour of New York City. Each successive generation of Mary Ann's family tended to do a little better educationally and occupationally. Mary Ann's father was a fireman, and her sister is a lawyer. Mary Ann does not think much about her Irish ancestry. She does attend Mass regularly, mostly because she likes the ritual and the connection with tradition. She has a vague interest in Ireland and admits she goes a little crazy on St. Patrick's Day, but otherwise, her energies are completely focused on her family and her job.

In one of her fourth-grade classes, Mary Ann took a liking to a young Native American student named George Snyder. George was born on a reservation in upstate New York, but his family moved to the city when he was a baby. The unemployment rate on the reservation often exceeded 50%, and George's father thought the city would offer a better chance for work. Mary Ann and George kept in touch after he left elementary school, and George stopped by occasionally for a chat. Then, when George was in high school, his father was laid off, and the family returned to the reservation. Shortly thereafter, George became rebellious, and his grades began to slip. He was arrested for shoplifting and later for selling drugs, spent some time in a state correctional facility, and never finished school. The last time Mary Ann saw him, she tried to persuade him to return to school or pursue a GED but got nowhere. She pointed out that he was still young and told him there were many things he could do in the future, that life was full of opportunities. He responded, "What's the use? I'm an Indian with a record—I've got no future."

George's parole officer is Hector Gonzalez. Hector's parents came to the United States from Mexico. Every year, they crossed the border to join the stream of agricultural migrant laborers and then returned to their village in Mexico at the end of the season. With the help of a cousin, Hector's father eventually got a job as a cabdriver in New York City, where Hector was raised. Hector's mother never learned much English but worked occasionally in a garment factory located in her neighborhood. Hector thinks of himself as American but is interested in his parents' home village back in Mexico, where most of his extended family still lives. Hector is bilingual and has visited the village several times. His grandmother still lives there, and he calls her once a month.

Hector worked his way through college in 7 years. After 10 years as a parole officer, he is becoming increasingly burned out and discouraged, especially about young men such as George. "There are no jobs in the city, no real opportunities. What's the point of working with these guys if all they have the chance to do is hustle dope?"

Hector regularly has lunch at a restaurant around the corner from his office. Two of the three managers of the restaurant are white, most of the waitresses are black, and the kitchen staff is Latino. One of the bus boys who often clears Hector's table is in the country illegally. He left his home village in Guatemala 5 years ago, traveled the length of Mexico on freight trains and on foot and crossed the border through the desert of Southern Arizona. He lives in a tiny apartment with five others and sends 40% of his wages to his family back in Guatemala. He enjoys living in the United States but is not particularly interested in legalizing his status: His most fervent wish is to go home, get married, and start a family.

The restaurant is in a building owned by a corporation headed by William Buford III, a white American. The Bufords have been a part of New York's high society for generations. The family invests the bulk of its fortune in real estate and owns land and buildings throughout the New York metropolitan area. The Bufords have a three-story luxury townhouse in Manhattan but rarely go into town, preferring to spend their time on their rural Connecticut estate. William Buford attended the finest private schools and graduated from Harvard University. At age 57, he is semi-retired, plays golf twice a week, vacations in Europe, and employs a staff of five to care for himself and his family. He has little interest in the history of his family but knows that his ancestors came to America from England. Family legend has it that a distant relative played an important role in the Revolutionary War, but no one has ever bothered to investigate this claim.

These individuals belong to groups that vary along some of the most consequential dimensions within our society—ethnicity, race, immigration status, social class, gender, and religion—and their lives have been shaped by these affiliations (some more than others, of course). Similarly, our group memberships affect the ways others perceive us, the opportunities available to us, the way we think about ourselves, and our view of American society and the larger world. They affect our perception of what it means to be American.

THE INCREASING VARIETY OF AMERICAN MINORITY GROUPS

Trends and Questions

Our group memberships also shape the choices we make in the voting booth and in other areas of social life. We face important decisions that will affect our lives and the lives of countless millions, and we need to contemplate these choices systematically and thoroughly. We also need to be aware that members of different groups will evaluate these decisions in different ways. The issues will be filtered through the screens of divergent experiences, group histories, and present situations. The debates over which direction our society should take are unlikely to be meaningful or even mutually intelligible without some understanding of the variety of ways of being American.

Increasing Diversity

The choices about the future of our society are especially urgent because the diversity of U.S. society is increasing dramatically, largely due to high rates of immigration. Since the 1960s, the number of immigrants arriving in the United States each year has tripled and includes groups from all over the globe, literally (U.S. Department of Homeland Security, 2009).

Can our society deal successfully with this diversity of cultures, languages, and races? Concerns about increasing diversity are compounded by other long-standing minority issues and grievances that remain unresolved. For example, charts and graphs presented in Part III of this text document continuing gaps in income, poverty rates, and other measures of affluence and equality between minority groups and national norms. In fact, in many ways, the problems of African Americans, Native Americans, Hispanic Americans, and Asian Americans today are just as formidable as they were a generation ago.

As one way of gauging the dimensions of diversity in our nation, consider the changing makeup of U.S. society. Exhibit 1.1 presents the percentage of the total U.S. population in each of five groups. We will first consider this information "on its face" and analyze some of its implications. Then, we will consider (and question) the terms in which this information is framed.

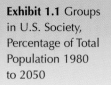

Exhibit 1.1 Groups in U.S. Society, Percentage of Total Population 1980 to 2050

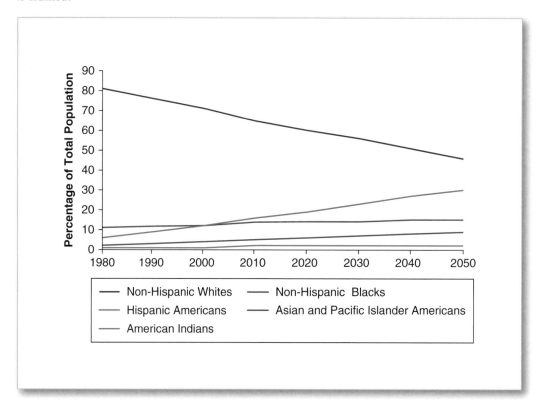

NOTE: "Hispanics" may be of any race.

SOURCE: U.S. Bureau of the Census (2008c).

The exhibit reports the actual relative sizes of the groups for 1980, 1990, and 2000 and the projected or estimated relative sizes through 2050. Note how the increasing diversity of U.S. society is reflected in the declining numerical predominance of non-Hispanic whites. As recently as 1980, more than 8 out of 10 Americans were members of this group, but, by the middle of this century, non-Hispanic whites will become a numerical minority. Several states (Texas, California, Hawaii, and New Mexico) are already "majority-minority," and seven more[1] are less than 60% white (*Wall Street Journal*, 2010). These states are a preview of what the entire nation will look like within several decades.

African Americans and American Indians are projected to remain stable in their relative size, but Hispanic Americans and Asian Americans and Pacific Islanders will grow dramatically. Asian and Pacific Islander groups composed only 2% of the population in 1980 but will grow to almost 10% by midcentury. The most dramatic growth, however, will be for Hispanic Americans, who became the largest minority group in 2002, surpassing African Americans. This group will grow to 30% of the population by midcentury.

The projections into the future are just educated guesses, of course, but they presage profound change for the United States. As this century unfolds, our society will grow more diverse racially, culturally, and linguistically. The United States will become less white, less European, and more like the world as a whole. Some see these changes as threats to traditional white, middle-class American values and lifestyles. Others see them as providing an opportunity for the emergence of other equally attractive and legitimate value systems and lifestyles.

What's in a Name?

Let's take a moment to reflect on the categories used in Exhibit 1.1. The group names I used are arbitrary, and none of these groups have clear or definite boundaries. We will use these terms because they are convenient, familiar, and consistent with the labels found in Census reports, much of the sociological research literature, and other sources of information. This does not mean that the labels are "true" in any absolute sense or equally useful in all circumstances. In fact, these group names have some serious shortcomings, several of which I note here.

First, the people within these groups are not necessarily similar to one another. Two people within any of these categories might be as different from each other as any two people selected from different categories. They may share some general, superficial physical or cultural traits, but they will also vary by social class, religion, gender, and in thousands of other ways. People classified as "Asian and Pacific Islander," for example, represent scores of different national and linguistic backgrounds (Japanese, Samoans, Vietnamese, Pakistanis, and so forth), and "American Indian or Alaska Native" includes people from hundreds of different tribal groups.

Also, the people within these categories do not necessarily think about themselves in terms of these labels. For example, a Hispanic American may think of herself more in national terms, as a Mexican or Cuban, or, even more specifically, she may identify with a particular region or village in her homeland. Thus, the labels often do not reflect the ways people think about who they are or where they come from. These statistical classifications do not necessarily reflect the everyday realities of the people in the category.

Third, even though the categories in Exhibit 1.1 are broad, they still provide no place for a number of groups. For example, where should we place Arab Americans and recent immigrants from Africa? These groups are relatively small in size (about 1 million people each), but there is no clear place for them in the categories listed in the exhibit. Should Arab Americans be classified as "Asian"? Should recent immigrants from Africa be placed in the same category as African Americans? Of course, we don't need to have a category for every single group and every person, but we should recognize that classification schemes such as the one used in this exhibit (and in many other contexts) have limited utility and application.

A related problem with this classification scheme will become increasingly apparent in the years to come: There are no categories for the growing number of mixed-race individuals. The number of "mixed" Americans is relatively small today—about 2% or 3% of the population (U.S. Bureau of the Census, 2008b)—but is likely to increase rapidly because of the growing number of marriages across group lines. The number of these marriages has increased more than 10 times over since 1960 and by a factor of three between 1980 and 2008 (U.S. Bureau of the Census, 2010d, Table 60). Obviously, the greater the number of mixed marriages, the greater the number of mixed Americans: One study estimates that 21% of the population will claim membership in this category by 2050 (Smith & Edmonston, 1997, p. 119).

Finally, we should note that these categories and group names are **social constructions**,[2] fabricated in particular historical circumstances and reflective of particular power relationships. For example, the group called "American Indians" today didn't exist prior to the period of European exploration and colonization of North America (and, in many ways, doesn't exist today). Before the arrival of Europeans, there were hundreds of separate societies spread across the North American continent, each with their own language and culture. American Indians thought of themselves primarily in terms of their tribe and had no sense of a common identity with (and little awareness of) the other peoples that inhabited North America. They became a group first in the perceptions of European conquerors, who stressed their similarities and cast them as an enemy or out-group. The fact that American Indians are often defined as a single group today reflects their defeat and subordination and their status as a minority group: They became the "others" in contrast to the dominant group. In the same way (although through different processes), African, Hispanic, and Asian Americans came to be seen as separate groups not by their own choices but as one outcome of an unequal interaction with white Americans. These groups have become "real," and much of this text is organized around a consideration of each of them (e.g., see the chapter titles in Part III). Nonetheless, we use the terms and labels as a convenience, not as a reflection of some unchangeable reality. These groups are real because they are seen as real from a particular perspective—that of the dominant group in this society: white Americans.

Questions About the Future, Sociology, and the Plan of This Book

Even though the labels used in Exhibit 1.1 are arbitrary, the trends displayed have important implications for the future of the United States. What kind of society are we becoming? What should it mean to be American? In the past, opportunity and success have been far more available to white Anglo-Saxon Protestant males than to members of other groups. Most of us, even the favored males such as William Buford III, would agree that this definition of American is far too narrow, but how inclusive should the definition be? Should we stress unity or celebrate diversity? How wide can the limits be stretched before national unity is threatened? How narrow can they be before the desire to preserve cultural and linguistic diversity is unjustly and unnecessarily stifled?

These first few pages have raised a lot of questions. The purpose of this book is to help you develop some answers and some thoughtful, informed positions on these issues. You should be aware from the beginning that the questions addressed here are complex and that the answers we seek are not obvious or easy. Indeed, there is no guarantee that we as a society will be able or willing to resolve all the problems of intergroup relations in the United States. However, we will never make progress in this area unless we confront the issues honestly and with an accurate base of knowledge and understanding. Certainly, these issues will not resolve themselves or disappear if they are ignored.

In the course of our investigation, we will rely on sociology and other social sciences for concepts, theory, and information. Chapters 1 to 3 introduce and define many of the ideas that will guide our investigation. Part II explores how relations between the dominant group and minority groups have evolved in American society. Part III analyzes the current situation of U.S. minority groups. In Part IV, the final section of the book, we explore many of the challenges and issues facing our society (and the world) and see what conclusions we can glean from our investigations and how they might shape the future.

What Does It Mean to Be an American?

In some ways, Butch is a typical American, a walking melting pot with a diverse ancestry. His multiple heritages symbolize the way Americans sometimes like to think of our society, as a blending of diversity, a unity forged from multiplicity. But are we really so flexible and accepting? Butch wonders if he really has a place in U.S. society. Like many people with multiple group memberships, he feels marginalized—partially a member of several groups but not fully accepted by any. According to projections, the number of people like Butch will increase in the future. What are the implications of this trend on the individual level, for identity and sense of belonging, and on the societal level, for unity and cohesion? Will we become more tolerant and accepting as people with multiple group memberships become more common? Will struggles like Butch's continue?

BUTCH'S STORY

Who am I? What race am I? What nationality am I? Where do I fit into American society? Where can I find total acceptance? For most of my 47 years, I have struggled to find answers to these questions. I am an American of multiracial descent and culture. In this aspect, I am not very different from many Americans. The difference for me is that I have always felt an urge to feel and live the intermingling of blood that runs through my veins. American society has a way of forcing multiracial and biracial people to choose one race over the other. I personally feel this pressure every time I have to complete an application form with instructions to check just one box for race category.

My own racial and cultural background consists of American Indian from two nations, Lahkota and Creek; African American; Italian American; and Puerto Rican. I am Spanish speaking, with some knowledge of the Lahkota language. Possessing such a diverse background has often placed me in a position to hear many insensitive and racist remarks from one group or another—obviously, I have often been the target. In the eyes of white Italian people, I am viewed as a black person. Blacks often view me as a weak and tainted half-breed. American Indians have either cautiously accepted or rejected me. The Puerto Rican community has offered the most acceptance.

A family tree would be next to impossible in our family, largely due to secrets (skeletons in the closet), question marks, and taboo subjects. The matriarch of our family was my maternal grandmother, Anna, who was half black and half Creek Indian. My paternal grandfather was Oglala Lahkota from the Pine Ridge Indian Reservation in South Dakota. He was called Jimbo, which was short for Jim Bull. I am told that my mother's father was an Italian immigrant who lived in a "Little Italy" neighborhood. My father's mother was black. Her husband, Jimbo, called her Pipe because she always smoked a pipe. So when all this finally sorted out, it looked like this: My mother, Laura, is one-fourth black, one-fourth Creek, and half Italian. My father is half black and half Oglala Lahkota.

The Italian side of our family was—and to a large extent remains—a mystery seldom discussed in our family. My mother and her siblings were born and raised in a "little Italy" neighborhood. At about the age of 12 or 13 years, I learned of our Italian ancestry. I received this information through one of our family historians, or storytellers, our Aunt June. Aunt June was one of my mother's younger sisters. Aunt June was fair skinned, with dark eyes and hair. . . .

We have fond memories of Aunt June babysitting for us on the weekends. . . . [She] would tell us old family stories of when she and her brothers and sisters were young children. Sometimes, [she] would cross the forbidden line and tell us things that my mother and her other sisters had secretly kept hidden. . . .

One day, Aunt June pulled out this old wallet-size photo of a dark-haired white man with a Hitler-style moustache. She said to me, "This is your grandfather, my father. You can keep this picture, but don't let my sisters know." [She] told me that my grandfather was an Italian immigrant from Calabria, Italy. . . . In some ways, learning about my grandfather helped me make sense of some things. Between the ages of 5 and 7 years, I began to perceive and question the differences in skin colors, which were quite evident in our family. My mother and Aunt June were fair skinned, while my aunts Candace and Lily were brown and olive. Their brother, Tony, had black skin.

So, as a child, I popped this question to my mother: "If Uncle Tony is your brother, then why is he so dark, and you are so white?" My mother responded with a quick, sharp slap to my face and told me, "It's not your business, and Tony is my brother, and that's that." As I was to learn . . . , this was just the beginning of hard questions to come with no easy answers.

WHAT IS A MINORITY GROUP?

Before we can begin to sort out the issues, we need common definitions and a common vocabulary for discussion. We begin with the term minority group. Taken literally, the mathematical connotation of this term is a bit misleading because it implies that minority groups are small. In reality, a minority group can be quite large and even can be a numerical majority of the population. Women, for example, are sometimes considered to be a separate minority group, but they are a numerical majority of the U.S. population. In South Africa, as in many nations created by European colonization, whites are a numerical minority (less than 10% of the population), but they have been by far the most powerful and affluent group and, despite recent changes, they retain their advantage in many ways.

Minority status has more to do with the distribution of resources and power than with simple numbers. The definition of minority group used in this book is based on Wagley and Harris (1958). According to this definition, a minority group has five characteristics:

1. The members of the group experience a pattern of disadvantage or inequality.

2. The members of the group share a visible trait or characteristic that differentiates them from other groups.

3. The minority group is a self-conscious social unit.

4. Membership in the group is usually determined at birth.

5. Members tend to marry within the group.

We will examine each of the defining characteristics here, and, a bit later, we will return to examine the first two—inequality and visibility—in greater detail, because they are the most important characteristics of minority groups.

The first and most important defining characteristic of a minority group is *inequality*—that is, some pattern of disability and disadvantage. The nature of the disability and the degree of disadvantage are variable and can range from exploitation, slavery, and genocide to slight irritants such as a lack of desks for left-handed students or a policy of racial exclusion at an expensive country club. (Note, however, that you might not agree the irritant is slight if you are a left-handed student awkwardly taking notes at a right-handed desk or if you are a golf aficionado who happens to be African American.)

Whatever its scope or severity, whether it extends to wealth, jobs, housing, political power, police protection, or health care, the pattern of disadvantage is the key characteristic of a minority group. Because the group has less of what is valued by society, the term *subordinate group* is sometimes used instead of *minority group*. The pattern of disadvantage is the result of the actions of another group, often in the distant past, that benefits from and tries to sustain the unequal arrangement. This group can be called the core group or the dominant group. The latter term is used most frequently in this book because it reflects the patterns of inequality and the power realities of minority group status.

The second defining characteristic of a minority group is some *visible trait* or characteristic that sets members of the group apart and that the dominant group holds in low esteem. The trait can be cultural (e.g., language, religion, speech patterns, or dress styles), physical (e.g., skin color, stature, or facial features), or both. Groups that are defined primarily by their cultural characteristics are called ethnic minority groups. Examples of such groups are Irish Americans and Jewish Americans. Groups defined primarily by their physical characteristics are racial minority groups, such as African Americans or Native Americans. Note that these categories overlap. So-called ethnic groups may have (or may be thought to have) distinguishing physical characteristics (for example, the stereotypical Irish red hair or Jewish nose), and racial groups commonly have (or are thought to have) cultural traits that differ from the dominant group (for example, differences in dialect, religious values, or cuisine).

These distinguishing traits set boundaries and separate people into distinct groups. The traits are outward signs that identify minority group members and help maintain the patterns of disadvantage. The dominant group has (or at one time had) sufficient power to create the distinction between groups and, thus, solidify a higher position for itself. These markers of group membership are crucial: Without these visible signs, it would be difficult or impossible to identify who was in which group, and the system of minority group oppression would soon collapse.[3]

It is important to realize that the characteristics that mark the boundaries between groups usually are not significant in and of themselves. They are selected for their visibility and convenience, and objectively, they may be quite trivial and unimportant. For example, scientists have concluded that skin color and other so-called racial traits have little scientific, evolutionary, medical, or biological importance. As we shall see, skin color is an important marker of group membership in our society because it was selected during a complex and lengthy historical process, not because it has any inherent significance. These markers are social constructions that become important because we attribute significance to them.

A third characteristic of minority groups is that they are *self-conscious social units*, aware of their differentiation from the dominant group and of their shared disabilities. This shared social status can provide the basis for strong intragroup bonds and a sense of solidarity and can lead to views of the world that are quite different from those of the dominant group and other minority groups: In some ways, minority and dominant groups can live in different cultural worlds. For example, public opinion polls frequently show vast differences between dominant and minority groups in their views of the seriousness and extent of discrimination in American society. Exhibit 1.2 shows persistent and sizeable gaps in the percentage of nationally representative samples of whites and blacks who agree that blacks and whites have equal job opportunities. As would be expected, given their different histories, experiences, and locations in the social structure, blacks have much more negative views of racial equality, even though both groups have become somewhat more optimistic over the years. Even after the election of President Barack Obama, the percentage of black Americans who perceived equal racial opportunity was about half the percentage of white Americans.

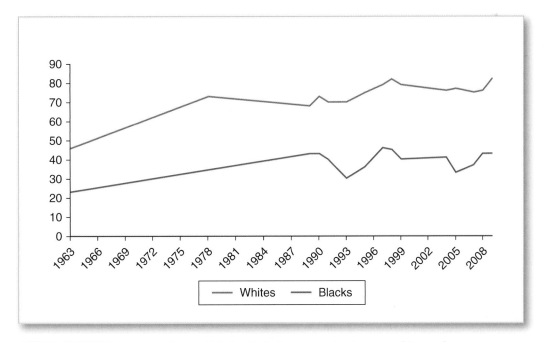

Exhibit 1.2 Percentages of White and Black Americans Who Believe That There Is Equal Opportunity in Their Community, 1963 to 2009

ACTUAL QUESTION: In general, do you think that blacks have as good a chance as white people in your community to get any kind of job for which they are qualified, or do you think they don't have as good a chance?

SOURCE: Gallup (2010).

A fourth characteristic of minority groups is that in general, membership is an ascribed status, or a status acquired at birth. The traits that identify minority group membership are typically not easy to change, and minority group status is usually involuntary and for life.

Finally, minority group members tend to *marry within their own groups*. This pattern can be voluntary, or the dominant group can dictate it. In fact, interracial marriages traditionally have been illegal in many states. Laws against miscegenation were declared unconstitutional only 40 years ago, in the late 1960s, by the U.S. Supreme Court (Bell, 1992).

This is a lengthy definition, but note how inclusive it is. Although it encompasses "traditional" minority groups such as African Americans and Native Americans, it also could be applied to other groups (with perhaps a little stretching). For instance, women arguably fit the first four criteria and can be analyzed with many of the same concepts and ideas that guide the analysis of other minority groups. Also, gay, lesbian, and transgendered Americans; disabled Americans; left-handed Americans; the aged; and very short, very tall, or very obese Americans could fit the definition of minority group without much difficulty. Although we should not be whimsical or capricious about definitions, it is important to note that the analyses developed in this book can be applied more generally than you might realize at first and may lead to some fresh insights about a wide variety of groups and people.

THE PATTERN OF INEQUALITY

As I mentioned earlier, the most important defining characteristic of minority group status is inequality. As documented in later chapters, minority group membership can affect access to jobs, education, wealth, health care, and housing. It is associated with a lower (often much lower) proportional share of valued goods and services and more limited (often much more limited) opportunities for upward mobility.

Stratification, or the unequal distribution of valued goods and services, is a basic feature of society. Every human society, except perhaps the simplest hunter-gatherer societies, is stratified to some degree; that is, the resources of the society are distributed so that some get more and others less of whatever is valued. Societies are divided into horizontal layers (or strata), often called social classes, which differ from one another by the amount of resources they command. Many criteria (such as education, age, gender, and talent) may affect a person's social class position and his or her access to goods and services. Minority group membership is one of these criteria, and it has had a powerful impact on the distribution of resources in the United States and many other societies.

This section begins with a brief consideration of theories about the nature and important dimensions of stratification. It then focuses on how minority group status relates to stratification. During the discussion, I identify several concepts and themes used throughout this book.

Theoretical Perspectives

Sociology and the other social sciences have been concerned with stratification and human inequality since the formation of the discipline in the 19th century. An early and important contributor to our understanding of the nature and significance of social inequality was Karl Marx, the noted social philosopher and revolutionary. Half a century later, a sociologist named Max Weber, a central figure in the development of the discipline, critiqued and elaborated on Marx's view of social inequality. Here, we also will consider the views of Gerhard Lenski, a contemporary sociologist whose ideas about the influence of economic and technological development on social stratification have considerable relevance when comparing societies and understanding the evolution of intergroup relations. We close with a consideration of the views of another contemporary sociologist, Patricia Hill Collins, who argues that we need to view class, racial, gender, and other inequalities as a single, interlocking pattern.

Karl Marx

Although best known as the father of modern communism, Karl Marx was also the primary architect of a political, economic, and social philosophy that has played a major role in world affairs for more than 150 years. Marxism is a complex theory of history and social change in which inequality is a central concept and concern.

Marx argued that the most important source of inequality in society was the system of economic production. More specifically, he focused on the means of production, or the materials, tools, resources, and organizations by which the society produces and distributes goods and services. In an agricultural society, the means of production include land, draft animals, and plows. In an industrial society, the means of production include factories, commercial enterprises, banks, and transportation systems, such as railroads.

All societies include two main social classes that struggle over the means of production. One class owns or controls the means of production, and in the case of an industrial society, Marx called this elite or ruling class the bourgeoisie. The other class is the working class, or the proletariat. Marx believed that conflict between these classes was inevitable and that the ultimate result of this class struggle would be the victory of the working class, followed by the creation of a utopian society without exploitation, coercion, or inequality: in other words, a classless society.

Marxism has been extensively revised and updated over the past century and a half. Still, modern social science owes a great deal to Marx's views on inequality and his insights on class struggle and social conflict. As you shall see, Marxism remains an important body of work and a rich source of insight into group relations in industrial society.

Max Weber

One of Marx's major critics was Max Weber, a German sociologist who did most of his work around the turn of the 20th century. Weber thought that Marx's view of inequality was too narrow. Marx saw social class as a matter of economic position or relationship to the means of production, but Weber argued that inequality was more complex and included dimensions other than just the economic. Individuals could be members of the elite in some ways but not in others. For example, an aristocratic family that has fallen on hard financial times might belong to the elite in terms of family lineage but not in terms of wealth. To use a more contemporary example, a major figure in the illegal drug trade could enjoy substantial wealth but be held in low esteem otherwise.

Weber expanded on Marx's view of inequality by identifying three separate stratification systems. First, economic inequality is based on ownership or control of property, wealth, and income. This is similar to Marx's concept of class, and in fact, Weber used the term *class* to identify this form of inequality.

A second system of stratification revolves around differences in prestige, or the amount of honor, esteem, or respect given to us by others. Class position is one factor that affects the amount of prestige enjoyed by a person. Other factors might include family lineage,

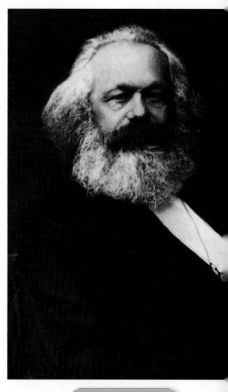

Photo 1.1

Karl Marx (1818–1883) was one of the founders of sociology and the author of *The Communist Manifesto*

© Michael Nicholson/ CORBIS.

athletic ability, and physical appearance. In the United States and other societies, prestige is affected by the groups to which people belong, and members of minority groups typically receive less prestige than members of the dominant group. The difference between prestige and class can be illustrated by Shirley Umphlett, one of the Americans introduced earlier. As a minority group member with an economically rewarding career, she is ranked higher on one dimension of stratification (class or control of property, wealth, and income) but lower on another (status or amount of prestige).

Weber's third stratification system is power, or the ability to influence others, make an impact on the decision-making process of society, and pursue and protect one's self-interest and achieve one's goals. One source of power is a person's standing in politically active organizations, such as labor unions or pressure groups, which lobby state and federal legislatures. Some politically active groups have access to great wealth and can use their riches to promote their causes. Other groups may rely more on their size and their ability to mobilize large demonstrations to achieve their goals. Political groups and the people they represent vary in their abilities to affect the political process and control decision making; that is, they vary in the amount of power they can mobilize.

Typically, these three dimensions of stratification go together: Wealthy, prestigious groups will be more powerful (more likely to achieve their goals or protect their self-interest) than low-income groups or groups with little prestige. It is important to realize, however, that power is a separate dimension: Even very impoverished groups have sometimes found ways to express their concerns and pursue their goals.

Gerhard Lenski

Gerhard Lenski is a contemporary sociologist who follows Weber and distinguishes between class (or property), prestige, and power. Lenski expands on Weber's ideas, however, by analyzing stratification in the context of societal evolution or the level of development of a society (Nolan & Lenski, 2004). He argues that the nature of inequality (the degree of inequality or the specific criteria affecting a group's position) is closely related to subsistence technology, the means by which the society satisfies basic needs such as hunger and thirst. A preindustrial agricultural society relies on human and animal labor to generate the calories necessary to sustain life. Inequality in this type of society centers on control of land and labor because they are the most important means of production at that level of development.

In a modern industrial society, however, land ownership is not as crucial as ownership of manufacturing and commercial enterprises. At the industrial level of development, control of capital is more important than control of land, and the nature of inequality will change accordingly.

The United States and other societies recently have entered still another stage of development, often referred to as *postindustrial society*. In this type of society, economic growth is powered by developments in new technology,

computer-related fields, information processing, and scientific research. In the postindustrial era, economic success will be closely related to specialized knowledge, familiarity with new technologies, and education in general (Chirot, 1994, p. 88; see also Bell, 1973).

These changes in subsistence technology, from agriculture to industrialization to the "information society," alter the stratification system. As the sources of wealth, success, and power change, so do the relationships between minority and dominant groups. For example, the shift to an information-based, "hi-tech," postindustrial society means that the advantages conferred by higher levels of education will be magnified and that groups that have less access to schooling are likely to fall even lower in the stratification system.

Patricia Hill Collins

Sociologist Patricia Hill Collins calls for a new approach to the study of inequality and group relations. She argues that it is insufficient to examine the dimensions of inequality—class, race, and gender—separately or one at a time. Rather, they need to be seen as interlocked and mutually reinforcing. Traditionally, inequality tends to be viewed by social scientists as a series of dichotomies: elite vs. masses, powerful vs. powerless, men vs. women, blacks vs. whites, and so forth. Intersectionality theorists urge us to analyze how these statuses are linked to one another and form a "matrix of domination." For example, white Americans should not be seen as simply the "dominant group," undifferentiated and homogenous. Some segments of this group, such as women or poor whites, may occupy a privileged status in terms of their race but be subordinate in others, as defined by their gender or economic status. In the same way, minority groups are internally differentiated along lines of class and gender and members of some segments are more privileged than others. Who is the oppressed and who is the oppressor changes across social contexts, and people can occupy both statuses simultaneously.

Photo 1.4

Patricia Hill Collins is an important contemporary contributor to the ongoing attempts by American social scientists to analyze minority-dominant relations.

All groups experience some relative degree of advantage and disadvantage, and Hill urges us to focus on how the separate systems of domination and subordination crosscut and overlap one another, how opportunity and individual experience is shaped by the matrix of domination. In this text, one of our main concerns will be to explore how minority group experience is mediated by class and gender, but you should be aware that this approach can be applied to many other dimensions of power and inequality, including disability, sexual preference, and religion.

Minority Group Status and Stratification

The theoretical perspectives we have just reviewed raise three important points about the connections between minority group status and stratification. First, as already noted, minority group status affects access to wealth and income, prestige, and power. A society in which minority groups systematically receive less of these valued goods is stratified, at least partly, by race and ethnicity. In the United States, minority group status has been and continues to be one of the most important and powerful determinants of life chances, health and wealth, and success. These patterns of inequality are documented and explored in Part III, but even casual observation of U.S. society will reveal that minority groups control proportionately fewer resources and that minority group status and stratification are intimately and complexly intertwined.

Second, although social classes and minority groups are correlated, they are separate social realities. The degree to which one is dependent on the other varies from group to group. Mary Ann O'Brien, the Irish American schoolteacher introduced at the beginning of this chapter, belongs to a group that today enjoys considerable social mobility, or easy access to opportunities, even though the Irish faced extensive discrimination in the past. Although her ethnicity may not matter much these days, her gender can still be an extremely consequential factor in shaping her life chances. As stressed by the intersectionality approach, degrees of domination and subordination are variable and all groups are subdivided by cross-cutting lines of differentiation.

Social class and minority group status are different dimensions of inequality, and they can vary independently. Some members of a minority group can be successful economically, wield great political power, or enjoy high prestige even though the vast majority of their group languishes in poverty and powerlessness. Each minority group is internally divided by systems of inequality based on class, status, or power, and in the same way, members of the same social class may be separated by ethnic or racial differences.

The third point concerning the connections between stratification and minority groups brings us back to group conflict. Dominant-minority group relationships are created by struggle over the control of valued goods and services. Minority group structures (such as slavery) emerge so that the dominant group can control commodities such as land or labor, maintain its position in the stratification system, or eliminate a perceived threat to its well-being. Struggles over property, wealth, prestige, and power lie at the heart of every dominant-minority relationship. Karl Marx believed that all aspects of society and culture were shaped to benefit the elite or ruling class and to sustain the economic system that underlies its privileged position. The treatment of minority groups throughout American history provides a good deal of evidence to support Marx's point.

VISIBLE DISTINGUISHING TRAITS

In this section, we focus on the second defining characteristic of minority groups: the visible traits that denote membership. The boundaries between dominant and minority groups have been established along a wide variety of lines, including religion, language, and occupation. Here, we consider race and gender, two of the more physical and permanent—and, thus, more socially visible—markers of group membership.

Race

In the past, race has been widely misunderstood, but the false ideas and exaggerated importance attached to race have not been mere errors of logic, subject to debate and refutation. At various times and places, they have been associated with some of the greatest tragedies in human history: massive exploitation and mistreatment, slavery, and genocide. Many myths about race survive in the present, although perhaps in diluted or muted form, and it is important to cultivate accurate understandings (although the scientific knowledge that has accumulated about race is no guarantee that it will not be used to instigate or justify further tragedies in the future).

Thanks to advances in the sciences of genetics, biology, and physical anthropology, we know more about what race is and, more importantly, what it is not. We cannot address all the confusion in these few pages, but we can establish a basic framework and use the latest scientific research to dispel some of the myths.

Race and Human Evolution

Our species first appeared in East Africa about 100,000 years ago. Our ancient ancestors were hunters and gatherers who slowly wandered away from their ancestral region in search of food and other resources. Over the millennia, our ancestors slowly wandered across the entire globe, first to what is now the Middle East and then to Asia, Europe, Australia, and North and South America.

Human "racial" differences evolved during this period of dispersion, as our ancestors adapted, physically as well as culturally, to different environments and ecological conditions. For example, consider skin color, the most visible "racial" characteristic. Skin color is derived from a pigment called melanin. In areas with intense sunlight, at or near the equator, melanin screens out the ultraviolet rays of the sun that cause sunburn and, more significantly, protects against skin cancer. Thus, higher levels of melanin and darker skin colors are found in peoples who are adapted to equatorial ecologies.

In peoples adapted to areas with less intense sunlight, the amount of melanin is lower, and skin color is lighter. The lower concentration of melanin also may be an adaptation to a particular ecology. It maximizes the synthesis of vitamin D, which is important for the absorption of calcium and protection against disorders such as rickets. Thus, the skin color (amount of melanin) of any group balances the need for vitamin D and the need for melanin to protect against ultraviolet rays.

The map in Exhibit 1.3 shows the distribution of skin color. Note the rough correlation with proximity to the equator: Peoples with darker skin are generally found within 20 degrees of the equator, while peoples with lighter skin are found primarily in the Northern Hemisphere, in locales distant from tropical sunlight. Note also that our oldest ancestors were adapted to the equatorial sun of Africa. This almost certainly means that they were dark skinned (had a high concentration of melanin) and that lighter skin colors are the more recent adaptation.

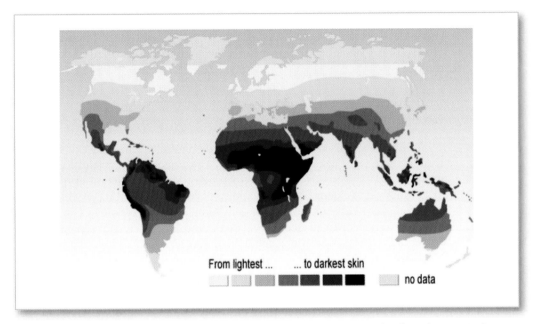

Exhibit 1.3 The Distribution of Skin Color

SOURCE: Emmanuelle Bournay, UNEP/GRID-Arendal, http://maps.grida.no/go/graphic/skin-colour-map-indigenous-people.

The period of dispersion and differentiation began to come to a close about 10,000 years ago when some of our hunting and gathering ancestors developed a new subsistence technology and settled down in permanent agricultural villages. Over the centuries, some of these settlements grew into larger societies and kingdoms and empires that conquered and absorbed neighboring societies, some of which differed culturally, linguistically, and racially from one another. The great agricultural empires of the past—Roman, Egyptian, Chinese, Aztec—united different peoples, reversed the process of dispersion and differentiation, and began a phase of consolidation and merging of human cultures and genetics. Over the next 10,000 years, human genes have been intermixed and spread around the globe, eliminating any "pure" races (if such ever existed). The differentiation created during the 90,000 years of dispersion was swamped by the consolidation that continues in the present. In our society, consolidation manifests itself in the increasing numbers of mixed-race folks, but similar patterns are common across the globe and throughout more recent human history. The consolidation phase accelerated beginning about 500 years ago with the expansion of European power that resulted in the exploration and conquest of much of the rest of the world.

Race and Western Traditions

The U.S. concept of race has its origins in Western Europe. Race became a matter of concern in the Western European tradition beginning in the 1400s when Europeans, aided by breakthroughs in navigation and ship design, began to travel to Africa, Asia, and, eventually, North and South America. They came into continuous contact with the peoples of these continents and became more aware of and curious about the physical differences they saw. Europeans also conquered, colonized, and sometimes destroyed the peoples and cultures they encountered. From the beginning, the European awareness of the differences between the races was linked to notions of inferior and superior (conquered vs. conquering) peoples. For centuries, the European tradition has been to see race in this political and military context and to intermix biological and physical variation with judgments about the relative merits of the various races. Racist thinking was used to justify military conquest, genocide, exploitation, and slavery. The toxic form of racism that bloomed during the expansion of European power continues to haunt the world today.

Race and Biology

While Europeans used race primarily to denigrate, reject, and exclude non-whites, there were also attempts to apply the principles of scientific research to the concept. These investigations focused on the construction of typologies or taxonomies, systems of classification that were intended to provide a category for every race and every person. Some of these typologies were quite elaborate and included scores of races and subraces. For example, the "Caucasian" race was often subdivided into Nordics (blond, fair-skinned Northern Europeans), Mediterraneans (dark-haired Southern Europeans), and Alpines (those falling between the first two categories).

One major limitation of these systems of classification was that the dividing lines between the so-called racial groups are arbitrary and blurred. There is no clear or definite point where, for example, "black" skin color stops and "white" skin color begins. The characteristics used to define race blend imperceptibly into one another, and one racial trait (skin color) can be blended with others (e.g., hair texture) in an infinite variety of ways. A given individual might have a skin color that is associated with one race, the hair texture of a second, the nasal shape of a third, and so forth. Even the most elaborate racial typologies could not handle the fact that many individuals fit into more than one category or none at all. Although people undeniably vary in their physical appearance, these differences do not sort themselves out in a way that permits us to divide people up like species of animals: The differences between the so-called human races are not at all like the differences between elephants and butterflies. The ambiguous and continuous nature of racial characteristics makes it impossible to establish categories that have clear, nonarbitrary boundaries.

Over the past several decades, rapid advances in genetics have provided additional information and new insights into race that continue to refute many racial myths and further undermine the validity of racial typologies. Perhaps the most important single finding of modern research is that genetic variation *within* the "traditional" racial groups is greater than the variation *between* those groups (American Sociological Association, 2003). In other words, any two randomly selected members of, say, the "black" race are likely to vary genetically from each other at least as much as they do from a randomly selected member of the "white" race. No single finding could be more destructive to traditional racial categories, which are, after all, supposed to group people into homogenous

Photo 1.5

© Peter Guttman/Corbis.

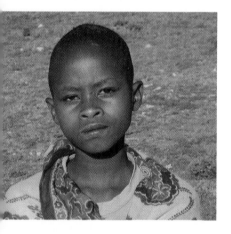

Photo 1.6

Taken by Rachel Walborn.

categories. Just as certainly, the traditional American perception of race based primarily on skin color has no scientific validity.

The Social Construction of Race

Despite its limited scientific usefulness, race continues to animate inter-group relations in the United States and around the world. It continues to be socially important and a significant way of differentiating among people. Race, along with gender, is one of the first things people notice about one another. In the United States, we still tend to see race as a simple, unambiguous matter of skin color alone and to judge everyone as belonging to one and only one group, ignoring the realities of multiple ancestry and ambiguous classification.

How can such an unimportant scientific concept retain its relevance? Because of the way they developed, Western concepts of race have a social as well as a biological or scientific dimension. To sociologists, race is a social construction and its meaning has been created and sustained not by science but by historical, social, economic, and political processes (see Omi & Winant, 1986; Smedley, 2007). For example, in Chapter 4, we will analyze the role of race in the creation of American slavery and will see that the physical differences between blacks and whites became important as a *result of* the creation of that system of inequality. The elites of colonial society needed to justify their unequal treatment of Africans and seized on the obvious difference in skin color, elevated it to a matter of supreme importance, and used it to justify the enslavement of blacks. In other words, the importance of race was socially constructed as the result of a particular historical conflict, and it remains important not because of objective realities but because of the widespread, shared social perception that it is important.

Gender

You already have seen that minority groups can be internally divided by social class and other factors. An additional source of differentiation is gender. Like race, gender has both a biological and a social component and can be a highly visible and convenient way of judging and sorting people. From birth, the biological differences between the sexes form the basis for different gender roles, or societal expectations about proper behavior, attitudes, and personality traits. In virtually all societies, including those at the advanced industrial stage, adult work roles tend to be separated by gender, and boys and girls are socialized differently in preparation for these roles. In hunter-gatherer societies, for example, boys typically train for the role of hunter, whereas girls learn the skills necessary for successful harvesting of vegetables, fruit, and other foodstuffs. Even in highly developed, modern societies, there is still a tendency for girls to learn nurturing skills while boys learn to be assertive and nonemotional.

Gender roles and relationships vary across time and from society to society, but gender and inequality usually have been closely related, and men typically claim more property, prestige, and power. Exhibit 1.4 provides some perspective on the variation in gender inequality across the globe. The map shows the distribution of a statistic called the gender development index, which measures the amount of inequality between men and women across a range of variables, including education, health, and income. As you can see, gender equality is generally highest in the more developed, industrialized nations of North America and Western Europe and lowest in the less developed, more agricultural nations of sub-Saharan Africa.

Photo 1.7

The children in Photos 1.5 to 1.7, an Inuit boy, a Masai girl from Kenya, and an American boy, suggest the enormous range of variation in human physical appearance. Only some of the differences between people are perceived to be "racial" and used to create minority groups.

Thinkstock/Jupiterimages.

Exhibit 1.4 Map of Gender Development Index Scores

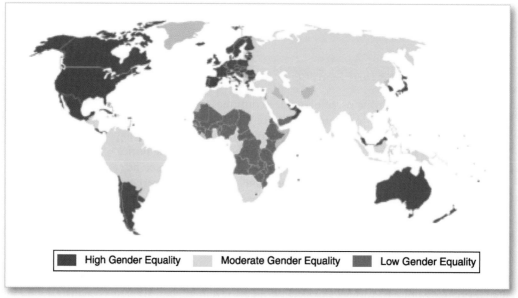

SOURCE: "Gender Development" (2011).

Although they rank relatively high on gender equality, the societies of Western Europe and North America have strong traditions of patriarchy, or male dominance. In a patriarchal society, men have more control over the economy and more access to leadership roles in religion, politics, and other institutions. In these societies, women possess many characteristics of a minority group (namely, a pattern of disadvantage based on group membership marked by a physical stigma). Thus, women could be, and in many ways should be, treated as a separate minority group.

In this book, however, rather than discussing women as a separate group, I will focus on the divergent experiences of men and women within each minority group. This approach will permit us to analyze the ways in which race, ethnicity, gender, and class combine, overlap, and cross-cut one another to form a "matrix of domination" (Hill-Collins, 1991, pp. 225–227). We will consider how the interests and experiences of females of different groups and classes coincide with and diverge from each other and from the men in their groups. For example, on some issues, African American females might have interests identical to those of white females and opposed to those of African American males. On other issues, the constellations of interests might be reversed. As you shall see, the experience of minority group membership varies by gender, and the way gender is experienced is not the same for every group.

History generally has been and is written from the standpoint of the "winners"—that is, those in power. The voices of minority groups generally have been repressed, ignored, forgotten, or trivialized. Much of the history of slavery in America, for instance, has been told from the viewpoint of the slave owners. Slaves were kept illiterate by law and had few mechanisms for recording their thoughts or experiences. A more balanced and accurate picture of slavery began to emerge only in the past few decades, when scholars began to dig beneath the written records and memoirs of the slave owners and reconstruct the experiences of African Americans from nonwritten materials such as oral traditions and the physical artifacts left by the slaves.

However, our understanding of the experiences of minority groups is often based almost entirely on the experiences of minority group males alone, and the experiences of minority group females are much less well-known and documented. If the voices of minority groups have been hushed, those of female minority group members have been virtually silenced. One of the important trends in contemporary scholarship is to adjust this skewed focus and systematically incorporate gender as a factor in the minority group experience (Baca Zinn & Thornton Dill, 1994; Espiritu, 1997).

The Social Construction of Gender

Social scientists see race as a social construction formulated in certain historical circumstances (such as the era of European colonialism) when it was needed to help justify the unequal treatment of nonwhite groups. What about gender? Is it also merely a social creation designed to rationalize the higher status of men and their easier access to power, prestige, and property? Exhibit 1.4 shows that all contemporary nations have some degree of gender inequality. Is this because—as many people believe—boys and men are "naturally" more aggressive and independent and girls and women are more emotional and expressive? What is the basis of these distinctions? What connection, if any, do they have with biology and genetics?

First of all, the traits commonly seen as "typical" of men or women—aggressiveness or emotional expressiveness, for example—are not discrete, separate categories. Every person has them to some degree, and, to the extent that gender differences exist at all, they are manifested not in absolutes but in averages, tendencies, and probabilities. Aggressiveness is often thought of as a male characteristic, but many women are more aggressive than many men. Likewise, emotionality tends to be associated with women, but many males are more expressive and emotional than many females. As was the case with racial differences, research has shown that there is more variation *within* categories than between—a finding that undermines the view that gender differences are genetic or biological (Basow, cited in Rosenblum & Travis, 2002).

Second, the fact that gender is a social construction is illustrated by the fact that what is thought to be "appropriate" gender behavior varies from time to time and society to society. The behavior expected of a female in Victorian England would be thoroughly out of place in 21st-century America, and the typical behavior of a contemporary male would be regarded as outrageously scandalous in Puritan America. This variability makes it difficult to argue that the differences between the genders are "hard-wired" in the genetic code: If they were, the variations would be nonexistent.

Third, the essentially social nature of gender roles is further illustrated by the relationship between subsistence technology and gender inequality. As we noted previously, our species evolved in East Africa and our ancestors relied on hunting and gathering to satisfy their need for food. They lived in small, nomadic bands that relied on cooperation and sharing for survival. Societies at this level of development typically divide adult labor roles by gender (with men hunting and women gathering), and, although they may tend toward patriarchy, women and women's work are highly valued and gender inequality is minimal. The subordination of women is more associated with settled agricultural communities, the first of which appeared in what is now the Middle East about 10,000 years ago. Survival in preindustrial farming societies requires the combined efforts of many people, and large families are valued as a cheap labor force. Women are consigned to household and domestic duties, with a strong emphasis on producing and raising children. Since the infant mortality rate in these societies is high (perhaps 50% or more), women spend much of their lives confined and secluded, pregnant or nursing young children, far removed from the possibility of contending for leadership roles in their communities.

Industrialization and urbanization, linked processes that began in the mid-1700s in Great Britain, changed the cost/benefit ratios for childbearing. The expenses associated with raising children increase in the city, and the nature of industrial work increasingly required education and literacy—qualities and abilities available to both genders. Thus, gender inequality probably reached its peak in preindustrial agrarian societies and has tended to decline as societies industrialize. It is no accident of timing that the push for gender equality and the women's liberation movement are associated with industrial societies and that gender equality is highest today in industrial and postindustrial societies (see Exhibit 1.4).

To be sure, biology shapes the production of personality and researchers are still exploring the possible links between genetics and gender roles (e.g., see Hopcroft, 2009; Huber, 2007; Udry, 2000), but the key to understanding gender is social and experiential (Booth, Granger, Mazur, & Kivligham, 2006, pp. 167–191). Gender, like race, is a social construction, especially when the supposed differences between men and women are treated as categorical, "natural," and fixed and then used to deny opportunity and equality to women.

KEY CONCEPTS IN DOMINANT-MINORITY RELATIONS

Whenever sensitive issues such as dominant-minority group relations are raised, the discussion turns to (or on) matters of prejudice and discrimination. We will be very much concerned with these subjects in this book, so we need to clarify what we mean by these terms. This section introduces and defines four concepts that will help you understand dominant-minority relations in the United States.

This book addresses how individuals from different groups interact, as well as relations among groups. Thus, we need to distinguish between what is true for individuals (the psychological level of analysis) and what is true for groups or society as a whole (the sociological level of analysis). Beyond that, we must attempt to trace the connections between the two levels of analysis.

We also need to make a further distinction on both the individual and the group levels. At the individual level, what people think and feel about other groups and how they actually behave toward members of that group may differ. A person might express negative feelings about other groups in private but deal fairly with members of the group in face-to-face interactions. Groups and entire societies may display this same kind of inconsistency. A society may express support for equality in its official documents or formal codes of law and simultaneously treat minority groups in unfair and destructive ways. An example of this kind of inconsistency is the contrast between the commitment to equality stated in the Declaration of Independence ("All men are created equal") and the actual treatment of black slaves, Anglo-American women, and Native Americans at that time.

At the individual level, social scientists refer to the "thinking/feeling" part of this dichotomy as prejudice and the "doing" part as discrimination. At the group level, the term ideological racism describes the "thinking/feeling" dimension and institutional discrimination describes the "doing" dimension. Exhibit 1.5 depicts the differences among these four concepts.

Exhibit 1.5 Four Concepts in Dominant-Minority Relations

Dimension	Level of Analysis	
	Individual	Group or Societal
Thinking/feeling	Prejudice	Ideological racism
Doing	Discrimination	Institutional discrimination

Prejudice

Prejudice is the tendency of an individual to think about other groups in negative ways, to attach negative emotions to those groups, and to prejudge individuals on the basis of their group memberships. Individual prejudice has two aspects: the cognitive, or thinking, aspect and the affective, or feeling, part. A prejudiced person thinks about other groups in terms of stereotypes (cognitive prejudice), generalizations that are thought to apply to group members. Examples of familiar stereotypes include notions such as "women are emotional," "Jews are stingy," "blacks are lazy," "the Irish are drunks," and "Germans are authoritarian." A prejudiced person also experiences negative emotional responses to other groups (affective prejudice), including contempt, disgust, arrogance, and hatred. People vary in their levels of prejudice, and levels of prejudice vary in the same person from one time to another and from one group to another. We can say that a person is prejudiced to the extent that he or she uses stereotypes in his or her thinking about other groups or has negative emotional reactions to other groups.

Generally, the two dimensions of prejudice are highly correlated with each other. However, they are also distinct and separate aspects of prejudice and can vary independently. One person may think entirely in stereotypes but feel no particular negative emotional response to any group. Another person may feel a strong aversion toward a group but be unable to articulate a clear or detailed stereotype of that group.

We should note here that individual prejudice, like all aspects of society, evolves and changes. In the past, American prejudice was strongly felt, baldly expressed, and laced with clear, detailed stereotypes. Today, in the modern atmosphere of "political correctness," prejudice tends to be expressed in subtle, indirect ways. For example, it might be manifested in code words, as when people disparage "welfare cheats" or associate criminality with certain minority groups. We will explore these modern forms of prejudice in Chapter 3, but we need to be clear that the relative absence of blatant stereotyping or the expression of strong public emotions against minority groups in modern society does not mean that we have eliminated individual prejudice in the United States.

Discrimination

Discrimination is defined as the unequal treatment of a person or persons based on group membership. An example of discrimination is an employer who decides not to hire an individual because he or she is African American (or Puerto Rican, Jewish, Chinese, etc.). If the unequal treatment is based on the group membership of the individual, the act is discriminatory.

Just as the cognitive and affective aspects of prejudice can be independent, discrimination and prejudice do not necessarily occur together. Even highly prejudiced individuals may not act on their negative thoughts or feelings. In social settings regulated by strong egalitarian codes or laws (e.g., restaurants and other public facilities), people who are highly bigoted in their private thoughts and feelings may abide by the codes in their public roles.

On the other hand, social situations in which prejudice is strongly approved and supported might evoke discrimination in otherwise unprejudiced individuals. In the Southern United States during the height of segregation or in South Africa during the period of state-sanctioned racial inequality called *apartheid*, it was usual and customary for whites to treat blacks in discriminatory ways. Regardless of a person's actual level of prejudice, he or she faced strong social pressure to conform to the official patterns of racial superiority and participate in acts of discrimination.

Ideological Racism

Ideological racism, a belief system that asserts that a particular group is inferior, is the group or societal equivalent of individual prejudice. These ideas and beliefs are used to legitimize or rationalize the inferior status of minority groups and are incorporated into the culture of a society and passed on from generation to generation during socialization.

Because it is a part of the cultural heritage, ideological racism exists apart from the individuals who inhabit the society at a specific time (Andersen, 1993, p. 75; See & Wilson, 1988, p. 227). An example of a racist ideology is the elaborate system of beliefs and ideas that attempted to justify slavery in the American South. The exploitation of slaves was "explained" in terms of the innate racial inferiority of blacks and the superiority of whites.

Distinguishing between individual prejudice and societal racist ideologies naturally leads to a consideration of the relationship between these two phenomena. We will explore this relationship in later chapters, but for now, I can make what is probably an obvious point:

People socialized into societies with strong racist ideologies are very likely to absorb racist ideas and be highly prejudiced. It should not surprise us that a high level of personal prejudice existed among whites in the antebellum American South or in other highly racist societies, such as South Africa. At the same time, we need to remember that ideological racism and individual prejudice are different things with different causes and different locations in the society. Racism is not a prerequisite for prejudice; prejudice may exist even in the absence of an ideology of racism.

Institutional Discrimination

The final concept is the societal equivalent of individual discrimination. Institutional discrimination refers to a pattern of unequal treatment based on group membership that is built into the daily operations of society, whether or not it is consciously intended. The public schools, the criminal justice system, and political and economic institutions can operate in ways that put members of some groups at a disadvantage.

Institutional discrimination can be obvious and overt. For many years following the Civil War, African Americans in the American South were prevented from voting by practices such as poll taxes and rigged literacy tests. For nearly a century, well into the 1960s, elections and elected offices in the South were confined to whites only. The purpose of this blatant pattern of institutional discrimination was widely understood by African American and white Southerners alike: It existed to disenfranchise the African American community and keep it politically powerless.

At other times, institutional discrimination may operate more subtly and without conscious intent. If public schools use aptitude tests that are biased in favor of the dominant group, decisions about who does and who does not take college preparatory courses may be made on racist grounds, even if everyone involved sincerely believes that they are merely applying objective criteria in a rational way. If a decision-making process has unequal consequences for dominant and minority groups, institutional discrimination well may be at work.

Note that although a particular discriminatory policy may be implemented and enforced by individuals, the policy is more appropriately thought of as an aspect of the operation of the institution as a whole. Election officials in the South during segregation did not and public school administrators today do not have to be personally prejudiced themselves to implement these discriminatory policies.

However, a major thesis of this book is that both racist ideologies and institutional discrimination are created to sustain the positions of dominant and minority groups in the stratification system. The relative advantage of the dominant group is maintained from day to day by widespread institutional discrimination. Members of the dominant group who are socialized into communities with strong racist ideologies and a great deal of institutional discrimination are likely to be personally prejudiced and to practice acts of individual discrimination routinely. The respective positions of dominant and minority groups are preserved over time through the mutually reinforcing patterns of prejudice, racism, and discrimination on both the individual and the institutional levels. Institutional discrimination is but one way in which members of a minority group can be denied access to valued goods and services, opportunities, and rights (such as voting). That is, institutional discrimination helps sustain and reinforce the unequal positions of racial and ethnic groups in the stratification system.

A White Male Reflects on Privilege

Tim Wise is a sociologist, lecturer, writer, and antiracism activist. In the passage below, he reflects on his whiteness and the fact that he has been accorded a higher status in this society simply because of his race. As he points out, it is usually minority group members who must consciously confront the realities of discrimination and racism: Whites tend to take their higher status for granted and ignore the ways in which society is organized to sustain their privilege. Although whites vary across a range of criteria—class, gender, region, and so forth—the group is connected by the privilege of whiteness, an advantage largely unexamined and unquestioned. Structures of racial privilege are largely invisible to whites because, unlike minority group members, they don't have to deal with the restrictions they impose. Institutionalized discrimination and racist cultural traditions conspire to make whiteness seem "normal," the standard against which "others" are contrasted and differentiated. From the white perspective, only nonwhites have race and ethnicity. In the same way, the limitations imposed by traditional gender roles can be invisible to males.

THE PRIVILEGES OF WHITENESS

When we first draw breath outside the womb, we inhale tiny particles of all that came before, both literally and figuratively. We are never merely individuals; we are never alone; we are always in the company, as uncomfortable as it sometimes can be, of others, the past, of history. We become part of that history just as surely as it becomes part of us. There is no escaping it, merely different levels of coping. . . .

Once born, I inherited my family and all that came with it. I also inherited my nation and all that came with that. And I inherited my "race" and all that came with that, too. In all three cases, the inheritance was far from inconsequential.

More than that, all three inheritances were intimately connected, intertwined in ways I could not possibly have understood at the time, but which are all too clear today. To be the child of Michael Julius Wise and Lucinda Anne (McLean) Wise meant something; to be born in the richest and most powerful nation on earth meant something; and to be white, especially in the United States, most assuredly meant something—a lot of things, truth be told. . . .

What does it mean to be white, especially in a nation created for the benefit of people like you? We [white people] don't often ask this question, mostly because we don't have to. Being a member of the majority, the dominant group, allows one to ignore how race shapes one's life. For those of us called white, whiteness simply is. Whiteness becomes, for us, the unspoken, uninterrogated norm, taken for granted, much as water can be taken for granted by a fish.

In high school, whites are sometimes asked to think about race, but rarely about whiteness. In my case, we read John Howard Griffin's classic book, *Black Like Me,* in which the author recounts his experiences in the Jim Crow South in 1959, after taking a drug that turned his skin brown and allowed him to experience apartheid for a few months from the other side of the color line.

It was a good book, especially for its time. Yet I can't help but find it a bit disturbing that it remains one of the most assigned volumes on summer reading lists dealing with race. That it continues to prove so popular signifies the extent to which race is considered a problem of the past . . . surely there are some more contemporary racial events students could discuss—not to mention the degree to which race is still viewed as something that can only be understood from the perspective of "the other." Whites are encouraged to think about race from the perspective of blacks, which is nice. Indeed, whites should listen to and learn from the stories of black and brown peoples—real black and brown people, not white men pretending to be black until the drugs wear off. But *Black Like Me* leaves another aspect of the discussion untouched: namely, the examination of the white experience.

Although whiteness may mean different things in different places and at different times, one thing I feel confident saying up front, without fear of contradiction, is that to be white in the United States, whether from the South, as I am, or from the North, West, or Midwest, whether one is rich or poor; male or female; Jew or Gentile; straight or gay, is to have certain common experiences based solely upon race. These experiences have to do with advantage, privilege (in the relative sense, vis-á-vis people of color), and belonging. We are, unlike people of color, born to belonging, and have rarely had to prove ourselves deserving of our presence here. . . .

While some might insist that whites have a wide range of experiences, and so, presumably, it isn't fair to make generalizations about whites as a group, this is a dodge, and not a particularly artful one at that. Of course we're all different, sort of like snowflakes, which come to think of it are also white. None of us have led the exact same life. But irrespective of one's particular history, all whites were placed above all persons of color when it came to the economic, social, and political hierarchies that were to form in the United States, without exception. This formal system of racial preference was codified in law from the 1600s until at least 1964, at which time the Civil Rights Act was passed, if not 1965, with the passage of the Voting Rights Act, or 1968, when our nation finally passed a law making racial housing discrimination illegal.

Prior to that time we didn't even pretend to be a nation based on equality. Or rather, we did pretend, but not very well; at least not to the point where the rest of the world believed it, or to the point where people of color in this country did. Most white folks believed it, but that's simply more proof of our privileged status. Our ancestors had the luxury of believing those things that black and brown folks could never take as givens: all that stuff about life, liberty, and the pursuit of happiness. Several decades later, whites can, indeed *must,* still believe it, while people of color have little reason to join the celebration, knowing as they do that there is still a vast gulf between who we say we are as a nation and people, and who we really are.

In other words, there is enough commonality about the white experience to allow us to make some general statements about whiteness and never be too far from the mark. Returning to the snowflake analogy: Although as with snowflakes, no two white people are exactly alike, it is also true that few snowflakes have radically different experiences from those of the average snowflake. Likewise, we know a snowflake when we see one, and in that recognition, we intuit, almost always correctly, something about its life experience.

SOURCE: Wise (2008, pp. 2–4).

A GLOBAL PERSPECTIVE

In the chapters that follow, we will focus on developing a number of concepts and theories and applying those ideas to the minority groups of the United States. However, it is important to expand our perspective beyond the experiences of just a single nation. Just as you would not accept an interview with a single person as an adequate test of a psychological theory, you should not accept the experiences of a single nation as proof for the sociological perspective developed in this text. Thus, we will take time, throughout this text, to apply our ideas to other societies and non-American minority groups. If the ideas and concepts developed in this text can help us make sense of these situations, we will have some assurance that they have some general applicability and that the dynamics of intergroup relations in the United States are not unique.

On another level, we must also take account of the ways in which group relations in the United States are shaped by economic, social, and political forces beyond our borders. As we will see, the experiences of this society cannot be understood in isolation. We are part of the global system of societies, and now, more than ever, we must systematically take account of the complex interconnections between the domestic and the international, particularly with respect to issues related to immigration. The world is indeed growing smaller, and we must see our society as one part of a larger system. The next section illustrates one connection between the global and the local.

Exhibit 1.6 The logo of the Samaritans

A Personal Experience With a Global Issue

SOURCE: © Green Valley/Sahuarita Samaritans.

Susan burst out her front door just as I drove up, yelling at me to get in her battered, 10-year-old Volvo. She had just gotten a call from a local church secretary about two migrants that needed help. She shared the scant information she had as we drove through suburban Tucson: The migrants had been walking through the desert of southern Arizona for the past 4 days, traveling north from Mexico, and had been spotted and pursued by two Minutemen. The migrants managed to duck into an arroyo, elude their pursuers, and find shelter in a church. They apparently had picked the church at random—or out of desperation—and, fortunately for them, the secretary who answered their knocks was sympathetic to their plight. She let them in, hid them in a nursery that was used only during Sunday services, and called Susan. When we got to the church, we entered through the back door as the Minutemen, driving a pickup truck with "Security" emblazoned on the doors, drove by the front. Several minutes later, the Border Patrol—perhaps alerted by the Minutemen—slowly drove by as well.

Susan is a member of Samaritans on the Border, a group of volunteers in southern

Arizona who aid migrants trying to cross the Sonora Desert and make their way from Mexico to Tucson, Phoenix, or other U.S. destinations (see Exhibit 1.6). I had met Susan and Michael, another Samaritan, the previous summer and was in Arizona to observe their program and learn more about immigration issues "on the ground."

The Samaritans have a simple goal—to reduce the number of migrant deaths—but they are addressing a small, local piece of a multifaceted and complex phenomenon. Emigration from Mexico to the United States and the human suffering the Samaritans are trying to reduce are the results of a constellation of forces, including the wall being constructed along the border and the increased efforts of U.S. authorities to stop migration, combined with continuing pressure to leave Mexico in search of a job—any job—in the north. These pressures have conspired to funnel migrant traffic through the trackless, forbidding desert of southern Arizona, one of the most physically challenging and demanding immigration routes. Thousands have died attempting this journey. Exhibit 1.7 displays one count of deaths in the desert for a 5-year period: Each red dot represents a migrant death. These include only the bodies that have been discovered, and, taking a longer view, they represent a small fraction of the deaths along the border between the mid-1990s and the present.

Everything the Samaritans do to assist migrants is legal, and they coordinate their activities with the Border Patrol and other law enforcement agencies. Susan and the other Samaritans maintain water supplies along the most likely migration routes and patrol the desert looking for people in trouble. When they find someone, they offer food and water, clothes and socks, and simple first aid. If the migrant is injured or simply too tired to go on, the Samaritans will alert the authorities (but only at the migrant's request) and wait with them until the Border Patrol arrives. The Samaritans are often alerted about migrant activity by people, such as the church secretary, who are sympathetic to their humanitarian goals.

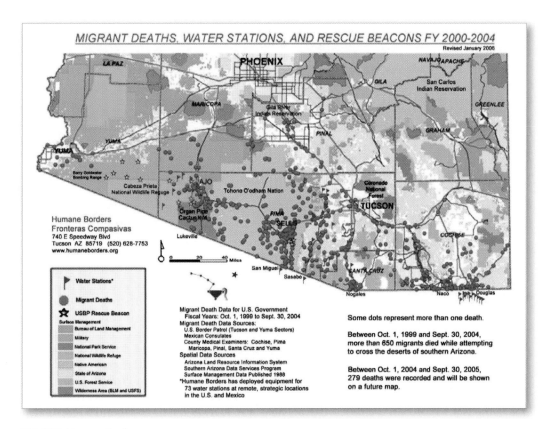

Exhibit 1.7 Deaths in the Desert, 2000 to 2004

SOURCE: Humane Borders.

When we got to the nursery, we found the migrants exhausted, hungry, sore, and frightened. Susan, in halting Spanish, gradually learned their story. Francisco, the older of the two, had lived in the United States for nearly a decade, worked in construction, and had a wife and two children in Phoenix. His wife was a U.S. citizen, but Francisco was not: He was what some call an "illegal alien" and, others, an "undocumented immigrant" or "unauthorized migrant." To Susan and me, he looked like someone who simply needed help.

Two weeks earlier, Francisco had returned to his village in southern Mexico—for the first time since he had left a decade earlier—to attend his father's funeral and had brought his younger brother, Ernesto, back with him. Ernesto had been unable to find work at home and decided to accompany Francisco back to the United States in hopes of finding a job and helping support the family. Ten years earlier, Francisco's journey had been financed by his kinfolk, who had saved for years to gather enough money to pay a guide (a *coyote*) to lead him across the border and through the desert. Now, continuing hard times in Mexico meant that there was no money to help the brothers. They crossed the border on their own, without a guide, in spite of the dangers. There are few markers in the trackless desert to help the inexperienced find their way, the terrain is extremely difficult, and water is nonexistent. Thorns, prickly cactus plants, loose rocks, hidden gullies, and other dangers threaten the unwary at every turn. The brothers knew they had to travel light and had brought only a few bottles of water and some snack bars for food. They had only the clothes on their backs to fight the cold desert nights (it was November, and the nightly temperatures had been in the 30s). In addition to the physical dangers, they had to avoid the drug traffickers, gangs, kidnappers, and assorted hoodlums and corrupt police on both sides of the border.

We gave them food and water and helped them doctor the blisters that had developed on their feet. The church secretary allowed them to use the shower and said she could keep the rest of the staff—not all of whom were sympathetic to migrants—out of the nursery area for the rest of the day. They rested for several hours, and then, when the coast seemed clear, they resumed their journey. We never heard if they made it to Phoenix.

Samaritans and Minutemen

The Samaritans are strongly opposed and deeply resented by many of their neighbors. Like Americans across the nation, many Arizonans regard migrants as dangerous criminals, threats to their communities, their jobs, and to U.S. culture. Individual Samaritans have been vilified by their neighbors and threatened with anonymous phone calls, and the group has been lambasted in letters to local papers, editorials, and stump speeches by politicians. One Samaritan, a minister, has had his Sunday morning church services picketed by the same lone protestor every week for years. The group is seen by many as hopelessly naïve and misguided, and they are often perceived to be aiding people that are—at least—unworthy.

Some of the opposition to the Samaritans is more organized, threatening, and potentially violent. Various groups called "Minutemen" also patrol the roads of southern Arizona, sometimes armed, and keep watch on the desert, but with the intent of deterring migration and returning migrants to their homelands. Some of the Minutemen destroy or befoul any Samaritan water supplies they discover. One Samaritan reports that she found a noose hanging in a tree near a water drop, an unmistakable sign of the attitudes of Minutemen (and many Arizonans and Americans) about migrants. The Minutemen are criticized as violent vigilantes who operate outside the law. They have been characterized as racists, and some branches of the group have been listed as hate groups by the Southern Poverty Law Center (http://www.splcenter.org/). As illustrated in Exhibit 1.8, they see themselves as protectors of the nation, stout defenders of the American Way, warriors willing to do what the federal and state authorities will not or cannot do. As so often in the past, the controversies over immigration in general and undocumented immigrants from Mexico in particular seem to bring out the best and worst of our society: altruistic humanitarianism and racist rejection.

Immigration, Concepts, Globalization, and This Text

We will explore immigration in detail in chapters to come. Here, we can use the topic to illustrate several of the concepts we have introduced in this chapter and make several points about the analysis to come.

Exhibit 1.8 Minuteman Logo

Immigration is a good preview of many of the issues we will deal with in this text for several reasons. First, we can use it to illustrate the sociological perspective. This means, in part, that we will always focus on the larger societal context in which individuals act. Our goal as sociologists is to analyze and understand the broad forces that create the situations in which men such as Francisco and Ernesto make the decision to leave their home and family for a dangerous and uncertain future in another country. Also, the sociological perspective means that our goal is to develop an objective view anchored in a careful review of relevant data and evidence. Of course, like many topics sociologists deal with, immigration can evoke strong feelings and intense emotions, and it is often a challenge to maintain an objective approach. Whether you are a Samaritan, a Minuteman, an ordinary citizen, or a trained sociologist, there are strong temptations to choose sides and hurl invectives at those with whom we disagree rather than to sift the facts and reason through the realities. Nonetheless, our analysis will seek to find its way through the emotions and opinions and anchor itself in objectively verified realities.

Our task is further complicated by the fact that the topics we confront are not only emotional, they are also complex and lack easy or obvious solutions. For example, some would consider the cases of Francisco and Ernesto clear cut: They are in the country illegally and should be immediately deported (or worse). Others might point out the economic realities of their situation: They are in the United States seeking economic survival, and the cost of deportation would be devastating, not only for them but for their families. In many ways, the brothers are victims who have been propelled unwillingly by economic and political forces beyond their control (or even their understanding). Still, as many would be quick to point out, there is no denying the myriad problems—in schools, neighborhoods, health care clinics, and scores of other locales—created by the population movement of which Francisco and Ernesto are a tiny part. The issues surrounding immigration have many levels and facets and can be seen from a variety of viewpoints. Our goal is to see issues in all their complexity, not make accusations or invent facile "solutions."

We can begin our analysis by applying some of the concepts we have introduced in this chapter. For example, we need to understand that one of the reasons that immigration issues stir up such intense emotions is because they tap the deep reservoirs of American prejudice and racism that have characterized this nation literally from its birth. This does not mean that people who oppose immigration or support the efforts to secure the southern border are racist: far from it. However, it is clear that many anti-immigrant sentiments resonate with the deep well of negative American feelings and stereotypes.

These traditions of prejudice and racism, in turn, stem from the fact that Mexican Americans have been a minority group since the early days of this nation, a history we will explore in detail in Chapter 8. They meet all five parts of our definition of a minority group, including a history of systematic discrimination (both individual and institutional) and a strong pattern of inequality. They have been labeled inferior on both racial and cultural terms, and the traditions of anti-Mexican prejudice and the stereotypes and feelings that attach to this group are well established.

Another cause of the intense reactions and emotions that surround immigration may be anxiety generated by the rising diversity of U.S. society documented in Exhibit 1.1. Many Americans see these trends as daily realities manifested in the changing complexions of their neighborhoods, the sounds of languages other than English in the streets, and the appearance of "exotic" foods at their grocery stores. They feel uneasy, and they are anxious that their vision of what America should be is being threatened: Cries of "I want my country back" are heard across the nation. These concerns are not simply the products of fevered racist minds and are expressed in the thinking of otherwise moderate citizens, newspaper columnists and intellectuals, academics and scholars (e.g., see Huntington, 2004). Many people are concerned about the "Hispanization" of America, that the rising tide of immigration threatens the primacy of the English language and Anglo culture. As we shall see, these are not new concerns or fears: They have been expressed over and over in the past, often in exactly the same terms being used today, as Americans have reacted to the arrival of immigrants. The fact that society has (more or less successfully) dealt with the challenges created by immigration in the past is not necessarily a comfort in the present. People wonder if it's different this time; if the world, the United States, and the nature of immigration are so different now that the experiences of the past are irrelevant.

Certainly, the world has changed. For one thing, globalization is linked with immigration in new ways. It is clear, for example, that immigration today must be understood in terms of changes that affect many nations and, indeed, the entire global system of societies. To illustrate, Mexico's economy has been disrupted by the North American Free Trade Agreement (NAFTA), which was implemented in 1994. NAFTA united the three North American nations into a single trading bloc and permitted goods and capital (but not people) to move freely between Canada, the United States, and Mexico. Among many other consequences, NAFTA opened Mexico to the importation of food products produced at very low cost by the agribusinesses of Canada and the United States. This cheap food (corn in particular) disrupted Mexican agriculture, and much of the rural Mexican population, including Francisco and Ernesto, found themselves unable to survive. Forced out of their traditional economic niche, millions have pursued the only survival strategy that seemed even remotely reasonable: migration to the North. Even the meanest job in the United States can pay many times more than the average Mexican wage. Of course, the grimmest calculation for many (including Francisco and Ernesto) is simply this: Even a very low-wage job in the United States is infinitely better than no wage at all.

We should also note that the United States is only one of many destinations for today's immigrants. The movement is generalized, and people are moving in huge numbers from less-developed nations to more-developed, affluent economies. The wealthy nations of Western Europe, including Germany, Ireland, France, and the Netherlands are also receiving large numbers of immigrants, and the citizens of these nations are concerned about jobs, communities, housing, language, and the integrity of the national culture in the same ways as Americans.

Finally, we need to see the issue in terms of the multigroup nature of U.S. society. Does the cheap labor provided by new immigrants threaten the jobs of the more economically vulnerable members of other groups? What, if anything, do other minority groups lose when immigrants gain a foothold in the American job structure? Should the grievances of groups such as African Americans—who have been a part of this society virtually from the beginning and have numerous unresolved, continuing grievances (as we shall see)—be given less attention because the society is focused on problems associated with the arrival of new groups? Where should we focus our attention? How should we prioritize the competing claims of all of America's groups (including white Americans)?

This chapter and this section raise a lot of questions. Let me assure you that this text will not answer them. However, by applying the sociological perspective and the concepts, theories, and body of research developed over the years, we can illuminate and clarify the issues and, in many cases, identify some approaches and ideas that are simply wrong and others that hold promise. Sociology can't answer all questions, but it does supply research tools and ideas that can help us think more clearly and with greater depth and nuance about the issues that face our society.

Birthright Citizenship: Who Should Be an American?

Who should be granted American citizenship? The United States is one of two advanced industrial nations to automatically confer citizenship on any baby born within its boundaries,[4] including babies born to undocumented immigrants. This policy is based on the 14th Amendment to the U.S. Constitution, passed shortly after the Civil War, which says, "All persons born or naturalized in the United States, and subject to the jurisdiction thereof, are citizens of the United States and of the State wherein they reside." The amendment was intended to guarantee the citizenship rights of ex-slaves, and the qualification that these citizens must be "subject to the jurisdiction" of the United States was specifically intended to exclude American Indians (who were seen, at the time, as being subject to the jurisdiction of their tribes and were not granted citizenship rights until the 1920s) and the children of foreign diplomats and visitors from other nations.

Birthright citizenship is one of the many issues that have split public opinion and generated the intensely emotional debates that emerge whenever immigration is discussed in this society. What is at stake here? Does this policy make sense? Is it too broad a definition of who should be an American? What are the costs of maintaining it? What message would be sent by repealing it? What are people really saying when they speak about issues such as this?

Following are several points of view on the issue. The first was posted at the website of the Federation for American Immigration Reform (FAIR), a national lobbying group that works to change national immigration policy and reduce the level of immigration. FAIR argues that U.S. citizens are being taken advantage of by unauthorized immigrants and that their babies add unjustly to an already heavy tax burden.

An opposing position is presented by demographer Jennifer Van Hook, who reports on the results of some research done under the sponsorship of the Migration Policy Institute, which describes itself as an "independent, nonpartisan, nonprofit think tank dedicated to the study of the movement of people worldwide." Van Hook uses population projections to argue that repeal of birthright citizenship would increase the size of the unauthorized immigrant population and create a large, permanent class of marginalized people, aliens to both the United States and to the native country of their ancestors. In effect, this group would be stateless, without full citizenship rights, and easily exploited.

A third point of view is presented by Martinez, Garcia, and Arons, who argue that the subtext of this debate is an emotional, racist, and sexist attack on immigrants. The authors are affiliated with the Center for American Progress, an organization dedicated to "improving the lives of Americans through progressive ideas and actions."

BIRTHRIGHT CITIZENSHIP IS TOO COSTLY

FAIR

The term *anchor baby* may be unfamiliar to most Americans, but it succinctly describes a troubling aspect of American immigration. An anchor baby is defined as an offspring of an illegal immigrant or other noncitizen, who under current legal interpretation becomes a United States citizen at birth. These children may instantly qualify for welfare and other state and local benefit programs. Additionally, . . . the child may sponsor other family members for entry into the United States when he or she reaches the age of 21. The sheer numbers are staggering. . . .

In Parkland Memorial Hospital Dallas, the second busiest maternity ward in the United States, 70% of the women giving birth were illegal aliens. That added up to 11,200 babies for which Medicaid kicked in 34.5 million dollars to deliver these babies, the feds another 9.5 million, and Dallas taxpayers tossed in 31.3 million. The average illegal patient is 25 years old and giving birth to her second anchor baby.

According to the [provision of the] 14th Amendment, in the case of illegal aliens, their native country has a claim of allegiance on the child. Therefore, some constitutional scholars argue that the completeness of the allegiance to the United States is impaired and logically precludes automatic citizenship. However, this issue never has been directly decided by the U.S. Supreme Court.

The Price We Pay

The nation's school system faces the economic burden of providing services to the millions of children born to illegal immigrants. In a 2004 United States General Accounting Office report, three states submitted their annual cost estimates of educating illegal children. The estimates provided ranged from 50 million dollars to 87.5 million in Pennsylvania and 932 million to 1.04 billion dollars in Texas. . . .

What Does This Mean?

Higher taxes: The federal government has control over immigration law for the United States. By not correcting this mis-application of the 14th Amendment, the funds that state and local governments must provide to anchor babies amounts to a virtual tax on U.S. citizens to subsidize illegal aliens.

Disrespect for the rule of law: Congress, by failing to act on legislation aimed at correcting the interpretation of citizenship by birth, in effect rewards law-breakers and punishes those who have chosen to follow the rules and immigrate legally.

The original intent of the 14th Amendment was clearly not to facilitate illegal aliens defying U.S. law and obtaining citizenship for their offspring, nor obtaining benefits at taxpayer expense. The United States is unusual in its offer to extend citizenship to anyone born on its soil. Other developed countries have changed their citizenship practice to eliminate the problems caused by the practice of birthright citizenship. The anchor baby problem has grown to such large proportions that the United States can no longer afford to ignore it. The logical first step for correcting the problem is for Congress to adopt legislation clarifying the meaning of the 14th Amendment.

SOURCE: FAIR (2010).

REPEALING BIRTHRIGHT CITIZENSHIP
WILL INCREASE THE UNAUTHORIZED POPULATION

*JENNIFER VAN HOOK, POPULATION RESEARCH INSTITUTE
AT PENNSYLVANIA STATE UNIVERSITY, WITH MICHAEL FIX, MIGRATION POLICY INSTITUTE*

Recently, debate has resurfaced over ending the grant of birthright citizenship to the children of unauthorized immigrants . . . as a way to reduce illegal immigration to the United States. Its proponents argue that unauthorized persons illegally migrate to the United States in order to give birth to children who can sponsor them for admission. These proposals, then, raise the question: What would happen to the U.S. unauthorized population if birthright citizenship were repealed? [We offer] an answer by [investigating various] scenarios involving the end of birthright citizenship in the future to U.S.-born children of unauthorized immigrants.

We conclude that if birthright citizenship were no longer granted to U.S.-born children of unauthorized immigrants, the unauthorized population likely would increase dramatically. An estimated 11 million unauthorized immigrants currently live in the United States; many giving birth to U.S.-born children. And these children grow up to have children of their own. Under a constitutional repeal of the birthright citizenship language of the 14th Amendment . . . , these U.S.-born descendants of unauthorized immigrants would be denied legal status in the United States, even though in all likelihood they would be thoroughly American in other respects. Their descendants, the third generation and higher, might have no claim to citizenship in the countries of their immigrant ancestors because they and their parents were not born in those countries. In short, the repeal of the 14th Amendment . . . would lead to the establishment of a permanent class of unauthorized persons.

How Large Would This Unauthorized Population Be?

To answer this question, we projected the size of the unauthorized population from 2010 to 2050, using standard demographic techniques and readily available data about immigrants. . . .

According to our projections, if the U.S.-born children of unauthorized immigrants were denied legal status, the unauthorized population would grow much larger. . . . Under current . . . law, the unauthorized population would remain constant at around 11 million. [If citizenship were denied to a child whose mother was unauthorized, the size of the unauthorized population would increase to] 19 million by 2050. This is 72% higher than the number under current law. . . .

The repeal of birthright citizenship would clearly affect immigrants and their children. What is less commonly understood is that the effects of repeal would be suffered by future U.S.-born generations—the descendants of today's immigrants—many of whom would have little to no connection with their ancestors' country of birth. . . .

The standard demographic projections presented here bring home several important facts that have been largely absent from emotional debates over the repeal of birthright citizenship. . . . One is that rather than shrink the size of the unauthorized population . . . , repeal would likely expand it—and expand it substantially. A second worrying finding is that repeal would set in motion a sizeable, self-perpetuating class of unauthorized immigrants for generations to come. This perpetuation of hereditary disadvantage based on the legal status of one's ancestors would be unprecedented in U.S. immigration law.

SOURCE: Van Hook (2010, pp. 2, 3, 6, 8).

THE BIRTHRIGHT CITIZENSHIP DEBATE IS SEXIST AND RACIST AND A THINLY VEILED ATTACK ON IMMIGRANT MOTHERS

GEBE MARTINEZ, ANN GARCIA, AND JESSICA ARONS

This election cycle, conservatives are intoxicated with immigrant bashing, particularly pregnant immigrant women and their children. Their tactic: change the U.S. Constitution to deny citizenship to babies born in this country to undocumented women. This is a cynical strategy that explicitly targets Latino communities—the fastest-growing segment of the electorate. These desperate politicians would rather get rid of these new voters than do the hard work of cultivating them. In their quest for power, they will do or say anything to get elected.

This is also an ugly strategy fueled by sexism and racism. It taps into a long history of population control—government efforts to curb growth among disfavored populations. . . . Conservatives' rhetoric on this issue is particularly insulting, likening the human birthing process to that of farm animals. "They come here to drop a child. It's called 'drop and leave,'" said Sen. Lindsey Graham (R-SC) during an interview on Fox News. . . . And Arizona State Senator Russell Pearce (R-Mesa)—the architect of S.B. 1070, the state's anti-immigrant law—conceded that his support for changing the Constitution is gender based. He circulated and publicly defended a statement by Al Garza, one of his constituents and a former top official of the Minutemen Civil Defense Corps, a group classified as a nativist extremist group by the Southern Poverty Law Center.

The e-mail Pearce defended reads, "If we are going to have an effect on the anchor baby racket, we need to target the mother. Call it sexist, but that's the way nature made it. Men don't drop anchor babies, illegal alien mothers do."

Pearce's amalgamation of legislative proposals would inexorably lead to ethnic profiling of pregnant women. . . . Ironically, many of the same politicians who have jumped on the citizenship denial bandwagon also claim to be "pro-life" and "pro-family." Yet they have no hesitation about splitting up families through harsh deportation policies or dehumanizing immigrant women and their children with their hateful rhetoric.

By portraying immigrant women as less than human—that they "drop" babies as animals drop their offspring— immigration opponents stir up fears that foreigners specifically come here to have children in order to derive citizenship from their children, or claim government benefits. Or, as Rep. Louie Gohmert (R-TX) has foolishly maintained, to "raise and coddle" future terrorists.

But the simple fact is that most immigrant women do not come to the United States to give birth. They come to work. A child cannot even petition for the parents to become citizens until the child is 21. What's more, undocumented immigrants never have been eligible for welfare benefits, and new legal immigrants to the United States became ineligible for services for the poor as a result of the 1996 welfare reform law President Bill Clinton signed.

Those wanting to maintain constitutional rights for citizen children of immigrants argued . . . that if birthright citizenship were removed, the policy would be difficult to carry out and mothers' health could be endangered. Moreover, health care professionals would be turned into immigration agents, and pregnant women who might not "look" like citizens would face stressful questioning or harassment at the borders. . . .

Hopefully, cooler heads will prevail. . . . Another conservative proposal, however, would deny pregnant foreigners permission to enter the United States. This, too, is wrong-headed and impossible to enforce. What do they suggest? Administering pregnancy tests to all women at the border? . . .

This politically manufactured issue is indeed ludicrous, but it is no laughing matter. It will take time to remind the public that the only "anchors" in this debate are the dead weights that refuse to act responsibly and fix our broken immigration system by enacting comprehensive immigration reform. Targeting women and children instead is a cowardly way out.

SOURCE: Martinez, Garcia, and Arons (2010).

DEBATE QUESTIONS TO CONSIDER

1. This chapter opened with some questions about what it means to be an American. How does the debate over birthright citizenship relate to this larger issue? How would each of the Americans introduced in "Some American Stories" relate to this debate? Can you predict their positions? How?

2. Is there a way of assessing the three arguments presented in this "Current Debate" that would go beyond mere partisanship? All three of the arguments cite facts and evidence. Which are most convincing? Why?

3. Can you relate these articles to some of the concepts introduced in this chapter? For example, where and how are these concepts used: inequality, gender, power, prejudice, and racism?

4. All three of these articles were located by searching the Internet. What are some of the dangers of doing "research" this way? How can you protect yourself against these threats? What would you want to know about these authors and their respective organizations as you assess their ideas? How could you find out?

5. Finally, after reading this chapter and considering these opinions, what are your views on the issue of birthright citizenship? Were you aware of the issue before reading these materials? Had you formed an opinion? If so, has your opinion changed? Why or why not? If the issue is new for you, what are your reactions? Either way, what else would you like to know about the issue? What questions occur to you? How could you answer them?

MAIN POINTS

- The United States faces enormous problems in dominant-minority relationships. Although many historic grievances of minority groups remain unresolved, our society is becoming increasingly diverse.
- The United States is a nation of immigrants, and many different groups and cultures are represented in its population.
- A minority group has five defining characteristics: a pattern of disadvantage, identification by some visible mark, awareness of its disadvantaged status, a membership determined at birth, and a tendency to marry within the group.
- A stratification system has three different dimensions (class, prestige, and power), and the nature of inequality in a society varies by its level of development. Minority groups and social class are correlated in numerous and complex ways.
- Race is a criterion widely used to identify minority group members. As a biological concept, race has been largely abandoned, but as a social category, race maintains a powerful influence on the way we think about one another.
- Minority groups are internally differentiated by social class, age, region of residence, and many other variables. In this book, I focus on gender as a source of variation within minority groups.
- Four crucial concepts for analyzing dominant-minority relations are prejudice, discrimination, ideological racism, and institutional discrimination.
- The public sociology assignments presented in the introduction to Part I give you several opportunities to apply some of the concepts presented in this chapter. Studying diversity in a local community will bring you face to face with the increasing diversity of U.S. society as well as some of the realities of inequality, discrimination, and racism. Assignments 2 and 3 can bring you into contact with expressions of dominant group stereotypes and other elements of prejudice and ideological racism. These assignments also relate to concepts and ideas introduced in Chapters 2 and 3.

STUDY SITE ON THE WEB

For chapter-specific resources, such as self-quizzes, videos, and flashcards, go to www.sagepub.com/healeyregc6e.

FOR FURTHER READING

Allport, Gordon. 1954. *The Nature of Prejudice.* Reading, MA: Addison-Wesley.

The classic work on individual prejudice

Baca Zinn, Maxine, & Thornton Dill, Bonnie (Eds.). 1994. *Women of Color in U.S. Society.* Philadelphia: Temple University Press.

A wide-ranging collection of articles examining the intersecting forces of race, class, and gender in the United States

Correspondents of *The New York Times.* 2001. *How Race Is Lived in America.* New York: Times Books.

An in-depth look at the continuing importance of race in American life conducted by correspondents of The New York Times. *Based on the Pulitzer-Prize winning television documentary*

Feagin, Joseph. 2001. *Racist America.* New York: Routledge.

A passionate analysis of the pervasiveness of racism and antiblack prejudice in America

Omi, Michael, & Winant, Howard. 1986. *Racial Formation in the United States from the 1960s to the 1980s.* New York: Routledge & Kegan Paul.

An adept analysis of the social and political uses of race

Smedley, Audrey. 1999. *Race in North American: Origin and Evolution of a Worldview.* Boulder, CO: Westview.

An analysis of the origins of the American view of race

Takaki, Ronald. 1993. *A Different Mirror: A History of Multicultural America.* Boston: Little, Brown.

A highly readable look at minority groups and cultural diversity in American life

QUESTIONS FOR REVIEW AND STUDY

1. What kind of society should the United States strive to become? In your view, does the increasing diversity of American society represent a threat or an opportunity? Should we acknowledge and celebrate our differences, or should we strive for more unity and conformity? What possible dangers and opportunities are inherent in increasing diversity? What are the advantages and disadvantages of stressing unity and conformity?

2. What groups should be considered "minorities"? Using each of the five criteria included in the definition presented in this chapter, should gay and lesbian Americans be considered a minority group? How about left-handed people or people who are very overweight? Explain and justify your answers.

3. What is a social construction? How do race and gender differ in this regard? What does it mean to say, "Gender becomes a social construction—like race—when it is treated as an unchanging, fixed difference and then used to deny opportunity and equality to women"?

4. Define and explain each of the terms in Exhibit 1.5. Cite an example of each from your own experiences. How does ideological racism differ from prejudice? Which concept is more sociological? Why? How does institutional discrimination differ from discrimination? Which concept is more sociological? Why?

INTERNET RESEARCH PROJECT

In this chapter, we discussed race—arguably the most consequential concept in the history of this nation (and the globe). To extend the discussion, we can utilize some readily available resources on the Internet. One very useful website (http://www.pbs.org/race/) was created to accompany a 2003 PBS-sponsored documentary titled "Race: The Power of an Illusion." The series is well worth viewing on its own, and the website includes a vast array of richly detailed insights on the phenomenon of race.

The single major point of the website (as in this text) is that race is a social construction, a cultural and political perception invented during particular historical eras, largely to justify and rationalize the differential treatment of others. Once established and passed from generation to generation, race becomes hugely consequential in the lives of all U.S. citizens—it becomes its own reality, shaping and controlling peoples' lives.

The website has six subsections, and you are encouraged to explore them all. As you do, look for answers to each of the questions below. Does this information change the way you think about race? How?

1. How is race a modern idea?

2. Is race biological?

3. How have ideas about race evolved and changed since ancient times?

4. What are some U.S. examples of how public policy has treated people differently based on race? What are some of the consequences?

5. How have definitions of black and white changed over the years? How have Census Bureau definitions of race changed? Why?

6. Try the "Sorting People" exercise and record your number of "correct" classifications here: ____. What does this exercise make you think about race as a concept? Can you accurately tell someone's race by looking at them? If not, what does this say about the concept of race?

7. Take the quiz under the "Human Diversity" tab, and record your number of correct answers here: ____. Was your information accurate? Where did you get this information?

8. Click on the "Explore Diversity" button under "Human Diversity" and explore the activities. Does this information support the idea that "race isn't biological"? How?

OPTIONAL GROUP DISCUSSION

Select three of the questions above to discuss with classmates. (NOTE: Your instructor may have more specific or different instructions.) Add your own topic if you wish. Bring your information and reactions from the website and the text to class, and be prepared to discuss the issues with your classmates. To aid the discussion, develop a concise statement or summary of what you learned and what you think was most important about the experience.

NOTES

1. These states are Arizona, Florida, Georgia, Maryland, Mississippi, Nevada, and New York.

2. Boldface terms in the text are defined in the Glossary at the end of the book.

3. A partial exception to this generalization, the Burakumin of Japan, is considered in Chapter 9.

4. Canada is the other.

2

Assimilation and Pluralism

From Immigrants to White Ethnics

We have room for but one flag, the American flag. . . . We have room for but one language here, and that is the English language . . . and we have room for but one loyalty and that is a loyalty to the American people.

—Theodore Roosevelt, 26th President of the United States, 1907

This chapter continues to look at the ways in which ethnic and racial groups in the United States relate to one another. Two concepts, assimilation and pluralism, are at the core of the discussion. Each includes a variety of possible group relations and pathways along which group relations might develop.

Assimilation is a process in which formerly distinct and separate groups come to share a common culture and merge together socially. As a society undergoes assimilation, differences among groups decrease. Pluralism, on the other hand, exists when groups maintain their individual identities. In a pluralistic society, groups remain separate, and their cultural and social differences persist over time.

In some ways, assimilation and pluralism are contrary processes, but they are not mutually exclusive. They may occur together in a variety of combinations within a particular society or group. Some groups in a society may be assimilating as others are maintaining (or even increasing) their differences. As we shall see in Part III, virtually every minority group in the United States has, at any given time, some members who are assimilating and others who are preserving or reviving traditional cultures. Some Native Americans, for example, are pluralistic. They live on or near reservations, are strongly connected to their heritage, and speak their native languages. Other Native Americans are very much assimilated into the dominant society: They live in urban areas, speak English only, and know relatively little about their traditional cultures. Both assimilation and pluralism are important forces in the everyday lives of Native Americans and most other minority groups.

American sociologists have been very concerned with these processes, especially assimilation. This concern was stimulated by the massive immigration from Europe to the United States that occurred between the 1820s and the 1920s. More than 31 million people crossed the Atlantic during this time, and a great deal of energy has been devoted to documenting, describing, and understanding the experiences of these immigrants and their descendants. These efforts have resulted in the development of a rich and complex literature that I will refer to as the "traditional" perspective on how newcomers are incorporated in U.S. society.

This chapter begins with a consideration of the traditional perspective on both assimilation and pluralism and a brief examination of several other possible group relationships. The concepts and theories of the traditional perspective are then applied to European immigrants and their descendants, and we develop a model of American assimilation based on these experiences. This model will be used in our analysis of other minority groups throughout the text and especially in Part III.

The United States is now experiencing its second mass immigration, which began in the mid-1960s, and a particularly important issue is whether the theories, concepts, and models based on the first mass immigration (from the 1820s to the 1920s) will apply to the second. The newest arrivals differ in many ways from those who came earlier, and ideas and theories based on the earlier experiences will not necessarily apply to the present. We will briefly note some of the issues in this chapter and explore them in more detail in the case study chapters in Part III.

Finally, at the end of this chapter, I briefly consider the implications of these first two chapters for the exploration of intergroup relations. By the end of this chapter, you will be familiar with many of the concepts that will guide us throughout this text as we examine the variety of possible dominant-minority group situations and the directions our society (and the groups within it) can take.

ASSIMILATION

We begin with assimilation because the emphasis in U.S. group relations historically has been on this goal rather than on pluralism. This section presents some of the most important sociological theories and concepts that have been used to describe and analyze the assimilation of the 19th-century immigrants from Europe.

Types of Assimilation

Assimilation is a general term for a process that can follow a number of different pathways. One form of assimilation is expressed in the metaphor of the "melting pot," a process in which different groups come together and contribute in roughly equal amounts to create a common culture and a new, unique society. People often think of the American experience of assimilation in terms of the melting pot. This view stresses the ways in which diverse peoples helped construct U.S. society and made contributions to American culture. The melting-pot metaphor sees assimilation as benign and egalitarian, a process that emphasizes sharing and inclusion.

Although it is a powerful image in our society, the melting pot is not an accurate description of how assimilation actually proceeded for American minority groups (Abrahamson, 1980, pp. 152–154). Some groups—especially the racial minority groups—have been largely excluded from the "melting" process. Furthermore, the melting-pot brew has had a distinctly Anglocentric flavor: "For better or worse, the white

Photo 2.1

Assimilation happens on many levels, including food. In this photo, a New York deli offers food from several ethnic traditions (Jewish, Italian, and Middle Eastern) brought together in a distinctly American venue.

© Envision/Corbis.

Anglo-Saxon Protestant tradition was for two centuries—and in crucial respects still is—the dominant influence on American culture and society" (Schlesinger, 1992, p. 28). Contrary to the melting-pot image, assimilation in the United States generally has been a coercive and largely one-sided process better described by the terms Americanization or Anglo-conformity. Rather than an equal sharing of elements and a gradual blending of diverse peoples, assimilation in the United States was designed to maintain the predominance of the English language and the British-type institutional patterns created during the early years of American society. The stress on Anglo-conformity as the central thrust of American assimilation is clearly reflected in the quote from President Roosevelt that opens this chapter. Many Americans today agree with Roosevelt: 77% of respondents in a recent survey—the overwhelming majority—agreed that "the United States should require immigrants to be proficient in English as a condition of remaining in the U.S." Interestingly, about 60% of Hispanic Americans (vs. 80% of non-Hispanic whites and 76% of blacks) also agreed with this statement (Carroll, 2007). We should note that the apparent agreement between whites and Hispanics on the need for immigrants to learn English may flow from very different orientations and motivations. For some whites, the response may mix prejudice and contempt with support for Americanization, while the Hispanic responses may be based on direct experience with the difficulties of negotiating the monolingual institutions of American society.

Under Anglo-conformity, immigrant and minority groups are expected to adapt to Anglo-American culture as a precondition to acceptance and access to better jobs, education, and other opportunities. Assimilation has meant that minority groups have had to give up their traditions and adopt Anglo-American culture. To be sure, many groups and individuals were (and continue to be) eager to undergo Anglo-conformity, even if it meant losing much or all of their heritage. For other groups, Americanization created conflict, anxiety, demoralization, and resentment. We assess these varied reactions in our examination of America's minority groups in Part III.

The "Traditional" Perspective on Assimilation: Theories and Concepts

American sociologists have developed a rich body of theories and concepts based on the assimilation experiences of the immigrants who came from Europe from the 1820s to the 1920s, and we shall refer to this body of work as the traditional perspective on assimilation. As you will see, the scholars working in this tradition have made invaluable contributions, and their thinking is impressively complex and comprehensive. This does not mean, of course, that they have exhausted the possibilities or answered (or asked) all the questions. Theorists working in the pluralist tradition and contemporary scholars studying the experiences of more recent immigrants have questioned many aspects of traditional assimilation theory and have made a number of important contributions of their own.

Robert Park

Many theories of assimilation are grounded in the work of Robert Park. He was one of a group of scholars who had a major hand in establishing sociology as a discipline in the United States in the 1920s and 1930s. Park felt that intergroup relations go through a predictable set of phases that he called a race relations cycle. When groups first come into contact (through immigration, conquest, etc.), relations are conflictual and competitive. Eventually, however, the process, or cycle, moves toward assimilation, or the "interpenetration and fusion" of groups (Park & Burgess, 1924, p. 735).

Park argued further that assimilation is inevitable in a democratic and industrial society. In a political system based on democracy, fairness, and impartial justice, all groups will eventually secure equal treatment under the law. In an industrial economy, people tend to be judged on rational grounds—that is, on the basis of their abilities and talents—and not by ethnicity or race. Park believed that as American society continued to modernize, urbanize, and industrialize, ethnic and racial groups would gradually lose their importance. The boundaries between groups would eventually dissolve, and a more "rational" and unified society would emerge (see also Geschwender, 1978, pp. 19–32; Hirschman, 1983).

Social scientists have examined, analyzed, and criticized Park's conclusions for years. One frequently voiced criticism is that he did not specify a time frame for the completion of assimilation, and therefore, his idea that assimilation is "inevitable" cannot be tested. Until the exact point in time when assimilation is deemed complete, we will not know whether the theory is wrong or whether we just have not waited long enough.

An additional criticism of Park's theory is that he does not describe the nature of the assimilation process in much detail. How would assimilation proceed? How would everyday life change? Which aspects of the group would change first?

Milton Gordon

To clarify some of the issues left unresolved by Park, we turn to the works of sociologist Milton Gordon, who made a major contribution to theories of assimilation in his book *Assimilation in American Life* (1964). Gordon broke down the overall process of assimilation into seven subprocesses; we will focus on the first three. Before considering these phases of assimilation, we need to consider some new concepts and terms.

Gordon makes a distinction between the cultural and the structural components of society. Culture encompasses all aspects of the way of life associated with a group of people. It includes language, religious beliefs, customs and rules of etiquette, and the values and ideas people use to organize their lives and interpret their existence. The social structure, or structural components of a society, includes networks of social relationships, groups, organizations, stratification systems, communities, and families. The social structure organizes the work of the society and connects individuals to one another and to the larger society.

It is common in sociology to separate the social structure into primary and secondary sectors. The primary sector includes interpersonal relationships that are intimate and personal, such as families and groups of friends. Groups in the primary sector are small. The secondary sector consists of groups and organizations that are more public, task oriented, and impersonal. Organizations in the secondary sector are often large and include businesses, factories, schools and colleges, and bureaucracies.

Now we can examine Gordon's earliest stages of assimilation, which are summarized in Exhibit 2.1.

Stage	Process
1. Acculturation	The group learns the culture of the dominant group, including language and values
2. Integration (structural assimilation) a. At the secondary level	Members of the group enter the public institutions and organizations of the dominant society
b. At the primary level	Members of the group enter the cliques, clubs, and friendship groups of the dominant society
3. Intermarriage (marital assimilation)	Members of the group marry with members of the dominant society on a large scale

Exhibit 2.1 Gordon's Stages of Assimilation

SOURCE: Adapted from Gordon (1964, p. 71). Reprinted by permission of Oxford University Press, Inc.

1. **Cultural Assimilation, or Acculturation.** Members of the minority group learn the culture of the dominant group. For groups that immigrate to the United States, acculturation to the dominant Anglo-American culture may include (as necessary) learning the English language, changing eating habits, adopting new value systems, and altering the spelling of the family surname.

2. Structural Assimilation, or Integration. The minority group enters the social structure of the larger society. Integration typically begins in the secondary sector and gradually moves into the primary sector. That is, before people can form friendships with members of other groups (integration into the primary sector), they must first become acquaintances. The initial contact between groups often occurs in public institutions such as schools and workplaces (integration into the secondary sector). The greater their integration into the secondary sector, the more nearly equal the minority group will be to the dominant group in income, education, and occupational prestige. Once a group has entered the institutions and public sectors of the larger society, according to Gordon, integration into the primary sector and the other stages of assimilation will follow inevitably (although not necessarily quickly). Measures of integration into the primary sector include the extent to which people have acquaintances, close friends, or neighbors from other groups.

3. Marital Assimilation, or Intermarriage. When integration into the primary sector becomes substantial, the basis for Gordon's third stage of assimilation is established. People are most likely to select spouses from among their primary relations, and thus, in Gordon's view, primary structural integration typically precedes intermarriage.

Gordon argued that acculturation was a prerequisite for integration. Given the stress on Anglo-conformity, a member of an immigrant or minority group would not be able to compete for jobs or other opportunities in the secondary sector of the social structure until he or she had learned the dominant group's culture. Gordon recognized, however, that successful acculturation does not automatically ensure that a group will begin the integration phase. The dominant group may still exclude the minority group from its institutions and limit the opportunities available to the group. Gordon argued that "acculturation without integration" (or Americanization without equality) is a common situation in the United States for many minority groups, especially the racial minority groups.

In Gordon's theory, movement from acculturation to integration is the crucial step in the assimilation process. Once that step is taken, all the other subprocesses will occur inevitably, although movement through the stages can be very slow. Gordon's idea that assimilation runs a certain course in a certain order echoes Park's conclusion regarding the inevitability of the process.

Almost 50 years after Gordon published his analysis of assimilation, some of his conclusions have been called into question. For example, the individual subprocesses of assimilation that Gordon saw as linked in a certain order are often found to occur independently of one another (Yinger, 1985, p. 154). A group may integrate before acculturating or combine the subprocesses in other ways. Also, many researchers no longer think of the process of assimilation as necessarily linear or one-way (Greeley, 1974). Groups (or segments thereof) may "reverse direction" and become less assimilated over time, revive their traditional cultures, relearn their old languages, or revitalize ethnic organizations or associations.

Nonetheless, Gordon's overall model continues to guide our understanding of the process of assimilation, to the point that a large part of the research agenda for contemporary studies of immigrants involves assessment of the extent to which their experiences can be described in Gordon's terms (Alba & Nee, 1997). In fact, Gordon's model will provide a major organizational framework for the case study chapters presented in Part III of this text.

Human Capital Theory

Why did some European immigrant groups acculturate and integrate more rapidly than others? Although not a theory of assimilation per se, human capital theory offers one possible answer to this question. This theory argues that status attainment, or the level of success achieved by an individual in society, is a direct result of educational levels, personal values and skills, and other individual characteristics and abilities. Education is seen as an investment in human capital, not unlike the investment a business might make in machinery or new technology. The greater the investment in a person's human capital, the higher the probability of success. Blau and Duncan (1967), in their pioneering statement of status attainment theory, found that even the relative advantage conferred by having a high-status father is largely mediated through education. In other words, high levels of affluence and occupational prestige are not so much a result of being born into a privileged status as they are the result of the superior education that affluence makes possible.

Why did some immigrant groups achieve upward mobility more rapidly than others? Human capital theory answers questions such as these in terms of the resources and cultural characteristics of the members of the groups, especially their levels of education and familiarity with English. Success is seen as a direct result of individual effort and the wise investment of personal resources. People or groups who fail have not tried hard enough, have not made the right kinds of educational investments, or have values or habits that limit their ability to compete.

More than most sociological theories, human capital theory is quite consistent with traditional American culture and values. Both tend to see success as an individual phenomenon, a reward for hard work, sustained effort, and good character. Both tend to assume that success is equally available to all and that the larger society is open and neutral in its distribution of rewards and opportunity. Both tend to see assimilation as a highly desirable, benign process that blends diverse peoples and cultures into a strong, unified whole. Thus, people or groups that resist Americanization or question its benefits are seen as threatening or illegitimate.

On one level, human capital theory is an important theory of success and upward mobility, and we will on occasion use the theory to analyze the experiences of minority and immigrant groups. On another level, the theory is so resonant with American "commonsensical" views of success and failure that we may tend to use it uncritically.

A final judgment on the validity of the theory will be more appropriately made at the end of the text, but you should be aware of the major limitations of the theory from the beginning. First of all, as an explanation of minority group experience, human capital theory is not so much "wrong" as it is incomplete. In other words, it does not take account of all the factors that affect mobility and assimilation. Second, as we shall see, the assumption that U.S. society is equally open and fair to all groups is simply wrong. We will point out other strengths and limitations of this perspective as we move through the text.

PLURALISM

Sociological discussions of pluralism often begin with a consideration of the work of Horace Kallen. In articles published in the Nation magazine in 1915, Kallen argued that people should not have to surrender their culture and traditions to become full participants in American society. He rejected the Anglo-conformist, assimilationist model and contended that the existence of separate ethnic groups, even with separate cultures, religions, and languages, was consistent with democracy and other core American values. In Gordon's terms, Kallen believed that integration and equality were possible without extensive acculturation and that American society could be a federation of diverse groups, a mosaic

Photo 2.3

© P Deliss/Godong/
Corbis.

Photo 2.4

© Richard T.
Nowitz/CORBIS.

of harmonious and interdependent cultures and peoples (Kallen, 1915a, 1915b; see also Abrahamson, 1980; Gleason, 1980).

Assimilation has been such a powerful theme in U.S. history that in the decades following the publication of Kallen's analysis, support for pluralism remained somewhat marginalized. In more recent decades, however, interest in pluralism and ethnic diversity has increased, in part because the assimilation predicted by Park (and implicit in the conventional wisdom of many Americans) has not materialized fully. Perhaps we simply have not waited long enough, but as the 21st century unfolds, distinctions among the racial minority groups in our society show few signs of disappearing, and, in fact, some members of these groups are questioning the very desirability of assimilation. Also, more surprising perhaps, white ethnicity maintains a stubborn persistence, although it continues to change in form and decrease in strength.

An additional reason for the growing interest in pluralism, no doubt, is the everyday reality of the increasing diversity of U.S. society, as reflected in Exhibit 1.1. Controversies over issues such as "English-only" policies, bilingual education, and welfare rights for immigrants are common and often bitter. Many Americans feel that diversity or pluralism has exceeded acceptable limits and that the unity of the nation is at risk (for example, visit http://www.us-english.org/, the homepage of a group that advocates for English-only legislation).

Finally, interest in pluralism and ethnicity in general has been stimulated by developments around the globe. Several nation-states have disintegrated into smaller units based on language, culture, race, and ethnicity. Recent events in India, the Middle East, Eastern Europe, the former U.S.S.R., Canada, and Africa, just to mention a few, have provided dramatic and often tragic evidence of how ethnic identities and enmities can persist across decades or even centuries of submergence and suppression in larger national units.

In contemporary debates, discussions of diversity and pluralism are often couched in the language of multiculturalism, a general term for a variety of programs and ideas that stress mutual respect for all groups and for the multiple heritages that have shaped the United States. Some aspects of multiculturalism are controversial and have evoked strong opposition. In many ways, however, these debates merely echo a recurring argument about the character of American society, a debate that will be revisited throughout this text.

Types of Pluralism

We can distinguish various types of pluralism by using some of the concepts introduced in the discussion of assimilation. Cultural pluralism exists when groups have not acculturated and each maintains its own identity. The groups might speak different languages, practice different religions, and have different value systems. The groups are part of the same society and might even live in adjacent areas, but in some ways, they live in different worlds. Some Native Americans are culturally pluralistic, maintaining their traditional languages and cultures and living on isolated reservations. The Amish, a religious community sometimes called the Pennsylvania Dutch, are also a culturally pluralistic group. They are committed to a way of life organized around farming, and they maintain a culture and an institutional life that is

separate from the dominant culture (see Hostetler, 1980; Kephart & Zellner, 1994; Kraybill & Bowman, 2001).

Following Gordon's subprocesses, a second type of pluralism exists when a group has acculturated but not integrated. That is, the group has adopted the Anglo-American culture but does not have full and equal access to the institutions of the larger society. In this situation, called structural pluralism, cultural differences are minimal, but the groups occupy different locations in the social structure. The groups may speak with the same accent, eat the same food, pursue the same goals, and subscribe to the same values, but they may also maintain separate organizational systems, including different churches, clubs, schools, and neighborhoods.

Under structural pluralism, groups practice a common culture but do so in different places and with minimal interaction across group boundaries. An example of structural pluralism can be found on any Sunday morning in the Christian churches of the United States. Not only are local parishes separated by denomination, they are also often identified with specific ethnic groups or races. What happens in the various churches—the rituals, expressions of faith, statements of core values and beliefs—is similar and expresses a common, shared culture. Structurally, however, this common culture is expressed in separate buildings, by separate congregations, and, often, by separate racial or ethnic groups.

A third type of pluralism reverses the order of Gordon's first two phases: integration without acculturation. This situation is exemplified by a group that has had some material success (measured by wealth or income, for example) but has not become Americanized (learned English, adopted American values and norms, etc.). Some immigrant groups have found niches in American society in which they can survive and occasionally prosper economically without acculturating much.

Two different situations can be used to illustrate this pattern. An enclave minority group establishes its own neighborhood and relies on a set of interconnected businesses, each of which is usually small in scope, for its economic survival. Some of these businesses serve the group, whereas others serve the larger society. The Cuban American community in South Florida and Chinatowns in many larger American cities are examples of ethnic enclaves. A similar pattern of adjustment, the middleman minority group, also relies on small shops and retail firms, but the businesses are more dispersed throughout a large area rather than concentrated in a specific locale. Some Chinese American communities fit this second pattern, as do Korean American greengroceries, Arab American markets, and Indian-American-owned motels (Portes & Manning, 1986). These types of minority groups are discussed further in Part III.

The economic success of enclave and middleman minorities is partly due to the strong ties of cooperation and mutual aid within their groups. The ties are based, in turn, on cultural bonds that would weaken if acculturation took place. In contrast to Gordon's idea that acculturation is a prerequisite to integration, whatever success these groups enjoy is due in part to the fact that they have not Americanized. Kim Park, whom we met in the first chapter, is willing to work in his uncle's grocery store for room and board and the opportunity to learn the business. His willingness to forgo a salary and subordinate his individual needs to the needs of the group reflects the strength of his relationship to family and kin. At various times and places, Jewish, Chinese, Japanese, Korean, and Cuban Americans have been enclave or middleman minorities (see Bonacich & Modell, 1980; Kitano & Daniels, 2001).

The situation of enclave and middleman minorities, integration without acculturation, can be considered either a type of pluralism (emphasizing the absence of acculturation) or a type of assimilation (emphasizing a high level of economic equality). Keep in mind that assimilation and pluralism are not opposites but can occur in a variety of combinations. It is best to think of acculturation, integration, and the other stages of assimilation (or pluralism) as independent processes.

OTHER GROUP RELATIONSHIPS

This book concentrates on assimilation and pluralism, but there are, of course, other possible group relationships and goals. Two commonly noted goals for minority groups are separatism and revolution (Wirth, 1945). The goal of separatism is for the group to sever all ties (political, cultural, and geographic) with the larger society. Thus, separatism goes well beyond pluralism. Native Americans have expressed both separatist and pluralist goals, and separatism also has been pursued by some African American organizations, such as the Black Muslims. In the contemporary world, there are separatist movements among groups in French Canada, Scotland, Chechnya, Cyprus, southern Mexico, Hawaii, and scores of other places.

A minority group promoting revolution seeks to switch places with the dominant group and become the ruling elite or create a new social order, perhaps in alliance with members of the dominant group. Although revolutionary activity can be found among some American minority groups (e.g., the Black Panthers), this goal has been relatively rare for minority groups in the United States. Revolutionary minority groups are more commonly found in situations such as those in colonial Africa, in which one nation conquered and controlled another racially or culturally different nation.

The dominant group may also pursue goals other than assimilation and pluralism, including forced migration or expulsion, extermination or genocide, and continued subjugation of the minority group. Chinese immigrants were the victims of a policy of expulsion, beginning in the 1880s, when the Chinese Exclusion Act (1882) closed the door on further immigration and concerted efforts were made to encourage those in the country to leave (see Chapter 9). Native Americans also have been the victims of expulsion. In 1830, all tribes living east of the Mississippi were forced to migrate to a new territory in the West (see Chapter 4). The most infamous example of genocide is the Holocaust in Nazi Germany, during which 6 million Jews were murdered. The dominant group pursues "continued subjugation" when, as with slavery in the antebellum South, it attempts to maintain a powerless and exploited position for the minority group. A dominant group may simultaneously pursue different policies with different minority groups and may, of course, change policies over time.

FROM IMMIGRANTS TO WHITE ETHNICS

In this section, we will explore the experiences of the minority groups that stimulated the development of the traditional perspective. A massive immigration from Europe began in the 1820s, and over the next century, millions of people made the journey from the Old World to the New. They came from every corner of the continent: Ireland, Greece, Germany, Italy,

Exhibit 2.2 Major European Sending Nations, Immigration to the United States, 1820–1920

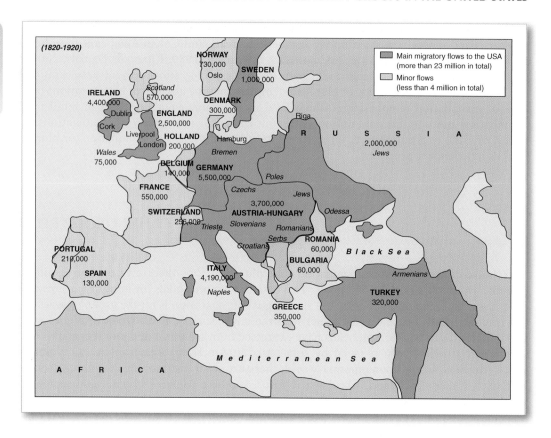

Poland, Portugal, Ukraine, Russia, and scores of other nations and provinces. They came as young men and women seeking jobs, as families fleeing religious persecution, as political radicals fleeing the police, as farmers seeking land and a fresh start, and as paupers barely able to scrape together the cost of the passage. They came as immigrants, became minority groups on their arrival, experienced discrimination and prejudice in all its forms, went through all the varieties and stages of assimilation and pluralism, and eventually merged into the society that had rejected them so viciously. Exhibit 2.2 shows the major European sending nations.

This first mass wave of immigrants shaped the United States in countless ways. When the immigration started in the 1820s, the United States was not yet 50 years old, an agricultural nation clustered along the East Coast. The nation was just coming into contact with Mexicans in the Southwest, immigration from China had not begun, slavery was flourishing in the South, and conflict with American Indians was intense and brutal. When the immigration ended in the 1920s, the population of the United States had increased from fewer than 10 million to more than 100 million, and society had industrialized, become a world power, and stretched from coast to coast—with colonies in the Pacific and the Caribbean.

It was no coincidence that European immigration, American industrialization, and the rise to global prominence occurred simultaneously. These changes were intimately interlinked, the mutual causes and effects of one another. Industrialization fueled the growth of U.S. military and political power, and the industrial machinery of the nation depended heavily on the flow of labor from Europe. By World War I, for example, 25% of the nation's total labor force was foreign-born, and more than half the workforce in New York, Detroit, and Chicago consisted of immigrant men. Immigrants were the majority of the workers in many important sectors of the economy, including coal mining, steel manufacturing, the garment industry, and meatpacking (Martin & Midgley, 1999, p. 15; Steinberg, 1981, p. 36).

In the sections that follow, we explore the experiences of these groups, beginning with the forces that caused them to leave Europe and come to the United States and ending with an assessment of their present status in American society.

Industrialization and Immigration

What forces stimulated this mass movement of people? Like any complex phenomenon, immigration from Europe had a multitude of causes, but underlying the process was a massive and fundamental shift in subsistence technology: the Industrial Revolution. I mentioned the importance of subsistence technology in Chapter 1. Dominant-minority relations are intimately related to the system a society uses to satisfy its basic needs, and they change as that system changes. The immigrants were pushed out of Europe as industrial technology wrecked the traditional agricultural way of life, and they were drawn to the United States by the jobs created by the spread of that very same technology. We will consider the impact of this fundamental transformation of social structure and culture in some detail.

Industrialization began in England in the mid-1700s, spread to other parts of Northern and Western Europe and then, in the 19th century, to Eastern and Southern Europe. As it rolled across the continent, the Industrial Revolution replaced people and animal power with machines and new forms of energy (steam, coal, and eventually oil), causing an exponential increase in the productive capacity of society. At the dawn of the Industrial Revolution, most Europeans lived in small, rural villages and survived by traditional farming practices that had changed very little over the centuries. The work of production was labor-intensive or done by hand or with the aid of draft animals. Productivity was low, and the tasks of food production and survival required the efforts of virtually the entire family working ceaselessly throughout the year.

Industrialization destroyed this traditional way of life as it introduced new technology, machines, and new sources of energy to the tasks of production. The new technology was capital-intensive or dependent on machine power, and it reduced the need for human labor in rural areas as it modernized agriculture. Also, farmland was consolidated into larger and larger tracts for the sake of efficiency, further decreasing the need for human laborers. At the same time, even as survival in the rapidly changing rural economy became more difficult, the rural population began to grow.

In response, peasants began to leave their home villages and move toward urban areas. Factories were being built in or near the cities, opening opportunities for employment. The urban population tended to increase faster than the job supply, however, and many migrants had to move on. Many of these former peasants responded to opportunities available in the New World, especially in the United States, where the abundance of farmland on the frontier kept people moving out of the cities and away from the East Coast, thereby sustaining a fairly constant demand for labor in the areas that were easiest for Europeans to reach. As industrialization took hold on both continents, the population movement to European cities and then to North America eventually grew to become the largest in human history (so far).

The timing of emigration from Europe followed the timing of industrialization. The first waves of immigrants, often called the "Old Immigration," came from Northern and Western Europe starting in the 1820s. A second wave, the "New Immigration," began arriving from Southern and Eastern Europe in the 1880s. Exhibit 2.3 shows both waves and the rates of legal immigration up to 2009. Note that the "new" immigration was much more voluminous than the "old" and that the number of immigrants declined drastically after the 1920s. We will explore the reasons for this decline later in this chapter and discuss in detail the more recent (post-1965) increase in immigration in Chapters 8 through 10.

Exhibit 2.3 Legal Immigration to the United States, 1820 to 2009

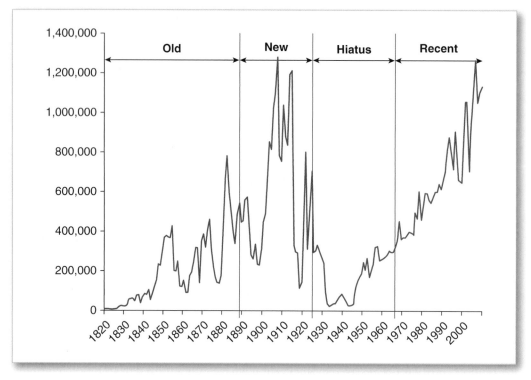

SOURCE: Department of Homeland Security, Yearbook of Immigration Statistics, 2009.

European Origins and Conditions of Entry

The immigrants from Europe varied from one another in innumerable ways. They followed a variety of pathways into the United States, and their experiences were shaped by their cultural and class characteristics, their countries of origin, and the timing of their arrival. Some groups encountered much more resistance than others, and different groups played different roles in the industrialization and urbanization of America. To discuss these diverse patterns systematically, I distinguish three subgroups of European immigrants: Protestants from Northern and Western Europe, the largely Catholic immigrant laborers from Ireland and from Southern and Eastern Europe, and Jewish immigrants from Eastern Europe. We look at these subgroups in roughly the order of their arrival. In later sections, we will consider other sociological variables (social class, gender) that further differentiated these groups.

Northern and Western Protestant Europeans

Northern and Western European immigrants included English, Germans, Norwegians, Swedes, Welsh, French, Dutch, and Danes. These groups were similar to the dominant group in their racial and religious characteristics and also shared many cultural values with the host society, including the Protestant Ethic—which stressed hard work, success, and individualism—and support for the principles of democratic government. These similarities eased their acceptance into a society that was highly intolerant of religious and racial differences until well into the 20th century, and these immigrant groups generally experienced a lower degree of ethnocentric rejection and racist disparagement than did the Irish and immigrants from Southern and Eastern Europe.

Northern and Western European immigrants came from nations that were just as developed as the United States. Thus, these immigrants tended to be more skilled and educated than other immigrant groups, and they often brought money and other resources with which to secure a comfortable place for themselves in their new society. Many settled in the sparsely populated

Photo 2.7

Until the Industrial Revolution, virtually the entire population of Europe lived in the countryside. This village scene depicts the crowds gathered on market day.

Midwest and in other frontier areas, where they farmed the fertile land that had become available after the conquest and removal of American Indians and Mexican Americans (see Chapter 4). By dispersing throughout the midsection of the country, they lowered their visibility and their degree of competition with dominant group members. Two brief case studies, first Norwegians and then Germans, outline the experiences of these groups.

Immigrants From Norway. Norway had a small population base, and immigration from this Scandinavian nation was never sizable in absolute numbers. However, "America Fever" struck here as it did elsewhere in Europe, and on a per capita basis, Norway sent more immigrants to the United States before 1890 than any other European nation except Ireland (Chan, 1990, p. 41).

The first Norwegian immigrants were moderately prosperous farmers searching for cheap land. They found abundant acreage in upper-Midwest states, such as Minnesota and Wisconsin, and then found that the local labor supply was too small to effectively cultivate the available land. Many turned to their homeland for assistance and used their relatives and friends to create networks and recruit a labor force. Thus, chains of communication and migration linking Norway to the Northern Plains were established, supplying immigrants to these areas for decades (Chan, 1990, p. 41). Today, a strong Scandinavian heritage is still evident in the farms, towns, and cities of the upper Midwest.

Immigrants From Germany. The stream of immigration from Germany was much larger than that from Norway, and German Americans left their mark on the economy, the political structure, and the cultural life of their new land. In the last half of the 19th century, at least 25% of the immigrants each year were German (Conzen, 1980, p. 406), and today, more Americans (about 15%) trace their ancestries to Germany than to any other country (Brittingham & de la Cruz, 2004).

The German immigrants who arrived earlier in the 1800s moved into the newly opened farmland and the rapidly growing cities of the Midwest, as had many Scandinavians. By

1850, large German communities could be found in Milwaukee, St. Louis, and other Midwestern cities (Conzen, 1980, p. 413). Some German immigrants followed the transatlantic route of the cotton trade between Europe and the southern United States and entered through the port of New Orleans, moving from there to the Midwest and Southwest.

German immigrants arriving later in the century were more likely to settle in urban areas, in part because fertile land was less available. Many of the city-bound German immigrants were skilled workers and artisans, and others found work as laborers in the rapidly expanding industrial sector. The double penetration of German immigrants into the rural economy and the higher sectors of the urban economy is reflected by the fact that by 1870, most employed German Americans were involved in skilled labor (37%) or farming (25%; Conzen, 1980, p. 413).

German immigrants took relatively high occupational positions in the U.S. labor force, and their sons and daughters were able to translate that relative affluence into economic mobility. By the dawn of the 20th century, large numbers of second-generation German Americans were finding their way into white-collar and professional careers. Within a few generations, German Americans had achieved parity with national norms in education, income, and occupational prestige.

Assimilation Patterns. By and large, assimilation for Norwegian, German, and other Protestant immigrants from Northern and Western Europe was consistent with the traditional views discussed earlier in this chapter. Although members of these groups felt the sting of rejection, prejudice, and discrimination, their movement from acculturation to integration and equality was relatively smooth, especially when compared with the experiences of racial minority groups. Their relative success and high degree of assimilation are suggested in Exhibits 2.6 and 2.7, presented later in this chapter.

Immigrant Laborers From Ireland and Southern and Eastern Europe

The relative ease of assimilation for Northern and Western Europeans contrasts sharply with the experiences of non-Protestant, less-educated, and less-skilled immigrants. These "immigrant laborers" came in two waves. The Irish were part of the Old Immigration that began in the 1820s, but the bulk of this group—Italians, Poles, Russians, Hungarians, Greeks, Serbs, Ukrainians, Slovaks, Bulgarians, and scores of other Southern and Eastern European groups—made up the New Immigration that began in the 1880s. Most of the immigrants in these nationality groups (like many recent immigrants to the United States) were peasants or unskilled laborers, with few resources other than their willingness to work. They came from rural, village-oriented cultures in which family and kin took precedence over individual needs or desires. Family life for them tended to be autocratic and male dominated, and children were expected to subordinate their personal desires and to work for the good of the family as a whole. Arranged marriages were common. This cultural background was less consistent with the industrializing, capitalistic, individualistic, Protestant, Anglo-American culture of the United States and was a major reason that these immigrant laborers experienced a higher level of rejection and discrimination than did the immigrants from Northern and Western Europe.

The immigrant laborers were much less likely to enter the rural economy than were the Northern and Western European immigrants. Much of the better frontier land already had been claimed by the time most new immigrant groups began to arrive, and a large number of them had been permanently soured on farming by the oppressive and exploitative agrarian economies from which they were trying to escape. They settled in the cities of the industrializing Northeast and found work in plants, mills, mines, and factories. They supplied the armies of laborers needed to power the Industrial Revolution in the United States, although their view of this process was generally from the bottom looking up. They arrived during the decades in which the American industrial and urban infrastructure was being constructed. They built roads, canals, and railroads, as well as the buildings that housed the machinery of industrialization. For example, the first tunnels of the New York City subway system were dug, largely by hand, by laborers from Italy. Other immigrants found work in the coal fields of Pennsylvania and West Virginia and the steel mills of Pittsburgh, and they flocked by the millions to the factories of the Northeast.

Like other low-skill immigrant groups, these newcomers took jobs in which strength and stamina were more important than literacy or skilled craftsmanship. In fact, the minimum level of skills required for employment actually declined as industrialization proceeded through its early phases. To keep wages low and take advantage of what seemed like an inexhaustible supply of cheap labor, industrialists and factory owners developed technologies and machines that required few skills and little knowledge of English to operate. As mechanization proceeded, unskilled workers replaced skilled workers in the workforce. Not infrequently, women and children replaced men because they could be hired for lower wages (Steinberg, 1981, p. 35).

Eventually, as the generations passed, the prejudice, systematic discrimination, and other barriers to upward mobility for the immigrant laborer groups weakened, and their descendants began to rise out of the working class. Although the first and second generations of these groups were largely limited to jobs at the unskilled or semiskilled level, the third and later generations rose in the American social class system. As Exhibits 2.6 and 2.7 show (later in this chapter), the descendants of the immigrant laborers achieved parity with national norms by the latter half of the 20th century.

Photo 2.8

Hester Street, circa 1900, was one of the main streets in the Lower East Side of New York City, the most famous American Jewish neighborhood.

From Library of Congress.

Eastern European Jewish Immigrants and the Ethnic Enclave

Jewish immigrants from Russia and other parts of Eastern Europe followed a third pathway into U.S. society. These immigrants were a part of the New Immigration and began arriving in the 1880s. Unlike the immigrant laborer groups, who were generally economic refugees and included many young, single males, Eastern European Jews were fleeing religious persecution and arrived as family units intending to settle permanently and become citizens. They settled in the urban areas of the Northeast and Midwest. New York City was the most common destination, and the Lower East Side became the best-known Jewish American neighborhood. By 1920, about 60% of all Jewish Americans lived in the urban areas between Boston and Philadelphia, with almost 50% living in New York City alone. Another 30% lived in the urban areas of the Midwest, particularly in Chicago (Goren, 1980, p. 581).

In Russia and other parts of Eastern Europe, Jews had been barred from agrarian occupations and had come to rely on the urban economy for their livelihoods. When they immigrated to the United States, they brought these urban skills and job experiences with them. For example, almost two thirds of immigrant Jewish men had been tailors and other skilled laborers in Eastern Europe (Goren, 1980, p. 581). In the rapidly industrializing U.S. economy of the early 20th century, they were able to use these skills to find work.

Other Jewish immigrants joined the urban working class and took manual labor and unskilled jobs in the industrial sector (Morawska, 1990, p. 202). The garment industry in particular became the lifeblood of the Jewish community and provided jobs to about one third of all Eastern European Jews residing in the major cities (Goren, 1980, p. 582). Women as well as men were involved in the garment industry. Jewish women, like the women of more recent immigrant laborer groups, found ways to combine their jobs and their domestic responsibilities. As young girls, they worked in factories and sweatshops, and after marriage, they did the same work at home, sewing precut garments together or doing other piecework such as wrapping cigars or making artificial flowers, often assisted by their children (Amott & Matthaei, 1991, p. 115).

Unlike most European immigrant groups, Jewish Americans became heavily involved in commerce and often found ways to start their own businesses and become self-employed. Drawing on their experience in the old country, many started businesses and small independent enterprises and developed an enclave economy. The Jewish neighborhoods were densely populated and provided a ready market for services of all kinds. Some Jewish immigrants became street peddlers or started bakeries, butcher and candy shops, or any number of other retail enterprises.

Capitalizing on their residential concentration and close proximity, Jewish immigrants created dense networks of commercial, financial, and social cooperation. The Jewish American enclave survived because of the cohesiveness of the group; the willingness of wives, children, and other relatives to work for little or no monetary compensation; and the commercial savvy of the early immigrants. Also, a large pool of cheap labor and sources of credit and other financial services were available within the community. The Jewish American enclave grew and provided a livelihood for many of the children and grandchildren of the immigrants (Portes & Manning, 1986, pp. 51–52). As has been the case with other enclave groups that we will discuss in future chapters, including Chinese Americans and Cuban Americans, economic advancement preceded extensive acculturation, and Jewish Americans made significant strides toward economic equality before they became fluent in English or were otherwise Americanized.

One obvious way in which an enclave immigrant group can improve its position is to develop an educated and acculturated second generation. The Americanized, English-speaking children of the immigrants used their greater familiarity with the dominant society and their language facility to help preserve and expand the family enterprise. Furthermore, as the second generation appeared, the American public school system was expanding, and education through the college level was free or inexpensive in New York City and other cities (Steinberg, 1981, pp. 128–138). There was also a strong push for the second and third generations to enter professions, and as Jewish Americans excelled in school, resistance to and discrimination against them increased. By the 1920s, many elite colleges and universities, such as Dartmouth, had established quotas that limited the number of Jewish students they would admit (Dinnerstein, 1977, p. 228). These quotas were not abolished until after World War II.

The enclave economy and the Jewish neighborhoods established by the immigrants proved to be an effective base from which to integrate into American society. The descendants of the Eastern European Jewish immigrants moved out of the ethnic neighborhoods years ago, and their positions in the economy—their pushcarts, stores, and jobs in the garment industry—have been taken over by more recent immigrants. When they left the enclave economy, many second- and third-generation Eastern European Jews did not enter the mainstream occupational structure at the bottom, as the immigrant laborer groups tended to do. They used the resources generated by the entrepreneurship of the early generations to gain access to prestigious and advantaged social class positions (Portes & Manning, 1986, p. 53). Studies show that Jewish Americans today, as a group, surpass national averages in income, levels of education, and occupational prestige (Sklare, 1971, pp. 60–69; see also Cohen, 1985; Massarik & Chenkin, 1973). The relatively higher status of Russian Americans shown in Exhibits 2.6 and 2.7 (later in this chapter) is due in part to the fact that many Jewish Americans are of Russian descent.

Entering the Promised Land

Mary Antin was born to a family of Russian Jews in 1881. She grew up in the Jewish ghetto of Polotzk (now in Belarus) and immigrated to the United States in 1894. Her family settled in the slums of Boston, and she was quickly identified as an outstanding student. Even though she spoke no English at her arrival, she was able to attend an elite high school and also attended Columbia University and Barnard College. In 1912, she published her memoir, The Promised Land, *which describes her childhood in Russia and her family's largely successful assimilation in American society. The book was immensely popular, perhaps because it presents her assimilation in generally positive terms. This passage describes her arrival in Boston and her first view of American society. Note how she consciously begins to absorb American culture, piece by piece.*

FIRST GLIMPSES OF AMERICAN SOCIETY

MARY ANTIN

Our initiation into American ways began with the first step on the new soil. My father had occasion to instruct or correct us even on the way from the pier to Wall Street, which journey we made crowded together in a rickety cab. He told us not to lean out of the windows, not to point, and explained the word "greenhorn." . . .

The first meal was an object lesson of much variety. My father produced several kinds of food, ready to eat, without any cooking, from little tin cans that had printing all over them. He attempted to introduce us to a queer, slippery kind of fruit, which he called "banana," but had to give it up for the time being. After the meal, he had better luck with a curious piece of furniture on runners, which he called "rocking-chair." There were five of us newcomers, and we found five different ways of getting into the American machine of perpetual motion; and as many ways of getting out of it. One born and bred to the use of a rocking-chair cannot imagine how ludicrous people can make themselves when attempting to use it for the first time. We laughed immoderately over our various experiments with the novelty, which was a wholesome way of letting off steam after the unusual excitement of the day.

In our flat, there was no bathtub. So in the evening of the first day my father conducted us to the public baths. As we moved along in a little procession, I was delighted with the illumination of the streets. So many lamps, and they burned until morning, my father said, and so people did not need to carry lanterns. In America, then, everything was free, as we had heard in Russia. Light was free; the streets were as bright as a synagogue on a holy day. . . .

Education was free. That subject my father had written about repeatedly, as comprising his chief hope for us children, the essence of American opportunity, the treasure that no thief could touch, not even misfortune or poverty. It was the one thing that he was able to promise us when he sent for us; surer, safer than bread or shelter. On our second day I was thrilled with the realization of what this freedom of education meant. A little girl from across the alley came and offered to conduct us to school. My father was out, but we five between us had a few words of English by this time. We knew the word *school*. We understood. This child, who had never seen us until yesterday, who could not pronounce our names, who was not much better dressed than we, was able to offer us the freedom of the schools of Boston! No application made, no questions asked, no examinations, rulings, exclusions; no machinations, no fees. The doors stood open for every one of us. The smallest child could show us the way.

This incident impressed me more than anything I had heard in advance of the freedom of education in America. It was a concrete proof—almost the thing itself. One had to experience it to understand it.

It was a great disappointment to be told by my father that we were not to enter upon our school career at once. It was too near the end of the term, he said. . . . Not that the time was really lost. . . . We had to visit the stores and be dressed from head to foot in American clothing; we had to learn the mysteries of the iron stove, the washboard, and the speaking-tube; we had to learn to trade with the fruit peddler through the window, and not to be afraid of the policeman; and, above all, we had to learn English. . . .

With our despised immigrant clothing we shed also our impossible Hebrew names; a committee of our friends, several years ahead of us in American experience, put their heads together and concocted American names for us all. Those of our real names that had no pleasing American equivalents they ruthlessly discarded . . . My mother, possessing a name that was not easily translatable, was punished with the undignified nickname of Annie. Fetchke, Joseph, and Deborah issued as Frieda, Joseph, and Dora, respectively. As for poor me, I was simply cheated. The name they gave me was hardly new. My Hebrew name being Maryashe . . . , my friends said that it would hold good in English as Mary; which was very disappointing, as I longed to possess a strange-sounding American name like the others.

SOURCE: Antin (1969, pp. 185–188).

Chains of Immigration

All the immigrant groups tended to follow "chains" established and maintained by the members of their groups. Some versions of the traditional assimilation perspective (especially human capital theory) treat immigration and status attainment as purely individual (psychological) matters. To the contrary, scholars have demonstrated that immigration to the United States was in large measure a group (sociological) phenomenon. Immigrant chains stretched across the oceans and were held together by the ties of kinship, language, religion, culture, and a sense of common peoplehood (Bodnar, 1985; Tilly, 1990). The networks supplied information, money for passage, family news, and job offers.

Here is how chain immigration worked (and continues to work today): Someone from a village in, say, Poland, would make it to the United States. The successful immigrant would send word to the home village, perhaps by hiring a letter writer. Along with news and stories of his adventures, he would send his address. Within months, another immigrant from the village, perhaps a brother or other relative, would show up at the address of the original immigrant. After his months of experience in the new society, the original immigrant could lend assistance, provide a place to sleep, help with job hunting, and orient the newcomer to the area.

Before long, others would arrive from the village in need of the same sort of introduction to the mysteries of America. The compatriots would tend to settle close to one another, in the same building or on the same block. Soon, entire neighborhoods were filled with people from a certain village, province, or region. In these ethnic enclaves, the old language was spoken and the old ways observed. Businesses were started, churches or synagogues were founded, families were begun, and mutual aid societies and other organizations were formed. There was safety in numbers and comfort and security in a familiar, if transplanted, set of traditions and customs.

Immigrants often responded to U.S. society by attempting to re-create as much of their old world as possible. Partly to avoid the harsher forms of rejection and discrimination and partly to band together for solidarity and mutual support, immigrants created their own miniature social worlds within the bustling metropolises of the industrializing Northeast and the West Coast. These Little Italys, Little Warsaws, Little Irelands, Greektowns, Chinatowns, and Little Tokyos were safe havens that insulated the immigrants from the larger society and allowed them to establish bonds with one another, organize a group life, pursue their own group interests, and have some control over the pace of their adjustment to American culture. For some groups and in some areas, the ethnic subcommunity was a short-lived phenomenon. For others (the Jewish enclave discussed earlier, for example), the neighborhood became the dominant structure of their lives, and the networks continued to function long after their arrival in the United States.

The Campaign Against Immigration: Prejudice, Racism, and Discrimination

Today, it may be hard to conceive of the bitterness and intensity of the prejudice that greeted the Irish, Italians, Poles, Jews, and other new immigrant groups. Even as they were becoming an indispensable segment of the American workforce, they were castigated, ridiculed, attacked, and disparaged. The Irish were the first immigrant laborers to arrive and, thus, the first to feel this intense prejudice and discrimination. Campaigns against immigrants were waged, Irish neighborhoods were attacked by mobs, and Roman Catholic churches and convents were burned. Some employers blatantly refused to hire the Irish, often advertising their ethnic preferences with signs that read "No Irish Need Apply." Until later-arriving groups pushed them up, the Irish were mired at the bottom of the job market. Indeed, at one time, they were referred to as the "niggers of Boston" (Blessing, 1980; Potter, 1973; Shannon, 1964).

Courtesy of Barbara Olney.

Photo 2.9

The campaign against immigrants was particularly strong in the job market. This sign blatantly expressed rejection of the Irish, but other groups were victimized as well.

Other groups felt the same sting of rejection as they arrived. Italian immigrants were particularly likely to be the victims of violent attacks, one of the most vicious of which took place in New Orleans in 1891. The city's police chief was assassinated, and rumors of Italian involvement in the murder were rampant. Hundreds of Italians were arrested, and 9 were brought to trial. All were acquitted. Anti-Italian sentiment was running so high, however, that a mob lynched 11 Italians while police and city officials did nothing (Higham, 1963).

Anti-Catholicism

Much of the prejudice against the Irish and the new immigrants was expressed as anti-Catholicism. Prior to the mid-19th century, Anglo-American society had been almost exclusively Protestant. Catholicism, with its celibate clergy, Latin masses, and cloistered nuns, seemed alien, exotic, and threatening. The growth of Catholicism, especially because it was associated with non-Anglo immigrants, raised fears that the Protestant religions would lose status. There were even rumors that the Pope was planning to move the Vatican to America and organize a takeover of the U.S. government.

Although Catholics were often stereotyped as single groups, they also varied along a number of dimensions. For example, the Catholic faith as practiced in Ireland differed significantly from that practiced in Italy, Poland, and other countries. Catholic immigrant groups often established their own parishes, with priests who could speak the old language. These cultural and national differences often separated Catholic groups, despite their common faith (Herberg, 1960).

Anti-Semitism

Jews from Russia and Eastern Europe faced intense prejudice and racism (or anti-Semitism) as they began arriving in large numbers in the 1880s. Biased sentiments and negative stereotypes of Jews have been a part of Western tradition for centuries and, in fact, have been stronger and more vicious in Europe than in the United States. For nearly two millennia, European Jews have been chastised and persecuted as the "killers of Christ" and stereotyped as materialistic moneylenders and crafty businessmen. The stereotype that links Jews and moneylending has its origins in the fact that in premodern Europe, Catholics were forbidden by the church to engage in usury (charging interest for loans). Jews were under no such restriction, and they filled the gap thus created in the economy. The ultimate episode in the long history of European anti-Semitism was, of course, the Nazi Holocaust, in which 6 million Jews died. European anti-Semitism did not end with the demise of the Nazi regime, and it remains a prominent concern throughout Europe and Russia.

ESTABLISHMENT DOES
WECLOME GUESTS OF
HEBREW PERSUASION

Before the mass immigration of Eastern European Jews began in the late 19th century, anti-Semitism in the United States was relatively mild, perhaps because the group was so small. As the immigration continued, anti-Jewish prejudice increased in intensity and viciousness, fostering the view of Jews as cunning but dishonest merchants. In the late 19th century, Jews began to be banned from social clubs and the boardrooms of businesses and other organizations. Summer resorts began posting notices: "We prefer not to entertain Hebrews" (Goren, 1980, p. 585).

By the 1920s and 1930s, anti-Semitism had become quite prominent among American prejudices and was being preached by the Ku Klux Klan and other extreme racist groups. Also, because many of the political radicals and labor leaders of the time were Jewish immigrants, anti-Semitism became fused with a fear of Communism and other anticapitalist doctrines. Some prominent Americans espoused anti-Semitic views, among them Henry Ford, the founder of Ford Motor Company; Charles Lindbergh, the aviator who was the first to fly solo across the Atlantic; and Father Charles Coughlin, a Catholic priest with a popular radio show (Selzer, 1972).

Anti-Semitism reached a peak before World War II and tapered off in the decades following the war, but as we shall see in Chapter 3, it remains part of U.S. society (Anti-Defamation League, 2000). Anti-Semitism also has a prominent place in the ideologies of a variety of extremist groups that have emerged in recent years, including "skinheads" and various contemporary incarnations of the Ku Klux Klan. Some of this targeting of Jews seems to increase during economic recession and may be related to the stereotypical view of Jewish Americans as extremely prosperous and materialistic.

Photo 2.10

Discrimination against ethnic groups extended far beyond the job market, as illustrated by this anti-Semitic sign.

A Successful Exclusion

The prejudice and racism directed against the immigrants also found expression in organized, widespread efforts to stop the flow of immigration. A variety of anti-immigrant organizations appeared almost as soon as the mass European immigration started in the 1820s. The strength of these campaigns waxed and waned, largely in harmony with the strength of the economy and the size of the job supply. Anti-immigrant sentiment increased in intensity, and the strength of its organized expressions increased during hard times and depressions and tended to soften when the economy improved. The campaign ultimately triumphed with the passage of the National Origins Act in 1924. This act drastically reduced the overall number of immigrants that would be admitted each year. The effectiveness of the numerical restrictions is clearly apparent in Exhibit 2.3.

The National Origins Act established a quota system that limited the number of immigrants that would be accepted each year from each sending nation, a system that was openly racist. For example, the size of the quota for European nations was based on the proportional representation of each nationality in the United States as of 1890. This year was chosen because it predated the bulk of the New Immigration and gave the most generous quotas to Northern and Western European nations. Immigration from Western Hemisphere nations was not directly affected by this legislation, but immigration from Asian nations was banned altogether. At this time, almost all parts of Africa were still the colonial possessions of various European nations and received no separate quotas. In other words, the quota for immigrants from Africa was zero.

The result was that the quota system allocated nearly 70% of the available immigration slots to the nations of Northern and Western Europe, despite the fact that immigration from those areas had largely ended by the 1920s. The National Origins Act was effective in reducing the volume of immigration, and by the time the Great Depression took hold of the American economy, the flow of newcomers had dropped to the lowest level in a century. The National Origins Act remained in effect until 1965.

PATTERNS OF ASSIMILATION

In this section, we will explore some of the common patterns in the process of assimilation followed by European immigrants and their descendants. These patterns have been well established by research conducted in the traditional perspective and are consistent with the model of assimilation developed by Gordon. They include assimilation by generation, ethnic succession, and structural mobility. We discuss each separately.

The Importance of Generations

People today—social scientists, politicians, and ordinary citizens—often fail to recognize the time and effort it takes for a group to become completely Americanized. For most European immigrant groups, the process took generations, and it was the grandchildren or the great-grandchildren (or even great-great-grandchildren) of the immigrants who finally completed acculturation and integration. Mass immigration from Europe ended in the 1920s, but the assimilation of some European ethnic groups was not completed until late in the 20th century.

Here is a rough summary of how assimilation proceeded for these European immigrants: The first generation, the actual immigrants, settled in ethnic neighborhoods, such as "Little Italy" in New York City, and made only limited movement toward acculturation and integration. They focused their energies on the network of family and social relationships encompassed within their own groups. Of course, many of them—most often the men—had to leave their neighborhoods for work and other reasons, and these excursions required some familiarity with the larger society. Some English had to be learned, and taking a job outside the neighborhood is, almost by definition, a form of integration. Nonetheless, the first generation lived and died largely within the context of the "old country," which had been re-created within the new.

The second generation, or the children of the immigrants, found themselves in a position of psychological or social marginality: They were partly ethnic and partly American but full members of neither group. They were born in America but in households and neighborhoods that were ethnic, not American. They learned the old language first and were socialized in the old ways. As they entered childhood, however, they entered the public schools, where they were socialized into the Anglo-American culture.

Very often, the world the second generation learned about at school conflicted with the world they inhabited at home. For example, the old country family values often expected children to subordinate their self-interests to the interests of their elders and of the family as a whole. Marriages were arranged by parents, or at least were heavily influenced by and subject to their approval. Needless to say, these expectations conflicted sharply with American ideas about individualism and romantic love. Differences of this sort often caused painful conflict between the ethnic first generation and their Americanized children.

As the second generation progressed toward adulthood, they tended to move out of the old neighborhoods. Their geographic mobility was often motivated by social mobility. They were much more acculturated than their parents, spoke English fluently, and enjoyed a wider range of occupational choices and opportunities. Discriminatory policies in education, housing, and the job market sometimes limited them, but they were upwardly mobile, and in their pursuit of jobs and careers, they left behind the ethnic subcommunity and many of the customs of their parents.

The members of the third generation, or the grandchildren of the immigrants, were typically born and raised in nonethnic settings. English was their first (and often their only) language, and their values and perceptions were thoroughly American. Although family and kinship ties with grandparents and the old neighborhood often remained strong, ethnicity for this generation was a relatively minor part of their daily realities and their self-images. Visits on weekends and holidays and family rituals revolving around the cycles of birth, marriage, and death—these activities might have connected the third generation to the world of their ancestors, but in terms of their everyday lives, they were American, not ethnic.

The pattern of assimilation by generation progressed as follows:

- The first generation began the process and was at least slightly acculturated and integrated.
- The second generation was very acculturated and highly integrated (at least into the secondary sectors of society).
- The third generation finished the acculturation process and enjoyed high levels of integration at both the secondary and the primary levels.

Exhibit 2.4 illustrates these patterns in terms of the structural assimilation of Italian Americans. The educational and occupational characteristics of this group converge with those of white Anglo-Saxon Protestants (WASPs) as the generations change. For example,

Exhibit 2.4 Some Comparisons Between Italians and WASPs

		Generation		
	WASPs*	First	Second	Third and Fourth
Percentage with some college	42.4	19.0	19.4	41.7
Average years of education	12.6	9.0	11.1	13.4
Percentage white collar	34.7	20.0	22.5	28.8
Percentage blue collar	37.9	65.0	53.9	39.0
Average occupational prestige	42.5	34.3	36.8	42.5
Percentage of "unmixed" Italian males marrying non-Italian females		21.9	51.4	67.3

SOURCE: Adapted from Alba (1985), Tables 5-3, 5-4, and 6-2. Data are originally from the NORC General Social Surveys, 1975–1980, and the Current Population Survey, 1979. Copyright © 1985 Richard D. Alba.

*White Anglo-Saxon Protestants (WASPs) were not separated by generation, and some of the differences between groups may be the result of factors such as age. That is, older WASPs may have levels of education more comparable to first-generation Italian Americans than WASPs as a whole.

the percentage of Italian Americans with some college shows a gap of more than 20 points between the first and second generations and WASPs. Italians of the third and fourth generations, though, are virtually identical to WASPs on this measure of integration in the secondary sector. The other differences between Italians and WASPs shrink in a similar fashion from generation to generation.

The first five measures of educational and occupational attainment in Exhibit 2.4 illustrate the generational pattern of integration (structural assimilation). The last comparison measures marital assimilation, or intermarriage. It displays the percentage of males of "unmixed," or 100%, Italian heritage who married females outside the Italian community. Note once more the tendency for integration, now at the primary level, to increase across the generations. The huge majority of first-generation males married within their group (only 21.9% married non-Italians). By the third generation, 67.3% of the males were marrying non-Italians.

Of course, this model of step-by-step, linear assimilation by generation fits some groups better than others. For example, immigrants from Northern and Western Europe (except for the Irish) were generally more similar, racially and culturally, to the dominant group and tended to be more educated and skilled. They experienced relatively easier acceptance and tended to complete the assimilation process in three generations or less.

In contrast, immigrants from Ireland and from Southern and Eastern Europe were mostly uneducated, unskilled peasants who were more likely to join the huge army of industrial labor that manned the factories, mines, and mills. These groups were more likely to remain at the bottom of the American class structure for generations and to have risen to middle-class prosperity only in the recent past. As mentioned earlier, Eastern European Jews formed an enclave and followed a distinctly different pathway of assimilation, using the enclave as a springboard to launch the second and third generations into the larger society (although their movements were circumscribed by widespread anti-Semitic sentiments and policies).

It is important to keep this generational pattern in mind when examining immigration to the United States today. It is common for contemporary newcomers (especially Hispanics) to be criticized for their "slow" pace of assimilation, but their "progress" takes on a new aspect when viewed in the light of the generational time frame for assimilation followed by European immigrants. Especially with modern forms of transportation, immigration can be very fast. Assimilation, on the other hand, is by nature slow.

Ethnic Succession

A second factor that shaped the assimilation experience is captured in the concept of ethnic succession, or the myriad ways in which European ethnic groups unintentionally affected one another's positions in the social class structure of the larger society. The overall pattern was that each European immigrant group tended to be pushed to higher social class levels and more favorable economic situations by the groups that arrived after them. As more experienced groups became upwardly mobile and began to move out of the neighborhoods that served as their "ports of entry," they were often replaced by a new group of immigrants who would begin the process all over again. Some neighborhoods in the cities of the Northeast served as the ethnic neighborhoods—the first safe havens in the new society—for a variety of successive groups. Some neighborhoods continue to fill this role today.

This process can be understood in terms of the second stage of Gordon's model: integration at the secondary level (see Exhibit 2.1) or entry into the public institutions and organizations of the larger society. Three pathways of integration tended to be most important for European immigrants: politics, labor unions, and the church. We will cover each in turn, illustrating with the Irish, the first immigrant laborers to arrive in large numbers, but the general patterns apply to all white ethnic groups.

Politics

The Irish tended to follow the Northern and Western Europeans in the job market and social class structure and were, in turn, followed by the wave of new immigrants. In many urban areas of the Northeast, they moved into the neighborhoods and took jobs left behind by German laborers. After a period of acculturation and adjustment, the Irish began to create their own connections with the mainstream society and improve their economic and social positions. They were replaced in their neighborhoods and at the bottom of the occupational structure by Italians, Poles, and other immigrant groups arriving after them.

As the years passed and the Irish gained more experience, they began to forge more links to the larger society, and, in particular, they allied themselves with the Democratic Party and helped construct the political machines that came to dominate many city governments in the 19th and 20th centuries. Machine politicians were often corrupt and even criminal, regularly subverting the election process, bribing city and state officials, using city budgets to fill the pockets of the political bosses and their cronies, and passing out public jobs as payoffs for favors and faithful service. Although not exactly models of good government, the political machines performed a number of valuable social services for their constituents and loyal followers. Machine politicians, such as Boss Tweed of Tammany Hall in New York City, could find jobs, provide food and clothing for the destitute, aid victims of fires and other calamities, and intervene in the criminal and civil courts.

Much of the power of urban political machines derived from their control of the city payroll. The leaders of the machines used municipal jobs and the city budget as part of a "spoils" system (as in "to the winner go the spoils") and as rewards for their supporters and allies. The faithful Irish party worker might be rewarded for service to the machine with a job in the police department (thus, the stereotypical Irish cop) or some other agency. Private businessmen might be rewarded with lucrative contracts to supply services or perform other city business.

The political machines served as engines of economic opportunity and linked Irish Americans to a central and important institution of the dominant society. Using the resources controlled by local government as a power base, the Irish (and other immigrant groups after them) began to integrate themselves into the larger society and carve out a place in the mainstream structures of American society, as illustrated in the following Narrative Portrait.

Labor Unions

The labor movement provided a second link between the Irish, other European immigrant groups, and the larger society. Although virtually all white ethnic groups had a hand in the creation and eventual success of the movement, many of the founders and early leaders were Irish. For example, Terence Powderly, an Irish Catholic, founded one of the first U.S. labor unions, and in the early years of the 20th century, about one third of union leaders were Irish, and more than 50 national unions had Irish presidents (Bodnar, 1985, p. 111; Brody, 1980, p. 615).

As the labor movement grew in strength and gradually acquired legitimacy, the leaders of the movement also gained status, power, and other resources, while the rank-and-file membership gained job security, increased wages, and better fringe benefits. The labor movement provided another channel through which resources, power, status, and jobs flowed to the white ethnic groups.

Because of the way in which jobs were organized in industrializing America, union work typically required communication and cooperation across ethnic lines. The American workforce at the turn of the 20th century was multiethnic and multilingual, and union leaders had to coordinate and mobilize the efforts of many different language and cultural groups to represent the interest of the workers as a social class. Thus, labor union leaders became important intermediaries between the larger society and European immigrant groups.

Ethnicity, Prejudice, and the Irish Political Machine

David Gray grew up a Welsh Protestant in the city of Scranton, Pennsylvania, during the 1930s and 1940s. At that time, this coal-mining town was split along ethnic lines, and Gray (1991) recounts in this memoir his gradual socialization into the realities of in-groups and out-groups. He also describes how Scranton's Irish Catholic community responded to the Great Depression of the 1930s and how they used the local political machine to protect their own. Gray reflects on the consequences of these experiences for his own personal prejudices and sense of social distance.

Gray eventually left Scranton and earned a PhD in sociology. He became a college professor and an accomplished and respected sociologist. Among his many admiring students was the author of this textbook, who grew up in Scranton's Irish Catholic community a generation after Gray.

SHADOW OF THE PAST

DAVID GRAY

C. Wright Mills (an American sociologist) [stressed] the intimate relationship of "history, social structure, and biography." Though he did not say so directly, the logic of Mills's position would surely indicate that, for self-knowledge, no biography is more important than one's own. Born within a social context not of our own making, subject to social forces we did not create, in retrospect, we attempt to understand. . . .

Personally, then, I did not ask to be born Welsh Protestant in Scranton, Pennsylvania. No more than Eddie Gilroy, with whom I attended . . . school, asked to be born Irish Catholic. But there we both were in the heart of the anthracite coal region . . . during the years of the Great Depression. . . . We were friends, good friends. During recess and after 3:00 p.m., he played second base and I played shortstop in the shrunken, dirt diamond in the schoolyard. . . . We thought we made a good double-play combination, and, beyond the baseball field, we respected and liked each other as well.

But, there was something wrong with Eddie Gilroy. At age 10 I didn't know exactly what it was. He didn't make many errors and we often shared whatever pennies we had . . . at the corner candy store. Still, there was something wrong with him—vague, general, apart from real experience, but true all the same.

His fundamental defect came into sharper focus at the age of 12. Sunday movies had just arrived in Scranton and . . . I wanted to go with Eddie and Johnny Pesavento [but] I couldn't.

"Why?"

"Because Protestants don't go to the movies on Sunday—nor play cards, football, or baseball."

"How come Eddie and Johnny can go?"

"They're Catholic."

No one quite used the word "immoral" but . . . anyone who attended Sunday movies was certainly close to sinful. And the implication was clear: If Catholics did such bad things on Sunday, they surely did a lot of bad things on other days as well.

No matter, then, that Gilroy might sacrifice for even a Protestant runner to go to second, or let you borrow his glove, or share his candy. . . . His Catholicism permeated his being, . . . muting his individual qualities. Eddie wasn't the point, his Catholicism was.

[The] deeply held beliefs . . . of the adult world were visited upon the young. Most often subtly . . . but persistently and effectively, little Welsh Protestant boys and girls learned that Catholics were somehow the enemy. . . .

Unfortunately, from their vantage point, the Welsh of Scranton were not the only ones in town. While they had come to the coal regions in large numbers, others, in even larger numbers, had come also. Irish, Italian, Polish, German, many from Eastern European countries, fewer who were Jewish—all constituted Scranton's ethnic portion of broader 19th-century immigrant waves. With [some] obvious exceptions, most were Catholic.

In this communal setting—a very ethnically and religiously distinct one—the Great Depression arrived with particular force. [The region suffered from massive unemployment and began to lose population as people left in search of work elsewhere.] The coal industry, upon which the economy of Northeastern Pennsylvania essentially rested, was gone. The private sector, initially hard-hit, did not recover [until after the 1960s]. The public sector consequently became the primary possibility for often meager, by no means high-paying jobs.

And the Irish, their political talents augmented by the fact that they were the largest single ethnic group in town, controlled political power. Allied with others of Catholic faith, the Irish did their best to take care of their religiously affiliated, politically important, own.

In Scranton's political life, the intimate relationship of religion, politics, and economics was clear for all to see. The mayor was Jimmy Hanlon, . . . the political boss, Mickey Lawlor, . . . McNulty ran the post office, and Judge Hoban the courts. From the mayor's office to trash collectors, with policemen, foremen, school teachers, truant officers, and dog catchers in between, the public payroll included the names of O'Neill, Hennigan, Lydon, Kennedy, Walsh, Gerrity, and O'Hoolihan. As the depression persisted, Welsh Protestants came to know (with reason but also as an act of faith) that Lewis, Griffiths, and Williams need not apply.

Pale shades of contemporary Northern Ireland, but with political power reversed. No shots were fired, perhaps because American democratic traditions compel accommodation and compromise. Nonetheless, among the Welsh, the general feeling of resentment on more than one occasion was punctuated with: "Those goddam Irish Catholics."

Whatever may have been true in pre-depression years, however tolerant or intolerant individuals may have been, . . . that Welsh sentiment was not at all limited to individuals guilty of irrational prejudice. It was communally shared. Jobs, homes, and lives were at stake, and religious affiliation was relevant to them all. Irish Catholic political power was a fact from which Welsh Protestant resentment followed. Prejudice there certainly was— deeply felt, poignantly articulated, subjectively often going beyond what facts would justify and, unfortunately, communicated to the young. . . .

The public sector was vulnerable to Irish Catholic control. The Welsh knew that. The private sector (banks, small businesses) simultaneously retained a diminished but tightened, now more consciously Protestant, ownership and/or control. Though the musically inclined Welsh never composed it, their regional battle hymn surely was: If Irish politicians were using their political power to control what they could, it was essential for Protestants to protect what they privately had.

SOURCE: Gray (1991).

Photo 2.11

Labor unions sometimes mixed ethnic groups. Note that the signs of these strikers are in Hebrew as well as English.

© Corbis.

Women were also heavily involved in the labor movement. Immigrant women were among the most exploited segments of the labor force, and they were involved in some of the most significant events in American labor history. For example, one of the first victories of the union movement occurred in New York City in 1909. The Uprising of the 20,000 was a massive strike of mostly Jewish and Italian women (many in their teens) against the garment industry. The strike lasted 4 months despite attacks by thugs hired by the bosses and abuses by the police and the courts. The strikers eventually won recognition of the union from many employers, a reversal of a wage decrease, and a reduction in the 56- to 59-hour week they were expected to work (Goren, 1980, p. 584).

One of the great tragedies in the history of labor relations in the United States also involved European immigrant women. In 1911, a fire swept through the Triangle Shirtwaist Company, a garment industry shop located on the 10th floor of a building in New York City. The fire spread rapidly, and the few escape routes were quickly cut off. About 140 young immigrant girls died, and many chose to leap to their deaths rather than be consumed by the flames. The disaster outraged the public, and the funerals of the victims were attended by more than a quarter of a million people. The incident fueled a drive for reform and improvement of work conditions and safety regulations (Amott & Matthaei, 1991, pp. 114–116; see also Schoener, 1967).

European immigrant women also filled leadership roles in the labor movement and served as presidents and in other offices, although usually in female-dominated unions. One of the most colorful union activists was Mother Jones, an Irish immigrant who worked tirelessly to organize miners:

Until she was nearly 100 years old, Mother Jones was where the danger was greatest—crossing militia lines, spending weeks in damp prisons, incurring the wrath of governors, presidents, and coal operators—she helped to organize the United Mine Workers with the only tools she felt she needed: "convictions and a voice." (Forner, 1980, p. 281)

Women workers often faced opposition from men as well as from employers. The major unions were not only racially discriminatory but also hostile to organizing women. For example, women laundry workers in San Francisco at the start of the 20th century were required to live in dormitories and work from 6 a.m. until midnight. When they applied to the international laundry workers union for a charter, they were blocked by the male members. They eventually went on strike and won the right to an 8-hour workday in 1912 (Amott & Matthaei, 1991, p. 117).

Religion

A third avenue of mobility for the Irish and other white ethnic groups was provided by religious institutions. The Irish were the first large group of Catholic immigrants and were, thus, in a favorable position to eventually dominate the church's administrative structure. The Catholic priesthood became largely Irish, and as they were promoted through the hierarchy, these priests became bishops and cardinals. The Catholic faith was practiced in different ways in different nations. As other Catholic immigrant groups began to arrive, conflict within the Irish-dominated church increased. Both Italian and Polish Catholic immigrants demanded their own parishes in which they could speak their own languages and celebrate their own customs and festivals. Dissatisfaction was so intense that some Polish Catholics broke with Rome and formed a separate Polish National Catholic Church (Lopata, 1976, p. 49).

The other Catholic immigrant groups eventually began to supply priests and other religious functionaries and to occupy leadership positions within the church. Although the church continued to be disproportionately influenced by the Irish, other white ethnic groups also used the Catholic Church as part of their power base for gaining acceptance and integration into the larger society.

Other Pathways

Besides party politics, the union movement, and religion, European immigrant groups forged other not-so-legitimate pathways of upward mobility. One alternative to legitimate success was offered by crime, a pathway that has been used by every ethnic group to some extent. Crime became particularly lucrative and attractive when Prohibition, the attempt to eliminate all alcohol use in the United States, went into effect in the 1920s. The criminalization of liquor failed to lower the demand, and Prohibition created a golden economic opportunity for those willing to take the risks involved in manufacturing and supplying alcohol to the American public.

Italian Americans headed many of the criminal organizations that took advantage of Prohibition. Criminal leaders and organizations with roots in Sicily, a region with a long history of secret antiestablishment societies, were especially important (Alba, 1985, pp. 62–64). The connection between organized crime, Prohibition, and Italian Americans is well-known, but it is not so widely recognized that ethnic succession operated in organized crime as it did in the legitimate opportunity structures. The Irish and Germans had been involved in organized crime for decades before the 1920s, and the Italians competed with these established gangsters and with Jewish crime syndicates for control of bootlegging and other criminal enterprises. The pattern of ethnic succession continued after the repeal of Prohibition, and members of groups newer to urban areas, including African Americans, Jamaicans, and Hispanic Americans, have recently challenged the Italian-dominated criminal "families."

Photo 2.12

The labor movement relied on women as well as men for its success. One of the most colorful labor leaders was Mother Jones, a tireless organizer of miners. Among the many quotable passages in her autobiography is this: "My address is like my shoes: it travels with me. I abide where there is a fight against wrong."

From Library of Congress.

Ethnic succession can also be observed in the institution of sports. Since the beginning of the 20th century, sports have offered a pathway to success and affluence that has attracted countless millions of young men. Success in many sports requires little in the way of formal credentials, education, or English fluency, and sports have been particularly appealing to the young men in minority groups that have few resources or opportunities.

For example, at the turn of the century, the Irish dominated the sport of boxing, but boxers from the Italian American community and other new immigrant groups eventually replaced them. Each successive wave of boxers reflected the concentration of a particular ethnic group at the bottom of the class structure. The succession of minority groups continues to this day, with boxing now dominated by African American and Latino fighters (Rader, 1983, pp. 87–106). A similar progression, or "layering," of ethnic and racial groups can be observed in other sports and in the entertainment industry.

The institutions of American society, both legitimate and illegal, reflect the relative positions of minority groups at a particular moment in time. Just a few generations ago, European immigrant groups dominated both crime and sports because they were blocked from legitimate opportunities. Now, the racial minority groups still excluded from the mainstream job market and mired in urban poverty are supplying disproportionate numbers of young people to these alternative opportunity structures.

Continuing Industrialization and Structural Mobility

We have already mentioned that dominant-minority relations tend to change along with changes in subsistence technology, and we can find an example of this relationship in the history of the European immigrant groups across the 20th century. Industrialization is a continuous process, and as it proceeded, the nature of work in America evolved and changed and created opportunities for upward mobility for the white ethnic groups. One important form of upward mobility throughout the 20th century, called structural mobility, resulted more from changes in the structure of the economy and the labor market than from any individual effort or desire to "get ahead."

Structural mobility is the result of the continuing mechanization and automation of the workplace. As machines replaced people in the workforce, the supply of manual, blue-collar jobs that had provided employment for so many first- and second-generation European immigrant laborers dwindled. At the same time, the supply of white-collar jobs increased, but access to the better jobs depended heavily on educational credentials. For white ethnic groups, a high school education became much more available in the 1930s, and college and university programs began to expand rapidly in the late 1940s, spurred in large part by the educational benefits made available to World War II veterans. Each generation of white ethnics, especially those born after 1925, was significantly more educated than the previous generation, and many were able to translate their increased human capital into upward mobility in the mainstream job market (Morawska, 1990, pp. 212–213).

The descendants of European immigrants became upwardly mobile not only because of their ambitions and efforts but also because of the changing location of jobs and the progressively greater opportunities for education available to them. Of course, the pace and timing of this upward movement was highly variable from group to group and place to place. Ethnic succession continued to operate, and the descendants of the most recent immigrants from Europe (Italians and Poles, for example) tended to be the last to benefit from the general upgrading in education and the job market. Still, structural mobility is one of the keys to the eventual successful integration of all white ethnic groups that is displayed in Exhibits 2.6 and 2.7 (later in this chapter). During these same years, the racial minority groups, particularly African Americans, were excluded from the dominant group's educational system and from the opportunity to compete for better jobs.

VARIATIONS IN ASSIMILATION

In the previous section, we discussed patterns that were common to European immigrants and their descendants. Now we address some of the sources of variation and diversity in assimilation, a complex process that is never exactly the same for any two groups. Sociologists have paid particular attention to the way that degree of similarity, religion, social class, and gender shaped the overall assimilation of the descendants of the mass European immigration. They have also investigated the way in which immigrants' reasons for coming to this country have affected the experiences of different groups.

Degree of Similarity

Since the dominant group consisted largely of Protestants with ethnic origins in Northern and Western Europe and especially in England, it is not surprising to learn that the degree of resistance, prejudice, and discrimination encountered by the different European immigrant groups varied in part by the degree to which they differed from these dominant groups. The most significant differences related to religion, language, cultural values, and, for some groups, physical characteristics. Thus, Protestant immigrants from Northern and Western Europe experienced less resistance than the English-speaking Catholic Irish, who in turn were accepted more readily than the new immigrants, who were both non–English speaking and overwhelmingly non-Protestant.

The preferences of the dominant group correspond roughly to the arrival times of the immigrants. The most similar groups immigrated earliest, and the least similar tended to be the last to arrive. Because of this coincidence, resistance to any one group of immigrants tended to fade as new groups arrived. For example, anti-German prejudice and discrimination never became particularly vicious or widespread (except during the heat of the World Wars), because the Irish began arriving in large numbers at about the same time. Concerns about the German immigrants were swamped by the fear that the Catholic Irish could never be assimilated. Then, as the 19th century drew to a close, immigrants from Southern and Eastern Europe—even more different from the dominant group—began to arrive and made concerns about the Irish seem trivial.

In addition, the New Immigration was far more voluminous than the Old Immigration (see Exhibit 2.3). Southern and Eastern Europeans arrived in record numbers in the early 20th century, and the sheer volume of the immigration raised fears that American cities and institutions would be swamped by hordes of what were seen as racially inferior, unassimilable immigrants (a fear with strong echoes in the present).

Thus, a preference hierarchy was formed in American culture that privileged Northern and Western Europeans over Southern and Eastern Europeans and Protestants over Catholics and Jews. These rankings reflect the ease with which the groups have been assimilated and made their way into the larger society. This hierarchy of ethnic preference is still a part of American prejudice, as we shall see in Chapter 3, although it is much more muted today than in the heyday of immigration.

Religion

A major differentiating factor in the experiences of the European immigrant groups, recognized by Gordon and other students of American assimilation, was religion. Protestant, Catholic, and Jewish immigrants lived in different neighborhoods, occupied different niches in the workforce, formed separate networks of affiliation and groups, and chose their marriage partners from different pools of people.

One important study that documented the importance of religion for European immigrants and their descendants (and also reinforced the importance of generations) was conducted by sociologist Ruby Jo Kennedy (1944). She studied intermarriage patterns in New Haven, Connecticut, over a 70-year period ending in the 1940s and found that the immigrant generation chose marriage partners from a pool whose boundaries were marked by ethnicity and religion. For example, Irish Catholics married other Irish Catholics, Italian Catholics married Italian Catholics, Irish Protestants married Irish Protestants, and so forth across all the ethnic and religious divisions she studied.

The pool of marriage partners for the children and grandchildren of the immigrants continued to be bounded by religion but not so much by ethnicity. Thus, later generations of Irish Catholics continued to marry other Catholics but were less likely to marry other Irish. As assimilation proceeded, ethnic group boundaries faded (or "melted"), but religious boundaries did not. Kennedy described this phenomenon as a triple melting pot: a pattern of structural assimilation within each of the three religious denominations (Kennedy, 1944, 1952).

Will Herberg (1960), another important student of American assimilation, also explored the connection between religion and ethnicity. Writing in the 1950s, he noted that the pressures of acculturation did not affect all aspects of ethnicity equally. European immigrants and their descendants were strongly encouraged to learn English, but they were not so pressured to change their religious beliefs. Very often, their religious faith was the strongest connection between later generations and their immigrant ancestors. The American tradition of religious tolerance allowed the descendants of the European immigrants to preserve this tie to their roots without being seen as "un-American." As a result, the Protestant, Catholic, and Jewish faiths eventually came to occupy roughly equal degrees of legitimacy in American society.

Thus, for the descendants of the European immigrants, religion became a vehicle through which their ethnicity could be expressed. For many members of this group, religion and ethnicity were fused, and ethnic traditions and identities came to have a religious expression. For example, Mary Ann O'Brien, the Irish American schoolteacher introduced in Chapter 1, attends Mass partly as a family matter and partly as a religious devotion. She does not know much about the Irish culture of her immigrant ancestors or about the adjustments and changes they had to make to survive in the United States. What she does know is that they were Catholic and that by observing the rituals of the church in the present, she is honoring her connections to the past. It is not just that she is Irish-Catholic-American but that—for her and millions of others—being Catholic is part of being Irish in America.

Social Class

Social class is a central feature of social structure, and it is not surprising that it affected the European immigrant groups in a number of ways. First, social class combined with religion to shape the social world of the descendants of the European immigrants. In fact, Gordon (1964) concluded that U.S. society in the 1960s actually incorporated not three, but four melting pots (one for each of the major ethnic/religious groups and one for black Americans), each of which were internally subdivided by social class. In his view, the most significant structural unit within American society was the ethclass, defined by the intersection of the religious, ethnic, and social class boundaries (e.g., working-class Catholic, upper-class Protestant, etc.). Thus, people were not "simply American," but tended to identify with, associate with, and choose their spouses from within their ethclasses.

Second, social class affected structural integration. The huge majority of the post-1880s European immigrants were working class, and because they "entered U.S. society at the bottom of the economic ladder, and . . . stayed close to that level for the next half century, ethnic history has been essentially working class history" (Morawska, 1990, p. 215; see also Bodnar, 1985). For generations, many groups of Eastern and Southern European immigrants did not acculturate to middle-class American culture, but to an urban working-class, blue-collar set of lifestyles and values. Even today, ethnicity for many groups remains interconnected with social class factors, and a familiar stereotype of white ethnicity is the hard-hat construction worker.

Gender

Anyone who wants to learn about the experience of immigration will find a huge body of literature incorporating every imaginable discipline and genre. The great bulk of this material, however, concerns the immigrant experience in general or focuses specifically on male immigrants. The experiences of female immigrants have been much less recorded and, hence, far less accessible. Many immigrant women came from cultures with strong patriarchal traditions, and they had much less access to leadership roles, education, and prestigious, high-paying occupations. As is the case with women of virtually all minority groups, the voices of immigrant women have been muted. The research that has been done, however, documents that immigrant women played multiple roles both during immigration and during the assimilation process. As would be expected in patriarchal societies, the roles of wife and mother were central, but immigrant women were involved in myriad other activities as well.

In general, male immigrants tended to precede women, and it was common for the males to send for the women only after they had secured lodging, jobs, and a certain level of stability. However, women immigrants' experiences were quite varied, often depending on the economic situation and cultural traditions of their home societies. In some cases, women were not only prominent among the "first wave" of immigrants but also began the process of acculturation and integration. During the 19th century, for example, a high percentage of Irish immigrants were young single women. They came to America seeking jobs and often wound up employed in domestic work, a role that permitted them to live "respectably" in a family setting. In 1850, about 75% of all employed Irish immigrant women in New York City worked as servants, and the rest were employed in textile mills and factories. As late as 1920, 81% of employed Irish-born women in the United States worked as domestics. Factory work was the second most prevalent form of employment (Blessing, 1980; see also Steinberg, 1981).

Because the economic situation of immigrant families was typically precarious, it was common for women to be involved in wage labor. The type and location of the work varied from group to group. Whereas Irish women were concentrated in domestic work and factories and mills, this was rare for Italian women. Italian culture had strong norms of patriarchy, and "one of the culture's strongest prohibitions was directed against contact between women and male strangers" (Alba, 1985, p. 53). Thus, acceptable work situations for Italian women were likely to involve tasks that could be done at home: doing laundry, taking in boarders, and doing piecework for the garment industry. Italian women who worked outside the home were likely to find themselves in single-sex settings among other immigrant women. Thus, women immigrants from Italy tended to be far less acculturated and integrated than those from Ireland.

Eastern European Jewish women represent a third pattern of assimilation. They were refugees from religious persecution, and most came with their husbands and children in intact family units. According to Steinberg (1981), "Few were independent bread-winners, and when they did work, they usually found employment in the . . . garment industry. Often they worked in small shops as family members" (p. 161).

Generally, immigrant women, like working-class women in general, were expected to work until they married, after which time it was expected that their husbands would support them and their children. In many cases, however, immigrant men could not earn enough to support their families, and their wives and children were required by necessity to contribute to the family budget. Immigrant wives sometimes continued to work outside the home, or they found other ways to make money. They took in boarders, did laundry or sewing, tended gardens, and were involved in myriad other activities that permitted them to contribute to the family budget and still stay home and attend to family and child-rearing responsibilities. A 1911 report on Southern and Eastern European households found that about half kept lodgers and that the income from this activity amounted to about 25% of the husbands' wages. Children also contributed to the family income by taking after-school and summertime jobs (Morawska, 1990, pp. 211–212). Compared with the men, immigrant women were more closely connected to home and family, less likely to learn to read or speak English or otherwise acculturate, and significantly more influential in preserving the heritage of their groups.

When they sought employment outside the home, they found opportunities in the industrial sector and in clerical and sales work, occupations that were quickly stereotyped as "women's work." Women were seen as working only to supplement the family treasury, and this assumption was used to justify a lower wage scale. Evans (1989) reports that in the late 1800s, "whether in factories, offices, or private homes . . . women's wages were about half of those of men" (p. 135).

Sojourners

Some versions of the traditional perspective and the "taken-for-granted" views of many Americans assume that assimilation is desirable and therefore desired. However, immigrant groups from Europe were highly variable in their interest in Americanization, a factor that greatly shaped their experiences.

Some groups were very committed to Americanization. Eastern European Jews, for example, came to America because of religious persecution and planned to make America their home from the beginning. They left their homeland in fear for their lives and had no plans and no possibility of returning. They intended to stay, for they had nowhere else to go. (The nation of Israel was not founded until 1948.) These immigrants committed themselves to learning English, becoming citizens, and familiarizing themselves with their new society as quickly as possible.

Other immigrants had no intention of becoming American citizens and, therefore, had little interest in Americanization. These sojourners, or "birds of passage," were oriented to the old country and intended to return once they had accumulated enough capital to be successful in their home villages or provinces. Because immigration records are not very detailed, it is difficult to assess the exact numbers of immigrants who returned to the old country (see Wyman, 1993). We do know, for example, that a large percentage of Italian immigrants were sojourners. It is estimated that although 3.8 million Italians landed in the United States between 1899 and 1924, around 2.1 million departed during the same interval (Nelli, 1980, p. 547).

THE DESCENDANTS OF THE IMMIGRANTS TODAY

Geographical Distribution

Exhibit 2.5 shows the geographical distribution of 15 racial and ethnic groups across the United States. The map displays the single largest group in each county. There is a lot of detail in the map, but for our purposes, we will focus on some of the groups mentioned in this chapter, including Norwegian, German, Irish, and Italian Americans (the Jewish population is too small to appear on this map).

First of all, the single largest ancestry group is German American, and this is reflected on the map in Exhibit 2.5 by the predominance of light blue from Pennsylvania to California. Note also how the map reflects the original settlement areas for this group, especially in the Midwest. Likewise, Norwegian Americans (light green) are numerically dominant in some

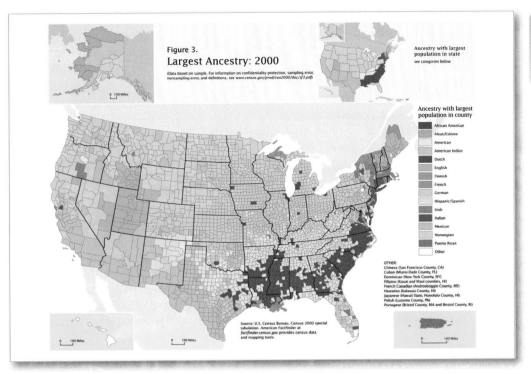

Figure 3.
Largest Ancestry: 2000

(Data based on sample. For information on confidentiality protection, sampling error, nonsampling error, and definitions, see www.census.gov/prod/cen2000/doc/sf3.pdf.)

Ancestry with largest
population in state
see categories below

Ancestry with largest
population in county

African American
Aleut/Eskimo
American
American Indian
Dutch
English
Finnish
French
German
Hispanic/Spanish
Irish
Italian
Mexican
Norwegian
Puerto Rican
Other

OTHER:
Chinese (San Francisco County, CA)
Cuban (Miami-Dade County, FL)
Dominican (New York County, NY)
Filipino (Kauai and Maui counties, HI)
French Canadian (Androscoggin County, ME)
Hawaiian (Kalawao County, HI)
Japanese (Hawaii State; Honolulu County, HI)
Polish (Luzerne County, PA)
Portuguese (Bristol County, MA and Bristol County, RI)

Source: U.S. Census Bureau, Census 2000 special
tabulation. American Factfinder at
factfinder.census.gov provides census data
and mapping tools.

Exhibit 2.5 Ancestry
With Largest Population
in Each County, 2000

SOURCE: Brittingham and de la Cruz (2004).

sections of the upper Midwest (e.g., Northwestern Minnesota and northern North Dakota), along with Finnish Americans (green), another Scandinavian group. Irish Americans (dark purple) and Italian Americans (dark blue) are also concentrated in their original areas of settlement, with the Irish in Massachusetts and Italians more concentrated around New York City.

Thus, almost a century after the end of mass immigration from Europe, many of the descendants of the immigrants have not wandered far from their ancestral locales. Of course, the map shows that the same point could be made for other groups, including blacks (concentrated in the "black belt" across the states of the old Confederacy), Mexican Americans (concentrated along the southern border from Texas to California), and Native Americans (their concentration in the upper Midwest, eastern Oklahoma, and the Southwest reflects the locations of the reservations into which they were forced after the end of the Indian wars).

Given all that has changed in American society over the past century—industrialization, population growth, urbanization, and massive mobility—the stable location of white ethnics (and other ethnic and racial groups) seems remarkable. Why aren't people distributed more randomly across the nation's landscape?

The stability is somewhat easier to explain for some groups. African Americans, Mexican Americans, and American Indians have been limited in their geographic as well as their social mobility by institutionalized discrimination, racism, and limited resources. We will examine the power of these constraints in detail in later chapters.

For white ethnics, on the other hand, the power of exclusion and rejection waned as the generations passed and the descendants of the immigrants assimilated and integrated. Their current locations are perhaps more a reflection of the idea (introduced in Chapter 1) that the United States is a nation of groups as well as individuals. Our group memberships, especially family and kin, exert a powerful influence on our decisions about where to live and work and, despite the transience and mobility of modern American life, can keep people connected to their relatives, the old neighborhood, their ethnic roots, and the sites of their ancestors' struggles.

Integration and Equality

Perhaps the most important point, for our purposes, about white ethnic groups (the descendants of the European immigrants) is that they are today on the verge of being completely assimilated. Even the groups that were the most despised and rejected in earlier years are acculturated, integrated, and thoroughly intermarried.

To illustrate this point, consider Exhibits 2.6 and 2.7, which illustrate the degree to which a variety of white ethnic groups had been integrated as long ago as 1990. The exhibits display data for 9 of the more than 60 white ethnic groups that people mentioned when asked to define their ancestries. The groups include the two largest white ethnic groups (German and Irish Americans) and seven more chosen to represent a range of geographic regions of origin and times of immigration (U.S. Bureau of the Census, 2008a).

The graphs show that by 1990, all 9 of the groups selected were at or above national norms ("all persons") for all measures of equality. There is some variation among the groups, of course, but Exhibit 2.6 shows that all exceeded the national averages for both high school and college education. Exhibit 2.7 shows that all 9 groups had dramatically lower poverty rates (see the line in the graph and refer to the right-hand axis for values), usually less than half the national average. The bars in Exhibit 2.7 show median household income (refer to the left-hand axis for values). All 9 groups exceed the national average, some—Russians, for example, many of whom are Jewish—by a considerable margin.

In other areas, the evidence for assimilation and equality is also persuasive. For example, the distinct ethnic neighborhoods that these groups created in American cities (Little Italy, Greektown, Little Warsaw, etc.) have faded away or been taken over by other groups, and the rate of intermarriage between members of different white ethnic groups is quite high. For example, based on data from the 1990 Census, about 56% of all married whites have spouses whose ethnic backgrounds do not match their own (Alba, 1995, pp. 13–14).

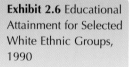

Exhibit 2.6 Educational Attainment for Selected White Ethnic Groups, 1990

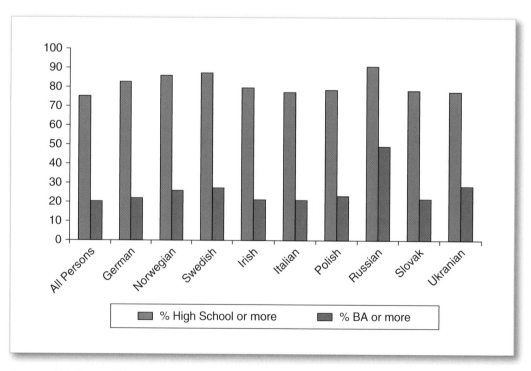

SOURCE: U.S. Bureau of the Census (2008a).

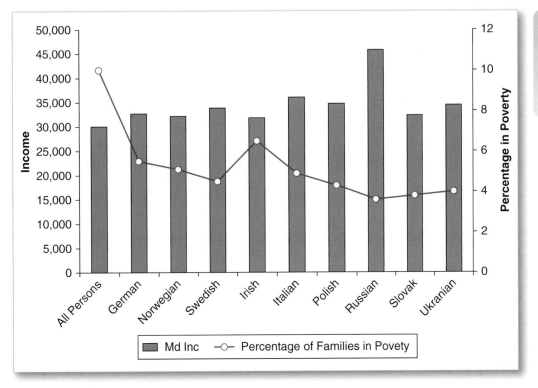

Exhibit 2.7 Median Household Income and Percentage of Families Living in Poverty for Selected White Ethnic Groups, 1990

SOURCE: U.S. Bureau of the Census (2008a).

The Evolution of White Ethnicity

Absorption into the American mainstream was neither linear nor continuous for the descendants of European immigrants. Over the generations, white ethnic identity sporadically reasserted itself in many ways, two of which are especially notable. First, there was a tendency for later generations to be more interested in their ancestry and ethnicity than were earlier generations. Marcus Hansen (1952) captured this phenomenon in his principle of third-generation interest: "What the second generation tries to forget, the third generation tries to remember" (p. 495). Hansen observed that the children of immigrants tended to minimize or de-emphasize ("forget") their ethnicity to avoid the prejudice and intolerance of the larger society and compete on more favorable terms for jobs and other opportunities. As they became adults and started families of their own, the second generation tended to raise their children in nonethnic settings, with English as their first and only language.

By the time the third generation reached adulthood, especially the "new" immigrant groups that arrived last, the larger society had become more tolerant of white ethnicity and diversity, and having little to risk, the third generation tried to reconnect with its grandparents and roots. These descendants wanted to remember their ethnic heritage and understand it as part of their personal identities, their sense of who they were and where they belonged in the larger society. Thus, interest in the "old ways" and the strength of the identification with the ancestral group was often stronger in the more Americanized third generation than in the more ethnic second. Ironically, of course, the grandchildren of the immigrants could not recover much of the richness and detail of their heritage because their parents had spent their lives trying to forget it. Nonetheless, the desire of the third generation to reconnect with its ancestry and recover its ethnicity shows that assimilation is not a simple, one-dimensional, or linear process. This process of ethnic recovery in later generations is illustrated in the biography of Mary Ann, the Irish Catholic introduced in Chapter 1, who attends Mass in part because she feels that the rituals connect her with her ancestors.

In addition to this generational pattern, the strength of white ethnic identity also responded to the changing context of American society and the activities of other groups. For example, in the late 1960s and early 1970s, there was a notable increase in the visibility of and interest in white ethnic heritage, an upsurge often referred to as the ethnic revival. The revival manifested itself in a variety of ways. Some people became more interested in their families' genealogical roots, and others increased their participation in ethnic festivals, traditions, and organizations. The "white ethnic vote" became a factor in local, state, and national politics, and appearances at the churches, meeting halls, and neighborhoods associated with white ethnic groups became almost mandatory for candidates for office. Demonstrations and festivals celebrating white ethnic heritages were organized, and buttons and bumper stickers proclaiming the ancestry of everyone from Irish to Italians were widely displayed. The revival was also endorsed by politicians, editorialists, and intellectuals (e.g., see Novak, 1973), reinforcing the movement and giving it additional legitimacy.

The ethnic revival may have been partly fueled, à la Hansen's principle, by the desire to reconnect with ancestral roots, even though most groups were well beyond their third generations by the 1960s. More likely, the revival was a reaction to the increase in pluralistic sentiment in society in general and the pluralistic, even separatist assertions of other groups. In the 1960s and 1970s, virtually every minority group generated a protest movement (Black Power, Red Power, Chicanismo, etc.) and proclaimed a recommitment to its own heritage and to the authenticity of its own culture and experience. The visibility of these movements for cultural pluralism among racial minority groups helped make it more acceptable for European Americans to express their own ethnicity and heritage.

Besides the general tenor of the times, the resurgence of white ethnicity had some political and economic dimensions that bring us back to issues of inequality and competition for resources. In the 1960s, a white ethnic urban working class made up largely of Irish and Southern and Eastern European groups still remained in the neighborhoods of the industrial Northeast and Midwest and still continued to breathe life into the old networks and traditions (see Glazer & Moynihan, 1970; Greeley, 1974). At the same time that cultural pluralism was coming to be seen as more legitimate, this ethnic working class was feeling increasingly threatened by minority groups of color. In the industrial cities, it was not unusual for white ethnic neighborhoods to adjoin black and Hispanic neighborhoods, putting these groups in direct competition for housing, jobs, and other resources.

Many members of the white ethnic working class saw racial minority groups as inferior and perceived the advances being made by these groups as unfair, unjust, and threatening. They also reacted to what they saw as special treatment and attention being accorded on the basis of race, such as school busing and affirmative action. They had problems of their own (the declining number of good, unionized jobs; inadequate schooling; and deteriorating city services) and felt that their problems were being given lower priority and less legitimacy because they were white. The revived sense of ethnicity in the urban working-class neighborhoods was in large part a way of resisting racial reform and expressing resentment for the racial minority groups. Thus, among its many other causes and forms, the revival of white ethnicity that began in the 1960s was fueled by competition for resources and opportunities. As we will see throughout this text, such competition commonly leads to increased prejudice and a heightened sense of cohesion among group members.

The Twilight of White Ethnicity?[1]

As the conflicts of the 1960s and 1970s faded and white ethnic groups continued to leave the old neighborhoods and rise in the class structure, the strength of white ethnic identity resumed its slow demise. Today, several more generations removed from the tumultuous 1960s, white ethnic identity has become increasingly nebulous and largely voluntary. It is

Photo 2.13

Will traditions such as Irish step dancing survive across the generations?

© Destinations/Corbis.

often described as symbolic ethnicity or as an aspect of self-identity that symbolizes one's roots in the "old country" but otherwise is minor. The descendants of the European immigrants feel vaguely connected to their ancestors, but this part of their identities does not affect their lifestyles, circles of friends and neighbors, job prospects, eating habits, or other everyday routines (Gans, 1979; Lieberson & Waters, 1988). For the descendants of the European immigrants today, ethnicity is an increasingly minor part of their identities that is expressed only occasionally or sporadically. For example, they might join in ethnic or religious festivals (e.g., St. Patrick's Day for Irish Americans, Columbus Day for Italian Americans), but these activities are seasonal or otherwise peripheral to their lives and self-images. The descendants of the European immigrants have choices, in stark contrast with their ancestors, members of racial minority groups, and recent immigrants: They can stress their ethnicity, ignore it completely, or maintain any degree of ethnic identity they choose. Many people have ancestors in more than one ethnic group and may change their sense of affiliation over time, sometimes emphasizing one group's traditions and sometimes another's (Waters, 1990).

In fact, white ethnic identity has become so ephemeral that it may be on the verge of disappearing altogether. For example, based on a series of in-depth interviews with white Americans from various regions of the nation, Gallagher (2001) found a sense of ethnicity so weak that it did not even rise to the level of "symbolic." His respondents were the products of ancestral lines so thoroughly intermixed and intermarried that any trace of a unique heritage from a particular group was completely lost. They had virtually no knowledge of the experiences of their immigrant ancestors or of the life and cultures of the ethnic communities they had inhabited, and for many, their ethnic ancestries were no more meaningful to them than their states of birth. Their lack of interest in and information about their ethnic heritage was so complete that it led Gallagher to propose an addendum to Hansen's principle: "What the grandson wished to remember, the great-granddaughter has never been told."

At the same time that more specific white ethnic identities are disappearing, they are also evolving into new shapes and forms. In the view of many analysts, a new identity is developing that merges the various "hyphenated" ethnic identities (German American, Polish American, etc.) into a single, generalized "European American" identity based on race and a common history of immigration and assimilation. This new identity reinforces the racial lines of separation that run through contemporary society, but it does more than simply mark group boundaries. Embedded in this emerging identity is an understanding, often deeply flawed, of how the white immigrant groups succeeded and assimilated in the past and a view, often deeply ideological, of how the racial minority groups should behave in the present. These understandings are encapsulated in "immigrant tales": legends that stress heroic individual effort and grim determination as key ingredients leading to success in the old days. These tales feature impoverished, victimized immigrant ancestors who survived and made a place for themselves and their children by working hard, saving their money, and otherwise exemplifying the virtues of the Protestant Ethic and American individualism. They stress the idea that past generations became successful despite the brutal hostility of the dominant group and with no government intervention, and they equate the historical difficulties faced by immigrants from Europe with those suffered by racial minority groups (slavery, segregation, attempted genocide, etc.). They strongly imply—and sometimes blatantly assert—that the latter groups could succeed in America by simply following the example set by the former (Alba, 1990; Gallagher, 2001).

These accounts mix versions of human capital theory and traditional views of assimilation with prejudice and racism. Without denying or trivializing the resolve and fortitude of European immigrants, equating their experiences and levels of disadvantage with those of African Americans, American Indians, and Mexican Americans is widely off the mark, as we shall see in the remainder of this text. These views support an attitude of disdain and lack of sympathy for the multiple dilemmas faced today by the racial minority groups and by many contemporary immigrants. They permit a more subtle expression of prejudice and racism and allow whites to use these highly distorted views of their immigrant ancestors as a rhetorical device to express a host of race-based grievances without appearing racist (Gallagher, 2001).

Alba (1990) concludes as follows:

The thrust of the [emerging] European American identity is to defend the individualistic view of the American system, because it portrays the system as open to those who are willing to work hard and pull themselves out of poverty and discrimination. Recent research suggests that it is precisely this individualism that prevents many whites from sympathizing with the need for African Americans and other minorities to receive affirmative action in order to overcome institutional barriers to their advancement. (p. 317)

What can we conclude? The generations-long journey from immigrant to white ethnic to European American seems to be drawing to a close. The separate ethnic identities are merging into a larger sense of "whiteness" that unites descendants of the immigrants with the dominant group and provides a rhetorical device for expressing disdain for other groups, especially African Americans.

CONTEMPORARY IMMIGRANTS: DOES THE TRADITIONAL PERSPECTIVE APPLY?

Does the traditional perspective—based as it is on the experiences of European immigrants and their descendants—apply to more recent immigrants? This is a key issue facing social scientists, government policymakers, and the general public today. Will contemporary immigrants duplicate the experiences of earlier groups? Will they acculturate before they integrate? Will religion, social class, and race be important forces in their lives? Will they take three generations to assimilate? More than three? Fewer? What will their patterns of intermarriage look like? Will they achieve socioeconomic parity with the dominant group? When? How?

Sociologists (as well as the general public and policymakers) are split in their answers to these questions. Some social scientists believe that the "traditional" perspective on assimilation does not apply and that the experiences of contemporary immigrant groups will differ greatly from those of European immigrants. They believe that assimilation today is fragmented or segmented and will have a number of different outcomes. Although some contemporary immigrant groups may integrate into the middle-class mainstream, others will find themselves permanently mired in the impoverished, alienated, and marginalized segments of racial minority groups. Still others may form close-knit enclaves based on their traditional cultures and become successful in the United States by resisting the forces of acculturation (Portes & Rumbaut, 2001, p. 45).

In stark contrast, other theorists believe that the traditional perspective on assimilation is still relevant and that contemporary immigrant groups will follow the established pathways of mobility and assimilation. Of course, the process will be variable from group to group and place to place, but even the groups that are today the most impoverished and marginalized will, in time, move into mainstream society.

How will the debate be resolved? We cannot say at the moment, but we can point out that this debate is reminiscent of the critique of Park's theory of assimilation. In both cases, the argument is partly about time: Even the most impoverished and segmented groups may find their way into the economic mainstream eventually, at some unspecified time in the future. There are also other levels of meaning in the debate, however, related to one's perception of the nature of modern U.S. society. Is U.S. society today growing more tolerant of diversity, more open and equal? If so, this would seem to favor the traditionalist perspective. If not, this trend would clearly favor those who argue for the segmented-assimilation hypothesis. Although we will not resolve this argument in this text, we will use the debate between the traditional and segmented views on assimilation as a useful framework as we consider the experiences of these groups (see Chapters 8, 9, and especially Chapter 10).

Implications for Examining Dominant-Minority Relations

Chapters 1 and 2 have introduced many of the terms, concepts, and themes that form the core of the rest of this text. Although the connections between the concepts are not simple, some key points can be made to summarize these chapters and anticipate the material to come.

First, minority group status has much more to do with power and the distribution of resources than with simple numbers or the percentage of the population in any particular category. We saw this notion expressed in Chapter 1 in the definition of minority group and in our exploration of inequality. The themes of inequality and differentials in status were also covered in our discussion of prejudice, racism, and discrimination. To understand minority relations, we must examine some basic realities of human society: inequalities in wealth, prestige, and the distribution of power. To discuss changes in minority group status, we must be prepared to discuss changes in the way society does business, makes decisions, and distributes income, jobs, health care, and opportunity.

A second area that we will focus on in the rest of the book is the question of how our society should develop. Assimilation and pluralism, with all their variations, define two broad directions. Each has been extensively examined and discussed by social scientists, by leaders and decision makers in American society, and by ordinary people from all groups and walks of life. The analysis and evaluation of these two broad directions is a thread running throughout this book.

Assimilation, Then and Now

Mario Puzo and Luis Rodriguez are both sons of immigrants, but they grew up in two very different Americas. Puzo, best known as the author of The Godfather, *grew up in the Italian American community, and his memoir of life in New York City in the 1930s illustrates some of the patterns at the heart of Gordon's theory of assimilation. Writing in the 1970s, Puzo remembers the days of his boyhood and his certainty that he would escape the poverty that surrounded him. Note also his view of (and gratitude for) an America that gave people (or at least white people) the opportunity to rise above the circumstances of their birth.*

Rodriguez paints a rather different picture of U.S. society. He grew up in the Los Angeles area in the 1950s and 1960s and was a veteran of gang warfare by the time he reached high school. His memoir, Always Running: La Vida Loca *(1993), illustrates the realities of segmented assimilation for contemporary immigrants. In this extract, he describes how his high school prepared Mexican American students for life. Contrast his despair with Puzo's gratitude. Which sector of American society is Rodriguez being prepared to enter?*

CHOOSING A DREAM: ITALIANS IN HELL'S KITCHEN

MARIO PUZO

In the summertime, I was one of the great Tenth Avenue athletes, but in the wintertime I became a sissy. I read books. At a very early age I discovered libraries. . . . My mother always looked at all this reading with a fishy Latin eye. She saw no profit in it, but since all her children were great readers, she was a good enough general to know she could not fight so pervasive an insubordination. And there may have been some envy. If she had been able to, she would have been the greatest reader of all.

My direct ancestors for a thousand years have most probably been illiterate. Italy, the golden land, . . . so majestic in its language and cultural treasures . . . has never cared for its poor people. My father and mother were both illiterates. Both grew up on rocky, hilly farms in the countryside adjoining Naples. . . . My mother was told that the family could not afford the traditional family gift of linens when she married, and it was this that decided her to emigrate to America. . . . My mother never heard of Michelangelo; the great deeds of the Caesars had not reached her ears. She never heard the great music of her native land. She could not sign her name.

And so it was hard for my mother to believe that her son could become an artist. After all, her one dream in coming to America had been to earn her daily bread, a wild dream in itself. And looking back, she was dead right. Her son an artist? To this day she shakes her head. I shake mine with her. America may be a Fascistic, warmongering, racially prejudiced country today. It may deserve the hatred of its revolutionary young. But what a miracle it once was!

What has happened here has never happened in any other country in any other time. The poor, who have been poor for centuries . . . whose children had inherited their poverty, their illiteracy, their hopelessness, achieved some economic dignity and freedom. You didn't get it for nothing, you had to pay a price in tears, in suffering, but why not? And some even became artists.

SOURCE: Puzo (1993). Reprinted by permission of Donadio & Olson, Inc. Copyright © 1993 Mario Puzo.

ALWAYS RUNNING: LA VIDA LOCA

LUIS RODRIGUEZ

Mark Keppel High School was a Depression-era structure with a brick and art deco facade and small, army-type bungalows in the back. Friction filled its hallways. The Anglo and Asian upper-class students from Monterey Park and Alhambra attended the school. They were tracked into the "A" classes; they were in the school clubs; they were the varsity team members and lettermen. They were the pep squad and cheerleaders.

But the school also took in the people from the Hills and surrounding community who somehow made it past junior high. They were mostly Mexican, in the "C" track (what were called the "stupid" classes). Only a few of these students participated in school government, in sports, or in the various clubs.

The school had two principal languages. Two skin tones and two cultures. It revolved around class differences. The white and Asian kids . . . were from professional, two-car households with watered lawns and trimmed trees. The laboring class, the sons and daughters of service workers, janitors, and factory hands lived in and around the Hills (or a section of Monterey Park called "Poor Side"). The school separated these two groups by levels of education: The professional-class kids were provided with college-preparatory classes; the blue-collar students were pushed into "industrial arts." . . .

If you came from the Hills, you were labeled from the start. I'd walk into the counselor's office and looks of disdain greeted me—one meant for a criminal, alien, to be feared. Already a thug. It was harder to defy this expectation than just accept it and fall into the trappings. It was a jacket I could try to take off, but they kept putting it back on. The first hint of trouble and the preconceptions proved true. So why not be an outlaw? Why not make it our own?

SOURCE: Rodriguez (1993).

Immigration, Emigration, and Ireland

Immigrating and adjusting to a new society are among the most wrenching, exciting, disconcerting, exhilarating, and heartbreaking of human experiences. Immigrants have recorded these feelings, along with the adventures and experiences that sparked them, in every possible media, including letters, memoirs, poems, photos, stories, movies, jokes, and music. These immigrant tales recount the traumas of leaving home, dealing with a new language and customs, coping with rejection and discrimination, and thousands of other experiences. The most poignant of these stories express the sadness of parting from family and friends, perhaps forever.

Peter Jones captured some of these feelings in his song *Kilkelly,* based on letters written nearly 150 years earlier by an Irish father to his immigrant son—Jones's great-grandfather—in the United States. Each verse of the song paraphrases a letter and includes news of the family and community left behind and also expresses, in simple but powerful language, the deep sadness of separation and the longing for reunion:

> *Kilkelly, Ireland, 18 and 90, my dear and loving son John*
>
> *I guess that I must be close on to 80,*
>
> *it's 30 years since you're gone.*
>
> *Because of all of the money you send me,*
>
> *I'm still living out on my own.*
>
> *Michael has built himself a fine house*
>
> *and Brigid's daughters have grown.*
>
> *Thank you for sending your family picture,*
>
> *they're lovely young women and men.*
>
> *You say that you might even come for a visit,*
>
> *what joy to see you again.*[2]

It is particularly appropriate to use an Irish song to illustrate the sorrows of immigration. Just as the United States has been a major receiver of immigrants for the past 200 years, Ireland has been a major supplier. Mass immigration from Ireland began with the potato famines of the 1840s and continued through the end of the 20th century, motivated by continuing hard times, political unrest, and unemployment. The sadness of Peter Jones's ancestors was repeated over and over as the youth of Ireland left for jobs in Great Britain, the United States, and hundreds of other places, never expecting to return. This mass immigration—along with the famines—cut the 1840 Irish population of 7 million in half, and today, the population is still only about 4 million.

History rarely runs in straight lines, however. At the turn of the 21st century, after nearly 200 years of supplying immigrants, Ireland (along with other nations of Northern and Western Europe) became a consumer. As displayed in Exhibit 2.8, the number of newcomers entering Ireland increased more than 5 times over between 1987 and 2006, to more than 100,000, and the number of people leaving decreased dramatically, to fewer than 25,000. In the most recent years, as the Irish economy soured and jobs became scarcer, immigration resumed its historic pattern and the number of newcomers dropped precipitously. Still, the patterns of immigration from the 1990s through 2007 are a remarkable reversal of a historic trend and beg for an explanation.

We should note, before turning to analysis, that the volume of in- and out-migration is minuscule compared with the United States, but the percentage of Ireland's population that is "non-Irish" (11%) is comparable to the percentage of the United States population that is foreign-born (13%; Central Statistics Office, Ireland, 2006).

What explains the influx of population from the 1990s to 2007? The answers are not hard to find. After decades of unemployment and depression, the Irish economy entered a boom phase in the early 1990s. Spurred by investments

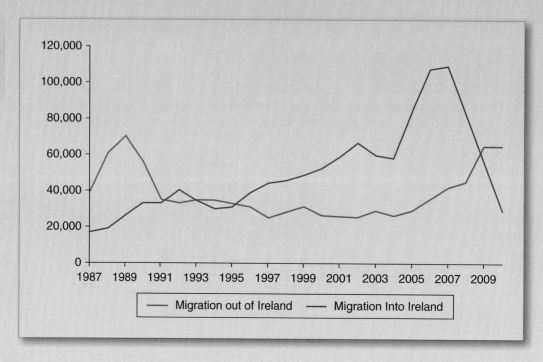

Exhibit 2.8
Immigration and
Emigration, Ireland,
1987 to 2010

120,000

100,000

80,000

60,000

40,000

20,000

0

1987 1989 1991 1993 1995 1997 1999 2001 2003 2005 2007 2009

—— Migration out of Ireland   —— Migration Into Ireland

from multinational corporations and the benefits of joining the European Economic Union, the Irish economy and the job supply have grown rapidly. The unemployment rate was less than 5% in 2006, and Ireland ranks 137th lowest out of 181 nations on this statistic ("Unemployment Rate," n.d.).

Irish nationals who had left Ireland to find work returned in large numbers, and people from Europe and other parts of the globe also arrived. In addition, Ireland received refugees and people seeking asylum. In 2010, for example, roughly 43% of immigrants were of Irish origin, 41% were from the United Kingdom or other nations of the European Union, and 15% were from "the rest of the world," a category that includes the Middle East, Nigeria, and various "trouble spots" around the globe (Central Statistics Office, Ireland, 2010). The immigration is changing the racial composition of Irish society. Although still a small minority of the total population, the number of Irish residents of African descent has increased by a factor of 7 since 1996, from fewer than 5,000 to more than 35,000. Also, the number of Irish of Asian descent increased by a factor of 6, from about 8,000 to about 47,000. Both groups are about 1% of the total population.

What awaits these newcomers when they arrive on the Emerald Isle? Will they be subjected to the Irish version of "Anglo-conformity"? Will Irish society become a melting pot? Will Gordon's ideas about assimilation be applicable to their experiences? Will their assimilation be segmented? Will the Irish, such immigrants themselves, be especially understanding and sympathetic to the traumas faced by the newcomers?

Although many Irish are sympathetic to the immigrants and refugees, others have responded with racist sentiments and demands for exclusion, reactions that ironically echo the rejection Irish immigrants in the United States experienced in the 19th century. Irish radio and TV talk shows commonly discuss issues of immigration and assimilation and frequently evoke prejudiced statements from the audience, and there are also reports of racism and discrimination.

The rejection of non-Irish newcomers was manifested in the passage of the Citizenship Amendment to the Irish Constitution, which was overwhelmingly supported (80% in favor) by the Irish electorate in June 2004. Prior to the passage of the amendment, any baby born in Ireland had the right to claim Irish citizenship. The amendment denied the right of citizenship to any baby that did not have at least one Irish parent and was widely interpreted as a hostile rejection of immigrants (see Fanning, 2003). One poll suggested that people supported the amendment because they believed there were simply too many immigrants in Ireland (Neissen, Schibel, & Thompson, 2005).

Like the United States, Ireland finds itself dealing with diversity and debating what kind of society it should become. It is too early to tell whether the Irish experience will parallel America's or whether the sociological concepts presented in this chapter will prove useful in analyzing the Irish immigrant experience. We can be sure, however, that the experience of the immigrants in Ireland will be laced with plentiful doses of the loneliness and longing experienced by Peter Jones's ancestors. Times have changed, but today's immigrants will yearn for Abuja, Riga, or Baku with the same melancholy experienced by previous waves of immigrants yearning for Kilkelly, Dublin, or Galway. Who knows what songs and poems will come from this?

THE POLITICAL TENSION BETWEEN LINGUISTIC ASSIMILATION AND PLURALISM IN FRANCE

PROFESSOR KAI HEIDEMANN

France is one of the most linguistically diverse nations in all of Europe. French is the sole official language—and most people speak some version of it—but there are also many linguistic minority groups within the nation. These can be split into three basic categories. The first category includes "transnational minority languages," or languages spoken by persons living along France's borders with other European nations, particularly Dutch (Flemish) and German in the north, Italian in the east, and Spanish to the south. The second category includes a wide variety of "diasporic" or "migrant" minority languages spoken by different ethnic groups who have migrated to France through the years. These include European languages linked to migration patterns dating back to the industrial era of the early 20th century (Italian, Polish, Portuguese, and Spanish) and numerous African and Asian languages linked to more recent postcolonial migration (Arabic, Armenian, Berber, Chinese, Turkish, Vietnamese, and Wolof). The third category consists of regional or autochthonous languages, including nine languages that have been spoken within France's modern-day borders for centuries: Alsatian, Basque, Breton, Catalan, Corsican, Occitan, and Provençal, as well as Yiddish and Romani. The people in this third category have tended to be the most active and vocal in seeking political rights and recognition for their cultures and languages.

As with many other democratic nations such as the United Kingdom and the United States, France's linguistic diversity often has been a source of heated public debate and political conflict. One particularly volatile area has been the issue of the use of language in the public education system. A key question in this context has been, Should the French state recognize and support minority languages as vehicles of instruction and learning in the public schools? Another concern has been the legal status and treatment of linguistic minorities within the French education system: Do linguistic minorities have the right to have their language supported in public schools? Should the schools work to prevent the loss of these languages?

Two competing types of orientations or "ideologies" have influenced the logic of language planning and policymaking in the French education system: assimilationism and pluralism.

On the one hand, from the standpoint of *assimilationism,* linguistic diversity has been viewed as a problem that should be minimized and suppressed within educational settings. From this perspective, the goal of public education is to achieve linguistic homogeneity so as to foster a strong sense of national unity as well as to ensure the use of French as the common language of communication. The motto of assimilationism in France can be interpreted as "one nation, one state, one language." [Note the echo of the quotation from President Roosevelt that opened this chapter.]

From this point of view, linguistic assimilation is seen as essential in providing all citizens of France with equality of opportunity and increased mobility, as well as for ensuring social cohesion, order, and progress. Moreover, proponents of linguistic assimilation also argue that the use of a minority language in public schools—such as Arabic or Basque—has a negative effect on the academic achievement and life chances of minority-language–speaking students by preventing them from fully and properly grasping French, the dominant language of society. A driving assumption behind assimilationism is that linguistic diversity must be minimized and controlled within education because multilingualism is a source of instability and conflict in French society. The inclusion of minority languages in public schools through bilingual education programs is often problematized as engendering a divisive form of ethnic "tribalism" or "nationalism." While people are free to speak other languages in their private lives, it is argued, France's public institutions should emphasize one single common language so as to uphold the indivisibility of the French Republic. Until the latter half of the 20th century, linguistic assimilationism was the unequivocally dominant position taken up by political authorities and educational policymakers in France, and minority languages, thus, generally have been excluded from the education system.

On the other hand, from the standpoint of *pluralism,* France's linguistic diversity has been viewed as a societal resource that should be recognized and supported within the education system rather than problematized and suppressed. The goal of public education from this perspective is to foster a multilingual nation wherein French citizens are free to use minority languages in public life. From this, it follows that France's linguistic minorities have a democratic right to have their languages represented within local schools. From this point of view, the emphasis is on the use of bi- or multilingual education programs that are explicitly designed to ensure acquisition of French as well as total proficiency and literacy in a minority language.

The pluralist position is basically a reaction to the long legacy of linguistic assimilationism in France. Its underlying assumption is that linguistic diversity becomes a source of political conflict only when the languages of minority groups are repressed and excluded. Educational policies that prohibit or place heavy restrictions on the use of minority languages in France are perceived as an injustice perpetrated against the speakers of these languages, who are often also racial and ethnic minorities. In contrast to supporters of linguistic assimilationism, proponents of pluralism also argue that an important goal of public schooling should be to foster comprehension in multiple languages. In addition to the utility of knowing multiple languages in an increasingly globalizing world society, it is argued that a multilingual citizenry will be more tolerant and understanding of ethnic and cultural difference and, thus, more likely to engage in the type of rational deliberation necessary for a healthy democracy. An important outcome attributed to the logic of pluralism is also the maintenance of minority languages, which have experienced high levels of language loss through the years. Although the basic ideas behind linguistic pluralism in education have become increasingly normalized in recent years—largely as a consequence of France's increased integration into the European Union—the logic of pluralism remains highly controversial in France.

English Only?

What role should learning English play in the process of adjusting to the United States? Should English language profi-ciency be a prerequisite for full inclusion in the society, as stated by President Roosevelt in 1907? Should English be made the official language of the nation? Does the present multiplicity of languages represent a danger for social cohesion and unity? Following are two reactions to these questions.

The first excerpt is from Mauro Mujica (2003), the chairman of U.S. English, Inc. (http://www.us-english.org/inc/), an immigrant himself and a passionate advocate for the unifying power of a single national language. His organization opposes efforts to recog-nize Spanish as an official second language (in part because of the expense and confusion that would ensue if all government documents, election ballots, street signs, etc., were published in both English and Spanish) and most forms of bilingual education. He is particularly concerned with stressing that the primary beneficiaries of learning English will be the immigrants.

An opposing point of view is presented by James Crawford, a writer and president of the Institute for Language and Education Policy (http://www.elladvocates.org/), who argues that making English the official language is an unnecessary assault on immi-grants and minority groups. He argues that the new immigrant groups are learning English rapidly—perhaps in two generations as opposed to the "traditional" three-generation pace—and that non-English languages are in danger of disappearing.

ENGLISH ONLY WILL SPEED THE ASSIMILATION OF IMMIGRANTS

MAURO MUJICA

[During my 11 years as chairman] of U.S. ENGLISH . . . I have encountered many myths about official English legislation. . . . A few of these myths were recently repeated in an opinion piece in the *Contra Costa Times*. [The author] . . . writes, ". . . the antibilingual education movement and the English-only movement could easily be labeled an anti-Spanish movement."

In that one sentence, [the author] repeats two of the most ridiculous myths about official English. There are other distortions as well. . . . Here are five of the most common myths about official English and the realities behind them.

Myth No. 1: Official English Is Anti-Immigrant

Declaring English the official language benefits all Americans, but it benefits immigrants most of all. Immigrants who speak English earn more money, do better in school, and have more career options than those who do not.

As an immigrant from Chile, I can testify that English proficiency is the most important gift we can give to newcomers. In fact, polls show that 70% of Hispanics and 85% of all immigrants support making English the official language of the United States. Learning English is the key to assimilating into the mainstream of American society. That is why our orga-nization, U.S. ENGLISH, Inc., advocates for English immersion classes for immigrant students and adults.

Myth No. 2: Official English Is "English Only"

Many far-left opponents of official English, such as the ACLU, refer to our legislation as "English Only." Official English simply requires that government conduct its business in English. It does not dictate what language must be spoken in the home, during conversations, cultural celebrations, or religious ceremonies. It does not prohibit the teaching of foreign languages. It does not affect private businesses or the services offered by them. In addition, HR 997 makes exceptions for emergency situations.

Myth No. 3: Today's Immigrants Are Learning English Just Like the Immigrants of Old

The United States has a rapidly growing population of people—often native-born—who are not proficient in English. The 2000 Census found that 21.3 million Americans (8% of the population) are classified as "limited English proficient," a 52% increase from 1990, and more than double the 1980 total. More than 5.6 million of these people were born in the United States. In states like California, 20% of the population is not proficient in English.

The Census also reports that 4.5 million American households are linguistically isolated, meaning that no one in the house-hold older than age 14 can speak English. These numbers indicate that the American assimilation process is broken. If not fixed, we will see our own "American Quebec" in the Southwestern United States and perhaps other areas of the country.

Myth No. 4: The Founding Fathers Rejected Making English the Official Language

English has been the language of our nation from its earliest days. In 1789, 90% of our nation's nonslave inhabitants were of English descent. Any notion that they would have chosen another language or used precious resources on print-ing documents in multiple languages lacks common sense.

The issue of an official language was never discussed at the Constitutional Convention, as the topic was not controversial enough to be debated. Even the Dutch colonies had been under English rule for more than a century. Contrary to popular belief, Congress never voted on a proposal to make German the official language. This myth is probably based on a 1794 bill to translate some documents into German (it was defeated).

Myth No. 5: In a Global Culture, an Official Language Is Anachronistic

Ninety-two percent of the world's countries (178 of 193) have at least one official language. English is the sole official language in 31 nations and has an official status in 20 other nations, including India, Singapore, the Philippines, Samoa, and Nigeria.

There has never been a language so widely spread in so short a time as English. It is the lingua franca of the modern world as much as Latin was the common tongue of the Roman Empire. Roughly one quarter of the world's population is already fluent or competent in English, and this number grows by the day.

English is the global language of business, communications, higher education, diplomacy, aviation, the Internet, science, popular music, entertainment, and international travel. Immigrants who don't know English not only lose out in the American economy but also in the global economy.

These are just some of the myths that must be corrected if we are to have a debate on a coherent language policy. This policy should be built on fact, not myth. Multilingual government is a disaster for American unity and results in billions of dollars in unnecessary government spending. We need only to look at Canada to see the problems that multilingualism can bring. HR 997 could be our last best chance to stop this process, and we cannot let distortions about official English sidetrack this legislation.

SOURCE: Mujica (2003).

FREQUENTLY ASKED QUESTIONS ABOUT OFFICIAL ENGLISH

JAMES CRAWFORD

Isn't bilingualism a threat to national unity, dividing people along language lines?

Language diversity is a fact of life throughout the world, the normal state of affairs in all but a few small countries. This has been equally true in the United States, where hundreds of immigrant and indigenous tongues have coexisted with English. About 380 languages are spoken by U.S. residents. . . .

As a marker of ethnic differences, language sometimes plays a role in ethnic conflicts. But diverse societies need not be divided societies. . . . For every Canada, where language differences have become politicized, there is a Switzerland, where four language groups have coexisted harmoniously for centuries, enjoying equal rights under their constitution.

Why has language been a source of tension in Canada?

Canada is a good example of the polarization that can result from generations of social inequality based on language. Before 1969, French-speaking citizens had limited access to government outside the province of Quebec. De facto English-only policies made them second-class Canadians. Official bilingualism, adopted that year, was a belated attempt to guarantee minority rights. Unfortunately, it came too late to head off Quebecois separatism in the 1970s. . . . The problem in Canada has not been language differences per se, but the use of language as a tool of ethnic domination.

Are policies to restrict languages other than English motivated by racism or nativism?

That has often been the case. Language-restrictionist laws are never just about language. Inevitably, they reflect attitudes toward—and authorize discrimination against—the speakers of certain languages.

[A] large percentage of the public favor making English the official language. . . . Does this mean most Americans are racist?

Yes, and no. Frequently, on first hearing about the official-English issue, monolingual Americans fail to see the downside. Many wonder, since English is so dominant in this country, whether it isn't already the official language. And if not, why not? This reaction is not surprising since—compared with citizens of many other nations—Americans have limited experience with the politics of language. But when the potential impact of [making English the official language] is explained, support drops off sharply.

Favoring English as the official language, in itself, should not be equated with racism. Yet racist attitudes—toward Latinos in particular—have been closely associated with this movement. U.S. English . . . was a spinoff from the immigration-restriction lobby.

[Does the spread of] immigrant languages . . . threaten the status of English . . . ?

English is in no way threatened in the United States. Certainly . . . it is now more common to hear other languages spoken. In the 2000 census, nearly one in five U.S. residents reported speaking a language other than English at home—although not to the exclusion of English. Less noticeable, perhaps, is a countertrend toward increasing bilingualism. Between 1980 and 2000, the number of minority language speakers doubled, but so did the number of this group who spoke English "very well."

For the children of immigrants, English proficiency is advancing especially fast. A long-term study of Hispanic and Asian teenagers found that 94% knew English well, while only 44% knew their parents' language well; 72% of second-generation youth said they preferred to speak English.

How does this pattern compare with rates of English acquisition in the past?

Today's immigrants are acquiring English more rapidly than ever before. . . . The data . . . show that it's languages other than English that are threatened in the United States today. Without the replenishing effects of immigration, most would soon die out.

. . . Owing to strict immigration quotas between 1924 and 1965, the foreign-born population of the United States declined from 14.7% in 1910 to 4.7% in 1970. As the number of non-English-speaking newcomers plummeted, second- and third-generation immigrants stopped speaking their ancestral languages. . . . This was the least diverse period, linguistically speaking, in American history.

Now that the proportion of foreign-born Americans has rebounded to its historic norm—11.1% in 2000—so has the use of non-English languages in American communities. To many people who came of age before the 1980s, today's level of bilingualism seems "abnormal." In fact, the atypical period was the mid-1900s.

Would it speed up English acquisition even more if government eliminated bilingual assistance programs?

Some people assume that if non-English speakers can read Social Security pamphlets or take driver's tests in their native language, they will have no incentive to learn English. Bilingual assistance programs supposedly convey the false notion that it's OK to live in the United States as monolingual speakers of Spanish or Chinese. Or they encourage immigrants to be lazy when it comes to language learning. In fact, no real evidence has ever been mustered to support such claims. . . .

Don't children learn English faster if they are "totally immersed" in English?

That was the assumption behind English-only school initiatives adopted in California (1998), Arizona (2000), and Massachusetts (2002). These laws established "structured immersion" programs intended to teach English to immigrant students in just one school year. But things have not worked out quite as planned:

- A 5-year study, commissioned by the California legislature, found no evidence that all-English immersion programs had improved academic outcomes for English learners in the state. In 2004 to 2005, only 9% of these students were reclassified as fluent in English—a rate that was virtually unchanged since the year before passage of the English-only law.
- Researchers at Arizona State University reported that 60% of English learners in Arizona made "no gain" in English in 2003 to 2004, while 7% actually lost ground; all were enrolled in English-only programs. Another ASU study found that the academic achievement gap between English learners and other students was widening.
- In Massachusetts, more than half the students were still limited in English after 3 years in structured English-immersion classrooms.

Isn't it important to send a message to immigrants that they are expected to learn our language?

People who face language barriers every day—on the job, in the supermarket, at the hospital—understand better than anyone the importance of proficiency in English in America. They don't need English-only laws to impress on them this reality. According to surveys by the Pew Hispanic Center, a substantial majority of Latinos agree that immigrants "have to speak English to say they are part of American society." Meanwhile, 92% say it is "very important" for immigrant children to be taught English—a higher percentage than non-Hispanic whites (87%) or blacks (83%).

Isn't there something to be said for the idea of uniting Americans through a common language?

Of all the arguments in favor of official English, this is probably the most hypocritical. Ever since the campaign emerged in the early 1980s, its main effect has been to divide communities. Whenever this debate flares up, the news media report outbreaks of language vigilantism, as local officials and individuals take it on themselves to enforce discriminatory policies, using slogans like "This is America—speak English!" . . .

While many English speakers may not see a problem, those targeted by English-only campaigns of language restrictions find them offensive and threatening. Opposing such legislation in his home state of Arizona, Senator John McCain asked: "Why would we want to pass [an] initiative that a significant portion of our population considers an assault on their heritage?" This is a question that English-only proponents have never been able to answer.

DEBATE QUESTIONS TO CONSIDER

1. What assumptions are these authors making about the role of language in the process of assimilation? What stage of Gordon's model of assimilation are they discussing? Do the authors believe that a group can adjust successfully to U.S. society without learning English?

2. What reaction might other groups (recent immigrants, African Americans, Native Americans, white ethnics) have to making Spanish an official second language? What stakes would they have in this policy issue?

3. As you think about the issue of bilingualism and multilingualism, see whether you can identify some social class aspects. Which economic classes would benefit from an English-only policy? Which economic classes would be hurt? How? Why?

4. Mujica argues that English is a global language and that non-English speakers are handicapped not only in the United States but also in the global economy. Crawford argues that proposals to make English an official language are unnecessary and insulting to immigrant groups. List the points made by each author side by side. Which argument seems more credible? What additional facts could clarify the debate? How could you collect such facts?

5. Would making Spanish an official second language threaten societal unity, as Mujica argues? Is the English-only movement a disguise for prejudice and intolerance? What evidence from this chapter and from your own experience can you cite to support these contradictory statements? How could the underlying debate be resolved?

MAIN POINTS

- Assimilation and pluralism are two broad pathways of development for intergroup relations. Assimilation and pluralism are in some ways contrary processes but may appear together in a variety of combinations.
- Two types of assimilation are the melting pot and Anglo-conformity. The latter historically has been the dominant value in the United States.
- Gordon theorized that assimilation occurs through a series of stages, with integration being the crucial stage. In his view, it is common for American minority groups, especially racial minority groups, to be acculturated but not integrated. Once a group has begun to integrate, all other stages will follow in order.
- In the past few decades, there has been increased interest in pluralism. There are three types of pluralistic situations: cultural, or full, pluralism; structural pluralism; and enclave, or middleman, minority groups.
- According to many scholars, white ethnic groups survived decades of assimilation, albeit in altered forms. New ethnic (and racial) minority groups continue to appear, and old ones change form and function as society changes. As the 21st century unfolds, however, white ethnicity may well be fading in salience for most people, except perhaps as a context for criticizing other groups.
- In the United States today, assimilation may be segmented and have outcomes other than equality with and acceptance into the middle class.
- Several opportunities for extending and applying the concepts and issues discussed in this chapter are presented in the Public Sociology Assignments listed in the introduction to Part I. How has your home community been affected by recent immigration? How was it shaped in the past by immigration? How commonly are the themes of ethnicity and diversity presented in TV portrayals of the family? How common are ethnic themes in the graffiti you can observe locally?

STUDY SITE ON THE WEB

For chapter-specific resources, such as self-quizzes, videos, and flashcards, go to www.sagepub.com/healeyregc6e.

FOR FURTHER READING

Alba, Richard. 1990. *Ethnic Identity: The Transformation of White America.* New Haven, CT: Yale University Press.

A useful analysis of the changing meanings of ethnic identity for the descendants of European immigrants

Alba, Richard, & Nee, Victor. 2003. *Remaking the American Mainstream: Assimilation and Contemporary Immigration.* Cambridge, MA: Harvard University Press.

Bean, Frank, & Stevens, Gillian. 2003. *America's Newcomers and the Dynamics of Diversity.* New York: Russell Sage.

Two recent works that argue that the "traditional" model of assimilation remains viable

Foner, Nancy. 2005. *In a New Land: A Comparative View of Immigration.* New York: NYU Press.

A masterful analysis of immigration across time and space

Gordon, Milton. 1964. *Assimilation in American Life.* New York: Oxford University Press.
Herberg, Will. 1960. *Protestant-Catholic-Jew: An Essay in American Religious Sociology.* New York: Anchor.

Two classic works of scholarship on assimilation, religion, and white ethnic groups

Perlman, Joel. 2005. *Italians Then, Mexicans Now.* New York: Russell Sage.

A detailed, intriguing, and rigorous comparison of immigrant groups from two different eras

Portes, Alejandro, & Rumbaut, Richard. 2001. *Ethnicities: Children of Immigrants in America.* New York: Russell Sage Foundation.
Portes, Alejandro, & Rumbaut, Rubén. 2001. *Legacies: The Story of the Immigrant Second Generation.* Berkeley: University of California Press.

Zhou, Min, & Bankston, Carl. 1998. *Growing Up American: How Vietnamese Children Adapt to Life in the United States.* New York: Russell Sage.

Three outstanding works analyzing the new immigrants and the concept of segmented assimilation

QUESTIONS FOR REVIEW AND STUDY

1. Summarize Gordon's model of assimilation. Identify and explain each stage and how the stages are linked together. Explain Exhibit 2.4 in terms of Gordon's model.

2. "Human capital theory is not so much wrong as it is incomplete." Explain this statement. What does the theory leave out? What are the strengths of the theory? What questionable assumptions does it make?

3. What are the major dimensions along which the experience of assimilation varies? Explain how and why the experience of assimilation can vary.

4. Define pluralism and explain the ways in which it differs from assimilation. Why has interest in pluralism increased? Explain the difference between and cite examples of structural and cultural pluralism. Describe enclave minority groups in terms of pluralism and in terms of Gordon's model of assimilation. How have contemporary theorists added to the concept of pluralism?

5. Define and explain segmented assimilation and explain how it differs from Gordon's model. What evidence is there that assimilation for recent immigrants is not segmented? What is the significance of this debate for the future of U.S. society? For other minority groups (e.g., African Americans)? For the immigrants themselves?

6. Do American theories and understandings of assimilation apply to Ireland?

INTERNET RESEARCH PROJECT

American society incorporates scores of ethnic and racial groups. In this exercise, you will use the U.S. Census to gather information about the relative assimilation of five different groups of your own choosing. One group can be your own—the group that you identify with (if you have one). Choose groups so that they include a variety of races, places of origin, and times of immigration (i.e., choose some that arrived before the 1920s restrictions and some that arrived more recently).

Get information by following these steps (**NOTE: The Census Bureau website is changing as the 2010 Census results become available. Go to the website for this book for updated instructions on how to access information**):

1. Go to the official U.S. Census Bureau website at www.census.gov.

2. Click on the "American FactFinder" tab on the left of the screen, and then click "factfinder.census.gov" on the right of the next screen. A new menu will open. Click on "American Community Survey" on the left of the screen.

3. Click the radio button next to "2007–2009 American Community Survey 3-Year Estimates."

4. Click "Selected Population Profiles" in the list on the right of the screen.

5. Click on "United States," and "Add" it to the "Current Geography Selections" window at the bottom of the screen. Click "Next."

6. The next screen has three tabs at the top: "Race or Ethnic Group," "Ancestry Group," and "Country of Birth." Disregard the third tab, but use the other two to select groups for this exercise.

   a. *Race or Ethnic Groups:* Under this tab, you will find whites, blacks, American Indians, Hispanics, and Asian and Pacific Islanders. You have many choices under this screen, but, in general, choose groups "alone or in combination with one or more races."

   b. *Ancestry Groups:* Under this tab, you will find ethnic groups not included in the first tab, including white ethnic groups (e.g., Irish and German), Arab Americans, sub-Saharan Africans, and non-Hispanic West Indian groups (e.g., Jamaicans).

7. After you have selected a group, click "Show Result," and the Selected Population Profile will appear with the characteristics of the total population listed on the left and your group on the right. For this exercise, ignore the "Margin of Error" column.

8. Scroll down the table until you get to "Place of Birth, Citizenship Status, and Year of Entry." Fill in the following table for your group. Scroll down a little more to see information on language, and use this to complete the table.

	Variables	TOTAL POPULATION	Groups				
			_____	_____	_____	_____	_____
1	Number foreign-born	38,090,166					
	% foreign-born who are						
	Male	50.2					
	Female	49.8					
2	% foreign-born who are naturalized citizens (Divide the number of foreign-born who are naturalized by the total number of foreign-born and multiply by 100)	42.9					
3	FOREIGN BORN: % THAT ENTERED U.S.						
	2000 or later	29.9					
	1990–1999	28.5					
	Before 1990	41.6					
4	LANGUAGE SPOKEN AT HOME AND ABILITY TO SPEAK ENGLISH						
	% English only	80.2					
	% who speak English less than "very well"	8.6					

QUESTIONS

1. How do these variables measure assimilation? What stage of Gordon's model (see Exhibit 2.1) do they relate to?

2. Which of your groups is most/least assimilated? Based on this chapter and what you know about these groups at this point, what factors might explain their relative position?

3. Compare the percentage of each group that entered the United States after 2000 with the percentage of the group that speaks only English. Do you see any trends here? Are the newest arrivals least likely to be speaking English only? Is there evidence that language acculturation is taking place?

OPTIONAL GROUP DISCUSSION

Bring the information on your five groups to class and compare with groups collected by others. Consider the issues raised in the questions above and in the chapter, and develop some ideas about why the groups are where they are relative to one another.

NOTES

1. This phrase comes from Alba (1990).

2. Copyright © Green Linnet Music 1983. Used with permission.

3

Prejudice and Discrimination

I've just recognized that, you know, all people have certain traits. The Jews have certain traits, the Irish have . . . for example, the Irish can't drink. What you always have to remember with the Irish is they get mean. Virtually every Irish I've known gets mean when he drinks. Particularly the real Irish. The Jews are just a very aggressive and abrasive and obnoxious personality.

[Bill Rogers says that blacks] are coming along, and that after all they are going to strengthen our country in the end because they are strong physically and some of them are smart. My own view is I think he's right if you're talking in terms of 500 years, . . . I think it's wrong if you're talking in terms of 50 years.

—Richard M. Nixon
37th President of the United States
February, 1973

Less than 40 years after President Nixon made these remarks during a casual chat in the Oval Office, the United States elected a black man to be its president. What does this mean—if anything—about American prejudice and discrimination? Some have argued that the election of President Barack Obama proves that prejudice, skin color, and group membership have become irrelevant in our society. Others, particularly social scientists, are less willing to pronounce the death of racism. Many argue that prejudice has not decreased so much as it has changed to subtler, more disguised and indirect forms. Which view is more supported by the evidence? Are prejudice and discrimination, whatever their form, still problems in America?

In this chapter, we explore these and a variety of other issues. Social scientists have developed an impressive array of theories and a huge volume of research on prejudice and discrimination, and we will review some of their most important conclusions and arguments. We begin by restating the difference between prejudice and discrimination and then explore the two dimensions of prejudice—affective and cognitive—in some detail. As we do so, we will examine some of the important individual-level theories of prejudice (see Exhibit 1.5). We will then cover some of the most important sociological perspectives on prejudice and discrimination. The emphasis will be on prejudice, but we will examine discrimination on a number of occasions in this chapter and in chapters to come. Toward the end of the chapter, we will return to the issues introduced above: How has American prejudice evolved and changed since President Nixon so casually disparaged Jewish, Irish, and black Americans four decades ago? We also consider the changing nature of sexism and conclude with a look at hate crimes, one of the most vicious manifestations of bigotry and antiminority emotion.

PREJUDICE AND DISCRIMINATION

Let's begin with definitions. Recall from Chapter 1 that prejudice is the tendency of individuals to think and feel in negative ways about members of other groups. Discrimination, on the other hand, is actual, overt, individual behavior. Although these concepts are obviously related, they do not always occur together or have a causal relationship with each other. Exhibit 3.1 presents four possible combinations of prejudice and discrimination in individuals. In two cases, the relationship between prejudice and discrimination is consistent. The "all-weather liberal" is not prejudiced and does not discriminate, whereas the "all-weather bigot" is prejudiced and does discriminate. The other two combinations, however, are inconsistent. The "fair-weather liberal" discriminates without being prejudiced, whereas the "timid bigot" is prejudiced but does not discriminate. These inconsistencies between attitudes and behavior are not uncommon and may be caused by a variety of social pressures, including the desire to conform to the expectations of others. They illustrate the fact that prejudice and discrimination can be independent of each other. Most of the material in this chapter is focused more on prejudice than on discrimination, but we will address the relationship between the two concepts on several occasions.

	Does Not Discriminate	Does Discriminate
Unprejudiced	Unprejudiced nondiscriminator (all-weather liberal)	Unprejudiced discriminator (fair-weather liberal)
Prejudiced	Prejudiced nondiscriminator (timid bigot)	Prejudiced discriminator (all-weather bigot)

Exhibit 3.1 Four Relationships Between Prejudice and Discrimination in Individuals

SOURCE: Adapted from Merton (1968).

Prejudice and discrimination can be subtle and discrete or open, dramatic, and violent.

© Abdul Aziz ibn Abdur Rahman / De/Demotix/ Demotix/Corbis.

PREJUDICE

American social scientists of all disciplines have researched prejudice from a variety of theoretical perspectives and have asked many different questions. One conclusion that has emerged is that prejudice has a variety of possible causes (some more psychological and individual, others more sociological and cultural) and can present itself in a variety of forms (some blatant and vicious, others subtle and indirect). One way to begin to approach this complex subject is by examining the two main dimensions of prejudice.

The Affective Dimension

Individual prejudice is partly a set of feelings or emotions that people attach to groups, including their own. The emotions can run a wide gamut from mild to intense. At one extreme, we might find relatively mild expressions of disparagement, such as "I don't care much for Italians" or President Nixon's remarks about the Irish. At the other, we might find the dreadful rage that accompanies a lynching or other hate crime. What makes these emotions part of prejudice is their generalized association with an entire group, often in the complete absence of any actual experience with group members, and their element of pre-judgment (which is, after all, the literal meaning of prejudice).

There are a number of psychological and social-psychological research traditions that focus on the emotional or affective aspect of prejudice. Here, we will briefly examine two of these theories: the scapegoat hypothesis and the theory of the authoritarian personality.

The Scapegoat Hypothesis

This theory links prejudice to feelings of frustration and aggression. People sometimes deal with personal failure or disappointment by expressing their anger against a substitute target (or scapegoat), not against the object or person that actually caused their frustration. For example, someone who has been demoted at work might attack his or her spouse rather than the boss, or a student who received a low grade on a test might "take it out" on a pet rather than on the professor. Generally speaking, the substitute targets (spouses or pets) will be less powerful than the actual cause of the frustration and may serve as a "safe" alternative to attacking bosses or professors.

From the standpoint of members of the dominant group, minority groups can make excellent substitute targets because they, by definition, control fewer power resources. In other words, minority groups are often selected as the recipients of anger and aggression that, for whatever reason, cannot be directed at the actual cause of a person's frustration. When released against a minority group, displaced aggression is expressed as or accompanied by prejudice.

Many researchers have produced scapegoating against minority groups in laboratory settings. In a typical experiment, subjects are purposely frustrated, perhaps by being asked to complete a task that the researchers have made sure is impossible. Then, the subjects are offered the opportunity to release their anger as prejudice, sometimes by completing a survey that measures their feelings about various minority groups. Many people respond to this situation with increased feelings of rejection and disparagement against other groups (see Berkowitz, 1978; Dollard, Miller, Doob, Mowrer, & Sears, 1939; Miller & Bugleski, 1948).

Outside the laboratory, the scapegoat theory has been proposed as an explanation for a variety of political, social, and economic events. For example, the theory has been applied to the rise of the Nazi Party in Germany in the 1930s. At that time, Germany was trying to cope with its defeat in World War I, a powerful economic recession, rampant unemployment, and horrific inflation. According to this line of analysis, the success of the extremely racist, violently anti-Semitic Nazi party was in part a result of its ability to capture these intense anxieties and fears and redirect them against Jews and other minorities (see Dollard et al., 1939). Along the same analytical lines, Hovland and Sears (1940) argued that the rate of lynching of African Americans in the South between 1882 and 1930 was correlated with fluctuations in cotton prices. Lynchings generally increased during hard times when the price of cotton was low and (presumably) frustrations were more widespread (for a different, more sociological view, see Beck & Clark, 2002, and Beck & Tolnay, 1990). Finally, scapegoating has been implicated in many hate crimes in the United States, including seemingly random attacks on Middle Easterners following the terrorist attacks of September 11, 2001. We will return to the topic of hate crimes at the end of this chapter.

The Theory of the Authoritarian Personality

This theory links prejudice to early childhood experiences and personality structure and argues that prejudice is produced by stern, highly punitive styles of parenting. On the surface, the children of authoritarian families respect and love their parents. Internally, however, they resent and fear their severe and distant parents. They can't consciously admit these negative feelings about their parents, so, instead, they scapegoat their fear and anger by expressing these emotions as prejudice against minority groups. Thus, prejudice provides people with authoritarian personalities a way of coping with their conflicted feelings for their parents.

The tradition of research on the authoritarian personality theory stretches back to before World War II and is supported by experiments and research projects that demonstrate a link between family structure, childhood experience, and prejudice (Adorno, Frenkel-Brunswick, Levinson, & Sanford, 1950). More recent research has examined the links between authoritarianism and gender roles (Peterson & Zurbriggen, 2010), child abuse (Rodriguez, 2010), attitudes toward international students (Charles-Toussaint & Crowson, 2010), and even leisure activities (Peterson & Pang, 2006).

Authoritarian personality theory has contributed to our understanding of individual prejudice, but it has been widely criticized for focusing solely on the internal dynamics of personality and not taking sufficient account of the social settings in which an individual is acting. Some individuals do use prejudice as a tool for handling their personality problems, but to fully understand prejudice, we need to see its connections with social structure, social class, and the context and history of group relations. The theory of the authoritarian personality is not "wrong" so much as it is incomplete. The sociological perspective, as we shall see, takes a broader approach and incorporates the social world in which the individual acts.

The Cognitive Dimension: Stereotypes

The cognitive dimension of prejudice includes stereotypes or ideas about the characteristics of other groups. Stereotypes are generalizations about groups of people that are exaggerated, overly simplistic, and resistant to disproof (Pettigrew, 1980, p. 822; see also Jones, 1997, pp. 164–202). Stereotypes stress a few traits and assume that these characteristics apply to all members of the group, regardless of individual characteristics. Highly prejudiced people will maintain their stereotypes even in the face of massive evidence that their views are wrong.

Virtually all Americans share a common set of images of the prominent ethnic, racial, and religious groups that make up U.S. society. These images include notions such as "Asians are clannish," "Jews are miserly," "Blacks are musical," and President Nixon's observation that "Irish are mean drunks." Less prejudiced people are probably familiar with these images but pay little attention to them, and they do not actually use them to judge the worth of others. More prejudiced people will think in stereotypes, apply them to all members of a group, make sweeping judgments about the worth of others, and even commit acts of violence based solely on another person's group identity.

For the prejudiced individual, stereotypes are an important set of cognitive categories. Once a stereotype is learned, it can shape perceptions to the point that the individual pays attention only to information that confirms that stereotype. Selective perception, the tendency to see only what one expects to see, can reinforce and strengthen stereotypes to the point that the highly prejudiced individual simply does not accept evidence that challenges his or her views. Thus, these overgeneralizations can become closed perceptual systems that screen out contrary information and absorb only the sensory impressions that ratify the original bias.

Types of Stereotypes and Dominant-Minority Relations

Stereotypes are, by definition, exaggerated overgeneralizations. At some level, though, even the most simplistic and derogatory stereotype can reflect some of the realities of dominant-minority group relationships. The content of a stereotype flows from the actual relationship between dominant and minority groups and is often one important way in which the dominant group tries to justify or rationalize that relationship.

For example, Pettigrew (1980) and others have pointed out two general stereotypes of minority groups. The first attributes extreme inferiority (e.g., laziness, irresponsibility, or lack of intelligence) to minority group members and tends to be found in situations (such as slavery) in which a minority group is being heavily exploited and held in an impoverished and powerless status by the dominant group. This type of stereotype is a rationalization that helps justify dominant group policies of control, discrimination, or exclusion.

The second type of stereotype is found when power and status differentials are less extreme, particularly when the minority group has succeeded in gaining some control over resources, has experienced some upward mobility, and has had some success in school and business. In this situation, credulity would be stretched too far to label the group "inferior," so their relative success is viewed in negative terms: They are seen as *too* smart, *too* materialistic, *too* crafty, *too* sly, or *too* ambitious (Pettigrew, 1980, p. 823; see also Simpson & Yinger, 1985, p. 101).

A team of psychologists has documented a similar pattern of stereotypes both in the United States and other nations. They find that perceptions of groups can be arrayed in a two-dimensional space defined by perceptions of competence and feelings of warmth. Interestingly, they include groups other than minority groups in their research. Exhibit 3.2 presents the results of multiple surveys of U.S. respondents, with clusters of scores indicating similar stereotypes. Among other findings, the researchers note two groups of ambivalent stereotypes: Some groups (e.g., the elderly, the disabled) are viewed as kind but helpless, while others (e.g., Jews, Asians) are seen as competent but cunning (Cuddy et al., 2009, p. 4). The latter stereotype echoes the characterization of groups that are seen as "too" successful, a pattern these researchers label as an "envious" prejudice. Note that African Americans and other racial minority groups fall in the same "moderately competent/moderately warm" cluster as, among others, gay men and Muslims and that "whites" are seen as more competent and warmer than the racial minorities but as less competent than the "envied" minority groups. Consistent with traditional American values, the lowest rated groups are the poor, welfare recipients, and the homeless—groups whose presumed characteristics are often seen as overlapping with those of African Americans.

Exhibit 3.2 American Stereotypes

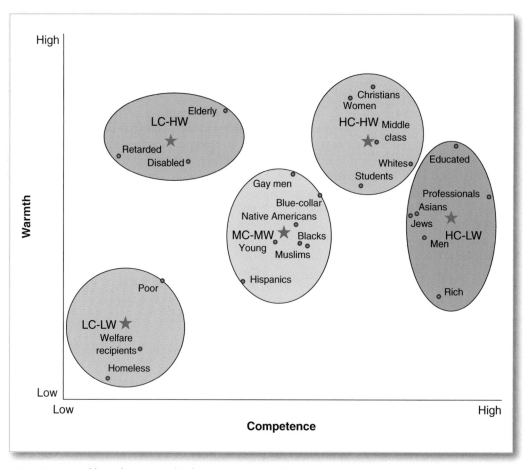

SOURCE: See Cuddy et al. (2009) and Fiske, Bergsieker, Russell, and Williams (2009).

While these patterns are important, you should also realize that stereotypes and prejudice can exist apart from the context of actual group relationships or the relative "success" of groups' social standing. Research shows that some individuals will readily stereotype groups about which they have little or no information. In fact, some individuals will express prejudice against groups that do not even exist! In one test, respondents were asked how closely they would associate with "Daniereans, Pireneans, and Wallonians"—all fictitious groups. A number of white respondents apparently reacted to the "foreign" sound of the names, rejected these three groups, and indicated that they would treat them about the same as other minority groups (Hartley, 1946). Clearly, the negative judgments about these groups were not made on the basis of personal experience or a need to rationalize some system such as slavery. The subjects were exhibiting a generalized tendency to reject minority groups of all sorts.

The Content of American Stereotypes

A series of studies with Princeton University undergraduates provides some interesting perspectives on the content of American stereotypes. Students were given a list of personality traits and asked to check those that applied to a number of different groups. The study was done first in 1933 and then repeated in 1951 and 1967 (Karlins, Coffman, & Walters, 1969). It is unusual to have comparable data covering such a long period of time, which makes these studies significant despite the fact that Princeton undergraduates are hardly a representative sample of American public opinion.

Several elements of these data are worth noting. First, the content of the stereotypes echoed American traditions well-known (although not necessarily endorsed) by all: The English were seen as sportsmanlike and conventional, Italians as passionate and musical, and Jews as shrewd and industrious. Second, the different types of stereotypes we previously discussed can be found in these results. Jews tended to be seen as successful ("intelligent") but pushy ("grasping"), whereas African Americans were seen as inferior ("lazy," "ignorant"). Third, in a recent readministration of the test (Fiske et al., 2009), the stereotypical traits ascribed to blacks included more positive traits ("loyal to family," "religious") as well as some elements of the traditional image ("musical") and some apparently negative elements ("loud").

Similar studies of stereotypical thinking have been conducted on other campuses in more recent years. Clark and Person (1982) measured white stereotypes of African Americans among undergraduates at two southeastern universities in the early 1980s. They found some continuity in the content of the stereotypes from earlier studies but also found that their subjects were more likely to characterize African Americans as having seemingly positive traits, such as "loyal to family." In contrast, a 1994 study conducted by Wood and Chesser found that white students at a large Midwestern university had more negative stereotypes of African Americans. The top five most common traits selected by the sample were uniformly negative and included "loud," "aggressive," and "lazy." This finding was echoed in a 1995 study at the University of Wisconsin that replicated the three Princeton University tests. Three of the top five most commonly selected traits for African Americans were similar to those selected by Princeton undergraduates—"rhythmic" (vs. "musical"), "low in intelligence" (vs. "ignorant"), and "lazy"—and two were new, "athletic" and "poor" (Devine & Elliot, 1995).

These studies are informative, but because they are based on college students, they may have little applicability to the attitudes of Americans in general. Fortunately, we can learn more about stereotypical thinking among Americans in general by reviewing research based on representative samples. One important study (Bobo & Kluegal, 1997) examined prejudice in the 1990s, and we can get a sense of how American stereotypes have changed by comparing their findings with results of a 2008 survey. In both years, respondents were asked to rate "the characteristics of people in a group" on a number of scales, including an "intelligent-unintelligent" scale and a "hardworking-lazy" scale. Results for white Americans are presented in Exhibits 3.3 and 3.4. The first exhibit displays perceptions of whites and blacks as "unintelligent," and the second does the same for perceptions of "laziness." In both years, more than 95% of the respondents answered the question, indicating that the willingness to label entire groups is widespread.

Exhibit 3.3 Perceptions of Whites and Blacks as Unintelligent, 1990 and 2008 (Whites Only)

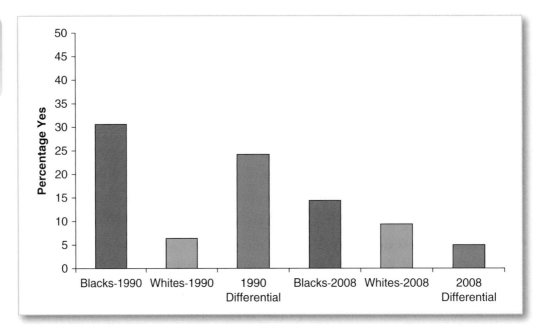

SOURCE: Adapted from Bobo and Kluegal (1997).

Exhibit 3.4 Perceptions of Blacks and Whites as Lazy, 1990 and 2008 (Whites Only)

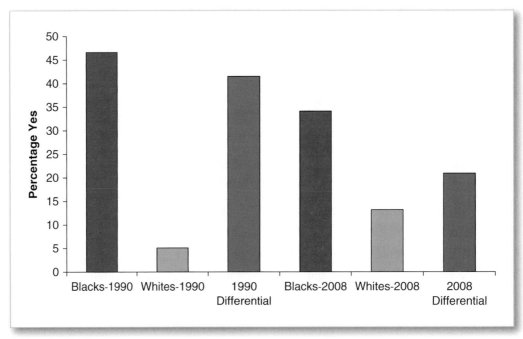

SOURCE: Adapted from Bobo and Kluegal (1997).

Let's begin by looking at the 1990 results for "unintelligent." About 30% of whites applied this term to blacks, but only about 5% applied it to their own group—a differential of almost 25%. We can think of the size of the differential as a measure of the strength of this aspect of the traditional antiblack stereotype (Bobo & Kluegal, 1997, p. 101). In 2008, the willingness to apply this negative trait to blacks was dramatically lower, as was the differential, and this result might be taken as evidence of the declining strength of antiblack stereotypes among whites.

Exhibit 3.4 presents a less optimistic picture. Compared with the stereotype of "unintelligent," the stereotype of black laziness was more widespread in 1990 (more than 45% of whites applied this characterization to blacks) and the differential was much larger. By 2008, the percentage of whites willing to apply this trait to blacks declined, as did the differential. Still, about a third of whites saw blacks as lazy, a result which indicates that this apect of the traditional, "negative" stereotype of blacks persists in American society.

Overall, these results support the idea that elements of traditional stereotypical thinking persist in the United States. The declines reflected in Exhibits 3.3 and 3.4 may reflect decreasing levels of prejudice or a growing unwillingness to verbalize prejudice, possibilities we will discuss later in this chapter.

Cognitive and Affective Dimensions of Stereotypes

Remember that individual prejudice has an affective dimension in addition to the cognitive. Robert Merton (1968), a prominent American sociologist, makes this distinction between dimensions dramatically. Merton analyzed stereotypical perceptions of Abraham Lincoln, Jews, and Japanese. In the following passage, he argues that the three "stereotypes" are identical in content but vastly different in emotional shading:

> The very same behavior undergoes a complete change of evaluation in its transition from the in-group Abe Lincoln to the out-group Abe Cohen or Abe Kurokawa. Did Lincoln work far into the night? This testifies that he was industrious, resolute, perseverant, and eager to realize his capacities to the full. Do the out-group Jews or Japanese keep these same hours? This only bears witness to their sweatshop mentality, their ruthless undercutting of American standards, their unfair competitive practices. Is the in-group hero frugal, thrifty, and sparing? Then the out-group villain is stingy, miserly, and penny-pinching. All honor is due to the in-group Abe for his having been smart, shrewd, and intelligent, and, by the same token, all contempt is owing the out-group Abes for their being sharp, cunning, crafty, and too clever by far. (p. 482)

The stereotype of all three Abes is identical; what varies is the affect, or the emotional tone, reflected in the descriptive terms. Thus, the same stereotype evokes different emotional responses for different groups or in different individuals.

Intersections of Race, Gender, and Class

The affective and cognitive dimensions of prejudice vary not only by race and ethnicity but also by gender and class, the major axes that define minority group experience. For example, the stereotypes and feelings attached to black males differ from those attached to black females, and feelings about lower-class Mexican Americans may vary dramatically from those attributed to upper-class members of the same group. Some of this variation was captured in a study that asked white students at Arizona State University about their perceptions of women (Weitz & Gordon, 1993). Sharp distinctions were found between "women in

Images and feelings about other groups vary by gender and social class.

Thinkstock/Creatas.

general" (a label that, to the students, apparently signified white women) and African American women in particular. When asked to select traits for "American women in general," the responses were overwhelmingly positive and included "intelligent," "sensitive," and "attractive." Of the 10 most commonly selected traits, only 2 ("materialistic" and "emotional") might have had some negative connotations.

The students selected very different terms to describe African American women. The single most commonly selected trait was "loud," and only 22% of the sample saw African American women as "intelligent." Of the 10 most commonly selected traits, 5 (e.g., "talkative," "stubborn") seemed to have at least some negative affect attached to them.

A study by sociologist Edward Morris further illustrates how race, gender, and class can intersect in shaping feelings and thoughts of other groups (Morris, 2005). He studied an urban high school and focused on how various types of students were perceived and disciplined by school administrators and faculty. Morris found that consistent with the notion of a "matrix of domination" mentioned in Chapter 1, stereotypes varied "not just through gender, or just through race, or just through class, but through all of these at once" (p. 44). For example, black boys were seen by school administrators and faculty as "too" masculine, extremely aggressive, dangerous, and in need of careful watching. Black girls, in contrast, were seen as not feminine enough, too loud and aggressive, and in need of being molded into more compliant and deferential females. Other groups in the school—Latinas, Asian males, white males and females—were also the objects of clear sets of stereotypes and feelings and tended to be subjected to forms of discipline that, ultimately, tended to reproduce the systems of inequality in the larger society.

SOCIOLOGICAL CAUSES OF PREJUDICE

Prejudice is a complex phenomenon with multiple causes and manifestations. In this section, we will focus on a macro-sociological approach and examine theories that stress the causes of prejudice that are related to culture, social structure, and group relationships.

The Role of Group Competition

Every form of prejudice—even the most ancient—started at some specific point in history. If we go back far enough in time, we can find a moment that predates antiblack prejudice, anti-Semitism, negative stereotypes about Native Americans or Hispanic Americans, or antipathy against Asian Americans. What sorts of conditions create prejudice? The one common factor that seems to account for the origin of all prejudices is competition between groups—some episode in which one group successfully dominates, takes resources from, or eliminates a threat from some other group. The successful group becomes the dominant group, and the other group becomes the minority group.

Why is group competition associated with the emergence of prejudice? Typically, prejudice is more a result of the competition than a cause. Its role is to help mobilize emotional energy for the contest; justify rejection and attack; and rationalize the structures of domination, such as slavery or segregation, that result from the competition. Groups react to the competition and to the threat presented by other groups with antipathy and stereotypes about the "enemy" group. Prejudice emerges from the heat of the contest but then can solidify and persist for years (even centuries) after the end of the conflict. In chapters to come—and particularly in Chapter 4—we will often focus on the relationships between group competition and prejudice.

Robber's Cave

The relationship between prejudice and competition has been demonstrated in a variety of settings and situations ranging from labor strikes to international war to social psychology labs. In the chapters to come, we will examine the role of prejudice during the creation of slavery in North America, as a reaction to periods of high immigration, and as an accompaniment to myriad forms of group competition. Here, to illustrate our central point about competition and prejudice, we will examine a classic experiment from the sociological literature. The Robber's Cave experiment was conducted in the 1950s at a summer camp for 11- and 12-year-old boys.

The camp director, social psychologist Muzafer Sherif, divided the campers into two groups, the Rattlers and the Eagles (Sherif, Harvey, White, Hood, & Sherif, 1961). The groups lived in different cabins, and the staff continually pitted them against each other in a wide range of activities. Games, sports, and even housekeeping chores were set up on a competitive basis. As the competition intensified, the groups developed and expressed negative feelings (prejudice) against each other. Competition and prejudicial feelings grew quite intense and were manifested in episodes of name calling and raids on the "enemy" group.

Sherif attempted to reduce the harsh feelings he had created by bringing the campers together in various pleasant situations featuring food, movies, and other treats. But the rival groups only used these opportunities to express their enmity. Sherif then came up with some activities that required the members of the rival groups to work cooperatively with each other. For example, the researchers deliberately sabotaged some plumbing to create an "emergency" that required the efforts of everyone to resolve. As a result of these cooperative activities, intergroup "prejudice" declined, and eventually, friendships were formed across groups.

In the Robber's Cave experiment, as in many actual group relationships, prejudice (negative feelings and stereotypes about other campers) arose to help mobilize feelings and to justify rejection and attacks, both verbal and physical, against the out-group. When group competition was reduced, the levels of prejudice abated and eventually disappeared, again demonstrating that prejudice is caused by competition, not the other way around.

Although the Robber's Cave experiment illustrates our central point, we must be cautious in generalizing from these results. The experiment was conducted in an artificial environment with young boys (all white) who had no previous acquaintance with one another and no history of grievances or animosity. Thus, these results may be only partially generalizable to group conflicts in the real world. Nonetheless, Robber's Cave illustrates a fundamental connection between group competition and prejudice that we will observe repeatedly in the chapters to come. Competition and the desire to protect resources and status and to defend against threats from other groups are the primary motivations for the construction of traditions of prejudice and structures of inequality that benefit the dominant group.

Theoretical Perspectives on Group Competition and Prejudice: Power/Conflict Models

Many theorists have examined the dynamics of group competition and its connection with prejudice and discrimination. Here we examine three of the most influential sociological perspectives on this topic.

Marxist Analysis

In Chapter 1, Marxism was discussed as a theory of social inequality. One of the tenets of Marxism is that the elites who control the means of production in a society also control the ideas and intellectual activity of the society. Ideologies and belief systems are shaped to support the dominance of the elites, and these ideologies and belief systems change when new elites come into control: "What else does the history of ideas prove, than that intellectual production changes in character in proportion as material production is changed? The ruling ideas of each age have been the ideas of its ruling class" (Marx & Engels, 1848/1967, p. 102).

Elite classes who subordinate or exploit a minority group will develop and institutionalize ideologies to justify or "explain" the arrangement. The history of the United States (and many other nations) includes numerous situations in which prejudice was used to help sustain the control of elite classes. For example, slave owners in the South used antiblack prejudice to attempt to control perceptions and justify the exploitation of the slaves. If it were commonly believed that blacks were inferior and too irresponsible to care for themselves, the constraints of slavery would seem less oppressive and unjust. People who did not benefit directly from slavery might not oppose the institution if they accepted the idea of black inferiority.

The slave owners also attempted to use Christianity to "brainwash" the slaves into accepting their powerless status. The exposure of slaves to religion was carefully controlled and emphasized those aspects of Christianity that stress the virtues of meekness and humility and promise rewards—but only in heaven. Thus, religion was used to stress obedience and to focus the attention of the slaves on the next life, not on the misery and injustice of this life.

In a more industrial example, the history of the United States for the past 150 years is replete with instances of struggle between the capitalists who control the means of production (factories, mills, mines, banks, etc.) and workers. Early in the 20th century, it was common for industrialists to try to weaken labor unions by splitting the working class along racial lines. The greater the extent to which black and white workers fought each other, the less likely there would be a unified uprising against the capitalist class. The capitalist class controlled the racially mixed working class by following a strategy of "divide and conquer" (Cox, 1948; Reich, 1986).

Split Labor Market Theory

This theory agrees with the Marxist idea that prejudice and racist ideologies serve the interest of a specific class, but it identifies a different beneficiary. In split labor market theory, there are three actors in the economic sector of an industrial society. First are the elites, the capitalists who own the means of production. The other two groups are segments of the working class. The labor market is divided (or split) into higher-priced labor and cheaper labor. It is in the economic self-interest of the capitalist class to use cheaper labor whenever possible. Recent immigrants and minority groups often fill the role of cheaper labor.

Higher-priced labor (usually consisting of members of the dominant group) will attempt to exclude cheaper labor from the marketplace whenever it can. Such efforts include barring minority groups from labor unions, violent attacks on minority group communities, support for discriminatory laws, and efforts to exclude groups from the United States entirely. Prejudice is used by higher-priced labor to arouse and mobilize opposition to the cheaper labor pool represented by the minority group. The economic nature of the competition and the economic self-interests of higher-priced labor are obscured by appeals to racial or cultural unity against the "threat" represented by the minority group. The major beneficiary of prejudice is not the capitalist class but the more powerful elements of the working class (Bonacich, 1972; Bonacich & Modell, 1980).

Group Interests

A similar line of analysis was begun by American sociologist Herbert Blumer (1958), who argued that prejudice is activated when groups feel that they are threatened by groups they see as beneath them (see also Bobo & Tuan, 2006). The dominant group—which, by definition, has the highest status in a society—is particularly likely to use prejudice as a weapon when it feels that its privileges, its sense of entitlement and high position, are in peril. We saw in Chapter 1 that sociologist Max Weber argued that there are three separate stratification systems in society: property (the economic system that includes jobs and income), power (control of decision making and the political institution at all levels), and prestige (the allocation of honor, esteem, and respect). Perceived threat could involve any of these dimensions or any combination of the three.

An example of these dynamics can be found in the reaction of many Southern (and other) whites to the black Civil Rights Movement of the 1950s and 1960s. We will discuss this era of race relations in some detail in Chapter 6, but, for now, we can point out that the Civil Rights movement challenged the Southern system of race-based privilege that was institutionalized during slavery and perpetuated during segregation, a system that granted even the lowest-status white a position superior to all blacks. Prejudice was an important part of the attempt by whites to resist the racial change demanded by the civil rights movement. Politicians and other leaders of the white community used the most vicious stereotypes (e.g., those that depicted black men as sexual threats to white women) and the most negative emotional rhetoric to motivate whites to attempt to defeat demands for racial equality and an end to segregation. Sometimes, prejudice was used to foment or justify violence—bombings, lynchings, and beatings—but even milder forms of resistance were motivated by the perceived need to maintain the higher position of whites in the South and protect their racial privilege and advantages.

Contemporary examples of how prejudice has been used to help defend group position are not difficult to locate. For example, many Americans today feel threatened by immigration (particularly undocumented immigrants), the rising tide of diversity (see Exhibit 1.1), and various global threats, including the rise of China. Predictably, politicians and media figures of all persuasions have exploited—and perhaps intensified—these feelings, particularly in election campaign ads designed (sometimes blatantly) to mobilize people's fears, prejudices, and sense of threat. One widely criticized example comes from the 2010 election campaign of Senator David Vitter of Louisiana. He accused his opponent of being soft on illegal immigration and border security, and his campaign ran a TV ad in which immigrants are shown sneaking across the border and being welcomed with checks, limousine rides, and other benefits, presumably the result of the policies advocated by his opponent (see http://www.youtube.com/watch?v=9uvp0Jljh6U for the ad). Vitter won the election by a wide margin.

Summary and Limitations

These theories share the conclusion that prejudice flows from struggles to control or expand a group's share of scarce resources. The primary beneficiary of prejudice is sometimes the elite class (e.g., capitalists, plantation owners, high-status groups) and sometimes another segment of the dominant group (e.g., higher-priced labor). In general, though, these perspectives agree that prejudice exists because someone or some group gains by it.

These points are persuasive and help us understand why prejudice originates in the first place, but they cannot account for prejudice in all its forms. No theory can explain everything, especially something as complex as prejudice. The origins of prejudice can be found in culture, socialization, family structure, and personality development, as well as in politics and economics. As the authoritarian personality theory reminds us, prejudice can have important psychological and social functions independent of group power relationships.

To illustrate these limitations, consider an analysis of attitudes toward immigrants. Consistent with the idea that prejudice is stimulated by group competition, Burns and Gimpel (2000) found that opposition to immigration is greater when times are hard and people feel economically threatened. However, they also found that anti-immigration prejudice cannot be explained by economics alone and that it persists even when economic conditions improve, a finding consistent with the idea that prejudice is shaped by cultural and personality factors in addition to conflict over scarce resources.

THE PERSISTENCE OF PREJUDICE

Prejudice originates in group competition of some sort but often outlives the conditions of its creation. It can persist, full-blown and intense, long after the episode that sparked it has faded from memory. How does prejudice persist through time?

The Vicious Cycle

In his classic analysis of American race relations, *An American Dilemma*, Swedish economist Gunnar Myrdal (1944/1962) proposed the idea that prejudice is perpetuated through time by a self-fulfilling prophecy or a vicious cycle of prejudice, as illustrated in Exhibit 3.5. The dominant group uses its power to force the minority group into an inferior status, such as slavery, as shown in the diagram in Area 1. Partly to motivate the construction of a system of racial stratification and partly to justify its existence, individual prejudice and racist belief systems are invented and accepted by the dominant group, as shown in Area 2. Individual prejudices are reinforced by the everyday observation of the minority group's inferior status. The fact that the minority group is impoverished, enslaved, or otherwise exploited confirms and strengthens the attribution of inferiority. The belief in inferiority motivates further discrimination and unequal treatment, as shown in Area 3 of the diagram, which reinforces the inferior status, which validates the prejudice and racism, which justifies further discrimination, and so on. Over a few generations, a stable, internally reinforced system of racial inferiority becomes an integral, unremarkable, and (at least for the dominant group) accepted part of everyday life.

Exhibit 3.5 Myrdal's Vicious Cycle

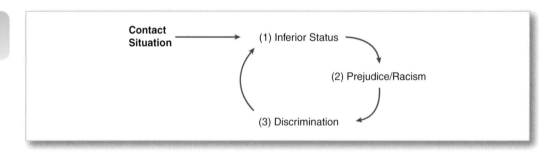

Culture is conservative, and once created, prejudice will be sustained over time just like any set of attitudes, values, and beliefs. Future generations will learn prejudice in the same way and for the same reasons that they learn any other aspect of their culture. Thus, prejudice and racism come to us through our cultural heritage as a package of stereotypes, emotions, and ideas. We learn which groups are "good" and which are "bad" in the same way we learn table manners and religious beliefs (Pettigrew, 1958, 1971, p. 137; Simpson & Yinger, 1985, pp. 107, 108). When prejudice is part of the cultural heritage, individuals learn to think and feel negatively toward other groups as a routine part of socialization. Much of the prejudice expressed by Americans—and the people of many other societies—is the normal result of typical socialization in families, communities, and societies that are, to some degree, racist. Given our long history of intense racial and ethnic exploitation, it is not surprising that Americans continue to manifest antipathy toward and stereotypical ideas about other groups.

Prejudice in Children

The idea that prejudice is learned during socialization is reinforced by studies of the development of prejudice in children. Research generally shows that children become aware of group differences (e.g., black vs. white) at an early age, perhaps as early as 6 months (Katz, 2003, p. 898). By age 3 or younger, they recognize the significance and the permanence of racial groups and can accurately classify people on the basis of skin color and other cues (Brown, 1995, pp. 121–136; Katz, 1976, p. 126). Once the racial or group categories are mentally established, children begin the process of learning the "proper" attitudes and stereotypes to associate with the various groups, and both affective and cognitive prejudice begin to grow at an early age.

It is important to note that children can acquire prejudice even when parents and other caregivers do not teach it overtly or directly. Adults control the socialization process and valuable resources (food, shelter, praise), and children are motivated to seek their approval and conform to their expectations (at least in the early years). There are strong pressures on the child to learn and internalize the perceptions of the older generation, and even a casual comment or an overheard remark can establish or reinforce negative beliefs or feelings about members of other groups (Ashmore & DelBoca, 1976). Children need not be directly instructed about presumed minority group characteristics; it is often said that racial attitudes are "caught and not taught."

Research also shows that children are actively engaged in their learning and that their levels of prejudice reflect their changing intellectual capabilities. Children as young as 5 to 6 months old can make some simple distinctions (e.g., by gender or race) between categories of people. The fact that this capability emerges so early in life suggests that it is not simply a response to adult teaching. "Adults use categories to simplify and make sense of their environment; apparently children do the same" (Brown, 1995, p. 126). Gross, simplistic distinctions between people may help very young children organize and understand the world around them. The need for such primitive categorizations may decline as the child becomes more experienced in life and more sophisticated in his or her thinking. Doyle and Aboud (1995), for example, found that prejudice was highest for younger children and actually decreased between kindergarten and the third grade. The decline was related to increased awareness of racial similarities (as well as differences) and diverse perspectives on race (see also Black-Gutman & Hickson, 1996; Bronson & Merryman, 2009; Brown, 1995, pp. 149–159; Powlishta, Serbin, Doyle, & White, 1994; Van Ausdale & Feagin, 2001). Thus, changing levels of prejudice in children may reflect an interaction between children's changing mental capacities and their environment rather than a simple or straightforward learning of racist cultural beliefs or values.

Social Distance Scales: The Cultural Dimensions of Prejudice

Further evidence for the cultural nature of prejudice is provided by research on the concept of social distance, which is related to prejudice but is not quite the same thing. Social distance is the degree of intimacy that a person is willing to accept in his or her relations with members of other groups. On this scale, the most intimate relationship is close kinship, and the most distant is exclusion from the country. The Seven Degrees of Social Distance, as specified by Emory Bogardus (1933), the inventor of the scale, are as follows:

1. To close kinship by marriage

2. To my club as personal chums

3. To my street as neighbors

4. To employment in my occupation

5. To citizenship in my country

6. As visitors only to my country

7. Would exclude from my country

Research using social distance scales demonstrates that Americans rank other groups in similar ways across time and space. The consistency indicates a common frame of reference or set of perceptions, a continuity of vision possible only if perceptions have been standardized by socialization in a common culture.

Exhibit 3.6 presents some results of seven administrations of the scale to samples of Americans from 1926 to 2001. The groups are listed by the rank order of their scores for

Exhibit 3.6 Social Distance Scores

Group	1926	1946	1956	1966	1977	1993	2001
English	1	3	3	2	2	2	4
American Whites	2	1	1	1	1	—	1
Canadians	3	2	2	3	3	—	3
Irish	5	4	5	5	7	1	5
Germans	7	10	8	10	11	10	8
Norwegians	10	7	10	7	12	8	—
Russians	13	13	24	24	29	13	20
Italians	14	16	12	8	5	3	2
Poles	15	14	13	16	18	12	14
American Indians	18	20	18	18	10	16	12
Jews	19	19	16	15	15	15	11
Mexicans	21	24	28	28	26	18	25
Japanese	22	30	26	25	25	19	22
Filipinos	23	23	21	21	24	—	16
African Americans	24	29	27	29	17	17	9
Turks	25	25	23	26	28	22	—
Chinese	26	21	25	22	23	20	17
Koreans	27	27	30	27	30	21	24
Asian Indians	28	28	29	30	27	—	26
Vietnamese	—	—	—	—	—	—	28
Muslims	—	—	—	—	—	—	29
Arabs	—	—	—	—	—	—	30
Mean (all scores)	2.14	2.12	2.08	1.92	1.93	1.43	1.44
Range	2.85	2.57	1.75	1.56	1.38	1.07	0.87
Total Number of Groups Included	28	30	30	30	30	24	30
Correlation With 1926 Rankings	—	.95	.93	.90	.84	.92	.76

SOURCES: 1926 through 1977—Smith and Dempsey (1983, p. 588); 1993—Kleg and Yamamoto (1998) and Parrillo (2003).

NOTE: Values in the table are ranks for that year. To conserve space, some groups and ranks have been eliminated.

Key:
Red = Northern and Western Europeans
Blue = Southern and Eastern Europeans
Black = "nonwhites"

1926. In that year, the sample expressed the least social distance from the English and the most distance from Asian Indians. Whereas the average social distance score for the English was 1.02, indicating virtually no sense of distance, the average score for Indians was 3.91, indicating a distance between "to employment in my occupation" and "to my street as neighbors."

Note, first of all, the stability in the rankings. The actual scores (not shown) generally decrease from decade to decade, indicating less social distance and presumably a decline in prejudice over the years. The group rankings, however, tend to be the same year after year. This stability is clearly displayed in the bottom row of the table, which shows correlations between the group rankings for each year and the 1926 ranking. If any of the lists of scores had been identical, the statistic in this row would have shown its maximum value of 1.00. Although they weaken over time, the actual correlations approach the maximum value of 1.00 and indicate that the rank order of the groups from year to year is substantially the same. Considering the changes that society experienced between 1926 and 2001 (the Great Depression; World War II, the Korean War, Vietnam, and the cold war with the U.S.S.R.; the civil rights movement; the resumption of large-scale immigration, etc.), this overall continuity in group rankings is remarkable.

Second, note the nature of the ranking: Groups with origins in Northern and Western Europe are ranked highest, followed by groups from Southern and Eastern Europe, with racial minorities near the bottom. These preferences reflect the relative status of these groups in the U.S. hierarchy of racial and ethnic groups, which, in turn, reflect the timing of immigration and the perceived "degree of difference" with the dominant group (see Chapter 2). The rankings also reflect the relative amount of exploitation and prejudice directed at each group over the course of U.S. history.

Although these patterns of social distance scores support the general point that prejudice is cultural, this body of research has some important limitations. The respondents were generally college students from a variety of campuses, not representative samples of the population, and the differences in actual scores from group to group are sometimes very small. Still, the stability of the patterns cannot be ignored: The top groups are always Northern European, Poles and Jews are always ranked in the middle third, and Koreans and Japanese always fall in the bottom third. African Americans and American Indians were also ranked toward the bottom until the most recent rankings.

Finally, note how the relative positions of some groups change with international and domestic relations. For example, both Japanese and Germans fell in the rankings at the end of World War II (1946). Comparing 1966 with 1946, Russians fell and Japanese rose, reflecting changing patterns of alliance and enmity in the global system of societies. The dramatic rise of Native Americans and African Americans since the 1966 ranking may reflect declining levels of overt prejudice in American society. In 2001, the scale was administered in the weeks following the terrorist attacks on September 11, and the low ranking of Arabs reflects the societal reaction toward those traumatic events.

How do we explain the fact that group rankings generally are so stable from the 1920s to 2001? The stability strongly suggests that Americans view the various groups through the same culturally shaped lens. A sense of social distance, a perception of some groups as "higher" or "better" than others, is part of the cultural package of intergroup prejudices we acquire from socialization into American society. The social distance patterns illustrate the power of culture to shape individual perceptions and preferences and attest to the fundamentally racist nature of American culture.

The power of culture to shape our perceptions is illustrated in the next Narrative Portrait.

The Cultural Sources of Prejudice

In The Crazy Ladies of Pearl Street, *best-selling novelist Trevanian (2005) recounts his experiences growing up Irish Catholic in a poor neighborhood in Albany, New York, in the 1930s. In the passage below, he recounts how his mother, Ruby LaPointe, decided to apply for public assistance after her husband had abandoned them. Trevanian, then a boy of 8, advises her to enlist the assistance of Mr. Kane, the local grocer who has already extended them credit to buy food and other essentials. The young Trevanian sees Mr. Kane as kindly and full of good humor. His mother focuses on another part of his identity: Mr. Kane is Jewish, and this dominates how she sees him.*

For the author, his mother is powerful, even heroic. She was the central character of his childhood, and he recounts in his memoir how she coped with daily disasters and rebounded from setback after setback, always determined to care for her children properly. She is also, as demonstrated in this passage, a product of her culture and her upbringing. She inherited a set of attitudes, images, and emotions about other groups and especially about Jews. Note her ability to see Mr. Kane and other Jews negatively: No matter what he says or does, her stereotypes are reinforced. Her view of Mr. Kane exemplifies how selective perception can sift through evidence and experience and turn positives into negatives.

THE CRAZY LADIES OF PEARL STREET

TREVANIAN

Here's how things were: We were marooned on this slum street in this strange city where we didn't know anybody and nobody gave a damn about us, and we had only a little more than five bucks to our name. But we weren't beaten. Not by a damn sight. Nobody beats Ruby Lucille LaPointe! No, sir! . . . Her pride had never let her seek public assistance, and it burned her up to have to do so now, but she . . . couldn't let pride stand in the way of us kids having food on the table. There must be agencies and people that she could turn to, just until we were on our feet again. First she'd contact them and ask them for help . . . make them help us, goddammit! Then she'd look for work as a waitress. . . . But first, she had to find out the addresses of the welfare agencies. If only she knew someone she could ask about things like this.

"What about Mr. Kane?" I suggested.

"The grocery man? Oh, I don't know. I don't think we want any more favors from his sort."

" . . . His sort?"

She shrugged.

"But he's nice," I said. "And smart, too."

She thought about that for a moment. She didn't like being beholden to strangers, but . . . Oh, all right, she'd go over to thank him for giving us credit. That was just common courtesy. And maybe while she was there she'd . . . "You know, come to think of it, this Mr. Kane of yours just might help us out because if he doesn't, we won't be able to pay what we owe him. You can only count on these people if there's something in it for them."

"He'd help us anyway. He's nice." . . .

She often said, and honestly believed, that she was not prejudiced—well, except in the case of Italian mobsters and drunken Irish loafers and stupid Poles and snooty Yankee Protestants, but then who wasn't? Among the cultural scars left by her early years in convent school was a stereotypical view of "the people who slew Jesus." "On the other hand," she said, always wanting to be fair, "I served some very nice Jewish people in Lake George Restaurant last season. They always chose my station. Real good tippers. But then they had to be, didn't they? To make up for things."

I accompanied her across the street, and Mr. Kane spent half the morning looking up the appropriate welfare agencies and using the pay phone at the back of his shop to call people and make appointments for my mother. . . . I looked up at my mother to give her an "I told you he was nice" look, and I was surprised to see tears standing in her eyes. . . . She confessed [to Mr. Kane] that she didn't know what she would do if somebody didn't help her. . . .

She thanked him for his help, but now there was a chill in her tone. I could tell that she was ashamed of having broken down before this stranger. As we crossed the street back to [the apartment] she told me that I must always be careful with these people.

"But Mr. Kane was just trying to be . . ."

"They have a way of worming things out of you."

"He wasn't worming any—"

"You just be careful what you tell them, and that's final. Period!"

Later that month, when we were able to begin paying something against our slate, my mother felt vindicated in her mistrust of "these people." She discovered that Mr. Kane had charged her a nickel for each call he made on her behalf. I explained that this was only fair because he had put a nickel into the slot for each call, but she waved this aside, saying she was sure he made a little something on each call. Why else would he have a phone taking up space in his shop? No, they work every angle, these people. . . .

SOURCE: Trevanian (2005, pp. 31–33). Copyright © 2005 by Trevanian. Used by permission of Crown Publishers, a division of Random House, Inc.

Situational Influences

As a final point in our consideration of the persistence of prejudice, we should note the importance of the social situation in which attitudes are expressed and behavior occurs. What people think and what they do is not always the same. Even intense prejudice may not translate into discriminatory behavior, and discrimination is not always accompanied by prejudice (refer back to Exhibit 3.1).

One of the earliest demonstrations of the difference between what people think and feel (prejudice) and what they actually do (discrimination) was provided by sociologist Robert LaPiere (1934). In the 1930s, he escorted a Chinese couple on a tour of the United States. At that time, Chinese and other Asians were the victims of widespread discrimination and exclusion, and anti-Chinese prejudice was quite high, as demonstrated by the scores in Exhibit 3.6. However, LaPiere and his companions dined in restaurants and stayed in hotels without incident for the entire trip and experienced discrimination only once.

Six months later, LaPiere wrote to every establishment the group had patronized and inquired about reservations. He indicated that some of the party were Chinese and asked if that would be a problem. Of those establishments that replied (about half), 92% said that they would not serve Chinese and would be unable to accommodate the party.

Why the difference? Although not a definitive or particularly sophisticated method of data gathering (for example, there was no way to tell whether the correspondents were the same persons LaPiere and his associates had dealt with in person), this episode exemplifies the difference between saying and doing and the importance of taking the situation into account. On LaPiere's original visit, anti-Asian prejudice may well have been present but was not expressed to avoid making a scene. In a different situation, the more distant interaction of written correspondence, the restaurant and hotel staffs may have allowed their prejudice to be expressed in open discrimination because the potential for embarrassment was much less.

The situation a person is in shapes the relationship between prejudice and discrimination. In highly prejudiced communities or groups, the pressure to conform may cause relatively unprejudiced individuals to discriminate. For example, if an ethnic or racial or gender joke is told in a group of friends or relatives, all might join in the laughter. Even a completely unprejudiced person might crack a smile or register a slight giggle to avoid embarrassing or offending the person who told the joke.

On the other hand, situations in which there are strong norms of equal and fair treatment may stifle the tendency of even the most bigoted individual to discriminate. For example, if a community vigorously enforces antidiscrimination laws, even the most prejudiced merchant might refrain from treating minority group customers unequally. Highly prejudiced individuals may not discriminate so they can "do business" (or at least avoid penalties or sanctions) in an environment in which discrimination is not tolerated or is too costly.

Summary and Limitations

The theories and perspectives examined in this section help us understand how prejudice can persist through time. Prejudice becomes a part of the culture of a society and is passed along to succeeding generations along with other values, norms, and information.

Although cultural causes of prejudice are obviously important, considering only cultural factors may lead us to the mistaken belief that all members of the same society have similar levels of prejudice. On the contrary, no two people have the same socialization experiences or develop exactly the same prejudices (or any other attitude, for that matter). Differences in family structure, parenting style, school experiences, attitudes of peers, and a host of other factors affect the development of an individual's personality and attitude.

Furthermore, socialization is not a passive process; we are not neutral recipients of a culture that is simply forced down our throats. Our individuality, intelligence, and curiosity affect the nature and content of our socialization experiences. Even close siblings may have very different experiences and, consequently, different levels of prejudice. People raised in extremely prejudicial settings may moderate their attitudes as a result of experiences later in life, just as those raised in nonprejudiced settings may develop stronger biases as time passes.

The development of prejudice is further complicated by the fact that, in the United States, we also learn egalitarian norms and values as we are socialized. Gunnar Myrdal was referring to this contrast when he titled his landmark study of race relations in the United States *An American Dilemma.* We learn norms of fairness and justice along with norms that condone or even demand unequal treatment based on group membership. Typically, people develop more than one attitude about other groups, and these multiple attitudes are not set in concrete. They can change from time to time and place to place, depending on the situation and a variety of other variables. The same point could be made about other attitudes besides prejudice; people have an array of attitudes, beliefs, and values about any particular subject, and some of them are mutually contradictory.

RECENT TRENDS: TRADITIONAL PREJUDICE AND MODERN RACISM

One of the questions we asked at the beginning of this chapter concerned recent trends in prejudice. Is prejudice still a problem in the United States? There is a great deal of evidence documenting a decline in "traditional" prejudice: the blatant, overt feelings and ideas that have characterized American prejudice virtually from the birth of the nation and that were exemplified in the quotations from President Nixon that opened this chapter. Surveys and public opinion polls show that this type of prejudice is losing strength in the general population.

However, while some celebrate the decline in harsh, overt prejudice, some social scientists argue strongly that prejudice has *not* declined but, rather, has evolved into a more subtle, less obvious, but just as consequential form. This new form of prejudice has been called a number of things, including modern racism, symbolic racism, and colorblind racism, and there is considerable debate over its exact shape, extent, and—indeed—existence. However, even while the issues continue to be debated and researched, there is considerable evidence to support the conclusion that prejudice, even in it's more subtle and disguised forms, remains a potent force in American society.

In this section, we will first investigate and document the decline in traditional prejudice and consider some of the possible causes for this decline. Second, we will consider the nature of modern racism, the newer way of expressing antipathy for other groups.

Traditional Prejudice: Changing Attitudes?

Some of the strongest evidence that traditional prejudice is declining comes from public opinion polls. Surveys measuring prejudice have been administered to representative samples of U.S. citizens since the early 1940s, and these polls document a consistent decrease in support for prejudicial statements, as the data in Exhibit 3.7 indicate.

In 1942, the huge majority—a little more than 70%—of white Americans thought that black and white children should attend different schools. Forty years later, in 1982, support for separate schools had dropped to less than 10%. Similarly, support for the right of white people to maintain separate neighborhoods declined from 65% in 1942 to 18% in the early 1990s. In more recent decades, the percentage of white respondents who support laws against interracial marriage decreased from almost 40% in the early 1970s to about 10% in 2002, and the percentage that believe blacks are inferior fell from 26% to less than 10% between the early 1970s and 2010.

The overall trend is unmistakable: There has been a dramatic decline in support for prejudiced statements since World War II. In the early 1940s, most white Americans supported prejudiced views. In recent times, only a small minority expresses such views.

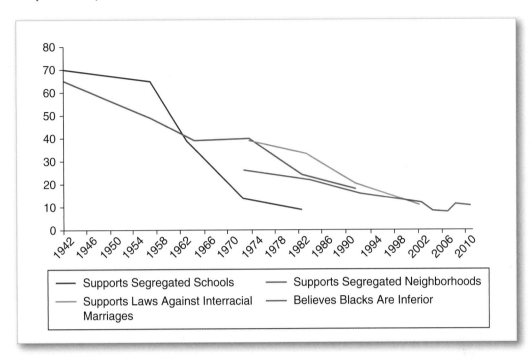

SOURCE: 1942, 1956, 1963—Hyman and Sheatsley (1964); 1972 through 2010—National Opinion Research Council (1972–2010).

NOTE: Results are accurate to within 3 or 4 percentage points.

Exhibit 3.7 Declining Antiblack Prejudice in the United States, 1942 to 2010 (White Americans Only)

Of course, these polls also show that prejudice has not vanished. A percentage of the white population continues to endorse highly prejudicial sentiments and opinions. Remember also that the polls show only what people *say* they feel and think, which might be different from what they truly believe.

Assuming that the overall trend displayed in these polls is reasonably valid, what causes might be important? Here, we investigate two possible independent variables: rising levels of education and increasing contact across racial lines.

Explaining the Decline of Traditional Prejudice 1: The Role of Education

One possible cause of declining prejudice is that Americans have become much more educated during the time period covered in Exhibit 3.7. Education frequently has been singled out as the most effective cure for prejudice and discrimination. Education, like travel, is said to "broaden one's perspective" and encourage a more sophisticated view of human affairs. People with higher levels of education are more likely to view other people in terms of their competence and abilities and not in terms of physical or ethnic characteristics. In some theories of assimilation (see Chapter 2), education is identified as one of the modernizing forces that will lead to a more rational, competency-based social system.

As shown in Exhibit 3.8, the percentage of the U.S. population with high school degrees increased more than 2.5 times between 1950 and 2008, from about 34% to 87%. In the same period, the percentage of the population with college degrees rose at an even faster rate (nearly 5 times), from about 6% to more than 29%. Could it be merely coincidental that prejudice declined so dramatically during the same time period?

Many studies have also found statistical correlations between an individual's level of prejudice and level of education. Exhibit 3.9 shows the relationships between various measures of prejudice and level of education for a representative sample of white Americans in the year 2010. These

Exhibit 3.8 Percentage of Population Age 25 and Older With High School and College Degrees, 1950 to 2008

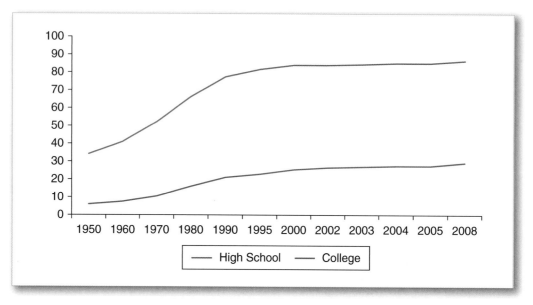

SOURCE: 1950—U.S. Bureau of the Census (1997); 1960 through 2008—U.S. Bureau of the Census (2010d, Table 225).

Exhibit 3.9 Prejudice by Level of Education, 2010 (Whites Only)

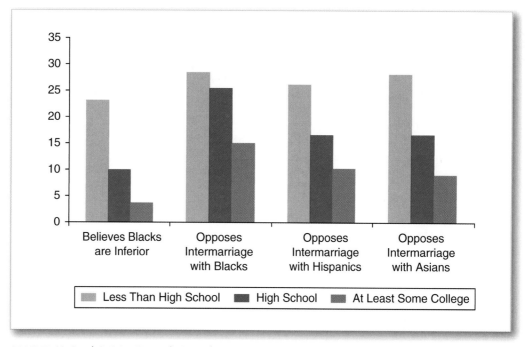

SOURCE: National Opinion Research Council (1972–2010).

graphs show that support for prejudiced responses declines as education increases. White respondents with less education express greater support for the belief that blacks are inferior, and they are more opposed to marriage across group lines with blacks, Hispanics, and Asians.

The correlation between increased education and decreased prejudice supports the common wisdom that education is the enemy of (and antidote to) prejudice, but we need to consider some caveats and qualifications before we come to any conclusions. First, correlation is not the same thing as causation, and just because education and prejudice change together over time and are statistically associated does not prove that one is causing the change in the other.

Perhaps people are still highly prejudiced and are simply hiding their true feelings from the public opinion pollsters, a trend that would be consistent with the arguments that traditional prejudice has morphed into modern racism. Second, the limited set of possible responses offered to respondents (e.g., "agree" or "disagree") might not record the full range, subtlety, or complexity of people's feelings. People typically have many attitudes about a subject, especially one as emotionally charged as prejudice. As we have seen, different situations may activate different sets of attitudes, and public opinion surveys may evoke more tolerant responses. The more educated are particularly likely to be aware of the "correct" responses and more likely to express socially acceptable opinions. The bottom line is that it is hard to determine how much of the apparent reduction in prejudice has been genuine and how much of it is due to conformity to the prevailing and fashionable attitudes of the day (see Jackman, 1978, 1981; Jackman & Muha, 1984; Smith & Seelbach, 1987; Weil, 1985).

Explaining the Decline of Traditional Prejudice 2: The Contact Hypothesis

Like education, contact and increased communication between groups often have been suggested as remedies for prejudice, misunderstandings, and hostile race and ethnic relations. A generic statement of this point of view might read something like this: "If only people would get together and really talk to one another, they would see that we're all the same, all human beings with hopes and dreams," and so on, and so forth. Such sentiments are common, and a number of organizations at all levels of society are devoted to opening and sustaining a dialogue between groups. How effective are such efforts? Does increased contact reduce prejudice? If so, under what conditions?

First of all, contact between groups is not, in and of itself, an immediate or automatic antidote for prejudice. Contact can have a variety of outcomes and can either reduce or increase prejudice, depending on the nature of the situation. When contact occurs under conditions in which groups have unequal status, such as during American slavery or segregation, prejudice is likely to be reinforced, not reduced. On the other hand, certain forms of intergroup contact do seem to reduce prejudice.

Photo 3.3

Contact across group lines in the classroom can fulfill all four conditions of the contact hypothesis.

Thinkstock/Creatas Images.

One theory that addresses the relationship between contact and prejudice is the equal status contact hypothesis. This theory specifies the conditions under which intergroup contact can reduce prejudice: Intergroup contact will tend to reduce prejudice when four conditions are filled: The groups must have (a) equal status and (b) common goals and must (c) interact intensively in noncompetitive, cooperative tasks and (d) have the active endorsement of authority figures (Pettigrew, 1998, pp. 66–67). Each of the four conditions is crucial to the reduction of prejudice.

1. *Equal Status.* Only in situations in which all groups have equal resources and prestige are people likely to view one another as individuals, not as representatives of their respective groups. When the people involved in intergroup contacts are unequal in status, they are more likely to sustain or even intensify their prejudice. During slavery, for example, there was a great deal of contact across racial lines because of the nature of agricultural work. These interactions between blacks and whites were conducted in a context of massive inequality, however, and the contact did not encourage (to say the least) an honest and open sharing of views. Under the system of segregation that followed slavery, the frequency of interracial contact actually declined as blacks and whites were separated into unequal communities. By World War II, segregation was so complete that whites and blacks hardly saw each other except in situations in which blacks were clearly lower in status (Woodward, 1974, p. 118).

2. *Common Goals.* The most effective contact situations for reducing prejudice are those in which members of different groups come together in a single group with a common goal. Examples of such settings include athletic teams working for victories; study groups of students helping one another prepare for tests; and community groups organized to build a playground, combat crime, raise money for cancer research, and so forth.

3. *Intergroup Cooperation and Intensive Interaction.* If contact is to reduce prejudice, it must occur in an atmosphere free from threat or competition between groups. When intergroup contact is motivated by competition for scarce resources, prejudice tends to increase and may even be accompanied by hatred and violence. Recall the Robber's Cave experiment and the levels of prejudice that were manufactured in that situation. If contact is to have a moderating effect on attitudes, it must occur in a setting where there is nothing at stake, no real (or imagined) resource that might be allocated differently as a result of the contact. If people are bound together by cooperative behavior across group lines and are motivated to achieve a common goal, they are much more likely to come to regard one another as individuals, not as caricatures or stereotypical representatives of their groups.

Furthermore, the contact has to be more than superficial. The situation must last for a significant length of time, and the participants must be fully involved. Standing next to each other at a bus stop or eating at adjoining tables in a restaurant does not meet this criterion; people of different groups must deal with each other face-to-face and on a personal level.

4. *Support of Authority, Law, or Custom.* The greater the extent to which contact takes place with strong support from authority figures (politicians, teachers, ministers, etc.) and is supported by moral codes and values, the more likely it is to have a positive impact on intergroup attitudes.

One of the most persuasive and interesting illustrations of the contact hypothesis is the Robber's Cave experiment, discussed earlier in this chapter (Sherif et al., 1961). As you recall, rival groups of campers were placed in competitive situations and became prejudiced as a result. It was not until the researchers created some situations in which the rival groups had to actively cooperate to achieve some common goals that prejudice began to decline. Contact, in and of itself, did not affect intergroup attitudes. Only contact that required the goal-oriented cooperation of equals in status reduced the prejudice that the staff had created through competition.

The Robber's Cave experiment provides dramatic support for the contact hypothesis, but we must be cautious in evaluating this evidence. The experiment was conducted in a "pristine" environment in which the campers had no prior acquaintance with one another and brought no backlog of grievances and no traditions of prejudice to the situation.

The study illustrates and supports the contact hypothesis but cannot prove the theory. For additional evidence, we turn to everyday life and more realistic intergroup contact situations.

In another classic study, Deutsch and Collins (1951) studied the antiblack prejudices of white residents of public housing projects. This study is significant because Deutsch and Collins were able to eliminate the problem of self-selection. In other studies, participation in the contact situation is typically voluntary. The people who volunteer for experiments in interracial contacts are usually not very prejudiced in the first place or at least are more open to change. Thus, any change in prejudice might be due to the characteristics of the people involved, not to the contact situation itself. By contrast, in the Deutsch and Collins study, some of the white participants were randomly assigned to live close to black families. The participants had no control over their living arrangement and, thus, were not self-selected for lower prejudice or openness to change.

A total of four public housing projects were studied. In two of the projects, black and white families were assigned to separate buildings or areas. In the remaining two, dwelling units were assigned regardless of race, and black and white families lived next to one another. As a result of proximity, the white subjects in these two housing projects had higher rates of contact with their black neighbors than did the white families assigned to "segregated" units.

The researchers interviewed the mothers of the white families and found that those living in the integrated projects were less racially prejudiced and much more likely to interact with their African American neighbors than those living in the segregated setting. Deutsch and Collins (1951) concluded that the higher volume of interracial contact had led to lower prejudice.

More recent studies have been based on surveys administered to large, representative samples of black and white Americans and have generally supported the contact hypothesis. Sigelman and Welch (1993, p. 793), for example, report that the professional research literature is generally consistent with the predictions of the contact hypothesis. (For more on the contact hypothesis, see Aberson, Shoemaker, & Tomolillo, 2004; Damico & Sparks, 1986; Dixon, 2006; Dixon & Rosenbaum, 2004; Ellison & Powers, 1994; Forbes, 1997; Katz & Taylor, 1988; Miller & Brewer, 1984; Pettigrew, 1998; Pettigrew & Tropp, 2006; Powers & Ellison, 1995; Smith, 1994; Wittig & Grant-Thompson, 1998; Yancey, 1999, 2007.)

Recent Trends in Intergroup Contact

Since the 1950s, concerted attempts have been made to reduce discrimination against minority groups in virtually every American social institution. In Gordon's (1964) terms, these efforts increased structural assimilation or integration (see Chapter 2) and provided opportunities for dominant and minority group members to associate with one another. Compared with the days of slavery and segregation, there is considerably more contact across group lines today in schools and colleges, workplaces, neighborhoods, and social gatherings.

Some of this increased contact has reduced prejudice. In other instances, contact situations that seem on paper to be likely to reduce prejudice have had no effect or have actually made matters worse. For example, schools and universities across the country have been officially integrated for decades, but these situations do not always lead to increased acceptance and the growth of friendships across group boundaries. The groups involved—whites, African Americans, Latinos, Asians, or Native Americans—sometimes minimize face-to-face interaction and contact across the social dividing lines. To illustrate, you need only visit the cafeteria of many university campuses during mealtime and observe how the seating pattern follows group lines. (For a view of intraracial interactions on racially diverse campuses, see Cowan, 2005.)

The contact hypothesis offers a possible explanation for this pattern of separation within integration. The student body in many schools and colleges is organized along lines that meet some, but not all, of the conditions necessary for a contact situation to lower prejudice. Even when students from the various racial and ethnic groups are roughly equal in status, they do not engage in many cooperative activities that cross group lines. Classrooms themselves are typically competitive and individualistic; students compete for grades and recognition on a one-by-one basis. Cooperation among students (either within or across groups) is not required and is not, in fact, particularly encouraged. The group separation and the lack of opportunities for cooperation often extend beyond the classroom into clubs, sports, and other activities (for an application of the contact hypothesis to high school sports teams, see Brown, Brown, Jackson, Sellers, & Manuel, 2003).

The separation might be reduced and positive contacts increased by encouraging cooperative activities between members of different groups—for example, by imitating the plumbing "emergency" fabricated during the Robber's Cave experiment. One successful attempt to increase cooperation and positive contact was made using a cooperative learning technique called the jigsaw method (Aronson & Gonzalez, 1988).

In this experiment, the students in a fifth-grade class were divided into groups. A certain learning task was divided into separate parts, like a jigsaw puzzle. Researchers ensured that each jigsaw group included both dominant and minority group children. Each student in the jigsaw group was responsible for learning one part of the lesson and then teaching his or her piece to the other students. Everyone was tested on all the pieces, not just his or her own. Each study group needed to make sure that everyone had all the information necessary to pass the test. This goal could be achieved only through the cooperation of all members of the group.

Unlike typical classroom activities, the jigsaw method satisfies all the characteristics for a positive contact experience: Students of equal status are engaged in a cooperative project in which mutual interdependence is essential for the success of all. As Aronson and Gonzalez point out, the students do not need to be idealistic, altruistic, or motivated by a commitment for this method to work. Rather, the students are motivated by pure self-interest; without the help of every member of their group, they cannot pass the test (Aronson & Gonzalez, 1988, p. 307). As we would expect under true equal status contact, the results of the jigsaw method included reductions in prejudice (p. 307; see also Aronson & Patnoe, 1997. For a website devoted to this teaching method, see http://olc.spsd.sk.ca/de/PD/coop/page4.html).

Limitations of the Contact Hypothesis

The contact hypothesis is supported by evidence from a variety of sources. However, it would be a mistake to conclude that all that is necessary to reduce prejudice further is to contrive more equal status contact situations. In many cases, the reduction in prejudice resulting from contact is situation specific; that is, the changed attitudes in one situation (e.g., the workplace) do not necessarily generalize to other situations (e.g., neighborhoods). Both prejudice and discrimination are situational, and stereotypes can be astonishingly resilient perceptual categories. Nonetheless, although this strategy is not a panacea, equal status cooperative contact does seem to have an effect in reducing prejudice and discrimination.

The Contact Hypothesis and European Prejudice

Much of the research on the contact hypothesis has been conducted in the United States. How will the theory fare in other societies? Rather well, according to sociologist Lauren McLaren (2003). Professor McLaren used data from representative samples of citizens drawn from 17 European societies to study anti-immigrant sentiment.

As has the United States, European nations have experienced a sharp increase in immigration over the past decades, and there is considerable concern about the impact of these newcomers. Some Europeans wish to exclude immigrants completely, while others want to help newcomers find their way into their new societies. What social factors might explain these varying responses?

One possibility is that people with greater equal status contacts with immigrants will be more tolerant and less likely to support expulsion. Another possibility is that Europeans who feel the most threatened by immigrants will be the most supportive of exclusion, an idea consistent with theories that link prejudice to group competition. Professor McLaren considered both of these possibilities and used statistical techniques to assess which explanation is more powerful.

Attitudes toward legal immigrants were measured on a 5-point scale that ranged from very open and positive views ("Legal immigrants should be allowed to naturalize") to very negative views ("Immigrants should all be sent back to where they came from"). The higher the score on this scale, the more negative the view.

Equal status contact was measured by a question about whether the respondent had "no, some, or many" friends among immigrant groups, and feelings of threat were measured by two sets of items, one measuring perceived threat to "personal life circumstances" (e.g., losing one's job) and one measuring broader threats to the society (e.g., the perception that immigrants increase the unemployment rate) and culture (e.g., the view that immigrant religions threaten "our way of life") (McLaren, 2003, p. 919).

McLaren found significant differences in support for expulsion by the number of immigrant friends in 16 of the 17 nations tested (the exception was Greece). Some illustrative results for 10 of the 17 nations are shown in Exhibit 3.10. For each nation, the average score for the respondents with "no friends" (the blue bar in Exhibit 3.10) was higher than the average score for respondents with "some friends" (red bar), and the latter score was generally higher than the score for people with "many friends" (green bar). This pattern is very (but not perfectly) consistent with the predictions of the equal status contact hypothesis.

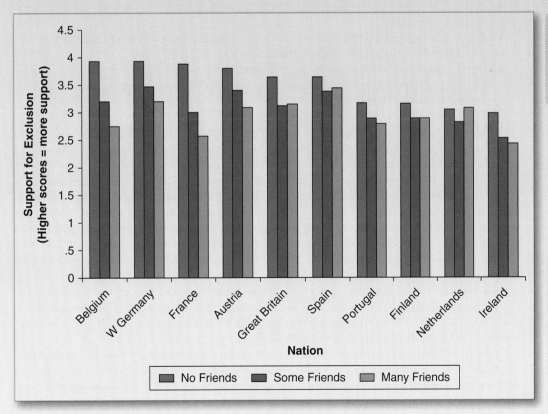

Exhibit 3.10 Support for Exclusion by Friendships With Immigrants, Results for 10 Nations

Professor McLaren also found that support for expulsion increased with the sense of threat felt by the respondent. Which was stronger, sense of threat or degree of contact? Contact still reduced support for exclusion even among those who felt a high level of threat, and the two factors had roughly equal strength in predicting support for expulsion. Thus, our confidence in the equal status contact hypothesis is increased by its strong performance in a non-U.S. arena.

Modern Racism: The New Face of Prejudice?

A number of scholars are investigating the idea that, rather than declining, prejudice is simply changing forms. They have been researching new forms of prejudice variously called symbolic, colorblind, or modern racism. Whatever the label, this form of prejudice is a more subtle, complex, and indirect way of expressing negative feelings toward minority groups and opposition to change in dominant-minority relations (see Bobo, 1988, 2001; Bonilla-Silva, 2001, 2006; Kinder & Sears, 1981; Kluegel & Smith, 1982; McConahy, 1986; Sears, 1988. For a review, see Quillian, 2006).

According to sociologist Eduardo Bonilla-Silva, one of the leading scholars in this area, the new form of prejudice is often expressed in seemingly neutral language or "objective" terms. For example, the modern racist might attribute the underrepresentation of people of color in high status positions to cultural rather than biological factors ("*They* don't emphasize education enough") or explain continuing residential and school segregation by the "natural" choices people make ("*They* would rather be with their own kind"). This kind of thinking rationalizes the status quo and permits dominant group members to live in segregated neighborhoods and send their children to segregated schools without guilt or hesitation (Bonilla-Silva, 2006, p. 28). It obscures the myriad, not-so-subtle social forces that created segregated schools, neighborhoods, and other manifestations of racial inequality in the first place and maintain them in the present.

Although modern racism has been defined in a variety of ways, it tends to be consistent with some tenets of the traditional assimilation perspective discussed in Chapter 2, especially human capital theory and the Protestant Ethic: the traditional American value system that stresses individual responsibility and the importance of hard work. One useful conception identifies three components of modern racism:

- There is no longer any serious or important racial, ethnic, or religious discrimination in American society.
- Any remaining racial or ethnic inequality is the fault of members of the minority group, who simply are not working hard enough.
- Demands for preferential treatment or affirmative action for minorities are unjustified. Minority groups (especially African Americans) have already gotten more than they deserve (Sears & Henry, 2003).

Modern racism tends to "blame the victim" and see group inequality as the result of the behavior or values of minority groups, not as the result of powerful historical processes and policies of the dominant group.

To illustrate the difference between traditional and modern racism, consider the results of a recent public opinion survey administered to a representative sample of Americans (National Opinion Research Council, 1972–2010). Respondents were asked to choose from among four explanations of why black people, on the average, have "worse jobs, income, and housing than white people." Respondents could choose as many explanations as they wanted.

One explanation, consistent with traditional or overt antiblack prejudice, attributes racial inequality to the genetic or biological inferiority of African Americans ("The differences are mainly because blacks have less inborn ability to learn"). About 9% of the white respondents chose this explanation. A second explanation attributes continuing racial inequality to discrimination and a third to the lack of opportunity for an education. Of white respondents, 32% chose the former, and 46% chose the latter.

A fourth explanation, consistent with modern racism, attributes racial inequality to a lack of effort by African Americans ("The differences are because most blacks just don't have the motivation or willpower to pull themselves up out of poverty"). Of the white respondents, 49% chose this explanation, the most popular of the four.

Thus, the survey found support for the idea that racial inequality was the result of discrimination and lack of educational opportunities, views that are consistent with the analysis presented in this book, and relatively little support for traditional antiblack prejudice based on genetic or biological stereotypes. However, the single most widely endorsed explanation was that the root of the problem of continuing racial inequality lies in the African American community, not the society as a whole. Modern racism asserts that African Americans could solve their problems themselves but are not willing to do so. As we have seen, modern racism deflects attention away from centuries of oppression and continuing institutional discrimination in modern society. It stereotypes African Americans and other minority groups and encourages the expression of negative attitudes against them (but without invoking the traditional images or stereotypes).

Researchers have consistently found that modern racism is correlated with opposition to policies and programs intended to reduce racial inequality (Bobo, 2001, p. 292; Quillian, 2006). In the survey summarized earlier, for example, respondents who blamed continuing racial inequality on the lack of motivation or willpower of blacks—the "modern racists"— were the least likely to support government help for blacks and comparable to the traditional racists (those who chose the "inborn ability" explanation) in their opposition to interracial marriage (see Exhibit 3.11).

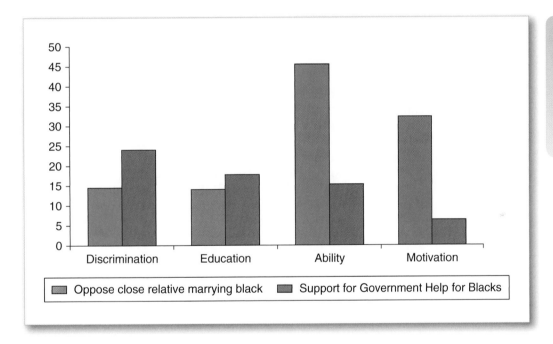

Exhibit 3.11 Support for Government Help for Blacks and Opposition to Interracial Marriage by Explanation of Racial Inequality, 2010 (Whites Only)

Exhibit 3.12 shows that the respondents' view of the causes of racial inequality is also associated with the perception of blacks as lazy. Only about 30% of those who chose the "discrimination" or "education" explanations attributed laziness to blacks, while about 65% (double the percentage) of the traditional racists agreed with the laziness perception. Of the modern racists, slightly less than half agreed with the perception of laziness, a percentage much closer to that of traditional racists than to those of the other explanations.

In the view of many researchers, modern racism has taken the place of traditional or overt prejudice. If this view is correct, the "report card" on progress in the reduction of racial hostility in the United States must be rather mixed. On one hand, we should not understate the importance of the fading of blatant, overt prejudice. On the other hand, we cannot ignore the evidence that antiblack prejudice has changed in form rather than declined in degree. Subtle and diffuse prejudice is probably preferable to the blunt and vicious variety, but it should not be mistaken for its demise. In fact, there is considerable reason to believe that "old-fashioned," blatant racism lives on and, in some ways, is thriving. This possibility is considered in the last section of this chapter.

Exhibit 3.12 Perception of Blacks as Lazy by Explanation for Racial Inequality, 2010 (Whites Only)

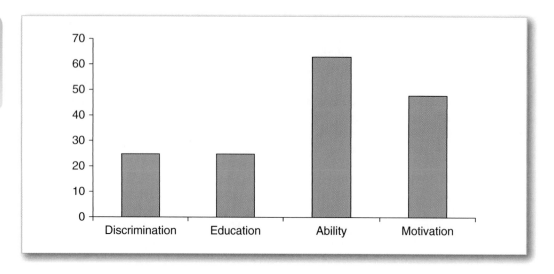

Limitations

As many critics have pointed out, theories of modern racism seem to confound prejudice with political conservatism. One of the classic tenets of American conservatism, for example, is that government should be minimal in size and scope. So, in Exhibit 3.11, when people object to "government help for blacks," are they expressing prejudice or are they stating their commitment to a particular theory of government? The survey item measures *both* beliefs about blacks and beliefs about the proper role of government, and it is difficult to isolate the prejudice component (Quillian, 2006, p. 313). Perhaps the problem is methodological and researchers need to do a better job of separating the two components, or perhaps the problem is that racism has become so thoroughly intermixed with some forms of political conservatism that it can't (or shouldn't) be separated.

HAS SEXISM MODERNIZED?

In the view of many analysts, sexism (negative feelings and stereotypes based on gender) and prejudice are closely related, part of the same set of perceptions that disparages, labels, and rejects out-groups. If so, sexism, like racism, should be evolving into more "modern" (more subtle and indirect) forms. A number of researchers have been investigating this possibility and have found substantial similarities between modern racism and sexism. Also, they have compiled evidence that modern sexism is related to lack of support for (or interest in) women's rights, gender equality, and "women's issues" (e.g., sexual harassment).

Modern sexism, in parallel to modern racism, asserts that

- there is no longer any serious discrimination against women,
- women (specifically, feminists) are pushing their agenda too hard, and
- programs such as affirmative action are unwarranted and give women unfair advantages over men (Swim & Cohen, 1997, p. 105; Swim, Mallett, & Stangor, 2004; Tougas, Rupert, & Joly, 1995, p. 843).

The modern sexist, as does the modern racist, has negative feelings but expresses them indirectly and symbolically. The old-fashioned sexist believes that gender inequality is natural and even desirable; the modern sexist denies the existence of sexual discrimination and inequality and trivializes or dismisses the concerns of women. Modern sexism is harder to detect and measure, in part because it is often expressed in the language of equality and fairness. For example, the modern sexist might express opposition to affirmative action programs for women by arguing that such programs are unfair to men rather than by invoking notions of female inferiority or incompetence (Beaton, Tougas, & Joly, 1996).

Before considering modern sexism further, we should pause to address the assertion that gender inequality is a thing of the past in U.S. society. In the chapters to come, we will present evidence that documents the lower (often, much lower) status of female minority group members. Here, we will compare the overall status of all men and women in terms of inequalities of income. Exhibit 3.13 shows median income for full-time, year-round workers of both sexes and documents a persistent, though generally shrinking, gender gap. In 1955, women earned about 65% of what men earned. In the years following, this percentage actually declined and then began to rise in the 1980s, a trend which continued nearly to the present. The gap shrank to its historic minimum in 2005, when women earned 79% of what men earned, but then grew slightly. In 2009, women earned 76% of what men earned. Contrary to the assertion that the United States has achieved gender equality, these results document the persistence of a substantial gender gap in income.

Why do women continue to earn less than men do? This is a complex question that would require the analysis of many factors (e.g., the changing American economy and the career choices made by men and women) to answer fully. However, research findings suggest that modern sexism is one important factor in the continued maintenance of gender inequality.

The studies indicate that modern sexists are less likely to perceive instances of sexist discrimination and more likely to dismiss complaints of sexism as trivial (e.g., see Barreto & Ellemers, 2005; Cameron, 2001; Swim et al., 2004). Also, modern sexists were less likely to identify instances of sexist discrimination and more likely to use sexist language. Another

Exhibit 3.13 Income for Full-Time, Year-Round Workers by Gender, 1955 to 2009 (in 2009 Dollars)

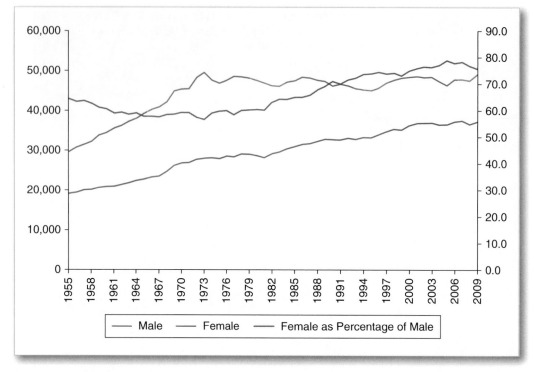

SOURCE: U.S. Bureau of the Census (2010e).

NOTE: Read income on left-hand axis and percentage on right-hand axis.

study (Swim & Cohen, 1997) examined reactions to several situations involving charges of sexual harassment (e.g., an offer to trade career assistance for sexual favors and a work situation in which male employees displayed sexually explicit photos or made sexual comments to female employees). The subjects in the study, all male, were asked to judge the seriousness of these various scenarios. Subjects who scored higher on modern sexism were less likely to classify the incidents as sexual harassment, had less sympathy for victims, were more likely to see the female victims as overreacting, and were less likely to recommend harsh punishments for perpetrators.

Modern sexism shapes perceptions and attitudes, desensitizes people to the damage that can be caused by sexually hostile work environments, and predisposes them to be unsympathetic to programs designed to reduce gender inequality. Thus, gender attitudes appear to be becoming "modernized" along with racial prejudice. Gender inequality remains a pervasive reality in modern American society and is perpetuated in part by attitudes of modern sexism that allow people to express opposition to the changing role of women without appearing to be blatantly or overtly sexist.

HATE CRIMES

Hate crimes are attacks or other acts of intimidation motivated by the group membership of the victim or victims. Victims can be chosen randomly and are often strangers to their assailants: They are chosen as representatives of a group, not because of who they are as individuals. These crimes are expressions of hatred or disdain, strong prejudice, and blatant racism and are not committed for profit or gain. In recent years, they have included assaults, arson against black churches, vandalism of Jewish synagogues, cross burnings, nooses prominently tied to office doors of black university professors, and other acts of intimidation and harassment. Furthermore, a number of violent, openly racist extremist groups—skinheads, the Ku Klux Klan (KKK), White Aryan Resistance (WAR), the Minutemen, and Aryan Nations—have achieved widespread notoriety and have a prominent presence not only in some communities but also on the Internet.

Hate crimes can include extreme violence and even murder. For example, consider two incidents that occurred in the late 1990s. In one, James Byrd, a black man, was beaten and dragged behind a pickup truck for miles by three white men until he died. In the other, college student Mathew Shepard was beaten and tied to a fence post and left to die. His assailants selected him as a victim in part because they thought he was gay.

Less violent hate crimes can have chilling effects on their victims. Consider the activity of William White, the leader of an American neo-Nazi group. In December of 2008, Mr. White was indicted by a federal Grand Jury on seven counts of committing hate crimes involving harassment and intimidation. Among the counts were these:

1. Mr. White allegedly tried to prevent two African American tenants from testifying in a court case against their landlord. He mailed letters to them that displayed the letterhead of his Nazi group and that read, in part, "I . . . know your type of slum nigger, and I wanted you to know that your actions have not been missed by the white community . . . and we know that you are and will never be anything other than a dirty parasite . . . and that our patience with you and the government that coddles you runs thin."

2. Mr. White allegedly threatened to injure a Canadian lawyer who advocated against illegal activities of white supremacists in Canada. White posted a message on the Internet in which he said that the lawyer "should be drug into the street and shot, after appropriate trial by a revolutionary tribunal of Canada's white activists. It won't be hard to do, he can be found, easily, at his home at [here, he cited the lawyer's home address]. . . . He must be killed. Find him at home and let him know you agree."

3. Mr. White allegedly threatened the African American mayor of a town in New Jersey. White called the mayor's home and spoke with his wife, telling her that he knew where she lived and was going to put a swastika in her front yard. White then sent an e-mail to the mayor that read:

> I recently read of the racism you've faced in New Jersey, and I wanted to make something perfectly clear: You are a nigger unworthy to govern over any white man; and, Fuck you. You've gotten exactly what you deserve from your constituents. Unfortunately, the days when white men would simply . . . run the nigger officials out with tar and feathers are past. However, your incidents give me hope that perhaps we shall see them again.
>
> PS: we know where you live. I just spoke to your wife. I hope you got my message.

Do hate crimes contradict the notion that blatant prejudice is on the decline? Do they balance the shift to modern racism with an opposite shift to overt, violent racism? What causes these attacks? What are the implications?

As we will see in chapters to come, racial violence, hate crimes, and extremist racist groups are hardly new to the United States. Violence between whites and nonwhites began in the earliest days of this society (e.g., conflicts with Native Americans, the kidnapping and enslavement of Africans) and has continued, in one form or another, to the present. Contemporary racist attacks and hate crimes, in all their manifestations, have deep roots in the American past.

Also, racist and extremist groups are no strangers to American history. The KKK, for example, was founded almost 150 years ago, shortly after the Civil War, and has since

Photo 3.5

Racist groups, such as the KKK, are still active in the United States, especially in the South.

© Daniel Lainé/ CORBIS.

played a significant role in local and state politics and in everyday life at various times and places—and not just in the South. During the turbulent 1920s, the Klan reached what was probably the height of its popularity. It had a membership in the millions and was said to control openly many U.S. senators, governors, and local politicians.

Are hate crimes increasing or decreasing? It's difficult to answer this question, though the FBI (Federal Bureau of Investigation) has been collecting and compiling information on hate crimes for more than a decade. Not all localities report these incidents or classify them in the same way, and perhaps more important, not all hate crimes are reported. Thus, the actual volume of hate crimes may be many times greater than the "official" rate compiled by the FBI (for a recent analysis, see Fears, 2007).

Keeping these sharp limitations in mind, here is some of what is known. Exhibit 3.14 reports the breakdown of hate crimes in 2009 and shows that most incidents were motivated by race. In the great majority (71%) of these racial cases, blacks were the target group. Most of the religious incidents (70%) involved Jewish victims, and most of the antiethnic attacks were against Hispanics (62%). The great majority (63%) of the attacks motivated by the sexual orientation of the victims were directed against male homosexuals (FBI, 2010).

Exhibit 3.15 shows the number of hate crimes by the group membership of victims since the mid-1990s. In two of the four cases (race and religion), the number of crimes has decreased at least slightly, but in the two others (sexual orientation and ethnicity), the trend is up. However, because our information on these crimes is so partial and untrustworthy, it is best not to make any hard-and-fast conclusions.

Hate crimes and hate groups are not limited to a particular region. The Southern Poverty Law Center (SPLC) tracks hate groups and hate crimes around the nation and estimates that there were 751 hate groups (defined as groups that "have beliefs or practices that attack or malign an entire class of people, typically for their immutable characteristics") active in the United States in 2006 (SPLC, 2010b). These groups include the KKK, various skinhead and

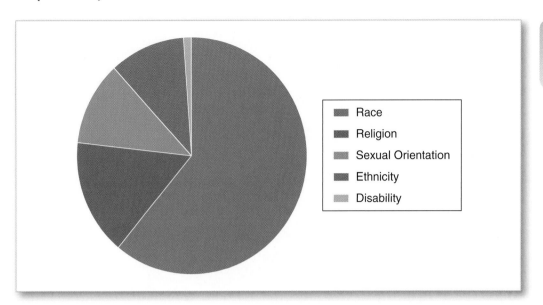

Exhibit 3.14 Hate Crimes by Target Group, 2009

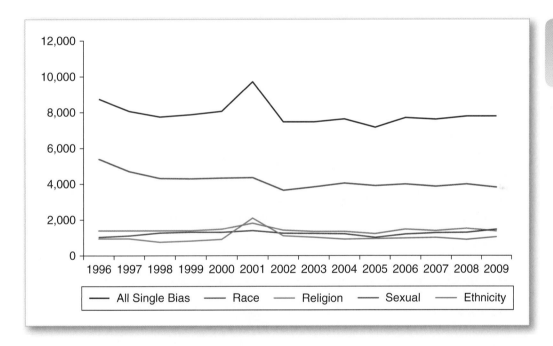

Exhibit 3.15 Number of Hate Crimes by Target Group, 1996 to 2009

white power groups, and black groups such as the Nation of Islam. The SPLC maintains a map at its website showing the locations of the known hate groups (see Exhibit 3.16). The map shows that although the greatest concentration is in the Southeast, Texas, and California, hate groups are spread across the nation and can be found in all states.

What causes hate crimes? According to some analysts, there are two main types of hate crimes. Many hate crimes are motivated by "thrill seeking" or the quest for excitement. These offenses are often committed by groups that search out random victims in gay bars, synagogues, or minority neighborhoods. The second common type of hate crime is "defensive": the

Exhibit 3.16
Distribution of Hate
Groups, 2009

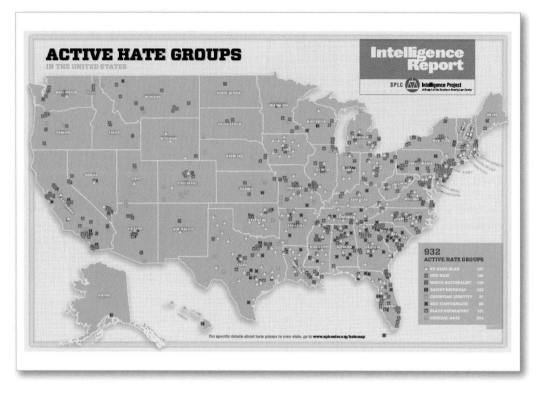

SOURCE: SPLC (2010b).

Photo 3.6

This lynching took
place in the central
square of a town in
Indiana in 1930.

© Bettmann/Corbis.

perpetrators feel that their territory has been invaded or that members of the other group are threatening their resources or status. They strike to punish or expel the invaders, recover their rightful share of resources, or restore their prestige (Gerstenfeld, 2004, pp. 73–75).

One possible explanation for at least some hate crimes is that they are fueled by perceived threats, frustration and fear, and anger and scapegoating. Some white Americans believe that minority groups are threatening their position in society and making unfair progress at their expense. They feel threatened by what they perceive to be an undeserved rise in the status of minority groups and fear that they may lose their jobs, incomes, neighborhoods, and schools to what they see as "inferior" groups.

Given the nature of American history, it is logical to suppose that the white Americans who feel most threatened and angriest are those toward the bottom of the stratification system: lower-class and working-class whites. It seems significant, for example, that the three murderers of James Byrd were unemployed ex-convicts with low levels of education and few prospects for economic success (at least in the conventional economy). On a broader scale, there is evidence that males from these classes commit the bulk of hate crimes and are the primary sources of membership for the extremist racist groups (Schafer & Navarro, 2004). In the eyes of the perpetrators, attacks on minorities may represent attempts to preserve status and privilege. Some of these dynamics are illustrated in the Narrative Portrait at the end of this section.

The connection between social class and hate crimes might also reflect some broad structural changes in the economy. The United States has been shifting from an industrial, manufacturing economy to a postindustrial, information-processing economy since the mid-20th century. We will examine this transition in depth in later chapters, but here, we will note that this economic change has meant a decline in the supply of secure, well-paying, blue-collar jobs. Many manufacturing jobs have been lost to other nations with cheaper workforces; others have been lost to automation and mechanization. The tensions resulting from the decline in desirable employment opportunities for people with lower levels of education have been exacerbated by industry downsizing, increasing inequality in the class structure, and rising costs of living. These economic forces have squeezed the middle and lower ranges of the dominant group's class system, creating considerable pressure and frustration, some of which may be expressed by scapegoating directed at immigrants and minority groups.

The idea that many hate crimes involve scapegoating is also supported by the spontaneous, unplanned, and highly emotional nature of these crimes. Consider how these themes of economic dislocation and scapegoating are illustrated in the murder of Vincent Chin, a frequently cited example of an American hate crime. Chin, who was Chinese American, was enjoying a final bachelor fling in a bar in a working-class Detroit neighborhood in June 1982 when he was confronted by two drunken autoworkers who blamed Japanese auto companies for their unemployment. Making no distinction between Chinese and Japanese (or American and Japanese), the autoworkers attacked and murdered Chin with a baseball bat. Apparently, any Asian would have served as a scapegoat for their resentment and anger (Levin & McDevitt, 1993, p. 58; see also U.S. Commission on Civil Rights, 1992, pp. 25–26).

Several studies also support the idea that hate crimes are motivated at least in part by scapegoating. One study found that at the state level, the rate of hate crimes increased as unemployment rose and as the percentage of the population between 15 and 19 years old increased. Also, the rate fell as average wages rose (Medoff, 1999, p. 970; see also Jacobs & Wood, 1999). Another study, based on county-level data gathered in South Carolina, found a correlation between white-on-black hate crimes and economic competition (D'Alessio, Stolzenberg, & Eitle, 2002). Finally, Arab Americans were victimized by a rash of violent attacks after September 11, 2001 (Ibish, 2003). These patterns are exactly what one would expect if the perpetrators of hate crimes tended to be young men motivated by a sense of threat and economic distress.

The Dynamics of Racial Hatred

As a teenager, Brian Patterson was on a fast track to hell. The product of a ruptured home and a racist father, Patterson in the late 1980s fell in with neo-Nazi skinheads and other racist groups [and was actively involved in a number of hate crimes]. When he [found himself] homeless, alone, angry, and abusing drugs and booze at age 18, a stranger, [a black man] stepped in . . . and rescued him. The crossing of their paths made an indelible impression on Patterson, who has fully rejected racism and hate. Now 38, Patterson . . . still is struggling to make a living and build a life . . . but he is at peace knowing his days of hate are behind him. He'd like to find Alfred and thank him, but no one knows what happened to Patterson's dark angel.

THE MAKING (AND UNMAKING) OF A SKINHEAD

INTERVIEW BY ROBERT STEINBACK

Where were you reared and where did this story start?

I was born in Tupelo, Mississippi. . . . My dad was racist, very racist. All of his friends and everybody that I was around was racist. . . . He was in the Klan. So was my grandfather and pretty much everybody I grew up knowing. [My father] . . . was violent. He liked to fight.

So violence was a part of life?

Yeah, it was routine. We were raised to be tough. Not to each other, but to outsiders and what [we] didn't agree with. We were raised to do violence. . . . Around age 9, me and my brother and my mother moved to Pensacola, Florida. Mama said she moved to get away from my father. . . . I wound up going back to Tupelo at 11. I went and lived with my father until I was 15. That's where [the hate] really took root. During that time, I really got indoctrinated. All of the kids in the area were indoctrinated into that way of thinking. We went to Klan rallies, and we loved it. We thought it was great. . . .

These Klan rallies were just like campfire parties to you?

Exactly. I . . . compare it to kind of a youth program. . . . I think they took the idea from Hitler Youth-type shit, you know. Get them while they're young.

Why did you leave Tupelo the second time?

Well, at 15, . . . I started experimenting, doing a little drugs and drinking. My dad, he was real strict. . . . I wound up back in Florida. . . . So I'm basically on the streets from 15 to 18. You got the punk rock scene and the skinhead scene, and that's where I wound up. I moved back and forth from Pensacola to Mobile, Alabama . . . just drifting back and forth with the crowd. The skinhead scene was pretty big in Mobile. . . . We had National White Resistance and WAR, White Aryan Resistance. The Klan was real big there, too. . . . I had fallen in with a violent group of skinheads. There were things that I did that I'm not proud of and I'll have to carry with me for the rest of my life. I never killed anybody; I never robbed a store or anything like that. But there was fighting. There was a lot of fighting, a lot of beatings.

Beatings of strangers?

Gang violence. Mostly gang confrontations. You could call them turf wars, I guess. You know, trying to keep blacks out of the neighborhoods that were predominantly white.

So it was white gang against nonwhite gang? . . .

Right. We tried to get along with the other white kids, and of course, indoctrinate them. There's where I met Bill Riccio. . . . I helped him set up that camp that he had in Alabama. I was part of that group. *[Editor's note: Bill Riccio, a former Klan chaplain and neo-Nazi, was the head of a racist skinhead group called the Aryan Youth Front in the late 1980s and early '90s. Riccio . . . set up a backwoods camp he called "the WAR House"—for White Aryan Resistance. It was equal parts skinhead recruiting station, clubhouse, and crash pad. It was home base for Riccio's "toy soldiers," white teenaged boys, many of them runaways, whom he plied with beer while indoctrinating them in racial hatred and Hitler worship. . . .]*

Did you personally do things that you now regret having done?

Just mainly fighting. . . . Beating black kids. We would go into a black neighborhood, or a neighborhood that was being encroached upon by black gangs. . . . We'd ambush them. . . . On one occasion, I hurt somebody pretty bad. I cracked his head open pretty good. He never saw it coming. . . .

Do you still have memories of that? . . .

I think about it all the time. Every time I see a young kid, I think about it. . . . It's a terrible thing to have to think about that you did to somebody. I'm not proud of it, but that's something I have to live with. . . .

But then you found yourself alone. How did that happen?

I . . . basically wound up by myself and stuck on Pensacola Beach. They left me there. . . . We got into it, and they left me. . . . I'm footin' it. No money, no food. . . . I'm just kind of drifting around and getting food stamps, whatnot, getting a little help . . . at the shelter. I was afraid to stay in the city because there I am, a racist sporting Doc Martens and suspenders and dirty clothes and little Nazi patches. . . . I went to the country. I went to where there were some woods. . . . I got no food; I got no money; it's cold. I got no winter clothes, no blanket. So I'm sleeping in this patch of woods by this lodge . . . and a baseball field and a little concession stand. I'm like, "Okay, nobody's going to see me here." And honestly, I'm thinking, "I'm going to break in this place and find some food." That's why I bedded down there.

How close to the edge were you that night?

I was thinking heavy thoughts by that time, brother. I was thinking, "I'm going to do whatever it takes from this point on to feed myself. . . . The next motherfucker I come across is going to get it." . . . That was like the crossroads right there.

What happened when morning arrived?

I wake up, and I smell food. And there's a blanket on me. I look up, and I'm like, "What in the fuck is going on here?" . . . There's this black guy. . . . He's . . . got a fire built. This dude has done throwed a blanket on me. He sees my bald head. He sees my red suspenders and my red shoelaces in my boots and my Nazi patch. This dude sees this. He still goes back to his house and gets a blanket and some food and brings it back to me, covers me up with this blanket. Builds a fire and heats up some stew. He's a country-ass black dude, mind you, but he was a Muslim . . . a real Muslim. I didn't know this until later, of course. But I wake up and he's sitting there cooking me something to eat.

Who was the man?

His name was Alfred. . . . He was determined to help me. . . . He helped me out with food and gave me some clothes. . . . He tried to get me in on the Muslim thing, but I've never been real religious. . . . But it wasn't the religion that won me over; it was his kindness. It was the way this man helped me despite what I was. It probably saved my life. Had he not been there, there's no telling what I would have done. . . .

How did your life change?

I got a job and started going to school. I got my GED and went to college for about a year and a half. Of course, I still had a little problem with drugs at that time. But the racism, man, that was gone. I mean, it just melted it right away when I met that guy. It just changed my world.

Did you run into any of your old pals in Mobile?

Yeah. . . . It was tense, because you don't get out of those groups. They abandoned me, too, so the way I looked at it was, "Y'all turned your back on me. And there's this guy I don't even know, a black guy. He's supposed to be my enemy, and this dude is feeding me and . . . showing me kindness, so y'all can just fuck off. You want to do something to me, bring it." I didn't have any trouble with them physically, but there were a lot of threats. . . . I'm not afraid to tell people . . . because . . . people need to know what to look out for. Keep your kids close and don't let them fall into that trap because that's who they're after—little white kids that feel like they don't belong to anything.

SOURCE: SPLC (2010a).

THE SOCIOLOGY OF PREJUDICE

We can summarize this chapter by considering the key points of the sociological approach to prejudice.

1. Prejudice has its origins in competition between groups, and it is more a result of that competition than a cause. It is created at a certain time in history to help mobilize feelings and emotional energy for competition and to rationalize the consignment of a group to minority status. It then is absorbed into the cultural heritage and is passed on to later generations as part of their taken-for-granted world, where it helps shape their perceptions and reinforce the very group inferiority that was its original cause.

2. Changes in the social environment, rising levels of education, or changing forms of intergroup contact will have relatively little impact on some types of prejudice. Prejudice that is caused by scapegoating or authoritarian personality structures, for example, is motivated by processes internal to the individual and may not respond to changes in the environment. It may be difficult to reduce these types of prejudice and impossible to eliminate them altogether. A more realistic goal might be to discourage their open expression. The greater the extent to which culture, authority figures, and social situations discourage prejudice, the more likely it will be that even people with strong personality needs for prejudice can be turned into prejudiced nondiscriminators, or "timid bigots" (see Exhibit 3.1).

3. Culture-based or "traditional" prejudice can be just as extreme as personality-based prejudice. This type of prejudice differs not in intensity but in the degree to which it is resistant to change. A person who acquires prejudice from being socialized in racist environments should be more open to change than the authoritarian personality and more responsive to education and contact with members of other groups. To create more "all-weather liberals," situations that encourage or reward prejudice and discrimination must be minimized, and public opinion, the views of community and societal leaders, and the legal code must all promote tolerance. The reduction in overt prejudice over the past five or six decades, documented in Exhibit 3.7, is probably mainly due to a decline in traditional prejudice.

4. Intergroup conflict produces vicious, even lethal, prejudice and discrimination, but the problems here are inequality and access to resources and opportunity, not prejudice. Group conflicts and the prejudices they stimulate will continue as long as society is stratified along the lines of race, ethnicity, and gender. Efforts to decrease hostile attitudes without also reducing inequality and exploitative relationships treat the symptoms rather than the disease.

5. Reducing prejudice will not necessarily change the situation of minority groups. The fundamental problems of minority group status are inequality and systems of institutional discrimination and privilege that sustain the advantages of dominant groups. Prejudice is *a* problem, but it is not *the* problem. Reducing prejudice will not, by itself, eliminate minority group poverty or unemployment or end institutional discrimination in schools or in the criminal justice system.

6. Individual prejudice and discrimination are not the same as racism and institutional discrimination (see Chapter 1), and any one of these variables can change independently of the others. Thus, we should not confuse the recent reductions in overt, traditional prejudice with the resolution of American minority group problems. Prejudice is only part of the problem and, in many ways, not the most important part.

These points are reflected in some key trends of the past several decades: Ethnic and racial inequalities persist (and may be increasing) despite the declines in overt prejudice. The verbal rejection of extreme or overt prejudice has been replaced by the subtleties of modern racism combined with an unwillingness to examine the social, political, and economic forces that sustain minority group inequality and institutional discrimination. Unless there are significant changes in the structure of the economy and the distribution of opportunities, we may have reached the limits of tolerance in America.

A Postracial America?

The election of Barack Obama to the presidency of the United States truly was an extraordinary event: A majority-white society with a long record of racial oppression and exploitation elected a black man to be its leader. The significance and meaning of this election will be debated for decades to come. Here, we will consider the possibility that Obama's victory signaled the end of prejudice and racism as important forces in American society.

The commentaries that follow continue to examine the transition from the "traditional," overt and blatant prejudice of America's past to the more subtle forms of what we have called "modern" racism. Columnist John McWhorter downplays the importance of prejudice in contemporary American society and argues that Obama's victory should be seen in the context of a society that, for the most part, has overcome its racist past. In sharp contrast, sociologists Feagin and Wingfield argue that racism remains the dominant perspective in American society, even though it has grown softer and more muted. Far from signaling the end of prejudice and racism, Obama's victory was due to the ability of his campaign to package him in ways that did not threaten whites or the dominance of the white racial perspective.

THE END OF RACISM?

JOHN MCWHORTER

I lost the ability to even conceive of Barack Obama not becoming president [months before the election]. Yet . . . many have told me I was missing . . . "The Role That Racism Still Plays In This Country." For months now, for example, newspaper stories quoting working-class whites refusing Obama their vote because of his color have been showing us what is still "out there." And never mind polls where whites surmised that their friends wouldn't vote for a black man, subconsciously associated black faces with negative terms, and so on. The big bad "out there."

All of this has been a manifestation of how people "in here" consider it a duty to stress that racism is not entirely extinct, despite Condoleezza, Tiger, and the massive black middle class. The implication is that we seek an America in which none of us even notice color.

The question is whether the total eclipse of racism is either possible or necessary. It is neither, and Barack Obama's victory is a lesson in how the word *racism* has drifted beyond its core meaning into something more calisthenic than proactive.

It was one thing when legalized segregation and disenfranchisement were outlawed in the mid-60s. This was a massive undertaking, but people devoted their lives—sometimes literally—to making it happen.

It was something else when, in the wake of this, racism became socially taboo in most segments of American society. Sure, there are lapses. But . . . there has been a seismic shift in America's racial relations since the 60s. . . . The very fact that it is news that there remain people who wouldn't vote for a black man shows that we live in a different world than 40 years ago.

The new frontier, however, is apparently people's individual psychologies: Not only must we not legislate racism or socially condone it, but no one is to even privately feel it.

The problem is we can't entirely reach people's feelings. . . . An America where nobody harbors racist sentiment? The very notion goes against everything we know about human hardwiring: Distrust of the other is inherent to our cognition. . . .

How do we reach everybody? Do we mean overcoming bias so thoroughly that a test looking for what's "out there" would not still reveal it? It's a utopian pipe dream.

Now, if this racism of the scattered and subliminal varieties were the obstacle to achievement that Jim Crow and open bigotry were, then we would have a problem. But [on election day], we saw that this "out there" brand of racism cannot keep a black man out of the White House.

Might it not be time to allow that our obsession with how unschooled and usually aging folk feel in their hearts about black people has become a fetish? Sure, there are racists. There are also rust and mosquitoes, and there always will be. Life goes on.

I know—what about "societal" racism? Well, if we can now relax about the backward folk "out there," then maybe Obama in the White House can help open up an honest discussion about the role racism does not play in black communities' problems.

Obama has come in for some criticism for not putting forth a "black" agenda—i.e., one designed to combat "racism" in various ways. It's because he knows that paradigm has no useful application to our times. . . .

America has problems and our new president knows it. However, is America's main problem still "the color line" as W. E. B. Du Bois put it 105 years ago? The very fact that the president is now black is a clear sign that it is no longer our main problem, and that we can, even as morally informed and socially concerned citizens, admit it.

There is nothing at all "unreal" about this. It is, after all, what we were supposed to be working toward. We must embrace it.

SOURCE: McWhorter (2008).

A POSTRACIAL UNITED STATES?

ADIA WINGFIELD AND JOE FEAGIN

By early 2008 it was increasingly clear that Senator Obama was the first viable black candidate for the U.S. presidency, and journalists increasingly began to discuss or assert the view that U.S. society was now a postracial society. . . .

After Obama's election in November 2008, the increase in emphasis on the United States being postracial was striking. . . . This perspective, often vehemently defended, was in many ways a relabeled soft version of the old white racial frame [or racist perspective] . . . that . . . views the United States as a society where "race" and racism are significantly receding and are no longer important to an increasingly "colorblind" society. In this commonplace framing, overtly racist commentary is usually replaced with conceptions of African Americans and other people of color that are subtly coded and stereotyped, particularly in public exchanges. African Americans and other people of color who behave according to white norms and accept this white framing are deemed more acceptable to whites. Even so, . . . whites are viewed as culturally superior, and whiteness is still centrally, if more subtly, asserted in everyday interactions and institutional operations.

The postracial perspective articulated by mainstream white commentators and academics since President Obama's election has [several] major elements: an emotion-laden accent on the decade-old idea of a major decline in racism; the emotion-laden idea that Obama is white-assimilated, acceptable, mixed-race, and thus less black (or not really black). . . .

Numerous mainstream commentators, especially in the media, have . . . portrayed the election as evidence that there is no significant racism left in the United States. For example, the country's leading business newspaper, the Republican-oriented *Wall Street Journal,* has asserted that Obama's election is a tribute to how open, democratic, and nonracist the country now is:

> A man of mixed race has now reached the pinnacle of U.S. power only two generations since the end of Jim Crow. This is a tribute to American opportunity, and it is something that has never happened in another Western democracy—notwithstanding European condescension about "racist" America.

After crowing about U.S. moral superiority over European countries, the white-framed editorial added this pointed commentary:

> While Mr. Obama lost among white voters, as most modern Democrats do, his success is due in part to the fact that he also muted any politics of racial grievance. . . . One promise of his victory is that perhaps we can put to rest the myth of racism as a barrier to achievement in this splendid country. Mr. Obama has a special obligation to help do so.[1]

Here an apparently white editorial writer has explicitly noted the point . . . that Obama ran a successful campaign because he did not engage in the "politics of racial grievance." That is, Obama ran to fit within the soft, colorblind version of the white frame, and this writer praises that effort. In addition, this writer emphasizes that a few African Americans have recently served in highly visible federal government positions . . . , and this token reality should be viewed as an indication that white racism is no longer a barrier to high achievement. More than that, the writer calls on President Obama to lead the effort to kill the "myth of racism," an old effort that white leaders have engaged in for centuries—that is, ferreting out a few black individuals, endowing them with economic and social rewards as well as high visibility, and getting them to whitewash the reality of systemic racism by contending that it is a nonissue. Note too that the irony in this argument about a "myth of racism" is lost on this writer, who earlier admitted that most whites did *not* vote for the first "mixed race" presidential candidate even in an era of extreme economic crisis created substantially by a Republican administration. . . .

Before and after his election, indeed during most of the long 2007–2008 campaign, many commentators have focused on "who" Obama really is in terms of racial credentials. . . . Much of the primary and general election season involved the efforts of political competitors, media analysts, and voters to define and redefine Senator Obama. Often these attempts took the form of coded or overtly racialized terms and imagery. The "man of mixed race" theme that the *Wall Street Journal* writer above articulated is one that has been developed by numerous interpreters of the presidential election. . . . Substantial debates have raged over just "how black" Senator Obama really was. We have previously noted that during the election reporters, and numbers of white supporters, accented questions about whether Obama should be viewed as black, white, biracial, or some other mix. Some of these concerns focused on his racial identity, while others were aimed at his complex cultural and family backgrounds.

This debate has continued since the general election. . . . In the United States, . . . powerful whites mostly control how Americans of color are racially identified, especially in public places. Americans of color cannot independently assert a racial identity and realistically expect most whites—including employers, teachers, police officers, and other government officials—to respect and accept that personal identity choice. Not surprisingly, thus, Obama has regularly described himself as black. Various efforts to remake him into something he is not—i.e., a white, almost-white, or not-really-black candidate—fit well into white racial framing that attributes primarily negative characteristics to black Americans, or emphasizes that traits like intelligence, decisiveness, and articulateness are qualities more readily associated with white men than with black men. Blackness is so negatively viewed within that centuries-old [white racial] frame that many whites feel it necessary to view Obama as an "exception to his race" and to highlight his positive characteristics as ones that are really more "white" in nature, while recognizing his blackness as something limited to his physical features only. By performing the visual sleight of hand that erases Obama's blackness, whites are then able to reinforce the idea that his positive characteristics are linked to—and a consequence of—his imagined "whiteness." As such, his triumphs, successes, bearing, and background become appropriated as something that whites can symbolically own, without any need to *challenge* the racist idea that these positive features are alien to blackness. . . . Ultimately, the idea that Obama's intelligence, background, and behavior run counter to his blackness and are best understood as exceptional rather than typical qualities for a black American strongly indicate fallacies in the "postracial America" argument. . . .

SOURCE: Wingfield and Feagin (2010).

DEBATE QUESTIONS TO CONSIDER

1. This chapter mentions several different causes of prejudice, including personality structures, culture or tradition, and group competition. Which type of prejudice is McWhorter discussing? How do you know?

2. Which of the forms of prejudice discussed in the chapter is most consistent with the "white racial frame" discussed by Wingfield and Feagin? How do you know?

3. Consider the notion of a "postracial" society. What characteristics would such a society have? Does the United States have these characteristics? If not, is it moving closer to or away from these characteristics?

4. Evaluate McWhorter's argument that racism is no longer much of a problem and that "we live in a different world than 40 years ago." Is this view convincing? Is it an expression of "modern" racism? What additional information would you need to answer these questions?

5. Are Feagin and Wingfield arguing that Obama's victory *sustains* white racism? Did Obama win because he chose not to challenge prejudice or emphasize his race or concentrate on racial issues? How was Obama framed as an "exception" to the dominant stereotypes of African Americans?

6. After reviewing the arguments stated here and the information you have absorbed in this course, consider the proposition that the United States is now "postracial." What evidence for and against this proposition can you cite? Finally, is the proposition true or false (or some combination of true and false)?

MAIN POINTS

- Prejudice is the tendency to think and feel negatively about the members of other groups. Discrimination refers to negative acts of behavior motivated by a person's group membership. Prejudice has at least two dimensions: the cognitive and the affective.
- Prejudice takes multiple forms and can have a variety of causes, and no one theory can account for the entirety of the phenomenon. However, all forms of prejudice seem to have their origins in group conflict over scarce resources.
- Once created, prejudice can become part of culture, handed down across the generations by socialization and reinforced by the everyday realities of minority group inequalities. The likelihood that prejudice or discrimination will be expressed depends heavily on the situation the individual is in.
- Traditional, overt forms of prejudice have lost strength in U.S. society over the past several decades. This decline in prejudice may be the result of higher levels of education and greater equal status contact across group lines.
- Contrary to the idea that prejudice is decreasing, many researchers argue that it is merely changing form. Modern racism combines subtle intergroup antipathy with low support for programs that address the situations of minority groups. Sexism also appears to be modernizing.
- Hate crimes and hate groups are a continuing reminder that the most vicious forms of prejudice and discrimination have not disappeared from U.S. society. These acts may be linked to scapegoating and the perception of less-educated young males that their position is threatened by the undeserved increase in the status of American minority groups.

STUDY SITE ON THE WEB

For chapter-specific resources, such as self-quizzes, videos, and flashcards, go to **www.sagepub.com/ healeyregc6e.**

FOR FURTHER READING

Allport, Gordon. 1954. *The Nature of Prejudice*. Reading, MA: Addison-Wesley.

A classic work in the field; a comprehensive summary of theory and research

Bonacich, Edna, & Modell, John. 1980. *The Economic Basis of Ethnic Solidarity: Small Business in the Japanese American Community*. Berkeley: University of California Press.

Split labor market theory applied to the Japanese American community

Bonilla-Silva, Eduardo. 2006. *Racism without Racists: Color-Blind Racism and the Persistence of Racial Inequality in the United States* (2nd ed.). Lanham, MD: Rowman & Littlefield.

One of the most important treatments of modern (or "colorblind") racism

Feagin, Joe, & O'Brien, Eileen. 2004. *White Men on Race: Power, Privilege, and the Shaping of Cultural Consciousness*. Boston: Beacon.

An analysis of the sometimes subtle expression of racial sentiment among elite white males

Levin, Jack, & McDevitt, Jack. 2002. *Hate Crimes Revisited: America's War on Those Who Are Different*. Boulder, CO: Westview.

An important sociological analysis of hate crimes

Wingfield, Adia, & Feagin, Joe. 2010. *Yes We Can: White Racial Framing and the 2008 Presidential Campaign*. New York: Routledge.

One of the most important analyses of Obama's election

Yancey, George. 2007. *Interracial Contact and Social Change*. Boulder, CO: Lynne Rienner.

A thin volume that presents a comprehensive and largely positive assessment of the contact hypothesis

QUESTIONS FOR REVIEW AND STUDY

1. Distinguish between prejudice and discrimination and explain clear examples of both. Explain the different dimensions of prejudice and differentiate between them. What are stereotypes? What forms do stereotypes take? How are stereotypes formed and maintained?

2. Explain the various causes of prejudice, including the theoretical perspectives presented in this chapter. Explain and evaluate the research evidence that has been presented. Which theories seem most credible in terms of evidence? Why? Try to think of an incident—from your own experience, the news, or popular culture—that illustrates each theory.

3. How does prejudice persist through time? What are children taught about other groups? What were you taught by your parents? How did this compare with what you learned from friends? How would your socialization experience have changed if you had been raised in another group? Have your views been changed by education or intergroup contact? How?

4. Is prejudice really decreasing, or are the negative emotions and attitudes changing into modern racism? What evidence is most persuasive in leading you to your conclusion? Why?

5. Interpret the information presented in Exhibit 3.11. Does this exhibit support the notion that modern racism is an important cause of resistance to racial change? How?

6. What forms of prejudice are involved in hate crimes? What are the roles of group competition and scapegoating? Develop an explanation for hate crimes based on these connections.

INTERNET RESEARCH PROJECT: IMPLICIT PREJUDICE

In this chapter, prejudice has been treated as a set of attitudes, opinions, stereotypes, feelings, and emotions that people express in their everyday conversations and that can be measured by surveys such as the social distance scale. A group of psychologists have developed a very different approach to the topic: They believe that people have a largely unconscious and unspoken set of attitudes toward other groups that affects their thinking, feelings, and actions (Greenwald et al., 2002; Greenwald & Banaji, 1995). These implicit or hidden prejudices are acquired during socialization and shape our relationships with other groups even though we may not be aware of it. This form of prejudice can exist even in people who have no conscious prejudice and who behave in nondiscriminatory ways.

Do you have an implicit negative reaction to other groups? You can find out by taking the Implicit Association Test (IAT) at the Project Implicit website (https://implicit.harvard.edu/implicit/). Click on the "Demonstration" button, click the "Go to the Demonstration Tests" link, and then click "I wish to proceed" after reading the preliminary information and the disclaimer. Take several of the tests, including the Race test.

Also, go to the "Background Information" page (https://implicit.harvard.edu/implicit/demo/background/index.jsp) and read more about the origins and interpretation of IAT scores and browse the "Answers to Frequently Asked Questions about the IAT" page to get more information.

After taking the tests and gathering some perspective on the IAT, consider these questions.

QUESTIONS

1. What is an "implicit" attitude? How does implicit prejudice differ from affective prejudice, stereotypes, social distance, and modern racism?

2. If the test shows you have a preference for one group over another, does this mean that you are prejudiced against the less-preferred group? Do you feel that the test accurately reflects your feelings and ideas? Why or why not? (*Remember that your implicit and explicit, or conscious, attitudes can be quite different.*)

3. Research using the IAT reveals that many white Americans have a preference for whites over blacks. Why do you think this is so? What aspects of American culture might create and sustain this preference?

4. Which of the situations listed below would be *most* affected by a person's implicit attitudes? Why?
   a. Friendship choices in a multigroup elementary school classroom
   b. Friendship choices in a multigroup high school or university
   c. Reactions to hearing that a friend is dating a member of another racial or ethnic group
   d. Reactions to a news story that a minority group male raped and killed a dominant group female
   e. Reactions to a news story that a dominant group male raped and killed a minority group female
   f. Choices between political candidates who are from different racial or ethnic groups
   g. Support for controversial policies such as affirmative action
   h. Hiring decisions involving applicants from a variety of groups
   i. Choices about which neighborhoods to live in
   j. Choices in a "shoot/don't shoot" situation involving a white police officer and a possibly armed black male suspect. How about if the suspect was a white female?

5. If the IAT shows that you have a group preference you would rather NOT have, what are some things you could do to change yourself?

OPTIONAL GROUP DISCUSSION

Select three of the questions above to discuss with classmates. (NOTE: Your instructor may have more specific or different instructions.) Add your own questions or topics if you wish. Individual students should NOT reveal their IAT scores during these discussions. To aid the discussion, bring a summary of what you learned about the IAT to class. What was the most important thing you learned from taking the IAT?

NOTES

1. *Wall Street Journal.* 2008. "President-Elect Obama: The Voters Rebuke Republicans for Economic Failure," November 5. Retrieved December 28, 2008, from http://online.wsj.com/article/SB122586244657800863.html.

PART II

THE EVOLUTION OF DOMINANT-MINORITY RELATIONS IN THE UNITED STATES

Chapter 4 The Development of Dominant-Minority Group Relations in Preindustrial America: The Origins of Slavery

Chapter 5 Industrialization and Dominant-Minority Relations: From Slavery to Segregation and the Coming of Postindustrial Society

The chapters in Part II explore several questions: Why do some groups become minorities? How and why do dominant-minority relations change over time? These questions are more than casual or merely academic. Understanding the dynamics that created and sustained prejudice, racism, discrimination, and inequality in the past will build understanding about group relations in the present and future, and such understanding is crucial if we are ever to deal effectively with these problems.

Both chapters in Part II use African Americans as the primary case study. Chapter 4 focuses on the preindustrial United States and the creation of slavery but also considers the fate of American Indians and Mexican Americans during the same time period. Chapter 5 analyzes the changes in group relations that were caused by the industrial revolution and focuses on the shift from slavery to segregation for African Americans and their migration out of the South. Throughout the 20th century, industrial technology continued to evolve and shape American society and group relationships. We begin to explore the consequences of these changes in Chapter 5, and we continue the investigation in the case studies of contemporary minority groups in Part III.

The concepts introduced in Part I are used throughout Chapters 4 and 5, and some important new concepts and theories are introduced as well. By the end of Part II, you will be familiar with virtually the entire conceptual framework that will guide us through the remainder of this text.

A NOTE ON THE MORALITY AND THE HISTORY OF MINORITY RELATIONS IN AMERICA: GUILT, BLAME, UNDERSTANDING, AND COMMUNICATION

Very often, when people confront the kind of material presented in the next few chapters, they react on a personal level. Some might feel a sense of guilt for America's less-than-wholesome history of group relations. Others might respond with anger about the injustice

IMAGE: Getty/Fernando Bueno.

and unfairness that remains in American society. Still others might respond with denial or indifference and might argue that the events discussed in Chapters 4 and 5 are so distant in time that they have no importance or meaning today.

These reactions—guilt, anger, denial, and indifference—are common, and I ask you to consider them. First, the awful things I will discuss did happen, and they were perpetrated largely by members of a particular racial and ethnic group: white Europeans and their descendants in America. No amount of denial, distancing, or disassociation can make these facts go away. African Americans, American Indians, Mexican Americans, and other groups were victims, and they paid a terrible price for the early growth and success of white American society.

Second, the successful domination and exploitation of these groups were made easier by the cooperation of members of each of the minority groups. The slave trade relied on agents and slavers that were black Africans, some American Indians aided and abetted the cause of white society, and some Mexicans helped cheat other Mexicans. There is plenty of guilt to go around, and Euro-Americans do not have a monopoly on greed, bigotry, or viciousness. Indeed, some white Southerners opposed slavery and fought for the abolition of the "peculiar institution." Many of the ideas and values on which the United States was founded (justice, equality, liberty) had their origins in European intellectual traditions, and minority group protest has often involved little more than insisting that the nation live up to these ideals. Segments of the white community were appalled at the treatment of American Indians and Mexicans. Some members of the dominant group devoted (and sometimes sacrificed) their lives to end oppression, bigotry, and racial stratification.

My point is to urge you to avoid, insofar as is possible, a "good-guy/bad-guy" approach to this subject matter. Guilt, anger, denial, and indifference are common reactions to this material, but these emotions do little to advance understanding, and often they impede communication between members of different groups. I believe that an understanding of America's racial past is vitally important for understanding the present. Historical background provides a perspective for viewing the present and allows us to identify important concepts and principles that we can use to disentangle the intergroup complexities surrounding us.

The goal of the chapters to come is not to make you feel any particular emotion. I will try to present the often ugly facts neutrally and without extraneous editorializing. As scholars, your goal should be to absorb the material, understand the principles, and apply them to your own life and the society around you—not to indulge yourself in elaborate moral denunciations of American society, develop apologies for the past, or deny the realities of what happened. By dealing objectively with this material, we can begin to liberate our perspectives and build an understanding of the realities of American society and American minority groups.

ABOUT THE PUBLIC SOCIOLOGY ASSIGNMENTS

In the Part II public sociology assignments, you will look for patterns of racial, ethnic, and gender relations in some surprising places: the children's book section of your local library and a local diner. The realities of group relations established in the early days of this society and perpetuated to the present are pervasive and can shape the social realities of every nook and cranny of society.

PUBLIC SOCIOLOGY ASSIGNMENTS

Linda M. Waldron

ASSIGNMENT 1: RACE AND GENDER IN CHILDREN'S BOOKS

Following the civil rights and women's movements, it might seem logical that publishing companies would begin putting out children's books that provide a more accurate and diverse portrayal of characters for our young readers. The task of this assignment is to see whether or not this is the case.

Step 1

Visit the children's section of a local public library. Pick a sample of 20 books to examine. Although you could conduct a convenience sample by simply grabbing the first 20 books you come across, consider taking a couple of extra minutes to be a little more systematic, which will help you get a more representative sample. First, pick one section of the shelving area and count all the books on the shelves. Determine your sampling interval by simply dividing the total population of books by 20. (For example, if there are 200 books, your sampling interval will be every 10th book.) Then, pick a random book to start with and proceed from there by picking every nth book until you have pulled 20 books from the shelves.

Step 2

Create a tally sheet to study the race, ethnicity, and gender of each book's main character. In each row, list the book title and the year of publication. In the columns, include such categories as "male" and "female," as well as different race and ethnic categories (i.e., white, African American, Hispanic, etc.).

Step 3

After you have gone through a couple of books, you may need to adjust your tally sheet to include such categories as "unknown"—for instance, when the main character is an animal and you can't determine the race. Maybe you need to differentiate between male children, male teens, and male adults. Perhaps an extra row is needed for books that have more than one main character.

Step 4

When you are done examining all 20 books, add up your columns and develop some general findings. How many main characters were male? Female? White? African American? Consider putting the list of books in order by publication date. Do you find that things have changed over time?

Step 5

Take it one step further by selecting a small sample of the books to examine more qualitatively. Read each book. Consider the story line, word choice, and dialogue, as well as the pictures. What are the race, ethnicity, and gender of the other characters in the book? What is the relationship between the main character and the supporting characters? What roles do these characters have? What adjectives are used to describe the characters and their actions? What are the storylines about?

Step 6

Identify stereotypes that are perpetuated in the books. Do female characters seem helpless and in need of a smart male character to help them solve a mystery? Are white characters given the role of the leader or boss in the book? Do Hispanic characters all know how to speak Spanish? Do dads work jobs and moms bake cookies? Also, consider how stereotypes are confronted in the books. Taken as a whole, do you think the book does a better job reifying or challenging stereotypes?

Step 7

Share your findings with the reference librarian. Ask the librarian what she or he thinks about the changing nature of race, ethnicity, and gender in children's books. Has she or he noticed any trends in children's books, or perhaps trends in the book choices of children and which books they are more apt to check out?

Step 8

Finally, consider what your findings may suggest about the socialization of children. What messages are young children being given about race and ethnic relations or the meaning of gender? What do you think is more important, the *number* of characters that exist or *how* each character was represented? In the end, do you think it is more important to have an equal representation of male and female characters, or do you think it is more important to have characters that challenge stereotypes?

ASSIGNMENT 2: THE LOCAL DINER

The local diner has a long history in American culture. Emerging in the Northeast in the latter part of the 19th century, diners constituted little more than horse-drawn lunch carts initially established to serve blue-collar workers during the Industrial Revolution (Anderson, 2008). Following World War II, this predominantly masculine space began to transform as women began to enter the workforce in larger numbers, serving as both middle-class consumers and cheap labor for restaurant owners (Anderson, 2008). Also, diners have a history of racial and ethnic segregation that may influence their status today, which can further be impacted by immigration. Keep an eye out for insights into how these forces may shape the everyday interactions in the diner.

Today, although the nostalgic version of the 1950s diner may no longer exist, most towns and cities still have some semblance of the local diner. Some continue to be places that serve working-class men lunch, whereas others offer coffee to the CEO on her way to catch the morning train into the city or french fries to a group of teenagers after dark. This assignment requires you to embark on an ethnographic investigation of the American diner.

Step 1

Locate a locally owned diner that has been in your community for at least a decade, and pick a time of day to observe that is most appropriate for the setting. This may require you to go to the diner and find out how long it has been in business and if it tends to get busy during breakfast, lunch, dinner, or late night.

Step 2

Investigate the guidelines for conducting research with your university's Institutional Review Board. Although projects of this scope may be exempt from board approval, it still is important to understand and follow the protocol for conducting ethical research that is laid out by your institution.

Step 3

Ethnography is a qualitative research design that requires you to take detailed notes to gather rich descriptions of people in everyday life, so you will need to buy a small notebook to take notes. (It's best to use a notebook instead of a computer, since this will be a less intrusive method of note taking.) For this assignment, you will take on the role of a participant observer, which means that you will let people at the diner know you are conducting research. Although there are cons to this approach (see discussion of limitations in Step 9), the pros are that notes help increase your level of accuracy in description and, since people know you are conducting research, they may volunteer to tell you relevant information or allow you to informally interview them, which will help you gather richer, more detailed notes.

Step 4

Pick three days to observe your site. On the first day, simply observe and take jottings. Jottings are your own brief shorthand notes that help you recall details about the atmosphere, events, people, and conversations you observe, which you will later use to write up more extensive field notes. Limit your observation time to 1 hour, since it will take you almost twice as long to type these notes as it did to conduct the observation—as a general rule, for every hour you observe, you will have five pages of typed field notes.

Step 5

Once you leave the setting, immediately type up your field notes so everything will still be fresh in your memory. Field notes are essentially a minute-to-minute account of your observation. The more detail, the better! Use complete sentences, write things down in chronological order, and avoid subjective statements. For example, instead of saying a customer was "sloppy," describe the clothes they were wearing, their demeanor, the style of their hair, the dirt under their fingernails, etc. The more detail you give, the more objective your notes will be.

Step 6

Start to look for some initial themes by coding your first set of field notes. Coding is simply a process that allows you to analyze your data in terms of certain variables. After you are done typing your field notes, print them out; as you read through them, write possible codes in the margin. For the purpose of this assignment, begin with demographic variables such as race, ethnicity, gender, age, and social class. This will help you start to see patterns emerge. For example, maybe you'll start to notice that only male patrons sit at the counters or that most of the workers are white. Try also to develop your own codes. This can be anything from a code titled "food" or "music" to one called "nostalgia" or "gossip." This process will not only help you systematically see patterns of behavior but will likely also introduce some unanswered questions about your site that you can investigate during your next visit.

Step 7

Follow the same process of taking jottings and field notes during your next two days of observation, but this time, don't be afraid to informally interview workers or patrons. This should help you answer some of the questions you have. In particular, try to find people to talk with who have either been working at the diner for a long time or patronizing it for years. This will allow you to get much more insight into the history and background of the diner than you would get if you only observed.

Step 8

Start to look for relationships between codes. What is the relationship between gender and work roles? How does ethnicity factor into the selection of menu items? How does the price of food influence the social class of the patrons? How have the demographics of the diner patrons changed over the past several decades? How does the diner represent a part of American culture?

Step 9

Write a one- to two-page paper with your initial findings. Discuss the limitations of your research, including your role as participant observer, and how you might fix these problems if you were to continue with this research project. This should include a discussion of reactivity—how the participants of your study may have modified their behavior because they knew they were being observed—and reflexivity—how your own identity may have influenced what you observed and how you interpreted these observations.

Resources

Anderson, Erin R. 2008. "Who's name's on the awning?" Gender, entrepreneurship, and the American diner. *Gender, Place, and Culture* 15(4): 395–410.

4

The Development of Dominant-Minority Group Relations in Preindustrial America

The Origins of Slavery

No man can put a chain about the ankle of his fellow man without at last finding the other end fastened about his own neck.

—Frederick Douglass (1818–1895)
ex-slave, abolitionist, orator, author
Washington, D.C. 1883

From the first settlements in the 1600s until the 19th century, most people living in what was to become the United States relied directly on farming for food, shelter, and other necessities of life. In an agricultural society, land and labor are central concerns, and the struggle to control these resources led directly to the creation of minority group status for three groups: African Americans, American Indians, and Mexican Americans. Why did the colonists create slavery? Why were Africans enslaved but not American Indians or Europeans? Why did American Indians lose their land and most of their population by the 1890s? How did the Mexican population in the Southwest become "Mexican Americans"? How did the experience of becoming a subordinated minority group vary by gender?

In this chapter, the concepts introduced in Part I will be used to answer these questions. Some new ideas and theories will also be introduced, and by the end of the chapter, we will have developed a theoretical model of the process that leads to the creation of a minority group. The creation of black slavery in colonial America, arguably the single most significant event in the early years of this nation, will be used to illustrate the process of minority group creation. We will also consider the subordination of American Indians and Mexican Americans—two more historical events of great significance—as additional case studies. We will follow the experiences of African Americans through the days of segregation (Chapter 5) and into the contemporary era (Chapter 6). The story of the development of minority group status for American Indians and Mexican Americans will be picked up again in Chapters 7 and 8, respectively.

Two broad themes underlie this chapter and, indeed, the remainder of the text:

1. The nature of dominant-minority group relations at any point in time is largely a function of the characteristics of the society as a whole. The situation of a minority group will reflect the realities of everyday social life and particularly the subsistence technology (the means by which the society satisfies basic needs, such as food and shelter). As explained by Gerhard Lenski (see Chapter 1), the subsistence technology of a society acts as a foundation, shaping and affecting every other aspect of the social structure, including minority group relations.

2. The contact situation—the conditions under which groups first come together—is the single most significant factor in the creation of minority group status. The nature of the contact situation has long-lasting consequences for the minority group and the extent of racial or ethnic stratification, the levels of racism and prejudice, the possibilities for assimilation and pluralism, and virtually every other aspect of the dominant-minority relationship.

THE ORIGINS OF SLAVERY IN AMERICA

By the early 1600s, Spanish explorers had conquered much of Central and South America, and the influx of gold, silver, and other riches from the New World had made Spain a powerful nation. Following Spain's lead, England proceeded to establish its presence in the Western Hemisphere, but its efforts at colonization were more modest than those of Spain. By the early 1600s, only two small colonies had been established: Plymouth, settled by pious Protestant families, and Jamestown, populated primarily by males seeking their fortunes.

By 1619, the British colony at Jamestown, Virginia, had survived for more than a decade. The residents of the settlement had fought with the local natives and struggled continuously to eke out a living from the land. Starvation, disease, and death were frequent visitors, and the future of the enterprise continued to be in doubt.

In August of that year, a Dutch ship arrived. The master of the ship needed provisions and offered to trade his only cargo: about 20 black Africans. Many of the details of this transaction have been lost, and we probably will never know exactly how these people came to be chained in the hold of a ship. Regardless, this brief episode was a landmark event in the formation of what would become the United States. In combination with the strained relations between the English settlers and American Indians, the presence of these first few Africans raised an issue that never has been fully resolved: How should different groups in this society relate to one another?

The colonists at Jamestown had no ready answer. In 1619, England and its colonies did not practice slavery, so these first Africans were probably incorporated into colonial society as indentured servants, contract laborers who are obligated to serve a master for a specific number of years. At the end of the indenture, or contract, the servant became a free citizen. The colonies depended heavily on indentured servants from the British Isles for labor, and

SLAVERS REVENGING THEIR LOSSES.

Livingstone (1874, p. 62).

Scene in the Hold of the "Blood-Stained Gloria." (Middle Passage.)

Drake (1860, p. 28). Library of Congress, Prints and Photographs Division, LC-USZ62-30818.

Photos 4.1 & 4.2

To provide labor for American plantations, slaves were kidnapped from their villages in Africa and marched to the sea, a journey that sometimes covered hundreds of miles. They were loaded aboard slave ships and packed tightly below decks. The "Middle Passage" across the Atlantic could take months.

this status apparently provided a convenient way of defining the newcomers from Africa, who were, after all, treated as commodities and exchanged for food and water (see Exhibit 4.1 for a map of slave trade from Africa).

The position of African indentured servants in the colonies remained ambiguous for several decades. American slavery evolved gradually and in small steps; in fact, there was little demand for African labor during the years following 1619. By 1625, there still were only 23 blacks in Virginia, and that number had increased to perhaps 300 by midcentury (Franklin & Moss, 1994, p. 57). In the decades before the dawn of slavery, we know that some African indentured servants did become free citizens. Some became successful farmers

Exhibit 4.1 The African Diaspora

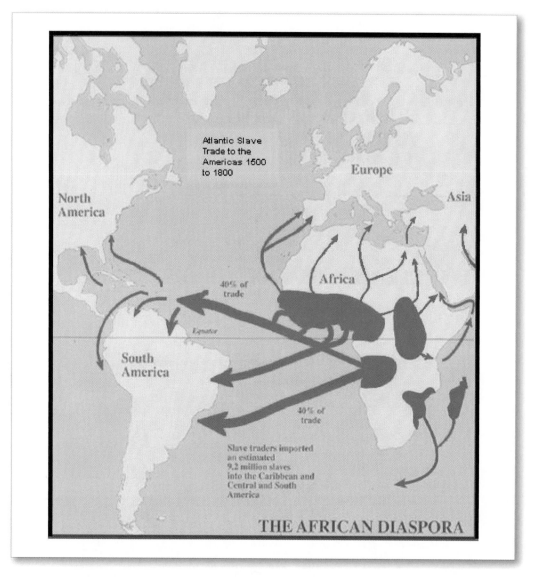

NOTE: The size of the arrows is proportional to the number of slaves. Note that the bulk went to South America and that there were also flows to Europe and Asia.

SOURCE: From Williams. *Macmillan Encyclopedia of World Slavery*, 1E. © 1998 Gale, a part of Cengage Learning, Inc. Reproduced by permission. www.cengage.com/permissions.

and landowners and, like their white neighbors, purchased African and white indentured servants themselves (Smedley, 2007, p. 104). By the 1650s, however, many African Americans (and their offspring) were being treated as the property of others, or in other words, as slaves (Morgan, 1975, p. 154).

It was not until the 1660s that the first laws defining slavery were enacted. In the century that followed, hundreds of additional laws were passed to clarify and formalize the status of Africans in colonial America. By the 1750s, slavery had been clearly defined in law and in custom, and the idea that a person could own another person—not just the labor or the energy or the work of a person, but the actual person—had been thoroughly institutionalized.

What caused slavery? The gradual evolution of and low demand for indentured servants from Africa suggest that slavery was not somehow inevitable or preordained. Why did the colonists deliberately create this repressive system? Why did they reach out all the way to Africa for their slaves? If they wanted to create a slave system, why didn't they enslave the American Indians nearby or the white indentured servants already present in the colonies?

The Labor Supply Problem

American colonists of the 1600s saw slavery as a solution to several problems they faced. The business of the colonies was agriculture, and farm work at this time was labor-intensive, performed almost entirely by hand. The Industrial Revolution was two centuries in the future, and there were few machines or labor-saving devices available to ease the everyday burden of work. A successful harvest depended largely on human effort.

As colonial society grew and developed, a specific form of agricultural production began to emerge. The plantation system was based on cultivating and exporting crops such as sugar, tobacco, and rice on large tracts of land using a large, cheap labor force. Profit margins tended to be small, so planters sought to stabilize their incomes by keeping the costs of production as low as possible. Profits in the labor-intensive plantation system could be maximized if a large, disciplined, and cheap workforce could be maintained by the landowners (Curtin, 1990; Morgan, 1975).

At about the same time the plantation system began to emerge, the supply of white indentured servants from the British Isles began to dwindle. Furthermore, the white indentured servants who did come to the colonies had to be released from their indenture every few years. Land was available, and these newly freed citizens tended to strike out on their own. Thus, landowners who relied on white indentured servants had to deal with high turnover rates in their workforces and faced a continually uncertain supply of labor.

Attempts to solve the labor supply problem by using American Indians failed. The tribes closest to the colonies were sometimes exploited for manpower. However, by the time the plantation system had evolved, the local tribes had dwindled in numbers as a result of warfare and disease. Other Indian nations across the continent retained enough power to resist enslavement, and it was relatively easy for American Indians to escape back to their kinfolk.

This left black Africans as a potential source of manpower. The slave trade from Africa to the Spanish and Portuguese colonies of South America had been established in the 1500s and could be expanded to fill the needs of the British colonies as well. The colonists came to see slaves imported from Africa as the most logical, cost-effective way to solve their vexing shortage of labor. The colonists created slavery to cultivate their lands and generate profits, status, and success. The paradox at the core of U.S. society had been established: The construction of a social system devoted to freedom and individual liberty "in the New World was made possible only by the revival of an institution of naked tyranny foresworn for centuries in the Old" (Lacy, 1972, p. 22).

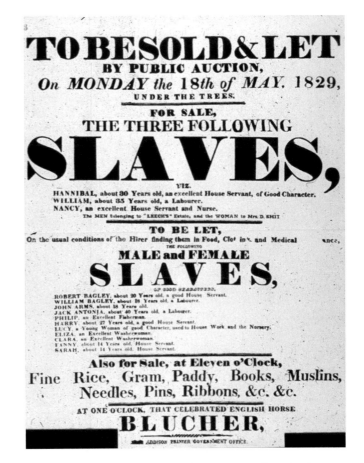

Poster Announcing Sale and Rental of Slaves, Saint Helena (South Atlantic), 1829. http://hitchcock.itc.virginia.edu/Slavery.

Photo 4.3

Slaves were regarded as commodities to be bought and sold.

The Contact Situation

The conditions under which groups first come into contact determine the immediate fate of the minority group and shape intergroup relations for years to come. We discussed the role of group competition in creating prejudice in Chapter 3. Here, I expand on some of these ideas by introducing two theories that will serve as analytical guides in understanding the contact situation.

The Noel Hypothesis

Sociologist Donald Noel (1968) identifies three features of the contact situation that in combination lead to some form of inequality between groups. The Noel hypothesis states: *If two or more groups come together in a contact situation characterized by ethnocentrism, competition, and a differential in power, then some form of racial or ethnic stratification will result* (p. 163; italics added). If the contact situation has all three characteristics, some dominant-minority group structure will be created.

Noel's first characteristic, ethnocentrism, is the tendency to judge other groups, societies, or lifestyles by the standards of one's own culture. Ethnocentrism is probably a universal component of human society, and some degree of ethnocentrism is essential to the maintenance of social solidarity and cohesion. Without some minimal level of pride in and loyalty to one's own society and cultural traditions, there would be no particular reason to observe the norms and laws, honor the sacred symbols, or cooperate with others in doing the daily work of society.

Regardless of its importance, ethnocentrism can have negative consequences. At its worst, it can lead to the view that other cultures and peoples are not just different, but inferior. At the very least, ethnocentrism creates a social boundary line that members of the groups involved will recognize and observe. When ethnocentrism exists in any degree, people will tend to sort themselves out along group lines and identify characteristics that differentiate "us" from "them."

Competition is a struggle over a scarce commodity. As we saw in Chapter 3, competition between groups often leads to harsh negative feelings (prejudice) and hostile actions (discrimination). In competitive contact situations, the victorious group becomes the dominant group, and the losers become the minority group. The competition may center on land, labor, jobs, housing, educational opportunities, political office, or anything else that is mutually desired by both groups or that one group has and the other group wants. Competition provides the eventual dominant group with the motivation to establish superiority. The dominant group serves its own interests by ending the competition and exploiting, controlling, eliminating, or otherwise dominating the minority group.

The third feature of the contact situation is a differential in power between the groups. Power, as you recall from Chapter 1, is the ability of a group to achieve its goals even in the face of opposition from other groups. The amount of power commanded by a group is a function of three factors. First, the size of the group can make a difference, and all other things being equal, larger groups are more powerful. Second, in addition to raw numbers, the degree of organization, discipline, and the quality of group leadership can make a difference in the ability of a group to pursue its goals. A third component of power is resources: anything that can be used to help the group achieve its goals. Depending on the context, resources might include anything from land to information to money. The greater the number and variety of resources at the disposal of a group, the greater that group's potential ability to dominate other groups. Thus, a larger, better-organized group with more resources at its disposal will generally be able to impose its will on smaller, less-well-organized groups with fewer resources. The Noel hypothesis is diagrammed in Exhibit 4.2.

Exhibit 4.2 A Model of the Establishment of Minority Group Status

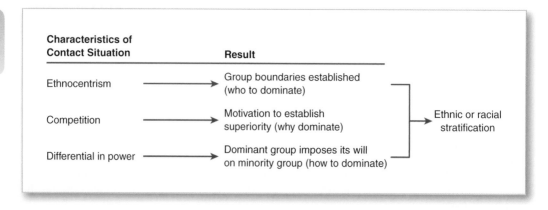

Characteristics of Contact Situation	Result	
Ethnocentrism	→ Group boundaries established (who to dominate)	
Competition	→ Motivation to establish superiority (why dominate)	→ Ethnic or racial stratification
Differential in power	→ Dominant group imposes its will on minority group (how to dominate)	

Note the respective functions of each of the three factors in shaping the contact situation and the emergence of inequality. If ethnocentrism is present, the groups will recognize their differences and maintain their boundaries. If competition is also present, the group that eventually dominates will attempt to maximize its share of scarce commodities by controlling or subordinating the group that eventually becomes the "minority" group. The differential in power allows the dominant group to succeed in establishing a superior position. Ethnocentrism tells the dominant group whom to dominate, competition tells the dominant group why it should establish a structure of dominance, and power is how the dominant group's will is imposed on the minority group.

The Noel hypothesis can be applied to the creation of minority groups in a variety of situations. We will also use the model to analyze changes in dominant-minority structures over time.

The Blauner Hypothesis

The contact situation also has been analyzed by sociologist Robert Blauner (1972), in his book *Racial Oppression in America*. Blauner identifies two different initial relationships—colonization and immigration—and hypothesizes that *minority groups created by colonization will experience more intense prejudice, racism, and discrimination than those created by immigration. Furthermore, the disadvantaged status of colonized groups will persist longer and be more difficult to overcome than the disadvantaged status faced by groups created by immigration.*

Colonized minority groups, such as African Americans, are forced into minority status by the superior military and political power of the dominant group. At the time of contact with the dominant group, colonized groups are subjected to massive inequalities and attacks on their cultures. They are assigned to positions, such as slave status, from which any form of assimilation is extremely difficult and perhaps even forbidden by the dominant group. Frequently, members of the minority group are identified by highly visible racial or physical characteristics that maintain and reinforce the oppressive system. Thus, minority groups created by colonization experience harsher and more persistent rejection and oppression than do groups created by immigration.

Immigrant minority groups are at least in part voluntary participants in the host society. That is, although the decision to immigrate may be motivated by extreme pressures, such as famine or political persecution, immigrant groups have at least some control over their destinations and their positions in the host society. As a result, they do not occupy positions that are as markedly inferior as those of colonized groups. They retain enough internal organization and resources to pursue their own self-interests, and they commonly experience more rapid acceptance and easier movement to equality. The boundaries between groups are not so rigidly maintained, especially when the groups are racially similar. In discussing European immigrant groups, for example, Blauner (1972) states that entering into American society

> involved a degree of choice and self-direction that was for the most part denied to people of color. Voluntary immigration made it more likely that . . . European . . . ethnic groups would identify with America and see the host culture as a positive opportunity. (p. 56)

Acculturation and, particularly, integration were significantly more possible for European immigrant groups than for the groups formed under conquest or colonization.

Blauner stresses that the initial differences between colonized and immigrant minority groups have consequences that persist long after the original contact. For example, based on measures of equality—or integration into the secondary sector, the second step in Gordon's model of assimilation (see Chapter 2)—such as average income, years of education, and unemployment rate, descendants of European immigrants are equal with national norms today (see Chapter 2 for specific data). In contrast, descendants of colonized and conquered groups (e.g., African Americans) are, on the average, below the national norms on virtually all measures of equality and integration (see Chapters 6–9 for specific data).

Blauner's two types of minority groups lie at opposite ends of a continuum, but there are intermediate positions between the extremes. Enclave and middleman minorities (see Chapter 2) often originate as immigrant groups who bring some resources and, thus, have more opportunities than colonized minority groups to carve out places for themselves in the host society. Unlike European groups, however, many of these minorities are also racially distinguishable, and certain kinds of opportunities may be closed to them. For instance, U.S. citizenship was expressly forbidden to immigrants from China until World War II. Federal laws restricted the entrance of Chinese immigrants, and state and local laws restricted their opportunities for education, jobs, and housing. For these and other reasons, the Asian immigrant experience cannot be equated with European immigrant patterns (Blauner, 1972, p. 55). Because they combine characteristics of both the colonized and the immigrant minority group experience, we can predict that in terms of equality, enclave and middleman minority groups will occupy an intermediate status between the more assimilated white ethnic groups and the colonized racial minorities.

Blauner's typology has proved to be an extremely useful conceptual tool for the analysis of U.S. dominant-minority relations, and it is used extensively throughout this text. In fact, the case studies that compose Part III of this text are arranged in approximate order from groups created by colonization to those created by immigration. Of course, it is difficult to measure such things as the extent of colonization objectively or precisely, and the exact order of the groups is somewhat arbitrary.

The Creation of Slavery in the United States

The Noel hypothesis helps explain why colonists enslaved black Africans instead of white indentured servants or American Indians. First, all three groups were the objects of ethnocentric feelings on the part of the elite groups that dominated colonial society. Black Africans and American Indians were perceived as being different on religious as well as racial grounds. Many white indentured servants were Irish Catholics, criminals, or paupers. They not only occupied a lowly status in society but were perceived as different from the British Protestants who dominated colonial society.

Second, competition of some sort existed between the colonists and all three groups. The competition with American Indians was direct and focused on control of land. Competition with indentured servants, white and black, was more indirect; these groups were the labor force that the landowners needed to work on their plantations and become successful in the New World.

Noel's third variable, differential in power, is the key variable that explains why Africans were enslaved instead of the other groups. During the first several decades of colonial history, the balance of power between the colonists and American Indians was relatively even and, in fact, often favored American Indians (Lurie, 1982, pp. 131–133). The colonists were outnumbered, and their muskets and cannons were only marginally more effective than bows and spears. The American Indian tribes were well-organized social units capable of sustaining resistance to and mounting reprisals against the colonists, and it took centuries for the nascent United States to finally defeat American Indians militarily.

White indentured servants, on the one hand, had the advantage of being preferred over black indentured servants (Noel, 1968, p. 168). Their greater desirability gave them bargaining power and the ability to negotiate better treatment and more lenient terms than black indentured servants. If the planters had attempted to enslave white indentured servants, this source of labor would have dwindled even more rapidly.

	Three Causal Factors		
Potential Sources of Labor	**Ethnocentrism**	**Competition**	**Differential in Power**
White indentured servants	Yes	Yes	No
American Indians	Yes	Yes	No
Black indentured servants	Yes	Yes	Yes

Exhibit 4.3 The Noel Hypothesis Applied to the Origins of Slavery

Africans, on the other hand, had become indentured servants by force and coercion. In Blauner's terms, they were a colonized group that did not freely choose to enter the British colonies. Thus, they had no bargaining power. Unlike American Indians, they had no nearby relatives, no knowledge of the countryside, and no safe havens to which to escape. Exhibit 4.3 summarizes the impact of these three factors on the three potential sources of labor in colonial America.

Paternalistic Relations

Recall the first theme stated at the beginning of this chapter: The nature of intergroup relationships will reflect the characteristics of the larger society. The most important and profitable unit of economic production in the colonial South was the plantation, and the region was dominated by a small group of wealthy landowners. A society with a small elite class and a plantation-based economy will often develop a form of minority relations called paternalism (van den Berghe, 1967; Wilson, 1973). The key features of paternalism are vast power differentials and huge inequalities between dominant and minority groups, elaborate and repressive systems of control over the minority group, caste-like barriers between groups, elaborate and highly stylized codes of behavior and communication between groups, and low rates of overt conflict. Each of these characteristics will be considered in turn.

As slavery evolved in the colonies, the dominant group shaped the system to fit its needs. To solidify control of the labor of their slaves, the plantation elite designed and enacted an elaborate system of laws and customs that gave masters nearly total legal power over slaves. In these laws, slaves were defined as chattel, or personal property, rather than as persons, and they were accorded no civil or political rights. Slaves could not own property, sign contracts, bring lawsuits, or even testify in court (except against another slave). The masters were given the legal authority to determine almost every aspect of a slave's life, including work schedules, living arrangements, diets, and even names (Elkins, 1959; Franklin & Moss, 1994; Genovese, 1974; Jordan, 1968; Stampp, 1956).

The law permitted the master to determine the type and severity of punishment for misbehavior. Slaves were forbidden by law to read or write, and marriages between slaves were not legally recognized. Masters could separate husbands from wives and parents from children if it suited them. Slaves had little formal decision-making ability or control over their lives or the lives of their loved ones.

In colonial America, slavery became synonymous with race. Race, slavery, inferiority, and powerlessness became intertwined in ways that, according to many analysts, still affect the ways black and white Americans think about one another (Hacker, 1992). Slavery was a caste system, or closed stratification system. In a caste system, there is no mobility between social positions, and the social class you are born into (your ascribed status) is permanent. Slave status was for life and was passed on to any children a slave might have. Whites, no matter what they did, could not become slaves.

Interaction between members of the dominant and minority groups in a paternalistic system is governed by a rigid, strictly enforced code of etiquette. Slaves were expected to

Photo 4.4

The prosperity of southern plantation owners was based on the labor of black slaves.

© Bettmann/CORBIS.

show deference and humility and visibly display their lower status when interacting with whites. These rigid behavioral codes made it possible for blacks and whites to work together, sometimes intimately, sometimes for their entire lives, without threatening the power and status differentials inherent in the system. Plantation and farm work required close and frequent contact between blacks and whites, and status differentials were maintained socially rather than physically.

The frequent but unequal interactions allowed the elites to maintain a pseudotolerance, an attitude of benevolent despotism, toward their slaves. Their prejudice and racism were often expressed as positive emotions of affection for their black slaves. The attitude of the planters toward their slaves was often paternalistic and even genteel (Wilson, 1973, pp. 52–55).

For their part, black slaves often could not hate their owners as much as they hated the system that constrained them. The system defined slaves as pieces of property owned by their masters—yet they were, undeniably, human beings. Thus, slavery was founded, at its heart, on a contradiction.

> The master learned to treat his slaves both as property and as men and women, the slaves learned to express and affirm their humanity even while they were constrained in much of their lives to accept their status as chattel. (Parish, 1989, p. 1)

The powerlessness of slaves made it difficult for them to openly reject or resist the system. Slaves had few ways in which they could directly challenge the institution of slavery or their position in it. Open defiance was ineffective and could result in punishment or even death. In general, masters would not be prosecuted for physically abusing their slaves.

One of the few slave revolts that occurred in the United States illustrates both the futility of overt challenge and the degree of repression built into the system. In 1831, in Southampton County, Virginia, a slave named Nat Turner led an uprising during which 57 whites were killed. The revolt was starting to spread when the state militia met and routed the growing slave army. More than 100 slaves died in the armed encounter, and Nat Turner and 13 others were later executed. Slave owners and white southerners in general were greatly alarmed by the uprising and consequently tightened the system of control over slaves, making it even more repressive (Franklin & Moss, 1994, p. 147). Ironically, the result of Nat Turner's attempt to lead slaves to freedom was greater oppression and control by the dominant group.

Others were more successful in resisting the system. Runaway slaves were a constant problem for slave owners, especially in the states bordering the free states of the North. The difficulty of escape and the low likelihood of successfully reaching the North did not deter thousands from attempting the feat, some of them repeatedly. Many runaway slaves received help from the Underground Railroad, an informal network of safe houses supported by African Americans and whites involved in abolitionism, the movement to abolish slavery. These escapes created colorful legends and heroic figures, including Frederick Douglass, Sojourner Truth, and Harriet Tubman. The Narrative Portrait in this chapter presents the experiences of two ex-slaves who eventually escaped to the North.

Besides running away and open rebellion, slaves used the forms of resistance most readily available to them: sabotage, intentional carelessness, dragging their feet, and work slow-downs. As historian Peter Parish (1989) points out, it is difficult to separate "a natural desire to avoid hard work [from a] conscious decision to protest or resist" (p. 73), and much of this behavior may fall more into the category of noncooperation than of deliberate political rebellion. Nonetheless, these behaviors were widespread and document the rejection of the system by its victims.

On an everyday basis, the slaves managed their lives and families as best they could. Most slaves were neither docile victims nor unyielding rebels. As the institution of slavery developed, a distinct African American experience accumulated, and traditions of resistance and accommodation developed side by side. Most slaves worked to create a world for themselves within the confines and restraints of the plantation system, avoiding the more vicious repression as much as possible while attending to their own needs and those of their families. An African American culture was forged in response to the realities of slavery and was manifested in folklore, music, religion, family and kinship structures, and other aspects of everyday life (Blassingame, 1972; Genovese, 1974; Gutman, 1976).

The Dimensions of Minority Group Status

The situation of African Americans under slavery can be more completely described by applying some of the concepts developed in Part I.

Power, Inequality, and Institutional Discrimination

The key concepts for understanding the creation of slavery are power, inequality, and institutional discrimination. The plantation elite used its greater power resources to consign black Africans to an inferior status. The system of racial inequality was implemented and reinforced by institutionalized discrimination and became a central aspect of everyday life in the antebellum South. The legal and political institutions of colonial society were shaped to benefit the landowners and give them almost total control over their slaves.

Prejudice and Racism

What about the attitudes and feelings of the people involved? What was the role of personal prejudice? How and why did the ideology of antiblack racism start? As we discussed in Chapter 3, individual prejudice and ideological racism are not so important as causes of the creation of minority group status but are more the results of systems of racial inequality (Jordan, 1968, p. 80; Smedley, 2007, pp. 100–104). The colonists did not enslave black indentured servants because they were prejudiced or because they disliked blacks or thought them inferior. The decision to enslave black Africans was an attempt to resolve a labor supply problem. The primary roles of prejudice and racism in the creation of minority group status are to rationalize and "explain" the emerging system of racial and ethnic advantage (Wilson, 1973, pp. 76–78).

Prejudice and racism help mobilize support for the creation of minority group status and help stabilize the system as it emerges. Prejudice and racism can provide convenient and convincing justifications for exploitation. They can help insulate a system such as slavery from questioning and criticism and make it appear reasonable and even desirable. Thus, the intensity, strength, and popularity of antiblack southern racism actually reached its height almost 200 years after slavery began to emerge. During the early 1800s, the American abolitionist movement brought slavery under heavy attack, and in response, the ideology of antiblack racism was strengthened (Wilson, 1973, p. 79). The greater the opposition to a system of racial stratification or the greater the magnitude of the exploitation, the greater the need of the beneficiaries and their apologists to justify, rationalize, and explain.

Once created, dominant group prejudice and racism become widespread and common ways of thinking about the minority group. In the case of colonial slavery, antiblack beliefs and feelings became part of the standard package of knowledge, understanding, and truths shared by members of the dominant group. As the decades wore on and the institution of slavery solidified, prejudice and racism were passed on from generation to generation. For succeeding generations, antiblack prejudice became just another piece of information and perspective on the world learned during socialization. Antiblack prejudice and racism began as part of an attempt to control the labor of black indentured servants, became embedded in early American culture, and were established as integral parts of the socialization process for succeeding generations (see Myrdal's "vicious cycle" in Chapter 3).

These conceptual relationships are presented in Exhibit 4.4. Racial inequality arises from the contact situation, as specified in the Noel hypothesis. As the dominant-minority relationship begins to take shape, prejudice and racism develop as rationalizations. Over time, a vicious cycle develops as prejudice and racism reinforce the pattern of inequality between groups, which was the cause of prejudice and racism in the first place. Thus, the Blauner hypothesis states, the subordination of colonized minority groups is perpetuated through time.

Exhibit 4.4 A Model for the Creation of Prejudice and Racism

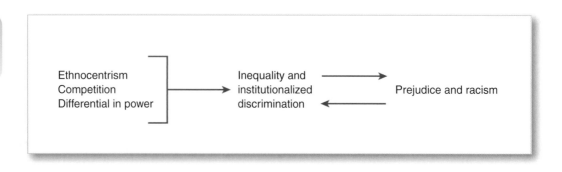

Ethnocentrism
Competition
Differential in power

Inequality and institutionalized discrimination

Prejudice and racism

A Slave's Life

The memoirs of two escaped slaves, Henry Bibb and Harriet Jacobs, illustrate some of the features of southern slavery. Bibb was married and had a child when he escaped to the North, where he spent the rest of his life working for the abolition of slavery. The passage printed here gives an overview of his early life and expresses his commitment to freedom and his family. He also describes some of the abuses he and his family suffered under the reign of a particularly cruel master. Bibb was unable to rescue his daughter from slavery and agonizes over leaving her in bondage.

Harriet Jacobs grew up as a slave in Edenton, North Carolina, and in this excerpt, she recounts some of her experiences, especially the sexual harassment she suffered at the hand of her master. Her narrative illustrates the dynamics of power and sex in the "peculiar institution" and the very limited options she had for defending herself from the advances of her master. She eventually escaped from slavery by hiding in her grandmother's house for nearly 17 years and then making her way to the North.

NARRATIVE OF THE LIFE AND ADVENTURES OF HENRY BIBB

HENRY BIBB

I was born May 1815, of a slave mother, in Shelby County, Kentucky, and was claimed as the property of David White. I was brought up . . . or, more correctly speaking, I was flogged up; for where I should have received moral, mental, and religious instruction, I received stripes without number, the object of which was to degrade and keep me in subordination. . . . The first time I was separated from my mother, I was young and small. . . . I was . . . hired out to labor for various persons and all my wages were expended for the education of [my master's daughter]. It was then I first commenced seeing and feeling that I was a wretched slave, compelled to work under the lash without wages, and often without clothes to hide my nakedness. . . .

All that I heard about liberty and freedom . . . I never forgot. Among other good trades I learned the art of running away to perfection. I made a regular business of it, and never gave it up, until I had broken the bands of slavery, and landed myself safely in Canada, where I was regarded as a man, and not a thing.

[Bibb describes his childhood and adolescence, his early attempts to escape to the North, and his marriage to Malinda.] Not many months [later] Malinda made me a father. The dear little daughter was called Mary Frances. She was nurtured and caressed by her mother and father. . . . Malinda's business was to labor out in the field the greater part of her time, and there was no one to take care of poor little Frances. . . . She was left at the house to creep under the feet of an unmerciful old mistress, Mrs. Gatewood (the owner's wife). I recollect that [we] came in from the field one day and poor little Frances came creeping to her mother smiling, but with large tear drops standing in her dear little eyes. . . . Her little face was bruised black with the whole print of Mrs. Gatewood's hand. . . . Who can imagine the feelings of a mother and father, when looking upon their infant child whipped and tortured with impunity, and they placed in a situation where they could afford it no protection? But we were all claimed and held as property; the father and mother were slaves!

On this same plantation, I was compelled to stand and see my wife shamefully scourged and abused by her master; and the manner in which this was done was so violent and inhuman that I despair in finding decent language to describe the bloody act of cruelty. My happiness or pleasure was all blasted; for it was sometimes a pleasure to be with my little family even in slavery. I loved them as my wife and child. Little Frances was a pretty child; she was quiet, playful, bright, and interesting. . . . But I could never look upon the dear child without being filled with sorrow and fearful apprehensions, of being separated by slaveholders, because she was a slave, regarded as property. . . . But Oh! When I remember that my daughter, my only child, is still there, . . . it is too much to bear. If ever there was any one act of my life as a slave, that I have to lament over, it is that of being a father and a husband to slaves. I have the satisfaction of knowing that I am the father of only one slave. She is bone of my bone, and flesh of my flesh; poor unfortunate child. She was the first and shall be the last slave that ever I will father, for chains and slavery on this earth.

SOURCE: Osofsky (1969, pp. 54–65, 80–81).

LIFE AS A SLAVE GIRL

HARRIET JACOBS

During the first years of my service in Dr. Flint's family, I was accustomed to share some indulgences with the children of my mistress. Though this seemed to me no more than right, I was grateful for it, and tried to merit the kindness by the faithful discharge of my duties. But I now entered on my fifteenth year—a sad epoch in the life of a slave girl. My master began to whisper foul words in my ear. Young as I was, I could not remain ignorant of their import. I tried to treat them with indifference or contempt. The master's age, my extreme youth, and the fear that misconduct would be reported to my grandmother made me bear this treatment for many months.

He was a crafty man, and resorted to many means to accomplish his purposes. Sometimes he had stormy, terrific ways, that made his victims tremble; sometimes he assumed a gentleness that he thought must surely subdue. Of the two, I preferred his stormy moods, although they left me trembling. He tried his utmost to corrupt the pure principles my grandmother had instilled. He peopled my young mind with unclean images, such as only a vile monster could think of. I turned from him with disgust and hatred. But he was my master. I was compelled to live under the same roof with him, where I saw a man forty years my senior daily violating the most sacred commandments of nature. He told me I was his property; that I must be subject to his will in all things. My soul revolted against the mean tyranny. But where could I turn for protection? No matter whether the slave girl be as black as ebony or as fair as her mistress. In either case, there is no shadow of law to protect her from insult, from violence, or even from death; all these are inflicted by fiends who bear the shape of men. The mistress, who ought to protect the helpless victim, has no other feelings towards her but those of jealousy and rage. The degradation, the wrongs, the vices that grow out of slavery, are more than I can describe. They are greater than you would willingly believe. Surely, if you credited on half the truths that are told you concerning the helpless millions suffering in this cruel bondage, you at the north would not help tighten the yoke. You surely would refuse to do for the master, on your own soil, the mean and cruel work which trained bloodhounds and the lowest class of whites do for him at the south.

SOURCE: "The Trials of Girlhood," reprinted by permission of the publishers from *Incidents in the Life of a Slave Girl: Written by Herself* by Harriet A. Jacobs, edited and with an Introduction by Jean Fagan Yellin, pp. 27–30, Cambridge, Mass.: Harvard University Press, Copyright © 1987, 2000 by the President and Fellows of Harvard College.

Assimilation

There is an enormous literature on American slavery, and research on the nature and meaning of the system continues to this day. Many issues remain unsettled, however, and one of the more controversial, consequential, and interesting of these concerns the effect of slavery on the slaves.

Apologists for the system of slavery and some historians of the South writing early in the 20th century accepted the rationalizations inherent in antiblack prejudice and argued that slavery was actually beneficial for black Africans. According to this view, British-American slavery operated as a "school for civilization" (Phillips, 1918) that rescued savages from the jungles of Africa and exposed them to Christianity and Western civilization. Some argued that slavery was benevolent because it protected slaves from the evils and exploitation of the factory system of the industrial North. These racist views were most popular a century ago, early in the development of the social sciences. Since that time, scholars have established a number of facts (e.g., Western Africa, the area from which most slaves came, had been the site of a number of powerful, advanced civilizations) that make this view untenable by anyone but the most dedicated racist thinkers.

At the opposite extreme, slavery has been compared to Nazi concentration camps and likened to a "perverted patriarchy" that brainwashed, emasculated, and dehumanized slaves, stripping them of their heritage and culture. Historian Stanley Elkins (1959) provocatively argued this interpretation, now widely regarded as overstated, in his book *Slavery: A Problem in American Institutional and Intellectual Life*. Although his conclusions might be overdrawn, Elkins's argument and evidence are important for any exploration of the nature of American slavery. In fact, much of the scholarship on slavery since the publication of Elkins's book has been an attempt to refute or at least modify the points he made.

Still a third view of the impact of slavery maintains that through all the horror and abuse of enslavement, slaves retained a sense of self and a firm anchor in their African traditions. This point of view stresses the importance of kinship, religion, and culture in helping African Americans cope and has been presented most poignantly in Alex Haley's (1976) semifictional family history, *Roots*, but it is also represented in the scholarly literature on slavery since Elkins (see Blassingame, 1972; Genovese, 1974).

The debate over the impact of slavery continues (see the "Current Debates" section at the end of this chapter), and we cannot hope to resolve the issues here. However, it is clear that African Americans, in Blauner's terms, were a "colonized" minority group who were extensively—and coercively—acculturated. Language acculturation began on the slave ships, where different tribal and language groups were mixed together to inhibit communication and lower the potential for resistance and revolt (Mannix, 1962).

The plantation elite and their agents needed to communicate with their workforce and insisted on using English. Within a generation or two, African language use died out. Some scholars argue that some African words and language patterns persist to the present day, but even if this is true, the significance of this survival is trivial compared with the coerced adoption of English. To the extent that culture depends on language, Africans under slavery experienced massive acculturation.

Acculturation through slavery was clearly a process that was forced on African Americans. Because they were a colonized minority group and unwilling participants in the system, they had little choice but to adjust to the conditions established by the plantation elite as best they could. Their traditional culture was suppressed, and their choices for adjustment to the system were sharply constrained. Black slaves developed new cultural forms and social relationships, but they did so in a situation with few options or choices (Blauner, 1972, p. 66). The extent to which any African cultural elements survived the institution of slavery is a matter of some controversy, but given the power differentials inherent in the system, African Americans had few choices regarding their manner of adjustment.

Gender Relations

Southern agrarian society developed into a complex social system stratified by race and gender as well as by class. The plantation elite, small in number but wealthy and politically powerful, was at the top of the structure. Most whites in the South were small farmers, and relatively few of them owned slaves. In 1860, for example, only 25% of all southern whites owned slaves (Franklin & Moss, 1994, p. 123).

The principal line of differentiation in the antebellum South was, of course, race, which was largely synonymous with slave versus nonslave status. Each of the racial groups was, in turn, stratified by gender. White women were subordinate to the males of the plantation elite, and the slave community echoed the patriarchal pattern of southern society, except that the degree of gender inequality among blacks was sharply truncated by the fact that slaves had little autonomy and few resources. At the bottom of the system were African American female slaves. Minority women are generally in double jeopardy, oppressed through their gender as well as their race. For black female slaves, the constraints were triple: "Black in a white society, slave in a free society, women in a society ruled by men, female slaves had the least formal power and were perhaps the most vulnerable group of antebellum America" (White, 1985, p. 15).

The race and gender roles of the day idealized southern white women and placed them on a pedestal. A romanticized conception of femininity was quite inconsistent with the roles women slaves were required to play. Besides domestic roles, female slaves also worked in the fields and did their share of the hardest, most physically demanding, least "feminine" farm work. Southern ideas about feminine fragility and daintiness were quickly abandoned when they interfered with work and the profit to be made from slave labor (Amott & Matthaei, 1991, p. 146).

Reflecting their vulnerability and powerlessness, women slaves were sometimes used to breed more slaves to sell. They were raped and otherwise abused by the males of the dominant group. John Blassingame (1972) expressed their vulnerability to sexual victimization:

Many white men considered every slave cabin a house of ill-fame. Often through "gifts" but usually by force, white overseers and planters obtained the sexual favors of black women. Generally speaking, the women were literally forced to offer themselves "willingly" and receive a trinket for their compliance rather than a flogging for their refusal. (p. 83)

Note the power relationships implicit in this passage: Female slaves had little choice but to feign willing submission to their white owners.

The routines of work and everyday life differed for male and female slaves. Although they sometimes worked with the men, especially during harvest time, women more often worked in sex-segregated groups organized around domestic as well as farm chores. In addition to working in the fields, they attended the births and cared for the children of both races, cooked and cleaned, wove cloth and sewed clothes, and did the laundry. The women often worked longer hours than the men, doing housework and other chores long after the men retired (Robertson, 1996, p. 21; White, 1985, p. 122).

The group-oriented nature of their tasks gave female slaves an opportunity to develop same-sex bonds and relationships. Women cooperated in their chores, in caring for their children, in the maintenance of their quarters, and in myriad other domestic and family chores. These networks and interpersonal bonds could be used to resist the system. For example, slave women sometimes induced abortions rather than bring more children into bondage. They often controlled the role of midwife and were able to effectively deceive slave owners and disguise the abortions as miscarriages (White, 1985, pp. 125–126). The networks of relationships among the female slaves provided mutual aid and support for everyday problems, solace and companionship during the travails of a vulnerable and exploited existence, and some ability to buffer and resist the influence and power of the slave owners (Andersen, 1993, pp. 164–165).

Slaves in the American system were brutally repressed and exploited, but females were even more subordinated than males. Also, their oppression and exclusion sharply differentiated female slaves from white females. The white "Southern Belle"—chaste, untouchable, and unremittingly virtuous—had little in common with African American women under slavery.

THE CREATION OF MINORITY STATUS
FOR AMERICAN INDIANS AND MEXICAN AMERICANS

Two other groups became minorities during the preindustrial period. In this section, we will review the dynamics of these processes and make some comparisons with African Americans. As you will see, both the Noel and Blauner hypotheses provide some extremely useful insights into these experiences.

American Indians

As Europeans began to penetrate the New World, they encountered hundreds of societies that had lived on this land for thousands of years. American Indian societies were highly variable in culture, language, size, and subsistence technology. Some were small, nomadic hunter-gatherer bands, whereas others were more developed societies in which people lived in settled villages and tended large gardens. Regardless of their exact nature, the inexorable advance of white society eventually devastated them all. Contact began in the East and established a pattern of conflict and defeat for American Indians that continued until the last of the tribes were finally defeated in the late 1800s. The continual expansion of white society into the West allowed many settlers to fulfill their dreams of economic self-sufficiency, but American Indians, who lost not only their lives and their land but also much of their traditional way of life, paid an incalculable price.

Photo 4.5

Most American Indians lived in small bands and relied on hunting and gardening for their subsistence.

From Library of Congress.

An important and widely unrecognized point about American Indians is that there is no such thing as the American Indian. Rather, there were—and are—hundreds of different tribes or nations, each with its own language, culture, home territory, and unique history. There are, of course, similarities from tribe to tribe, but there are also vast differences between, for example, the forest-dwelling tribes of Virginia, who lived in longhouses and cultivated gardens, and the nomadic Plains tribes, who relied on hunting to satisfy their needs. Each tribe was and remains a unique blend of language, values, and social structure. Because of space constraints, we will not always be able to take all these differences into account. Nonetheless, it is important to be aware of the diversity and sensitive to the variety of peoples and histories subsumed within the general category of American Indian.

A second important point is that many American Indian tribes no longer exist or are vastly diminished in size. When Jamestown was established in 1607, it is estimated that there were anywhere from 1 million to more than 10 million American Indians living in what became the United States. By 1890, when the Indian Wars finally ended, the number of American Indians had fallen to fewer than 250,000. By the end of the nearly 300-year-long "contact situation," American Indian populations had declined by 75% or more (Wax, 1971, p. 17; see also McNickle, 1973).

Very little of this population loss was due directly to warfare and battle casualties. The greatest part was caused by European diseases brought over by the colonists and by the destruction of the food supplies on which American Indian societies relied. American Indians died by the thousands from measles, influenza, smallpox, cholera, tuberculosis, and a variety of other infectious diseases (Wax, 1971, p. 17; see also Oswalt & Neely, 1996; Snipp, 1989). Traditional hunting grounds and garden plots were taken over by the expanding American society, and game such as the buffalo was slaughtered to the point of extinction. The result of the contact situation for American Indians very nearly approached genocide.

American Indians and the Noel and Blauner Hypotheses

We have already used the Noel hypothesis to analyze why American Indians were not enslaved during the colonial era. Their competition with whites centered on land, not labor, and the Indian nations were often successful in resisting domination (at least temporarily). As American society spread to the West, competition over land continued, and the growing power, superior technology, and greater resource base of the dominant group gradually pushed American Indians to near extinction.

Various attempts were made to control the persistent warfare, the most important of which occurred before independence from Great Britain. In 1763, the British Crown ruled that the various tribes were to be considered "sovereign nations with inalienable rights to their land" (see Lurie, 1982; McNickle, 1973; Wax, 1971). In other words, each tribe was to be treated as a nation-state, like France or Russia, and the colonists could not simply expropriate tribal lands. Rather, negotiations had to take place, and treaties of agreement had to be signed by all affected parties. The tribes had to be compensated for any loss of land.

This policy was often ignored but was continued by the newborn federal government after the American Revolution. The principle of sovereignty is important because it established a unique relationship between the federal government and American Indians. The fact that white society ignored the policy and regularly broke the treaties gives American Indians legal claims against the federal government that are also unique.

East of the Mississippi River, the period of open conflict was brought to a close by the Indian Removal Act of 1830, which dictated a policy of forced emigration to the tribes. The law required all eastern tribes to move to new lands west of the Mississippi. Some of the affected tribes went without resistance, others fought, and still others fled to Canada rather than move to the new territory. Regardless, the Indian Removal Act "solved" the Indian problem in the East. The relative scarcity of American Indians in the eastern United States continues to the present, and the majority of American Indians live in the western two thirds of the nation.

In the West, the grim story of competition for land, accompanied by rising hostility and aggression, repeated itself. Wars were fought, buffalo were killed, territory was expropriated, atrocities were committed on both sides, and the fate of the tribes became more and more certain. By 1890, the greater power and resources of white society had defeated the Indian nations. All the great warrior chiefs were dead or in prison, and almost all American Indians were living on reservations controlled by agencies of the federal government. The reservations consisted of land set aside for the tribes by the government during treaty negotiations. Often, these lands were not the traditional homelands and were hundreds or even thousands of miles away from what the tribe considered to be "home." It is not surprising that the reservations were usually on undesirable, often worthless land.

The 1890s mark a low point in American Indian history, a time of great demoralization and sadness. The tribes had to find a way to adapt to reservation life and new forms of subordination to the federal government. Although elements of the tribal way of life have survived, the tribes were impoverished and without resources and had little ability to pursue their own interests.

American Indians, in Blauner's terms, were a colonized minority group who faced high levels of prejudice, racism, and discrimination. Like African Americans, they were controlled by paternalistic systems (the reservations) and in a variety of ways were coercively accultur- ated. Furthermore, according to Blauner, the negative consequences of colonized minority group status will persist long after the contact situation has been resolved. As we will see in Chapter 8, there is a great deal of evidence to support this prediction.

Gender Relations

In the centuries before contact with Europeans, American Indian societies distributed resources and power in a wide variety of ways. At one extreme, some American Indian soci- eties were highly stratified, and many practiced various forms of slavery. Others stressed equality, sharing of resources, and respect for the autonomy and dignity of each individual, including women and children (Amott & Matthaei, 1991, p. 33). American Indian societies were generally patriarchal and followed a strict gender-based division of labor, but this did not necessarily mean that women were subordinate. In many tribes, women held positions of great responsibility and controlled the wealth. For example, among the Iroquois (a large and powerful federation of tribes located in the Northeast), women controlled the land and the harvest, arranged marriages, supervised the children, and were responsible for the appointment of tribal leaders and decisions about peace and war (Oswalt & Neely, 1996, pp. 404–405). It was not unusual for women in many tribes to play key roles in religion, politics, warfare, and the economy. Some women even became highly respected warriors and chiefs (Amott & Matthaei, 1991, p. 36).

Gender relations were affected in a variety of ways during the prolonged contact period. In some cases, the relative status and power of women rose. For example, the women of the Navajo tribe (located mainly in what is now Arizona and New Mexico) were traditionally responsible for the care of herd animals and livestock. When the Spanish introduced sheep and goats into the region, the importance of this sector of the subsistence economy increased, and the power and status of women grew along with it.

In other cases, women were affected adversely. The women of the Great Plains tribes, for example, suffered a dramatic loss as a result of contact. The sexual division of labor in these tribes was that women were responsible for gardening, whereas men handled the hunting. When horses were introduced from Europe, the productivity of the male hunters was greatly increased. As their economic importance increased, males became more dominant and women lost status and power. Women in the Cherokee nation—a large tribe whose original homelands were in the Southeast—similarly lost considerable status and power under the pressure to assimilate. Traditionally, Cherokee land was cultivated, controlled, and passed down from generation to generation by the women. This matrilineal pattern was abandoned in favor of the European pattern of male ownership when the Cherokee attempted (futilely, as it turned out) to acculturate and avoid relocation under the Indian Removal Act of 1830 (Evans, 1989, pp. 12–18).

Summary

By the end of the contact period, the surviving American Indian tribes were impoverished, powerless, and clearly subordinate to white society and the federal government. Like African Americans, American Indians were sharply differentiated from the dominant group by race, and, in many cases, the tribes were internally stratified by gender. As was the case with African American slaves, the degree of gender inequality within the tribes was limited by their overall lack of autonomy and resources.

Hawaii

In 1788, while American Indians and whites continued their centuries-long struggle, white Europeans first made contact with the indigenous people of Hawaii. The contact situation and the system of group relations that evolved on the island nation provide an interesting and instructive contrast with the history of American Indians.

In Hawaii, contact was not immediately followed by conquest and colonization. Early relations between Europeans and Hawaiians were organized around trade and commerce, not competition over the control of land or labor. Also, Hawaiian society was large and highly developed, and it had sufficient military strength to protect itself from the relatively few Europeans who came to the islands in the early days. Thus, two of the three conditions stated in the Noel hypothesis for the emergence of a dominant-minority situation were not present in the early days of European-Hawaiian contact and, consistent with the hypothesis, overt structures of conquest or dominance did not emerge until decades after first contact.

Contact with Europeans did bring other consequences, of course, including smallpox and other diseases to which native Hawaiians had no immunity. Death rates began to rise, and the population of native Hawaiians, which numbered about 300,000 in 1788, fell to fewer than 60,000 a century later (Kitano & Daniels, 1995, p. 137). White Europeans gradually turned the land to commercial agriculture, and by the mid-1800s, white planters had established large sugar plantations, an enterprise that is extremely labor-intensive and that often has been associated with systems of enforced labor and slavery (Curtin, 1990). By that time, however, there were not enough native Hawaiians to fill the demand for labor, and the planters began to recruit abroad, mostly in China, Portugal, Japan, Korea, Puerto Rico, and the Philippines. Native Hawaiians continued to shrink in numbers and were gradually pushed off their land and to the margins of the emerging society.

The white plantation owners came to dominate the island economy and political structure. Other groups, however, were not excluded from secondary structural assimilation. Laws banning entire groups from public institutions or practices such as school segregation are unknown in Hawaiian history. Americans of Japanese ancestry, for example, are very powerful in politics and have produced many of the leading Hawaiian politicians. Most other groups have taken advantage of the relative openness of Hawaiian society and have carved out niches for themselves in the institutional structure.

In the area of primary structural assimilation, rates of intermarriage among the various groups are much higher than on the mainland, reflecting openness to intimacy across group lines that has characterized Hawaii since first contact. In particular, Native Hawaiians have intermarried freely with other groups (Kitano & Daniels, 1995, pp. 138–139).

Unlike the mainland society, Hawaii has no history of the most blatant and oppressive forms of group domination, racism, and legalized discrimination. Still, all is not perfect in this reputed racial paradise, and there is evidence of continuing ethnic and racial stratification, as well as prejudice and discrimination. In particular, Native Hawaiians today retain their minority group status. The group is quite small and numbers about 150,000, an increase from the historic lows of the 19th century but still only about 12% of the state's population and a tiny minority of the U.S. population.

On the other hand, Native Hawaiians compare favorably with both American Indians and black Americans in terms of education, income, and poverty (see Exhibit 4.6). This relatively higher status today is consistent with both the Noel

Photo 4.6

A male dancer prepares for the Hula. Many elements of traditional Hawaiian culture survived the contact period.

© Richard A. Cooke/Corbis.

and Blauner hypotheses: They were not subjected to the harsh conditions (slavery, segregation, near genocide, and massive institutional discrimination) of the other two groups. Although they compare favorably with the two colonized and conquered groups, Native Hawaiians tend to be the poorest of the various ethnic and racial groups on the island, and a protest movement of Native Hawaiians that stresses self-determination and the return of illegally taken land has been in existence since at least the 1960s.

Exhibit 4.5 Map of the Hawaiian Islands

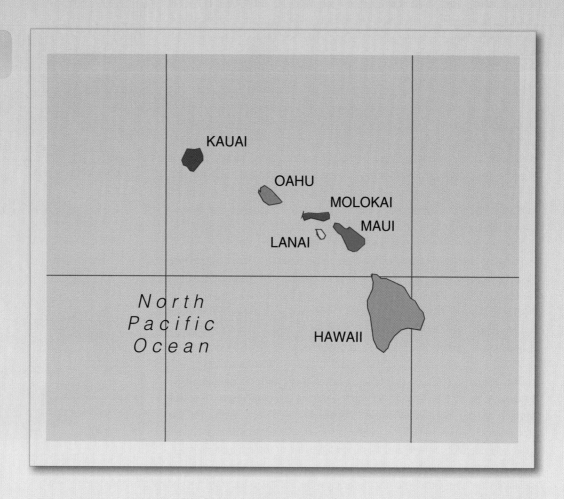

Exhibit 4.6 Native Hawaiians Compared With Total Population, Black Americans, and American Indians, 2009

Indicator	Total U.S. Population	Native Hawaiians	Black Americans	Native Americans
Percentage high school graduate or more	84.9	89.3	85.3	80.6
Percentage college graduate or more	27.8	16.2	24.4	16.0
Median household income	$51,369	$60,164	$39,447	$38,411
Percentage of families in poverty	9.9	9.9	20.4	18.8

SOURCE: U.S. Bureau of the Census (2009a).

NOTE: Black Americans and Native Americans are "Alone and in Combination."

Mexican Americans

As the population of the United States increased and spread across the continent, contact with Mexicans inevitably occurred. Spanish explorers and settlers had lived in what is now the southwestern United States long before the wave of American settlers broke across this region. For example, Santa Fe, New Mexico, was founded in 1598, nearly a decade before Jamestown. As late as the 1820s, Mexicans and American Indians were almost the sole residents of the region.

In the early 1800s, four areas of Mexican settlement had developed, roughly corresponding to what was to become Texas, California, New Mexico, and Arizona. These areas were sparsely settled, and most Mexicans lived in what was to become New Mexico (Cortes, 1980, p. 701). The economy of the regions was based on farming and herding. Most people lived in villages and small towns or on ranches and farms. Social and political life was organized around family and the Catholic Church and tended to be dominated by an elite class of wealthy landowners.

Photo 4.7

Mexican labor has been vital for the development of the Southwest.

From Library of Congress.

Texas

Some of the first effects of U.S. expansion to the West were felt in Texas early in the 1800s. Mexico was no military match for its neighbor to the north, and the farmland of East Texas was a tempting resource for the cotton-growing interests in the American South. Anglo-Americans began to immigrate to Texas in sizable numbers in the 1820s, and by 1835, they outnumbered Mexicans 6 to 1. The attempts by the Mexican government to control these immigrants were clumsy and ineffective and eventually precipitated a successful revolution by the Anglo-Americans, with some Mexicans also joining the rebels. At this point in time, competition between Anglos and Texans of Mexican descent (called Tejanos) was muted by the abundance of land and opportunity in the area. Population density was low, fertile land was readily available for all, and the "general tone of the time was that of intercultural cooperation" (Alvarez, 1973, p. 922).

Competition between Anglo-Texans and Tejanos became increasingly intense. When the United States annexed Texas in the 1840s, full-scale war broke out and Mexico was defeated. Under the Treaty of Guadalupe Hidalgo in 1848, Mexico ceded much of the Southwest to the United States. In the Gadsden Purchase of 1853, the United States acquired the remainder of the territory that now composes the southwestern United States. As a result of these treaties, the Mexican population of this region had become, without moving an inch from their traditional villages and farms, both a conquered people and a minority group.

Following the war, intergroup relations continued to sour, and the political and legal rights of the Tejano community were often ignored in the hunger for land. Increasingly impoverished and powerless, the Tejanos had few resources with which to resist the growth of Anglo-American domination. They were badly outnumbered and stigmatized by the recent Mexican military defeat. Land that had once been Mexican increasingly came under Anglo control, and widespread violence and lynching reinforced the growth of Anglo dominance (Moquin & Van Doren, 1971, p. 253).

California

In California, the Gold Rush of 1849 spurred a massive population movement from the East. Early relations between Anglos and Californios (native Mexicans in the state) had been relatively cordial, forming the basis for a multiethnic, bilingual state. The rapid growth of an Anglo majority after statehood in 1850 doomed these efforts, however, and the Californios, like the Tejanos, lost their land and political power.

Laws were passed encouraging Anglos to settle on land traditionally held by Californios. In such situations, the burden was placed on the Mexican American landowners to show that their deeds were valid. The Californios protested the seizure of their land but found it difficult to argue their cases in the English-speaking, Anglo-controlled court system. By the mid-1850s, a massive transfer of land to Anglo-American hands had taken place in California (Mirandé, 1985, pp. 20–21; see also Pitt, 1970).

Other laws passed in the 1850s made it increasingly difficult for Californios to retain their property and power as Anglo-Americans became the dominant group as well as the majority of the population. The area's Mexican heritage was suppressed and eliminated from public life and institutions such as schools and local government. For example, in 1855, California repealed a requirement in the state constitution that all laws be published in Spanish as well as English (Cortes, 1980, p. 706). Anglo-Americans used violence, biased laws, discrimination, and other means to exploit and repress Californios, and the new wealth generated by gold mining flowed into Anglo hands.

Arizona and New Mexico

The Anglo immigration into Arizona and New Mexico was less voluminous than that into Texas and California, and both states retained Mexican numerical majorities for a number of decades. In Arizona, most of the Mexican population were immigrants themselves, seeking work on farms, on ranches, in the mines, and on railroads. The economic and political structures of the state quickly came under the control of the Anglo population.

Only in New Mexico did Mexican Americans retain some political power and economic clout, mostly because of the relatively large size of the group and their skill in mobilizing for political activity. New Mexico did not become a state until 1912, and Mexican Americans continued to play a prominent role in governmental affairs even after statehood (Cortes, 1980, p. 706).

Thus, the contact situation for Mexican Americans was highly variable by region. Although some areas were affected more rapidly and more completely than others, the ultimate result was the creation of minority group status for Mexican Americans (Acuña, 1999; Alvarez, 1973; McLemore, 1973; McWilliams, 1961; Moore, 1970; Stoddard, 1973).

Mexican Americans and the Noel and Blauner Hypotheses

The causal model we have applied to the origins of slavery and the domination of American Indians also provides a way of explaining the development of minority group status for Mexican Americans. Ethnocentrism was clearly present from the very first contact between Anglo immigrants and Mexicans. Many American migrants to the Southwest brought with them the prejudices and racism they had acquired with regard to African Americans and American Indians. In fact, many of the settlers who moved into Texas came directly from the South in search of new lands for the cultivation of cotton. They readily transferred their prejudiced views to at least the poorer Mexicans, who were stereotyped as lazy and shiftless (McLemore, 1973, p. 664). The visibility of group boundaries was heightened and reinforced by physical and religious differences. Mexicans were "racially" a mixture of Spaniards and American Indians, and the differences in skin color and other physical characteristics provided a convenient marker of group membership. In addition, the vast majority of

Mexicans were Roman Catholic, whereas the vast majority of Anglo-Americans were Protestant.

Competition for land began with the first contact between the groups. However, for many years, population density was low in the Southwest, and the competition did not immediately or always erupt into violent domination and expropriation. Nonetheless, the loss of land and power for Mexican Americans was inexorable, although variable in speed.

The size of the power differential between the groups was variable and partly explains why domination was established faster in some places than others. In both Texas and California, the subordination of the Mexican American population followed quickly after a rapid influx of Anglos and the military defeat of Mexico. Anglo-Americans used their superior numbers and military power to acquire control of the political and economic structures and expropriate the resources of the Mexican American community. In New Mexico, the groups were more evenly matched in size, and Mexican Americans were able to retain a measure of power for decades.

Unlike the case of American Indians, however, the labor as well as the land of the Mexicans was coveted. On cotton plantations, ranches, and farms, and in mining and railroad construction, Mexican Americans became a vital source of inexpensive labor. During times of high demand, this labor force was supplemented by workers who were encouraged to emigrate from Mexico. When demand for workers decreased, these laborers were forced back to Mexico. Thus began a pattern of labor flow that continues to the present.

As in the case of African Americans and American Indians, the contact period clearly established a colonized status for Mexican Americans in all areas of the Southwest. Their culture and language were suppressed even as their property rights were abrogated and their status lowered. In countless ways, they, too, were subjected to coercive acculturation. For example, California banned the use of Spanish in public schools, and bullfighting and other Mexican sports and recreational activities were severely restricted (Moore, 1970, p. 19; Pitt, 1970). In contrast to African Americans, however, Mexican Americans were in close proximity to their homeland and maintained close ties with villages and families. Constant movement across the border with Mexico kept the Spanish language and much of the Mexican heritage alive in the Southwest. Nonetheless, 19th-century Mexican Americans fit Blauner's category of a colonized minority group, and the suppression of their culture was part of the process by which the dominant culture was established.

Anglo-American economic interests benefited enormously from the conquest of the Southwest and the colonization of the Mexican people. Growers and other businessmen came to rely on the cheap labor provided by Mexican Americans and immigrant and day laborers from Mexico. The region grew in affluence and productivity, but Mexican Americans were now outsiders in their own land and did not share in the prosperity. In the land grab of the 1800s and the conquest of the indigenous Mexican population lies one of the roots of Mexican American relations with the dominant U.S. society today.

Gender Relations

Prior to the arrival of Anglo-Americans, Mexican society in the Southwest was patriarchal and maintained a clear gender-based division of labor. These characteristics tended to persist after the conquest and the creation of minority group status.

Most Mexican Americans lived in small villages or on large ranches and farms. The women devoted their energies to the family, child rearing, and household tasks. As Mexican Americans were reduced to a landless labor force, women along with men suffered the economic devastation that accompanied military conquest by a foreign power.

The kinds of jobs available to the men (mining, seasonal farm work, railroad construction) often required them to be away from home for extended periods of time, and women, by default, began to take over the economic and other tasks traditionally performed by males.

Poverty and economic insecurity placed the family structures under considerable strain. Traditional cultural understandings about male dominance and patriarchy became moot when the men were absent for long periods of time and the decision-making power of Mexican American women increased. Also, women were often forced to work outside the household for the family to survive economically. The economics of conquest led to increased matriarchy and more working mothers (Becerra, 1988, p. 149).

For Mexican American women, the consequences of contact were variable even though the ultimate result was a loss of status within the context of the conquest and colonization of the group as a whole. Like black female slaves, Mexican American women became the most vulnerable part of the social system.

COMPARING MINORITY GROUPS

American Indians and black slaves were the victims of the explosive growth of European power in the Western Hemisphere that began with Columbus's voyage in 1492. Europeans needed labor to fuel the plantations of the mid-17th-century American colonies and settled on slaves from Africa as the most logical, cost-effective means of resolving their labor supply problems. Black Africans had a commodity the colonists coveted (labor), and the colonists subsequently constructed a system to control and exploit this commodity.

To satisfy the demand for land created by the stream of European immigrants to North America, the threat represented by American Indians had to be eliminated. Once their land was expropriated, American Indians ceased to be of much concern. The only valuable resource they possessed—their land—was under the control of white society by 1890, and American Indians were thought to be unsuitable as a source of labor.

Mexico, like the United States, had been colonized by a European power—in this case, Spain. In the early 1800s, the Mexican communities in the Southwest were a series of outpost settlements, remote and difficult to defend. Through warfare and a variety of other aggressive means, Mexican citizens living in this area were conquered and became an exploited minority group.

African Americans, American Indians, and Mexican Americans, in their separate ways, became involuntary players in the growth and development of European and, later, American economic and political power. None of these groups had much choice in their respective fates; all three were overpowered and relegated to an inferior, subordinate status. Many views of assimilation (such as the "melting pot" metaphor discussed in Chapter 2) have little relevance to these situations. These minority groups had little control over their destinies, their degree of acculturation, or even their survival as groups. These three groups were coercively acculturated in the context of paternalistic relations in an agrarian economy. Meaningful integration (structural assimilation) was not a real possibility, especially for African Americans and American Indians. In Milton Gordon's (1964) terms (see Chapter 2), we might characterize these situations as "acculturation without integration" or structural pluralism. Given the grim realities described in this chapter, Gordon's terms seem a little antiseptic, and Blauner's concept of colonized minority groups seems far more descriptive.

Mexico, Canada, and the United States

In this chapter, we argued that dominant-minority relations are profoundly shaped by the contact situation and by the characteristics of the groups involved (especially their subsistence technologies). We saw how these factors shaped relations with Native Americans and Mexican Americans and how they led British colonists to create a system of slavery to control the labor of African Americans. How do the experiences of the Spanish and the French in the Western Hemisphere compare with those of the British in what became the United States? What roles did the contact situation and subsistence technology play in the development of group relations in these two neighbors of the United States?[1]

The Spanish were the first of the three European nations to invade the Western Hemisphere, and they conquered much of what is now Central and South America about a century before Jamestown was founded. In 1521, they defeated the Aztec Empire, located in what is now central Mexico. The Aztec Empire was large, highly organized, and complex. The Emperor ruled over scores of subject nations, each with its own language and identity, and the great majority of his subjects were peasants or agricultural laborers who farmed small plots of land owned by members of the elite classes, to whom they paid rents. Peasants are a fundamental part of any labor-intensive, preindustrial agrarian society and were just as common in Spain as they were among the Aztecs.

When the Spanish defeated the Aztecs, they destroyed their cities, their temples, and their leadership (the emperor, the nobility, priests, etc.). They did not destroy the Aztec social structure; rather, they absorbed it and used it for their own benefit. For example, the Aztec Empire had financed its central government by collecting taxes and rents from citizens and tribute from conquered tribes. The Spanish simply grafted their own tax collection system onto this structure and diverted the flow from the Aztec elite classes (which they had, at any rate, destroyed) to themselves (Russell, 1994, pp. 29–30).

The Spanish tendency to absorb rather than destroy operated at many levels. For example, Aztec peasants became Spanish (and then Mexican) peasants, occupying roughly the same role in the new society that they had in the old, save for paying their rents to different landlords. There was also extensive interbreeding between the Spanish and the conquered tribes of Mexico, but, unlike the situation in the English colonies, the Spanish recognized the resultant racial diversity and developed an elaborate system for classifying people by race. They recognized as many as 56 racial groups, including whites, **mestizos** (mixed European-Indian), and mulattoes (mixed European-African) (Russell, 1994, p. 35). The society that emerged was highly race conscious, and race was highly correlated with social class: The elite classes were white, and the lower classes were nonwhite. However, the large-scale intermarriage and the official recognition of mixed-race peoples did establish the foundation for a racially mixed society. Today, the huge majority of the Mexican population is mestizo, although there remains a very strong correlation between race and class, and the elite positions in the society tend to be monopolized by people of "purer" European ancestry.

The French began to colonize Canada at about the same time the English established their colonies further south. The dominant economic enterprise in the early days was not farming, but trapping and the fur trade. The French developed a lucrative trade in this area by allying themselves with some American Indian tribes. The Indians produced the furs and traded them to the French, who, in turn, sold them on the world market. Like the Spanish in Mexico, the French in Canada tended to link to and absorb Native American social structures. There was also a significant amount of intermarriage between the French and Native Americans, resulting in a mixed-race group, called Metis, who had their own identities and, indeed, their own settlements along the Canadian frontier (Russell, 1994, p. 39).

Note the profound differences in these three contact situations between Europeans and Native Americans. The Spanish confronted a large, well-organized social system and found it expeditious to adapt Aztec practices to their own benefit. The French developed an economy that required cooperation with at least some of the Native American tribes they encountered, and they, too, found benefits in adaptation. The tribes encountered by the English were much smaller and much less developed than the Aztecs, and there was no particular reason for the English to adapt to or absorb these social structures. Furthermore, because the business of the English colonies was agriculture (not trapping), the competition at the heart of the contact situation was for land, and American Indians were seen as rivals for control of that most valuable resource. Thus, the English tended to confront and exclude American Indians, keeping them on the outside of their emerging society and building strong boundaries between their own "civilized" world and the "savages" that surrounded them. The Spanish and French colonists had to adapt their societies to fit with American Indians, but the English faced no such restraints. They could create their institutions and design their social structure to suit themselves (Russell, 1994, p. 30).

As we have seen, one of the institutions created in the English colonies was slavery based on African labor. Slavery was also practiced in New Spain (Mexico) and New France (Canada), but the institution evolved in very different ways in those colonies and never assumed the importance that it did in the United States. Why? As you might suspect, the answer has a lot to do with the nature of the contact situation. Like the English colonists, both the Spanish and French attempted large-scale agricultural enterprises that might have created a demand for imported slave labor. In the case of New Spain, however, there was a ready supply of Native American peasants available to fill the role played by blacks in the English colonies. Although Africans became a part of the admixture that shaped modern Mexico racially and socially, demand for black slaves never matched that of the English colonies. Similarly, in Canada, slaves from Africa were sometimes used, but farmers there tended to rely on the flow of labor from France to fill their agricultural needs. The British opted for slave labor from Africa over indentured labor from Europe, and the French made the opposite decision.

Another difference among the three European nations that helps explain the divergent development of group relations is their relative levels of modernization. Compared with England, Spain and France were more traditional and feudalistic in their cultures and social structures. Among other things, this meant that they had to shape their agricultural enterprises in the New World around the ancient social relations between peasants and landlords they brought from the Old World. Thus, the Spanish and French colonists were limited in their actions by these ancient customs, traditions, and understandings. Such old-fashioned institutions were much weaker in England, and, thus, the English colonists were much freer to design their social structure to suit their own needs. Whereas the Spanish and French had to shape their colonial societies to fit both American Indian social patterns and European traditions, the English could improvise and attend only to their own needs and desires. The closed, complex, and repressive institution of American slavery—designed and crafted from scratch in the New World—was one result.

Finally, we should note that many of the modern racial characteristics of these three neighboring societies were foreshadowed in their colonial origins (e.g., the greater concentration of African Americans in the United States and the more racially intermixed population of Mexico). The differences run much deeper than race alone, of course, and include differences in class structure and relative levels of industrialization and affluence. For our purposes, however, this brief comparison of the origins of dominant-minority relations underscores the importance of the contact situation in shaping group relations for centuries to come.

CURRENT DEBATES

How Did Slavery Affect the Origins of African American Culture?

A debate over the impact of slavery on African American culture began in the 1960s and continues to the present day. Stanley Elkins, in his 1959 book Slavery: A Problem in American Institutional and Intellectual Life, *laid down the terms of the debate. Elkins concluded that African American culture in the United States was created in response to the repressive plantation system and in the context of brutalization, total control of the slaves by their owners, and dehumanization. He argued that black culture was "made in America," but in an abnormal, even pathological social setting. The plantation was a sick society that dominated and infantilized black slaves. The dominant reality for slaves—and the only significant other person in their lives—was the master. Elkins described the system as a "perverted patriarchy" that psychologically forced the slaves to identify with their oppressors and to absorb the racist values at the core of the structure.*

Elkins's book has been called "a work of great intellectual audacity, based on a methodology which has little connection with conventional historical research and arriving at conclusions which were challenging or outrageous, according to one's point of view" (Parish, 1989, p. 7). The book stimulated an enormous amount of controversy and research on the impact of slavery and the origins of African American culture. This body of research developed new sources of evidence and new perspectives and generally concluded that African American culture is a combination of elements, some from the traditional cultures of Africa and others fabricated on the plantation. The selection that follows the one by Elkins, from the work of historian William Piersen, illustrates this argument and focuses on West African and African American family customs.

A third view is presented in an excerpt from the writings of Deborah Gray White. She argues that most scholarly work on slavery is written from the perspective of the male slave only, to the point of excluding the female experience. In the passage from her 1985 book Ar'n't I a Woman? Female Slaves in the Plantation South, *she also addresses the problems of research in the area of minority group females and summarizes some of what has been learned from recent scholarship on the impact of slavery.*

All three of these views are consistent with Blauner's idea that the cultures of colonized minority groups are attacked and that the groups are forcibly acculturated. Elkins's argument is the most extreme in that it sees African American culture as fabricated entirely in response to the demands of enslavement and the fearful, all-powerful figure of the master.

SLAVERY CREATED AFRICAN AMERICAN CULTURE

STANLEY ELKINS

Both [the Nazi concentration camps and the American slave plantations] were closed systems from which all standards based on prior connections had been effectively detached. A working adjustment to either system required a childlike conformity, a limited choice of "significant other." Cruelty per se cannot be considered the primary key to this; of far greater importance was the simple "closedness" of the system, in which all lines of authority descended from the master and in which alternative social bases that might have supported alternative standards were systematically suppressed. The individual, consequently, for his very psychic security, had to picture his master in some way as the "good father," even when, as in the concentration camp, it made no sense at all.

For the Negro child, in particular, the plantation offered no really satisfactory father image other than the master. The "real" father was virtually without authority over his child, since discipline, parental responsibility, and control of rewards and punishments all rested in other hands; the slave father could not even protect the mother of his children.

From the master's viewpoint, slaves had been defined in law as property, and the master's power over his property must be absolute. . . . Absolute power for him meant absolute dependency for the slave—the dependency not of the developing child but of the perpetual child. For the master, the role most aptly fitting such a relationship would naturally be that of father.

SOURCE: Elkins (1959, pp. 130–131).

AFRICAN AMERICAN CULTURE WAS CREATED BY AN INTERPLAY OF ELEMENTS FROM AFRICA AND AMERICA

WILLIAM D. PIERSEN

In the colonial environment, . . . [African and European] traditions were fused. . . . The result was an unprecedented and unintended new multicultural American way of life. . . . [Africans] had little choice [but this] adjustment was not as difficult . . . as we might suppose: The cultures of Africa and Europe were both dominated by the rhythms and sensibilities of a premodern, agricultural way of life shaped more by folk religion than by science, and domestic responsibilities were relatively similar on both continents. . . .

One of the greatest sacrifices that faced the new African Americans was the loss of the extended families that had structured most social relationships in Africa. . . . [African marriage customs were usually polygynous (permitting more than one wife) and patrilineal (tracing ancestry through the male side).] With marriage, most African Americans seem . . . to have settled quickly into Euro-American style, monogamous nuclear families that trace inheritance bilaterally through the lines of both parents. Nonetheless, colonial naming choices show the continuing importance of African ideas of kinship among African Americans, for black children were more commonly . . . named after recently deceased relatives, a practice rooted in the African belief of rebirth across generations. . . .

African Americans . . . tried to rebuild as best they could the social cohesion once provided by the now missing extended families of Africa. [They] tried to duplicate some of the kinship . . . functions . . . by forging close relationships with their countrymen and shipmates from the Middle Passage. . . . [Many] treated both the blacks and whites that lived with them . . . as a kind of artificial kin. . . .

In North America many white colonials soon gave up traditional European village residence patterns to move out individually on the land, but African Americans, when they had the choice, generally preferred to stay together. . . . Such communalism [was] a reflection of the value that Africans and African Americans put on collective living.

In West Africa kin groups gathered in their housing together in large compounds that featured centralized open spaces devoted to social functions and collective recreation. Husbands and wives within the compounds usually had their own separate family quarters. . . . In colonial African American housing the old ways were maintained. . . . [In early-18th-century Virginia] most slaves lived in clusterings of more than 10 people. In these quarters, black social life was centered not on the interior of the small dark sleeping structures but outside on the common space devoted to social functions.

SOURCE: Piersen (1996).

THE EXPERIENCES OF FEMALE SLAVES HAVE BEEN UNDER-RESEARCHED AND UNDER-REPORTED

DEBORAH GRAY WHITE

Stanley Elkins began [the debate] by alleging that the American slave master had such absolute power and authority over the bondsman that the slave was reduced to childlike dependency. "Sambo," Elkins argued, was more than a product of southern fantasy. He could not be dismissed as a "stereotype."

Elkins' thesis had a profound effect upon the research and writing of the history of slavery. The direction that the research took, however, was in large part predetermined because Elkins' slavery defined the parameters of the debate. In a very subtle way these parameters had more to do with the nature of male slavery than with female slavery. . . .

John Blassingame's *The Slave Community* is a classic, but much of it deals with male status. For instance, Blassingame stressed the fact that many masters recognized the male as the head of the family. He observed that during courtship, men flattered women and exaggerated their prowess. There was, however, little discussion of the reciprocal activities of slave women. Blassingame also described how slave men gained status in the family and slave community, but did not do the same for women. . . .

The reality of slave life gives us reason to suspect that we do black women a disservice when we rob them of a history that placed them at the side of their men in their race's struggle for freedom. The present study takes a look at slave women and argues that they were not submissive, subordinate, or prudish, and they were not expected to be so. Women had different roles from those of men, and they also had a great deal in common with their African foremothers, who held positions not inferior but complementary to those of men. . . .

Source material on the general nature of slavery exists in abundance, but it is very difficult to find source material about slave women in particular. Slave women are everywhere, yet nowhere. . . .

The source problem is directly related to what was and still is the black woman's condition. Every economic and political index demonstrated the black woman's virtual powerlessness in American society. A consequence of the double jeopardy and powerlessness is the black woman's invisibility. . . .

The history of slavery has come a long way. We have learned that race relations were never so clear-cut as to be solely a matter of white over black, but that in the assimilation of culture, in the interaction of blacks and whites, there were gray areas and relationships more aptly described in terms of black over white. We have also begun to understand that despite the brutality and inhumanity, or perhaps because of it, a distinct African American culture based on close-knit kinship relationships grew and thrived, and that it was this culture that sustained black people through many trials before and after emancipation.

SOURCE: From *Ar'nt I a Woman?: Female Slaves in the Plantation South* by Deborah Gray White. Copyright © 1985 by Deborah Gray White. Used by permission of W. W. Norton & Company, Inc.

DEBATE QUESTIONS TO CONSIDER

1. Why is the origin of African American culture an important issue? What difference does it make today? If you believe Elkins is correct, what are the implications for dealing with racial inequality in the present? Could a culture that was created under a pathological system and a sick society be an adequate basis for the pursuit of equality and justice today? Is Elkins's thesis a form of blaming the victim? Is it a way of blaming the present inequality of the black community on an "inadequate" culture, thus absolving the rest of society from blame?

2. If you agree with Piersen's or White's viewpoints, what are the implications for how African Americans think about their history and about themselves? What difference does it make if your roots are in Africa or in colonial Virginia or, as White and Piersen argue, in both?

3. What does White add to the debate? What are some of the challenges in researching the experiences of female slaves? How did the experiences of female slaves differ from those of male slaves?

MAIN POINTS

- Dominant-minority relations are shaped by the characteristics of society as a whole, particularly by subsistence technology. The contact situation is the single most important factor in the development of dominant-minority relations.
- The Noel hypothesis states that when a contact situation is characterized by ethnocentrism, competition, and a differential in power, ethnic or racial stratification will result. In colonial America, Africans were enslaved instead of white indentured servants or American Indians because only they fit all three conditions. American slavery was a paternalistic system.
- Prejudice and racism are more the results of systems of racial and ethnic inequality than they are the causes. They serve to rationalize, "explain," and stabilize these systems.
- The competition with American Indians centered on control of the land. American Indian tribes were conquered and pressed into a paternalistic relationship with white society. American Indians became a colonized minority group and were subjected to forced acculturation.
- Mexican Americans were the third minority group created during the preindustrial era. Mexican Americans competed with white settlers over both land and labor. Like Africans and American Indians, Mexican Americans were a colonized minority group subjected to forced acculturation.
- Conquest and colonization affected men and women differently. Women's roles changed, and they sometimes were less constrained by patriarchal traditions. These changes were always in the context of increasing powerlessness and poverty for the group as a whole, however, and minority women have been doubly oppressed by their gender roles as well as their minority group status.
- How long do patterns of ethnic and racial stratification persist? The two public sociology assignments presented in the introduction to Part II give you an opportunity to research this question in your local library and a diner of your choosing.

STUDY SITE ON THE WEB

For chapter-specific resources, such as self-quizzes, videos, and flashcards, go to **www.sagepub.com/ healeyregc6e.**

FOR FURTHER READING

Acuña, Rodolfo. 1999. *Occupied America* (4th ed.). New York: Harper & Row.

   Examines a broad sweep of Mexican American experiences and argues that their status is comparable to that of other colonized groups

Brown, Dee. 1970. *Bury My Heart at Wounded Knee.* New York: Holt, Rinehart, & Winston.

   An eloquent and moving account of the conquest of American Indians

Genovese, Eugene D. 1974. *Roll, Jordan, Roll.* New York: Pantheon.
Gutman, Herbert G. 1976. *The Black Family in Slavery and Freedom.* New York: Vintage.
Levine, Lawrence. 1977. *Black Culture and Black Consciousness.* New York: Oxford University Press.
Rawick, George P. 1972. *From Sundown to Sunup: The Making of the Black Community.* Westport, CT: Greenwood.
Stuckey, Sterling. 1987. *Slave Culture: Nationalist Theory and the Foundations of Black America.* New York: Harper & Row.

   Five vital sources on the origins and psychological and cultural impact of slavery in America

McWilliams, Carey. 1961. *North from Mexico: The Spanish-Speaking People of the United States.* New York: Monthly Review.

   A classic overview of the historical development of Mexican Americans

Mirandé, Alfredo. 1985. *The Chicano Experience: An Alternative Perspective.* Notre Dame, IN: University of Notre Dame Press.

   A passionate argument for a new sociological approach to the study of Mexican Americans, including many useful insights into Mexican American family structures, the problem of crime, and other areas

Nabakov, Peter (Ed.). 1999. *Native American Testimony* (Rev. ed.). New York: Penguin.

   A collection of valuable and insightful American Indian accounts of the past 500 years

Wax, Murray. 1971. *Indian Americans: Unity and Diversity.* Englewood Cliffs, NJ: Prentice Hall.

   A compact and informative analysis of the history and present situation of American Indians

QUESTIONS FOR REVIEW AND STUDY

1. State and explain the two themes presented at the beginning of the chapter. Apply each to the contact situations between white European colonists, African Americans, American Indians, and Mexican Americans. Identify and explain the key differences and similarities among the three situations.

2. Explain what a plantation system is and why this system of production is important for understanding the origins of slavery in colonial America. Why are plantation systems usually characterized by (a) paternalism, (b) huge inequalities between groups, (c) repressive systems of control, (d) rigid codes of behavior, and (e) low rates of overt conflict?

3. Explain the Noel and Blauner hypotheses and explain how they apply to the contact situations covered in this chapter. Explain each of the following key terms: *ethnocentrism, competition, power, colonized minority group*, and *immigrant minority group*. How did group conflict vary when competition was over land rather than over labor?

4. Explain the role of prejudice and racism in the creation of minority group status. Do prejudice and racism help cause minority group status, or are they caused by minority group status? Explain.

5. Compare and contrast gender relations in regard to each of the contact situations discussed in this chapter. Why do the relationships vary?

6. What does it mean to say that under slavery, acculturation for African Americans was coerced? What are the implications for assimilation, inequality, and African American culture?

7. Compare and contrast the contact situations of Native Hawaiians and American Indians. What were the key differences in their contact situations, and how are these differences reflected in the groups' current situations?

8. Compare and contrast the contact situations in colonial America, Canada, and Mexico. What groups were involved in each situation? What was the nature of the competition, and what were the consequences?

INTERNET RESEARCH PROJECT: MODERN SLAVERY

Americans today might look at slavery as a distant relic of history, remote and bizarre. The idea that a person could be owned by another person, defined as a piece of property, and bought and sold like livestock probably seems alien to people who live in a culture devoted to individual happiness and personal well-being. Yet, this ancient institution can still be found around the world, on every continent, in societies at every level of development, and in the United States.

In this project, you will use sources of information readily available on the Internet to gather facts and estimate the volume and scope of modern slavery. You will also collect some case studies or personal examples of slavery, analyze the nature of the practice today, compare it to American slavery, and find out what is being done to combat the practice. This project will also provide an opportunity to review some of the important points and ideas presented in this chapter.

To begin, consider the list of questions below. Next, visit the websites listed here and search for answers to the questions. Also, search the Internet for additional sources that may help you develop an understanding of modern slavery. (NOTE: Your instructor may have additional or different instructions for gathering information.) As you search the Internet, remember that you will need to practice a healthy skepticism about the information, ideas, and arguments that you find—including the information on the websites listed here. Of course, you should always be careful and critical when doing research, but, as you know, the Internet includes unregulated sites that present incomplete, deeply biased, or false information, and an extra note of caution is justified. Also, recognize at the outset that many of the facts you gather (e.g., the number of people currently enslaved) will be approximations and, in some cases, mere guesswork.

Questions for Research and Discussion

1. Scope and volume
    a. List and consider the definitions of slavery or involuntary servitude that you find. Which seem to be the most useful? Why?
    b. About how many people are currently enslaved or in a condition of involuntary servitude? (*You might want to cite both high and low estimates.*)
    c. Describe this population in terms of gender, age, race, and nationality. What percentage are women? Children?
    d. Where in the world—what regions or nations—are modern slaves most numerous or common?
    e. For the slave population that is transported across national lines, what are the major sending areas or nations and what are the most important destination areas and nations?

2. Experiences
    a. How are people being enslaved today? What is the role of debt bondage? How often are coercion and violence used? How do these practices vary across different types of slavery (e.g., sex trafficking vs. involuntary labor)?

   b. Find three to five case studies of people who have been victimized by modern slavery and write brief summaries of these situations.

   c. Sociologically, what do these people have in common? That is, what important social characteristics (age, gender, social class, race, and ethnicity) do they share?

3. Dynamics and causes
   a. American slavery was shaped by the level of development and labor-intensive subsistence technology of the colonial era. Identify and explain similar factors that shape modern slavery.
   b. Can you apply elements of the Noel hypothesis to modern slavery? Does ethnocentrism, prejudice, or sexism play a role? How? Do modern slaves have resources or abilities that are being competed for? What role does power play in shaping and maintaining these practices?

4. Markets: supply and demand
   a. What roles do modern slaves play in the job market? What economic niches are being filled? Who profits? Who loses? Describe the dominant-minority group situations you find in your search for facts.

5. Enforcement efforts, legal considerations, human rights
   a. Find at least three national and international programs aimed at stopping modern slavery and describe what they are doing. How effective are these efforts? How might they be improved?
   b. What specific human rights are at stake here? Is slavery illegal? Where? By what authority?

Websites for This Project

1. http://www.freetheslaves.net—*Homepage for "Free the Slaves"; includes information, resources for teachers, and a description of the organization's efforts to combat modern slavery*

2. http://www.ijm.org—*Homepage for the International Justice Mission, a Christian advocacy and activist group dedicated to combating slavery*

3. http://www.state.gov/g/tip/rls/tiprpt—*U.S. Department of State's annual "Trafficking in Persons Report"; can be downloaded in PDF format*

OPTIONAL GROUP DISCUSSION

Bring your findings to class and discuss with classmates. Focus your discussion on comparing and contrasting modern and colonial American slavery, especially the roles of ethnocentrism and power, subsistence technology, demand and supply, human rights, and enforcement efforts. (NOTE: Your instructor may have more specific or different instructions.)

NOTES

1. This section is largely based on Russell (1994).

5

Industrialization and Dominant-Minority Relations

From Slavery to Segregation and the Coming of Postindustrial Society

Racial stratification is a moving target.

—Douglas Massey, sociologist[1]

One theme stated at the beginning of Chapter 4 was that a society's subsistence technology shapes dominant-minority group relations. A corollary of this theme, explored in this chapter, is that *dominant-minority group relations change as the subsistence technology changes.* We saw in Chapter 4 that dominant-minority relations in the formative years of the United States were profoundly shaped by agrarian technology and the desire to control land and labor. The agrarian era ended in the 1800s, and the United States has experienced two major transformations in subsistence technology since that time, each of which has transformed dominant-minority relations and required the creation of new structures and processes to maintain racial stratification and white privilege.

The first transformation, the industrial revolution, began in the early 19th century when machine-based technologies began to develop, especially in the North. In the agrarian era, work was labor-intensive, done by hand or with the aid of draft animals. During industrialization, work became capital-intensive and machines replaced people and animals.

Photo 5.1

Early in the industrial revolution, work was done by hand. The original subway tunnels in New York City were dug with pick and shovel, largely by Italian immigrants.

© Corbis.

The new industrial technology rapidly increased the productivity and efficiency of the U.S. economy and quickly began to change all other aspects of society, including the nature of work, politics, communication, transportation, family life, birthrates and death rates, the system of education, and, of course, dominant-minority relations. The groups that had become minorities during the agrarian era (African Americans, American Indians, and Mexican Americans) faced new possibilities and new dangers, but industrialization also created new minority groups, new forms of exploitation and oppression, and, for some, new opportunities to rise in the social structure and succeed in America. In this chapter, we will explore this transformation and illustrate its effects on the status of African Americans, focusing primarily on the construction of Jim Crow segregation in the South. The impact of industrialization on other minority groups will be considered in the case studies presented in Part III.

The second transformation in subsistence technology brings us to more recent times. In the mid-20th century, the United States (and other advanced industrial societies) entered the postindustrial era, also called deindustrialization. This shift in subsistence technology was marked by (1) a decline in the manufacturing sector of the economy and a decrease in the supply of secure, well-paid, blue-collar, manual-labor jobs, and (2) an expansion in the service and information-based sectors of the economy and an increase in the relative proportion of white-collar and "high-tech" jobs. Like the 19th-century industrial revolution, these changes have profound implications for every aspect of modern society, not just for dominant-minority relations. Indeed, every characteristic of American society—work, family, politics, popular culture—is being transformed as the subsistence technology continues to develop and modernize. In the latter part of this chapter, we examine this most recent transformation in general terms and point out some of its implications for minority groups. We will examine some new concepts—especially the concept of modern institutional discrimination—to help us understand group relations in this new era, and we will also establish some important groundwork for the case studies in Part III, in which we consider the implication of postindustrial society for America's minority groups in detail.

Exhibit 5.1 summarizes the characteristics of the three major subsistence technologies considered in this text. As U.S. society moved through these stages, group relations changed and the target of racial stratification continuously moved.

Technology	Key Trends and Characteristics	Dates
Agrarian	Labor-intensive agriculture. Control of land and labor are central.	1607 to early 1800s
Industrial	Capital-intensive manufacturing. Machines replace animal and human labor.	Early 1800s to mid-1900s
Postindustrial	Shift away from manufacturing to a service economy. The "information society."	Mid-1900s to the present

Exhibit 5.1 Three Subsistence Technologies and the United States

INDUSTRIALIZATION AND THE SHIFT FROM PATERNALISTIC TO RIGID COMPETITIVE GROUP RELATIONS

The Industrial Revolution began in England in the mid-1700s and spread from there to the rest of Europe, to the United States, and eventually to the rest of the world. The key innovations associated with this change in subsistence technology were the application of machine power to production and the harnessing of inanimate sources of energy, such as steam and coal, to fuel the machines. As machines replaced humans and animals, work became many times more productive, the economy grew, and the volume and variety of goods produced increased dramatically.

In an industrial economy, the close, paternalistic control of minority groups found in agrarian societies becomes irrelevant. Paternalistic relationships such as slavery are found in societies with labor-intensive technologies and are designed to organize and control a large, involuntary, geographically immobile labor force. An industrial economy, in contrast, requires a workforce that is geographically and socially mobile, skilled, and literate. Furthermore, with industrialization comes urbanization, and close, paternalistic controls are difficult to maintain in a city.

Thus, as industrialization progresses, agrarian paternalism tends to give way to a rigid competitive group system (see Exhibit 5.6). Under this system, minority group members are freer to compete for jobs and other valued commodities with dominant group members, especially the lower-class segments of the dominant group. As competition increases, the threatened members of the dominant group become more hostile, and attacks on the minority groups tend to increase. Whereas paternalistic systems seek to directly dominate and control the minority group (and its labor), rigid competitive systems are more defensive in nature. The threatened segments of the dominant group seek to minimize or eliminate minority group encroachment on jobs, housing, or other valuable goods or services (van den Berghe, 1967; Wilson, 1973).

Paternalistic systems such as slavery required members of the minority group to be active, if involuntary, participants. In contrast, in rigid competitive systems, the dominant group seeks to handicap the minority group's ability to compete effectively or, in some cases, eliminate competition from the minority group altogether. We have already considered an example of a dominant group attempt to protect itself from a threat. As you recall, the National Origins Act was passed in the 1920s to stop the flow of cheaper labor from Europe and protect jobs and wages (see Chapter 2). In this chapter, we consider dominant group attempts to keep African Americans powerless and impoverished—to maintain black-white racial stratification—as society shifted from an agricultural to an industrial base.

THE IMPACT OF INDUSTRIALIZATION ON THE RACIAL STRATIFICATION OF AFRICAN AMERICANS: FROM SLAVERY TO SEGREGATION

Industrial technology began to transform American society in the early 1800s, but its effects were not felt equally in all regions. The northern states industrialized first, while the South remained primarily agrarian. This economic diversity was one of the underlying causes of the regional conflict that led to the Civil War. Because of its more productive technology, the North had more resources and defeated the Confederacy in a bloody war of attrition. Slavery was abolished, and black-white relations in the South entered a new era when the Civil War ended in April 1865.

The southern system of race relations that ultimately emerged after the Civil War was designed in part to continue the control of African American labor institutionalized under slavery. It was also intended to eliminate any political or economic threat from the African American community. This rigid competitive system grew to be highly elaborate and inflexible, partly because of the high racial visibility and long history of inferior status and powerlessness of African Americans in the South and partly because of the particular needs of southern agriculture. In this section, we look at black-white relations from the end of the Civil War through the ascendance of segregation in the South and the mass migration of African Americans to the cities of the industrializing North.

Reconstruction

The period of Reconstruction, from 1865 to the 1880s, was a brief respite in the long history of oppression and exploitation of African Americans. The Union army and other agencies of the federal government, such as the Freedman's Bureau, were used to enforce racial freedom in the defeated Confederacy. Black southerners took advantage of the Fifteenth Amendment to the Constitution, passed in 1870, which states that the right to vote cannot be denied on the grounds of "race, color, or previous condition of servitude." They registered to vote in large numbers and turned out on Election Day, and some were elected to high political office. Schools for the former slaves were opened, and African Americans purchased land and houses and founded businesses.

The era of freedom was short, however, and Reconstruction began to end when the federal government demobilized its armies of occupation and turned its attention to other matters. By the 1880s, the federal government had withdrawn from the South, Reconstruction was over, and black southerners began to fall rapidly into a new system of exploitation and inequality.

Reconstruction was too brief to change two of the most important legacies of slavery. First, the centuries of bondage left black southerners impoverished, largely illiterate and uneducated, and with few power resources. When new threats of racial oppression appeared, African Americans found it difficult to defend their group interests. These developments are consistent with the Blauner hypothesis: Colonized minority groups face greater difficulties in improving their disadvantaged status because they confront greater inequalities and have fewer resources at their disposal.

Second, slavery left a strong tradition of racism in the white community. Antiblack prejudice and racism originated as rationalizations for slavery but had taken on lives of their own over the generations. After two centuries of slavery, the heritage of prejudice and racism was thoroughly ingrained in southern culture. White southerners were predisposed by this cultural legacy to see racial inequality and exploitation of African Americans as normal and desirable. They were able to construct a social system based on the assumption of racial inferiority after Reconstruction ended and the federal government withdrew.

De Jure Segregation

The system of race relations that replaced slavery in the South was de jure segregation, sometimes referred to as the Jim Crow system. Under segregation, the minority group is physically and socially separated from the dominant group and consigned to an inferior position in virtually every area of social life. The phrase de jure ("by law") means that the system is sanctioned and reinforced by the legal code; the inferior status of African Americans was actually mandated or required by state and local laws. For example, southern cities during this era had laws requiring African Americans to ride at the back of the bus. If an African American refused to comply with this seating arrangement, he or she could be arrested.

De jure segregation came to encompass all aspects of southern social life. Neighborhoods, jobs, stores, restaurants, and parks were segregated. When new social forms, such as movie theaters, sports stadiums, and interstate buses, appeared in the South, they, too, were quickly segregated.

The logic of segregation created a vicious cycle. The more African Americans were excluded from the mainstream of society, the greater their objective poverty and powerlessness became. The more inferior their status and the greater their powerlessness, the easier it was to mandate more inequality. High levels of inequality reinforced racial prejudice and made it easy to use racism to justify further separation. The system kept turning on itself, finding new social niches to segregate and reinforcing the inequality that was its starting point. For example, at the height of the Jim Crow era, the system had evolved to the point that some courtrooms maintained separate Bibles for African American witnesses to swear on. Also, in Birmingham, Alabama, it was against the law for blacks and whites to play checkers and dominoes together (Woodward, 1974, p. 118).

What were the causes of this massive separation of the races? Once again, the concepts of the Noel hypothesis prove useful. Because strong antiblack prejudice was already in existence when segregation began, we do not need to account for ethnocentrism. The post-Reconstruction competition between the racial groups was reminiscent of the origins of slavery in that black southerners had something that white southerners wanted: labor. In addition, a free black electorate threatened the political and economic dominance of the elite segments of the white community. Finally, after the withdrawal of federal troops and the end of Reconstruction, white southerners had sufficient power resources to end the competition on their own terms and construct repressive systems of control for black southerners.

The Origins of De Jure Segregation

Although the South lost the Civil War, its basic class structure and agrarian economy remained intact. The plantation elite remained the dominant class, and they were able to use their power to build a system of racial stratification to replace slavery.

Control of Black Labor. The plantation elite retained ownership of huge tracts of land, and cotton remained the primary cash crop in the South. As was the case before the Civil War, the landowners needed a workforce to farm the land. Because of the depredations and economic disruptions of the war, the old plantation elite were short on cash and liquid capital and could not always hire workers for wages. In fact, almost as soon as the war ended, southern legislatures attempted to force African Americans back into involuntary servitude by passing a series of laws known as the "Black Codes." Only the beginning of Reconstruction and the active intervention of the federal government halted the implementation of this legislation (Geschwender, 1978, p. 158; Wilson, 1973, p. 99).

The plantation elite solved their manpower problem this time by developing a system of sharecropping, or tenant farming. The sharecroppers worked the land, which was actually owned by the planters, in return for payment in shares of the profit when the crop was taken to market. The landowner would supply a place to live and food and clothing on credit. After the harvest, tenant and landowner would split the profits (sometimes very unequally), and the tenant's debts would be deducted from his share. The accounts were kept by the landowner, who could cheat and take advantage of the tenant with great impunity. With few or no political and civil rights, black sharecroppers found it difficult to keep unscrupulous white landowners honest. The landowner could inflate the indebtedness of the sharecropper and claim that he was still owed money even after profits had been split. Under this system, sharecroppers had few opportunities to improve their situations and could be bound to the land until their "debts" were paid off (Geschwender, 1978, p. 163).

By 1910, more than half of all employed African Americans worked in agriculture, and more than half of the remainder (25% of the total) worked in domestic occupations, such as maid or janitor (Geschwender, 1978, p. 169). The manpower shortage in southern agriculture was solved, and the African American community once again found itself in a subservient status. At the same time, the white southern working class was protected from direct job competition with African Americans. As the South began to industrialize, white workers were able to exclude black workers and reserve the better-paying jobs using a combination of whites-only labor unions and strong antiblack laws and customs. White workers took advantage of the new jobs created by industrialization, while black southerners remained a rural peasantry, excluded from participation in the modernizing job structure.

In some sectors of the changing southern economy, the status of African Americans actually fell lower than it had been during slavery. For example, in 1865, 83% of the artisans in the South were African Americans; by 1900, this percentage had fallen to 5% (Geschwender, 1978, p. 170). The Jim Crow system confined African Americans to the agrarian and domestic sectors of the labor force, denied them the opportunity for a decent education, and excluded them from politics. The system was reinforced by still more laws and customs that drastically limited the options and life opportunities available to black southerners.

Political and Civil Rights Under Jim Crow. A final force behind the creation of de jure segregation was political. As the 19th century drew to a close, a wave of agrarian radicalism known as populism spread across the country. This anti-elitist movement was a reaction to changes in agriculture caused by industrialization. The movement attempted to unite poor whites and blacks in the rural South against the traditional elite classes. The economic elite were frightened by the possibility of a loss of power and split the incipient coalition between whites and blacks by fanning the flames of racial hatred. The strategy of "divide and conquer" proved to be effective (as it often has both before and since this time), and the white elite classes in states throughout the South eliminated the possibility of future threats by depriving African Americans of the right to vote (Woodward, 1974).

The disenfranchisement of the black community was accomplished by measures such as literacy tests, poll taxes, and property requirements. The literacy tests were officially justified as promoting a better-informed electorate but were shamelessly rigged to favor white voters. The requirement that voters pay a tax or prove ownership of a certain amount of property could also disenfranchise poor whites, but again, the implementation of these policies was racially biased.

The policies were extremely effective, and by the early 20th century, the political power of the southern black community was virtually nonexistent. For example, as late as 1896 in Louisiana, there were more than 100,000 registered African American voters and African American voters were a majority in 26 parishes (counties). In 1898, the state adopted a new constitution containing stiff educational and property requirements for voting unless the voter's father or grandfather had been eligible to vote as of January 1, 1867. At that time, the Fourteenth and Fifteenth Amendments, which guaranteed suffrage for black males, had not yet been passed. Such "grandfather clauses" made it easy for white males to register while disenfranchising blacks. By 1900, only about 5,000 African Americans were registered to vote in Louisiana, and African American voters were not a majority in any parish. A similar decline occurred in Alabama, where an electorate of more than 180,000 African American males was reduced to 3,000 by provision of a new state constitution. This story repeated itself throughout the South, and African American political powerlessness was a reality by 1905 (Franklin & Moss, 1994, p. 261).

This system of legally mandated racial privilege was approved by the U.S. Supreme Court, which ruled in the case of *Plessy v. Ferguson* (1896) that it was constitutional for states to require separate facilities (schools, parks, etc.) for African Americans as long as the separate facilities were fully equal. The southern states paid close attention to "separate" but ignored "equal."

Reinforcing the System

Under de jure segregation, as under slavery, the subordination of the African American community was reinforced and supplemented by an elaborate system of racial etiquette. Everyday interactions between blacks and whites proceeded according to highly stylized and rigidly followed codes of conduct intended to underscore the inferior status of the African American community. Whites were addressed as "Mister" or "Ma'am," whereas African Americans were called by their first names or, perhaps, by an honorific title such as "Aunt," "Uncle," or "Professor." Blacks were expected to assume a humble and deferential manner, remove their hats, cast their eyes downward, and enact the role of the subordinate in all interactions with whites. If an African American had reason to call on anyone in the white community, he or she was expected to go to the back door.

These expectations and "good manners" for black southerners were systematically enforced. Anyone who ignored them ran the risk of reprisal, physical attacks, and even death by lynching. During the decades in which the Jim Crow system was being imposed, there were thousands of lynchings in the South. From 1884 until the end of the century, lynchings averaged almost one every other day (Franklin & Moss, 1994, p. 312). The bulk of this violent terrorism was racial and intended to reinforce the system of racial advantage or punish real or imagined transgressors. Also, various secret organizations, such as the Ku Klux Klan, engaged in terrorist attacks against the African American community and anyone else who failed to conform to the dictates of the system.

Increases in Prejudice and Racism

As the system of racial advantage formed and solidified, levels of prejudice and racism increased (Wilson, 1973, p. 101). The new system needed justification and rationalization, just as slavery did, and antiblack sentiment, stereotypes, and ideologies of racial inferiority grew stronger. At the start of the 20th century, the United States in general—not just the South—was a very racist and intolerant society. This spirit of rejection and scorn for all out-groups coalesced with the need for justification of the Jim Crow system and created an especially negative brand of racism in the South.

The "Great Migration"

Although African Americans lacked the power resources to withstand the resurrection of southern racism and oppression, they did have one option that had not been available under slavery: freedom of movement. African Americans were no longer legally tied to a specific master or to a certain plot of land. In the early 20th century, a massive population movement out of the South began. Slowly at first, African Americans began to move to other regions of the nation and from the countryside to the city. The movement increased when hard times hit southern agriculture and slowed down during better times. It has been said that African Americans voted against southern segregation with their feet.

As Exhibits 5.2 and 5.3 show, an urban black population living outside the South is a 20th-century phenomenon. A majority of African Americans continue to live in the South, but the group is more evenly distributed across the nation and much more urbanized than a century ago.

The significance of this population redistribution is manifold. Most important, perhaps, was the fact that by moving out of the South and from rural to urban areas, African Americans moved from areas of great resistance to racial change to areas of lower resistance. In the northern cities, for example, it was far easier to register and to vote. Black political

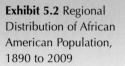

Exhibit 5.2 Regional Distribution of African American Population, 1890 to 2009

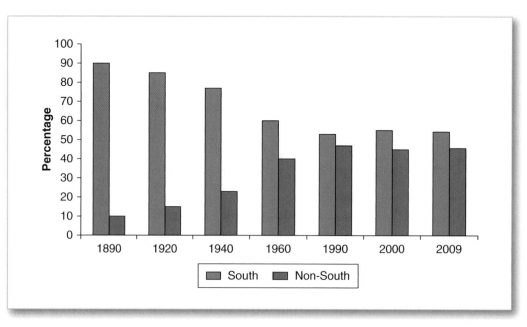

SOURCE: 1890 to 1960—Geschwender (1978); 1990—Heaton, Chadwick, & Jacobson (2000); 2000, 2009—U.S. Bureau of the Census (2009b).

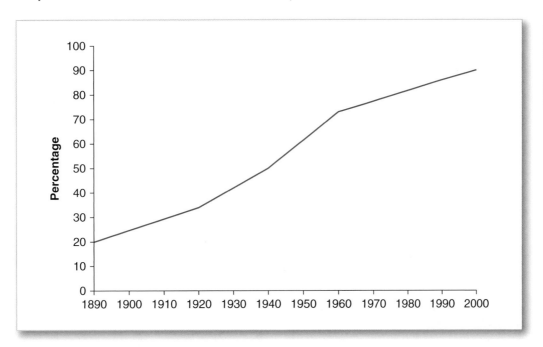

SOURCE: 1890 to 1960—Geschwender (1978); 1970, 1980, 1990—Pollard and O'Hare (1999, p. 27); 2000—U.S. Bureau of the Census (2000d).

Exhibit 5.3 Percentage of African American Population Living in Urban Areas, 1890 to 2000

power began to grow and eventually provided many of the crucial resources that fueled the civil rights movement of the 1950s and 1960s.

Life in the North

What did African American migrants find when they got to the industrializing cities of the North? There is no doubt that life in the North was better for the vast majority of African American migrants. The growing northern African American communities relished the absence of Jim Crow laws and oppressive racial etiquette, the relative freedom to pursue jobs, and the greater opportunities to educate their children. Inevitably, however, life in the North fell far short of utopia. Many aspects of African American culture—literature, poetry, music—flourished in the heady new atmosphere of freedom, but on other fronts, northern African American communities faced massive discrimination in housing, schools, and the job market. Along with freedom and such cultural flowerings as the Harlem Renaissance came black ghettos and new forms of oppression and exploitation. We will explore these events and the workings of what has been called segregation de facto in Chapter 6.

Competition With White Ethnic Groups

It is useful to see the movement of African Americans out of the South in terms of their resultant relationships with other groups. Southern blacks began to move to the North at about the same time as the "New Immigration" from Europe (see Chapter 2) began to end. By the time substantial numbers of black southerners began arriving in the North, European immigrants and their descendants had had years, decades, and even generations to establish themselves in the job markets, political systems, labor unions, and neighborhoods of the North. Many of the European ethnic groups also had been the victims of discrimination and rejection, and, as we discussed in Chapter 2, their hold on economic

Photos 5.4 & 5.5

Writers Langston
Hughes and Claude
McKay were leading
figures in the
Harlem
Renaissance.

© Corbis.

security and status was tenuous for much of the 20th century. Frequently, they saw the newly arriving black migrants as a threat to their status, a perception that was reinforced by the fact that industrialists and factory owners often used African Americans as strike-breakers and scabs during strikes. The white ethnic groups responded by developing defensive strategies to limit the dangers presented by these migrants from the South. They tried to exclude African Americans from their labor unions and other associations and limit their impact on the political system. They also attempted, often successfully, to maintain segregated neighborhoods and schools (although the legal system outside the South did not sanction overt de jure segregation).

This competition led to hostile relations between black southern migrants and white ethnic groups, especially the lower- and working-class segments of those groups. Ironically, however, in another chapter of the ethnic succession discussed in Chapter 2, the newly arriving African Americans actually helped white ethnic groups become upwardly mobile. Dominant-group whites became less contemptuous of white ethnic groups as their alarm over the presence of African Americans increased. The greater antipathy of the white community toward African Americans made the immigrants more desirable and, thus, hastened their admission to the institutions of the larger society. For many white ethnic groups, the increased tolerance of the larger society coincided happily with the coming of age of the more educated and skilled descendants of the original immigrants, further abetting the rise of these groups in the U.S. social class structure (Lieberson, 1980).

For more than a century, each new European immigrant group had helped push previous groups up the ladder of socioeconomic success and out of the old, ghettoized neighborhoods. Black southerners got to the cities after immigration from Europe had been curtailed, and no newly arrived immigrants appeared to continue the pattern of succession for northern African Americans. Instead, American cities developed concentrations of low-income blacks who were economically vulnerable and politically weak and whose position was further solidified by antiblack prejudice and discrimination (Wilson, 1987, p. 34).

THE KITCHENETTE

Richard Wright (1908–1960), one of the most powerful writers of the 20th century, lived through and wrote about many of the social changes discussed in this chapter. He grew up in the South during the height of the Jim Crow system, and his passionate hatred for segregation and bigotry is expressed in his major works, Native Son *(1940) and the autobiographical* Black Boy *(1945). In 1941, Wright helped produce* 12 Million Black Voices, *a folk history of African Americans. A combination of photos and brief essays, the work is a powerful commentary on three centuries of oppression.*

The following selection is adapted from "Death on the City Pavement," which expresses Wright's view of the African American [black] migration out of the South, a journey he himself experienced. This bittersweet migration often traded the harsh, rural repression of the South for the overcrowded, anonymous ghettos of the North. Housing discrimination, both overt and covert, confined African American migrants to the least desirable, most overcrowded areas of the city—in many cases, the neighborhoods that had first housed immigrants from Europe. Unscrupulous landlords subdivided buildings into the tiniest possible apartments ("kitchenettes"), and as impoverished newcomers who could afford no better, African American migrants were forced to cope with overpriced, substandard housing as best they could. Much of this passage, incidentally, could have been written about any 20th-century minority group.

DEATH ON THE CITY PAVEMENT

RICHARD WRIGHT

A war sets up in our emotions: One part of our feelings tells us it is good to be in the city, that we have a chance at life here, that we need but turn a corner to become a stranger, that we need no longer bow and dodge at the sight of the Lords of the Land. Another part of our feelings tells us that, in terms of worry and strain, the cost of living in the kitchenettes is too high, that the city heaps too much responsibility on us and gives too little security in return. . . .

The kitchenette, with its filth and foul air, with its one toilet for thirty or more tenants, kills our black babies so fast that in many cities twice as many of them die as white babies. . . .

The kitchenette scatters death so widely among us that our death rate exceeds our birthrate, and if it were not for the trains and autos bringing us daily into the city from the plantations, we black folk who dwell in northern cities would die out entirely over the course of a few years. . . .

The kitchenette throws desperate and unhappy people into an unbearable closeness of association, thereby increasing latent friction, giving birth to never-ending quarrels of recrimination, accusation, and vindictiveness, producing warped personalities.

The kitchenette injects pressure and tension into our individual personalities, making many of us give up the struggle, walk off and leave wives, husbands, and even children behind to shift for themselves. . . .

The kitchenette reaches out with fingers of golden bribes to the officials of the city, persuading them to allow old firetraps to remain standing and occupied long after they should have been torn down.

The kitchenette is the funnel through which our pulverized lives flow to ruin and death on the city pavement, at a profit.

SOURCE: Wright (1988, pp. 105–111).

THE ORIGINS OF BLACK PROTEST

As I pointed out in Chapter 4, African Americans have always resisted their oppression and protested their situation. Under slavery, however, the inequalities they faced were so great and their resources so meager that the protest was ineffective. With the increased freedom

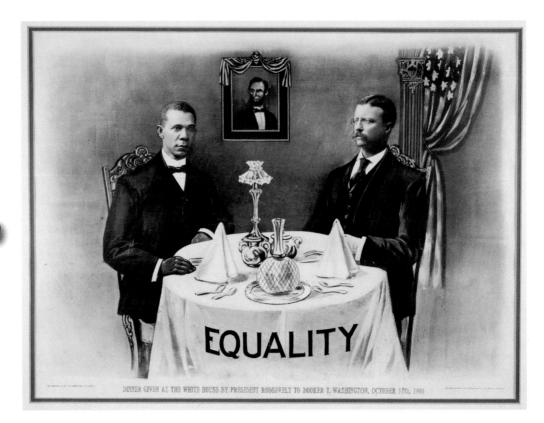

Photo 5.6

Booker T. Washington, the most renowned African American of his time, dines with President Theodore Roosevelt.

© David J. & Janice L. Frent Collection/ Corbis.

that followed slavery, a national African American leadership developed and spoke out against oppression and founded organizations that eventually helped lead the fight for freedom and equality. Even at its birth, the black protest movement was diverse and incorporated a variety of viewpoints and leaders.

Booker T. Washington was the most prominent African American leader prior to World War I. Washington had been born in slavery and was the founder and president of Tuskegee Institute, a college in Alabama dedicated to educating African Americans. His public advice to African Americans in the South was to be patient, to accommodate to the Jim Crow system for the time being, to raise their levels of education and job skills, and to take full advantage of whatever opportunities became available. This nonconfrontational stance earned Washington praise and support from the white community and widespread popularity in the nation. Privately, he worked behind the scenes to end discrimination and implement full racial integration and equality (Franklin & Moss, 1994, pp. 272–274; Hawkins, 1962; Washington, 1965).

Washington's most vocal opponent was W. E. B. Du Bois, an intellectual and activist who was born in the North and educated at some of the leading universities of the day. Among his many other accomplishments, Du Bois was part of a coalition of blacks and white liberals who founded the National Association for the Advancement of Colored People (NAACP) in 1909. Du Bois rejected Washington's accommodationist stance and advocated immediate pursuit of racial equality and a direct assault on de jure segregation. Almost from the beginning of its existence, the NAACP filed lawsuits that challenged the legal foundations of Jim Crow segregation (Du Bois, 1961). As we shall see in Chapter 6, this legal strategy was eventually successful and led to the demise of the Jim Crow system.

Washington and Du Bois may have differed on matters of strategy and tactics, but they agreed that the only acceptable goal for African Americans was an integrated, racially equal United States. A third leader who emerged early in the 20th century called for a very different approach to the problems of U.S. race relations. Marcus Garvey was born in Jamaica and immigrated to the United States during World War I. He argued that the white-dominated U.S. society was hopelessly racist and would never truly support integration and racial equality. He advocated separatist goals, including a return to Africa. Garvey founded the Universal Negro Improvement Association in 1914 in his native Jamaica and founded the first U.S. branch in 1916. Garvey's organization was popular for a time in African American communities outside the South, and he helped establish some of the themes and ideas of black nationalism and pride in African heritage that would become prominent again in the pluralistic 1960s (Essien-Udom, 1962; Garvey, 1969, 1977; Vincent, 1976).

These early leaders and organizations established some of the foundations for later protest movements, but prior to the mid-20th century, they made few actual improvements in the situation of African Americans in the North or South. Jim Crow was a formidable opponent, and the African American community lacked the resources to successfully challenge the status quo until the century was well along and some basic structural features of American society had changed.

APPLYING CONCEPTS

Acculturation and Integration

During this era of southern segregation and migration to the North, assimilation was not a major factor in the African American experience. Rather, the black-white relations of the time are better described as a system of structural pluralism combined with great inequality. Excluded from the mainstream but freed from the limitations of slavery, African Americans constructed a separate subsociety and subculture. In all regions of the nation, African Americans developed their own institutions and organizations, including separate neighborhoods, churches, businesses, and schools. Like immigrants from Europe in the same era, they organized their communities to cater to their own needs and problems and pursue their agenda as a group.

During segregation, a small African American middle class emerged based on leadership roles in the church, education, and business. A network of black colleges and universities was constructed to educate the children of the growing middle class, as well as other classes. Through this infrastructure, African Americans began to develop the resources and leadership that in the decades ahead would attack, head-on, the structures of racial inequality.

Gender and Race

For African American men and women, the changes wrought by industrialization and the population movement to the North created new possibilities and new roles. However, as African Americans continued to be the victims of exploitation and exclusion in both the North and the South, African American women continued to be among the most vulnerable groups in society.

Following Emancipation, there was a flurry of marriages and weddings among African Americans, as they were finally able to legitimatize their family relationships (Staples, 1988, p. 306). African American women continued to have primary responsibility for home and children. Historian Herbert Gutman (1976) reports that it was common for married women to drop out of the labor force and attend solely to household and family duties, because a working wife was too reminiscent of a slave role. This pattern became so widespread that it created serious labor shortages in many areas (Gutman, 1976; see also Staples, 1988, p. 307).

The former slaves were hardly affluent, however, and as sharecropping and segregation began to shape race relations in the South, women often had to return to the fields or to domestic work for the family to survive. One former slave woman noted that women "do double duty, a man's share in the field and a woman's part at home" (Evans, 1989, p. 121). During the bleak decades following the end of Reconstruction, southern black families and black women in particular lived "close to the bone" (Evans, 1989, p. 121).

In the cities and in the growing African American neighborhoods in the North, African American women played a role that in some ways paralleled the role of immigrant women from Europe. The men often moved north first and sent for the women after they had attained some level of financial stability or after the pain of separation became too great (Almquist, 1979, p. 434). In other cases, African American women by the thousands left the South to work as domestic servants; they often replaced European immigrant women, who had moved up in the job structure (Amott & Matthaei, 1991, p. 168).

In the North, discrimination and racism created constant problems of unemployment for the men, and families often relied on the income supplied by the women to make ends meet. It was comparatively easy for women to find employment, but only in the low-paying, less desirable areas, such as domestic work. In both the South and the North, African American women worked outside the home in larger proportions than did white women. For example, in 1900, 41% of African American women were employed, compared with only 16% of white women (Staples, 1988, p. 307).

In 1890, more than a generation after the end of slavery, 85% of all African American men and 96% of African American women were employed in just two occupational categories: agriculture and domestic or personal service. By 1930, 90% of employed African American women were still in these same two categories, whereas the corresponding percentage for employed African American males had dropped to 54% (although nearly all the remaining 46% were unskilled workers) (Steinberg, 1981, pp. 206–207). Since the inception of segregation, African American women have had consistently higher unemployment rates and lower incomes than African American men and white women (Almquist, 1979, p. 437). These gaps, as we shall see in Chapter 6, persist to the present day.

During the years following Emancipation, some issues did split men and women, within both the African American community and the larger society. Prominent among these was suffrage, or the right to vote, which was still limited to men only. The abolitionist movement, which had been so instrumental in ending slavery, also supported universal suffrage. Efforts to enfranchise women, though, were abandoned by the Republican Party and large parts of the abolitionist movement to concentrate on efforts to secure the vote for African American males in the South. Ratification of the Fifteenth Amendment in 1870 extended the vote, in principle, to African American men, but the Nineteenth Amendment enfranchising women would not be passed for another 50 years (Almquist, 1979, pp. 433–434; Evans, 1989, pp. 121–124).

South African Apartheid

Photo 5.7

Apartheid meant poverty and powerlessness for black South Africans.

© Jon Hrusa/epa/Corbis.

Photo 5.8

Nelson Mandela served nearly three decades in prison for his anti-apartheid activities. He was released in 1990 and was elected president of South Africa in 1994.

© Louise Gubb/CORBIS SABA.

Systems of legally sanctioned racial segregation can be found in many nations and historical eras, but perhaps the most infamous system—called **apartheid**—was constructed in South Africa (see Exhibit 5.4). As in the United States, South African segregation was intended to control the labor of the black population and eliminate all political and economic threats from the group. A small minority of whites (less than 15% of the population for much of the 20th century) dominated the black African population and enjoyed a level of race-based privilege rarely equaled in the history of the world. Today, although enormous problems of inequality and racism remain, South Africa has officially dismantled the machinery of racial oppression, has enfranchised nonwhites, and has elected three black presidents.

Some background will illuminate the dynamics of the system. Europeans first came into contact with Southern Africa in the 1600s, at about the time the British were establishing colonies in North America. First to arrive were the Dutch, who established ports on the coast to resupply merchant ships for the journey between Asia and Europe. Some of the Dutch moved into the interior to establish farms and sheep and cattle ranches. The "trekkers," as they were called, regularly fought with indigenous black Africans and with tribes moving into the area from the North. These interracial conflicts were extremely bloody and resulted in enslavement for some black Africans, genocide for others, and a gradual push of the remaining black Africans into the interior. In some ways, this contact period resembled that between European Americans and Native Americans, and in other ways, it resembled the early days of the establishment of black slavery in North America.

In the 1800s, South Africa became a British colony, and the new governing group attempted to grant more privileges to blacks. These efforts stopped far short of equality, however, and South Africa continued to evolve as a racially divided, white-dominated society into the 20th century. The white community continued to be split between people of Dutch (Boers) and English descent, and hostilities erupted into violence on a number of occasions. In 1899, British and Dutch factions fought each other in the Boer War, a bitter, intense struggle that widened and solidified the divisions between the two white communities. Generally, the descendants of the Dutch have been more opposed to racial change than have the descendants of the British.

In 1948, the National Party, the primary political vehicle of the Afrikaans, or Dutch, segment of the white community, came into control of the state. As the society modernized and industrialized, there was growing concern about controlling

Exhibit 5.4 Map of
Africa Showing South
Africa

the majority black population. Under the leadership of the National Party, the system of apartheid was constructed to firmly establish white superiority. In Afrikaans, *apartheid* means "separate" or "apart"; the basic logic of the system was to separate whites and blacks in every area of life: schools, neighborhoods, jobs, buses, churches, and so forth. Apartheid resembled the Jim Crow system of segregation in the United States, except it was even more repressive, elaborate, and unequal.

Although the official government propaganda claimed that apartheid would permit blacks and whites to develop separately and equally, the system was clearly intended to solidify white privilege and black powerlessness. By keeping blacks poor and powerless, white South Africans created a pool of workers who were both cheap and docile. Whites of even modest means could afford the luxuries of personal servants, and employers could minimize their payrolls and their overhead. Of the dominant-minority situations considered in this text, perhaps only American slavery rivals apartheid for its naked, unabashed subjugation of one group for the benefit of another.

Note that the coming of apartheid reverses the relationship between modernization and control of minority groups in the United States. As the United States industrialized and modernized, group relations evolved from paternalistic (slavery) to rigid competitive forms (de jure segregation), with the latter representing a looser form of control over the minority group. In South Africa after 1948, group relations became more rigid, and the structures of control became stronger and more oppressive. Why the difference?

Just as U.S. southerners attempted to defend their privileged status and resist the end of de jure segregation in the 1950s and 1960s, white South Africans were committed to retaining their status and the benefits it created. Although South Africans of British descent tended to be more liberal in matters of race than those of Dutch descent, both groups were firmly committed to white supremacy. Thus, unlike the United States, in which there was almost constant opposition to racial oppression in any form—slavery or segregation—there was little internal opposition among South African whites to the creation of apartheid.

Furthermore, South African blacks in the late 1940s were comparatively more powerless than blacks in the United States at the same time. Although South African black protest organizations existed, they were illegal and had to operate underground or from exile and under conditions of extreme repression. In the United States, in contrast, blacks living outside the South were able to organize and pool their resources to assist in the campaign against Jim Crow, and these activities were protected (more or less) by the national commitment to civil liberties and political freedom.

A final difference between the two situations has to do with numbers. Whereas in the United States, blacks are a numerical minority, they were the great majority of the population in South Africa. Part of the impetus for establishing the rigid system of apartheid was the fear among whites that they would be "swamped" by the numerical majority unless black powerlessness was perpetuated. The difference in group size helped contribute to what has been described as a "fortress" mentality among some white South Africans: the feeling that they were defending a small (but luxurious) outpost surrounded and besieged by savage hordes who threatened their immediate and total destruction. This strong sense of threat among whites and the need to be vigilant and constantly resist the least hint of racial change made the system seem impregnable and perpetual to many observers.

Apartheid lasted about 40 years. Through the 1970s and 1980s, changes within South Africa and in the world in general built up pressure against the system. Internally, protests against apartheid by blacks began in the 1960s and continued to build in intensity. The South African government responded to these protests with violent repression, and thousands died in the confrontations with police and the army. Nonetheless, anti-apartheid activism continued to attack the system from below.

Apartheid also suffered from internal weaknesses and contradictions. For example, jobs were strictly segregated, along with all other aspects of South African society. In a modern, industrial economy, however, new types of jobs are continually being created, and old jobs are continually lost to mechanization and automation, making it difficult to maintain simple, caste-like rules about who can do what kinds of work. Also, many of the newer jobs required higher levels of education and special skills, and the number of white South Africans was too small to fill the demand. Thus, some black South Africans were slowly rising to positions of greater affluence and personal freedom even as the system attempted to coerce and repress the group as a whole.

Internationally, pressure on South Africa to end apartheid was significant. Other nations established trade embargoes and organized boycotts of South African goods. South Africa was officially banned from the Olympics and other international competitions. Although many of these efforts were more symbolic than real and had only minor impact on everyday social life, they sustained an outcast status for South Africa and helped create an atmosphere of uncertainty among its economic and political elite.

In the late 1980s, these various pressures made it impossible to ignore the need for reform any longer. In 1990, F. W. de Klerk, the leader of the National Party and the prime minister of the nation, began a series of changes that eventually ended apartheid. He lifted the ban on many outlawed black African protest organizations, and perhaps most significantly, he released Nelson Mandela from prison. Mandela was the leader of the African National Congress (ANC), one of the oldest and most important black organizations, and he had served a 27-year prison term for actively protesting apartheid. Together, de Klerk and Mandela helped ease South Africa through a period of rapid racial change that saw the franchise being extended to blacks, the first open election in South African history, and in 1994, Mandela's election to a 5-year term as president. In 1999, Mandela was replaced by Thabo M. Mbeke, another black South African. Mbeke was reelected in 2004 but was ousted in September 2008 after a bitter struggle with ANC rival Jacob Zuma, who became president in 2009. Zuma is a charismatic figure with strong support among the rank and file of the party, but his standing has been compromised by allegations of corruption, charges of rape, and other scandals.

The future of South Africa remains unclear. Although the majority black population now has political power, deep racial divisions remain. In many urban and white areas, South Africa maintains a first-world infrastructure, but the black population continues to live in third-world poverty. For example, South Africa hosted the 2010 soccer World Cup and expanded airports, improved roads, and built hotels and stadiums to provide first-class facilities for the hordes of fans that witnessed the matches. While the World Cup was generally regarded as a triumph for South Africa, much of the black population continues to live in apartheid-era townships—pockets of deep, grinding poverty with no running water or sewage, poor or nonexistent medical care, and grossly overcrowded and understaffed schools. To illustrate, the average annual income (in U.S. dollars) for white households in 2006 was about $38,000, while black households averaged about $5,000 (Statistics South Africa, 2008, p. 9).

The problems of racial and class inequality facing South Africa are enormous, and this experiment in racial reform might still fail. However, should it succeed in meeting these challenges, the dramatic transition away from massive racism and institutionalized discrimination could provide a model of change for other racially divided societies.

INDUSTRIALIZATION, THE SHIFT TO POSTINDUSTRIAL SOCIETY, AND DOMINANT-MINORITY GROUP RELATIONS: GENERAL TRENDS

The processes of industrialization that began in the 19th century continued to shape the larger society and dominant-minority relations throughout the 20th century. Today, the United States bears little resemblance to the society it was a century ago. The population has more than tripled in size and has urbanized even more rapidly than it has grown. New organizational forms (bureaucracies, corporations, multinational businesses) and new technologies (nuclear power, computers) dominate everyday life. Levels of education have risen, and the public schools have produced one of the most literate populations and best-trained workforces in the history of the world.

Minority groups also grew in size during this period, and most became even more urbanized than the general population. Minority group members have come to participate in an increasing array of occupations, and their average levels of education have also risen. Despite these real improvements, however, virtually all U.S. minority groups continue to face racism, poverty, discrimination, and exclusion. As industrialization proceeded, the mechanisms for maintaining racial stratification also evolved, morphing into forms that are subtle, indirect, but, in their way, as formidable as Jim Crow segregation.

In this section, I outline the social processes that began in the industrial era and continue to shape the postindustrial stage. I note the ways in which these processes have changed American society and examine some of the general implications for minority groups. I then summarize these changes in terms of a transition from the rigid competitive Jim Crow era to a new stage of group relations called fluid competitive relations. The treatment here is broad and intended to establish a general framework for the examination of the impacts of industrialization and deindustrialization on group relations in the case studies that compose Part III of this text.

Urbanization

We have already noted that urbanization made close, paternalistic controls of minority groups irrelevant. For example, the racial etiquette required by southern de jure segregation, such as African Americans deferring to whites on crowded sidewalks, tended to disappear in the chaos of an urban rush hour.

Besides weakening dominant group controls, urbanization also created the potential for minority groups to mobilize and organize large numbers of people. As stated in Chapter 1, the sheer size of a group is a source of power. Without the freedom to organize, however, size means little, and urbanization increased both the concentration of populations and the freedom to organize.

Occupational Specialization

One of the first and most important results of industrialization, even in its earliest days, was an increase in occupational specialization and the variety of jobs available in the workforce. The growing needs of an urbanizing population increased the number of jobs available in the production, transport, and sale of goods and services. Occupational specialization was also stimulated by the very nature of industrial production. Complex manufacturing processes could be performed more efficiently if they were broken down into the narrower component tasks. It was easier and more efficient to train the workforce in the simpler, specialized jobs. Assembly lines were invented, work was subdivided, the division of labor became increasingly complex, and the number of different occupations continued to grow.

The sheer complexity of the industrial job structure made it difficult to maintain rigid, caste-like divisions of labor between dominant and minority groups. Rigid competitive forms of group relations, such as Jim Crow segregation, became less viable as the job market became more diversified and changeable. Simple, clear rules about which groups could do which jobs disappeared. As the more repressive systems of control weakened, job opportunities for minority group members sometimes increased. However, as the relationships between group memberships and positions in the job market became more blurred, conflict between groups also increased. For example, as we have noted, African Americans moving from the South often found themselves in competition for jobs with members of white ethnic groups, labor unions, and other elements of the dominant group.

Bureaucracy and Rationality

As industrialization continued, privately owned corporations and businesses came to have workforces numbering in the hundreds of thousands. Gigantic factories employing thousands of workers became common. To coordinate the efforts of these huge workforces, bureaucracy became the dominant form of organization in the economy and, indeed, throughout the society.

Bureaucracies are large-scale, impersonal, formal organizations that run "by the book." They are governed by rules and regulations (i.e., "red tape") and are "rational" in that they attempt to find the most efficient ways to accomplish their tasks. Although they typically fail to attain the ideal of fully rational efficiency, bureaucracies tend to recruit, reward, and promote employees on the basis of competence and performance (Gerth & Mills, 1946).

The stress on rationality and objectivity can counteract the more blatant forms of racism and increase the array of opportunities available to members of minority groups. Although they are often nullified by other forces (see Blumer, 1965), these antiprejudicial tendencies do not exist at all or are much weaker in preindustrial economies.

The history of the concept of race illustrates the impact of rationality and scientific ways of thinking. Today, virtually the entire scientific community regards race as a biological triviality, a conclusion based on decades of research. This scientific finding undermined and contributed to the destruction of the formal systems of privilege based solely on race (e.g., segregated school systems) and traditional prejudice, which is based on the assumption that race is a crucial personal characteristic.

Growth of White-Collar Jobs and the Service Sector

Industrialization changed the composition of the labor force. As work became more complex and specialized, the need to coordinate and regulate the production process increased, and as a result, bureaucracies and other organizations grew larger still. Within these organizations, white-collar occupations—those that coordinate, manage, and deal with the flow of paperwork—continued to expand. As industrialization progressed, mechanization and automation reduced the number of manual or blue-collar workers, and white-collar occupations became the dominant sector of the job market in the United States.

Photo 5.9

Some new service jobs, such as staffing help centers, have been outsourced to nations with cheaper labor, including India.

Getty/ImagesBazaar.

The changing nature of the workforce can be illustrated by looking at the proportional representation of three different types of jobs:

1. **Extractive (or primary) occupations** are those that produce raw materials, such as food and agricultural products, minerals, and lumber. The jobs in this sector often involve unskilled manual labor, require little formal education, and are generally low paying.

2. **Manufacturing (or secondary) occupations** transform raw materials into finished products ready for sale in the marketplace. Like jobs in the extractive sector, these blue-collar jobs involve manual labor, but they tend to require higher levels of skill and are more highly rewarded. Examples of occupations in this sector include the assembly line jobs that transform steel, rubber, plastic, and other materials into finished automobiles.

3. **Service (or tertiary) occupations** do not produce "things"; rather, they provide services. As urbanization increased and self-sufficiency decreased, opportunities for work in this sector grew. Examples of tertiary occupations include police officer, clerk, waiter, teacher, nurse, doctor, and cabdriver.

The course of industrialization is traced in the changing structure of the labor market depicted in Exhibit 5.5. In 1840, when industrialization was just beginning in the United States, most of the workforce (70%) was in the extractive sector, with agriculture being the dominant occupation. As industrialization progressed, the manufacturing, or secondary, sector grew, reaching a peak after World War II. Today, in the postindustrial era, the large majority of U.S. jobs are in the service, or tertiary, sector.

This shift away from blue-collar jobs and manufacturing since the 1960s is sometimes referred to as deindustrialization or discussed in terms of the emergence of postindustrial society. The U.S. economy has lost millions of unionized, high-paying factory jobs since the 1960s, and the downward trend continues. The industrial jobs that sustained so many generations of American workers have moved to other nations where wages are considerably

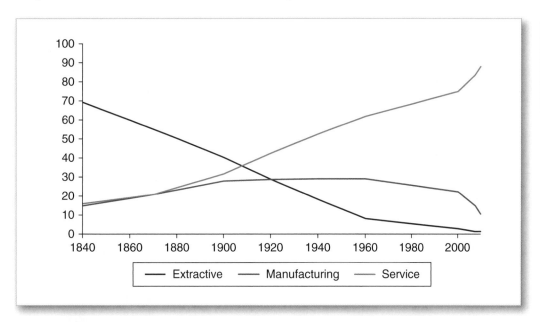

SOURCE: 1840 to 1990—Adapted from Lenski, Nolan, and Lenski (1995); 2002—Calculated from U.S. Bureau of the Census (2005, pp. 385–388); 2005—Calculated from U.S. Bureau of the Census (2007b, pp. 388–391); 2009—Calculated from U.S. Bureau of the Census (2011d, pp. 393–395).

Exhibit 5.5 The Changing U.S. Workforce: The Distribution of Jobs From 1840 to 2009

lower than in the United States or have been eliminated by robots or other automated manufacturing processes (see Rifkin, 1996).

The changing structure of the job market helps clarify the nature of intergroup competition and the sources of wealth and power in society. Job growth in the United States today is largely in the service sector, and these occupations are highly variable. At one end are low-paying jobs with few, if any, benefits or chances for advancement (e.g., washing dishes in a restaurant). At the upper end are high-prestige, lucrative positions, such as Supreme Court justice, scientist, and financial analyst. The new service sector jobs are either highly desirable technical, professional, or administrative jobs with demanding entry requirements (e.g., physician or nurse) or low-paying, low-skilled jobs with few benefits and little security (e.g., receptionist, nurse's aide). For the last half century, job growth in the United States has been either in areas in which educationally deprived minority group members find it difficult to compete or in areas that offer little compensation, upward mobility, or security. As we will see in Part III, the economic situation of contemporary minority groups reflects these fundamental trends.

The Growing Importance of Education

Education has been an increasingly important prerequisite for employability in the United States and in other advanced industrial societies. A high school or, increasingly, a college degree has become the minimum entry-level requirement for employment. However, opportunities for high-quality education are not distributed equally across the population. Some minority groups, especially those created by colonization, have been systematically excluded from the schools of the dominant society, and today, they are less likely to have the educational backgrounds needed to compete for better jobs.

Access to education is a key issue for all U.S. minority groups, and the average educational levels of these groups have been rising since World War II. Still, minority children continue to be much more likely to attend segregated, underfunded, deteriorated schools and to receive inferior educations (see Orfield & Lee, 2007).

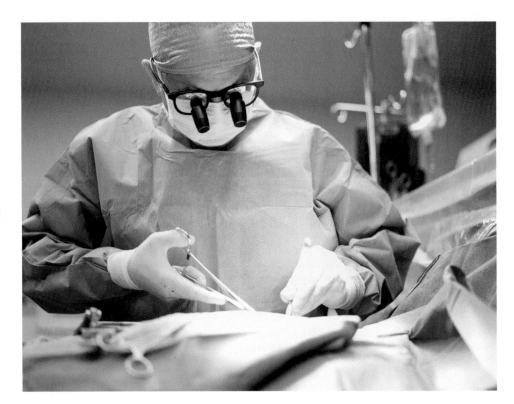

Photos 5.10 & 5.11

The U.S. job market is segmented with more desirable, higher-prestige jobs, such as surgeon in the primary sector, and low-paid, less prestigious jobs, such as fast-food worker in the secondary sector.

Getty/Reza Estakhrian.

Getty/Justin Sullivan.

A Dual Labor Market

The changing composition of the labor force and increasing importance of educational credentials has split the U.S. labor market into two segments or types of jobs. The primary labor market includes jobs usually located in large, bureaucratic organizations. These positions offer higher pay, more security, better opportunities for advancement, health and retirement benefits, and other amenities. Entry requirements include college degrees, even when people with fewer years of schooling could competently perform the work.

The secondary labor market, sometimes called the competitive market, includes low-paying, low-skilled, insecure jobs. Many of these jobs are in the service sector. They do not represent a career and offer little opportunity for promotion or upward mobility. Very often, they do not offer health or retirement benefits, have high rates of turnover, and are part-time, seasonal, or temporary.

Many American minority groups are concentrated in the secondary job market. Their exclusion from better jobs is perpetuated not so much by direct or overt discrimination as by their lack of access to the educational and other credentials required to enter the primary sector. The differential distribution of educational opportunities, in the past as well as in the present, effectively protects workers in the primary sector from competition from minority groups.

Globalization

Over the past century, the United States became an economic, political, and military world power with interests around the globe. These worldwide ties have created new minority groups through population movement and have changed the status of others. Immigration to this country has been considerable for the past three decades. The American economy is one of the most productive in the world, and jobs, even those in the low-paying secondary sector, are the primary goals for millions of newcomers. For other immigrants, this country continues to play its historic role as a refuge from political and religious persecution.

Many of the wars, conflicts, and other disputes in which the United States has been involved have had consequences for American minority groups. For example, both Puerto Ricans and Cuban Americans became U.S. minority groups as the result of processes set in motion during the Spanish-American War of 1898. Both World War I and World War II created new job opportunities for many minority groups, including African Americans and Mexican Americans. After the Korean War, international ties were forged between the United States and South Korea, and this led to an increase in immigration from that nation. In the 1960s and 1970s, the military involvement of the United States in Southeast Asia led to the arrival of Vietnamese, Cambodians, Hmong, and other immigrant and refugee groups from that region.

Dominant-minority relations in the United States have been increasingly played out on an international stage as the world has effectively "shrunk" in size and become more interconnected by international organizations, such as the United Nations; by ties of trade and commerce; and by modern means of transportation and communication. In a world in which two thirds of the population is nonwhite and many important nations (such as China, India, and Nigeria) are composed of peoples of color, the treatment of racial minorities by the U.S. dominant group has come under increased scrutiny. It is difficult to preach principles of fairness, equality, and justice—which the United States claims as its own—when domestic realities suggest an embarrassing failure to fully implement these standards. Part of the pressure for the United States to end blatant systems of discrimination such as de jure segregation came from the desire to maintain a leading position in the world.

Postindustrial Society and the Shift From Rigid to Fluid Competitive Relationships

The coming of postindustrial society brought changes so fundamental and profound that they are often described in terms of a revolution: from an industrial society, based on manufacturing, to a postindustrial society, based on information processing and computer-related or other new technologies. As the subsistence technology evolved, so did American dominant-minority relations. The rigid competitive systems (such as Jim Crow) associated with earlier phases of industrialization gave way to fluid competitive systems of group relations. In fluid competitive relations, formal or legal barriers to competition—such as Jim Crow laws or apartheid—no longer exist. Both geographic and social mobility are greater, and the limitations imposed by minority group status are less restrictive and burdensome. Rigid caste systems of stratification, in which group membership determines opportunities, adult statuses, and jobs, are replaced by more open class systems, in which there are weaker relationships between group membership and wealth, prestige, and power. Because fluid competitive systems are more open and the position of the minority group is less fixed, the fear of competition from minority groups becomes more widespread for the dominant group, and intergroup conflict increases. Exhibit 5.6 compares the characteristics of the three systems of group relations.

Compared with previous systems, the fluid competitive system is closer to the American ideal of an open, fair system of stratification in which effort and competence are rewarded and race, ethnicity, gender, religion, and other "birthmarks" are irrelevant. However, as we will see in chapters to come, race and ethnicity continue to affect life chances and limit opportunities for minority group members even in fluid competitive systems. As suggested by the Noel

Exhibit 5.6
Characteristics of Three Systems of Group Relationships

| | Systems of Group Relations | | |
| | **Paternalistic** | **Competitive** | |
		Rigid	**Fluid**
Subsistence Technology:	Agrarian	Industrial	Postindustrial
Stratification	**Caste**. Group determines status.	**Mixed**. Elements of caste and class. Status largely determined by group.	**Variable**. Status strongly affected by group. Inequality varies within groups.
Division of labor	**Simple**. Determined by group.	**More complex**. Job largely determined by group, but some sharing of jobs by different groups.	**Most complex**. Group and job are less related. Complex specialization and great variation within groups.
Contact between groups	**Common**, but statuses unequal.	**Less common** and mostly unequal.	**More common**. Highest rates of equal status contact.
Overt intergroup conflict	**Rare**.	**More common**.	**Common**.
Power differential	**Maximum**. Minority groups have little ability to pursue self-interests.	**Less**. Minority groups have some ability to pursue self-interests.	**Least**. Minority groups have more ability to pursue self-interests.

SOURCE: Based on Farley (2000, p. 109).

hypothesis, people continue to identify themselves with particular groups (ethnocentrism), and competition for resources continues to play out along group lines. Consistent with the Blauner hypothesis, the minority groups that were formed by colonization remain at a disadvantage in the pursuit of opportunities, education, prestige, and other resources.

GENDER INEQUALITY IN A GLOBALIZING, POSTINDUSTRIAL WORLD

Deindustrialization and globalization are transforming gender relations along with relations between racial and ethnic groups. Everywhere, even in the most patriarchal, male-dominated societies, women are moving away from their traditional wife and mother roles, taking on new responsibilities, and facing new challenges. Some women are also encountering new dangers and new forms of exploitation that perpetuate their lower status and extend it into new areas.

Trends in the United States

In the United States, the transition to a postindustrial society has changed gender relations and the status of women on a number of levels. Women and men are now equal in terms of levels of education (U.S. Bureau of the Census, 2011d, p. 149), and the shift to fluid competitive group relations has weakened the barriers to gender equality along with those to racial equality, although formidable barriers remain. The changing role of women is also shaped by other characteristics of a modern society: smaller families, high divorce rates, and rising numbers of single mothers who must work to support their children as well as themselves. Here, we will look at the ways in which the shift to a postindustrial subsistence technology has raised the status of women relative to that of men and then examine some of the barriers and challenges that remain.

One of the most fundamental changes in U.S. gender relations has been the increasing participation of women in the paid labor force, a change that is related both to demographic trends (e.g., lower birthrates) and to changing aspirations. Women are now employed at almost the same levels as men. In 2009, for example, 64% of single women (vs. about 68% of single men) and about 61% of married women (vs. about 76% of married men) had jobs outside the home (U.S. Bureau of the Census, 2011d, p. 384). Furthermore, between 1970 and 2009, participation in the workforce of married women with children increased from a little less than 40% to almost 70% (U.S. Bureau of the Census, 2011d, p. 385).

One reflection of changing aspirations is that U.S. women are entering a wider variety of careers. In the past, women were largely concentrated in a relatively narrow range of female-dominated jobs, such as nurse and elementary school teacher. Exhibit 5.7 focuses on four pairs of careers and illustrates both the traditional pattern and recent changes. Each pair includes a female-dominated occupation and a comparable but higher-status, more lucrative, traditionally male-dominated occupation. While the "women's" careers remain largely female, the percentage of females in higher-status occupations has increased dramatically (even though, except for university professor, the more lucrative careers remain disproportionately male).

Photo 5.12

Women are increasingly entering traditionally male professions.

© Bill Varie/Corbis.

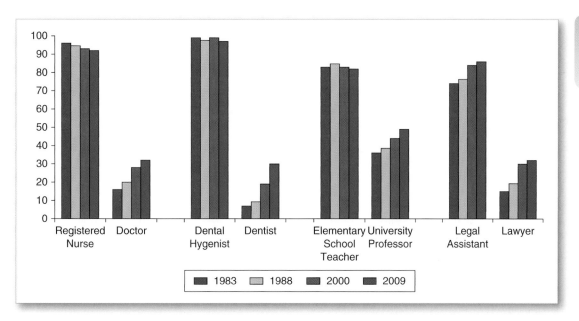

Exhibit 5.7 Percentage Female in Selected Occupations, 1983 to 2009

SOURCE: 1983—Calculated from U.S. Bureau of the Census (2005 pp. 383–385); 1988—Calculated from U.S. Bureau of the Census (1990, pp. 389–391); 2000—Calculated from U.S. Bureau of the Census (2001 pp. 379–382); 2009—Calculated from U.S. Bureau of the Census (2011d, pp. 393–396).

We saw in Exhibit 3.13 that the gender gap in income has decreased over the past few decades but has not disappeared. On the average, women today earn about 76% of what men earn, up from about 65% fifty years ago. The relative increase in women's income is due partly to their movement into more lucrative careers, as reflected in Exhibit 5.7. Another cause of women's rising income is that some of the occupations in which women are highly concentrated have benefited from deindustrialization and the shift to a service economy. For example, job opportunities in the finance, insurance, and real-estate sector have expanded rapidly since the 1960s, and, because women workers tend to be concentrated in these areas, this has tended to elevate average salaries for women in general (Farley, 1996, pp. 95–101).

A third reason for the narrowing gender income gap has more to do with men's wages than women's. Before deindustrialization began to transform U.S. society, men monopolized the more desirable, higher-paid, unionized jobs in the manufacturing sector. For much of the 20th century, these blue-collar jobs paid well enough to subsidize a comfortable lifestyle, a house in the suburbs, and vacations, with enough money left over to save for a rainy day or for the kids' college. However, when deindustrialization began, many of these desirable jobs were lost to automation and to cheaper labor forces outside the United States and were replaced, if at all, by low-paying jobs in the service sector. The result, reflected in Exhibit 3.13, is that while women's wages have increased steadily since the 1950s, men's wages have not.

These large-scale, macrolevel forces have tended to raise the status of women and narrow the income gap, but they have not equalized gender relations. Far from it! For example, although women and men are now equal in terms of education, women tend to get lower returns on their investment in human capital. Exhibit 5.8 compares men and women who were full-time workers in 2009 and shows a wage gap at every level of education. Wages rise as education rises for both sexes, but the wage gap tends to increase as education increases. The least-educated women earned 78% of what the least-educated men earned, and women with a high-school education earned 74% of what comparably educated men earned. The most-educated women, college graduates, earned only 73% of what the most-educated men earned.

Exhibit 5.8 Median Earnings for Full-Time, Year-Round Workers by Gender and Level of Education, 2009

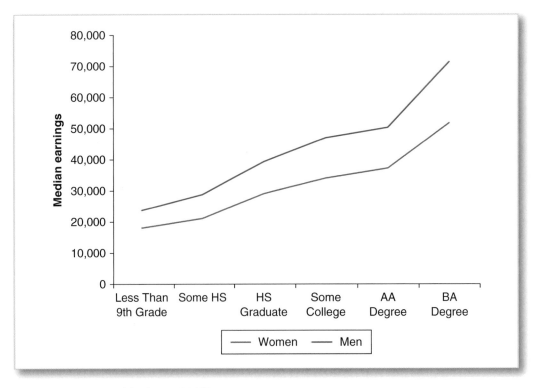

SOURCE: U.S. Bureau of the Census (2010b).

Furthermore, the gender wage gap persists across occupational areas. Exhibit 5.9 compares men and women in 10 types of occupations in 2009 and, like Exhibit 5.8, shows a substantial wage gap. The gap is largest for sales jobs (63%) and transportation (70%) and lowest for maintenance (92%) and office support jobs (87%).

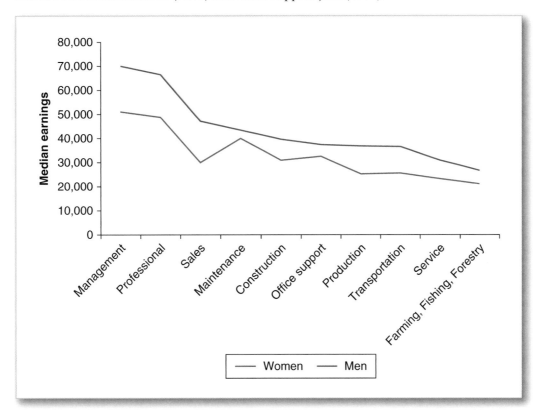

Exhibit 5.9 Median Earnings for Full-Time, Year-Round Workers by Gender and Type of Occupation, 2009

SOURCE: U.S. Bureau of the Census (2010c).

The continuing gender income gap is related to the continuing concentration of women in less-well-paid occupations illustrated in Exhibit 5.7, a result of outright occupational discrimination and a pervasive pressure to funnel young women into "appropriate" jobs. This pattern is also a result of the choices women make to balance the demands of their jobs with their family obligations. Whereas men are expected to make a total commitment to their jobs and careers, women have been expected to find ways to continue to fulfill their domestic roles even while working full-time, and many "female" jobs offer some flexibility in this area (Shelton & John, 1996). For example, some women become elementary school teachers because the job offers long summer breaks, which can help women meet their child-care and other family responsibilities. This pattern of gender occupational segregation testifies to the persistence of minority status for women and the choices they make to reconcile the demands of career and family.

Women, along with minority groups in general, are also limited by the glass ceiling, or the discriminatory practices that limit opportunities to rise to higher levels in their careers, qualify for promotions, and earn higher salaries. These practices are, today, usually subtle, unspoken, and unwritten, but effective in maintaining gender inequality—including income inequality. Decisions about promotions or raises will not overtly mention gender, but the glass ceiling is maintained, for example, by giving women less access to key mentors or sponsors and fewer opportunities for training and other experiences needed to qualify for higher-level jobs (Federal Glass Ceiling Commission, 1995, p. 8; Ridgeway, 2011, pp. 109–117).

One recent cross-national study demonstrated the reality of gender discrimination in business. The researchers followed a group of men and women who held MBAs from prestigious universities and found that the women in the sample started in lower positions, earned less over the course of their careers, and were far less likely to rise to the top of their companies (Carter & Silva, 2010). Another recent study of the Fortune 500 largest corporations found that women were woefully underrepresented among top business leaders and absent from the executive suites and boardrooms. Women made up almost half the total workforce in these companies but accounted for only about 15% of executive officers and board members and less than 8% of top earners (Soares, Combopiano, Regis, Shur, & Wong, 2010).

Global Trends

How have deindustrialization and globalization affected women around the world? In part, these trends parallel those in the United States. According to the United Nations (2010a), indicators such as rising education levels for women and lower rates of early marriage and childbirth show that women around the world are moving out of their traditional (and often highly controlled and repressed) status. Levels of education for women are rising worldwide, and women are approaching educational parity with men, although progress has been slowed by the recent global economic crisis. Women are entering the labor force in unprecedented numbers virtually everywhere, and they now make up about 40% of the paid global workforce. Still, women are concentrated in lower-status, less-lucrative, and more-insecure jobs everywhere (United Nations, 2010a, pp. 20–23).

Although the status of women is generally rising, the movement away from traditional gender roles also brings exposure to new forms of exploitation. Around the globe, women have become a source of cheap labor, often in jobs that have been recently exported from the U.S. economy. For example, many manufacturing jobs formerly held by men in the United States have migrated just south of the border to Mexico, where they are held by women. Maquiladoras are assembly plants built by corporations (often headquartered in

Photo 5.13

This woman, working as a prostitute in Bangkok, Thailand, is part of an international sex industry that often depends on impoverished women and children.

© Andrew Holbrooke/ Corbis.

the United States) to take advantage of the plentiful supply of working-class females who will work for low wages and in conditions that would not be tolerated in the United States.

The weakening of traditional gender roles has increased women's vulnerability in other areas as well. A global sex trade in prostitution and pornography is flourishing and accounts for a significant portion of the economy of Thailand, the Philippines, and other nations. This international industry depends on impoverished women (and children) pushed out of the subsistence rural economy by industrialization and globalization and made vulnerable to exploitation by their lack of resources and power (Poulan, 2003. See also Ehrenreich & Hochschild, 2004; Kristof & WuDunn, 2010).

Across all these changes and around the globe, women commonly face the challenge of reconciling their new work demands with their traditional family responsibilities. Also, women face challenges and issues such as sexual harassment and domestic violence, which clearly differentiate their status from that of men. In this context, minority group women face a double disadvantage because the issues they face as women are complicated by the barriers created by racial and ethnic prejudice and discrimination. As we shall see in Part III, minority group and immigrant women often form the poorest, most vulnerable, and exploited groups in U.S. society and around the globe.

MODERN INSTITUTIONAL DISCRIMINATION

Virtually all American minority groups continue to lag behind national averages in income, employment, and other measures of equality, despite the greater fluidity of group relations, the end of legal barriers such as Jim Crow laws, the dramatic declines in overt prejudice (see Chapter 3), and the introduction of numerous laws designed to ensure that all people are treated without regard to race, gender, or ethnicity. After all this change, shouldn't there be less minority group inequality and racial stratification?

As we saw in Chapter 3, many Americans attribute the persisting patterns of inequality to the minority groups' lack of willpower or motivation to get ahead. In the remaining chapters of this text, however, I argue that the major barriers facing minority groups in postindustrial, post-Jim Crow America are pervasive, subtle, but still powerful forms of discrimination, which together can be called modern institutional discrimination.

As you recall from Chapter 1, institutional discrimination is built into the everyday operation of the social structure of society. The routine procedures and policies of institutions and organizations are arranged so that minority group members are automatically put at a disadvantage. In the Jim Crow era in the South, for example, African Americans were deprived of the right to vote by overt institutional discrimination and could acquire little in the way of political power.

The forms of institutional discrimination that persist in the present are more subtle and difficult to document than the blatant, overt customs and laws of the Jim Crow system. In fact, they are sometimes unintentional or unconscious and are manifested more in the results for minority groups than in the intentions or prejudices of dominant group members. Modern institutional discrimination is not necessarily linked to prejudice, and the decision makers who implement it may sincerely think of themselves as behaving rationally and in the best interests of their organizations.

The Continuing Power of the Past

Many forces conspire to maintain racial stratification in the present. Some are the legacies of past discriminatory practices. Consider, for example, past-in-present institutional discrimination, which involves practices in the present that have discriminatory consequences because of some pattern of discrimination or exclusion in the past (Feagin & Feagin, 1986, p. 32). One form of this discrimination is found in workforces organized around the principle of seniority. In these systems, which are quite common, workers who have been on the job longer have higher incomes; more privileges; and other benefits, such as longer vacations. The "old-timers" often have more job security and are designated in official, written policy as the last to be fired or laid off in the event of hard times. Workers and employers alike may think of the privileges of seniority as just rewards for long years of service, familiarity with the job, and so forth.

Personnel policies based on seniority may seem perfectly reasonable, neutral, and fair. However, they can have discriminatory results in the present because in the past, members of minority groups and women were excluded from specific occupations by racist or sexist labor unions, discriminatory employers, or both. As a result, minority group workers and women may have fewer years of experience than dominant group workers and men and may be the first to go when layoffs are necessary. The adage "last hired, first fired" describes the situation of minority group and female employees who are more vulnerable not because of some overtly racist or sexist policy but because of the routine operation of the seemingly neutral principle of seniority.

Racial differences in homeownership provide a second example of the myriad ways in which the past shapes the present and maintains the moving target of racial stratification. Today, about 73% of non-Hispanic whites own their own homes, and these houses have a median value of $193,000. In contrast, only 46% of non-Hispanic blacks are homeowners, and the median value of their homes is $139,000 (U.S. Bureau of the Census, 2009a). Homeownership is an important source of family wealth because home equity can be used to establish credit; finance businesses, other purchases, and investments; and fund education and other sources of human capital for the next generation. What is the origin of these huge differences in family wealth?

Part of the answer lies in events that date back 80 years. As you know, President Franklin D. Roosevelt's administration responded to the Great Depression of the 1930s, in part, by instituting the New Deal: a variety of programs that provided assistance to distressed Americans. What is not so widely known is that these programs were racially discriminatory and provided few or no benefits to African Americans (Massey, 2007, p. 60. See also Katznelson, 2005; Lieberman, 1998). One of the New Deal programs was administered by the Federal Housing Administration (FHA): The agency offered low-interest mortgages and made homeownership possible for millions of families. However, the FHA sanctioned racially restrictive covenants that forbid whites to sell to blacks and helped institutionalize the practice of "redlining" black neighborhoods, which prevented banks from making home loans in these areas. Together, these and other discriminatory practices effectively excluded black Americans from homeownership (Massey, 2007, pp. 60–61; Massey & Denton, 1993, pp. 53–54). Thus, another racial divide was created that, over the generations, has helped countless white families develop wealth and credit but made it impossible for black families to qualify for homeownership, the "great engine of wealth creation" (Massey, 2007, p. 61).

More broadly, racial residential segregation—which is arguably the key factor in preserving racial stratification in the present—provides another illustration of modern institutional discrimination. The overt, Jim Crow-era laws and customs that created racially segregated neighborhoods and towns in the past were abolished decades ago, and racial discrimination in selling and renting houses has been illegal since the passage of the Fair Housing Act in 1968. However, blacks continue to be concentrated in all- or mostly black neighborhoods, many of which are also characterized by inadequate services and high levels of poverty and crime. How is racial residential segregation maintained in an era of fair housing laws?

Some of the practices that preserve racial residential segregation have been documented by audit studies. In this technique, black and white (and sometimes Latino and Asian) customers are prepared with carefully matched background credentials (education, employment and credit histories, and finances) and sent to test the market for racial fairness. Characteristically, the black customer is steered away from white neighborhoods, required to furnish greater down payments or deposits, charged higher interest rates, or otherwise discouraged from a successful sale or rental. Sometimes, the black customer may be told that a unit is already sold or rented, or otherwise given false or misleading information.

The result is that blacks are discouraged from breaking the housing color line, but not directly, blatantly, or in ways that clearly violate the fair housing laws. The gatekeepers (real-estate agents, landlords, mortgage bankers) base their behavior not on race per se but on characteristics associated with race—accent, dialect, home address, and so forth—to make decisions about what levels of service and responsiveness to provide to customers. Sociologist Douglas Massey has even demonstrated racially biased treatment based on the use of "Black English" in telephone contacts (Massey, 2000, p. 4).

Audit studies have also documented racial discrimination in the job market (e.g., see Bertrand & Mullainathan, 2004). Other forms of modern institutional discrimination include the use of racially and culturally biased standardized tests in school systems, the pattern of drug arrests that sends disproportionate numbers of black teenage boys and young men to jail and prison (see Chapter 6 for more on this), and decisions by businesspeople to move their operations away from center-city neighborhoods. Part of what makes modern institutional discrimination so challenging to document is that race, ethnicity, or gender may not be a conscious or overt part of these decision-making processes. Still, the results are that blacks and other minorities—in the past as in the present—are filtered away from opportunities and resources, and the moving target of racial stratification is maintained, even in the new age of a supposedly colorblind society.

Modern institutional discrimination routinely places black Americans in less desirable statuses in education, residence and homeownership, jobs, the criminal justice system—indeed, across the entire expanse of the socioeconomic system. The result is racial stratification maintained not by monolithic Jim Crow segregation or slavery but by a subtle and indirect system that is the "new configuration of inequality" (Katz & Stern, 2008, p. 100). We will apply the concept of modern institutional discrimination throughout the case study chapters in Part III of this text.

Affirmative Action

By its nature, modern institutional discrimination is more difficult to identify, measure, and eliminate. Some of the most heated disputes in recent group relations have concerned public policy and law in this area. Among the most controversial issues is affirmative action, a group of programs that attempts to reduce the effects of past discrimination or increase diversity in the workplace or in schools. In the 1970s and 1980s, the Supreme Court found that programs designed to favor minority employees as a strategy for overcoming past discrimination were constitutional (e.g., *Firefighters Local Union No. 1784 v. Stotts*, 1984; *Sheet Metal Workers v. EEOC*, 1986; *United Steelworkers of America, AFL-CIO-CLC v. Weber*, 1979). Virtually all these early decisions concerned blatant policies of discrimination, which are becoming increasingly rare as we move further away from the days of Jim Crow. Even so, the decisions were based on narrow margins (votes of 5 to 4) and featured acrimonious and bitter debates. More recently, the Supreme Court narrowed the grounds on which such past grievances could be redressed and dealt serious blows to affirmative action programs (e.g., *Adarand Constructors Inc. v. Pena*, 1995).

A Case of Discrimination?

The most recent case involving affirmative action programs in the work place is *Ricci v. DeStefano*, which involved firefighters in New Haven, Connecticut. In 2003, the city administered a test for promotion in the city's fire department. More than 100 people took the test, but no African American scored high enough to qualify for promotion. The city decided to throw out the test results on the grounds that its dramatically unequal racial results strongly suggested that it was biased against African Americans. This decision is consistent with the concept of "disparate impact": If a practice has unequal results, federal policy and court precedents tend to assume that the practice is racially biased. The city feared that using these possibly "tainted" test scores might result in lawsuits by black and other minority firefighters. Instead, a lawsuit was filed by several white and Hispanic firefighters who *had* qualified for promotion, claiming that invalidating the test results amounted to reverse racial discrimination. In yet another 5–4 ruling, the Supreme Court ruled in favor of the white plaintiffs in 2009.

This case illustrates some of the difficult issues that accompany attempts to address modern institutional discrimination. The issue in *Ricci v. DeStefano* is not overt, Jim Crow discrimination but, rather, a test that might be discriminatory in its results, although not in its intent. New Haven was attempting to avoid racial discrimination: How far do employers need to go to ensure racial fairness? Should policies and procedures be judged by the outcomes or their intents? What does "fairness" and "equal treatment" mean in a society in which minority groups have only recently won formal equality and still have lower access to quality schooling and jobs in the mainstream economy? Did the city of New Haven go too far in its attempt to avoid discrimination (five of the Supreme Court Justices thought so)? Can there be a truly fair, race-neutral policy for employment and promotion in the present when opportunities and resources have been allocated on the basis of race for so long in the past? If the problem is color-coded, can the solution be color neutral?

Higher Education and Affirmative Action

Colleges and universities have been another prominent battleground for affirmative action programs. Since the 1960s, many institutions of higher education have implemented programs to increase the number of minority students on campus at both the undergraduate and graduate levels, sometimes admitting minority students who had lower grade point averages or test scores than those of dominant group students who were turned away. In general, advocates of these programs have justified them in terms of redressing the discriminatory practices of the past or increasing diversity on campus and making the student body a more accurate representation of the surrounding society. To say the least, these programs have been highly controversial and the targets of frequent lawsuits, some of which have found their way to the highest courts in the land.

Recent decisions by the Supreme Court have limited the application of affirmative action to colleges and universities. In two lawsuits involving the University of Michigan in 2003 (*Grutter v. Bollinger* and *Gratz v. Bollinger*), the Supreme Court held that the university's law school *could* use race as one criterion in deciding admissions but that undergraduate admissions *could not* award an automatic advantage to minority applicants. In other words, universities could take account of an applicant's race but only in a limited way, as one factor among many.

In the spring of 2007, the court further narrowed the scope of affirmative action in a ruling that involved two public school systems (*Parents Involved in Community Schools v. Seattle School District No. 1* and *Meredith v. Jefferson County (Ky.) Board of Education*). At issue were the plans in Seattle and Louisville to further racial integration and diversity in their schools despite the extensive residential segregation in their areas. Students were assigned to schools partly on the basis of race, and the Court ruled that these plans violated the equal protection clause of the Constitution (Bames, 2007).

The Future of Affirmative Action

What lies ahead for affirmative action? On one hand, there seems to be a clear trend in court decisions to narrow the scope and applicability of these programs. Also, there is little public support for affirmative action, especially for programs that are perceived as providing specific numerical quotas in jobs or university admissions for minority groups. For example, a representative sample of Americans was asked in a 2010 survey if they supported "preferential hiring and promotion of blacks." Only 12% of white respondents expressed support, and, more surprising perhaps, preferential hiring was supported by less than half of black respondents (National Opinion Research Council, 1972–2010).

On the other hand, although white (and many minority-group) Americans object to fixed quotas or preferences, there is support for programs that expand the opportunities available to minority groups, including enhanced job training, education, and recruitment in minority communities (Wilson, 2009, p. 139). Programs of this sort are more consistent with traditional ideologies and value systems that stress individual initiative, personal responsibility, and equality of opportunity. Also, many businesses and universities are committed to the broad principles of affirmative action—the need to address past injustices and the importance of providing diversity in the workplace and classroom—and they are likely to sustain their programs (to the extent allowed by court decisions and legislation) into the future. By and large, it seems that affirmative action programs, especially those that stress equality of opportunity, will continue in some form, perhaps quite limited, into the foreseeable future.

SOCIAL CHANGE AND MINORITY GROUP ACTIVISM

This chapter has focused on the continuing Industrial Revolution and its impact on minority groups in general and black-white relations in particular. For the most part, changes in group relations have been presented as the results of the fundamental transformation of the U.S. economy from agrarian to industrial to postindustrial. However, the changes in the situation of African Americans and other minority groups did not "just happen" as society modernized. Although the opportunity to pursue favorable change was the result of broad structural changes in American society, the realization of these opportunities came from the efforts of the many who gave their time, their voices, their resources, and sometimes their lives in pursuit of racial justice in America. Since World War II, African Americans often have been in the vanguard of protest activity, and we focus on the contemporary situation of this group in the next chapter.

CURRENT DEBATES

Reparations

Should African Americans be compensated for the losses they suffered as a result of their kidnapping from Africa, their centuries of slavery, and their continuing oppression under de jure segregation? What, if anything, does American society owe for the centuries of uncompensated labor performed by African Americans and the oppression and coerced inequality of the Jim Crow era? Should present-day Americans be held accountable for the actions of their ancestors? What about the families and businesses that grew rich from the labor of African Americans (and other minorities) in the past? To what extent are they responsible for the continuing racial gaps in income and wealth documented in this chapter?

The idea of reparations has been placed on the national agenda in a variety of forms, including bills proposed to the U.S. Congress and apologies for slavery issued by several states and corporations. A reparations lawsuit was filed in 2002 against a number of large corporations that allegedly benefited directly from slavery, and the lawsuit remained active until a petition to the Supreme Court was denied in 2007. Also, a number of university campuses across the nation have held demonstrations and teach-ins on the issue.

In the excerpts below, Joe Feagin and Eileen O'Brien (1999), while arguing for reparations, place the issue in a historical context. David Horowitz, a conservative journalist, presents a case against reparations. His points are disputed by Ernest Allen and Robert Chrisman in an article taken from The Black Scholar, *a prominent journal devoted to the writings and thoughts of African Americans.*

REPARATIONS FOR AFRICAN AMERICANS IN HISTORICAL CONTEXT

JOE FEAGIN AND EILEEN O'BRIEN

Many discussions of reparation for African Americans seem to suggest that such compensation is a wild idea well beyond conventional U.S. practice or policy. This is not, however, the case. The principle of individual and group compensation for damages done by others is accepted by the federal government and the larger society in regard to some claims, but only grudgingly and incompletely for others, such as those by African Americans who have been harmed by racial oppression. For example, recent anticrime legislation, in the form of the Victims of Crime Act, codifies the principle of compensation for victims of crime. In addition, as a nation, we now expect corporations to compensate the deformed children of mothers who took drugs without knowing their consequences. . . . The fact that those who ran the corporation in the initial period of damage are deceased does not relieve the corporation from having to pay compensation to those damaged later on from the earlier actions. Injured children can sue for redress many years later. Clearly, in some cases monetary compensation for past injustices is accepted and expected.

Long after the Nazi party had been out of power and most of its leaders had grown old or died, the U.S. government continued to press the German government to make tens of billions of dollars in reparations to the families of those killed in the Holocaust and to the state of Israel.

In recent years, the federal government has grudgingly agreed to (modest) reparations for those Japanese Americans who were interned during World War II. Federal courts have also awarded nearly a billion dollars in compensatory damages to Native American groups whose lands were stolen in violation of treaties. Significantly, however, these slow moves to compensate some victims of racial oppression have not extended, even modestly, to African Americans. . . .

In his 1946 book, *The World and Africa*, W. E. B. Du Bois argued that the poverty in Europe's African colonies was "a main cause of wealth and luxury in Europe" (1965, p. 37). Du Bois argued that the history of African colonization is omitted from mainstream histories of European development and wealth. A serious understanding of European wealth must center on the history of exploitation and oppression in Africa, for the resources of Africans were taken to help create Europe's wealth. To a substantial degree, Europeans were rich because Africans were poor. Africa's economic development—its resources, land, and labor—had been and was being sacrificed to spur European economic progress.

In our view, a similar argument is applicable to the development of the wealth and affluence of the white population in the United States. From its first decades, white-settler colonialism in North America involved the extreme exploitation of enslaved African Americans.

European colonists built up much wealth by stealing the labor of African Americans and the land of Native Americans.

Racial oppression carried out by white Americans has lasted for nearly four centuries and has done great damage to the lives, opportunities, communities, and futures of African Americans. The actions of white Americans over many generations sharply reduced the income of African Americans and, thus, their economic and cultural capital. Legal segregation in the South, where most African Americans resided until recent decades, forced black men and women into lower-paying jobs or into unemployment, where they could not earn incomes sufficient to support their families adequately, much less to save. In the 1930s, two thirds of African Americans still lived in the South. They were still firmly entrenched in the semislavery of legal segregation, which did not allow the accumulation of wealth. Significant property holding was not even available as a possibility to a majority of African Americans until the late 1960s. . . .

Most whites do not understand the extent to which the racial oppression of the past continues to fuel inequalities in the present. Although affirmative action programs (where they still exist) attempt to redress discrimination by increasing job or educational opportunities for African Americans in a few organizations, such programs do little to address the large-scale wealth inequality between black and white Americans. All the "equal opportunity" programs and policies one could envisage would not touch the assets of whites who long ago reaped the benefits of not being subjected to legal segregation during the United States' most prosperous economic times in the 19th and 20th centuries. . . .

Wealth transmission is a critical factor in the reproduction of racial oppression. Given the nature of whites' disproportionate share of America's wealth and the historical conditions under which it was acquired—often at the expense of African Americans—it is of little significance that legal discrimination and segregation do not exist today. The argument that "Jim Crow is a thing of the past" misses the point, because the huge racial disparities in wealth today are a direct outgrowth of the economic and social privileges one group secured unfairly, if not brutally, at the expense of another group.

TEN REASONS WHY REPARATIONS FOR SLAVERY IS A BAD IDEA FOR BLACKS—AND RACIST TOO

DAVID HOROWITZ

1. There is no single group clearly responsible for . . . slavery.

[Besides white Europeans and Americans] Black Africans and Arabs were responsible for enslaving the ancestors of African Americans. [Also,] there were 3,000 black slave owners in the antebellum United States. Are reparations to be paid by their descendants, too?

2. There is no one group that benefited exclusively from slavery.

The claim for reparations is premised on the false assumption that only whites have benefited. . . . If slave labor created wealth for Americans, then obviously it has created wealth for black Americans as well, including the descendants of slaves. The GNP of black America is so large that it makes the African American community the 10th most prosperous "nation" in the world. American blacks on average enjoy per capita incomes in the range of 20 to 50 times that of blacks living in any of the African nations from which they were kidnapped.

3. Only a tiny minority of white Americans ever owned slaves, and others gave their lives to free them.

Only one of five [people] in antebellum South ever owned slaves. . . . Why should the descendants [of non-slave owners] owe a debt? What about the descendants of the 350,000 Union soldiers who died to free the slaves? They gave their lives. What possible moral principle would ask them to pay (through their descendants) again?

4. America today is a multiethnic nation, and most Americans have no connection . . . to slavery.

The two great waves of American immigration occurred after 1880 and then after 1960. What rationale would require Vietnamese boat people, Russian refuseniks, Iranian refugees, and Armenian victims of the Turkish persecution, Jews, Mexicans, Greeks, or Polish, Hungarian, Cambodian and Korean victims of Communism, to pay reparations to American blacks?

5. The historical precedents . . . do not apply, and the claim is based on race not injury.

The historical precedents generally invoked to justify the reparations claim are payments to Jewish survivors of the Holocaust, Japanese Americans, and African American victims of racial experiments in Tuskegee, or racial outrages in Rosewood and Oklahoma City. But in each case, the recipients . . . were the direct victims of the injustice or their immediate families. [Reparations for slavery would be paid] to people who were not immediately affected and whose sole qualification . . . would be racial. As has already been pointed out, during the slavery era, many blacks were free men or slave owners themselves, yet the reparations claimants make no distinction between the roles blacks actually played. . . .

6. The reparations argument is based on the unfounded claim that all African American descendants of slaves suffer from the economic consequences of slavery and discrimination.

No evidence . . . has . . . proved that living individuals have been adversely affected by a slave system that was ended over 150 years ago. But there is plenty of evidence the [current] hardships . . . were hardships that individuals could and did overcome. The black middle class in America is a prosperous community that is now larger in absolute terms than the black underclass. Does its existence not suggest that economic adversity is the result of failures of individual character rather than the lingering after-effects of racial discrimination . . . ?

7. The reparations claim is one more attempt to turn African Americans into victims.

The renewed sense of grievance—which is what the claim for reparations will inevitably create—is neither a constructive nor a helpful message for black leaders to be sending to their communities. . . . To focus the social passions of African Americans on what some Americans may have done to their ancestors . . . is to burden them with a crippling sense of victimhood. How are the millions of refugees from tyranny and genocide who are now living in America going to receive these claims . . . except as demands for special treatment . . . that is only necessary because some blacks can't seem to locate the ladder of opportunity within reach of others—many less privileged than themselves?

8. Reparations to African Americans have already been paid.

Since the passage of the Civil Rights Acts and the advent of the Great Society in 1965, trillions of dollars . . . have been paid to African Americans in the form of welfare benefits and racial preferences (in contracts, job placements, and educational admissions)—all under the rationale of redressing historic racial grievances. . . .

9. What about the debt blacks owe to America?

In [slavery's entire] existence, there never was an antislavery movement until white Christians—Englishmen and Americans—created one. If not for . . . white Englishmen and Americans, the slave trade would not have been brought to an end. If not for the sacrifices of white soldiers and a white American president who gave his life to sign the Emancipation Proclamation, blacks in America would still be slaves. If not for the dedication of Americans of all ethnicities and colors to a society based on the principle that all men are created equal, blacks in America would not enjoy the highest standard of living of blacks anywhere in the world. . . . They would not enjoy the greatest freedoms and the most thoroughly protected individual rights anywhere. Where is the gratitude of black America and its leaders for those gifts?

10. The reparations claim is a separatist idea that sets African Americans against the nation that gave them freedom.

Blacks were here before the Mayflower. Who is more American than the descendants of African slaves? For the African American community to isolate itself even further from America is to embark on a course whose implications are troubling. . . . African-Americans have an enormous stake in their country and its heritage. It is this heritage that is really under attack by the reparations movement. . . . The American idea needs the support of its African American citizens [and] it is this idea that led to the principles and institutions that have set African Americans—and all of us—free.

SOURCE: Horowitz (2001).

TEN REASONS: A RESPONSE TO DAVID HOROWITZ

ERNEST ALLEN AND ROBERT CHRISMAN

1. There is no single group clearly responsible for the crime of slavery.

Horowitz's first point . . . can only lead to two conclusions: (1) Societies are not responsible for their actions, and (2) since "everyone" was responsible for slavery, no one was responsible. While diverse groups on different continents certainly participated in the trade, the principal responsibility for . . . that trade and . . . slavery . . . rests with European and American individuals and institutions. . . . The evidence is overwhelming that the vast majority of black slaveholders were free men who purchased members of their families or who acted out of benevolence.

2. There is no single group that benefited exclusively from slavery.

. . . Who benefited primarily from slavery? Those who were responsible for the [system] . . . also received the primary benefits. . . . New England slave traders, merchants, bankers, and insurance companies all profited from the slave trade. . . . The free labor provided by slavery was central to the growth of industry in Western Europe and the United States. . . . Slaveholders benefited primarily . . . , of course, . . . but the sharing of the proceeds of slave exploitation spilled across class lines within white communities as well. . . . Even poor whites benefited from the legal advantage they enjoyed over all blacks as well as from the psychological advantage of having a group beneath them.

3. Only a tiny minority of white Americans ever owned slaves, and others gave their lives to free them.

[We dealt with the first part of this argument above]. Most white Union troops were drafted. . . . [Moreover], Horowitz's focus on what he mistakenly considers to be the overriding, benevolent aim of white union troops in the Civil War obscures the role that blacks themselves played in their own liberation. . . .

4. Most living Americans have no connection (direct or indirect) to slavery.

As Joseph Anderson . . . observed, "the arguments for reparations aren't made on the basis of whether every white person directly gained from slavery. The arguments are made on the basis that slavery was institutionalized and protected by law in the United States. As the government is an entity that survives generations, its debts and obligations survive the lifespan of any particular individuals . . ." (*San Francisco Chronicle*, March 26, 2001, p. A21). . . . Passage of time does not negate the responsibility of government in crimes against humanity. . . . The U.S. government is not the same government as it was in the pre-Civil War era, yet its debts and obligations from the past are no less relevant today.

5. The historical precedents used to justify the reparations claim do not apply, and the claim itself is based on race not injury.

Slavery was inflicted upon a people designated as a race. The descendants of that people—still socially constructed as a race today—continue to suffer the institutional legacies of slavery. . . . To attempt to separate the issue of so-called race from that of injury in this instance is pure sophistry. For example, the criminal (in)justice system today largely continues to operate as it did under slavery—for the protection of white citizens against black "outsiders." Although no longer inscribed in law, this very attitude is implicit to processes of law enforcement, prosecution, and incarceration, guiding the behavior of police, prosecutors, judges, juries, wardens, and parole boards. Hence, African Americans continue to experience higher rates of incarceration than do whites charged with similar crimes, endure longer sentences for the same classes of crimes perpetrated by whites, and . . . receive far less consideration by parole boards when being considered for release. . . .

6. The reparations argument is based on the unfounded claim that all African American descendants of slaves suffer from the economic consequences of slavery and discrimination.

Most blacks suffered and continue to suffer the economic consequences of slavery and its aftermath. . . . [*NOTE: See the racial income gap documented in Chapter 6*.] [Data on] financial worth, which reflects . . . the wealth handed down within families from generation to generation, [make] the figures appear much starker. . . . [*NOTE: See the racial wealth gap documented in Chapter 6*.]

7. The reparations claim is one more attempt to turn African Americans into victims. It sends a damaging message to the African American community.

What is a victim? Black people have certainly been victimized, but acknowledgment of that fact is not a case of "playing the victim" but of seeking justice. There is no validity to Horowitz's comparison between black Americans and victims of oppressive regimes who have voluntarily immigrated to these shores. Further, many members of those populations . . . direct their energies for redress toward the governments of their own oppressive nations—which is precisely what black Americans are doing. . . . The damage lies in the systematic treatment of black people in the U.S., not their claims against those who initiated this damage and their spiritual descendants who continue its perpetuation.

8. Reparations to African Americans have already been paid.

. . . "Welfare benefits and racial preferences" are not reparations. The welfare system was set in place in the 1930s to alleviate the poverty of the Great Depression, and more whites than blacks received welfare. So-called "racial preferences" come not from benevolence but from lawsuits by blacks against white businesses, government agencies, and municipalities which practice racial discrimination.

9. What about the debt blacks owe to America?

Horowitz's assertion that [white Christians led the antislavery movement] . . . only demonstrates his ignorance concerning the formidable efforts of blacks to free themselves. Led by black Toussaint L'Ouverture, the Haitian revolution of 1793 overthrew the French slave system, created the first black republic in the world. . . . Slave insurrections and conspiracies such as those of Gabriel (1800), Denmark Vesey (1822), and Nat Turner (1831) were potent sources of black resistance; black abolitionists such as Harriet Tubman, Frederick Douglass, Richard Allen, Sojourner Truth, Martin Delany, David Walker, and Henry Highland Garnet waged an incessant struggle against slavery. . . . Black Americans were in no ways the passive recipients of freedom from anyone. . . .

   The idea of black debt to U.S. society is a rehash of the Christian missionary argument of the 17th and 18th centuries: Because Africans were considered heathens, it was therefore legitimate to enslave them and drag them in chains to a Christian nation. Following their . . . conversion, their moral and material lot were improved, for which black folk should be eternally grateful. . . . Please excuse the analogy, but if someone chops off your fingers and then hands them back to you, should you be "grateful" for having received your mangled fingers, or enraged that they were chopped off in the first place?

10. The reparations claim is a separatist idea that sets African Americans against the nation that gave them freedom.

Again, Horowitz reverses matters. Blacks are already separated from white America in . . . income, family wealth, housing, legal treatment, education, and political representation. . . . To ignore such divisions, and then charge those who raise valid claims against society with promoting divisiveness, offers a classic example of "blaming the victim." And we have already refuted the spurious point that African Americans were the passive recipients of benevolent white individuals or institutions which "gave" them freedom.

SOURCE: Allen and Chrisman (2001, pp. 49–55).

DEBATE QUESTIONS TO CONSIDER

1. Feagin and O'Brien justify reparations for African Americans, in part, by making comparisons to other situations in which victimized groups have been compensated. Are the situations they cite truly comparable to slavery and segregation? If so, what characteristics make the situations comparable? If not, explain the key differences that make the comparisons invalid.

2. Compare the arguments of Horowitz and Allen and Chrisman point by point. For each point, which side of the argument seems more convincing? For each point, what additional information would be necessary to clarify the argument?

3. How would Feagin and O'Brien respond to Horowitz's fifth and sixth points? Would they agree with the rebuttals to these points framed by Allen and Chrisman? What additional points might they make in this argument?

4. What about Horowitz's seventh point regarding victimhood? Is his argument convincing? Why or why not? Do Allen and Chrisman provide a convincing response? Why or why not? What additional points or evidence could be brought to bear to settle this point?

5. Should women also be compensated for their centuries of exclusion from the workplace and politics? Which of Horowitz's points would be most fitting in a debate over reparations for women? How would Allen and Chrisman respond?

MAIN POINTS

- Group relations change as the subsistence technology and the level of development of the larger society change. As nations industrialize and urbanize, dominant-minority relations change from paternalistic to rigid competitive forms.
- In the South, slavery was replaced by de jure segregation, a system that combined racial separation with great inequality. The Jim Crow system was motivated by a need to control labor and was reinforced by coercion and intense racism and prejudice.
- Black southerners responded to segregation in part by moving to northern urban areas. The northern African American population enjoyed greater freedom and developed some political and economic resources, but a large concentration of low-income, relatively powerless African Americans developed in the ghetto neighborhoods.
- In response to segregation, the African American community developed a separate institutional life centered on family, church, and community. An African American middle class emerged, as well as a protest movement.
- African American women remain one of the most exploited groups. Combining work with family roles, African American females were employed mostly in agriculture and domestic service during the era of segregation.
- Industrialization continued throughout the 20th century and has profoundly affected dominant-minority relations. Urbanization, specialization, bureaucratization, and other trends have changed the shape of race relations, as have the changing structure of the occupational sector and the growing importance of education. Group relations have shifted from rigid to fluid competitive. Modern institutional discrimination is one of the major challenges facing minority groups.

STUDY SITE ON THE WEB

For chapter-specific resources, such as self-quizzes, videos, and flashcards, go to **www.sagepub.com/healeyregc6e.**

FOR FURTHER READING

Bluestone, Barry, & Harrison, Bennet. 1982. *The Deindustrialization of America*. New York: Basic Books.

The classic analysis of the shift from a manufacturing to a service-based, information society

Feagin, Joe R., & Feagin, Clairece Booher. 1986. *Discrimination American Style: Institutional Racism and Sexism*. Malabar, FL: Robert E. Krieger.

A comprehensive and provocative look at modern institutional discrimination

Geschwender, James A. 1978. *Racial Stratification in America*. Dubuque, IA: William C. Brown.

Pincus, Fred. 2003. *Reverse Discrimination: Dismantling the Myth*. Boulder, CO: Lynne Reiner.

A compact, masterful review of the myths and realities surrounding affirmative action

Wilson, William J. 1973. *Power, Racism, and Privilege: Race Relations in Theoretical and Sociohistorical Perspectives*. New York: Free Press.

Woodward, C. Vann. 1974. *The Strange Career of Jim Crow* (3rd ed.). New York: Oxford University Press.

Three outstanding analyses of black-white relations in the United States, with a major focus on the historical periods covered in this chapter

QUESTIONS FOR REVIEW AND STUDY

1. A corollary to two themes from Chapter 4 is presented at the beginning of Chapter 5. How exactly does the material in this chapter illustrate the usefulness of this corollary?

2. Explain paternalistic and rigid competitive relations and link them to industrialization. How does the shift from slavery to de jure segregation illustrate the dynamics of these two systems?

3. What was the "Great Migration" to the North? How did it change American race relations?

4. Explain the transition from rigid competitive to fluid competitive relations and explain how this transition is related to the coming of postindustrial society. Explain the roles of urbanization, bureaucracy, the service sector of the job market, and education in this transition.

5. What is modern institutional discrimination? How does it differ from "traditional" institutional discrimination? Explain the role of affirmative action in combating each.

6. Explain the impact of industrialization and globalization on gender relations. Compare and contrast these changes with the changes that occurred for racial and ethnic minority groups.

7. Explain the relevance of the quotation that opens this chapter. How is racial stratification a "moving target"? Could the same statement be applied to gender inequality? How?

8. What efforts have been made on your campus to combat modern institutional discrimination? How effective have these programs been?

INTERNET RESEARCH PROJECT

In this project, you will extend the treatment of de jure segregation in this chapter by visiting a website titled "The Rise and Fall of Jim Crow" (http://www.pbs.org/wnet/jimcrow/index.html). The website is related to a documentary series, which can be ordered from the website and is well worth viewing.

The website has five subsections, and you should explore each and take the "Jim Crow Quiz" under the "Tools & Activities" link. As you browse the site, find answers to each of the questions below. (NOTE: Your instructor may have different or additional questions.)

QUESTIONS

1. What "strange fruit" did Billie Holiday sing about?

2. In what year did Louisiana ban marriages between "white persons and persons of color?"

3. What state, in 1876, provided that schools could be segregated if there were 15 or more "colored" children?

4. In Florida in 1909, what was the fine for "occupying" a train car other than the one designated for one's race?

5. In what year was Wilberforce University in Ohio founded? Who was Wilberforce? What was the mission of this institution?

6. What were the following people best known for? Where did they live and what were their dates of birth and death?
   a. Sidney Bechet
   b. Madam C. J. Walker
   c. Ida B. Wells
   d. Walter White
   e. Ned Cobb

7. What was the Brownsville Affair of 1906? How does this incident illustrate the dynamics of the Jim Crow era?

8. Why is the *Plessy v. Ferguson* Supreme Court decision important? What was its relationship to the Jim Crow system? What events led to this decision?

9. What happened during the Red Summer of 1919? How do these events illustrate the dynamics of the Jim Crow system and American race relations in general?

10. What was the relevance of the following organizations for Jim Crow?
    a. The Democratic Party
    b. The Populist Party
    c. The National Urban League
    d. The Brotherhood of Sleeping Car Porters

REACTIONS

Using the information and insights you gathered from the website, along with the material in this chapter, write an essay in which you explain the legal, political, economic, and social dimensions of Jim Crow segregation, citing specific examples. How did the system control blacks, institutionalize racial stratification, and sustain the privilege of whites? (*Your instructor may have more specific or different instructions.*)

OPTIONAL GROUP DISCUSSION

Discuss what you learned from the website and this chapter with a group of your classmates. Use your reaction essay to help guide your thoughts and focus the discussion. You might organize the discussion around questions such as the following. (NOTE: Your instructor may have more specific or different instructions.)

1. Why did de jure segregation happen? What was at stake? Who gained and who lost? Be sure to discuss class and gender differences in connection with these issues.

2. How was the Jim Crow system sustained across time? What was the role of prejudice and racism? Subsistence technology? Law and custom? How was violence used to enforce the system? What organizations were involved in the creation and persistence of segregation?

3. What does it mean to call this system "rigid competitive"? How did it differ from the paternalistic system of slavery?

4. How did the black community react to segregation? What means of resistance and escape were available? Were they effective? Why or why not?

5. Why did de jure segregation end? What macrolevel changes in subsistence technology made segregation untenable? Why?

NOTES

1. Massey (2007, p. 54).

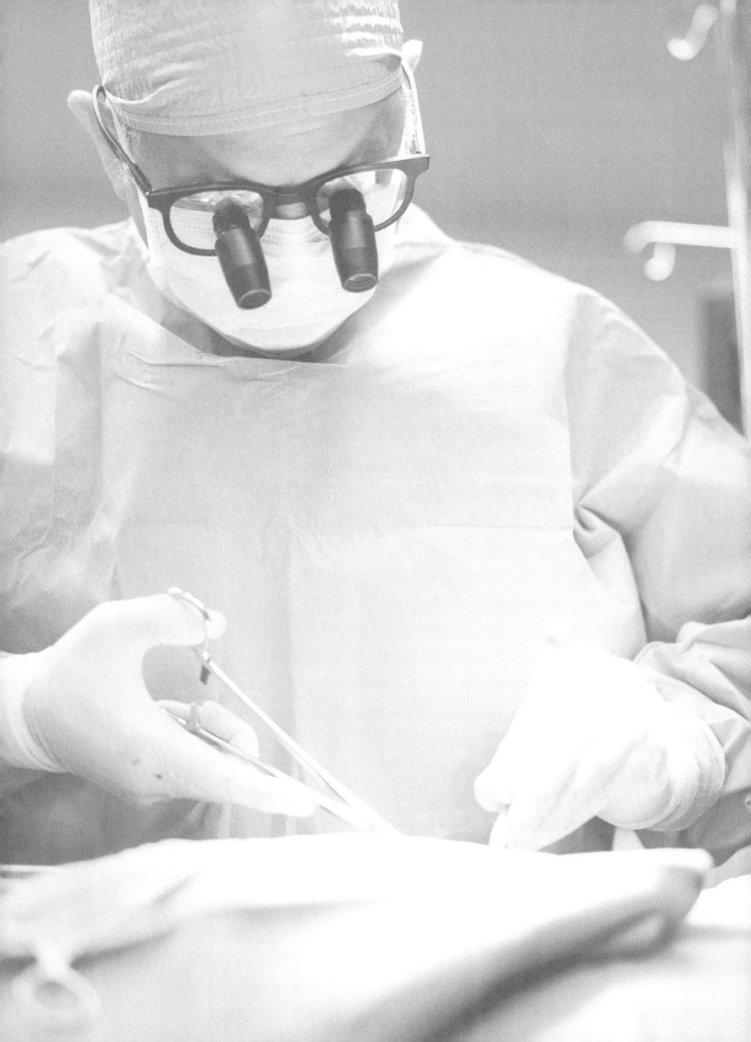

PART III

UNDERSTANDING DOMINANT-MINORITY RELATIONS IN THE UNITED STATES TODAY

Chapter 6 African Americans: From Segregation to Modern Institutional Discrimination and Modern Racism

Chapter 7 American Indians: From Conquest to Tribal Survival in a Postindustrial Society

Chapter 8 Hispanic Americans: Colonization, Immigration, and Ethnic Enclaves

Chapter 9 Asian Americans: "Model Minorities"?

UNDERSTANDING DOMINANT-MINORITY RELATIONS IN THE UNITED STATES TODAY

In Part III, we turn to contemporary intergroup relations. The emphasis is on the present situation of American minority groups, but the recent past is also investigated to see how present situations developed. We explore the ways minority and dominant groups respond to changing American society and to each other and how minority groups define and pursue their own self-interests in interaction with other groups, American culture and values, and the institutions of the larger society.

The themes and ideas developed in the first two parts of this text will continue to be central to the analysis. For example, the case studies are presented in an order that roughly follows the Blauner hypothesis: Colonized groups are presented first, and we end with groups created by immigration. Also, we will continue to rely on the concepts of the Noel hypothesis to analyze and explain contemporary dominant-minority patterns.

The history and present conditions of each minority group are unique, and no two groups have had the same experiences. To help identify and understand these differences, the concepts developed in the first two parts of this text and a common comparative frame of reference are used throughout Part III. We stress assimilation and pluralism; inequality and power; and prejudice, racism, and discrimination. For ease of comparison, the final sections of Chapters 6 through 9 use the same headings and subheadings, in the same order. Much of the conceptual frame of reference employed in these case studies can be summarized in seven themes. The first six themes are based on material from previous chapters; the last is covered in the forthcoming chapters.

IMAGE: Getty/Dimitri Vervitsiotis.

1. Consistent with the Noel hypothesis, the present conditions of America's minority groups reflect their contact situations, especially the nature of their competition with the dominant group (e.g., competition over land vs. competition over labor) and the size of the power differential between groups at the time of contact.

2. Consistent with the Blauner hypothesis, minority groups created by colonization experience economic and political inequalities that have lasted longer and been more severe than those experienced by minority groups created by immigration.

3. Power and economic differentials and barriers to upward mobility are especially pronounced for groups identified by racial or physical characteristics, as opposed to cultural or linguistic traits.

4. Consistent with the themes stated in Chapters 4 and 5, dominant-minority relations reflect the economic and political characteristics of the larger society and change as those characteristics change. Changes in the subsistence technology of the larger society are particularly consequential for dominant-minority relations. The shift from a manufacturing to a service economy (deindustrialization) is one of the key factors shaping dominant-minority relations in the United States today.

5. As we saw in Chapter 3, the "mood" of the dominant group over the past four decades combines a rejection of blatant racism with the belief that the modern United States is nondiscriminatory and that success is attainable for all who are willing to work hard enough. It is also common for dominant group Americans to believe that further reforms of the larger society or special programs or treatment for minorities are unnecessary and unjustified. Efforts to address contemporary minority group problems must deal with the pervasive "modern racism" of the dominant group.

6. The development of group relations, both in the past and for the future, can be analyzed in terms of assimilation (more unity) and pluralism (more diversity). Group relations in the past (e.g., the degree of assimilation permitted or required of the minority group) reflected mainly dominant group needs and wishes. Although the pressure for Americanization remains considerable, there is more flexibility and variety in group relations today.

7. Since World War II, minority groups have gained significantly more control over the direction of group relationships. This trend reflects the decline of traditional prejudice in the larger society and the successful efforts of minority groups to protest, resist, and change patterns of exclusion and domination. These successes have been possible in large part because American minority groups have increased their share of political and economic resources.

PUBLIC SOCIOLOGY ASSIGNMENTS

LINDA M. WALDRON

ASSIGNMENT 1: SCHOOL CAFETERIAS AND RACE RELATIONS

In 1999, social psychologist Beverly Tatum Daniels published a bestselling book whose title posed a rather provocative question: *Why Are All of the Black Kids Sitting Together? And*

Other Discussions of Race. Daniels' interest in this question began when considering her own childhood experience, growing up as an African American girl who attended a predominantly white school. She grew interested in why, today—despite the racial diversity of schools and progress in race relations—children still tend to self-segregate by race and ethnicity. Her book draws on racial identity theory to consider the process by which children develop meaning and significance in relation to a particular race or ethnic group, a process that she argues happens in a social and cultural context involving not just our family and friends but larger structures of politics, media, and the history of our society. This assignment requires you to consider whether or not "all the black kids are sitting together" in your own school's cafeteria.

Step 1

Get a sense of what the overall racial breakdown of your school is. Using your school's website, look up some demographic information about the student population. At minimum, most schools will provide percentages of the basic racial and ethnic categories (i.e., white, African American, Hispanic, Asian American, Native American). If you cannot find this information on your school's website, consider visiting the National Center for Education Statistics website (http://nces.edu.gov), which provides institutional profiles of every school in the United States under the "School, College, and Library Search" link.

Step 2

Visit your site before you begin any observations and create a diagram that represents the seating chart of the cafeteria. You may want to recreate this on your computer and make several copies of it so you can easily take notes on the seating patterns of the people you are observing.

Step 3

Pick a typical mealtime (breakfast, lunch, or dinner) to observe a cafeteria at your school for several days. If your school has more than one cafeteria—for example, one in each dorm—consider observing multiple sites.

Step 4

Spend 1 hour each day taking notes of the race and ethnicity of the students in relationship to their seating patterns. Keep in mind, your observations should be unobtrusive; so the race or ethnicity you identify for each person you observe will be somewhat flawed since it will be based on your *perception* of the individual's race rather than on actual knowledge of his or her identity. In addition to keeping track of the race and ethnicity of individuals at each table, try to take notes on anything else that seems significant, such as the gender of the individuals, clothing, or conversations that people may be having.

Step 5

Try to quantify your results to see if there is a relationship between race and ethnicity and seating patterns. If it appears that everyone at the table knows one another, then use the number of tables as your base of observation for calculating some simple frequencies. If not, try to determine the overall number of groups and use that as your base of observation.

Consider how many groups of people are sitting in interracial groupings. How large or small are the interracial groups compared with the monoracial groups? (For example, maybe there is only one group of interracial cohorts, but this group has 12 people in it, as opposed to tables of monoracial cohorts that have only 2 or 3 people.) What is the race or ethnicity of people who appear to be sitting alone? Since people often get up and down during a meal-time, it may be useful to pick just one moment in time to do this. For example, at 11 a.m., of the 10 tables observed, 5 appeared to have mixed racial groups, 2 appeared to be all white, 2 appeared to be all black, and 1 appeared to be all Hispanic.

Step 6

Use your knowledge of the school to consider *why* students may be sitting together, *beyond* race. For example, did it seem as though one table was a group of freshmen that might be sitting together just because they were all from the same dorm? Was one table a group of students who appeared to be studying for a big final exam? Was another table a group of basketball players or fraternity members?

Step 7

What did you learn about the self-segregation of students by race and ethnicity? Does it seem to exist at your school? What surprised you the most about what you observed?

Step 8

Consider the relationships among all the data you collected. How might the sheer number of students of each racial or ethnic group at your school influence how students decide to sit together? Is there a relationship between the athletic recruiting at your school and minority student enrollment? Were there some organizations on campus that seemed to foster better interracial relations than others?

Step 9

Think about the possible limitations of your observations. (Hint: I already mentioned one in Step 4.) Also, consider both the positive and negative reasons why race and ethnicity might influence how and why people interact at your school.

ASSIGNMENT 2: EDUCATIONAL TESTING GAPS

In an effort to address growing concerns over educational inequality, the No Child Left Behind Act (NCLB) now mandates that schools monitor and report on the progress of several subgroups of students, including major racial and ethnic groups, students with disabilities, economically disadvantaged students, and limited English proficient students. They must also report scores based on gender and migrant status, although these categories are not factored into the Adequate Yearly Progress report. What this means is that in order for schools to pass their yearly progress report, they need not only to demonstrate that the entire student population is learning, but they must show evidence that these subgroups of students are also succeeding.

As research suggests, students of color and low-income students are much more likely than their white and middle-class counterparts to attend overcrowded schools, be taught by unqualified teachers, drop out of school, be tracked into remedial classes, and not attend college. The purpose of this provision is to hold schools accountable for failing to meet the needs of minority and at-risk students, although certainly critics contend that this mandate doesn't necessarily measure effective teaching and learning, or why the achievement gap continues to persist. This assignment requires you to investigate these issues further.

Step 1

Pick either your hometown school or a local school district to study for this project. Begin by accessing the school's latest NCLB report card. Although this is public information, states provide this information in different places. You might begin by searching your state's Department of Education website, as well as the website for the individual school or local board of education. You can also gain valuable insight by visiting the National Center for Education Statistics' website (http://nces.ed.gov).

Step 2

Look for "proficient" and "advanced" rates or percentage of students who "meet or exceed target" for the entire school as well as rates that are disaggregated by various subgroups. At a minimum, you should be able to find language arts literacy and math scores, although some districts may provide science scores as well.

Step 3

Compare your school's test scores to the rest of the school district. For example, if you are investigating a high school, see what the scores look like for the elementary and middle schools that feed into that high school. Are test scores getting better or worse as students progress in school? Or, if there are several high schools in the area, how does your school fare in comparison with the others?

Step 4

Try to find other indicators of achievement that your school has made available. This might include graduation rates, dropout rates, SAT scores, or teacher qualifications.

Step 5

Summarize your findings in a one-page paper. How successful is your school in meeting the needs of different racial and ethnic groups, economically disadvantaged students, and limited English proficient students?

Step 6

Investigate this issue further by interviewing teachers and administrators at the school. This part of the project may require you to go through your university's Institutional Review Board (IRB) for Protection of Human Subjects to ensure ethical research practices. Even if your school does not require IRB approval for this level of research, make sure you follow the best practices set forth by your university's IRB. This includes explaining the benefits of the project to your participants, letting them know that it is a confidential interview and you will take certain measures to protect their identity, and explaining to them any risks that may be involved in answering your questions.

If possible, ask permission to record the interview so you can guarantee accuracy with the participant's responses. Otherwise, take detailed notes during the interview and be sure to transcribe it immediately in order to recall as much detail as possible.

Step 7

Develop a standard set of 8 to 10 open-ended interview questions that address the NCLB mandate as well as the specific results of your investigation into test scores at the school. Open-ended questions generally begin with *how* or *what*. For example, "How do you as a teacher prepare your students for standardized tests?" "What are some challenges that different racial and ethnic groups face at your school?" "How have the new NCLB provisions changed the way you teach?" Asking "how" and "what" questions generally helps you avoid leading questions and provides an avenue for understanding your participants' perspectives on education inequality and the NCLB test results.

Step 8

Treat this as a semistructured interview. This means you will ask the same set of questions to each participant to provide consistent and systematic results, yet you can also ask follow-up questions that allow you to probe for more answers.

Step 9

Transcribe your interviews and look for patterns of responses among your participants. How do teachers understand educational inequality among different racial and ethnic groups at their school? What is the principal's perspective on NCLB's new provisions for reporting test scores, and how does it compare with the teachers' perspectives? How do these educators explain the results of their school's NCLB report card?

Write a thank you letter to your participants for the time they devoted to your research project.

Step 10

Consider the benefits and limitations of this NCLB mandate. What did you learn about the academic achievement gap at your school? How does this provision highlight continuing issues of educational inequity? How is this mandate problematic? What other methods for measuring success or failure of minority students were suggested by your teachers and administrators? What progress has your school made to address the achievement gap of minority and economically disadvantaged students? What further work is still needed?

Use your findings to write a two- to three-page report to share with educators throughout the school district to help them better understand and deal with education inequality.

ASSIGNMENT 3: LITERACY VOLUNTEER

Illiteracy in the United States used to be quite common. In the latter part of the 19th century and beginning of the 20th century, about 20% of all Americans and 80% of African Americans were illiterate. The standard for literacy at this time was pretty basic though. In

1840, the U.S. Census Bureau asked individuals only if they could read or write a simple sentence; those who said "yes" were classified as literate. Today, a much more complex understanding of literacy exists, so it is likely that by today's standard, an even larger percentage of people in the 1900s would be classified as illiterate.

Although literacy rates have improved significantly and the gap between black and white literacy has narrowed, the United States still faces many challenges when it comes to literacy.

In 2003, the U.S. Department of Education conducted the National Assessment of Adult Literacy (NAAL), which provides one of the most comprehensive assessments of literacy rates to date. The project studied adults ages 16 and older, including inmates living in federal and state prisons, and found that about 14% of adults had *below* basic prose literacy skills. This means that around 30 million Americans are functionally illiterate and have only the simplest literacy skills: the ability to sign one's name or fill out a bank deposit slip. Unfortunately, there are still about 11 million adults who are nonliterate—lacking the ability to communicate, read, or write even the simplest sentence, word, or in some cases, letter of the alphabet.

Certain subgroups continue to face a higher risk of illiteracy. These include African Americans and Hispanics, as well as people who did not graduate from high school, people with disabilities, the elderly, and people for whom English is a second language. There are some obvious problems associated with low literacy rates. Illiterate individuals struggle to stay in school, pay their bills, and read the label on their prescription pill bottle or a book to their child. They also face higher unemployment rates, tend to make lower salaries than their literate counterparts, and are more likely to engage in criminal activity or be incarcerated. In fact, about 70% of all inmates are at or below a basic literacy level, and almost 1 in 5 are completely illiterate.

This assignment asks you to face this challenge directly by working in your community to help solve the problem of illiteracy.

Step 1

Begin by trying to gain an understanding of the different ways that literacy is measured. NAAL breaks literacy down into three areas: prose, document, and quantitative. Visit the NAAL website (http://nces.ed.gov/naal/) to learn more about what it means to have below basic, basic, intermediate, and proficient literacy skills.

Step 2

Learn about literacy rates in your community. The NAAL website allows you to search both city and state rates (http://nces.ed.gov/naal/estimates/index.aspx). How does your community fare in terms of literacy?

Step 3

Identify a nonprofit or faith-based organization in your community that is working with adults who are struggling with communicating, reading, or writing in English. This might include programs that target recent immigrants or English as a second language (ESL) learners. If you cannot find an organization, contact your local school district. Many schools provide adult education classes or ESL classes for parents or other community members.

Step 4

Contact the local organization with which you hope to volunteer and meet with the person in charge of volunteers. Keep in mind many organizations might require training before they allow you to volunteer. Others may ask that you commit to a certain number of service hours. This is to protect the people they serve and to avoid problems associated with volunteers coming and going.

Step 5

Tutoring is just one form of service you might provide, so don't limit yourself if you feel uncomfortable tutoring or the organization does not provide this type of service. The organization may need your help in other ways, such as organizing a book drive, putting together a fundraising event, or raising awareness in the community. Be open to the multiple ways you might help fight the problem of illiteracy.

Step 6

Keep a reflective journal for each day of service. You should include at least one of these elements in your journal entries:

- *Successes of the day*: What went efficiently or was enjoyable? Reflect on why it was successful.
- *Challenges of the day*: What tasks were inefficient, awkward, or frustrating? Reflect on why they were challenging.
- *Connection to the course*: Did anything happen that relates to course topics, concepts, or theories?
- *Connection to your career*: Are you learning things that might help you in your future career?

Step 7

Write a final paper about your experience. Unlike your journal, which is more of a summary of each day, analyze and reflect critically on the significant issues raised in your volunteer experience. Evaluate any crucial issues you learned about illiteracy in your community. Consider what you learned from this experience and why it is important—to you personally and to the broader society. Finally, consider how you can use what you have learned from this experience as you embark on both your college and future career.

Step 8

Congratulate yourself for making a difference in improving the lives of people in your community!

ASSIGNMENT 4: SURVIVAL AND PROMOTION OF ENDANGERED LANGUAGES

Many sociologists and anthropologists argue that without language, there can be no culture. Language binds people together, facilitates cooperation and education among groups of people, and is the avenue for sharing and sustaining stories, songs, religion, rituals, and norms of a society.

This piece of culture is in danger though. Over the past 500 years, about half of all languages have become extinct. Today, the United Nations estimates that there are about 6,000 languages in existence but that nearly half will disappear by the end of the century.

The disappearance of a language most often represents a broader power struggle in society. Throughout history, dominant groups have tried to suppress language as a method of oppression and control of indigenous people in particular. For example, in 1870, the U.S. government began forcing Native Americans into boarding schools, demanding that they leave their families behind and relinquish their indigenous language for English. This policy to assimilate, written as an effort to "civilize" "savage" people, institutionalized racist practices against Native Americans. Many Native Americans have given accounts of abuse and hostility that they faced in boarding schools, an experience that stripped them of their language but also of their identity and culture.

Throughout the world, war, ethnic cleansing, and compulsory education continue to destroy languages and, essentially, the cultures of oppressed people. This assignment will help you understand and appreciate the importance of saving endangered languages.

Step 1

The United Nations Educational, Scientific, and Cultural Organization (UNESCO) has spearheaded efforts to identity and revitalize dying languages. Begin by visiting UNESCO's website (www.unesco.org) and searching for the "Endangered languages" page. Read up on the importance of linguistic diversity and the type of projects the United Nations is undertaking to maintain language vitality.

Step 2

Locate the "Interactive Atlas of the World's Languages in Danger" on UNESCO's website. Pick a country that you would like to investigate and see how many languages are considered vulnerable, endangered, or extinct. Click on the interactive map to learn more about each language. Pick one of the vulnerable or endangered languages to explore further.

Step 3

Find out everything you can about the language you picked. Although UNESCO will provide basic information about the location where the language is spoken and approximately how many people who speak this language are still alive, move your search beyond UNESCO to learn everything you can about the location, people, and history of the language. In particular, try to find out why this language is becoming extinct. UNESCO provides a "Resources" link that includes websites and online resources, but you should use the Internet and your school's library to gather as much information as you can.

Step 4

Since many disappearing languages exist only through oral tradition, many linguists are trying to record disappearing languages. Try to see if you can find an audio file of the language you picked. *National Geographic* has a channel on YouTube called "Enduring Voices" that might provide a good starting point for your search.

Step 5

Whether or not you are able to find an audio file of the language, look for an expert you can interview about it. This might include an academic who studies the topic, an official at the U.S. embassy for the language's country of origin, or even your friend's grandmother who grew up in that country. You will likely have to conduct this as a phone interview, rather than in person. Ask if you can record the interview so you can include it in your presentation.

Step 6

Create a presentation to share with your class on the endangered language that you researched. In an effort to make this presentation as engaging as possible, try to include as much audio and visual content as you can find.

The goals of this presentation should be to (1) inform your audience about the significance of the language you studied, (2) teach your audience about the people and place from which this language comes, (3) identify why and how this language has become endangered, and (4) convince the audience that language preservation is intricately tied to the preservation of culture.

Step 7

Since there are thousands of languages and not a lot is known about many of them, share your findings with the public. Return to one of the websites or educational centers you visited during your search for information. E-mail a copy of your presentation to a person in charge. You never know, your presentation may provide much-needed research on an endangered language and may help increase the likelihood that the language you studied will remain in existence.

6

African Americans

From Segregation to Modern Institutional Discrimination and Modern Racism

When America catches a cold, African Americans get pneumonia.

—Traditional folk saying

A century ago, African Americans were primarily a southern, rural peasantry, victimized by de jure segregation, exploited by the sharecropping system of agriculture, and blocked from the better-paying industrial and manufacturing jobs in urban areas. Segregation had disenfranchised them and stripped them of the legal and civil rights they had briefly enjoyed during Reconstruction. As we saw in Chapter 5, the huge majority of African Americans had limited access to quality education, few political rights, few occupational choices, and few means of expressing their grievances to the larger society or the world.

Today, African Americans are highly urbanized, dispersed throughout the United States, and represented in every occupation. The single most significant sign of the progress African Americans have made is, without question, the election of Barack Obama to the presidency of the United States, but members of the group are visible across the board at the highest levels of American society: from the Supreme Court to corporate boardrooms to the most prestigious universities. Some of the best-known, most successful, most respected (and wealthiest) people in the world have been African Americans: Martin Luther King Jr., Malcolm X, Michael Jordan, Jesse Jackson, Bill Cosby, Toni Morrison, Maya Angelou, Muhammad Ali, Oprah Winfrey, Barbara Jordan, Colin Powell, and Condoleezza Rice, to name just a few. Furthermore, some of the most important and prestigious American corporations (including Merrill Lynch, American Express, and Time Warner) have been led by African Americans.

Compared with 100 years ago, the situation of black Americans today is obviously much improved. The journey to racial equality and a truly colorblind society is, however, far from accomplished. As we shall see in this chapter, a large percentage of black Americans remain on the margins of society: excluded, segregated, and victimized by persisting inequalities in opportunity, education, health care, housing, and jobs. Even the more fortunate segments of the black community remain in a tenuous situation: They have fewer resources to fall back on in hard times and weaker connections to the sources of power and privilege. The glittering success stories of the few obscure the continuing struggles of the many, and racism, prejudice, and discrimination continue to be significant problems. The greater vulnerability of the group is captured in the quote that opens this chapter: Hard times for America can mean disaster for black Americans.

To understand black-white relations in the present, we must deal with the watershed events of the recent past: the end of de jure segregation, the triumph (and limitations) of the civil rights movement of the 1950s and 1960s, the urban riots and Black Power movement of the 1960s, and the continuing racial divisions within U.S. society since the 1970s. Behind these events, we can see the powerful pressures of industrialization and modernization, the shift from rigid to fluid competitive group relations, deindustrialization and modern institutional discrimination, changing distributions of power and forms of intergroup competition, the shift from traditional prejudice to modern racism, and new ideas about assimilation and pluralism. Black-white relations changed as a direct result of protest, resistance, and the concerted actions of thousands of individuals, both black and white.

THE END OF DE JURE SEGREGATION

As a colonized minority group, African Americans entered the 20th century facing extreme inequality, relative powerlessness, and sharp limitations on their freedom. Their most visible enemy was the system of de jure segregation in the South, the rigid competitive system of group relations that controlled the lives of most African Americans.

Why and how did de jure segregation come to an end? Recall from Chapter 5 that dominant-minority relationships change as the larger society and its subsistence technology change. As the United States industrialized and urbanized during the 20th century, a series of social, political, economic, and legal processes were set in motion that ultimately destroyed Jim Crow segregation.

The mechanization and modernization of agriculture in the South had a powerful effect on race relations. As farm work became less labor-intensive and machines replaced people, the need to maintain a large, powerless workforce declined (Geschwender, 1978, pp. 175–177). Thus, one of the primary motivations for maintaining Jim Crow segregation and the sharecropping system of farming lost force.

In addition, the modernization of southern agriculture helped spur the migration northward and to urban areas, as we discussed in Chapter 5. Outside the rural South, African Americans found it easier to register to vote and pursue other avenues for improving their situations. The weight of the growing African American vote was first felt in the 1930s and was large enough to make a difference in local, state, and even national elections by the 1940s. In 1948, for example, President Harry Truman recognized that he could not be reelected without the support of African American voters. As a result, the Democratic Party adopted a civil rights plank in the party platform—the first time since Reconstruction that a national political party had taken a stand on race relations (Wilson, 1973, p. 123).

The weight of these changes accumulated slowly, and no single date or specific event marks the end of de jure segregation. The system ended as it had begun: gradually and in a series of discrete episodes and incidents. By the mid-20th century, resistance to racial change was weakening, and the power resources of African Americans were increasing. This enhanced freedom and strength fueled a variety of efforts that sped the demise of Jim Crow segregation. Although a complete historical autopsy is not necessary here, a general under-standing of the reasons for the death of Jim Crow segregation is essential for an understand-ing of modern black-white relations.

Wartime Developments

One of the first successful applications of the growing stock of black power resources occurred in 1941, as the United States was mobilizing for war against Germany and Japan. Despite the crisis atmosphere, racial discrimination was common, even in the defense industry. A group of African Americans, led by labor leader A. Philip Randolph, head of the Brotherhood of Sleeping Car Porters, threatened to march on Washington to protest the discriminatory treatment.

To forestall the march, President Franklin D. Roosevelt signed Executive Order No. 8802, banning discrimination in defense-related industries, and created a watchdog federal agency, the Fair Employment Practices Commission, to oversee compliance with the new antidis-criminatory policy (Franklin & Moss, 1994, pp. 436–437; Geschwender, 1978, pp. 199–200). President Roosevelt's actions were significant in two ways. First, a group of African Americans not only had their grievances heard at the highest level of society but also succeeded in getting what they wanted. Underlying the effectiveness of the planned march was the rising political and economic power of the African American community outside the South and the need to mobilize all segments of the population for a world war. Second, the federal government made an unprecedented commitment to fair employment rights for African Americans. This alliance between the federal government and African Americans was tentative, but it foreshadowed some of the dynamics of racial change in the 1950s and 1960s.

The Civil Rights Movement

The **civil rights movement** was a multifaceted campaign to end legalized segregation and ameliorate the massive inequalities faced by African Americans. The campaign lasted for decades and included lawsuits and courtroom battles as well as protest marches and demon-strations. We begin our examination with a look at the movement's successful challenge to the laws of racial segregation.

Brown v. Board of Education of Topeka

Undoubtedly, the single most powerful blow to de jure segregation was delivered by the U.S. Supreme Court in *Brown v. Board of Education of Topeka* in 1954. The Supreme Court reversed the *Plessy v. Ferguson* decision of 1896 and ruled that racially separate facilities are inherently unequal and therefore unconstitutional. Segregated school systems—and all other forms of legalized racial segregation—would have to end. The landmark Brown decision was the culmination of decades of planning and effort by the National Association for the Advancement of Colored People (NAACP) and individuals such as Thurgood Marshall, the NAACP's chief counsel (who was appointed to the Supreme Court in 1967).

The strategy of the NAACP was to attack Jim Crow by finding instances in which the civil rights of an African American had been violated and then bringing suit against the relevant governmental agency. These lawsuits were intended to extend far beyond the spe-cific case being argued. The goal was to persuade the courts to declare segregation uncon-stitutional not only in the specific instance being tried but in all similar cases. The Brown (1954) decision was the ultimate triumph of this strategy. The significance of the Supreme Court's decision was not that Linda Brown—the child in whose name the case was argued—would attend a different school or even that the school system of Topeka, Kansas, would be integrated. Instead, the significance was in the rejection of the principle of de jure segregation

in the South and, by implication, throughout the nation. The Brown decision changed the law and dealt a crippling blow to Jim Crow segregation.

The blow was not fatal, however. Southern states responded to the Brown (1954) decision by stalling and mounting campaigns of massive resistance. Jim Crow laws remained on the books for years. White southerners actively defended the system of racial privilege and attempted to forestall change through a variety of means, including violence and intimidation. The Ku Klux Klan (KKK), largely dormant since the 1920s, reappeared along with other racist and terrorist groups, such as the White Citizens' Councils. White politicians and other leaders competed with one another to express the most adamant statements of racist resistance (Wilson, 1973, p. 128). One locality, Prince Edward County in central Virginia, chose to close its public schools rather than integrate. The schools remained closed for 5 years. During that time, the white children attended private, segregated academies, and the county provided no education at all for African American children (Franklin, 1967, p. 644).

Nonviolent Direct Action Protest

The principle established by Brown (1954) was assimilationist: It ordered the educational institutions of the dominant group to be opened up freely and equally to all. Southern states and communities overwhelmingly rejected the principle of equal access and shared facilities. Centuries of racist tradition and privilege were at stake, and considerable effort would be required to overcome southern defiance and resistance. The central force in this struggle was a protest movement, the beginning of which is often traced to Montgomery, Alabama, where on December 1, 1955, Rosa Parks, a seamstress and NAACP member, rode the city bus home from work, as she usually did. As the bus filled, she was ordered to surrender her seat to a white male passenger. When she refused, the police were called and Rosa Parks was jailed for violating a local segregation ordinance.

Although Mrs. Parks was hardly the first African American to be subjected to such indignities, her case stimulated a protest movement in the African American community, and a boycott of the city buses was organized. Participants in the boycott set up car pools, shared taxis, and walked (in some cases, for miles) to and from work. They stayed off the buses for more than a year, until

Freedom riders staging a sit-in at a bus terminal.

© Bettmann/Corbis.

victory was achieved and the city was ordered to desegregate its buses. The Montgomery boycott was led by the Reverend Martin Luther King Jr., the new minister of a local Baptist church.

From these beginnings sprang the protest movement that eventually defeated de jure segregation. The central strategy of the movement involved **nonviolent direct action**, a method by which the system of de jure segregation was confronted head-on, not in the courtroom or in the state legislature but in the streets. The movement's principles of nonviolence were adopted from the tenets of Christianity and from the teachings of Mohandas K. Gandhi, Henry David Thoreau, and others. Dr. King expressed the philosophy in a number of books and speeches (King, 1958, 1963, 1968). Nonviolent protest was intended to confront the forces of evil rather than the people who happened to be doing evil, and it attempted to win the friendship and support of its enemies rather than to defeat or humiliate them. Above all, nonviolent protest required courage and discipline; it was not a method for cowards (King, 1958, pp. 83–84).

The movement used different tactics for different situations, including sit-ins at segregated restaurants, protest marches and demonstrations, prayer meetings, and voter registration drives. The police and terrorist groups such as the KKK often responded to these protests with brutal repression and violence, and protesters were routinely imprisoned, beaten, and attacked by police dogs. The violent resistance sometimes escalated to acts of murder, including the 1963 bombing of a black church in Birmingham, Alabama, which took the lives of four little girls, and the 1968 assassination of Dr. King. Resistance to racial change in the South was intense. It would take more than protests and marches to end de jure segregation, and the U.S. Congress finally provided the necessary tools (see D'Angelo, 2001; Killian, 1975; King, 1958, 1963, 1968; Morris, 1984).

Landmark Legislation

The successes of the protest movement, combined with changing public opinion and the legal principles established by the Supreme Court, coalesced in the mid-1960s to stimulate the passage of two laws that, together, ended Jim Crow segregation. In 1964, at the urging of President Lyndon B. Johnson, the U.S. Congress passed the Civil Rights Act of 1964, banning discrimination on the grounds of race, color, religion, national origin, or gender. The law applied to publicly owned facilities such as parks and municipal swimming pools, businesses and other facilities open to the public, and any programs that received federal aid. Congress followed this up with the Voting Rights Act in 1965, also initiated by President Johnson, which required that the same standards be used to register all citizens in federal, state, and local elections. The act banned literacy tests, whites-only primaries, and other practices that had been used to prevent African Americans from registering to vote. This law gave the franchise back to black southerners and laid the groundwork for increasing black political power. This landmark federal legislation, in combination with court decisions and the protest movement, finally succeeded in crushing Jim Crow.

The Success and Limitations of the Civil Rights Movement

Why did the civil rights movement succeed? A comprehensive list of reasons would be lengthy, but we can cite some of the most important causes of its success, especially those consistent with the general points about dominant-minority relations that have been made in previous chapters.

First, the continuing industrialization and urbanization of the society as a whole—and the South in particular—weakened the Jim Crow, rigid competitive system of minority group control and segregation. We made this point in Chapter 5 when we discussed the impact of the changing subsistence technology and the end of paternalistic controls (see Exhibit 5.6).

Second, following World War II, the United States enjoyed a period of prosperity that lasted into the 1960s. Consistent with the Noel hypothesis, this was important because it reduced the intensity of intergroup competition, at least outside the South. During prosperous times, resistance to change tends to weaken. If the economic "pie" is expanding, the "slices" claimed by minority groups can increase without threatening the size of anyone else's portions, and the prejudice generated during intergroup competition (a la Robber's Cave, Chapter 3) is held in check. Thus, these "good times" muted the sense of threat experienced in the dominant group by the demands for equality made by the civil rights movement.

Third, some of the economic prosperity found its way into African American communities and increased their pool of economic and political resources. Networks of independent, African-American-controlled organizations and institutions, such as churches and colleges, were created or grew in size and power. The increasingly elaborate infrastructure of the black community included protest organizations, such as the NAACP (see Chapter 5), and provided material resources, leadership, and "people power" to lead the fight against segregation and discrimination.

Fourth, the goals of the civil rights movement were assimilationist; the movement embraced the traditional American values of liberty, equality, freedom, and fair treatment. It demanded civil, legal, and political rights for African Americans, rights available to whites automatically. Thus, many whites did not feel threatened by the movement because they saw it as consistent with mainstream American values, especially in contrast with the intense, often violent resistance of southern whites.

Fifth, the perceived legitimacy of the goals of the movement also opened up the possibility of alliances with other groups (white liberals, Jews, college students). The support of others was crucial because black southerners had few resources of their own other than their numbers and their courage. By mobilizing the resources of other, more powerful groups, black southerners forged alliances and created sympathetic support that was brought to bear on their opposition.

Finally, widespread and sympathetic coverage from the mass media, particularly television, was crucial to the success of the movement. The oft-repeated scenario of African Americans being brutally attacked while demonstrating for their rights outraged many Americans and reinforced the moral consensus that eventually rejected "traditional" racial prejudice along with Jim Crow segregation (see Chapter 3).

The southern civil rights movement ended de jure segregation but found it difficult to survive the demise of its primary enemy. The confrontational tactics that had been so effective against the Jim Crow system proved less useful when attention turned to the actual distribution of jobs, wealth, political power, and other valued goods and services. Outside the South, the allocation of opportunity and resources always had been the central concern of the African American community. Let's take a look at these concerns.

DEVELOPMENTS OUTSIDE THE SOUTH

De Facto Segregation

Chapter 5 discussed some of the difficulties encountered by African Americans as they left the rural South. Discrimination by labor unions, employers, industrialists, and white ethnic groups was common. Racial discrimination outside the South was less overt but was still pervasive, especially in housing, education, and employment.

The pattern of racial separation and inequality outside the South is often called **de facto segregation**: segregation resulting from what seems to be, at first glance, the voluntary choices of dominant and minority group members alike. As opposed to the Jim Crow system in the South or apartheid in South Africa, there are no public laws mandating racial separation and it is often assumed that de facto segregation "just happened" as people and groups made decisions about where to live and work or that it resulted from some benign tendency of people to be "with their own kind."

On the contrary, de facto segregation was quite intentional and is best thought of as de jure segregation in thin disguise. Racial segregation outside the South was the direct result of intentionally racist decisions made by governmental and quasi-governmental agencies, such as real-estate boards, school boards, and zoning boards (see Massey & Denton, 1993, pp. 74–114). De facto segregation was created when local and state authorities actively colluded with private citizens behind the scenes, ignored racist practices within their jurisdiction, and "simply refrained from enforcing black social, economic, and political rights so that private discriminatory practices could do their work" (Massey, 2007, p. 57). For example, shortly after World War I, the real-estate board in the city of Chicago adopted a policy that required its members, on penalty of "immediate expulsion," to enforce racial residential segregation (Cohen & Taylor, 2000, p. 33). The city itself passed no Jim Crow laws, but the end result was the same: Black Americans were consigned to a separate and unequal status.

African Americans outside the South faced more poverty, higher unemployment, and lower-quality housing and schools than did whites, but there was no clear equivalent of Jim Crow to attack or blame for these patterns of inequality. Thus, the triumphs of the Civil Rights movement had little impact on their lives. In the 1960s, the African American community outside the South expressed its frustration over the slow pace of change in two ways: urban unrest and a movement for change that rose to prominence as the civil rights movement faded.

Urban Unrest

In the mid-1960s, the frustration and anger of urban African American communities erupted into a series of violent uprisings. The riots began in the summer of 1965 in Watts, a neighborhood in Los Angeles, California, and over the next 4 years, virtually every large black urban community experienced similar outbursts. Racial violence was hardly a new phenomenon in America. Race riots had existed as early as the Civil War, and various time periods had seen racial violence of considerable magnitude. The riots of the 1960s were different, however. Most race riots in the past had been attacks by whites against blacks, often including the invasion and destruction of African American neighborhoods (e.g., see D'Orso, 1996; Ellsworth, 1982). The urban unrest of the 1960s, in contrast, consisted largely of attacks by blacks against the symbols of their oppression and frustration. The most obvious targets were white-owned businesses operating in black neighborhoods and the police, who were seen as an army of occupation and whose excessive use of force was often the immediate precipitator of riots (Conot, 1967; National Advisory Commission, 1968).

The Black Power Movement

The urban riots of the 1960s were an unmistakable sign that the problems of race relations had not been resolved with the end of Jim Crow segregation. Outside the South, the problems were different and called for different solutions. Even as the civil rights movement was celebrating its victory in the South, a new protest movement rose to prominence. The **Black Power movement** was a loose coalition of organizations and spokespersons that encompassed a variety of ideas and views, many of which differed sharply from those of the civil rights movement. Some of the central ideas included racial pride ("Black is beautiful" was a key slogan of the day), interest in African heritage, and Black Nationalism. In contrast to the assimilationist goals of the civil rights movement, Black Power groups worked to increase African American control over schools, police, welfare programs, and other public services operating in black neighborhoods.

Most adherents of the Black Power movement felt that white racism and institutional discrimination, forces buried deep in the core of American culture and society, were the primary causes of racial inequality in America. Thus, if African Americans were ever to be truly empowered, they would have to liberate themselves and do it on their own terms. Some Black Power advocates specifically rejected the goal of assimilation into white society, arguing that integration would require blacks to become part of the very system that had for centuries oppressed, denigrated, and devalued them and other peoples of color.

The Nation of Islam

The themes of Black Power voiced so loudly in the 1960s were decades, even centuries, old. Marcus Garvey had popularized many of these ideas in the 1920s, and they were espoused and further developed by the Nation of Islam, popularly known as the Black Muslims, in the 1960s.

The Black Muslims, one of the best-known organizations within the Black Power movement, were angry, impatient, and outspoken. They denounced the hypocrisy, greed, and racism of American society and advocated staunch resistance and racial separation. The Black Muslims did more than talk, however. Pursuing the goals of autonomy and self-determination, they worked hard to create a separate, independent African American economy within the United States. They opened businesses and stores in African American neighborhoods and tried to deal only with other Muslim-owned firms. Their goal was to develop the African American community economically and supply jobs and capital for expansion solely by using their own resources (Essien-Udom, 1962; Lincoln, 1961; Malcolm X, 1964; Wolfenstein, 1993).

The Nation of Islam and other black power groups distinguished between racial separation and racial segregation. The former is a process of empowerment whereby a group becomes stronger as it becomes more autonomous and self-controlled. The latter is a system of inequality in which the African American community is powerless and is controlled by the dominant group. Thus, the Black Power groups were working to find ways in which African Americans could develop their own resources and deal with the dominant group from a more powerful position, a strategy similar to that followed by minority groups that form ethnic enclaves (see Chapter 2).

The best-known spokesman for the Nation of Islam was Malcolm X, one of the most charismatic figures of the 1960s. Malcolm X forcefully articulated the themes of the Black Power movement. Born Malcolm Little, he converted to Islam and joined the Nation of Islam while serving a prison term. He became the chief spokesperson for the Black Muslims and a well-known but threatening figure to the white community. After a dispute with Elijah Muhammad, the leader of the Nation of Islam, Malcolm X founded his own organization, in which he continued to express and develop the ideas of Black Nationalism. Like so many other protest leaders of the era, Malcolm X was assassinated, in 1965.

Black power leaders such as Malcolm X advocated autonomy, independence, and a pluralistic direction for the African American protest movement. They saw the African American community as a colonized, exploited population in need of liberation from the unyielding racial oppression of white America, not integration into the system that was the source of its oppression.

PROTEST, POWER, AND PLURALISM

The Black Power Movement in Perspective

By the end of the 1960s, the riots had ended and the most militant and dramatic manifestations of the Black Power movement had faded. In many cases, the passion of Black Power activists had been countered by the violence of the police and other agencies, and many of the most powerful spokespersons of the movement were dead; others were in jail or in exile. The nation's commitment to racial change wavered and weakened as other concerns, such as the Vietnam War, competed for attention. Richard M. Nixon was elected president in 1968 and made it clear that his administration would not ally itself with the black protest movement. Pressure from the federal government for racial equality was reduced. The boiling turmoil of the mid-1960s faded, but the idea of Black Power had become thoroughly entrenched in the African American community.

In some part, the pluralistic themes of Black Power were a reaction to the failure of assimilation and integration in the 1950s and 1960s. Laws had been passed; court decisions had been widely publicized; and promises and pledges had been made by presidents, members of Congress, ministers, and other leaders. For many African Americans, though, little had changed. The problems of their parents and grandparents continued to constrain and limit their lives and, as far into the future as they could see, the lives of their children. The pluralistic Black Power ideology was a response to the failure to go beyond the repeal of Jim Crow laws and fully implement the promises of integration and equality.

Black Nationalism, however, was, and remains, more than simply a reaction to a failed dream. It was also a different way of defining what it means to be black in America. In the context of black-white relations in the 1960s, the Black Power movement served a variety of purposes. First, along with the civil rights movement, it helped carve out a new identity for African Americans. The cultural stereotypes of black Americans (see Chapter 3) stressed laziness, irresponsibility, and inferiority. This image needed to be refuted, rejected, and buried. The black protest movements supplied a view of African Americans that emphasized power, assertiveness, seriousness of purpose, intelligence, and courage.

Second, Black Power served as a new rallying cry for solidarity and unified action. Following the success of the civil rights movement, these new themes and ideas helped focus attention on "unfinished business": the black-white inequalities that remained in U.S. society.

Finally, the ideology provided an analysis of the problems of American race relations in the 1960s. The civil rights movement had, of course, analyzed race relations in terms of integration, equality of opportunity, and an end to exclusion. After the demise of Jim Crow, that analysis became less relevant. A new language was needed to describe and analyze the continuation of racial inequality. Black Power argued that the continuing problems of U.S. race relations were structural and institutional, not individual or legal. To take the next steps toward actualizing racial equality and justice would require a fundamental and far-reaching restructuring of society. Ultimately, white Americans, as the beneficiaries of the system, would not support such restructuring. The necessary energy and commitment had to come from African Americans pursuing their own self-interests.

The nationalistic and pluralistic demands of the Black Power movement evoked defensiveness and a sense of threat in white society. By questioning the value of assimilation and celebrating a separate African heritage equal in legitimacy with white European heritage, the Black Power movement questioned the legitimacy and worth of Anglo-American values. In fact, many Black Power spokespersons condemned Anglo-American values fiercely and openly and implicated them in the creation and maintenance of a centuries-long system of racial repression. Today, almost 50 years after the success of the civil rights movement, assertive and critical demands by the African American community continue to be perceived as threatening.

Gender and Black Protest

Both the civil rights movement and the Black Power movement tended to be male dominated. African American women were often viewed as supporters of men rather than as equal partners in liberation. Although African American women were heavily involved in the struggle, they were often denied leadership roles or decision-making positions in favor of men. In fact, the women in one organization, the Student Nonviolent Coordinating Committee, wrote position papers to protest their relegation to lowly clerical positions and the frequent references to them as "girls" (Andersen, 1993, p. 284). The Nation of Islam emphasized female subservience, imposing a strict code of behavior and dress for women and separating the sexes in many temple and community activities. Thus, the battle against racism and the battle against sexism were separate struggles with separate and often contradictory agendas, as the black protest movement continued to subordinate women (Amott & Matthaei, 1991, p. 177).

When the protest movements began, however, African American women were already heavily involved in community and church work, and they often used their organizational skills and energy to further the cause of black liberation. In the view of many, African American women were the backbone of the movement, even if they were often relegated to less glamorous but vital organizational work (Evans, 1979).

Photo 6.3

Fannie Lou Hamer speaks out at the Democratic Party convention in 1964.

© Bettmann/Corbis.

Fannie Lou Hamer of Mississippi, an African American who became a prominent leader in the black liberation movement, illustrates the importance of the role played by women. Born in 1917 to sharecropper parents, Hamer's life was so circumscribed that until she attended her first rally at the beginning of the civil rights movement, she was unaware that blacks could—even theoretically—register to vote. The day after the rally, she quickly volunteered to register:

> I guess I'd had any sense I'd a-been a little scared, but what was the point of being scared? The only thing they could do to me was kill me and it seemed like they'd been trying to do that a little bit at a time ever since I could remember. (Evans, 1989, p. 271)

As a result of her activism, Hamer lost her job, was evicted from her house, and was jailed and beaten on a number of occasions. She devoted herself entirely to the civil rights movement and founded the Freedom Party, which successfully challenged the racially segregated Democratic Party and the all-white political structure of the State of Mississippi (Evans, 1979; Hamer, 1967).

Much of the energy that motivated black protest was forged in the depths of segregation and exclusion, a system of oppression that affected all African Americans. Not all segments of the community had the same experience; the realities faced by the black community were, as always, differentiated by class as well as gender. A flavor of life in the Jim Crow South is presented in the Narrative Portrait in this chapter.

Growing Up Black and Female in the Jim Crow South

Feminist intellectual bell hooks was born in Kentucky in the 1950s, at the height of the Jim Crow system. Her family was rural and poor, but she rose from these humble beginnings to earn her doctorate in English. She has written more than 20 books and has devoted her life to a passionate critique of white supremacy, capitalism, and patriarchy. The name under which she writes is a pseudonym, and she does not capitalize it, to stress that her ideas are more important than her name or any other aspect of her identity. She teaches at City College of New York. What class, gender, and other differentiating factors can you identify in the passage? What is the young bell hooks learning about herself and her world?

BONE BLACK

bell hooks

We live in the country. We children do not understand that that means we are among the poor. We do not understand that the outhouses behind many of the houses are still there because running water came here long after they had it in the city. We do not understand that our playmates who are eating laundry starch do so not because the white powder tastes so good but because they are sometimes without necessary food. We do not understand that we wash with the heavy, unsmelling, oddly shaped pieces of homemade lye soap because real soap costs money. We never think about where lye soap comes from. We only know we want to make our skin itch less—that we do not want our mouths to be washed out with it. Because we are poor, because we live in the country, we go to the country school—the little white wood-frame building where all the country kids come. They come from miles and miles away. They come so far because they are black. As they are riding the school buses they pass school after school where children who are white can attend without being bused, without getting up in the wee hours of the morning, sometimes leaving home in the dark.

We are not bused. The school is only a mile or two away from our house. We get to walk. We get to wander aimlessly in the road—until a car comes by. We get to wave at the buses. They are not allowed to stop and give us a ride. We do not understand why. . . .

School begins with chapel. There we recite the Pledge of Allegiance to the Flag. We have no feeling for the flag but we like the words; said in unison, they sound like a chant. We then listen to a morning prayer. We say the Lord's Prayer. It is the singing that makes morning chapel the happiest moment of the day. It is there I learn to sing "Red River Valley." It is a song about missing and longing. I do not understand all the words, only the feeling—warm wet sorrow, like playing games in spring rain. After chapel we go to classrooms.

In the first grade the teacher gives tasting parties. She brings us different foods to taste so that we can know what they are like because we do not eat them in our homes. All of us eagerly await the Fridays when the tasting party will begin. . . .

Mama tells us that most of that food we taste isn't good to eat all the time, that it is a waste of money. We do not understand money. We do not know that we are all poor. We cannot visit many of the friends we make because they live miles and miles away. We have each other after school.

Here at the country school we must always work to raise money—selling candy, raffle tickets, having shows for which tickets are sold. Sold to our parents, neighbors, friends, people without money who are shamed into buying little colored paper they cannot afford, tickets that will help keep the school going. The people with lots of money can buy many tickets—can show that they are "big time." Their flesh is often the color of pigs in the storybook. Somehow they have more money because they are lighter, because their flesh turns pink and pinker, because they dye their hair blond, red, to emphasize the light, lightness of their skin. We children think of them as white. We are so confused by this thing called Race.

We learn about color with crayons. We learn to tell the difference between white and pink and a color they call Flesh. The flesh-colored crayon amuses us. Like white it never shows up on the thick Manila paper they give us to draw on, or on the brown paper sacks we draw on at home. Flesh we know has no relationship to our skin, for we are brown and brown and brown like all good things. And we know that pigs are not pink or white like these flesh people. We secretly love pigs, especially me. I like to watch them lie in the mud, covering themselves in the cool red mud that is like clay, that is flaming red hot like dirt on fire. I like to watch them eat—to feed them. For some weeks now I have been feeding them the coal that is our way of keeping warm in winters. I give them little pieces at a time to hear the crunching sound. I want to give them all the tickets to eat so no one will have to sell them, so mama will not have to complain about the way it adds to her worries that she must now sell tickets. The pigs are disgusted by the tickets. Even when I prod them with a stick they only turn away. They would rather eat coal.

I must sell tickets for a Tom Thumb wedding, one of the school shows. It isn't any fun for children. We get to dress up in paper wedding clothes and go through a ceremony for the entertainment of the adults. The whole thing makes me sick but no one cares. Like every other girl I want to be the bride but I am not chosen. It has always to do with money. The important roles go to the children whose parents have money to give, who will work hard selling tickets. I am lucky to be a bridesmaid, to wear a red crepe paper dress made just for me. I am not thrilled with such luck. I would rather not wear a paper dress, not be in a make-believe wedding. They tell me that I am lucky to be lighter skinned, not black black, not dark brown, lucky to have hair that is almost straight, otherwise I might not be in the wedding at all, otherwise I might not be so lucky.

This luck angers me and when I am angry things always go wrong. We are practicing in our paper dresses, walking down the aisle while the piano music plays a wedding march. We are practicing to be brides, to be girls who will grow up to be given away. My legs would rather be running, itch to go outdoors. My legs are dreaming, adventurous legs. They cannot walk down the aisle without protest. They go too fast. They go too slow. They make everything slow down. The girl walking behind me steps on the red dress; it tears. It moves from my flesh like wind moving against the running legs. I am truly lucky now to have this tear. I hope they will make me sit, but they say No we would not think of taking you out of the show. They know how much every girl wants to be in a wedding. The tear must be mended. The red dress like a woman's heart must break silently and in secret.

SOURCE: hooks (1996, pp. 4–9).

Race in Another America

Traditional antiblack prejudice in the United States includes an array of stereotypes alleging biological inferiority and laziness along with feelings of contempt and dislike. These ideas and emotions reflect the particular history of black-white relations in the United States, especially the centuries of slavery and decades of legally sanctioned racial inferiority. Other nations, even close neighbors to the United States, have different experiences, different histories, different cultures, and different sets of stereotypes and emotions.

One of the key characteristics of traditional U.S. antiblack prejudice is a simple "two-race" view: Everyone belongs to one and only one race, and a person is either black or white. This perception is a legacy of the assumption of black inferiority that was at the heart of both U.S. slavery and Jim Crow segregation in the South. The southern states formalized the racial dichotomy in law as well as custom with the "one-drop rule": Any trace of black ancestry, even "one drop" of African blood, meant that a person was legally black and subject to all the limitations of extreme racial inequality.

This two-race model continues in the present, and many Americans continue to insist on a single racial category for everyone, regardless of actual racial inheritance. This rigid perception will be challenged by the increases in racial inter-marriage and the number of mixed-race individuals, but, in fact, "racial mixing" always has been a part of the U.S. experience, and there always have been people of mixed-race heritage. In the past, especially under slavery, interracial unions were generally coercive, and following the one-drop rule, the offspring were classified, socially and legally, as black. This nation has a long history of ignoring the reality that people can be both black and white.

The U.S. perception of race contrasts sharply with the racial sensibilities in many other nations. Throughout Central and South America, for example, race is perceived as a continuum of possibilities and combinations, not as a simple split between white and black. This does not mean that these societies are egalitarian, racially open utopias. To the contrary, they incorporate a strong sense of status and position and clear notions of who is higher and who is lower. However, other factors, especially social class, are considered more important than race as criteria for judging and ranking other people. In fact, social class can affect perceptions of skin color to the extent that people of higher status can be seen as "whiter" than those of lower status, regardless of actual skin color.

One interesting comparison is between the United States and Brazil, the largest nation in South America. The racial histories of Brazil and the United States run parallel in many ways, and prejudice, discrimination, and racial inequality are very much a part of Brazilian society, past and present. Like other Central and South Americans, however, Brazilians recognize many gradations of skin color and the different blends that are possible in people of mixed-race heritage. Commonly used terms in Brazil include *branco* (white), *moreno* (brown), *moreno claro* (light brown), *claro* (light), *pardo* (mixed race), and *negro* and *preto* (black). Some reports count scores of Brazilian racial categories, but Telles (2004, p. 82) reports that fewer than 10 are in common use. Still, this system is vastly more complex than the traditional U.S. perception of race.

Why the differences in racial perception? Why does Brazil have a more open-ended, less rigid system than the United States? This issue cannot be fully explored in these few paragraphs, but we can make the point that the foundation for this perception was laid in the distant past. The Portuguese, the colonial conquerors of Brazil, were mostly single males, and they took brides from other racial groups. These intermarriages produced a large class of mixed-race people. Also, slavery was not so thoroughly equated with race in Brazil as it was in North America. Although slave status was certainly regarded as undesirable and unfortunate, it did not carry the same presumption of racial inferiority as in North America, where slavery, blackness, and inferiority were tightly linked in the dominant ideology, an equation with powerful echoes in the present. Also, after slavery ended, Brazil did not go through a period of legalized racial segregation like the Jim Crow system in the U.S. South or apartheid in South Africa. Thus, there was less need politically, socially, or economically to divide people into rigid groups in Brazil.

I should stress that Brazil is not a racial utopia, as is sometimes claimed. Prejudice is an everyday reality, the legacy of slavery is strong, and there is a high correlation between skin color and social status. Black Brazilians have much higher illiteracy, unemployment, and poverty rates and are much less likely to have access to a university education. Whites dominate the more prestigious and lucrative occupations and the leadership positions in the economy and in politics, whereas blacks are concentrated at the bottom of the class system, with mixed-race people in between (Kuperman, 2001, p. 25). It would be difficult to argue that race prejudice in Brazil is less intense than in the United States. On the other hand, given the vastly different perceptions of race in the two societies, we can conclude that Brazilian prejudice has a different content and emotional texture and reflects a different contact situation and national history.

BLACK-WHITE RELATIONS SINCE THE 1960S: ISSUES AND TRENDS

Black-white relations have changed over the past five decades, of course, but the basic outlines of black inequality and white dominance have persisted. To be sure, some progress has been made in integrating society and eliminating racial inequality. The election of Barack Obama—unimaginable just a few decades ago (and maybe a few years ago)—stands as one unmistakable symbol of racial progress, a breakthrough so stunning that it has led many to conclude that America is now "postracial" and that people's fates are no longer connected to the color of their skin, an argument that is easily refuted by a consideration of the trends and statistics presented in this chapter.

Without denying the signs of progress, the situation of the African American community today has stagnated on many dimensions, and the problems that remain are deep-rooted and inextricably mixed with the structure and functioning of modern American society. As was the case in earlier eras, racism and racial inequality today cannot be addressed apart from the trends of change in the larger society, especially changes in subsistence technology. This section examines the racial separation that continues to characterize so many areas of U.S. society and applies many of the concepts from previous chapters to present-day black-white relations.

Continuing Separation

More than 40 years ago, a presidential commission charged with investigating black urban unrest warned that the United States was "moving towards two societies, one black, one white, separate and unequal" (National Advisory Commission, 1968). We could object to the commission's use of the phrase "moving towards," with its suggestion that U.S. society was at one time racially unified, but the warning still seems prophetic. Without denying the progress toward integration that has been made, African Americans and white Americans continue to live in worlds that are, indeed, separate and unequal.

Each group has committed violence and hate crimes against the other, but the power differentials and the patterns of inequality that are the legacy of our racist past guarantee that African Americans will more often be seen as "invaders" pushing into areas where they do not belong and are not wanted. Sometimes, the reactions to these perceived intrusions are immediate and bloody, but other, subtler attempts to maintain the exclusion of African Americans continue to be part of everyday life, even at the highest levels of society. For example, in a lawsuit reminiscent of Jim Crow days, a national restaurant chain was accused of discriminating against African American customers by systematically providing poor service. In 2004, the company agreed to pay $8.7 million to settle the lawsuit (McDowell, 2004). In another example, Texaco, in 1996, was sued for discrimination by several of its minority employees. The case was settled out of court after a tape recording of company executives plotting to destroy incriminating documents and making racist remarks was made public (Eichenwald, 1996).

Many African Americans mirror the hostility of whites, and as the goals of full racial equality and justice continue to seem remote, frustration and anger continue to run high. While Obama's election and inauguration stirred strong optimism and positive attitudes toward the future in the black community, the more typical mood is pessimistic (recall our discussion of public opinion poll results and the differences in black and white perceptions of U.S. race relations from Chapter 1).

The discontent and frustration has been manifested in violence and riots; the most widely publicized example was the racial violence that began with the 1991 arrest and beating of Rodney King by police officers in Los Angeles. The attack on King was videotaped and shown repeatedly on national and international news, and contrary to the expectations of most who saw the videotape, the police officers were acquitted of almost all charges in April 1992. On hearing word of the acquittals, African American communities in several cities erupted in violence. The worst disturbance occurred in the Watts section of Los Angeles, where 58 people lost their lives and millions of dollars of property was damaged or destroyed (Wilkens, 1992).

In some ways, the riot following the 1992 King verdict was different from the riots of the 1960s. The more recent event was multiracial and involved Hispanics as well as African Americans. In fact, most of the 58 fatalities were from these two groups. Also, many of the businesses looted and burned were owned by Korean Americans, and many of the attacks were against whites directly, as in the beating of truck driver Reginald Denny (also, ironically, captured on videotape).

In other ways, the events were similar. Both were spontaneous and expressed diffuse but bitter discontent with the racial status quo. Both signaled the continuing racial inequality, urban poverty and despair, and the reality of separate nations, unequal and hostile. (For more on these urban uprisings, see Gooding-Williams, 1993.)

The Criminal Justice System and African Americans

No area of race relations is more volatile and controversial than the relationship between the black community and the criminal justice system. There is considerable mistrust and resentment of the police among African Americans, and the perception that the entire criminal justice system is stacked against them is common. These perceptions are not without justification: The police and other elements of the criminal justice system have a long tradition of abuse, harassment, and mistreatment of black citizens. The perception of the police as the

Photo 6.4

A Los Angeles policeman guards stores against looters in 1992.

© Peter Turnley/ CORBIS.

enemy and the entire criminal justice system as an occupying force remains widespread. For example, a 2008 nationally representative poll found that only 12% of black respondents—as opposed to 42% of white respondents—had a "great deal" of confidence that local police would treat blacks and whites equally. Furthermore, 67% of blacks—versus only 32% of whites—thought that the American justice system was biased against blacks (Gallup, 2008).

The great majority of social science research in this area has documented the continuing bias of the criminal justice system, at all levels, against African Americans (and other minorities). In a comprehensive summary of this research, Rosich (2007) concludes that, while blatant and overt discrimination has diminished over the past few decades, the biases that remain have powerful consequences for the black community, even though they often are more subtle and harder to tease out. Even slight acts of discrimination against blacks can accumulate over the stages of processing in the criminal justice system and result in large differences in racial outcomes (Rosich, 2007). The magnitude of these racial differences is documented by a report that found that, while African Americans make up 16% of all young people, they account for 28% of juvenile arrests, 34% of those formally processed by the courts, and 58% of those sent to adult prison (National Council on Crime and Delinquency, 2007, p. 37). Civil rights advocates and other spokespersons for the black community charge that there is a dual justice system in the U.S. and that blacks, adults as well as juveniles, are more likely to receive harsher treatment than are whites charged with similar crimes.

Perhaps the most important manifestation of these biases is that black males are much more likely than white males to be involved in the criminal justice system, and in many communities, a third or more of young African American men are under the supervision of the system: in jail or prison or on probation or parole (Mauer & Huling, 2000, p. 417). This phenomenal level of imprisonment is largely the result of a national "get tough" policy on drugs, especially on crack cocaine, that began in the 1980s. Crack cocaine is a cheap form of the drug, and the street-level dealers who have felt the brunt of the national antidrug campaign have been disproportionately young African American males from less affluent areas. Some see this crackdown as a not-so-subtle form of racial discrimination. For example, federal laws require a mandatory prison term of 5 years for possession of 5 grams of crack cocaine, a drug much more likely to be dealt by poor blacks. In contrast, comparable levels of sentencing for dealing powder cocaine—the more expensive form of the drug—are not reached until the accused possesses a minimum of 500 grams (Rosich, 2007).

Exhibit 6.1 shows the differential drug arrest rates for blacks and whites. Note the spike in arrest rates for blacks in the late 1980s—when the "war on drugs" began—and the continuing large racial gap since that time. It should be stressed that there is considerable evidence that blacks and whites use illegal drugs at roughly the same rate: The difference in arrest rates does not reflect a proportional difference in use (National Center for Health Statistics, 2010, p. 235). The African American community suffered a double victimization from crack cocaine: first from the drug itself and then from the so-called "war on drugs."

The nature of the relationship between the African American community and the criminal justice system is further documented in two recent studies. The first (Pettit & Western, 2004) focused on men born between 1965 and 1969 and found that 3% of whites, compared with 20% of blacks, had been imprisoned by the time they were 30 years old. Also, the study found that education was a key variable affecting the probability of imprisonment: Nearly 60% of African American men in this cohort who had not completed high school went to prison. The second study (Pew Charitable Trust, 2008) found that black men were imprisoned at far higher rates than white men: While less than 1% of all white men are in prison, the rate for black men is 7%. Furthermore, 11% of black men aged 20 to 34 are imprisoned.

On another level, more pervasive if less dramatic, is the issue of racial profiling: the police use of race as an indicator when calculating whether a person is suspicious or dangerous (Kennedy, 2001, p. 3). The tendency to focus more on blacks and disproportionately to stop, question, and follow them is a form of discrimination that generates resentment and increases the distrust (and fear) many African Americans feel toward their local police

Exhibit 6.1 Drug Arrest Rates by Race (Arrests per 100,000 Population), 1980 to 2007

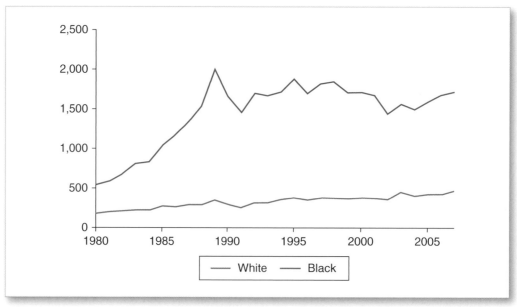

SOURCE: National Center for Health Statistics (2010).

forces. According to some, humiliating encounters with police (for example, being stopped and questioned for "driving while black") are virtually a rite of passage for black men (Kennedy, 2001, p. 7). According to one national survey, more than half of all black men and 25% of black females feel that they have been unfairly stopped by police (Morin & Cottman, 2001; see also Weitzer & Tuch, 2005).

The charges of racial profiling and discrimination in the war against drugs can be controversial, but these patterns sustain the ancient perceptions of African Americans as dangerous outsiders, and they feed the tradition of resentment and anger toward the police in the African American community.

Increasing Class Inequality

As black Americans moved out of the rural South and as the repressive force of de jure segregation receded, social class inequality within the African American population increased. Since the 1960s, the black middle class has grown, but black poverty continues to be a serious problem.

The Black Middle Class

A small African American middle class, based largely on occupations and businesses serving only the African American community, had been in existence since before the Civil War (Frazier, 1957). Has this more affluent segment benefited from increasing tolerance in the larger society, civil rights legislation, and affirmative action programs? Is the African American middle class growing in size and affluence?

The answers to these questions are not entirely clear, but research strongly suggests that the size and affluence of the African American middle class is less than is often assumed. For example, one study (Kochhar, 2004) found that between 1996 and 2002, the percentage

of blacks that could be considered middle and upper class never exceeded 25% of the black population. The comparable figure for whites was almost 60%. Thus, by this definition, the black middle and upper class were less than half the size of the white middle and upper class.

Another recent study (Oliver & Shapiro, 2006) indicates that the African American middle class is not only smaller but also much less affluent. The researchers studied racial differences in wealth, which includes not only income but all other financial assets: the value of houses, cars, savings, other property, and so forth. Exhibit 6.2 compares the wealth of blacks and whites, using two different definitions of "middle class" and two different measures of "wealth." Middle-class status is defined, first, in terms of level of education, with a college education indicating middle-class status, and, second, in terms of occupation, with a white-collar occupation indicating middle-class status. Wealth is defined first in terms of net worth, which includes all assets (houses, cars, and so forth) minus debt. The second measure, net financial assets, is the same as net worth but excludes the value of a person's investments in home and cars. This second measure is a better indicator of the resources that are available to invest in educating the next generation or financing new businesses (Oliver & Shapiro, 2006, pp. 60–62).

Photo 6.6

Some African Americans are among the best-known and most affluent people in the world. Here, Oprah Winfrey, possibly the richest woman in the world, endorses Senator Barack Obama for the presidency of the United States for 2008.

© Dennis Van Tine/Retna Ltd./Corbis.

Exhibit 6.2 Wealth by Definition of Middle Class by Race

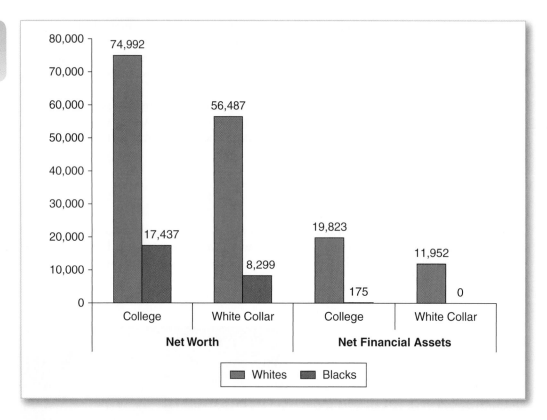

SOURCE: Oliver and Shapiro (2006, p. 96).

By either definition, the black middle class is at a distinct disadvantage. There are huge differentials in net worth between blacks and whites and even greater differences in net financial assets. Note, in fact, that the figure for net financial assets of blacks in white-collar occupations is exactly zero. Once their equity in houses and cars is subtracted out, they are left with no wealth at all—a statistic that strongly underscores the greater precariousness of middle-class standing for blacks. (For other studies that document the lower size and affluence of the black middle class, see Avery & Rendall, 2002; Pollard & O'Hare, 1999; Shapiro, 2004.)

These economic differences are due partly to discrimination in the present and partly to the racial gaps in income, wealth, and economic opportunity inherited from past generations. As suggested by the concept of net financial assets in Exhibit 6.2, economically more-advantaged white families have passed along a larger store of resources, wealth, and property to the present generation. Thus, the greater economic marginality of the African American middle class today is a form of "past-in-present" institutional discrimination (see Chapter 5). It reflects the greater ability of white parents (and grandparents) to finance higher education and to subsidize business ventures and home mortgages (Oliver & Shapiro, 2006).

Not only is their economic position more marginal, but middle-class African Americans commonly report that they are unable to escape the narrow straitjacket of race. No matter what their level of success, occupation, or professional accomplishments, race continues to be seen as their primary defining characteristic in the eyes of the larger society (Benjamin, 2005; Cose, 1993; Hughes & Thomas, 1998). Without denying the advances of some, many analysts argue that the stigma of race continues to set sharp limits on the life chances of African Americans.

There is also a concern that greater class differentiation may decrease solidarity and cohesion within the African American community. There is greater income inequality among African Americans than ever before, with the urban poor at one extreme and some of the wealthiest, most recognized figures in the world at the other: millionaires, celebrities, business moguls, politicians, and sports and movie stars. Will the more affluent segment of the African American community disassociate itself from the plight of the less fortunate and move away from the urban neighborhoods, taking with it its affluence, articulateness, and leadership skills? If this happens, it would reinforce the class division and further seal the fate of impoverished African Americans, who are largely concentrated in urban areas.

Urban Poverty

African Americans have become an urban minority group, and the fate of the group is inextricably bound to the fate of America's cities. The issues of black-white relations cannot be successfully addressed without dealing with urban issues, and vice versa.

As we saw in Chapter 5, automation and mechanization in the workplace have eliminated many of the manual-labor jobs that sustained city dwellers in earlier decades (Kasarda, 1989). The manufacturing, or secondary, segment of the labor force has declined in size, and the service sector has continued to expand (see Exhibit 5.5). The more desirable jobs in the service sector have more and more demanding educational prerequisites. The service sector jobs available to people with lower educational credentials pay low wages, often less than the minimum necessary for the basics, including food and shelter, and offer little in the way of benefits, security, and links to more rewarding occupations. This form of past-in-present institutional discrimination constitutes a powerful handicap for colonized groups such as African Americans, who have been excluded from educational opportunities for centuries.

Photo 6.7

Children in "the ghetto."

© Daniel Lainé/ CORBIS.

Furthermore, many of the blue-collar jobs that have escaped automation have migrated away from the cities. Industrialists have been moving their businesses to areas where labor is cheaper, unions have less power, and taxes are lower. This movement to the suburbs, to the Sunbelt, and offshore has been devastating for the inner city. Poor transportation systems, the absence of affordable housing outside the center city, and outright housing discrimination have combined to keep urban poor people of color confined to center-city neighborhoods, distant from opportunities for jobs and economic improvement (Feagin, 2001, pp. 159–160; Kasarda, 1989; Massey & Denton, 1993).

Sociologist Rogelio Saenz (2005) recently analyzed the situation of blacks in the 15 largest metropolitan areas in the nation and found that they are much more likely than whites to be living in highly impoverished neighborhoods, cut off from the "economic opportunities, services, and institutions that families need to succeed" (p. 1). Saenz found that the greater vulnerability and social and geographical isolation of blacks is pervasive, however, and includes not only higher rates of poverty and unemployment but also large differences in access to cars and even phones, amenities taken for granted in the rest of society. In the areas studied by Saenz, blacks were as much as 3 times as likely not to have a car (and, thus, no means to get to jobs outside center-city areas) and as much as 8 times as likely not to have a telephone.

Some of these industrial and economic forces affect all poor urbanites, not just minority groups or African Americans in particular. The dilemma facing many African Americans is in some part not only racism or discrimination; the impersonal forces of evolving industrialization and social class structures contribute as well. However, when immutable racial stigmas and centuries of prejudice (even disguised as modern racism) are added to these economic and urban developments, the forces limiting and constraining many African Americans become extremely formidable.

For the past 60 years, the African American poor have been increasingly concentrated in narrowly delimited urban areas ("the ghetto") in which the scourge of poverty has been compounded and reinforced by a host of other problems, including joblessness, high rates of school dropout, crime, drug use, teenage pregnancy, and welfare dependency. These increasingly isolated neighborhoods are fertile grounds for the development of oppositional cultures, which reject or invert the values of the larger society. The black urban counterculture may be most visible in music, fashion, speech, and other forms of popular culture, but it is also manifest in widespread lack of trust in the larger society and whites in particular. An **urban underclass**, barred from the mainstream economy and the primary labor force and consisting largely of poor African Americans and other minority groups of color, has become a prominent and perhaps permanent feature of the American landscape (Kasarda, 1989; Massey & Denton, 1993; Wilson, 1987, 1996, 2009).

Consider the parallels and contrasts between the plight of the present urban underclass and black southerners under de jure segregation:

- In both eras, a large segment of the African American population was cut off from opportunities for success and growth.
- In the earlier era, African Americans were isolated in rural areas; now, they are isolated in urban areas, especially center cities.
- In the past, escape from segregation was limited primarily by political and legal restrictions and blatant racial prejudice; escape from poverty in the present is limited by economic and educational deficits and a more subtle and amorphous prejudice.

The result is the same: Many African Americans remain as a colonized minority group—isolated, marginalized, and burdened with a legacy of powerlessness and poverty.

Modern Institutional Discrimination

The social processes that maintain racial inequality in the present are indirect and sometimes difficult to document and measure. They often flow from the patterns of blatant racial discrimination in the past but are not overtly racial in the present. They operate through a series of cumulative effects that tend to filter black Americans into less desirable positions in education, housing, the criminal justice system, and the job market. Consider two instances where racial class inequalities are perpetuated: one by employment networks that were closed in the past and remain shut today and the other reflecting the greater vulnerability of the black community to economic hardships in the larger society.

Closed Networks and Racial Exclusion

The continuing importance of race as a primary factor in the perpetuation of class inequality is dramatically illustrated in a recent research project. Royster (2003) interviewed black and white graduates of a trade school in Baltimore. Her respondents had completed the same curricula and earned similar grades. In other words, they were nearly identical in terms of the credentials they brought to the world of work. Nonetheless, the black graduates were employed less often in the trades for which they had been educated, had lower wages, got fewer promotions, and experienced longer periods of unemployment. Virtually every white graduate found secure and reasonably lucrative employment. The black graduates, in stark contrast, usually were unable to stay in the trades and became, instead, low-skilled, low-paid workers in the service sector.

What accounts for these differences? Based on extensive interviews with the subjects, Royster (2003) concluded that the differences could not be explained by training or by personality characteristics. Instead, she found that what really mattered was not "what you know" but "who you know." The white graduates had access to networks of referrals and recruitment that linked them to the job market in ways that simply were not available to black graduates. In their search for jobs, whites were assisted more fully by their instructors and were able to use intraracial networks of family and friends, connections so powerful that they "assured even the worst [white] troublemaker a solid place in the blue-collar fold" (p. 78).

Needless to say, these results run contrary to some deeply held American values, most notably the widespread, strong support for the idea that success in life is due to individual effort, self-discipline, and the other attributes enshrined in the Protestant Ethic. The strength of this faith is documented in a recent survey that was administered to a representative sample of adult Americans. The respondents were asked whether they thought people got ahead by hard work, luck, or a combination of the two. Fully 69% of the sample chose "hard work," and another 20% chose "hard work and luck equally" (National Opinion Research Council, 1972–2010). This overwhelming support for the importance of individual effort is echoed in human capital theory and many "traditional" sociological perspectives on assimilation (see Chapter 2).

Royster's results demonstrate that American faith in the power of hard work alone is simply wrong. To the contrary, access to jobs is controlled by networks of personal relationships that are decidedly not open to everyone. These subtle patterns of exclusion and closed intraracial networks are more difficult to document than the blatant discrimination that was at the core of Jim Crow segregation, but they can be just as devastating in their effects and just as powerful as mechanisms for perpetuating racial gaps in income and employment.

The Differential Impact of Hard Times

According to the quote that opened this chapter, African Americans are more likely to suffer the more virulent form of any illness—economic or otherwise—that strikes society: They will tend to feel the impact earlier, experience higher levels of distress, and be the last to recover. The recent downturn in the U.S. economy has affected almost everyone in one way or another: Americans everywhere have suffered from job loss, increasing poverty, home foreclosures, loss of health care coverage, and other disasters. How has the recession affected the black community?

Consider the unemployment rate, which generally runs twice as high for blacks as for whites. During the recession, the rate rose for all groups, but, as displayed in Exhibit 6.3, it rose earlier for blacks, rose at a steeper angle to a much higher peak, and leveled off and began to fall later than for whites. The highest rate for whites was 8.8, a little more than half the peak rate of 16.5 for blacks. The white unemployment rate leveled off and began to fall in early 2010. The rate for blacks dipped several months later but rose again before declining in late 2010. These hard times affected all groups, across the board, but created a deeper economic hole for black Americans.

Exhibit 6.3 Monthly Unemployment Rates by Race, January 2001 Through February 2011

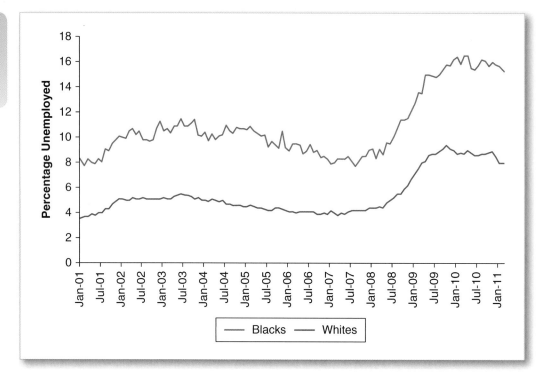

SOURCE: U.S. Bureau of Labor Statistics (2011).

A similar pattern of greater difficulty for black Americans has affected homeownership over recent years. As we saw in Chapter 5, homeownership is a crucial source of wealth for the average American since home equity can be used to finance businesses, retirement, education, and for scores of other purposes: Income enables families to get along, but financial assets such as homeownership help families get ahead, escape poverty, and become socially mobile (Oliver & Shapiro, 2008, p. A9). The financial advantages of homeownership are particularly important for black Americans because of the long history of racial economic inequality and discrimination in the housing market.

A recent report (Oliver & Shapiro, 2008) found that black Americans and other minority groups of color, compared with whites, were more than 3 times as likely to be victimized by toxic, so-called "subprime" home loans and more than twice as likely to suffer foreclosure as a result. These home loans were new financial instruments that enabled many previously ineligible people to qualify for home mortgages. The loans were especially marketed to more vulnerable populations by predatory lenders and had hidden costs, higher interest rates, and other features that made keeping up with payments difficult. The result of the housing market's collapse was "the greatest loss of financial wealth" in the African American community (p. A11). Thus, a group that was already more vulnerable and economically marginal suffered the greatest proportional loss—an economic collapse that will take years to recover from—and, again, we see that the economic difficulties of the larger society create the biggest holes for minority groups. These societal disasters are not shared equally by everyone; they are especially severe for the groups that are the most vulnerable and have the most tenuous connections with prosperity and affluence. Thus, racial inequality persists decades after the end of blatant, direct, state-supported segregation.

The Family Institution and the Culture of Poverty

The nature of the African American family institution has been a continuing source of concern and controversy. On one hand, some analysts see the African American family as structurally

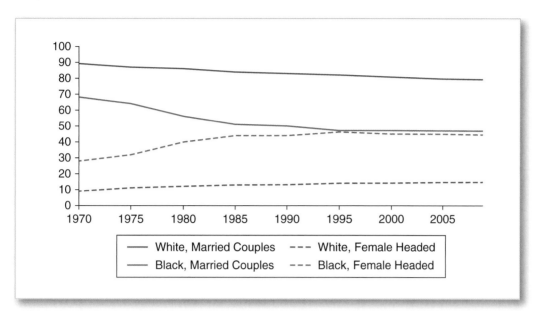

Exhibit 6.4 Percentage of Family Households With Married Couples and Headed by Females, 1970 to 2009

SOURCE: 1977—U.S. Bureau of the Census (1978, p. 43); 2007—U.S. Bureau of the Census (2007b, p. 56).

weak, a cause of continuing poverty and a variety of other problems. No doubt the most famous study in this tradition was the Moynihan (1965) report, which focused on the higher rates of divorce, separation, desertion, and illegitimacy among African American families and the fact that black families were far more likely to be female headed than were white families. Moynihan concluded that the fundamental barrier facing African Americans was a family structure that he saw as crumbling, a condition that would perpetuate the cycle of poverty entrapping African Americans (p. iii). Today, many of the differences between black and white family institutions identified by Moynihan are even more pronounced. Exhibit 6.4, for example, compares the percentage of households headed by females (black and white) with the percentage of households headed by married couples. (Note that the trends seem to have stabilized since the mid-1990s.)

The line of analysis implicit in the Moynihan (1965) report locates the problem of urban poverty in the characteristics of the African American community, particularly in the African American family. These structures are "broken" in important ways and need to be "fixed." This argument is consistent with the **culture of poverty theory**, which argues that poverty is perpetuated by the particular characteristics of the poor. Specifically, poverty is said to encourage **fatalism** (the sense that one's destiny is beyond one's control) and an orientation to the present rather than the future. The desire for instant gratification is a central trait of the culture of poverty, as opposed to the ability to defer gratification, which is thought to be essential for middle-class success. Other characteristics include violence, school failure, authoritarianism, and high rates of alcoholism and family desertion by males (Lewis, 1959, 1965, 1966. For a recent reprise of the debate over the culture of poverty concept, see Steinberg, 2011; Small, Harding, & Lamont, 2010).

The culture of poverty theory leads to the conclusion that the problem of urban poverty would be resolved if female-headed family structures and other cultural characteristics correlated with poverty could be changed. Note that this approach is consistent with the traditional assimilationist perspective and human capital theory: The poor have "bad" or inappropriate values. If they could be equipped with "good" (i.e., white, middle-class) values, the problem would be resolved.

An opposed perspective, more consistent with the concepts and theories that underlie this text, sees the matriarchal structure of the African American family as the result of urban poverty—rather than a cause—and a reflection of pervasive, institutional racial discrimination and the scarcity of jobs for urban African American males. In impoverished African American urban neighborhoods, the supply of men able to support a family is reduced by high rates of unemployment, incarceration, and violence, and these conditions are, in turn, created by the concentration of urban poverty and the growth of the "underclass" (Massey & Denton, 1993; Wilson, 1996, 2009). Thus, the burden of child rearing tends to fall on females, and female-headed households are more common than in more-advantaged neighborhoods.

Female-headed African American families tend to be poor, not because they are weak in some sense but because of the lower wages accorded to women in general and to African American women in particular, as documented in Exhibit 6.5. Note that black female workers have the lowest wages throughout the time period. Also note that the gap between black women and white men has narrowed over the years. In 1955, black women earned about a third of what white men earned. In 2009, the gap stood at about 65% (after shrinking to just under 70% in 2005), largely because male wages (for blacks as well as whites) have been relatively flat since the 1970s, while women's wages (again for whites and blacks) have risen. This pattern reflects the impact of deindustrialization: the shift away from manufacturing, which has eliminated many good blue-collar jobs, and the rise of employment sectors in which women tend to be more concentrated. A similar pattern was documented in Exhibit 3.13, which compared the wages of all full-time, year-round workers by sex.

Exhibit 6.5 Median Incomes for Full-Time, Year-Round Workers by Race and Sex, 1955 to 2009 (in 2009 Dollars)

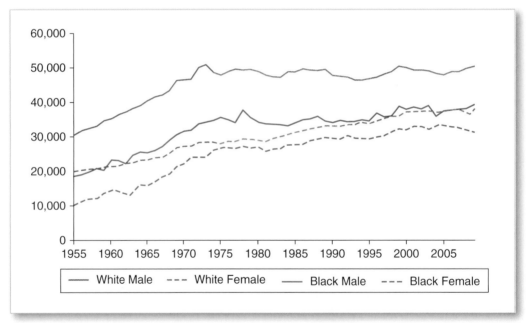

SOURCE: U.S. Bureau of the Census (2010e).

The poverty associated with black, female-headed households reflects the interactive effects of sexism and racism on black women, not some weakness in the black family. African American urban poverty is the result of the complex forces of past and present institutional discrimination, American racism and prejudice, the precarious position of African American women in the labor force, and continuing urbanization and industrialization. The African American family is not in need of "fixing," and the attitudes and values of the urban underclass are more the results of impoverishment than they are the causes. The solution to African American urban poverty lies in fundamental changes in the urban industrial economy and sweeping alterations in the distribution of resources and opportunities.

Mixed Race and New Racial Identities

As we have discussed, Americans traditionally see race as a simple dichotomy: People are either black or white, with no intermediate categories. In the past, the social convention of the "one-drop rule" meant that people of mixed racial descent were classified as black. To illustrate, consider the story of Gregory Williams (known then as Billy), a white boy growing up in the segregated South in the late 1940s and early 1950s (Williams, 1995). When Billy was 10, his father revealed that he was "half-colored." Under the one-drop rule, that made Billy black. Billy at first refused to believe: "I'm not colored, I'm white! I look white! I've always been white! I go to the 'whites only' school, 'whites only' movie theaters, and 'whites only' swimming pool" (p. 34). Gradually, he came to realize that his life—not just his life chances and his relations with others but his very identity—had been transformed by the revelation of his father's race.

In the past, mixed-race people like Gregory Williams had few choices: Others classified him as black, and the rigid social conventions of the day forced him to accept that identity, with all its implications. Today, four decades after the formal end of Jim Crow segregation, Americans are confronting the limitations of this dichotomous racial convention. People of mixed-race descent are increasing in number and, in fact, are some of the most prominent and well-known people in society. President Barack Obama is an obvious example of a highly visible mixed-race person, but others include Tiger Woods, the professional golfer (who defines himself—tongue in cheek—as Cablanasian: Caucasian, black, American Indian, and Asian), vocalist Mariah Carey, Yankee baseball star Derek Jeter, and actress Halle Berry.

How do people of multiracial descent define themselves today? How are they defined by others? Have the old understandings of race become irrelevant? Is there still pressure to place people in one and only one group? There has been a fair amount of research on this issue, and we can begin to formulate some ideas.

One important study illustrates some of the possible identities for mixed-race individuals. Rockquemore and Brunsma (2008; Brunsma, 2005) interviewed a sample of several hundred mixed-race college students, confining their attention to people who had one white and one black parent. They found that today, unlike the situation faced by Gregory Williams, the meaning of mixed-race identity is conceptually complex and highly variable (Rockquemore & Brunsma, 2008, p. 50). They identified four main categories that their respondents used to understand their biracialism, and I present these in order from most to least common. However, the sample they assembled was not representative, and there is no reason to assume that these same percentages would characterize all biracial Americans.

1. The most common racial identity in the sample was the *border identity*. These respondents (58% of the sample) didn't consider themselves to be either black or white. They defined themselves as members of a third, separate category that is linked to both groups but is unique in itself. One respondent declared, "I'm not black, I'm biracial" (Rockquemore & Brunsma, 2008, p. 43). The authors make a further distinction:

   a. Some border identities are "validated" or recognized and acknowledged by others. These respondents see themselves as biracial, and they are also seen that way by family, friends, and the community.

   b. Other border identities are "unvalidated" by others. These individuals see themselves as biracial but are classified by others as black. For example, one respondent said, "I consider myself biracial, but I experience the world as a black person" (p. 45). This disconnect may be the result of the persistence of traditional dichotomous racial thinking and the fact that some people lack the category of "biracial" in their thinking. According to the authors, people in this category are of special interest because of the tensions created by the conflict between their self-image and the way they are defined by others.

2. The second most common identity in the sample was the *singular identity*. These individuals saw themselves not as biracial but as exclusively black (13%) or exclusively

white (3%). As the case of Gregory Williams illustrated, the singular black identity is most consistent with American traditional thinking about race. The authors argue that the fact that this identity was *not* the most common in their sample illustrates the complexity of racial identity for biracial people today.

3. A third identity was the *transcendent identity* (15%). The respondents in this category rejected the whole notion of race, along with the traditional categories of black and white, and insisted that they should be seen as unique individuals and not placed in a category, especially since those categories carry multiple assumptions about character, personality, intelligence, attitudes, and a host of other characteristics. Respondents with the transcendent identity were in a constant battle to avoid classification in our highly race-conscious society. One respondent's remarks are illustrative:

> I'm just John, you know? . . . I'm a good guy, just like me for that. . . . When I came here (to college), it was like I was almost forced to look at other people as being white, black, Asian, or Hispanic. And so now, I'm still trying to go, "I'm just John," but uh, you gotta be something. (p. 49)

4. The final racial identity is the least common (4%) but perhaps the most interesting. The authors describe the racial identity of these individuals as *protean*, or changing as the individual moves from group to group and through the various social contexts of everyday life. There are different "ways of being" in groups of blacks versus groups of whites, and individuals with the protean racial identity slip effortlessly from one mode to the next and are accepted by both groups as insiders. The authors point out that most people adjust their *behavior* to different situations (e.g., a fraternity party vs. a family Thanksgiving dinner), but these individuals also change their *identity* and adjust who they are to different circumstances. Respondents with the protean identity felt empowered by their ability to fit in with different groups and felt they were endowed with a high degree of "cultural savvy" (p. 47). In our increasingly diverse, multicultural, and multiracial society, the ability to belong easily to multiple groups may prove to be a unique strength.

What can we conclude? Racial identity, like so many other aspects of our society, is evolving and becoming more complex. Traditions such as the one-drop rule live on but in attenuated, weakened form. Also, racial identity, like other aspects of self-concept, can be situational or contingent on social context, not permanent or fixed. Given the world in which he lived, Gregory Williams had no choice but to accept a black racial identity. Today, in a somewhat more tolerant and pluralistic social environment, biracial people have choices and some space in which to carve out their own, unique identity. According to Rockquemore and Brunsma (2008), these identity choices are contingent on a number of factors, including personal appearance, but they are always made in the context of a highly race-conscious society with long and strong traditions of racism and prejudice.

Prejudice and Discrimination

Modern racism, the more subtle form of prejudice that seems to dominate contemporary race relations, was discussed in Chapter 3. Although the traditional, more overt forms of prejudice have certainly not disappeared, contemporary expressions of prejudice are often amorphous and indirect. For example, the widespread belief among whites that racial discrimination has been eliminated in the United States may be a way of blaming African Americans—rather than themselves or the larger society—for the continuing reality of racial inequality.

A parallel process of evolution from blunt and overt forms to more subtle and covert forms has occurred in patterns of discrimination. The clarity of Jim Crow has yielded to the ambiguity of modern institutional discrimination and the continuing legacy of past discrimination in the present.

The dilemmas of the African American urban underclass provide a clear, if massive, example of modern institutional discrimination. As long as American businesses and financial and political institutions continue to operate as they do, jobs will continue to migrate, cities will continue to lack the resources to meet the needs of their poorer citizens, and urban poverty will continue to sustain itself, decade after decade. The individual politicians, bankers, industrialists, and others who perpetuate and benefit from this system are not necessarily prejudiced and may not even be aware of these minority group issues. Yet their decisions can and do have profound effects on the perpetuation of racial inequality in America.

The effects of past discrimination on the present can be illustrated by the relatively low level of African American business ownership. From the beginning of slavery through the end of Jim Crow segregation in the 1960s, the opportunities for African Americans to start their own businesses were severely restricted (or even forbidden) by law. The black-owned businesses that did exist were confined to the relatively less affluent market provided by the African American community, a market they had to share with firms owned by dominant group members. At the same time, customs and laws prevented the black-owned businesses from competing for more-affluent white customers. The lack of opportunity to develop and maintain a strong business base in the past—and the consequent inability to accumulate wealth, experience, and other resources—limits the ability of African Americans to compete successfully for economic opportunities in the present (Oliver & Shapiro, 2001, p. 239). These limitations are reinforced, as we have seen, by the lower home equities of black Americans and the consequent lesser ability to amass the resources to finance new business ventures.

How can the pervasive problems of racial inequality be addressed in the present atmosphere of modern racism, low levels of sympathy for the urban poor, and subtle but powerful institutional discrimination? Many people advocate a "colorblind" approach to the problems of racial inequality: The legal and political systems should simply ignore skin color and treat everyone the same. This approach seems sensible to many people because, after all, the legal and overt barriers of Jim Crow discrimination are long gone and, at least at first glance, there are no obvious limits to the life chances of blacks.

In the eyes of others, a colorblind approach is doomed to failure: In order to end racial inequality and deal with the legacy of racism, society must follow race-conscious programs that explicitly address the problems of race and racism. Colorblind strategies amount to inaction: All we need to do to perpetuate (or widen) the present racial gap is nothing. This issue is taken up in the Current Debates section at the end of this chapter.

Assimilation and Pluralism

Acculturation

The Blauner hypothesis states that the culture of groups created by colonization will be attacked, denigrated, and, if possible, eliminated, and this assertion seems well validated by the experiences of African Americans. African cultures and languages were largely eradicated under slavery. As a powerless, colonized minority group, slaves had few opportunities to preserve their heritage even though traces of African homelands have been found in black language patterns, kinship systems, music, folk tales, and family legends (see Levine, 1977; Stuckey, 1987).

Cultural domination continued under the Jim Crow system, albeit through a different structural arrangement. Under slavery, slaves and their owners worked together and interracial contact was common. Under de jure segregation, intergroup contact diminished and blacks and whites generally became more separate. After slavery ended, the African American community had somewhat more autonomy (although still few resources) to define itself and develop a distinct culture.

The centuries of cultural domination and separate development have created a unique black experience in America. African Americans share language, religion, values, beliefs, and norms with the dominant society but have developed distinct variations on the general themes.

The acculturation process may have been slowed (or even reversed) by the Black Power movement. Beginning in the 1960s, on one hand, there has been an increased interest in African culture, language, clothing, and history, and a more visible celebration of unique African American experiences (e.g., Kwanzaa) and the innumerable contributions of African Americans to the larger society. On the other hand, many of those traditions and contributions have been in existence all along. Perhaps all that really changed was the degree of public recognition.

Secondary Structural Assimilation

Structural assimilation, or integration, involves two different phases. Secondary structural assimilation refers to integration in more public areas, such as the job market, schools, and political institutions. We can assess integration in this area by comparing residential patterns, income distributions, job profiles, political power, and levels of education of the different groups. Each of these areas is addressed in the next sections. We then discuss primary structural assimilation (integration in intimate associations, such as friendship and intermarriage).

Residential Patterns. After a century of movement out of the rural South, African Americans today are highly urbanized and much more spread out across the nation. As we saw in Chapter 5 (see Exhibits 5.2 and 5.3), about 90% of African Americans are urban and a slim majority of African Americans continue to reside in the South. About 37% of African Americans now live in the Northeast and Midwest, overwhelmingly in urban areas. Exhibit 6.6 clearly shows the concentration of African Americans in the states of the old Confederacy; the urbanized East Coast corridor from Washington, D.C., to Boston; the industrial centers of the Midwest; and, to a lesser extent, California.

Exhibit 6.6
Geographical Distribution of the African American Population, 2000

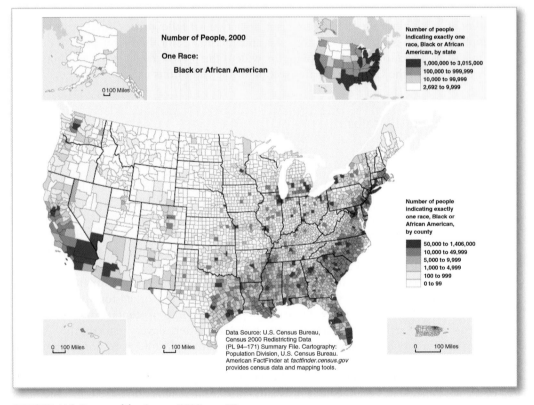

SOURCE: U.S. Bureau of the Census (2000c, p. 41).

Since Jim Crow segregation ended in the 1960s, residential integration has advanced slowly, if at all. Black and white Americans continue to live in separate areas, and racial residential segregation has been the norm across the nation. This pattern is reinforced by the fact that African Americans are more urbanized than whites and especially concentrated in densely populated center-city areas. Today, the extent of residential segregation varies around the nation, but African Americans continue to be residentially isolated, especially in the older industrial cities of the Northeast and Midwest and in the South.

Is racial residential segregation increasing or decreasing? Looking at the nation as a whole, the answer to this question is somewhat unclear because the studies that have been done use different methodologies, definitions, and databases and come to different conclusions (e.g., see Glaeser & Vigdor, 2001; Lewis Mumford Center, 2001). One illustrative study (Iceland, Weinberg, & Steinmetz, 2002) examined residential segregation within each of the four major regions of the United States. Exhibit 6.7 presents a measure of segregation called the dissimilarity index for African Americans for 1980, 1990, and 2000. This index indicates the degree to which a group is not evenly spread across neighborhoods or census tracts. Specifically, the index is the proportion of each group that would have to move to a different tract or area to achieve integration, and scores over 0.6 are considered to indicate extreme segregation.

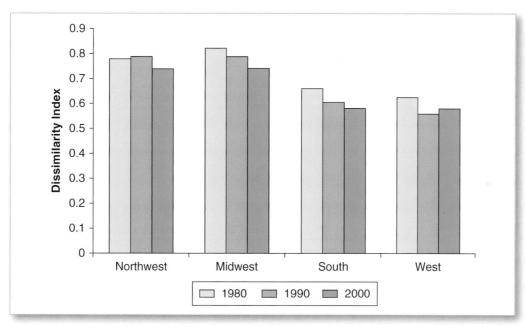

Exhibit 6.7 Racial Residential Segregation in 220 Metropolitan Areas, 1980 to 2000

SOURCE: Iceland, Weinberg, and Steinmetz (2002, p. 64).

In 1980, all regions scored at or above the 0.6 mark, with the highest levels of segregation found in the Midwest. By 2000, there were declines in all regions, and two (the South and West) had fallen slightly below the 0.6 mark. Thus, according to this study, racial residential segregation is declining but remains quite high across the nation. As we have seen, in Chapter 5 and earlier in this chapter, the continuing patterns of residential segregation are reinforced by a variety of practices, including racial steering (guiding clients to same-race housing areas) by realtors and barely disguised discrimination.

Contrary to popular belief among whites, an African American preference for living in same-race neighborhoods plays a small role in perpetuating these patterns. For example, one study of representative samples of African Americans from four major American cities (Atlanta, Boston, Detroit, and Los Angeles) found that African Americans overwhelmingly preferred to live in areas split 50/50 between blacks and whites (Krysan & Farley, 2002, p. 949).

Finally, the social class and income differences between blacks and whites are also relatively minor factors in perpetuating residential segregation, as the African American middle class is just as likely to be segregated as the African American poor (Stoll, 2004, p. 26. See also Dwyer, 2010).

School Integration. In 1954, the year of the landmark Brown desegregation decision, the great majority of African Americans lived in states operating segregated school systems. Compared with white schools, Jim Crow schools were severely underfunded and had fewer qualified teachers, shorter school years, and inadequate physical facilities. School integration was one of the most important goals of the civil rights movement in the 1950s and 1960s, and, aided by pressure from the courts and the federal government, considerable strides were made toward this goal for several decades. More recently, the pressure from the federal government has eased, and one recent report found that schools are being resegregated today at the fastest rate since the 1950s. For example, as displayed in Exhibit 6.8, schools in the Southern states actually reached their highest levels of racial integration in the late 1980s, more than 20 years ago, when 44% of black students attended white-majority schools. Since that time, this percentage has drifted downward and reached a low of 27% in 2005 (Orfield & Lee, 2007).

Exhibit 6.8 Percentage of Black Students Attending Majority-White Schools in the South, 1954 to 2005

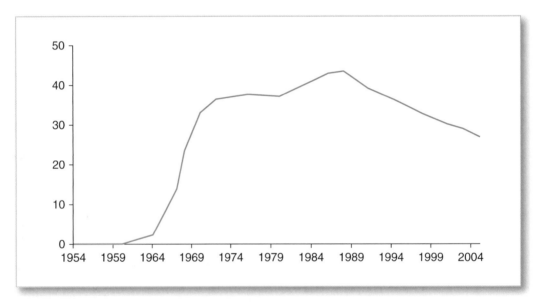

SOURCE: Orfield and Lee (2007).

Exhibit 6.9 shows the extent of school segregation for the nation as a whole in the 1993–1994 and 2005–2006 school years. Three indicators of school segregation are used. The first is the percentage of white and black students in majority-white schools, and the second is the percentage of each in "majority-minority" schools, or schools in which at least 51% of the student body is nonwhite. The third indicator is the percentage attending schools that are extremely segregated, in which minorities make up more than 90% of the student body.

Exhibit 6.9 clearly shows that the goal of racial integration in public schools has not been achieved. In both school years, the overwhelming majority of white students attended predominantly white schools, while the great majority of black students attended schools that were predominantly minority. The percentage of black students in "majority-minority" schools was higher in the 2005–2006 school year than in the 1993–1994 year, as was the percentage of black students in extremely segregated schools. The degree of racial isolation

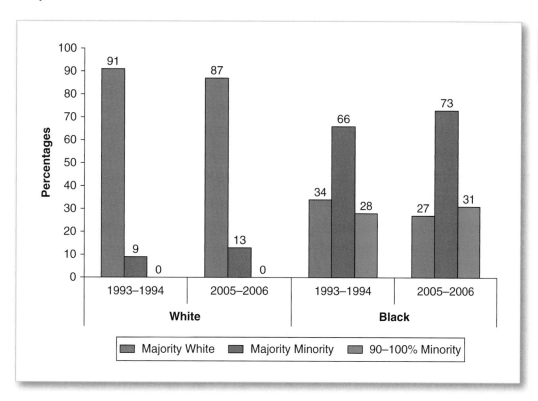

SOURCE: Fry (2007).

declined slightly between the two time periods as the percentage of white students in majority-white schools dropped from 91% to 87%. According to analyst Richard Fry (2007), this was due to a massive increase (55%) in Hispanic students in the schools, not an increase in black-white contacts (p. 1).

Underlying and complicating the difficulty of school integration is the widespread residential segregation mentioned previously. The challenges for school integration are especially evident in those metropolitan areas, such as Washington, D.C., that consist of a largely black-populated inner city surrounded by largely white-populated rings of suburbs. Even with busing, political boundaries would have to be crossed before the school systems could be substantially integrated. Without a renewed commitment to integration, American schools will continue to resegregate. This is a particularly ominous trend because it directly affects the quality of education. For example, years of research demonstrate that the integration of schools—by social class as well as by race—is related to improved test scores (Orfield & Lee, 2006).

In terms of the quantity of education, the gap between whites and blacks has generally decreased over the past several decades. Exhibit 6.10 displays the percentage of the population over 25 years old, by race and sex, who have high school diplomas. The racial gap has shrunk dramatically at the high school level, even though it has not disappeared. Of course, given the increasing demands for higher educational credentials in the job market, it is ironic that the nation has nearly achieved racial equality in high school education at a time when this credential matters less.

At the college level, the trends somewhat parallel the narrowing gap in levels of high school education, as shown in Exhibit 6.11. In 1960, white males held a distinct advantage over all other race/gender groups: They were about 3.5 times more likely than African American males to have a college degree. By 2007, the advantage of white males had shrunk, but they were still about 1.7 times more likely than black males and 1.5 times more likely than black females to have a college degree. These racial differences are larger with more-advanced degrees, however,[1] and differences such as these will be increasingly serious in an economy in which jobs more frequently require an education beyond high school.

Exhibit 6.10 Percentage of Persons Age 25 and Older Completing High School by Sex and Race, 1960 to 2009

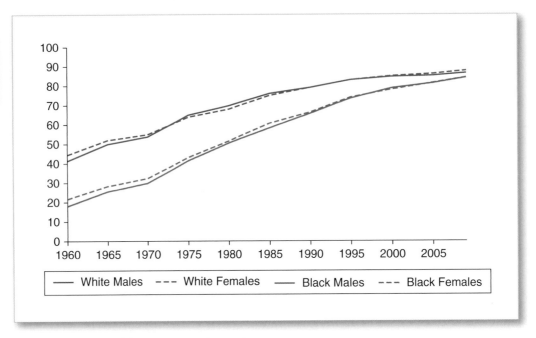

SOURCE: U.S. Bureau of the Census (2011d, p. 147).

Exhibit 6.11 Percentage of People 25 Years of Age and Older With College Degrees, 1960 to 2009

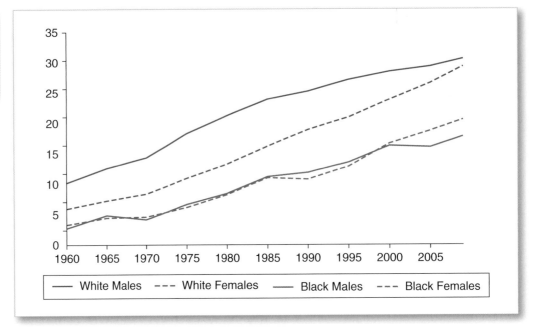

SOURCE: U.S. Bureau of the Census (2011d).

Political Power. Two trends have increased the political power of African Americans since World War II. One is the movement out of the rural South, a process that concentrated African Americans in areas in which it was easier to get people registered to vote. The first African American representative to the U.S. Congress (other than those elected during Reconstruction) was elected in 1928. By 1954, there were still only three African American members in the House of Representatives (Franklin, 1967, p. 614), and there are currently 41, about 9% of the total (U.S. Bureau of the Census, 2011d, p. 255). In 2004, Barack

Obama was elected to the U.S. Senate from the state of Illinois, the third African American senator since Reconstruction (the other two were Edward Brooke, R-Mass., who served two terms beginning in 1967, and Carol Mosely-Braun, D-Ill., who served one term beginning in 1993). When Senator Obama became president, his unexpired term was filled by Roland Burris, who was also African American. Burris decided not to seek reelection, and there are currently no African Americans in the U.S. Senate.

The number of African American elected officials at all levels of government increased from virtually zero at the turn of the 20th century to more than 9,000 in 2001 (U.S. Bureau of the Census, 2011d, p. 258). In Virginia in 1989, Douglas Wilder became the first African American to be elected to a state governorship, and both Colin Powell and Condoleezza Rice have served as secre-

Condoleezza Rice served as secretary of state, one of the highest governmental offices to be held by African Americans.

© Ron Sachs/CNP/ Sygma/Corbis.

tary of state, the highest governmental office—along with Supreme Court justice—ever held by African Americans, other than the presidency. African American communities are virtually guaranteed some political representation by their high degree of geographical concentration at the local level. Today, most large American cities, including Los Angeles, Chicago, Atlanta, New York, and Washington, D.C., have elected African American mayors.

The other trend is the dismantling of the institutions and practices that disenfranchised southern blacks during Jim Crow segregation (see Chapter 5). In particular, the Voting Rights Act of 1965 specifically prohibited many of the practices (poll taxes, literacy tests, and whites-only primaries) traditionally used to keep African Americans politically powerless. The effect of these repressive policies can be seen in the fact that as late as 1962, only 5% of the African American population of Mississippi and 13% of the African American population of Alabama were registered to vote (O'Hare, Pollard, Mann, & Kent, 1991, p. 33).

Since the 1960s, the number of African Americans in the nation's voting age population has increased from slightly less than 10% to about 13%. This increasing potential for political power was not fully mobilized in the past, however, and actual turnout generally has been much lower for blacks than for whites. In the hotly contested presidential races of 2000 and 2004, however, a variety of organizations (such as the NAACP) made a concerted and largely successful effort to increase turnout for African Americans. In both years, black turnout was comparable to that of whites. In the 2008 election, featuring African American Barack Obama against Republican John McCain, the black turnout (60.8%) was slightly larger than the white turnout (59.6%) (U.S. Bureau of the Census, 2011d, p. 260). Black voters have been a very important constituency for the Democratic Party and, even with lower turnout, figured prominently in the elections of John F. Kennedy in 1960, Jimmy Carter in 1976, and Bill Clinton in 1992 and 1996.

Jobs and Income. Integration in the job market and racial equality in income follow the trends established in many other areas of social life: The situation of African Americans has improved since the end of de jure segregation but has stopped well short of equality. Among males, whites are much more likely to be employed in the highest-rated and most lucrative occupational areas, whereas blacks are overrepresented in the service sector and in unskilled labor. Although huge gaps remain, we should also note that the present occupational distribution represents a rapid and significant upgrading, given the fact that as recently as the 1930s, the majority of African American males were unskilled agricultural laborers (Steinberg, 1981, pp. 206–207).

A similar improvement has occurred for African American females. In the 1930s, about 90% of employed African American women worked in agriculture or in domestic service (Steinberg, 1981, pp. 206–207). The percentage of African American women in these categories has dropped dramatically, and the majority of African American females are employed in the two highest occupational categories, although typically at the lower levels of these categories. For example, in the top-rated "managerial and professional" category, women are more likely to be concentrated in less-well-paid occupations, such as nurse or elementary school teacher (see Exhibit 5.7), whereas men are more likely to be physicians and lawyers.

The racial differences in education and jobs are reflected in a persistent racial income gap, as shown in Exhibit 6.12. In the early 1970s, black household income was about 58% of white household income. The gap remained relatively steady through the 1980s, closed during the boom years of the 1990s, and, since the turn of the century, has widened again. The gap was smallest in 2000 (68%) and, in the most recent year, has grown to 63%, reflecting the differential effects of the recession on minority groups of color, as we discussed previously.

Exhibit 6.12 Median Household Income by Race, 1967 to 2009 (in 2009 Dollars)

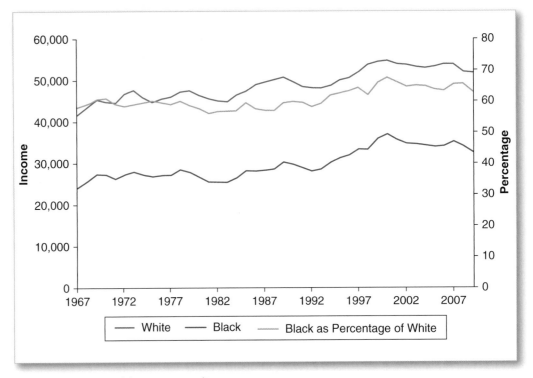

SOURCE: U.S. Bureau of the Census (2011b).

NOTE: Read income on left-hand axis and percentage on right-hand axis.

Exhibit 6.12 depicts the racial income gap in terms of the median, an average that shows the difference between "typical" white and black families. Exhibit 6.13 supplements this information by comparing the distribution of income within each racial group for 2009 and highlights the differences in the percentage of each group in low-, middle-, and upper-income categories. To read this graph, note that income categories are arrayed from top to bottom and that the horizontal axis has a zero point in the middle of the graph. The percentage of white households in each income category is represented by the bars to the left of the zero point, and the same information is presented for black households by the bars to the right of the center point.

Starting at the bottom, note that the bars representing black households are considerably wider than those for white households: This reflects the fact that black Americans are more concentrated in the lower income brackets. For example, 15.6% of black households had incomes of $10,000 or less, 2.5 times greater than the percentage of white households (6.2%) in this range.

As we move upward, note that there is a noticeable clustering for both black and white households in the $50,000 to $124,000 categories, income ranges that would be associated

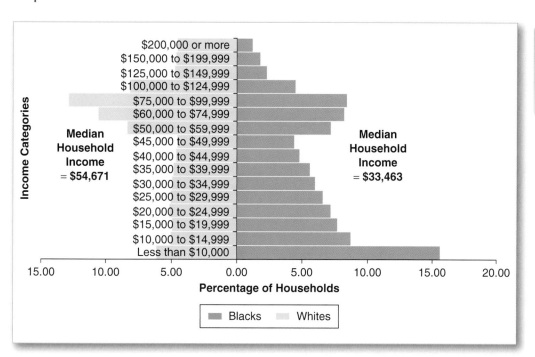

SOURCE: U.S. Bureau of the Census (2009a).

Exhibit 6.13
Distribution of Household Income for Whites and Blacks, 2009

with an upper-middle-class lifestyle. In this income range, however, it is the white households that are overrepresented: 40% of white households versus only 28% of black households had incomes in this range. The racial differences are even more dramatic in the two highest income ranges: More than 9% of white households had incomes greater than $150,000 versus only 3% of black households. Graphs such as this convincingly refute the notion, common among "modern racists" and many other Americans, that there are no important racial inequalities in the United States today.

Finally, poverty affects African Americans at much higher rates than it does white Americans. Exhibit 6.14 shows the percentage of white and black American families living below the federally established, "official" poverty level from 1967 through 2009. The poverty rate for African American families runs about 2.5 to 3 times greater than the rate for whites.

For most of this time period, poverty rates for both groups tended to decline and there was a dramatic decrease in black poverty during the 1990s. Since 2000, rates for both groups have drifted upward, especially in the most recent years. Tragically, the highest rates of poverty continue to be found among children, especially African American children. Note the increases in child poverty for both groups in the most recent years. Again, graphs such as this one convincingly refute the notion that serious racial inequality is a thing of the past for U.S. society.

Primary Structural Assimilation

Interracial contact in the more public areas of society, such as schools or the workplace, is certainly more common today, and as Gordon's model of assimilation predicts, this has led to increases in more intimate contacts across racial lines. For example, the percentage of African Americans who say they have "good friends" who are white increased from 21% in 1975 to 78% in 1994. Comparable increases have occurred for whites: In 1975, only 9% said they had "good friends" who were black, and that percentage rose to 73% in 1995 (Thernstrom & Thernstrom, 1997, p. 521).

One study looked at changing intimate relationships among Americans by asking a nationally representative sample about the people with whom they discuss "important matters." Although the study did not focus on black-white relations per se, the researchers did find that the percentage

Exhibit 6.14 Percentage of Families in Poverty, 1967 to 2009, and Percentage of Children in Poverty, 1974 to 2009

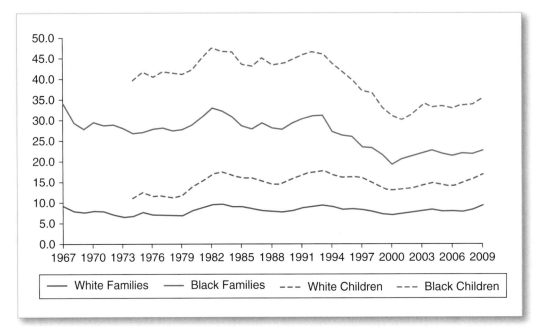

SOURCE: U.S. Bureau of the Census (2011c).

of whites who included African Americans as intimate contacts increased from 9% to more than 15% between 1984 and 2004 (McPherson, Smith-Lovin, & Brashears, 2006). While this increase would be heartening to those committed to a more integrated, racially unified society, these low percentages could also be seen as discouraging as they suggest that about 85% of white Americans maintain racially exclusive interpersonal networks of friends and acquaintances.

Another interesting study (Fisher, 2008) looked at interracial friendships on a sample of 27 college campuses across the nation. First-year students were interviewed at the end of their second semester and asked about the group membership of their 10 closest friends on campus. The study found that cross-group friendships were common but that white students had the least-diverse circles of friends. For whites, 76% of their friends were also white, a much higher percentage of in-group exclusiveness than Asian students (51%), Hispanic students (56%), and black students (27%). Obviously, these percentages reflect the racial composition of the campuses (all were majority white), but it is significant that cross-group choices were positively related to more tolerant attitudes and a history of having a friend from another group in high school. Most interesting, perhaps, was that cross-group choices were positively related to greater diversity on campus. This finding supports the contact hypothesis and Gordon's assertion that integration at the secondary level leads to integration at the primary level.

Consistent with the decline in traditional, overt prejudice, Americans are much less opposed to interracial dating and marriage today. A Gallup poll, for example, reports that 75% of white Americans express approval of black-white marriage, up from just 20% approval in 1968. The comparable percentage of blacks was 85%, up from 56% in 1968 (*Editor and Publisher*, 2007). Approval of interracial dating and marriage appears to be especially high among younger people: In a 2007 poll, 86% of Americans in the 18 to 29 age range approved of interracial marriage, as opposed to 30% of those aged 65 and older (Wellner, 2007).

Behavior appears to be following attitudes as the rates of interracial dating and marriage are increasing. A number of studies find that interracial dating is increasingly common (see Wellner, 2007), and marriages between blacks and whites are also increasing in number, although still a tiny percentage of all marriages. According to the U.S. Bureau of the Census (2011d), there were 65,000 black-white married couples in 1970 (including persons of Hispanic origin), about 0.10% of all married couples. By 2007, the number of black-white married couples had increased more than sevenfold, to 550,000, but this is still only about 0.90% of all married couples (p. 54).

Is the Glass Half Empty or Half Full?

The contemporary situation of African Americans is perhaps what might be expected for a group so recently "released" from exclusion and subordination. The average situation of African Americans improved vastly during the latter half of the 20th century in virtually every area of social life. As demonstrated by the data presented in this chapter, however, racial progress stopped well short of equality. In assessing the present situation, one might stress the improved situation of the group (the glass is half full) or the challenges that remain before full racial equality and justice are achieved (the glass is half empty). Perhaps the most reasonable approach is to recognize that in many ways, the overall picture of racial progress is "different" rather than "better" and that over the past century of change, a large percentage of the African American population has traded rural peasantry for urban poverty and now faces an array of formidable and deep-rooted problems.

The situation of African Americans is intimately intermixed with the plight of our cities and the changing nature of the labor force. It is the consequence of nearly 400 years of prejudice, racism, and discrimination, but it also reflects broader social forces, such as urbanization and industrialization. Consistent with their origin as a colonized minority group, the relative poverty and powerlessness of African Americans has persisted long after other groups (e.g., the descendants of the European immigrants who arrived between the 1820s and the 1920s) have achieved equality and acceptance. African Americans were enslaved to meet the labor demands of an agrarian economy, became a rural peasantry under Jim Crow segregation, were excluded from the opportunities created by early industrialization, and remain largely excluded from the better jobs in the emerging postindustrial economy.

Progress toward racial equality has slowed considerably since the heady days of the 1960s, and in many areas, earlier advances seem hopelessly stagnated. Public opinion polls indicate that there is little support or sympathy for the cause of African Americans (see Chapter 3). Traditional prejudice has declined only to be replaced by modern racism. In the court of public opinion, African Americans are often held responsible for their own plight. Biological racism has been replaced by indifference to racial issues or by blaming the victims.

Of course, in acknowledging the challenges that remain, we should not downplay the real improvements that have been made in the lives of African Americans. Compared with their forebears in the days of Jim Crow, African Americans today are on the average more prosperous and more politically powerful, and some are among the most revered of current popular heroes (the glass is half full). However, the increases in average income and education and the glittering success of the few obscure a tangle of problems for the many, problems that may well grow worse as America moves further into the postindustrial era. Poverty, unemployment, a failing educational system, residential segregation, subtle racism, and continuing discrimination continue to be inescapable realities for millions of African Americans. In many African American neighborhoods, crime, drugs, violence, poor health care, malnutrition, and a host of other factors compound these problems (the glass is half empty).

Given this gloomy situation, it should not be surprising to find significant strength in pluralistic, nationalistic thinking, as well as resentment and anger in the African American community. Black Nationalism and Black Power remain powerful ideas, but their goals of development and autonomy for the African American community remain largely rhetorical sloganeering without the resources to bring them to actualization.

The situation of the African American community in the early 21st century might be characterized as structural pluralism combined with inequality. The former characterization testifies to the failure of assimilation and the latter to the continuing effects, in the present, of a colonized origin. The problems that remain are less visible (or perhaps just better hidden from the average white middle-class American) than those of previous eras. Responsibility is more diffused, the moral certainties of opposition to slavery or to Jim Crow laws are long gone, and contemporary racial issues must be articulated and debated in an environment of subtle prejudice and low levels of sympathy for the grievances of African Americans. Urban poverty, modern institutional discrimination, and modern racism are less dramatic and more difficult to measure than an overseer's whip, a lynch mob, or a sign that says "Whites Only," but they can be just as real and just as deadly in their consequences.

Should the United States Be Colorblind?

Many people believe that U.S. society should officially ignore race and that the way to finally get past the injustices of the past is to treat everyone exactly the same in schools, jobs, politics, and every other American institution. This argument resonates strongly with fundamental American values and appeals to many as simple common sense: If we want to have a society in which only character matters—not race or skin color—we need to start treating people as individuals, not as representatives of groups. From this viewpoint, programs such as affirmative action perpetuate rather than solve the problems of racial inequality in America.

Others, a distinct minority of public opinion, feel that to ignore race is to perpetuate the inequalities of the past. Colorblindness leads not to a more equal and open society but, rather, simply perpetuates white privilege and dominance. The only way to end racial inequality is to build programs and policies that take explicit notice of race and confer an affirmative advantage on blacks and on other colonized, marginalized groups. Without a strong program to force employers to balance their workforces and to require college admission programs to seek out qualified minority candidates, the racial status quo will be perpetuated indefinitely.

The view that America needs to be colorblind is presented below in an interview with Ward Connerly, an African American and a prominent leader of anti-affirmative action programs in California and across the nation. The interview was published in The American Enterprise in 2003. The opposing view is presented by Ian F. Haney Lopez, a professor of law at the University of California at Berkeley and author of White by Law: The Legal Construction of Race (2006).

CREATING EQUAL: THE IMPORTANCE OF BEING COLORBLIND

WARD CONNERLY INTERVIEW

The American Enterprise (*TAE*): What are the biggest problems facing young black Americans today?

Connerly: The problems that face black Americans are really no different from the threats that face all young Americans. I would sum them up this way: How do we preserve a culture in which every American citizen is treated as an equal without regard to his race or color?

TAE: Is it easier to be a white person in America than a black person?

Connerly: Maybe, but that really should not be important. It certainly is a lot easier for a black person growing up today than it was 40 years ago. But that didn't stop blacks 40 years ago from overcoming their problems. And they didn't do it alone; the nation grew with them.

There is no obstacle in the way of any black kid or Latino kid today that is insurmountable. A lot of things that we present as barriers for black people are barriers that are created by expecting the worst. When you expect the worst you get it. So I don't think that the challenges facing black people once they step outside the prism of blackness are any greater than they are for anybody else.

TAE: There now exists a sizable, reasonably well-off generation of African Americans who have never faced legal discrimination. Is this group eventually going to conclude that affirmative action is no longer needed, and how soon do you think that might happen?

Connerly: There is indeed a sizable black middle class, and also a sizable group of very wealthy blacks. . . . But there's still an element of political correctness that stops black Americans from . . . saying, "We don't need affirmative action." That won't happen until the cultural and political waters are warmer for them to say that.

Today's successful blacks have taken advantage of opportunities that were there. They were prepared, worked hard, and made it. But it's not yet fashionable among blacks to say that. If you do, the wrath of the "professional" blacks—people for whom being black is their profession—will come down on you. If you're the CEO of a big company, you don't want Jesse Jackson and the Congressional Black Caucus ragging on you every day. So you just roll over—and let the Connerlys of the world do the dirty work.

TAE: So what do you think a modern civil rights movement should focus on?

Connerly: A modern civil rights movement should focus on making sure that every American understands that civil rights are not just for black people. They're for everybody. I think it's time for the conservative movement to conduct a friendly, or perhaps a hostile, takeover of the civil rights movement. . . . The next step, I think, is to articulate the absolute importance of deregulating race. Getting it out of the equation. Getting to the point where you no longer have to ask me about black people.

TAE: Tell us about the Racial Privacy Initiative.

Connerly: The Racial Privacy Initiative is aimed at breathing life into what I think is at the core of America—taking people from all around the globe who come here, and saying to them: Once you are fully here, you're just an American citizen, no more, no less. You have the same expectations, same privileges, same benefits as any other American citizen. You're not a black American citizen. You're not Irish. You're just an American. In the privacy of your own life you can celebrate anything you want to celebrate. But the government will not be a party to that. The government doesn't give a damn about whether you are black or white or whatever.

TAE: How hopeful are you that that is going to happen? It seems like racial identity politics has become very entrenched.

Connerly: Let's step back for a moment. Just a short 9 years ago . . . to even think of challenging affirmative action was unthinkable. Now affirmative action is on the ropes. . . .

TAE: Are public schools leaving black youths ill-prepared for competitive colleges? Isn't this one of the main factors creating the pressure for admission quotas by race?

Connerly: Yeah, I think that public schools are a large part of the problem. But you cannot dismiss the role of the family. Public schools provide lesson plans and homework assignments, and babysit the kids during the day. When kids get home it's the parents who make sure that they're learning. Before children have their first day in school they need to know their ABCs, and they need to be disciplined. In all too many black families, they have not been taught how to speak proper English. And therein lies the basic problem. A kid who comes to school speaking little proper English is severely handicapped.

   Many black kids . . . are taught that learning is a white man's game. Many of the black kids we are worried about are low-income kids; kids without parents who understand the importance of getting them prepared. These are not problems of their skin color, and the minute we say they're black that just translates into a whole different approach to how we deal with the problem. We think they're being discriminated against yadda, yadda, yadda, and we never get to the real core of the problem, which is that the kid is in a dysfunctional family setting where race isn't the real problem. . . .

TAE: Do you consider yourself black?

Connerly: It is a testimony to my endurance that I've sat through this interview, with nearly every question being about color, and I'm still civil at the end of it. My origin is of African descent, Choctaw Indian, French, and Irish. Two of my grandkids are all of that plus their grandmother, who is Irish, and their father, who is of German descent. And two other grandkids are all of those ingredients plus their mother, who is half Vietnamese.

So you see, for me, checking these racial-identification boxes is rather personal. I don't like it. I don't buy into it. I say I'm black for the sake of not spending the whole interview quarreling about classification. But I don't like it. I'm brown in color. What is black? It's a term we use because we're lazy. It's easier to put somebody into a box and use that as a shortcut for something. But it's not useful.

SOURCE: "Ward Connerly: Interview" (2003, pp. 18–22).

COLORBLINDNESS WILL PERPETUATE RACIAL INEQUALITY

IAN F. HANEY LOPEZ

How will race as a social practice evolve in the United States over the next few decades? The American public, and indeed many scholars, increasingly believe that the country is leaving race and racism behind. . . . My sense of our racial future differs. Not only do I fear that race will continue to fundamentally skew American society over the coming decades, but I worry that the belief in the diminished salience of race makes that more likely rather than less. . . . We find ourselves now in the midst of a racial era marked by what I term "colorblind white dominance," in which a public consensus committed to formal antiracism deters effective remediation of racial inequality, protecting the racial status quo while insulating new forms of racism and xenophobia.

We remain a racially stratified country, though for some that constitutes an argument for rather than against colorblindness. . . . For the first half of the 20th century, colorblindness represented the radical . . . aspiration of dismantling de jure racial subordination. . . . In the wake of the civil rights movement's limited but significant triumphs, the relationship between colorblindness and racial reform changed markedly. The greatest potency of colorblindness came to lie in preserving, rather than challenging, the racial status quo. When the end of explicit race-based subordination did not eradicate stubborn racial inequalities, progressives increasingly recognized the need for state and private actors to intervene along racial lines. Rather than call for colorblindness, they began to insist on the need for affirmative race-conscious remedies. In that new context, colorblindness appealed to those opposing racial integration. . . . Colorblindness provided cover for opposition to racial reform. . . .

Wielding the ideal of colorblindness as a sword, in the past three decades racial conservatives on the Supreme Court have increasingly . . . [cut] back on protections against racial discrimination as well as severely limiting race-conscious remedies. In several cases in the 1970s . . . the court ruled that the need to redress the legacy of segregation made strict colorblindness impossible. But as the 1980s went on . . . the court presented race as a phenomenon called into existence just when someone employed a racial term. Discrimination existed only [when] . . . someone used racial language. . . .

That approach ignores the continuing power of race as a society-altering category. The civil rights movement changed the racial zeitgeist of the nation by rendering illegitimate all explicit invocations of white supremacy, a shift that surely marked an important step toward a more egalitarian society. But it did not bring into actual existence that ideal, as white people remain dominant across virtually every social, political, and economic domain. . . . Those many in our society who are darker, poorer, more identifiably foreign will continue to suffer the poverty, marginalization, immiseration, incarceration, and exclusion historically accorded to those whose skin and other features socially mark them as nonwhite. . . . Racial hierarchy will continue as the links are strengthened between nonwhite identity and social disadvantage on the one hand, and whiteness and privilege on the other. . . .

Contemporary colorblindness . . . define[s] how people comprehend, rationalize, and act on race. [It] continues to retard racial progress. It does so for a simple reason: It focuses on the surface, on the bare fact of racial classification, rather than looking down into the nature of social practices. It gets racism and racial remediation exactly backward, and insulates new forms of race baiting.

White dominance continues with few open appeals to race. Consider the harms wrought by segregated schools today. Schools in predominantly white suburbs are far more likely to have adequate buildings, teachers, and books, while the schools serving mainly minority children are more commonly underfinanced, unsafe, and in a state of disrepair. Such harms accumulate, encouraging white flight to avoid the expected deterioration in schools and the violence that is supposedly second nature to "them," only to precipitate the collapse in the tax base that in fact ensures a decline not only in schools but also in a range of social services. Such material differences in turn buttress seemingly commonsense ideas about disparate groups, so that we tend to see pristine schools and suburbs as a testament to white accomplishment and values. When violence does erupt, it is laid at the feet of alienated and troubled teenagers, not a dysfunctional culture. Yet we see the metal detectors guarding entrances to minority schoolhouses (harbingers of the prison bars to come) as evidence not of the social dynamics of exclusion and privilege, but of innate pathologies. No one need talk about the dynamics of privilege and exclusion. No one need cite white-supremacist arguments nor openly refer to race—race exists in the concrete of our gated communities and barrios, in government policies and programs, in cultural norms and beliefs, and in the way Americans lead their lives. . . .

To break the interlocking patterns of racial hierarchy, there is no other way but to focus on, talk about, and put into effect constructive policies explicitly engaged with race. To be sure, inequality in wealth is a major and increasing challenge for our society, but class is not a substitute for a racial analysis—though, likewise, racial oppression cannot be lessened without sustained attention to poverty. It's no accident that the poorest schools in the country warehouse minorities, while the richest serve whites; the national education crisis reflects deeply intertwined racial and class politics. One does not deny the imbrication of race and class by insisting on the importance of race-conscious remedies: The best strategies for social repair will give explicit attention to race as well as to other sources of inequality, and to their complex interrelationship. . . .

Contemporary colorblindness loudly proclaims its antiracist pretensions. To actually move toward a racially egalitarian society, however, requires that we forthrightly respond to racial inequality today. The alternative is the continuation of colorblind white dominance. As Justice Harry Blackmun enjoined in defending affirmative action in Bakke: "In order to get beyond racism, we must first take account of race. There is no other way."

SOURCE: Lopez (2006a).

DEBATE QUESTIONS TO CONSIDER

1. What assumptions does Connerly make about the overall fairness of American society? Are there any similarities between his position and human capital theory (see Chapter 2)? Judging from the evidence presented in this chapter, how credible is his statement that young black Americans face essentially the same problems as all young Americans? Is he thinking about all African Americans? Middle-class African Americans? Male as well as female African Americans? How close is the United States to Connerly's "Racial Privacy Initiative"?

2. What, according to Lopez, would be the consequences of official colorblindness? Would the progress toward racial equality that has been made be reversed? How is colorblindness a disguised form of white domination?

3. Which author(s) directly addresses "past-in-present" discrimination? How?

4. Which of these two positions is most appealing to you? If you agree with Connerly, how would you combat modern institutional discrimination? If you agree with Lopez, how would you respond to the charge that programs such as affirmative action are a form of "reverse discrimination"?

MAIN POINTS

- At the beginning of the 20th century, the racial oppression of African Americans took the form of a rigid competitive system of group relations, de jure segregation. This system ended because of changing economic and political conditions, changing legal precedents, and a mass movement of protest initiated by African Americans.
- The U.S. Supreme Court decision in *Brown v. Board of Education of Topeka* (1954) was the single most powerful blow struck against legalized segregation. A nonviolent direct action campaign was launched in the South to challenge and defeat segregation. The U.S. Congress delivered the final blows to de jure segregation in the 1964 Civil Rights Act and the 1965 Voting Rights Act.
- Outside the South, the concerns of the African American community centered on access to schooling, jobs, housing, health care, and other opportunities. African Americans' frustration and anger were expressed in the urban riots of the 1960s. The Black Power movement addressed the massive problems of racial inequality remaining after the victories of the civil rights movement.
- Black-white relations since the 1960s have been characterized by continuing inequality, separation, and hostility, along with substantial improvements in status for some African Americans. Class differentiation within the African American community is greater than ever before.
- The African American family has been perceived as weak, unstable, and a cause of continuing poverty. Culture of poverty theory attributes poverty to certain characteristics of the poor. An alternative view sees problems such as high rates of family desertion by men as the result of poverty, rather than the cause.
- Antiblack prejudice and discrimination are manifested in more subtle, covert forms (modern racism and institutional discrimination) in contemporary society.
- African Americans are largely acculturated, but centuries of separate development have created a unique black experience in American society.
- Despite real improvements in their status, the overall secondary structural assimilation of African Americans remains low. Evidence of racial inequalities in residence, schooling, politics, jobs, income, unemployment, and poverty is massive and underlines the realities of the urban underclass.
- In the area of primary structural assimilation, interracial interaction and friendships appear to be rising. Interracial marriages are increasing, although they remain a tiny percentage of all marriages.
- Compared with their situation at the start of the 20th century, African Americans have made considerable improvements in quality of life. The distance to true racial equality remains enormous.

STUDY SITE ON THE WEB

For chapter-specific resources, such as self-quizzes, videos, and flashcards, go to **www.sagepub.com/healeyregc6e.**

FOR FURTHER READING

Correspondents of *The New York Times.* 2001. *How Race is Lived in America.* New York: Times Books.

> *A comprehensive investigation by reporters of* The New York Times *on how race is lived in the everyday lives of ordinary Americans*

Feagin, Joe. 2001. *Racist America: Roots, Current Realities, and Future Reparations.* New York: Routledge.

Hacker, Andrew. 1992. *Two Nations: Black and White, Separate, Hostile, Unequal.* New York: Scribner's.

> *Two readable overviews of contemporary black-white relations*

Massey, Douglas, & Denton, Nancy. 1993. *American Apartheid: Segregation and the Making of the Underclass.* Cambridge, MA: Harvard University Press.

> *Argues powerfully that residential segregation is the key to understanding urban black poverty*

Morris, Aldon D. 1984. *The Origins of the Civil Rights Movement.* New York: Free Press.

Smelser, N., Wilson, W., & Mitchell, F. (Eds.). 2001. *America Becoming: Racial Trends and Their Consequences.* Washington, DC: National Academy Press.

> *A two-volume collection of articles by leading scholars that presents a comprehensive analysis of black-white relations in America*

Williams, Juan. 1987. *Eyes on the Prize: America's Civil Rights Years, 1954–1965.* New York: Penguin.

> *Indispensible sources on the southern civil rights movement*

Wilson, William J. 2009. *More Than Just Race: Being Black and Poor in the Inner City.* New York: W. W. Norton.

> *The latest publication of one of the most important authorities on race in the United States*

Wingfield, Adia, & Feagin, Joe. 2010. *Yes We Can? White Racial Framing and the 2008 Presidential Campaign.* New York: Routledge.

> *An important analysis of the racial dynamics of Obama's election campaign*

QUESTIONS FOR REVIEW AND STUDY

1. What forces led to the end of de jure segregation? To what extent was this change a result of broad social forces (e.g., industrialization), and to what extent was it the result of the actions of African Americans acting against the system (e.g., the southern civil rights movement)? By the 1960s and 1970s, how had the movement for racial change succeeded, and what issues were left unresolved? What issues remain unresolved today?

2. Describe the differences between the southern civil rights movement and the Black Power movement. Why did these differences exist? How are the differences related to the nature of de jure versus de facto segregation? Do these movements remain relevant today? How?

3. How does gender affect contemporary black-white relations and the African American protest movement? Is it true that African American women are a "minority group within a minority group"? How?

4. Evaluate the accuracy of the quote that opened this chapter. Use the information, data, and analysis to evaluate the quote. Is it true? Exaggerated? Untrue? What other kinds of information would be needed for a fuller assessment of the quote? How could you get this information?

5. What are the implications of increasing class differentials among African Americans? Does the greater affluence of middle-class blacks mean they are no longer a part of a minority group? Will future protests by African Americans be confined only to working-class and lower-class blacks?

6. Regarding contemporary black-white relations, is the glass half empty or half full? Considering the totality of evidence presented in this chapter, which of the following statements would you agree with? Why? (1) American race relations are the best they've ever been; racial equality has been essentially achieved (even though some problems remain), or (2) American race relations have a long way to go before society achieves true racial equality.

INTERNET RESEARCH PROJECT

In this exercise, you will use U.S. Census data to gather information about the total population, African Americans, and two white ethnic groups of your own choosing. You will then use course concepts to assess and analyze this information and place it in the context of this text. *Visit the website for this text for instructions on finding the information needed to complete the table below.*

		Total Population	African Americans	White Ethnic Groups	
				_____	_____
1	Number				
2	% of total population	_____			
3	% with bachelor's degree				
4	% unemployed				
5	Median household income				
6	% of all families in poverty				
7	% living in owner-occupied houses				
8					
9					

QUESTIONS

1. What stage of Gordon's model of assimilation (see Exhibit 2.1) do these variables measure?

2. Review the Blauner hypothesis (see Chapter 4). Do the patterns you observe in the data you've collected conform to the predictions of the hypothesis? How?

3. Review the themes stated at the beginning of Chapter 4 and the "corollary" stated at the beginning of Chapter 5. How do the patterns you've observed in the table above relate to the contact situation and changing subsistence technologies?

4. Review the concepts of modern institutional discrimination and past-in-present discrimination introduced in Chapter 5 and applied in this chapter. How do the patterns you've observed in the table above relate to these concepts?

OPTIONAL GROUP DISCUSSION

Bring the information on your groups to class and compare with the information collected by others. Consider the issues raised in the question above and in the chapter and develop some ideas about why the groups are where they are relative to one another and the total population.

NOTES

1. For example, in 2009, whites were 1.7 times more likely than blacks to have a Master's degree and 2.7 times more likely to have a PhD (U.S. Bureau of the Census, 2010b).

7

American Indians

From Conquest to Tribal Survival in a Postindustrial Society

If you go into any office in Congress, and [if they] are still operating on the . . . sports team level, they are not the ones who are going to make great Indian policy. . . . People don't make good and lasting and thorough policy for cartoons, or mascots, or disembodied heads.

—Suzan Shown Harjo, Indian activist[1]

We discussed the contact period for American Indians in Chapter 4. As you recall, this period began in the earliest colonial days and lasted nearly 300 years, ending only with the final battles of the Indian Wars in the late 1800s. The Indian nations fought for their land and to preserve their cultures and ways of life. The tribes had enough power to win many battles, but they eventually lost all the wars. The superior resources of the burgeoning white society made the eventual defeat of American Indians inevitable, and by 1890, the last of the tribes had been conquered, their leaders had been killed or were in custody, and their people were living on government-controlled reservations.

Early in the 20th century, American Indians were, in Blauner's (1972) terms, a conquered and colonized minority group. Like the slave plantations, the reservations were paternalistic systems that controlled American Indians with federally mandated regulations and government-appointed Indian agents. For most of the 20th century, as Jim Crow segregation, Supreme Court decisions, industrialization, and urbanization shaped the status of other minority groups, American Indians subsisted on the fringes of development and change—marginalized, relatively powerless, and isolated. Their links to the larger society were weaker and, compared with African Americans, white ethnic groups, and other minorities, they were less affected by the forces of social and political evolution. While other minority groups maintained a regular presence in the national headlines, American Indians have been generally ignored and unnoticed, except perhaps as mascots for sports teams, including the Washington Redskins, Atlanta

Braves, and Cleveland Indians. As Harjo points out in the quote that opens this chapter, it is unlikely that a group recognized mainly as a stereotype would be accorded favorable or realistic treatment. The issue of Indian sports team mascots is addressed in the Current Debates section at the end of this chapter.

The very last years of the 20th century witnessed some improvement in the status of American Indians in general, and some tribes, especially those with casinos and other gaming establishments, made notable progress toward parity with national standards. Also, the tribes are now more in control of their own affairs, and many have effectively used their increased autonomy and independence to address problems in education, health, joblessness, and other areas. Despite this progress, however, large gaps remain between American Indians and the dominant group in virtually every area of social and economic life, and American Indians living on reservations are among the poorest groups in U.S. society.

In this chapter, we will bring the history of American Indians up to the present and explore both recent progress and persisting problems. Some of the questions we address include the following: What accounts for the lowly position of this group for much of the past 100 years? How can we explain the improvements in the most recent decades? Now, early in the 21st century, what problems remain, and how does the situation of American Indians compare with that of other colonized and conquered minority groups? What are the most promising strategies for closing the remaining gaps between American Indians and the larger society?

SIZE OF THE GROUP

How many Indians are there? There are several different answers to this question, partly because of the way census information is collected and partly because of the social and subjective nature of race and group membership. The most current answers come from the American Community Survey, conducted every year by the U.S. Bureau of the Census since the last full census in 2000. This survey provides estimates for the number of American Indians and Alaska Natives (AIAN) and for some of the larger tribes.

The task of determining the size of the group is also complicated by the way the census collects information on race. As you recall, beginning with the 2000 Census, people were allowed to claim membership in more than one racial category. If we define "American Indians" as consisting of people who identify themselves *only* as American Indian (listed under "Alone" in Exhibit 7.1), we will get one estimate of the size of the group. If we use a broader definition and include people who claim mixed racial ancestry (listed under "Alone or in Combination" in the exhibit), our estimate of group size will be much larger.

At any rate, Exhibit 7.1 shows that there were almost 5 million people who claimed at least some American Indian or Alaska Native ancestry but only about half that number if we confine the group to people who selected one race only. By either count, the group is a tiny minority (about 1%) of the total population of the United States. Exhibit 7.1 also presents information for American Indians and Alaska Natives separately, for the 10 largest tribal groupings of American Indians and for the three largest tribal groups of Alaska Natives.

American Indians have been growing rapidly over the past several decades, but this fact needs to be seen in the full context of American Indian history. As I mentioned in Chapter 4, in 1492, there were at least 1 million American Indians living in what is now the continental ("lower 48") United States (Snipp, 1992, p. 354). Losses suffered during the contact period reduced the population to fewer than 250,000 by 1900, a loss of at least 75%. Recent population growth has restored the group to its pre-Columbian size. As displayed in Exhibit 7.2, growth was slow in the early decades of the 20th century but much more rapid in recent decades. The more recent growth is largely the result of changing definitions of race in the larger society and a much greater willingness of people to claim Indian ancestry, a pattern that again underscores the basically social nature of race (Thornton, 2001, p. 137).

	Alone (One Race)	Alone or in Combination (Two or More Races)
ALL AMERICAN INDIANS AND ALASKA NATIVES	2,446,895	4,738,073
AMERICAN INDIANS	1,992,034	3,668,451
Ten Largest Tribal Groupings for American Indians		
Cherokee	265,005	1,030,220
Navaho	303,814	353,393
Choctaw	84,885	203,830
Sioux	116,603	193,497
Chippewa	110,264	176,787
Blackfeet	26,032	135,300
Apache	64,734	134,478
Iroquois	46,943	98,138
Pueblo	72,270	91,242
Creek	36,936	83,839
ALASKA NATIVE	108,865	152,715
Three Largest Tribal Groupings for Alaska Natives		
Eskimo	54,076	67,923
Tlingit-Haida	NA	24,593
Alaskan Athabascan	NA	23,325

Exhibit 7.1 American Indians and Alaska Natives

SOURCE: Adapted from U.S. Bureau of the Census (2007a); Ogunwole (2006).

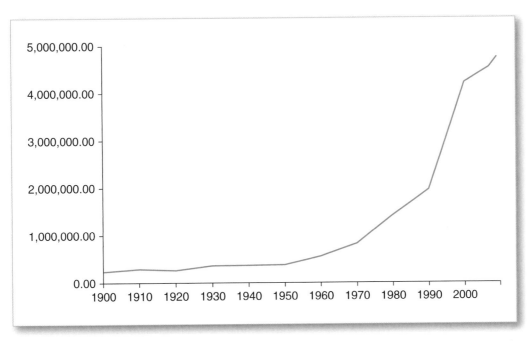

Exhibit 7.2 Population of American Indians and Alaska Natives, 1900 to 2009

SOURCE: 1900 to 1990—Thornton (2001, p. 142); 2000—U.S. Bureau of the Census (2007b, p. 14); 2006—U.S. Bureau of the Census (2007a).

AMERICAN INDIAN CULTURES

The dynamics of American Indian and Anglo-American relationships have been shaped by the vast differences in culture, values, and norms between the two groups. These differences have hampered communication in the past and continue to do so in the present. A comprehensive analysis of American Indian cultures is well beyond the scope of this text, but the past experiences and present goals of the group can be appreciated only with some understanding of their views of the world.

We must note here, as we did in Chapter 4, that there were (and are) hundreds of different tribes in what is now the United States—each with its own language and heritage—and that a complete analysis of American Indian culture would have to take this diversity into account. However, some patterns and cultural characteristics are widely shared across the tribes, and we will concentrate on these similarities.

Before exploring the content of their culture, we should note that most Native American tribes that existed in what is now the United States relied on hunting and gathering to satisfy their basic needs, although some cultivated gardens as well. This is important because, as noted by Lenski (see Chapter 1), societies are profoundly shaped by their subsistence technology.

Hunting-and-gathering societies often survive on the thin edge of hunger and want. They survive by stressing cultural values such as sharing and cooperation and by maintaining strong bonds of cohesion and solidarity. As you will see, American Indian societies are no exception to this fundamental survival strategy.

The relatively lower level of development of Native Americans is reflected in what is perhaps their most obvious difference with people in Western cultures: their ideas about the relationship between human beings and the natural world. In the traditional view of many American Indian cultures, the universe is a unity. Humans are simply a part of a larger reality, no different from or more important than other animals, plants, trees, and the earth itself. The goal of many American Indian tribes was to live in harmony with the natural world, not "improve" it or use it for their own selfish purposes—views that differ sharply from Western concepts of development, commercial farming, and bending the natural world to the service of humans. The gap between the two worldviews is evident in the reaction of one American Indian to the idea that his people should become farmers: "You ask me to plow the ground. . . . Shall I take a knife and tear my mother's bosom? You ask me to cut grass and make hay . . . but how dare I cut my mother's hair?" (Brown, 1970, p. 273).

The concept of private property, or the ownership of things, was not prominent in American Indian cultures and was, from the Anglo-American perspective, most notably absent in conceptions of land ownership. The land simply existed, and the notion of owning, selling, or buying it was foreign to American Indians. In the words of Tecumseh, a chief of the Shawnee, a man could no more sell the land than the "sea or the air he breathed" (Josephy, 1968, p. 283).

As is typical at the hunting-and-gathering level of development, American Indian cultures and societies also tended to be more oriented toward groups (e.g., the extended family, clan, or tribe) than toward individuals. The interests of the self were subordinated to those of the group, and child-rearing practices strongly encouraged group loyalty (Parke & Buriel, 2002). Cooperative, group activities were stressed over those of a competitive, individualistic nature. The bond to the group was (and is) so strong that "students go hungry rather than ask their parents for lunch money, for in asking they would be putting their needs in front of the group's needs" (Locust, 1990, p. 231).

Many American Indian tribes were organized around egalitarian values that stressed the dignity and worth of every man, woman, and child. Virtually all tribes had a division of labor based on gender, but women's work was valued, and women often occupied far more important positions in tribal society than was typical for women in Anglo-American society. In many of the American Indian societies that practiced gardening, women controlled the land. In other tribes, women wielded considerable power and held the most important political and religious offices. Among the Iroquois, for example, a council of older women appointed the chief of the tribe and made decisions about when to wage war (Amott & Matthaei, 1991, pp. 34–35).

These differences in values, compounded by the power differentials that emerged, often placed American Indians at a disadvantage when dealing with the dominant group. The American Indians' conception of land ownership and their lack of experience with deeds, titles, contracts, and other Western legal concepts often made it difficult for them to defend their resources from Anglo-Americans. At other times, cultural differences led to disruptions of traditional practices, further weakening American Indian societies. For example, Christian missionaries and government representatives tried to reverse the traditional American Indian division of labor, in which women were responsible for the gardening. In the Western view, only males did farm work. Also, the military and political representatives of the dominant society usually ignored female tribal leaders and imposed Western notions of patriarchy and male leadership on the tribes (Amott & Matthaei, 1991, p. 39).

RELATIONS WITH THE FEDERAL GOVERNMENT AFTER THE 1890s

By the end of the Indian Wars in 1890, American Indians had few resources with which to defend their self-interests. In addition to being confined to the reservations, the group was scattered throughout the western two thirds of the United States and split by cultural and linguistic differences. Politically, the power of the group was further limited by the fact that the huge majority of American Indians were not U.S. citizens and that most tribes lacked a cultural basis for understanding representative democracy as practiced in the larger society.

Economically, American Indians were among the most impoverished groups in society. Reservation lands were generally of poor quality, traditional food sources such as buffalo and other game had been destroyed, and traditional hunting grounds and gardening plots had been lost to white farmers and ranchers. The tribes had few means of satisfying even their most basic needs. Many became totally dependent on the federal government for food, shelter, clothing, and other necessities.

Prospects for improvement seemed slim. Most reservations were in remote areas, far from sites of industrialization and modernization, and American Indians had few of the skills (knowledge of English, familiarity with Western work habits and routines) that would have enabled them to compete for a place in the increasingly urban and industrial American society of the early 20th century. Off the reservations, racial prejudice and strong intolerance limited them. On the reservations, they were subjected to policies designed either to maintain their powerlessness and poverty or to force them to Americanize. Either way, the future of American Indians was in serious jeopardy, and their destructive relations with white society continued in peace as they had in war.

Reservation Life

As would be expected for a conquered and still hostile group, the reservations were intended to closely supervise American Indians and maintain their powerlessness. Relationships with the federal government were paternalistic and featured a variety of policies designed to coercively acculturate the tribes.

Paternalism and the Bureau of Indian Affairs

The reservations were run not by the tribes but by an agency of the federal government: the U.S. Bureau of Indian Affairs (BIA) of the U.S. Department of the Interior. The BIA and its local superintendent controlled virtually all aspects of everyday life, including the reservation budget, the criminal justice system, and the schools. The BIA (again, not the tribes) even determined tribal membership.

The traditional leadership structures and political institutions of the tribes were ignored as the BIA executed its duties with little regard for, and virtually no input from, the people it supervised. The BIA superintendent of the reservations "ordinarily became the most powerful influence on local Indian affairs, even though he was a government employee, not responsible to the Indians but to his superiors in Washington" (Spicer, 1980, p. 117). The superintendent controlled the food supply and communications to the world outside the reservation. This control was used to reward tribal members who cooperated and to punish those who did not.

Coercive Acculturation:
The Dawes Act and Boarding Schools

Consistent with the Blauner hypothesis, American Indians on the reservations were subjected to coercive acculturation or forced Americanization. Their culture was attacked, their languages and religions were forbidden, and their institutions were circumvented and undermined. The centerpiece of U.S. Indian policy was the Dawes Allotment Act of 1887, a deeply flawed attempt to impose white definitions of land ownership and transform American Indians into independent farmers by dividing their land among the families of each tribe. The intention of the act was to give each Indian family the means to survive like their white neighbors.

Although the law might seem benevolent in intent (certainly thousands of immigrant families would have been thrilled to own land), it was flawed by a gross lack of understanding of American Indian cultures and needs, and in many ways, it was a direct attack on those cultures. Most American Indian tribes did not have a strong agrarian tradition, and little or nothing was done to prepare the tribes for their transition to peasant yeomanry. More important, American Indians had little or no concept of land as private property, and it was relatively easy for settlers, land speculators, and others to separate Indian families from the land allocated to them by this legislation. By allotting land to families and individuals, the legislation sought to destroy the broader kinship, clan, and tribal social structures and replace them with Western systems that featured individualism and the profit motive (Cornell, 1988, p. 80).

About 140 million acres were allocated to the tribes in 1887. By the 1930s, nearly 90 million of those acres—almost 65%—had been lost. Most of the remaining land was desert or otherwise nonproductive (Wax, 1971, p. 55). From the standpoint of the Indian Nations, the Dawes Allotment Act was a disaster and a further erosion of their already paltry store of resources (for more details, see Josephy, 1968; Lurie, 1982; McNickle, 1973; Wax, 1971).

Coercive acculturation also operated through a variety of other avenues. Whenever possible, the BIA sent American Indian children to boarding schools, sometimes hundreds of miles away from parents and kin, where they were required to speak English, convert to Christianity, and become educated in the ways of Western civilization. Consistent with the Blauner (1972) hypothesis, tribal languages, dress, and religion were forbidden, and to the extent that native cultures were mentioned at all, they were attacked and ridiculed. Children of different tribes were mixed together as roommates to speed the acquisition of English. When school was not in session, children were often boarded with local white families, usually as unpaid domestic helpers or farmhands, and prevented from visiting their families and revitalizing their tribal ties (Hoxie, 1984; Spicer, 1980; Wax, 1971).

American Indians were virtually powerless to change the reservation system or avoid the campaign of acculturation. Nonetheless, they resented and resisted coerced Americanization, and many languages and cultural elements survived the early reservation period, although often in altered form. For example, the traditional tribal religions remained vital through the period despite the fact that by the 1930s, the great majority of Indians had affiliated with one Christian faith or another. Furthermore, many new religions were founded, some combining Christian and traditional elements (Spicer, 1980, p. 118). Narrative Portrait in this chapter gives an intimate account of the dynamics of coercive acculturation.

Civilize Them With a Stick

In recent decades, boarding schools for American Indian children have been much improved. Facilities have been modernized and faculties upgraded. The curriculum has been updated and often includes elements of American Indian culture and language. Still, it was not that long ago that coercive acculturation at its worst was the daily routine.

In the following passage, Mary Crow Dog, a member of the Sioux tribe who became deeply involved in the Red Power movement that began in the 1960s, recalls some of the horrors of her experiences at a reservation boarding school. As you read her words, keep in mind that she was born in 1955 and started school in the early 1960s, just a generation or two ago.

LAKOTA WOMAN

MARY CROW DOG

It is almost impossible to explain to a sympathetic white person what a typical old Indian boarding school was like; how it affected the Indian child suddenly dumped into it like a small creature from another world, helpless, defenseless, bewildered, trying desperately to survive and sometimes not surviving at all. Even now, when these schools are so much improved, when . . . the teachers [are] well-intentioned, even trained in child psychology—unfortunately the psychology of white children, which is different from ours—the shock to the child upon arrival is still tremendous. . . .

In the traditional Sioux family, the child is never left alone. It is always surrounded by relatives, carried around, enveloped in warmth. It is treated with the respect due to any human being, even a small one. It is seldom forced to do anything against its will, seldom screamed at, and never beaten. . . . And then suddenly a bus or car arrives full of strangers, who yank the child out of the arms of those who love it, taking it screaming to the boarding school. The only word I can think of for what is done to these children is kidnapping. . . .

The mission school at St. Francis was a curse for our family for generations. My grandmother went there, then my mother, then my sisters and I. At one time or another, every one of us tried to run away. Grandma told me about the bad times she experienced at St. Francis. In those days they let students go home only for one week every year. Two days were used up for transportation, which meant spending just 5 days out of every 365 with her family. . . . My mother had much the same experiences but never wanted to talk about them, and then there was I, in the same place. . . . Nothing had changed since my grandmother's days. I have been told that even in the '70s they were still beating children at that school. All I got out of school was being taught how to pray. I learned quickly that I would be beaten if I failed in my devotions or, God forbid, prayed the wrong way, especially prayed in Indian to Wakan Tanka, the Indian creator. . . .

My classroom was right next to the principal's office and almost every day I could hear him swatting the boys. Beating was the common punishment for not doing one's homework, or for being late to school. It had such a bad effect upon me that I hated and mistrusted every white person on sight, because I met only one kind. It was not until much later that I met sincere white people I could relate to and be friends with. Racism breeds racism in reverse.

The Indian Reorganization Act

By the 1930s, the failure of the reservation system and the policy of forced assimilation had become obvious to all who cared to observe. The quality of life for American Indians had not improved, and there was little economic development and fewer job opportunities on the reservations. Health care was woefully inadequate, and education levels lagged far behind national standards.

The plight of American Indians eventually found a sympathetic ear in the administration of Franklin D. Roosevelt, who was elected president in 1932, and John Collier, the man he appointed to run the BIA. Collier was knowledgeable about American Indian issues and concerns and was instrumental in securing the passage of the Indian Reorganization Act (IRA) in 1934.

This landmark legislation contained a number of significant provisions for American Indians and broke sharply with the federal policies of the past. In particular, the IRA rescinded the Dawes Act of 1887 and the policy of individualizing tribal lands. It also provided means by which the tribes could expand their landholdings. Many of the mechanisms of coercive Americanization in the school system and elsewhere were dismantled. Financial aid in various forms and expertise were made available for the economic development of the reservations. In perhaps the most significant departure from earlier policy, the IRA proposed an increase in American Indian self-governance and a reduction of the paternalistic role of the BIA and other federal agencies.

Although sympathetic to American Indians, the IRA had its limits and shortcomings. Many of its intentions were never realized, and the empowerment of the tribes was not unqualified. The move to self-governance generally took place on the dominant group's terms and in conformity with the values and practices of white society. For example, the proposed increase in the decision-making power of the tribes was contingent on their adoption of Anglo-American political forms, including secret ballots, majority rule, and written constitutions. These were alien concepts to those tribes that selected leaders by procedures other than popular election (e.g., leaders might be chosen by councils of elders) or that made decisions by open discussion and consensus building (i.e., decisions required the agreement of everyone with a voice in the process, not a simple majority). The incorporation of these Western forms illustrates the basically assimilationist intent of the IRA.

The IRA had variable effects on American Indian women. In tribes that were male dominated, the IRA gave women new rights to participate in elections, run for office, and hold leadership roles. In other cases, new political structures replaced traditional forms, some of which, as in the Iroquois culture, had accorded women considerable power. Although the political effects were variable, the programs funded by the IRA provided opportunities for women on many reservations to receive education and training for the first time. Many of these opportunities were oriented toward domestic tasks and other traditionally Western female roles, but some prepared American Indian women for jobs outside the family and off the reservation, such as clerical work and nursing (Evans, 1989, pp. 208–209).

In summary, the Indian Reorganization Act of 1934 was a significant improvement over prior federal Indian policy but was bolder and more sympathetic to American Indians in intent than in execution. On one hand, not all tribes were capable of taking advantage of the opportunities provided by the legislation, and some ended up being further victimized. For example, in the Hopi tribe, located in the Southwest, the act allowed a Westernized group of American Indians to be elected to leadership roles, with the result that dominant group firms were allowed to have access to the mineral resources, farmland, and water rights controlled by the tribe. The resultant development generated wealth for the white firms and their Hopi allies, but most of the tribe continued to languish in poverty (Churchill, 1985, pp. 112–113). On the other hand, some tribes prospered (at least comparatively speaking) under the IRA. One impoverished, landless group of Cherokee in Oklahoma acquired land, equipment, and expert advice through the IRA, and between 1937 and 1949, they developed a prosperous, largely debt-free farming community (Debo, 1970, pp. 294–300). Many tribes remained suspicious of the IRA, and by 1948, fewer than 100 tribes had voted to accept its provisions.

The Termination Policy

The IRA's stress on the legitimacy of tribal identity seemed "un-American" to many. There was constant pressure on the federal government to return to an individualistic policy that encouraged (or required) Americanization. Some viewed the tribal structures and communal-property-holding patterns as relics of an earlier era and as impediments to modernization and development. Not so incidentally, some elements of dominant society still coveted the remaining Indian lands and resources, which could be more easily exploited if property ownership were individualized.

In 1953, the assimilationist forces won a victory when Congress passed a resolution calling for an end to the reservation system and to the special relationships between the tribes and the federal government. The proposed policy, called termination, was intended to get the federal government "out of the Indian business." It rejected the IRA and proposed a return to the system of private land ownership imposed on the tribes by the Dawes Act. Horrified at the notion of termination, the tribes opposed the policy strongly and vociferously. Under this policy, all special relationships—including treaty obligations—between the federal government and the tribes would end. Tribes would no longer exist as legally recognized entities, and tribal lands and other resources would be placed in private hands (Josephy, 1968, pp. 353–355).

About 100 tribes, most of them small, were terminated. In virtually all cases, the termination process was administered hastily, and fraud, misuse of funds, and other injustices were common. The Menominee of Wisconsin and the Klamath on the West Coast were the two largest tribes to be terminated. Both suffered devastating economic losses and precipitous declines in quality of life. Neither tribe had the business or tax base needed to finance the services (e.g., health care and schooling) formerly provided by the federal government, and both were forced to sell land, timber, and other scarce resources to maintain minimal standards of living. Many poor American Indian families were forced to turn to local and state agencies, which placed severe strain on welfare budgets. The experience of the Menominee was so disastrous that at the concerted request of the tribe, reservation status was restored in 1973 (Deloria, 1969, pp. 60–82; McNickle, 1973, pp. 103–110; Raymer, 1974). The Klamath reservation was restored in 1986 (Snipp, 1996, p. 394).

Relocation and Urbanization

At about the same time the termination policy came into being, various programs were established to encourage American Indians to move to urban areas. The movement to the city had already begun in the 1940s, spurred by the availability of factory jobs during World War II. In the 1950s, the movement was further encouraged with assistance programs and by the declining government support for economic development on the reservation, the most dramatic example of which was the policy of termination (Green, 1999, p. 265). Centers for American Indians were established in many cities, and various services (e.g., job training, housing assistance, English instruction) were offered to assist in the adjustment to urban life. The urbanization of the American Indian population is displayed in Exhibit 7.3. Note the rapid increase in the movement to the city that began in the 1950s. Almost 60% of all American Indians are now urbanized, and since 1950, Indians have urbanized faster than the general population. Nevertheless, American Indians are still the least urbanized minority group. The population as a whole is about 80% urbanized; in contrast, African Americans (see Exhibit 5.3) are about 90% urbanized.

As with African Americans, American Indians arrived in the cities after the mainstream economy had begun to deemphasize blue-collar or manufacturing jobs. Because of their relatively low average levels of educational attainment and their racial and cultural differences, American Indians in the city tended to encounter the same problems experienced by African Americans and other minority groups of color: high rates of unemployment, inadequate housing, and all the other travails of the urban underclass.

Exhibit 7.3
Urbanization of American Indians, 1900 to 2000

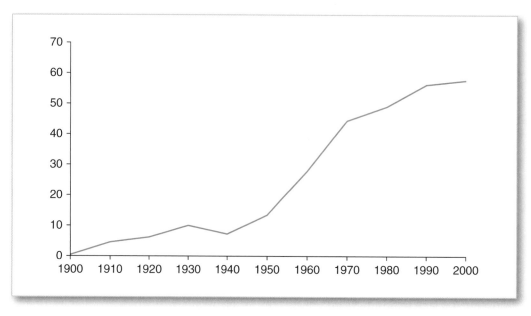

SOURCE: 1900 to 1990: Thornton (2001, p. 142); 2000—U.S. Bureau of the Census (2000a).

Photo 7.1

Indians often live in more deteriorated, less desirable urban areas.

Getty/William F. Campbell.

American Indian women also migrated to the city in considerable numbers. The discrimination, unemployment, and poverty of the urban environment often made it difficult for the men of the group to fulfill the role of breadwinner; thus, the burden of supporting the family tended to fall on the women. The difficulties inherent in combining child rearing and a job outside the home are compounded by isolation from the support networks provided by extended family and clan back on the reservations. Nevertheless, one study found that American Indian women in the city continue to practice their traditional cultures and maintain the tribal identity of their children (Joe & Miller, 1994, p. 186).

American Indians living in the city are, on average, better off than those living on reservations, where unemployment can reach 80% or even 90%. The improvement is relative, however. Although many individual Indians prosper in the urban environment, income figures for urban Indians as a whole are comparable to those for African Americans and well below those for whites. American Indian unemployment rates run much higher than the national average. For example, in the first half of 2010, unemployment for all American Indians was about 15%, comparable to the rate for African Americans (see Exhibit 6.3) and 67% higher than that for whites (Austin, 2010). Thus, a move to the city often means trading rural poverty for the urban variety, with little net improvement in life chances.

American Indians will probably remain more rural than other minority groups for years to come. Despite the poverty and lack of opportunities for schooling and jobs, the reservation offers some advantages in services and lifestyle. On the reservation, there may be opportunities for political participation and leadership roles that are not available in the cities, where American Indians are a tiny minority. Reservations also offer kinfolk, friends, religious services, and tribal celebrations (Snipp, 1989, p. 84). Lower levels of education, work experience, and financial resources combine with the prejudice, discrimination, and racism of the larger society to lower the chances of success in the city and will probably sustain a continuing return to the reservations.

Although the economic benefits of urbanization have been slim for the group as whole, other advantages have accrued from life in the city. It was much easier to establish networks of friendship and affiliation across tribal lines in the cities, and urban Indians have been one of the sources of strength and personnel for a movement of protest that began early in the 20th century. Virtually all the organizational vehicles of American Indian protest have had urban roots.

Self-Determination

The termination policy aroused so much opposition from American Indians and was such an obvious disaster that the pressure to push tribes to termination faded in the late 1950s, although the act itself was not repealed until 1975. Since the 1960s, federal Indian policy has generally returned to the tradition set by the IRA. Termination and forced assimilation continue to be officially rejected, and within limits, the tribes have been granted more freedom to find their own way, at their own pace, of relating to the larger society.

Several federal programs and laws have benefited the tribes during the past few decades, including the antipoverty and "Great Society" campaigns launched in the 1960s. In 1970, President Richard Nixon affirmed the government's commitment to fulfilling treaty obligations and the right of the tribes to self-governance. The Indian Self-Determination and Education Assistance Act was passed in 1975. This legislation increased aid to reservation schools and American Indian students and increased tribal control over the administration of the reservations, from police forces to schools to road maintenance.

The Self-Determination Act primarily benefited the larger tribes and those that had well-established administrative and governing structures. Smaller and less-well-organized tribes have continued to rely heavily on the federal government (Snipp, 1996, p. 394). Nonetheless, in many cases, this new phase of federal policy has allowed American Indian tribes to plot their own courses free of paternalistic regulation, and just as important, it gave them the tools and resources to address their problems and improve their situations. Decision making was returned to local authorities, who were "held more accountable to local needs, conditions, and cultures than outsiders" (Taylor & Kalt, 2005, p. xi).

In the view of many, self-determination is a key reason for the recent improvements in the status of American Indians, and we will look at some of these developments after examining the American Indian protest movement.

PROTEST AND RESISTANCE

Early Efforts

As BIA-administered reservations and coercive Americanization came to dominate tribal life in the 20th century, new forms of Indian activism appeared. The modern protest movement was tiny at first and, with few exceptions, achieved a measure of success only in recent decades. In fact, the American Indian protest movement in the past was not so much unsuccessful as simply ignored. The movement has focused on several complementary goals: protecting American Indian resources and treaty rights, striking a balance between assimilation and pluralism, and finding a relationship with the dominant group that would permit a broader array of life chances without sacrificing tribal identity and heritage.

Formally organized American Indian protest organizations have existed since the 1910s, but the modern phase of the protest movement began during World War II. Many American Indians served in the military or moved to the city to take jobs in aid of the war effort and were thereby exposed to the world beyond the reservation. Also, political activism on the reservation, which had been stimulated by the IRA, continued through the war years, and the recognition that many problems were shared across tribal lines grew.

These trends helped stimulate the founding of the National Congress of American Indians (NCAI) in 1944. This organization was pantribal (i.e., included members from many different tribes); its first convention was attended by representatives of 50 different tribes and reservations (Cornell, 1988, p. 119). The leadership consisted largely of American Indians educated and experienced in the white world. However, the NCAI's program stressed the importance of preserving the old ways and tribal institutions as well as protecting Indian welfare. An early victory for the NCAI and its allies came in 1946 when an Indian Claims Commission was created by the federal government. This body was authorized to hear claims brought by the tribes with regard to treaty violations. The commission has settled hundreds of claims, resulting in awards of millions of dollars to the tribes, and it continues its work today (Weeks, 1988, pp. 261–262).

In the 1950s and 1960s, the protest movement was further stimulated by the threat of termination and by the increasing number of American Indians living in the cities who developed friendships across tribal lines. Awareness of common problems, rising levels of education, and the examples set by the successful protests of other minority groups also increased readiness for collective action.

Red Power

By the 1960s and 1970s, American Indian protest groups were finding ways to express their grievances and problems to the nation. The Red Power movement, like the Black Power movement (see Chapter 6), encompassed a coalition of groups, many considerably more assertive than the NCAI, and a varied collection of ideas, most of which stressed self-determination and pride in race and cultural heritage. Red Power protests included a "fish-in" in Washington State in 1965, an episode that also illustrates the nature of American Indian demands. The state of Washington had tried to limit the fishing rights of several different tribes on the grounds that the supply of fish was diminishing and needed to be protected. The tribes depended on fishing for subsistence and survival and argued that their right to fish had been guaranteed by treaties signed in the 1850s and that it was the pollution and commercial fishing of the dominant society that had depleted the supply of fish. They organized a "fish-in" in violation of the state's policy and were met by a contingent of police officers and other law officials. Violent confrontations and mass arrests ensued. Three years later, after a lengthy and expensive court battle, the tribes were vindicated, and the U.S. Supreme Court confirmed their treaty rights to fish the rivers of Washington State (Nabakov, 1999, pp. 362–363).

Another widely publicized episode took place in 1969, when American Indians from various tribes occupied Alcatraz Island in San Francisco Bay, the site of a closed federal prison. The protesters were acting on an old law that granted American Indians the right to reclaim abandoned federal land. The occupation of Alcatraz was organized in part by the American Indian Movement (AIM), founded in 1968. More militant and radical than the previously established protest groups, AIM aggressively confronted the BIA, the police, and other forces that were seen as repressive. With the backing of AIM and other groups, Alcatraz was occupied for nearly 4 years and generated a great deal of publicity for the Red Power movement and the plight of American Indians.

In 1972, AIM helped organize a march on Washington, D.C., called the "Trail of Broken Treaties." Marchers came from many tribes and represented both urban and reservation Indians. The intent of the marchers was to dramatize the problems of the tribes. The leaders demanded the abolition of the BIA, the return of illegally taken land, and increased self-governance for the tribes, among other things. When they reached Washington, some of the marchers forcibly occupied the BIA offices. Property was damaged (by which side is disputed), and records and papers were destroyed. The marchers eventually surrendered, but none of their demands were met. The following year, AIM occupied the village of Wounded Knee in South Dakota to protest the violation of treaty rights. Wounded Knee was the site of the last armed confrontation between Indians and whites in 1890 and was selected by AIM for its deep symbolic significance. The occupation lasted more than 2 months and involved several armed confrontations with federal authorities. Again, the protest ended without achieving any of the demands made by the Indian leadership (Olson & Wilson, 1984, pp. 172–175). Since the early 1970s, the level of protest activity has declined, just as it has for the African American protest movement. Lawsuits and court cases have predominated over dramatic, direct confrontations.

Photo 7.2

Indian activists occupy an abandoned missile base.

© Bettmann/Corbis.

Ironically, the struggle for Red Power encouraged assimilation as well as pluralism. The movement linked members of different tribes and forced Indians of diverse heritages to find common ground, often in the form of a "generic" American Indian culture. Inevitably, the protests were conducted in English, and the grievances were expressed in ways that were understandable to white society, thus increasing the pressure to acculturate even while arguing for the survival of the tribes. Furthermore, successful protest required that American Indians be fluent in English, trained in the law and other professions, skilled in dealing with bureaucracies, and knowledgeable about the formulation and execution of public policy. American Indians who became proficient in these areas thereby took on the characteristics of their adversaries (Hraba, 1994).

As the pantribal protest movement forged ties between members of diverse tribes, the successes of the movement and changing federal policy and public opinion encouraged a rebirth of commitment to tribalism and "Indianness." American Indians were simultaneously stimulated to assimilate (by stressing their common characteristics and creating organizational forms that united the tribes) and to retain a pluralistic relationship with the larger society (by working for self-determination and enhanced tribal power and authority). Thus, part of the significance of the Red Power movement was that it encouraged both pantribal unity and a continuation of tribal diversity (Olson & Wilson, 1984, p. 206). Today, American Indians continue to seek a way of existing in the larger society that merges assimilation with pluralism.

Exhibit 7.4 summarizes this discussion of federal policy and Indian protest. The four major policy phases since the end of overt hostilities in 1890 are listed on the left. The thrust of the government's economic and political policies are listed in the next two columns, followed by a brief characterization of tribal response. The last column shows the changing bases for federal policy, sometimes aimed at weakening tribal structures and individualizing American Indians and sometimes (including most recently) aimed at working with and preserving tribal structures.

Exhibit 7.4 Federal Indian Policy and Indian Response

Period	Economic Impact	Political Impact	Indian Response	Government Approach
Reservation: late 1800s to 1930s	Land loss (Dawes Act) and welfare dependency	Government control of reservation and coerced acculturation	Some resistance; growth of religious movements	Individualistic; creation of self-sufficient farmers
Reorganization (IRA): 1930s and 1940s	Stabilized land base and supported some development of reservation	Establish federally sponsored tribal governments	Increased political participation in many tribes; some pantribal activity	Incorporated tribes as groups; creation of self-sufficient "Americanized" communities
Termination and Relocation: late 1940s to early 1960s	Withdrawal of government support for reservations; promotion of urbanization	New assault on tribes, new forms of coercive acculturation	Increased pantribalism; widespread and intense opposition to termination	Individualistic; dissolved tribal ties and promoted incorporation into the modern, urban labor market
Self-Determination: 1960s to present	Developed reservation economies; increased integration of Indian labor force	Support for tribal governments	Greatly increased political activity	Incorporated tribes as self-sufficient communities with access to federal programs of support and welfare

SOURCE: Based on Cornell, Kalt, Krepps, and Taylor (1998, p. 5).

THE CONTINUING STRUGGLE FOR DEVELOPMENT IN CONTEMPORARY AMERICAN INDIAN–WHITE RELATIONS

Conflicts between American Indians and the larger society are far from over. Although the days of deadly battle are (with occasional exceptions) long gone, the issues that remain are serious, difficult to resolve, and, in their way, just as much matters of life and death. American Indians face enormous challenges in their struggle to improve their status, but largely as a result of their greater freedom from stifling federal control since the 1970s, they also have some resources, some opportunities, and a leadership that is both talented and resourceful (Bordewich, 1996, p. 11).

Natural Resources

Ironically, land allotted to American Indian tribes in the 19th century sometimes turned out to be rich in resources that became valuable in the 20th century. These resources include oil, natural gas, coal, and uranium, basic sources of energy in the larger society. In addition (and despite the devastation wreaked by the Dawes Act of 1887), some tribes hold title to water rights, fishing rights, woodlands that could sustain a lumbering industry, and wilderness areas that could be developed for camping, hunting, and other forms of recreation. These resources are likely to become more valuable as the earth's natural resources and undeveloped areas are further depleted in the future.

The challenge faced by American Indians is to retain control of these resources and to develop them for their own benefit. Threats to the remaining tribal lands and assets are common. Mining and energy companies continue to cast envious eyes on American Indian land, and other tribal assets are coveted by real-estate developers, fishermen (recreational as well as commercial), backpackers and campers, and cities facing water shortages (Harjo, 1996).

Some tribes have succeeded in developing their resources for their own benefit, in part because of their increased autonomy and independence since the passage of the 1975 Indian Self-Determination Act. For example, the White Mountain Apaches of Arizona own a variety of enterprises, including a major ski resort and a casino (Cornell & Kalt, 1998, pp. 3–4). On many other reservations, however, even rich stores of resources lie dormant, awaiting the right combination of tribal leadership, expertise, and development capital.

On a broader level, tribes are banding together to share expertise and negotiate more effectively with the larger society. For example, 25 tribes founded the Council of Energy Resource Tribes in 1975 to coordinate and control the development of the mineral resources on reservation lands. Since its founding, the council has successfully negotiated a number of agreements with dominant group firms, increasing the flow of income to the tribes and raising their quality of life (Cornell, 1988; Snipp, 1989). The council now encompasses more than 50 tribes and several Canadian First Nations (see their website at http://www.certred earth.com/ for more information).

Attracting Industry to the Reservation

Many efforts to develop the reservations have focused on creating jobs by attracting industry through such incentives as low taxes, low rents, and a low-wage pool of labor—not unlike the package of benefits offered to employers by less-developed nations in Asia, South America, and Africa. With some notable exceptions, these efforts have not been particularly successful (for a review, see Cornell, 2006; Vinje, 1996). Reservations are often so geographically isolated that transportation costs become prohibitive. The jobs that have materialized are typically low wage and have few benefits; usually, non-Indians fill the more lucrative managerial positions. Thus, the opportunities for building economic power or improving the standard of living from these jobs are sharply limited. These new jobs may transform "the welfare poor into the working poor" (Snipp, 1996, p. 398), but their potential for raising economic vitality is low.

To illustrate the problems of developing reservations by attracting industry, consider the Navajo, the second-largest American Indian tribe. The Navajo reservation spreads across Arizona, New Mexico, and Utah and encompasses about 20 million acres, an area a little smaller than either Indiana or Maine. Although the reservation seems huge on a map, much of the land is desert not suitable for farming or other uses. As they have for the past several centuries, the Navajo today rely heavily on the cultivation of corn and sheepherding for sustenance.

Most wage-earning jobs on the reservation are with the agencies of the federal government (e.g., the BIA) or with the tribal government. Tourism is large and growing, but the jobs available in that sector are typically low wage and seasonal. There are reserves of coal, uranium, and oil on the reservation, but these resources have not generated many jobs. In some cases, the Navajo have resisted the damage to the environment that would be caused by mines and oil wells because of their traditional values and respect for the land. When exploitation of these resources has been permitted, the companies involved often use highly automated technologies that generate few jobs (Oswalt & Neely, 1996, pp. 317–351).

Exhibits 7.5 and 7.6 contrast Navaho income, poverty, and education with those for non-Hispanic whites. The poverty rate for the Navaho is about 3 times greater than the rate for non-Hispanic whites, and they are far below national standards in terms of education. Educational achievement is even lower for members of the tribe living on the reservation, where only about 64% have finished high school (vs. 73% of all Navaho) (U.S. Bureau of the Census, 2009a). Also, median household income for the Navaho is less than 60% of household income for non-Hispanic whites.

Exhibit 7.5 Poverty and Education for Non-Hispanic White (NHW), All American Indians (AI), Navaho, and Choctaw

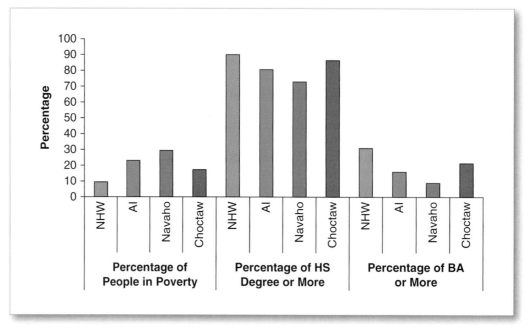

SOURCE: U.S. Bureau of the Census (2009a).

Exhibit 7.6 Median Household Income

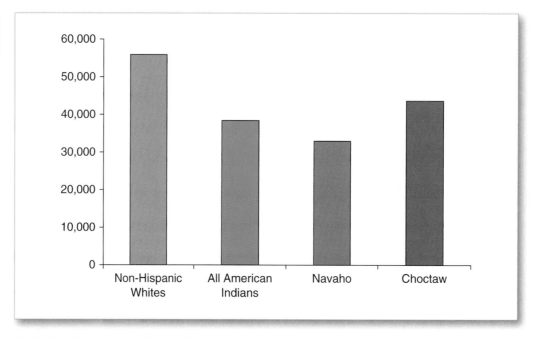

SOURCE: U.S. Bureau of the Census (2009a).

On the other hand, some tribes have managed to achieve relative prosperity by bringing jobs to their people. The Choctaw Nation of Mississippi, for example, has become one of the largest employers in the state. Tribal leaders have been able to attract companies such as Xerox and Harley-Davidson by promising (and delivering) high-quality labor for relatively low wages. Incomes have risen, unemployment is relatively low, and the tribe has built schools, hospitals, and a television station and administers numerous other services for its members (Bordewich, 1996, pp. 300–305). The poverty rate for the Choctaw is 40% lower than the Navaho rate (although still almost double the rate for non-Hispanic whites), and their educational levels are much closer to national standards. More than 21% of the Choctaw are college educated, more than double the rate for the Navaho. Median household income for the Choctaw is only about 80% of non-Hispanic whites but more than $10,000 greater than median income for the Navaho.

The Choctaw are not the most affluent tribe, and the Navajo are far from being the most destitute. They illustrate the mixture of partial successes and failures that typify efforts to bring prosperity to the reservations; together, these two cases suggest that attracting industry and jobs to the reservations is a possible—but difficult and uncertain—strategy for economic development.

It is worth repeating that self-determination, the ability of tribes to control development on the reservation, seems to be one of the important keys to success. Tribes such as the Choctaw are, in a sense, developing ethnic enclaves (see Chapter 2) in which they can capitalize on local networks of interpersonal relationships. As with other groups that have followed this strategy, success in the enclave depends on solidarity and group cohesion, not Americanization and integration (see Cornell, 2006).

Broken Treaties

For many tribes, the treaties signed with the federal government in the 19th century offer another potential resource. These treaties were often violated by white settlers, the military, state and local governments, the BIA, and other elements and agencies of the dominant group, and many tribes are pursuing this trail of broken treaties and seeking compensation for the wrongs of the past. For example, in 1972, the Passamaquoddy and Penobscot tribes filed a lawsuit demanding the return of 12.5 million acres of land—more than half the state of Maine—and $25 billion in damages. The tribes argued that this land had been illegally taken from them more than 150 years earlier. After 8 years of litigation, the tribes settled for a $25 million trust fund and 300,000 acres of land. Although far less than their original demand, the award gave the tribes control over resources that could be used for economic development, job creation, upgrading educational programs, and developing other programs that would enhance human and financial capital (Worsnop, 1992, p. 391).

Virtually every tribe has similar grievances, and if pursued successfully, the long-dead treaty relationship between the Indian nations and the government could be a significant fount of economic and political resources. Of course, lawsuits require considerable (and expensive) legal expertise and years of effort to bring to fruition. Because there are no guarantees of success, this avenue has some sharp limitations and risks.

Gaming and Other Development Possibilities

Another resource for American Indians is the gambling industry, the development of which was made possible by federal legislation passed in 1988. There are currently more than 400 tribes with gaming establishments (National Indian Gaming Commission, 2011), and the industry has grown many times over, from $212 million in revenues in 1988 (Spilde, 2001) to more than $26 billion in 2009 (National Indian Gaming Commission, n.d.). Exhibit 7.7 charts the growth of revenues from gaming on American Indian reservations from 1995 to 2009. In this time period, revenues have grown more than 5 times over.

Most operations are relatively small in scale. The 21 largest Indian casinos—about 5% of all Indian casinos—generate almost 40% of the total income from gaming, and the 71 smallest operations—about 17% of all Indian casinos—account for less than 1% of the income (National Indian Gaming Commission, 2011).

The single most profitable Indian gambling operation is the Foxwoods Casino in Connecticut, operated by the Pequot tribe. The casino is one of the largest in the world and generates more revenue than the casinos of Atlantic City. The profits from the casino are used to benefit tribal

Exhibit 7.7 Revenues From Gaming in American Indian Casinos, 1995 to 2009

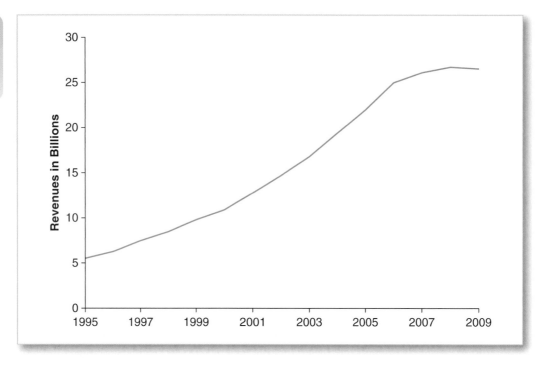

SOURCE: National Indian Gaming Commission (2011).

Photo 7.3

This Apache-owned facility combines a casino and a resort.

© Bob Rowan; Progressive Image/ CORBIS.

members in a variety of ways, including the repurchase of tribal lands, housing assistance, medical benefits, educational scholarships, and public services, such as a tribal police force (Bordewich, 1996, p. 110). Other tribes have used gambling profits to purchase restaurants and marinas and to finance the development of outlet malls, manufacturing plants, and a wide variety of other businesses and enterprises (Spilde, 2001).

The power of gaming to benefit the tribes is suggested by the information displayed in Exhibit 7.8. The table shows that on a number of indicators, both gaming and nongaming reservations enjoyed significant improvements in their quality of life in the last decade of the 20th century but that gaming reservations improved more rapidly. For example, all reservations increased their per capita income faster than the nation as a whole (+11%), but gaming reservations improved faster (+36%) than nongaming reservations (+21%).

Various tribes have sought other ways to capitalize on their freedom from state regulation and taxes. Some have established small but profitable businesses selling cigarettes tax-free. Also, because they are not subject to state and federal environmental regulations, some reservations are exploring the possibility of housing nuclear waste and other refuse of industrialization—a somewhat ironic and not altogether attractive use of the remaining Indian lands.

Clearly, the combination of increased autonomy, treaty rights, natural resources, and gambling means that American Indians today have an opportunity to dramatically raise their standards of living and creatively take control of their own destinies. Some tribes have enjoyed enormous benefits, but for others, these assets remain a potential waiting to be actualized. Without denying the success stories or the improvements in recent years, the lives of many American Indians continue to be limited by poverty and powerlessness, prejudice, and discrimination. We document these patterns in the next section.

Indicator	Nongaming	Gaming	U.S.
Per capita income	+21%	+36%	+11%
Family poverty	–7%	–12%	–1%
Unemployment	–2%	–5%	–1%
High school graduates	–1%	+2%	–1%
College graduates	+2%	+3%	+4%

SOURCE: Taylor and Kalt (2005, p. xi).

Exhibit 7.8 Various Indicators of Improvement on Gaming vs. Nongaming Reservations and Total U.S., 1990 to 2000

CONTEMPORARY AMERICAN INDIAN–WHITE RELATIONS

This section uses many of the terms and concepts we have developed over the first seven chapters to analyze the contemporary situation of American Indians. Compared with other groups, information about American Indians is scant. Nonetheless, a relatively clear picture emerges. The portrait stresses a mixed picture for this group: improvements for some tribes combined with continued colonization, marginalization, and impoverishment for others. Like African Americans, American Indians can be found at every status and income level in the United States, but Indians living on reservations continue as one of the most impoverished, marginalized groups in society. American Indians as a group face ongoing discrimination and exclusion and continue the search for a meaningful course between assimilation and pluralism.

Prejudice and Discrimination

Anti-Indian prejudice has been a part of American society from the beginning. Historically, negative feelings such as hatred and contempt have been widespread and strong, particularly during the heat of war, and various stereotypes of Indians have been common. One stereotype, especially strong during periods of conflict, depicts Indians as bloodthirsty, ferocious, cruel savages capable of any atrocity. The other image of American Indians is that of "the noble Red Man" who lives in complete harmony with nature and symbolizes goodwill and pristine simplicity (Bordewich, 1996, p. 34). Although the first stereotype tended to fade away as hostilities drew to a close, the latter image retains a good deal of strength in modern views of Indians found in popular culture and among environmentalist and "new age" spiritual organizations.

A variety of studies have documented continued stereotyping of Native Americans in the popular press, textbooks, the media, cartoons, and various other places (e.g., see Aleiss, 2005; Bird, 1999; Meek, 2006; Rouse & Hanson, 1991). In the tradition of "the noble Red Man," American Indians are often portrayed as bucks and squaws, complete with headdresses, bows, tepees, and other such "generic" Indian artifacts. These portrayals obliterate the diversity of American Indian culture and lifestyles. American Indians are often referred to in the past tense, as if their present situation were of no importance or, worse, as if they no longer existed. Many history books continue to begin the study of American history in Europe or with the "discovery" of America, omitting the millennia of civilization prior to the arrival of European explorers and colonizers. Contemporary portrayals of American Indians, such as in the movie *Dances with Wolves* (1990), are more sympathetic but still treat the tribes as part of a bucolic past forever lost, not as peoples with real problems in the present.

The persistence of stereotypes and the extent to which they have become enmeshed in modern culture is illustrated by continuing controversies surrounding nicknames for athletic teams (e.g., the Washington Redskins, the Cleveland Indians, and the Atlanta Braves) and the use of American Indian mascots, tomahawk "chops," and other practices offensive to many American Indians (see the Current Debates section at the end of this chapter for more). Protests have been staged at some athletic events to increase awareness of these derogatory depictions, but as was the case so often in the past, the protests have been attacked, ridiculed, or simply ignored.

There are relatively few studies of anti-Indian prejudices in the social science literature, and it is, therefore, difficult to characterize changes over the past several decades. We do not know whether there has been a shift to more symbolic or "modern" forms of anti-Indian racism, as there has been for antiblack prejudice, or whether the stereotypes of American Indians have declined in strength or changed in content.

One of the few records of national anti-Indian prejudice over time is that of social distance scale results (see Exhibit 3.6). When the scales were first administered in 1926, American Indians were ranked in the middle third of all groups (18th out of 28), at about the same level as Southern and Eastern Europeans and slightly above Mexicans, another colonized group. The ranking of American Indians remained stable until 1977, when there was a noticeable rise in their position relative to other groups. In the most recent polls, the social distance scores of American Indians fell (indicating less prejudice), but the relative ranking still placed them with other racial minority groups. These shifts may reflect a decline in levels of prejudice, a change from more overt forms to more subtle modern racism, or both. Remember, however, that the samples for the social distance research were college students for the most part and do not necessarily reflect trends in the general population (see also Hanson & Rouse, 1987; Smith & Dempsey, 1983).

Research is also unclear about the severity or extent of discrimination against American Indians. Certainly, the group's lower average levels of education limit their opportunities for upward mobility, choice of occupations, and range of income. This is a form of institutional discrimination in the sense that the opportunities to develop human capital are much less available to American Indians than to much of the rest of the population. In terms of individual discrimination or more overt forms of exclusion, there is simply too little evidence to sustain clear conclusions (Snipp, 1992, p. 363). The situation of American Indian women is also under-researched, but Snipp reports that like their counterparts in other minority groups and the dominant group, they "are systematically paid less than their male counterparts in similar circumstances" (p. 363).

The very limited evidence available from social distance scales suggests that overt anti-Indian prejudice has declined, perhaps in parallel with antiblack prejudice. A great deal of stereotyping remains, however, and demeaning, condescending, or negative portrayals of American Indians are common throughout the dominant culture. Institutional discrimination is a major barrier for American Indians, who have not had access to opportunities for education and employment.

Assimilation and Pluralism

In this section, we continue to assess the situation of American Indians today using the same conceptual framework used in Chapter 6.

Acculturation

Despite more than a century of coercive Americanization, many tribes have been able to preserve at least a portion of their traditional cultures. For example, many tribal languages continue to be spoken on a daily basis. Almost 20% of American Indians speak a language other than English at home, about the same percentage as the total population. Exhibit 7.9

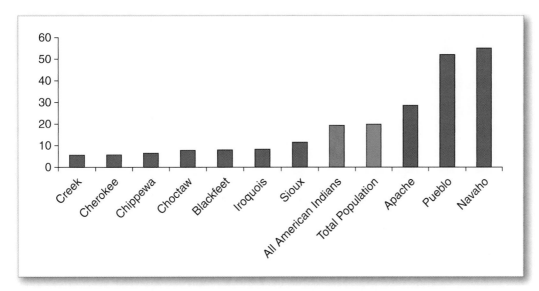

Exhibit 7.9 Percentage of Total Population, All American Indians, and 10 Largest Tribes That Speak a Language Other Than English at Home, 2009

SOURCE: U.S. Bureau of the Census (2011); American Community Survey (2007–2009).

suggests the extent of language preservation. For 6 of the 10 largest tribes, less than 10% of their members speak the tribal language at home. For some tribes, however, the picture is dramatically different. For example, more than 50% of all Navajo and Pueblo Indians speak the tribal language at home.

While some Native American languages have survived, it seems that even the most widely spoken of these languages is endangered. One study (Krauss, 1996) estimates that only about 11% of the surviving 200 languages are being taught by parents to their children in the traditional way, and most languages are spoken on a daily basis only by the older generation. If this pattern persists, Native American languages will disappear as the generations change. A number of tribes have instituted programs to try to renew and preserve their language, along with other elements of their culture, but the success of these efforts is uncertain (Schmid, 2001, p. 25).

Traditional culture is retained in other forms besides language. Religions and value systems, political and economic structures, and recreational patterns have all survived the military conquest and the depredations of reservation life, but each pattern has been altered by contact with the dominant group. Cornell (1987), for example, argues that although American Indians have been affected by the "American dream" of material success through hard, honest work, their individual values continue to reflect their greater orientation to the group rather than to the individual.

The tendency to filter the impact of the larger society through continuing, vital American Indian culture is also illustrated by the Native American Church. The Native American Church is an important American Indian religion, with more than 100 congregations across the nation.

This religion combines elements from both cultures, and church services freely mix Christian imagery and the Bible with attempts to seek personal visions by using peyote, a hallucinogenic drug. The latter practice is consistent with the spiritual and religious traditions of many tribes but clashes sharply with the laws and norms of the larger society. The difference in traditions has generated many skirmishes with the courts, and as recently as 2004, the right of the Native American Church to use peyote was upheld by the Supreme Court of Utah ("Utah Supreme Court," 2004).

American Indians have been more successful than African Americans in preserving their traditional cultures, a pattern that is partly explained by the differences in the relationship between each minority group and the dominant group. African Americans were exploited for

labor, whereas the competition with American Indians involved land. African cultures could not easily survive because the social structures that transmitted the cultures and gave them meaning were destroyed by slavery and sacrificed to the exigencies of the plantation economy.

In contrast, American Indians confronted the dominant group as tribal units, intact and whole. The tribes maintained integrity throughout the wars and throughout the reservation period. Tribal culture was indeed attacked and denigrated during the reservation era, but the basic social unit that sustained the culture survived, albeit in altered form. The fact that American Indians were placed on separate reservations, isolated from one another and the "contaminating" effects of everyday contact with the larger society, also abetted the preservation of traditional languages and culture (Cornell, 1990). The next Narrative Portrait illustrates the persistence of a distinct Indian culture and point of view.

The vitality of Indian cultures may have increased in the current atmosphere of greater tolerance and support for pluralism in the larger society, combined with increased autonomy and lower government regulation on the reservations. However, a number of social forces are working against pluralism and the continuing survival of tribal cultures. Pantribalism may threaten the integrity of individual tribal cultures as it represents American Indian grievances and concerns to the larger society. Opportunities for jobs, education, and higher incomes draw American Indians to more developed urban areas and will continue to do so as long as the reservations are underdeveloped. Many aspects of the tribal cultures can be fully expressed and practiced only with other tribal members on the reservations. Thus, many American Indians must make a choice between "Indian-ness" on the reservation and "success" in the city. The younger, more educated American Indians will be most likely to confront this choice, and the future vitality of traditional American Indian cultures and languages will hinge on which option is chosen.

Secondary Structural Assimilation

This section assesses the degree of integration of American Indians into the various institutions of public life, following the general outlines of the parallel section in Chapter 6.

An Indian View of White Civilization

Who's the savage? One stereotype of American Indians portrays them as "cruel, barbaric, and savage." Is it possible, however, that American Indians are more advanced than the dazzling sophisticates of urban America? In a 1972 interview, John Lame Deer, a Sioux, gives his view of the technologically advanced society that surrounds him. Through his words, we can hear the voices of the Indian cultures that have survived.

LISTENING TO THE AIR

JOHN LAME DEER

You have made it hard for us to experience nature in the good way by being part of it. Even here [a Sioux reservation in South Dakota] we are conscious that somewhere out in those hills there are missile silos and radar stations. White men always pick the few unspoiled, beautiful, awesome spots for these abominations. You have raped and violated these lands, always saying, "gimme, gimme, gimme," and never giving anything back. . . . You have not only despoiled the earth, the rocks, the minerals, all of which you call "dead" but which are very much alive; you have even changed the animals, . . . changed them in a horrible way, so no one can recognize them. There is power in a buffalo—spiritual, magic power—but there is no power in an Angus, in a Hereford.

There is power in an antelope, but not in a goat or a sheep, which holds still while you butcher it, which will eat your newspaper if you let it. There was great power in a wolf, even in a coyote. You made him into a freak—a toy poodle, a Pekinese, a lap dog. You can't do much with a cat, which is like an Indian, unchangeable. So you fix it, alter it, declaw it, even cut its vocal cords so you can experiment on it in a laboratory without being disturbed by its cries. . . .

You have not only altered, declawed, and malformed your winged and four-legged cousins; you have done it to yourselves. You have changed men into chairmen of boards, into office workers, into time-clock punchers. You have changed women into housewives, truly fearful creatures. . . . You live in prisons which you have built for yourselves, calling them "homes," offices, factories. We have a new joke on the reservations: "What is cultural deprivation?" Answer: "Being an upper-middle-class white kid living in a split-level suburban home with a color TV." . . .

I think white people are so afraid of the world they created that they don't want to see, feel, smell, or hear it. The feeling of rain or snow on your face, being numbed by an icy wind and thawing out before a smoking fire, coming out of a hot sweat bath and plunging into a cold stream, these things make you feel alive, but you don't want them anymore. Living in boxes that shut out the heat of the summer and the chill of winter, living inside a body that no longer has a scent, hearing the noise of the hi-fi rather than listening to the sounds of nature, watching some actor on TV have a make-believe experience when you no longer experience anything for yourself, eating food without taste—that's your way. It's no good.

Exhibit 7.10 Percentage of County Populations Choosing AIAN, Alone and in Combination, 2000

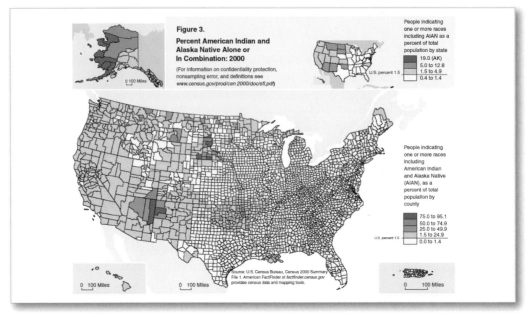

SOURCE: Ogunwole (2002).

Residential Patterns. Since the Indian Removal Act of 1830 (see Chapter 4), American Indians have been concentrated in the western two thirds of the nation, as illustrated in Exhibit 7.10, although some pockets of population still can be found in the East. The states with the largest concentrations of American Indians—California, New Mexico, and Arizona—together include about one third of all American Indians, and another 10% live in Oklahoma. American Indians belong to hundreds of different tribes, the 10 largest of which were listed in Exhibit 7.1.

Exhibit 7.11 provides some information about the levels of residential segregation of American Indians. The data in the exhibit are limited to metropolitan areas only. Since American Indians are such a small, rural group, Exhibit 7.11 is limited to only 13 metropolitan areas, most in the West. The Northeast is not included because of the small numbers of American Indians living in the metropolitan areas of that region. Residential segregation is measured using the dissimilarity index, the same statistic used in Exhibit 6.7 for African Americans.

Exhibit 7.11 Residential Segregation of American Indians, 1980 to 2000

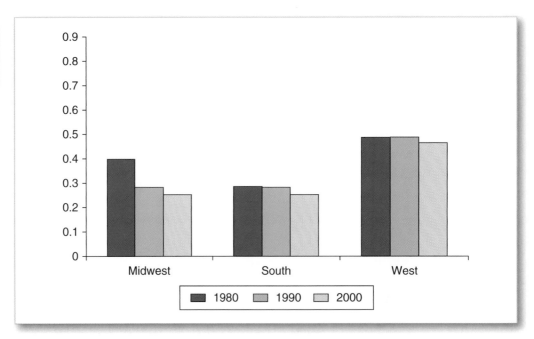

SOURCE: Iceland, Weinberg, and Steinmetz (2002, p. 23).

Although based on small numbers, the exhibit shows that residential segregation is much lower for American Indians than for African Americans (see Exhibit 6.7) and approaches the "high" range (0.6) only in the western region. Also, the level of residential segregation declined slightly between 1980 and 2000, but remember that more than a third of American Indians live on rural reservations where the levels of residential segregation are quite high.

School Integration and Educational Attainment. As a result of the combined efforts of missionaries and federal agencies, American Indians have had a long but not necessarily productive acquaintance with Western education. Until the past few decades, schools for American Indians were primarily focused on Americanizing children, not so much on educating them. For many tribes, the percentage of high school graduates has increased in the recent past, but American Indians as a whole are still somewhat below national levels. On the other hand, four of the largest tribes now exceed the national standard. The gap in college education is closing as well but remains large. None of the 10 largest tribes approaches the national norm on this variable. The differences in schooling are especially important because the lower levels of educational attainment limit mobility and job opportunities in the postindustrial job market. The educational levels of American Indians are displayed in Exhibit 7.12.

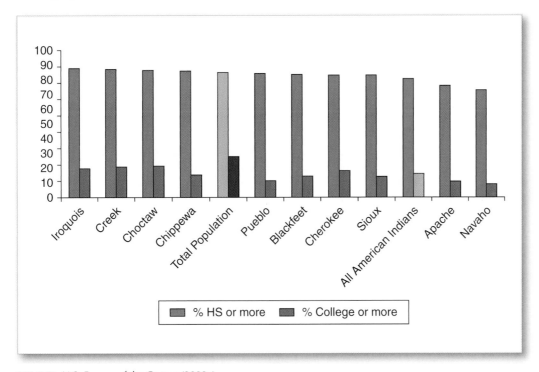

Exhibit 7.12
Educational Attainment for the Total Population, All American Indians, and 10 Largest Tribes, 2009

SOURCE: U.S. Bureau of the Census (2009a).

One positive development for the education of American Indians is the rapid increase in tribally controlled colleges. There are now 37 tribal colleges: All offer 2-year degrees, six offer 4-year degrees, and two offer Master's degrees. These institutions are located on or near reservations, and some have been constructed with funds generated in the gaming industry. They are designed to be more sensitive to the educational and cultural needs of the group, and tribal college graduates who transfer to 4-year colleges are more likely to graduate than other American Indian students (Pego, 1998; see also American Indian Higher Education Consortium, 2008).

Exhibit 7.13 displays the extent of school segregation for American Indians in the 1993–1994 and 2005–2006 school years, using the same measures as in Exhibit 6.9. American Indian schoolchildren are less segregated than their African American counterparts, but the degree of racial isolation is still substantial and is actually increasing. The percentage of American

Exhibit 7.13 School Integration, 1993–1994 and 2005–2006

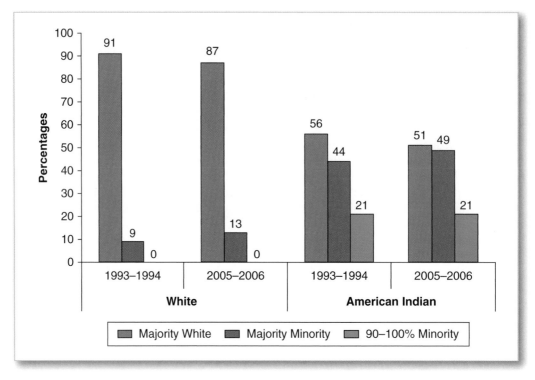

SOURCE: Fry (2007).

Indian children attending "majority-minority" schools increased from 44% to 49% between the two school years. The percentage in extremely segregated schools, on the other hand, held steady at 21%, about 10 percentage points lower than the corresponding figure for African American children.

Political Power. The ability of American Indians to exert power as a voting bloc or to otherwise directly affect the political structure is limited by group size; they are a tiny percentage of the electorate. Furthermore, their political power is limited by their lower average levels of education, language differences, lack of economic resources, and fractional differences within and between tribes and reservations. The number of American Indians holding elected office is minuscule, far less than 1% (Pollard & O'Hare, 1999). In 1992, however, Ben Nighthorse Campbell, of Colorado, a member of the Northern Cheyenne tribe, was elected to the U.S. Senate and served until 2005.

Jobs and Income. Some of the most severe challenges facing American Indians relate to work and income. The problems are especially evident on the reservations, where jobs traditionally have been scarce and affluence rare. As mentioned previously, the overall unemployment rate for all American Indians is about double the rate for whites. For Indians living on or near reservations, however, the rate is much higher, sometimes rising to 70% to 80% on the smaller, more isolated reservations (U.S. Bureau of the Census, 2009a).

Nationally, American Indians are underrepresented in the higher-status, more lucrative professions and overrepresented in unskilled labor and service jobs (U.S. Bureau of the Census, 2009a). As is the case for African Americans, American Indians who hold white-collar jobs are more likely than whites to work in relatively low-level occupations, such as typist or retail salesperson (Pollard & O'Hare, 1999).

The income data in Exhibit 7.14 show median household income in 2009 for the total U.S. population, all American Indians, and the 10 largest tribes. Overall, income for American Indians

Ben Cheyenne looks out over a reservation in South Dakota. Poverty, unemployment, and alcoholism continue to be major problems on many reservations.

© NewSport/Corbis.

is about 75% of national levels. There is a good deal of variability among the 10 largest tribes, but again, none approaches national norms. These incomes reflect lower levels of education as well as the interlocking forces of past discrimination and lack of development on many reservations. The rural isolation of much of the population and their distance from the more urbanized centers of economic growth limit possibilities for improvement and raise the likelihood that many reservations will remain the rural counterparts to urban underclass ghettos.

Exhibit 7.15 supplements the information in Exhibit 7.14 by displaying the distribution of income for American Indians and Alaska Natives (AIAN) compared with non-Hispanic whites.

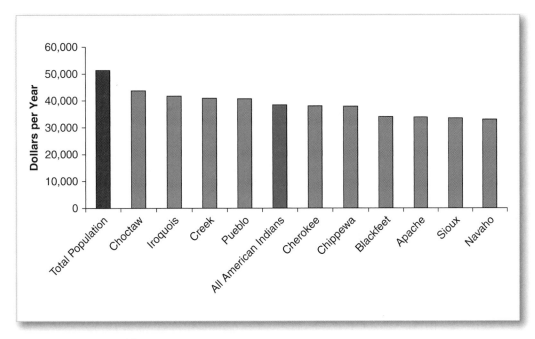

Exhibit 7.14 Median Household Income for Total Population, All American Indians, and 10 Largest Tribes, 2009

SOURCE: U.S. Bureau of the Census (2009a).

Exhibit 7.15

Distribution of Household Income for Non-Hispanic Whites (NHW) and American Indians and Alaska Natives (AIAN), 2009

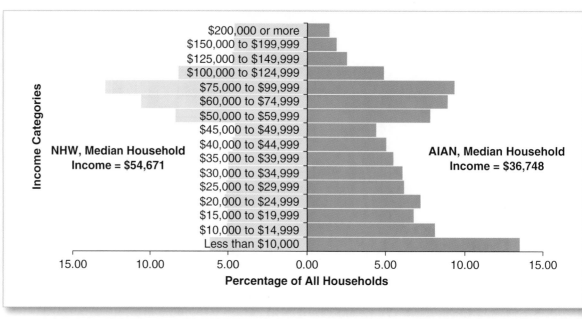

SOURCE: U.S. Bureau of the Census (2009a).

This type of graph was introduced in the chapter on African Americans and follows the same format as Exhibit 6.13. In both graphs, the pattern of income inequality is immediately obvious. Starting at the bottom, we see that like African Americans, AIAN are overrepresented in the lowest income groups. For example, almost 13% of AIAN have incomes less than $10,000—more than double the percentage for non-Hispanic whites (6%) in this range.

Moving up the figure through the lower and middle income brackets, we see that AIAN households continue to be overrepresented. As was the case with Exhibit 6.13, there is a notable clustering of both groups in the $50,000 to $100,000 categories, but it is whites who are overrepresented at these higher income levels: Almost a third of white households, compared with only 26% of AIAN households, are in these categories. The income differences between the groups are especially obvious at the top of the figure. More than 14% of white households versus 6% of AIAN households are in the top three income categories. Exhibit 7.15 also shows the median household income for both groups in 2009, and the difference of almost $18,000 further illustrates the lower socioeconomic level of American Indians.

Finally, Exhibit 7.16 shows the poverty levels for the total population, all American Indians, and the 10 largest tribes. The poverty rate for American Indian families is almost double the national rate, and 6 of the 10 largest tribes have an even higher percentage of families living in poverty. The poverty rates for children show a similar pattern, with very high rates for the Apache, Navajo, and Sioux.

Taken together, this information on income and poverty shows that despite the progress American Indians have made over the past several decades, a sizable socioeconomic gap persists.

Primary Structural Assimilation

Rates of out-marriage for American Indians are quite high compared with other groups, as displayed in Exhibit 7.17. For each of the past three census years, more than half of all married American Indians had spouses from another racial group, a much higher rate than any other group. This pattern is partly the result of the small size of the group. As less than 1% of the total population, American Indians are numerically unlikely to find dating and marriage partners within their own group, especially in those regions of the country and urban areas where the group is small in size. For example, an earlier study found that in New England, which has the lowest relative percentage of American Indians of any region, more

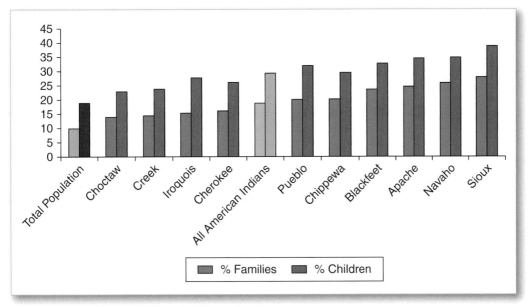

Exhibit 7.16 Poverty Levels for Families and for Children for Total Population, All American Indians, and 10 Largest Tribes, 2009

SOURCE: U.S. Bureau of the Census (2009a).

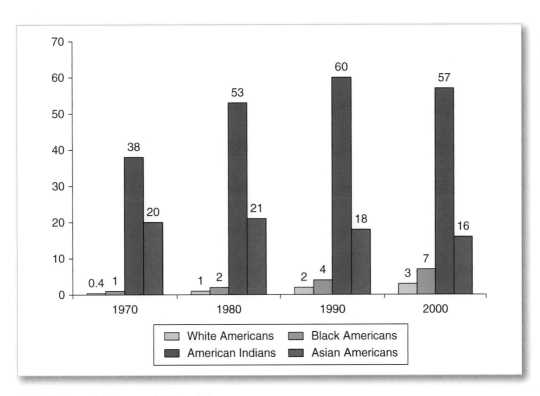

Exhibit 7.17 Interracial Marriage by Group: Percentage of Married People With Spouse of Another Race

SOURCE: Lee and Edmonston (2005, p. 12).

than 90% of Indian marriages were to partners outside the group. In the mountain states, which have a greater number of American Indians who are also highly concentrated on reservations, only about 40% of Indian marriages involved partners outside the group (Snipp, 1989, pp. 156–159). Also, the social and legal barriers to Indian-white intermarriages have been comparatively weak (Qian & Lichter, 2007).

COMPARING MINORITY GROUPS

Comparing the experiences of American Indians with those of other groups will further our understanding of the complexities of dominant-minority relationships and permit us to test the explanatory power of the concepts and theories that are central to this text. No two minority groups have had the same experiences, and our concepts and theories should help us understand the differences and the similarities. We will make it a point to compare groups in each of the chapters in this part of the text. We begin by comparing American Indians with African Americans.

First, note the differences in the stereotypes attached to the two groups during the early years of European colonization. While Indians were seen as cruel savages, African Americans under slavery were seen as lazy, irresponsible, and in constant need of supervision. The two stereotypes are consistent with the outcomes of the contact period. The supposed irresponsibility of blacks under slavery helped justify their subordinate, highly controlled status, and the alleged savagery of American Indians helped justify their near extermination by white society.

Second, both American Indians and African Americans were colonized minority groups, but their contact situations were governed by very different dynamics (competition for labor vs. land) and a very different dominant group agenda (the capture and control of a large, powerless workforce vs. the elimination of a military threat). These differing contact situations shaped subsequent relationships with the dominant group and the place of the groups in the larger society.

For example, consider the situations of the two groups a century ago. At that time, the most visible enemy for African Americans was de jure segregation, the elaborate system of repression in the South that controlled them politically, economically, and socially (see Chapters 5 and 6). In particular, the southern system of agriculture needed the black population—but only as a powerless, cheap workforce. The goals of African Americans centered on dismantling this oppressive system, assimilation, and equality.

American Indians, in contrast, were not viewed as a source of labor and, after their military defeat, were far too few in number and too dispersed geographically to constitute a political threat. Thus, there was little need to control them in the same way African Americans were controlled. The primary enemies of the tribes were the reservation system, various agencies of the federal government (especially the BIA), rural isolation, and the continuing attacks on their traditional cultures and lifestyles, which are typical for a colonized minority group. American Indians had a different set of problems, different resources at their disposal, and different goals in mind. They always have been more oriented toward a pluralistic relationship with the larger society and preserving what they could of their autonomy, their institutions, and their heritage. African Americans spent much of the 20th century struggling for inclusion and equality; American Indians were fighting to maintain or recover their traditional cultures and social structures. This difference in goals reflects the different histories of the two groups and the different circumstances surrounding their colonization.

PROGRESS AND CHALLENGES

What does the future hold for American Indians? Their situation has certainly changed over the past 100 years, but is it "better" or just "different," as is the case for large segments of the African American community? The answer seems to be a little of both, as the group grows in size and improves its status. To reach some conclusions, we will look at several aspects of the situation of American Indians and assess the usefulness of our theoretical models and concepts.

Since the 1960s, the decline of intolerance in society at large, the growth of pride in ancestry in many groups (e.g., Black Power), and the shift in federal government policy to encourage self-determination have all helped spark a reaffirmation of commitment to tribal cultures and traditions. As was the case with African Americans and the Black Power movement, the Red Power movement asserted a distinct and positive Indian identity, a claim for the equal validity of American Indian cultures within the broad framework of the larger society. During the same time period, the favorable settlements of treaty claims, the growth in job opportunities, and the gambling industry have enhanced the flow of resources and benefits to some reservations. In popular culture, American Indians have enjoyed a strong upsurge of popularity and sympathetic depictions. This enhanced popularity accounts for much of the growth in population size as people of mixed ancestry resurrect and reconstruct their Indian ancestors and their own ethnic identities.

Linear or simplistic views of assimilation do not fit the current situation or the past experiences of American Indians very well. Some American Indians are intermarrying with whites and integrating into the larger society; others strive to retain a tribal culture in the midst of an urbanized, industrialized society; and still others labor to use the profits from gaming and other enterprises for the benefit of the tribe as a whole. Members of the group can be found at every degree of acculturation and integration, and the group seems to be moving toward assimilation in some ways and away from it in others.

From the standpoint of the Noel and Blauner hypotheses, we can see that American Indians have struggled with conquest and colonization, experiences made more difficult by the loss of so much of their land and other resources and by the concerted, unrelenting attacks on their culture and language. The legacy of conquest and colonization was poor health and housing, an inadequate and misdirected education system, and slow (or nonexistent) economic development. For most of the 20th century, American Indians were left to survive as best they could on the margins of the larger society, too powerless to establish meaningful pluralism and too colonized to pursue equality.

Today, one key to further progress for some members of this group is economic development on reservation lands and the further strengthening of the tribes as functioning social units. Some tribes do have assets—natural resources, treaty rights, and the gambling industry—that could fuel development. However, they often do not have the expertise or the capital to finance the exploitation of these resources. They must rely, in whole or in part, on non-Indian expertise and white-owned companies and businesses. Thus, non-Indians, rather than the tribes, may be the primary beneficiaries of some forms of development (this would, of course, be quite consistent with American history). For those reservations for which gambling is not an option and for those without natural resources, investments in human capital (education) may offer the most compelling direction for future development.

Urban Indians confront the same patterns of discrimination and racism that confront other minority groups of color. Members of the group with lower levels of education and job skills face the prospects of becoming a part of a permanent urban underclass. More-educated and skilled American Indians share with African Americans the prospect of a middle-class lifestyle that is more partial and tenuous than that of comparable segments of the dominant group.

The situation of American Indians today is vastly superior to the status of the group a century ago, and this chapter has documented the notable improvements that have occurred since 1990. Given the depressed and desperate conditions of the reservations in the early 20th century, however, it would not take much to show an improvement. American Indians are growing rapidly in numbers and are increasingly diversified by residence, education, and degree of assimilation. Some tribes have made dramatic progress over the past several decades, but enormous problems remain, both on and off the reservations. The challenge for the future, as it was in the past, is to find a course between pluralism and assimilation, and pantribalism and traditional lifestyles that will balance the issues of quality of life against the importance of retaining an Indian identity.

Australian Aborigines and American Indians

The history of American Indians—their conquest and domination by a larger, more powerful society—has a number of parallels from around the globe, a reflection of the rise of European societies to power and their frequent conquest of indigenous societies in Africa, North and South America, and Asia. A comparative analysis of these episodes suggests that similar dynamics have come into play, even though each has its own unique history. To illustrate, we will use some of the concepts developed in this text to compare the impact of European domination on Australian Aborigines and the indigenous peoples of North America.

Australia came under European domination in the late 1700s, nearly two centuries after the establishment of Jamestown and the beginning of Anglo-American Indian relations. In spite of the time difference, however, the two contact situations shared many features. In both cases, the colonial power was Great Britain, and first contacts occurred in the preindustrial era (although Britain had begun to industrialize by the late 1700s). Also, the indigenous peoples of both North America and Australia were thinly spread across vast areas and were greatly inferior to the British in their technological development.

The Aboriginal peoples had lived in Australia for 50,000 years by the time the British arrived. Estimates of their population size vary, but there may have been as many as a million Aborigines at the time of contact with the British ("A Sorry Tale," 2000). They were organized into small, nomadic hunting-and-gathering bands and were generally much less developed than the tribes of North America, lacking the population base, social organization, and resources that would have permitted sustained resistance to the invasion of their land. There was plenty of violence in the contact situation, but unlike the situation in North America, there were no sustained military campaigns pitting large armies against each other.

The initial thrust of colonization was motivated by Great Britain's need for a place to send its convicts after losing the Revolutionary War to the fledgling United States. The European population in Australia grew slowly at first and consisted mostly of prisoners. The early economic enterprises centered on subsistence farming and sheepherding, not large-scale enterprises that required forced labor (at least not on the same scale as in North America).

Early relations between the English and the Aborigines were hostile and centered on competition for land. In their ethnocentrism, the invaders denied that the Aborigines had any claims to the land and simply pushed them aside or killed them if they resisted. As in the Americas, European diseases took their toll, and the indigenous population declined rapidly. Because they were not desired as laborers (although many became semi-unfree servants), they were pushed away from the areas of white settlement into the fringes of development, where they and their grievances could be ignored. As in North America, they were seen as "savages": a culture that would (and in the view of the emerging dominant group, should) wither away and disappear.

To the extent that there was contact with the larger society, it was often in the form of coercive acculturation. For example, throughout much of the 20th century, the Australian government, aided by various church organizations, actually removed children of mixed parentage from their Aboriginal mothers and placed them in orphanages. The idea behind this program was to give these children a chance to leave their Aboriginal culture behind, marry whites, and enter the larger society. This policy, abandoned only in the 1960s, resulted in the state-sponsored orphaning of thousands of Aboriginal children. Some of the angriest and most militant members of the current generation of Aborigines belong to this "stolen generation" (for a report on this program, see Australian Human Rights and Equal Opportunity Commission, 1997).

The contemporary situation of Australian Aborigines has many parallels with American Indians, as does their past. The group is largely rural and continues to live on land that is less desirable. After the initial—and dramatic—declines, their numbers have been increasing of late, partly because of higher birthrates and partly because of changing perceptions, growing sympathy for their plight, and increased willingness of people to claim their Aboriginal heritage. The population fell to a low of fewer than 100,000 at the start of the 20th century but is now put at 427,000, or about 2.5% of the total population (Australian Bureau of Statistics, 2009).

Just as in North America, there is a huge gap between the indigenous population and the rest of society on every statistic that measures quality of life, equality, and access to resources. Life expectancy for Aborigines is as much as 20 years lower than that of the general population, and their infant mortality rate is 2 to 3 times higher. They have much less access to health care, and Aboriginal communities are much more afflicted with alcoholism, suicide, and malnutrition than the general population. Unemployment rates are double the rate in the general population, average income is about 65% of the national average, and only about a third as many Aboriginal people (13.6%) as compared with the national population (34.4%) are in school at age 19 ("Asia: Original Sin," 2007; Brace, 2001; see also Australian Bureau of Statistics, 2002). The issues animating Aboriginal affairs have a familiar ring for anyone acquainted with the issues of American Indians. They include concerns for the preservation of Aboriginal culture, language, and identity; self-determination and autonomy; the return of lands illegally taken by the Anglo invaders; and an end to discrimination and unequal treatment.

Aboriginal relations are in flux, and the overall picture is mixed. For example, in 1998, the federal government of Australia was condemned by the United Nations Committee on the Elimination of Racial Discrimination for its handling of Aboriginal land claims. Australia is the only developed nation to have ever received this censure (Pilger, 2000). On the other hand, the opening ceremonies of the 2000 Olympic Games in Sydney featured a celebration of Aboriginal culture, dance, music, and art, and Aboriginal athlete Cathy Freeman lit the Olympic flame.

The Aboriginal peoples of Australia, like American Indians, face many—often overwhelming—challenges to securing a better future for themselves and their children. Their history and their present situation clearly validate both the Blauner and Noel hypotheses: They are a colonized minority group, victims of European domination, with all that that status implies.

Are Indian Sports Team Mascots Offensive?

American Indians face many challenges as they address persistent problems such as unemployment and poverty. Some of the issues they face are not about money and jobs but are, rather, symbolic and perceptual. How are American Indians seen by the larger society? What stereotypes linger in American popular culture? How might these stereotypes affect the ability of American Indians to argue their causes? If American Indians are seen primarily as exaggerated, stereotypical mascots, can they expect to generate much interest, support, or—as Harjo points out in the opening quote—realistic national policies?

The controversies over using Indian mascots for athletic teams illustrate these symbolic battles. Is there any real harm in using team names such as "Indians," "Seminoles," or "Braves"? Are people who object to these names carrying political correctness and sensitivity too far?

The excerpts below present both sides of this argument. Journalists Price and Woo, in the March 4, 2002, issue of Sports Illustrated (SI), *argue that the team names are not offensive to sports fans and, in fact, to most American Indians. The opposing point of view is presented by a group of five academics and Indian activists. They raise a number of issues about the* SI *article, including its use of polling and what they see as a profound bias on the part of the authors and the magazine. In this selection, their analysis of stereotypes and American Indians is presented.*

INDIAN SYMBOLS AND MASCOTS ARE NOT OFFENSIVE

S. L. PRICE AND ANDREA WOO

[The thorniest word problem in sports today is] the use of Native American names and mascots by high school, college, and professional teams. For more than 30 years the debate has been raging over whether names such as Redskins, Braves, Chiefs and Indians honor or defile Native Americans, whether clownish figures like the Cleveland Indians' Chief Wahoo have any place in today's racially sensitive climate, and whether the sight of thousands of non-Native Americans doing the tomahawk chop at Atlanta's Turner Field is mindless fun or mass bigotry. It's an argument that, because it mixes mere sports with the sensitivities of a people who were nearly exterminated, seems both trivial and profound. . . .

[The case of Betty Ann Gross, a member of the Sisseton-Wahpeton Sioux tribe] illustrates how slippery the issue can be. She grew up on a reservation in South Dakota and went to Sisseton High, a public school on the reservation whose teams are called the Redmen. Gross, 49, can't recall a time when people on the reservation weren't arguing about the team name, evenly divided between those who were proud of it and those who were ashamed. Gross recently completed a study that led the South Dakota state government to change the names of 38 places and landmarks around the state, yet she has mixed feelings on the sports issue. She wants Indian mascots and the tomahawk chop discarded, but she has no problem with team names like the Fighting Sioux (University of North Dakota) or even the Redskins. "There's a lot of division," Gross says. . . .

Although most Native American activists and tribal leaders consider Indian team names and mascots offensive, neither Native Americans in general nor a cross-section of U.S. sports fans agree. That is one of the findings of a poll conducted for *SI*. . . . The pollsters interviewed 351 Native Americans (217 living on reservations and 134 living off) and 743 fans. Their responses were weighted according to U.S. Census figures for age, race, and gender and for distribution of Native Americans on and off reservations. With a margin of error of ±4%, 83% of the Indians said that professional teams should not stop using Indian nicknames, mascots, or symbols, and 79% of the fans agreed with them. . . . When pollsters asked about the Washington Redskins, they found no great resentment toward the name. Instead, they again found agreement between Native Americans and fans (69% of the former and 74% of the latter do not object to the name). . . .

Regardless, the campaign to erase Indian team names and symbols nationwide has been a success. Though Native American activists have made little progress at the highest level of pro sports . . . their single-minded pursuit of the issue has literally changed the face of sports in the U.S. Since 1969 more than 600 school teams and minor league professional clubs have dropped nicknames deemed offensive by Native American groups. . . .

While those who support names such as Seminoles (Florida State) and [Atlanta] Braves can argue that the words celebrate Native American traditions, applying that claim to the Redskins is absurd. Nevertheless, Redskins vice president Karl Swanson says the name "symbolizes courage, dignity, and leadership and has always been employed in that manner"—conveniently ignoring the fact that in popular usage dating back four centuries, the word has been a slur based on skin color. . . . Many experts on Native American history point out that . . . the word *redskin* was first used by whites who paid and received bounties for dead Indians. . . .

However, what's most important, Swanson counters, is intent: Because the Redskins and their fans mean nothing racist by using the nickname, it isn't racist or offensive. Not so, says Suzan Harjo (a Native American activist): "There's no more derogatory word that's used against us . . . in the English language. . . . Everyone knows that it has never been an honorific. It's a terrible insult." . . .

That the name is offensive to Native Americans is easy for non-Natives to presume. It resonates when an Olympic hero and former Marine Corps captain such as Billy Mills (a Native American and a Gold Medal winner in the 1964 Olympics), who speaks out against Indian names and mascots at schools around the country, insists that a team named Redskins in the capital of the nation that committed genocide against Native Americans is the equivalent of a soccer team in Germany being called the Berlin Kikes.

Somehow that message is lost on most of Mills's fellow Native Americans. Asked if they were offended by the name Redskins, 75% of Native American respondents in *SI*'s poll said they were not, and even on reservations, where Native American culture and influence are perhaps felt most intensely, 62% said they weren't offended. . . . Only 29% of Native Americans . . . thought [the owner of the Redskins] should change his team's name. Such indifference implies a near total disconnect between Native American activists and the general Native American population on this issue. . . .

The Utes's experience with the University of Utah might serve as a model for successful resolution of conflicts over Indian nicknames. Four years ago the council met with university officials, who made it clear that they would change their teams' name, the Running Utes, if the tribe found it objectionable. . . . The council was perfectly happy to have the Ute name continue to circulate in the nation's sports pages. . . . Florida State, likewise, uses the name Seminoles for its teams with the express approval of the Seminole nation. . . . Like the Ute tribe, most Native Americans have no problem with teams using [Indian] names. . . .

SOURCE: Price and Woo (2002, pp. 66–73).

MASCOTS ARE OFFENSIVE

C. RICHARD KING, ELLEN J. STAUROWSKY, LAWRENCE BACA, LAUREL R. DAVIS, AND CORNEL PEWEWARDY

To fully understand both the *SI* article and ongoing controversy about mascots, one must grasp the history of Indian symbols in sports. . . . Native American mascots emerged (mainly) in the early 1900s, after [the end of military hostilities]. . . . These mascots were part of a larger phenomenon of increased prevalence of Native American images in U.S. popular culture, including Western movies, symbols for beer and butter, and art in homes. One of the reasons why most Americans find the mascots unremarkable . . . is because of the prevalence of similar images throughout U.S. popular culture. . . .

Historically, the most popular sport mascots have been animals associated with aggression (e.g., Tigers) and Native Americans (e.g., Indians, Chiefs, Braves, and so forth). Although other ethnic groups have been occasionally used as mascots, these mascots differ from Native American mascots in several ways: [these mascots] are often (a) a people that do not exist today (e.g., Spartans); (b) less associated with aggression (e.g., Scots); (c) selected by people from the same ethnicity (e.g., Irish Americans at Notre Dame); and (d) not mimicked to nearly the same degree.

Native American mascots emerged in a context in which many non-Native Americans were "playing Indian." Still today, children don "Indian" costumes at Halloween, "act like Indians" during "Cowboy and Indian" games, "become

Indian Princesses" at the YMCA, and perform "Indian rituals" at summer camps. Adults belong to organizations that involve learning "Indian ways" and performing "Indian rituals." Non-Native Americans have created an imaginary version of Indianness that they sometimes enact, and they expect real Native Americans to either ignore, affirm, or validate such myths and practices. Similar practices applied to other races/ethnicities, such as "playing black" or "playing Jewish," would not be accepted in our society today.

Activism against Native American mascots has been evident for more than 30 years. Since the early 1990s, this activism has become more widespread [and] emerged from Native American individuals, groups, and communities that work on a variety of other issues, such as treaty, economic, cultural, environmental, health, and educational issues. Although many U.S. citizens see the mascot issue as emerging "out of the blue," many Native American organizations see the elimination of such mascots as part of a larger agenda of reducing societal stereotyping about Native Americans (in the media, school curriculums, and so forth) and informing the public about the realities of Native American lives. An increase in accurate information about Native Americans is viewed as necessary for the achievement of other goals such as poverty reduction, educational advancements, and securing treaty rights.

Anti-mascot activists articulate many different arguments against the mascots. First, they assert that the mascots stereotype Native Americans as only existing in the past, having a single culture, and being aggressive fighters. Second, they hold that these stereotypes influence the way people perceive and treat Native Americans. Such imagery is seen as affecting Native American images of themselves, creating a hostile climate for many Native Americans, and preventing people from understanding current Native American realities, which affects public policy relative to Native Americans. Third, the activists state that no racial/cultural group should be mimicked (especially in regard to sacred items/practices), even if such mimicking is "culturally accurate." And fourth, they argue that Native Americans should have control over how they are represented. . . .

Native American mascots are rooted in the bloodthirsty savage stereotype, as it is this stereotype that is linked to desirable athletic qualities such as having a fighting spirit and being aggressive, brave, stoic, proud, and persevering. . . .

Of course, even [this] so-called positive stereotype [is] ultimately negative. [All] stereotypes fail to recognize diversity among the people who are being stereotyped. . . . Most people deny that they believe any racial stereotypes. . . . When we do notice our own stereotyping, it is often because our beliefs are very negative (e.g., believing that African Americans are criminal or Puerto Ricans are lazy). When our stereotypes are "positive" (e.g., Jews as good at business or Asians as smart), we tend to think that these beliefs are not stereotypical and thus not racist.

Sport mascots are based on what is today perceived as "positive" ideas about Native Americans: that they are brave, principled, persevering, good fighters. This "positive cast" to the mascot stereotype leads most to conclude that the mascots are not racist. In fact, it is this "positive cast" to the mascot stereotype that leads many mascot supporters to think that the mascots actually counter racism by "honoring" Native Americans. . . .

It is not surprising that some Native Americans embrace "positive" stereotypes of Native Americans, and thus that some are not critical of Native American mascots. There are several factors that encourage Native Americans to accept, internalize, celebrate, and even capitalize on, "positive" stereotypes of Native Americans. First, many people do not define so-called positive stereotypes as stereotypes or racist. In fact, a group that experiences a great deal of inequality may be especially attracted to any imagery that is positive, as such imagery might be a relief from the negative. Second, throughout much of U.S. history, Native people have faced intense pressures to acculturate and have been exposed to many of the same stereotypical images of Native Americans as non-Natives have. These pressures have certainly resulted in some Natives adopting "dominant/white/outsider views" of Native Americans. Third, given the destruction of Native economies and the resulting economic destitution, some Native people have turned to the marketing of their ethnicity, or an acceptable Hollywood version of their ethnicity, to survive, including teaching "Native spirituality" to non-Native Americans; selling Native jewelry and art; and managing Native tourist establishments.

In conclusion, to understand the Native American mascot issue, and the *SI* article, one needs to understand the social context surrounding the mascots. Most important, one must understand the historically rooted, but contemporarily alive, stereotypes of Native Americans. Native American mascots emerged from these stereotypes, and these mascots continue to reinforce these stereotypes. The continued prevalence of these stereotypes inhibits social changes that would better contemporary Native American lives.

SOURCE: King, Staurowsky, Baca, Davis, and Pewewardy (2002, pp. 381–403).

DEBATE QUESTIONS TO CONSIDER

1. Price and Woo argue that the majority of American Indians polled did not object to the use of Indian team mascots. How relevant is this point to the debate? Should questions such as these be decided by "popular vote," or are there deeper principles that should guide public policy? If so, what are those principles, and how should they be applied?

2. Price and Woo quote an official of the Washington Redskins franchise as arguing that the team uses the term to honor American Indians for their courage and dignity. Should "intent" matter in deciding whether a term is insulting or offensive? Who should decide these matters? The team? The tribes? Someone else?

3. What arguments do King et al. make about why these matters are important? What real harm comes from using Indian team mascots? Are their arguments convincing? Why or why not? What are "positive stereotypes," and how do they differ (if at all) from negative stereotypes? Are positive stereotypes less harmful than negative stereotypes?

4. Is there a gender dimension to these arguments? Price and Woo mention the controversy about a South Dakota high school using "Redmen" as a team name. What do you suppose the women's teams at this school were called? Lady Redmen? Redwomen? How is this handled on your campus? Are the women's athletic teams distinguished by adding the modifier "Lady" or "Women"? What issues arise from this (very common) pattern? How do these issues matter?

5. Ultimately, is all this just a matter of political correctness? What is at stake here (if anything)?

MAIN POINTS

- American Indian and Anglo-American cultures are vastly different, and these differences have hampered communication and understanding, usually in ways that harmed American Indians or weakened the integrity of their tribal structures.
- At the beginning of the 20th century, American Indians faced the paternalistic reservation system, poverty and powerlessness, rural isolation and marginalization, and the Bureau of Indian Affairs. American Indians continued to lose land and other resources.
- The Indian Reorganization Act of 1934 attempted to increase tribal autonomy and to provide mechanisms for improving the quality of life on the reservations. The policy of termination was proposed in the 1950s. The policy was a disaster, and the tribes that were terminated suffered devastating economic losses and drastic declines in quality of life.
- American Indians began to urbanize rapidly in the 1950s but are still less urbanized than the population as a whole. They are the least urbanized American minority group.
- The Red Power movement rose to prominence in the 1960s and had some successes but was often simply ignored. The Red Power movement was partly assimilationist even though it pursued pluralistic goals and greater autonomy for the tribes.
- Current conflicts between American Indians and the dominant group center on control of natural resources, preservation of treaty rights, and treaties that have been broken in the past. Another possible source of development and conflict is in the potentially lucrative gambling industry.
- There is some indication that anti-Indian prejudice has shifted to more "modern" forms. Institutional discrimination and access to education and employment remain major problems confronting American Indians.

- American Indians have preserved much of their traditional culture, although in altered form. The secondary structural assimilation of American Indians remains relatively low, despite recent improvements in quality of life for many tribes. Primary structural assimilation is comparatively high.
- Over the course of the past 100 years, American Indians have struggled from a position of powerlessness and isolation. Today, the group faces an array of problems similar to those faced by all American colonized minority groups of color as they try to find ways to raise their quality of life and continue their commitment to their tribes and to an Indian identity.

STUDY SITE ON THE WEB

For chapter-specific resources, such as self-quizzes, videos, and flashcards, go to **www.sagepub.com/ healeyregc6e**.

FOR FURTHER READING

Amott, Teresa, & Matthaei, Julie. 1991. I Am the Fire of Time: American Indian Women. In T. Amott & J. Matthaei (Eds.), *Race, Gender, and Work: A Multicultural History of Women in the United States* (pp. 31–62). Boston: South End.

A good overview of the history and present situation of American Indian women

Bordewich, Fergus. 1996. *Killing the White Man's Indian*. New York: Doubleday.

A comprehensive, dispassionate analysis of current problems and future possibilities

Brown, Dee. 1970. *Bury My Heart at Wounded Knee*. New York: Holt, Rinehart, & Winston.

A passionately written, highly readable account of the military defeat and establishment of dominance over American Indians

Deloria, Vine. 1969. *Custer Died for Your Sins*. New York: Macmillan.
Deloria, Vine. 1970. *We Talk, You Listen*. New York: Macmillan.
Deloria, Vine. 1995. *Red Earth, White Lies*. New York: Scribner's.

The three major works of the well-known American Indian activist, writer, and professor of Indian studies

The Harvard Project on American Indian Economic Development. 2008. *The State of the Native Nations*. New York: Oxford University Press.

A comprehensive look at economic development and other issues on reservations across the nation

Nabakov, Peter (Ed.). 1999. *Native American Testimony*. New York: Penguin.

A collection of personal accounts by American Indians from pre-Columbian times to the present day

Snipp, C. Matthew. 1989. *American Indians: The First of This Land*. New York: Russell Sage Foundation.

A valuable scholarly study covering a variety of aspects of the American Indian condition

QUESTIONS FOR REVIEW AND STUDY

1. What were the most important cultural differences between American Indian tribes and the dominant society? How did these affect relations between the two groups?

2. Compare and contrast the effects of paternalism and coercive acculturation on American Indians after the end of the contact period with those on African Americans under slavery. What similarities and differences existed in the two situations? Which system was more oppressive and controlling? How? How did these different situations shape the futures of the groups?

3. How did federal Indian policy change over the course of the 20th century? What effects did these changes have on the tribes? Which were more beneficial? Why? What was the role of the Indian protest movement in shaping these policies?

4. What options do American Indians have for improving their position in the larger society and developing their reservations? Which strategies seem to have the most promise? Which seem less effective? Why?

5. Compare and contrast the contact situations of American Indians, African Americans, and Australian Aborigines. What are the most crucial differences in the situations? What implications did these differences have for the development of each group's situation after the initial contact situation?

6. Characterize the present situation of American Indians in terms of acculturation and integration. How do they compare with African Americans? What factors in the experiences of the two groups might help explain contemporary differences?

7. What gender differences can you identify in the experiences of American Indians? How do these compare with the gender differences in the experiences of African Americans?

8. Given the information and ideas presented in this chapter, speculate about the future of American Indians. How likely are American Indian cultures and languages to survive? What are the prospects for achieving equality?

9. Given their small size and marginal status, recognition of their situations and problems continues to be a central struggle for American Indians (see the quote that opens this chapter). What are some ways that the group can build a more realistic, informed, and empathetic relationship with the larger society, the federal government, and other authorities? Are there lessons in the experiences of other groups or in the various protest strategies followed in the "Red Power" movement?

INTERNET RESEARCH PROJECT

In this exercise, you will use U.S. Census data and the Internet to gather information about the total population of all American Indians and two tribal groups of your choosing. This project adds to the information you gathered in Chapter 6. You can add the information for African Americans from the previous exercise and add data for the new variables in this exercise. You will then use course concepts to assess and analyze this information and place it in the context of this text. *Visit the website for this text for instructions on finding the information needed to complete the following table.*

		Total Population	African Americans	AIAN (AOIC)	American Indian Tribes	
					_____	_____
1	Number					
2	% of total population	———				
3	% married					
4	% with bachelor's degree					
5	% speak English less than "very well"					
6	% unemployed					
7	Median household income					
8	% of all families in poverty					
9	% living in owner-occupied houses					
10						
11						

QUESTIONS

1. Summarize what you found out in your search of the Internet about the two tribal groupings you selected.

2. What stage of Gordon's model of assimilation (see Exhibit 2.1) do the variables in the table measure?

3. According to Blauner (see Chapter 4), both American Indians and African Americans are "colonized or conquered" minority groups. Is their status in American society similar? What important differences do you see? Are these colonized groups higher or lower than the white ethnic groups you investigated in Chapter 4? Do these patterns agree with Blauner's predictions? How?

4. Review the themes stated at the beginning of Chapter 4 and the "corollary" stated at the beginning of Chapter 5. How do the patterns you've observed in the table above relate to the contact situation and changing subsistence technologies?

5. Review the concepts of modern institutional discrimination and past-in-present discrimination introduced in Chapter 5. How do the patterns you've observed in the table above relate to these concepts?

OPTIONAL GROUP DISCUSSION

Bring the information on your groups and tribe to class and compare with the information collected by others. Consider the issues raised in the questions above and in the chapter and develop some ideas about why the groups are where they are relative to one another and the total population.

NOTES

1. Harjo, Suzan Shown. 2007. Activism: Time to Change Native American References in Sports. In George Horse Capture, Duane Champagne, and Chandler Jackson (Eds.), *American Indian Nations: Yesterday, Today, and Tomorrow.* Lanham, MD: AltaMira. (Quote on p. 21)

8

Hispanic Americans

Colonization, Immigration, and Ethnic Enclaves

The Hispanic population... accounted for most (56%) of the nation's [population] growth from 2000 to 2010.

—Jeffrey Passel, D'Vera Cohn, and Mark Lopez
of the Pew Hispanic Center, 2011

Hispanic Americans are about 16% of the total population, which makes them the nation's largest minority group (African Americans are about 13% of the population). The group is concentrated in the Southwest, where there have been large Hispanic American communities for many years, but there are nine states—all in the Southeast except South Dakota—where the number of Latinos has more than doubled since 2000 (Passel, Cohn, & Lopez, 2011, p. 2). Communities throughout the nation are, for the first time, hearing Spanish spoken on their streets and finding "exotic" foods—tortillas, salsa, and refried beans—in their grocery stores. America is, once again, being reshaped and remade.

Of course, not all Hispanic American groups are newcomers. Some of these groups were in North America before the Declaration of Independence was signed, before slavery began, even before Jamestown was founded. The label "Hispanic American" includes a number of groups that are diverse and distinct from one another. These groups connect themselves to a variety of traditions; like the larger society, they are dynamic and changeable, unfinished and evolving. Hispanic Americans share a language and some cultural traits but do not generally think of themselves as a single social entity. Many identify with their national origin groups (e.g., Mexican American) rather than broader, more encompassing labels.

In this chapter, we look at the development of Hispanic American groups over the past century, examine their contemporary relations with the larger society, and assess their current status. We focus on the three largest Hispanic groups: Mexican Americans, Puerto Ricans, and Cuban Americans. Other, smaller groups will be covered in Chapter 10. Exhibit 8.1 displays some information on the size and growth of Hispanic Americans and the 10 largest

Latino groups as of 2009 (information on the size of these subgroups is not available from the 2010 Census at this writing). Mexican Americans, the largest single group, are 10% of the total U.S. population (and about two thirds of all Hispanic Americans), but the other groups are small in size. The relative sizes of the major subgroups of Latinos in the United States are displayed in Exhibit 8.2, and Exhibit 8.3 shows the countries of origin of the three largest Hispanic American groups.

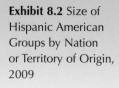

Exhibit 8.1 Size and Growth of All Hispanic Americans and 10 Largest Groups by Nation or Territory of Origin, 1990–2009

Country of Origin	1990	2000	2009	Growth (number of times larger, 1990–2009)	Percentage of Total Population, 2009
Mexico	13,496,000	20,641,000	30,533,408	2.3	10.0
Puerto Rico*	2,728,000	3,406,000	4,285,380	1.6	1.4
Cuba	1,044,000	1,242,000	1,643,908	1.6	< 1
Dominican Republic	520,521	799,768	1,295,746	2.5	< 1
El Salvador	565,081	708,741	1,595,385	2.8	< 1
Guatemala	268,779	372,487	991,906	3.7	< 1
Colombia	378,726	496,748	854,109	2.3	< 1
Honduras	131,066	217,569	600,821	4.6	< 1
Ecuador	191,198	260,559	572,159	3.0	< 1
Nicaragua	202,658	177,684	342,054	1.7	< 1
Total Hispanic	22,355,990	32,091,000	48,356,760	2.2	15.8%
Percentage of U.S. Population	9.0%	11.4%	15.8%		
Total U.S. Population	248,710,000	281,422,000	307,006,556	1.2	

SOURCES: 1990—U.S. Bureau of the Census (1990); 2000—U.S. Bureau of the Census (2000d); 2007—U.S. Bureau of the Census (2009a).

*Living on mainland only

Exhibit 8.2 Size of Hispanic American Groups by Nation or Territory of Origin, 2009

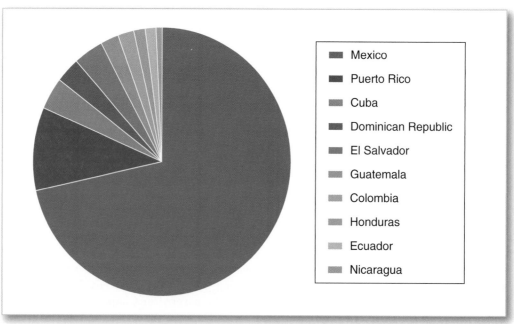

SOURCE: U.S. Bureau of the Census (2007a).

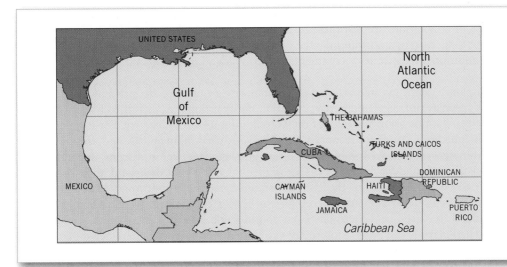

SOURCE: U.S. Bureau of the Census.

Exhibit 8.3 Points of Origin for Mexicans, Cuban Americans, and Puerto Ricans

Latinos are growing rapidly, partly because of their relatively high birthrates but mainly because of immigration. The number of Mexican Americans more than doubled between 1990 and 2009, and Hispanic groups in general are growing at rates above the national average. This growth is projected to continue well into the century, and Hispanic Americans will become an increasingly important part of life in the United States. Today, 16 out of every 100 Americans is Hispanic, but by 2050, this ratio is projected to double to 30 out of every 100 (see Exhibit 1.1). One result of these high rates of immigration is that the majority (in some cases, the great majority) of many Hispanic groups are first generation or foreign-born. The percentages are displayed in Exhibit 8.4.

It is appropriate to discuss Hispanic Americans at this point because they include both colonized and immigrant groups, and in that sense, they combine elements of the polar extremes of Blauner's typology of minority groups. We would expect that the Hispanic groups that were more colonized in the past would have much in common with African Americans and Native Americans today. Hispanic groups whose experiences lie closer to the

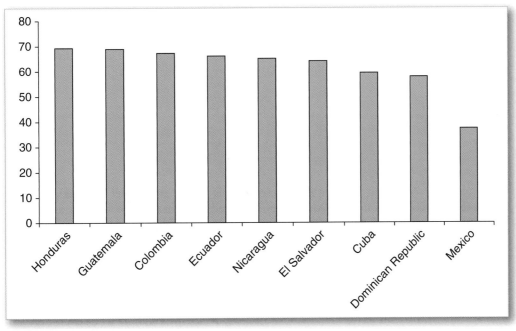

Exhibit 8.4 Percentage Foreign-Born by Country of Origin

SOURCE: U.S. Bureau of the Census (2009a).

"immigrant" end of the continuum would have different characteristics and follow different pathways of adaptation. We test these ideas by reviewing the histories of the groups and by analyzing their current status and degree of acculturation and integration.

Two additional introductory comments can be made about Hispanic Americans:

- Hispanic Americans are partly an ethnic minority group (i.e., identified by cultural characteristics such as language) and partly a racial minority group (i.e., identified by their physical appearance). Latinos bring a variety of racial backgrounds to U.S. society. For example, most Mexican Americans combine European and Native American ancestries and are identifiable by their physical traits as well as by their culture and language. Puerto Ricans, in contrast, are a mixture of white and black ancestry. The original inhabitants of the island, the Arawak and Caribe tribes, were decimated by the Spanish conquest, and the proportion of Native American ancestry is much smaller in Puerto Rico than it is in Mexico. Africans were originally brought to the island as slaves, and there has been considerable intermarriage between whites and blacks. The Puerto Rican population today varies greatly in its racial characteristics, combining every conceivable combination of white and African ancestry. Hispanic Americans are often the victims of racial discrimination in the United States. Racial differences often (but not always) overlap with cultural distinctions and reinforce the separation of Hispanic Americans from Anglo-American society. Even members of the group who are completely acculturated may still experience discrimination based on their physical appearance.

- As is the case with all American minority groups, labels and group names are important. The term Hispanic American is widely applied to this group and might seem neutral and inoffensive to non-Hispanics. In fact, a recent survey shows that the preferred designation varies widely by the primary language and generation of the respondent. About two thirds of Spanish speakers and first-generation (foreign-born) individuals prefer to identify themselves in terms of their countries of origin, while a slight majority of English speakers and third-generation Hispanics prefer to be called simply "American" (Pew Hispanic Center, 2005). An earlier study showed that a sizable majority (67%) of the group preferred the Hispanic label to being called Latino (Jones, 2001). At any rate, both the Hispanic and Latino labels are similar to American Indian in that they were invented and applied by the dominant group and may reinforce the mistaken perception that all Spanish-speaking peoples are the same. Also, the term *Hispanic* highlights Spanish heritage and language but does not acknowledge the roots of these groups in African and Native American civilizations. Further, the label is sometimes mistakenly applied to immigrant groups that bring French, Portuguese, or English traditions (e.g., Haitians, Brazilians, and Jamaicans, respectively). On the other hand, the Latino label stresses the common origins of these groups in Latin America and the fact that each culture is a unique blend of diverse traditions. In this chapter, the terms *Latino* and *Hispanic* are used interchangeably.

MEXICAN AMERICANS

We applied the Noel and Blauner hypotheses to this group in Chapter 4. Mexicans were conquered and colonized in the 19th century and used as a cheap labor force in agriculture, ranching, mining, railroad construction, and other areas of the dominant group economy in the Southwest. In the competition for control of land and labor, they became a minority group, and the contact situation left them with few power resources with which to pursue their self-interests.

By the dawn of the 20th century, the situation of Mexican Americans resembled that of American Indians in some ways. Both groups were small, numbering about 0.5% of the total population (Cortes, 1980, p. 702). Both differed from the dominant group in culture and language, and both were impoverished, relatively powerless, and isolated in rural areas distant from the centers of industrialization and modernization. In other ways, Mexican Americans resembled African Americans in the South in that they also supplied much of the labor power for the agricultural economy of their region, and both were limited to low-paying occupations and subordinate status in the social structure. All three groups were colonized and, at least in the early decades of the 20th century, lacked the resources to end their exploitation and protect their cultural heritages from continual attack by the dominant society (Mirandé, 1985, p. 32).

There were also some important differences in the situation of Mexican Americans and the other two colonized minority groups. Perhaps the most crucial difference was the proximity of the sovereign nation of Mexico. Population movement across the border was constant, and Mexican culture and the Spanish language were continually rejuvenated, even as they were attacked and disparaged by Anglo-American society.

Cultural Patterns

Besides language differences, Mexican American and Anglo-American cultures differ in many ways. Whereas the dominant society is largely Protestant, the overwhelming majority of Mexican Americans are Catholic, and the church remains one of the most important institutions in any Mexican American community. Religious practices also vary; Mexican Americans (especially men) are relatively inactive in church attendance, preferring to express their spiritual concerns in more spontaneous, less routinized ways.

In the past, everyday life among Mexican Americans was often described in terms of the "culture of poverty" (see Chapter 6), an idea originally based on research in several different Hispanic communities (see Lewis, 1959, 1965, 1966). This perspective asserts that Mexican Americans suffer from an unhealthy value system that includes a weak work ethic, fatalism, and other negative attitudes. Today, this characterization is widely regarded as exaggerated or simply mistaken. More recent research shows that the traits associated with the culture of poverty tend to characterize people who are poor and uneducated, rather than any particular racial or ethnic group. In fact, a number of studies show that there is little difference between the value systems of Mexican Americans and other Americans of similar length of residence in the United States, social class, and educational background (e.g., see Buriel, 1993; Moore & Pinderhughes, 1993; Pew Hispanic Center, 2005, p. 20; Valentine & Mosley, 2000).

Another area of cultural difference involves machismo, a value system that stresses male dominance, honor, virility, and violence. The stereotypes of the dominant group exaggerate the negative aspects of machismo and often fail to recognize that machismo can also be expressed through being a good provider and a respected father, as well as in other nondestructive ways. In fact, the concern for male dignity is not unique to Hispanics and can be found in many cultures in varying strengths and expressions, including Anglo-American. Thus, this difference is one of degree rather than kind (Moore & Pachon, 1985).

Compared with Anglo-Americans, Mexican Americans tend to place more value on family relations and obligations. Strong family ties can be the basis for support networks and cooperative efforts but can also conflict with the emphasis on individualism and individual success in the dominant culture. For example, strong family ties may inhibit geographical mobility and people's willingness to pursue educational and occupational opportunities distant from their home communities (Moore, 1970, p. 127).

These cultural and language differences have inhibited communication with the dominant group and have served as the basis for excluding Mexican Americans from the larger society. However, they also have provided a basis for group cohesion and unity that has sustained common action and protest activity.

Photo 8.1

Dancers celebrate Cinco de Mayo, Mexican Independence Day.

© Morton Beebe/Corbis.

The Meaning of Macho

Words as well as people can immigrate, and in both cases, the process can be transforming. In the following passage, Rose Guilbault (1993), a newspaper editor and columnist, reflects on the meaning of one term that has become central to the dominant group's view of Hispanic males. The image evoked by the term macho *changed from positive to negative as it found its way into American English, a process that reflects dominant-minority relations and partly defines them.*

AMERICANIZATION IS TOUGH ON "MACHO"

ROSE DEL CASTILLO GUILBAULT

What is macho? That depends on which side of the border you come from. . . . The negative connotations of macho in this country are troublesome to Hispanics.

The Hispanic macho is manly, responsible, hardworking, a man in charge, a patriarch. A man who expresses strength through silence. . . .

The American macho is a chauvinist, a brute, uncouth, loud, abrasive, capable of inflicting pain, and sexually promiscuous.

Quintessential macho models in this country are Sylvester Stallone, Arnold Schwarzenegger, and Charles Bronson. . . . They exude toughness, independence, masculinity. But a closer look reveals their machismo is really violence masquerading as courage, sullenness disguised as silence, and irresponsibility camouflaged as independence. . . .

In Spanish, macho ennobles Latin males. In English it devalues them. This pattern seems consistent with the conflicts ethnic minority males experience in this country. Typically the cultural traits other societies value don't translate as desirable characteristics in America.

I watched my own father struggle with these cultural ambiguities. He worked on a farm for 20 years. He laid down miles of irrigation pipe, carefully plowed long, neat rows in fields, . . . stoically worked 20-hour days during the harvest season, accepting the long hours as part of agricultural work. When the boss complained or upbraided him for minor mistakes, he kept quiet, even when it was obvious that the boss had erred.

He handled the most menial tasks with pride. At home he was a good provider. . . . Americans regarded my father as decidedly un-macho. His character was interpreted as non-assertive, his loyalty non-ambition, and his quietness, ignorance. I once overheard the boss's son blame him for plowing crooked rows. . . . My father merely smiled at the lie, knowing the boy had done it, . . . confident his good work was well-known. . . . Seeing my embarrassment, my father dismissed the incident, saying, "They're the dumb ones. Imagine me fighting with a kid."

I tried not to look at him with American eyes because sometimes the reflection hurt. . . .

In the United States, I believe it was the feminist movement of the early '70s that changed macho's meaning. Perhaps my generation of Latin women was in part responsible. I recall Chicanas complaining about the chauvinistic nature of Latin men and the notion they wanted their women barefoot, pregnant, and in the kitchen. The generalization that Latin men embodied chauvinistic traits led to this . . . twist of semantics. Suddenly a word that represented something positive in one culture became a negative stereotype in another. . . .

The impact of language in our society is undeniable. And the misuse of macho hints at a deeper cultural misunderstanding that extends beyond mere word definitions.

SOURCE: Guilbault (1993, pp. 163–165).

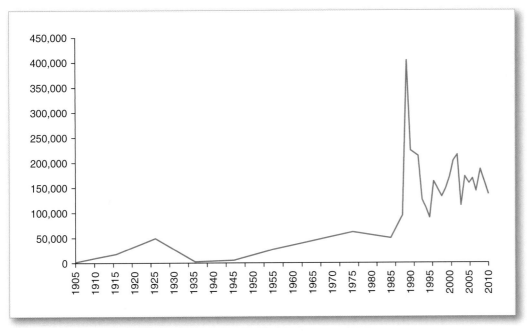

SOURCE: U.S. Department of Homeland Security (2010).

NOTE: The very high number of "immigrants" in the late 1980s and early 1990s was the result of people already in the United States legalizing their status under the provisions of the Immigration Reform and Control Act.

Exhibit 8.5 Legal Immigration From Mexico, 1905 to 2010

Immigration

Although Mexican Americans originated as a colonized minority group, their situation since the early 1900s (and especially since the 1960s) has been largely shaped by immigration. The numbers of legal Mexican immigrants to the United States are shown in Exhibit 8.5. The fluctuations in the rate of immigration can be explained by conditions in Mexico; the varying demand for labor in the low-paying, unskilled sector of the U.S. economy; broad changes in North America and the world; and changing federal immigration policy. As you will see, competition, one of the key variables in Noel's hypothesis, has shaped the relationships between Mexican immigrants and the larger American society.

Push and Pull

Like the massive wave of immigrants from Europe that arrived between the 1820s and the 1920s (see Chapter 2), Mexicans have been **pushed** from their homeland and toward the United States by a variety of sweeping changes, both domestic and global. European immigration was propelled by industrialization, urbanization, and rapid population growth. Mexican immigrants have been motivated by similarly broad forces, including continuing industrialization and globalization.

At the heart of the immigration lies a simple fact: The almost 2,000-mile-long border between Mexico and the United States is the longest continuous point of contact between a less developed and a more developed nation in the world. For the past century, the United States has developed faster than Mexico, moving from an industrial to a postindustrial society and sustaining a substantially higher standard of living. The continuing wage gap between the two nations has made even menial work in the North attractive to millions of Mexicans (and other Central and South Americans). Mexico has a large number of people who need work, and the United States offers jobs that pay more—often much more—than the wages available south of the border. Today, roughly 10% of the Mexican population lives in the United States. Just as the air flows from high to low pressure, people move from areas of lower to higher economic opportunities. The flow is not continuous, however, and has been affected by conditions in both the sending and receiving nations.

An Immigrant's Tale

The stories of Delfino and Florentino represent the experiences of thousands of immigrants—legal as well as undocumented—who have crossed the border into the United States over the past century. Driven by the poverty of their home villages and attracted by the allure of work in el Norte, they pay thousands of dollars to their guides and often risk their lives in pursuit of the dream of earning a decent wage. Many are sojourners who remain focused on the families they have left behind. They send millions of dollars home and are the main—or even the sole—support for their kin, the hope and lifeblood for perhaps scores of relatives.

DELFINO'S DREAM

SAM QUINONES

By early 2004, Delfino [who had left his Mexican village home years before and crossed the U.S. border illegally] had phony papers, a car, a shared house, a job, some English. It was then that his attention turned to other things. Back in Mexico, his family's 8-by-12-foot shack had been the most visible sign of its . . . low social standing. The shack had dirt floors, leaked rain, and left them unprotected from the cold. A girl's family once refused Florentino's [Delfino's brother] marriage proposal because that shack was all he could offer her.

Delfino began sending extra money home every month. . . . In the middle of 2004, the family moved its shack to one side—it took only a few men to lift it. On the site where the shack once stood, Delfino built the first house in his village ever paid for with dollars. It . . . had an indoor toilet, a kitchen, and concrete floors. The house was fronted by two smoked-glass windows so wide and tall that it looked as if the house wore sunglasses.

"I wanted it to look good when you pass," Delfino said, "and to have a nice view."

In Xocotla, nothing like it had ever been built so quickly by a youth so poor.

A few months later, Florentino [also in the United States illegally] arranged with his father to have a house built in the village [for himself]. . . . All this helped change their father [Lázaro]. He had stopped drinking and discovered Alcoholics Anonymous. He was now in his 40s and tired of waking up in the pig muck. . . . His sons could now send him money for construction materials and know he wouldn't spend it on booze. So within a year of Delfino's arrival in the United States, Lázaro was not only sober but supervising construction of first Delfino's house, and then Florentino's. . . .

Lázaro had never been the object of anyone's envy. He found that he liked it. He kept building those houses, telling everyone that he'd build until his sons in America told him to stop.

For a time, the Juárez brothers were the village's largest employers—spending close to 40 thousand dollars on labor and supplies. As Florentino's house went up, the family of the girl who'd refused his marriage proposal let it be known that they regretted their decision. When Delfino returned to Xocotla for a few months in late 2004, older men, who'd once laughed at his mohawked hair, came to him to borrow money.

"Now everyone says hello," said Delfino.

SOURCE: Quinones (2007, pp. 284–286).

Conditions in Mexico, Fluctuating Demand for Labor, and Federal Immigration Policy

Generally, for the past 100 years, Mexico has served as a reserve pool of cheap labor for the benefit of U.S. businesses, agricultural interests, and other groups, and the volume of immigration largely reflects changing economic conditions in the United States. Immigration increases with good times in the United States and decreases when times are bad, a pattern reinforced by the policies and actions of the federal government. The most important events in the complex history of Mexican immigration to the United States are presented in Exhibit 8.6, along with some comments regarding the nature of the event and its effects.

Prior to the early 1900s, the volume of immigration was generally low and largely unregulated. People crossed the border—in both directions—as the need arose, informally and without restriction. The volume of immigration and concern about controlling the border began to rise with the increase of political and economic turmoil in Mexico in the early decades of the 20th century but still remained a comparative trickle.

Dates	Event	Result	Effect on Immigration From Mexico
1910	Mexican Revolution	Political turmoil and unrest in Mexico	Increased
Early 20th century	Mexican Industrialization	Many groups (especially rural peasants) displaced	Increased
1920s	National Origins Act of 1924	Decreased immigration from Europe	Increased
1930s	Great Depression	Decreased demand for labor and increased competition for jobs leads to repatriation campaign	Decreased, many return to Mexico
1940s	World War II	Increased demand for labor leads to Bracero Guest Worker Program	Increased
1950s	Concern over illegal immigrants	Operation Wetback	Decreased, many return to Mexico
1965	Repeal of National Origins Act	New immigration policy gives high priority to close family of citizens	Increased (see Exhibit 8.5)
1986	Immigration Reform and Control Act	Illegal immigrants given opportunity to legalize status	Many illegal immigrants gain legal status
1994	NAFTA	Borders more open, many groups in Mexico (especially rural peasants) displaced	Increased
2007	Recession in the United States	Widespread unemployment in the United States, job supply shrinks	Decreased

Exhibit 8.6 Significant Dates in Mexican Immigration

Immigration increased in the 1920s when federal legislation curtailed the flow of cheap labor from Europe and then decreased in the 1930s when hard times came to the United States (and the world) during the Great Depression. Many Mexicans in the United States returned home during that decade, sometimes voluntarily, often by force. As competition for jobs increased, efforts began to expel Mexican laborers, just as the Noel hypothesis would predict. The federal government instituted a repatriation campaign aimed specifically at deporting illegal Mexican immigrants. In many localities, repatriation was pursued with great zeal, and the campaign intimidated many legal immigrants and native-born Mexican Americans into moving to Mexico. The result was that the Mexican American population of the United States declined by an estimated 40% during the 1930s (Cortes, 1980, p. 711).

When the depression ended and U.S. society began to mobilize for World War II, federal policy toward immigrants from Mexico changed once more as employers again turned to Mexico for workers. In 1942, the Bracero program was initiated to permit contract laborers, usually employed in agriculture and other areas requiring unskilled labor, to work in the United States for a limited amount of time. When their contracts expired, the workers were required to return to Mexico.

The Bracero program continued for several decades after the end of the war and was a crucial source of labor for the American economy. In 1960 alone, braceros supplied 26% of the nation's seasonal farm labor (Cortes, 1980, p. 703). The program generated millions of dollars of profit for growers and other employers because they were paying braceros much less than American workers would have received (Amott & Matthaei, 1991, pp. 79–80).

At the same time that the Bracero program permitted immigration from Mexico, other programs and agencies worked to deport undocumented (or illegal) immigrants, large numbers of whom entered the United States with the braceros. Government efforts reached a peak in the early 1950s with Operation Wetback, a program under which federal authorities deported almost 4 million Mexicans (Grebler, Moore, & Guzman, 1970, p. 521).

During Operation Wetback, raids on the homes and places of business of Mexican Americans were common, and authorities often ignored their civil and legal rights. In an untold number of cases, U.S. citizens of Mexican descent were deported along with illegal immigrants. These violations of civil and legal rights have been a continuing grievance of Mexican Americans (and other Latinos) for decades (Mirandé, 1985, pp. 70–90).

In 1965, the overtly racist national immigration policy incorporated in the 1924 National Origins Act (see Chapter 2) was replaced by a new policy that gave a high priority to immigrants who were family and kin of U.S. citizens. The immediate family (parents, spouses, and children) of U.S. citizens could enter without numerical restriction. Some numerical restrictions were placed on the number of immigrants from each sending country, but about 80% of these restricted visas were reserved for other close relatives of citizens. The remaining 20% of the visas went to people who had skills needed in the labor force (Bouvier & Gardner, 1986, pp. 13–15, 41; Rumbaut, 1991, p. 215).

Immigrants have always tended to move along chains of kinship and other social relationships, and the new policy reinforced those tendencies. The social networks connecting Latin America with the United States expanded, and the rate of immigration from Mexico increased sharply after 1965 (see Exhibit 8.5) as immigrants became citizens and sent for other family members.

Most of the Mexican immigrants, legal as well as undocumented, who have arrived since 1965 continue the pattern of seeking work in the low-wage, unskilled sectors of the labor market in the cities and fields of the Southwest. For many, work is seasonal or temporary. When the work ends, they often return to Mexico, commuting across the border as has been done for decades.

In 1986, Congress attempted to deal with illegal immigrants, most of whom were thought to be Mexican, by passing the Immigration Reform and Control Act. This legislation allowed illegal immigrants who had been in the country continuously since 1982 to legalize their status. According to the U.S. Immigration and Naturalization Service (1993, p. 17), about 3 million people—75% of them Mexican—have taken advantage of this provision, but the program did not slow the volume of illegal immigration. In 1988, at the end of the amnesty application period, there were still almost 3 million undocumented immigrants in the United States. In 2010, the number of undocumented immigrants was estimated at 11.2 million, down from a high of 12 million in 2006 (Passel & Cohn, 2011).

Recent Immigration From Mexico

Mexican immigration to the United States continues to reflect the differences in level of development and standard of living between the two societies. Mexico remains a much more agricultural nation and continues to have a much lower standard of living, as measured by average wages, housing quality, health care, or any number of other criteria. To illustrate, according to United Nations (2011) data, the per capita income of the United States ($45,230) is 4.5 times greater than the per capita income of Mexico ($9,964). Many Mexicans live in poverty, and the population continues to grow. Many people are unable to find a place in their home economy and are drawn to the opportunities for work provided by their affluent northern neighbor. Since the average length of schooling in their homeland is only about 7 years ("Education Statistics," 2011), Mexican immigrants bring much lower levels of job skills and compete for work in the lower levels of the U.S. job structure.

The impetus to immigrate has been reinforced by the recent globalization of the Mexican economy. In the past, the Mexican government insulated its economy from foreign competition with a variety of tariffs and barriers. These protections have been abandoned over the past several decades, and Mexico, like many less developed nations, has opened its doors to the world economy. The result has been a flood of foreign agricultural products (cheap corn in particular), manufactured goods, and capital, which, while helpful in some parts of the economy, has disrupted social life and forced many Mexicans, especially the poor and rural dwellers, out of their traditional way of life.

Probably the most significant changes to Mexican society have come from the North American Trade Agreement, or NAFTA. Starting in 1994, this policy united the three nations of North America in a single trading zone. U.S. companies began to move their manufacturing operations to Mexico, attracted by lower wages, less stringent environmental regulations, and weak labor unions. They built factories (called maquiladoras) along the border and brought many new jobs to the Mexican economy. However, other jobs—no longer protected from global competition—were lost, more than offsetting these gains, and Mexican wages actually declined after the implementation of NAFTA, increasing the already large number of Mexicans living in poverty. One analyst estimates that more than 2.5 million families have been driven out of the rural economy because they cannot compete with U.S. and Canadian agribusinesses (Faux, 2004).

Thus, globalization in general and NAFTA in particular have reinforced the long-term relationship between the two nations. Mexico, like other nations of the less developed "South," continues to produce a supply of unskilled, less-educated workers, while the United States, like other nations of the more developed and industrialized "North," provides a seemingly insatiable demand for cheap labor. Compared with what is available at home, the wages in *el Norte* are quite attractive, even when the jobs are at the margins of the mainstream economy or in the irregular, underground economy (e.g., day laborers paid off the books, illegal sweatshop jobs in the garment industry, and sex work) and even when the journey requires Mexican immigrants to break American laws, pay large sums of money to "coyotes" to guide them across the border, and live in constant fear of raids by *La Migra*. Predictably, when the U.S. economy faltered recently and the supply of jobs shrunk, the number of immigrants declined dramatically. Exhibit 8.7 displays the recent decline based on data compiled by the Pew Hispanic Center.

Photo 8.2

A California road sign warns motorists to watch for migrant workers crossing the highway.

© Christopher Morris/ Corbis.

The Continuing Debate Over Immigration Policy

Immigration has once again become a hotly debated issue in the United States. How many immigrants should be admitted? From which nations? With what skills? Should the relatives of U.S. citizens continue to receive a high priority? And, perhaps the issue that generates the most passion, what should be done about illegal immigrants? Virtually all of these questions—even those phrased in general, abstract terms—are mainly about the large volume of immigration from Mexico and the porous U.S. southern border.

Exhibit 8.7 Migration In and Out of Mexico, 2002 to 2009

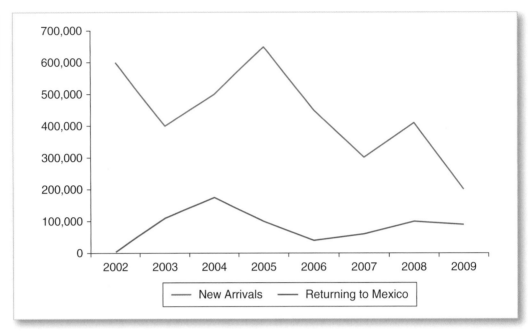

SOURCE: Passel and Cohn (2009).

Photo 8.3

These undocumented immigrants were apprehended by the Border Patrol and are being prepared for deportation. Many will attempt to return.

© Rick D'Elia/Corbis.

The federal government is attempting to reduce the flow by building a wall on the border with Mexico and beefing up the Border Patrol, with both increased personnel and more high-tech surveillance technology. Still, communities across the nation—not just in border states—are feeling the impact of Mexican immigration and wondering how to respond. Many citizens support extreme measures to close the borders— bigger, thicker walls and even the use of deadly force—while others ponder ways to absorb the newcomers without disrupting or bankrupting local school systems, medical facilities, or housing markets. The nation is divided on many of the issues related to immigration. Public opinion polls over the past decade (see Exhibit 8.8) show that about 40% to 50% of all Americans would like to lower the volume of immigration but that an almost equal percentage (30–40%) favor keeping the present level. A much smaller but steady 10% to 20% favor an increase in the rate of immigration.

A variety of reforms for immigration policy have been proposed and continue to be debated. One key issue is the treatment of illegal immigrants: Should the undocumented be summarily deported, or should some provision be made for them to legalize their status, as was done in the Immigration Reform and Control Act of 1986? If the latter, should the opportunity to attain legal status be extended to all or only to immigrants who meet certain criteria (e.g., those with steady jobs and clean criminal records)? Many feel that amnesty is unjust because immigrants who entered illegally have, after all, broken the law and should be punished. Others point to the economic contributions of these immigrants and the damage to the economy that would result from summary, mass expulsions. Still others worry

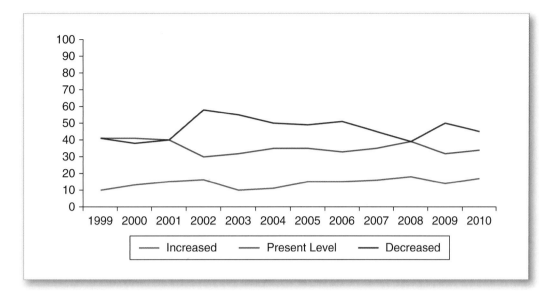

Exhibit 8.8 U.S. Public Opinion on Immigration, 1999 to 2010

SOURCE: Morales (2010).

about the negative impact illegal immigrants might be having on the job prospects for the less skilled members of the larger population, including the urban underclass that is disproportionately minority. We address some of these issues later in this chapter and in Chapters 9 and 10.

Immigration, Colonization, and Intergroup Competition

Three points can be made about Mexican immigration to the United States. First, the flow of population from Mexico was and is stimulated and sustained by powerful political and economic interests in the United States. Systems of recruitment and networks of communication and transportation have been established to routinize the flow of people and make it a predictable source of labor for the benefit of U.S. agriculture and other employers. The movement of people back and forth across the border was well established long before current efforts to regulate and control it. Depending on U.S. policy, this immigration is sometimes legal and encouraged and sometimes illegal and discouraged. Regardless of the label, the river of people has been steadily flowing for decades in response to opportunities for work in the North (Portes, 1990, pp. 160–163).

Second, Mexican immigrants enter a social system in which a colonized status for the group already has been established. The paternalistic traditions and racist systems that were established in the 19th century shaped the positions that were open to Mexican immigrants in the 20th century. Mexican Americans continued to be treated as a colonized group despite the streams of new arrivals, and the history of the group in the 20th century has many parallels with African Americans and American Indians. Thus, Mexican Americans might be thought of as a colonized minority group that happens to have a large number of immigrants or, alternatively, as an immigrant group that incorporates a strong tradition of colonization.

Third, this brief review of the twisting history of U.S. policy on Mexican immigration should serve as a reminder that levels of prejudice, racism, and discrimination increase as competition and the sense of threat between groups increases. The very qualities that make Mexican labor attractive to employers have caused bitter resentment among those segments of the Anglo population who feel that their own jobs and financial security are threatened. Often caught in the middle, Mexican immigrants and Mexican Americans have not had the resources to avoid exploitation by employers or rejection and discrimination by others. The ebb and flow of the efforts to regulate immigration (and sometimes even deport U.S. citizens of Mexican descent) can be understood in terms of competition, differentials in power, and prejudice.

Developments in the United States

As the flow of immigration from Mexico fluctuated with the need for labor, Mexican Americans struggled to improve their status. In the early decades of the 20th century, like other colonized minority groups, they faced a system of repression and control in which they were accorded few rights and had little political power.

Continuing Colonization

Throughout much of the 20th century, Mexican Americans have been limited to less-desirable, low-wage jobs. Split labor markets, in which Mexican Americans are paid less than Anglos for the same jobs, have been common. The workforce often has been further split by gender, with Mexican American women assigned to the worst jobs and receiving the lowest wages in both urban and rural areas (Takaki, 1993, pp. 318–319).

Men's jobs often took them away from their families to work in the mines and fields. In 1930, 45% of all Mexican American men worked in agriculture, with another 28% in unskilled nonagricultural jobs (Cortes, 1980, p. 708). The women were often forced by economic necessity to enter the job market; in 1930, they were concentrated in farm work (21%), unskilled manufacturing jobs (25%), and domestic and other service work (37%) (Amott & Matthaei, 1991, pp. 76–77). They were typically paid less than both Mexican American men and Anglo women. In addition to their job responsibilities, Mexican American women had to maintain their households and raise their children, often facing these tasks without a spouse (Baca Zinn & Eitzen, 1990, p. 84).

As the United States industrialized and urbanized during the century, employment patterns became more diversified. Mexican Americans found work in manufacturing, construction, transportation, and other sectors of the economy. Some Mexican Americans, especially those of the third generation or later, moved into middle- and upper-level occupations, and some began to move out of the Southwest. Still, Mexican Americans in all regions (especially recent immigrants) tended to be concentrated at the bottom of the occupational ladder. Women increasingly worked outside the home, but their employment was largely limited to agriculture, domestic service, and the garment industry (Amott & Matthaei, 1991, pp. 76–79; Cortes, 1980, p. 708).

Like African Americans in the segregated South, Mexican Americans were excluded from the institutions of the larger society by law and by custom for much of the 20th century. There were separate (and unequal) school systems for Mexican American children, and in many communities, Mexican Americans were disenfranchised and accorded few legal or civil rights. There were "whites-only" primary elections modeled after the Jim Crow system, and residential segregation was widespread. The police and the court system generally abetted or ignored the rampant discrimination against the Mexican American community. Discrimination in the criminal justice system and civil rights violations have been continual grievances of Mexican Americans throughout the century.

Protest and Resistance

Like all minority groups, Mexican Americans have attempted to improve their collective position whenever possible. The beginnings of organized resistance and protest stretch back to the original contact period in the 19th century, when protest was usually organized on a local level. Regional and national organizations made their appearance in the 20th century (Cortes, 1980, p. 709).

As with African Americans, Mexican Americans' early protest organizations were integrationist and reflected the assimilationist values of the larger society. For example, one of the earlier and more significant groups was the League of United Latin American Citizens (LULAC), founded in Texas in 1929. LULAC promoted Americanization and greater educational opportunities for Mexican Americans. The group also worked to expand civil and political rights and to increase equality for Mexican Americans. LULAC fought numerous court battles against discrimination and racial segregation (Moore, 1970, pp. 143–145).

The workplace has been a particularly conflictual arena for Mexican Americans. Split-labor market situations increased anti-Mexican American prejudice; some labor unions tried to exclude Mexican immigrants to the United States, along with immigrants from Asia and Southern and Eastern Europe (Grebler et al., 1970, pp. 90–93).

At the same time, Mexican Americans played important leadership roles in the labor movement. Since early in the century, Mexican Americans have been involved in union organizing, particularly in agriculture and mining. When excluded by Anglo labor unions, they often formed their own unions to work for the improvement of working conditions. As the 20th century progressed, the number and variety of groups pursuing the Mexican American cause increased. During World War II, Mexican Americans served in the armed forces, and, as with other minority groups, this experience increased their impatience with the constraints on their freedoms and opportunities. After the war ended, a number of new Mexican American organizations were founded, including the Community Service Organization in Los Angeles and the American GI Forum in Texas. Compared with older organizations such as LULAC, the new groups were less concerned with assimilation per se, addressed a broad range of community problems, and attempted to increase Mexican American political power (Grebler et al., 1970, pp. 543–545).

Chicanismo

The 1960s were a time of intense activism and militancy for Mexican Americans. A protest movement guided by an ideology called Chicanismo began at about the same time as the Black Power and Red Power movements. Chicanismo encompassed a variety of organizations and ideas, united by a heightened militancy and impatience with the racism of the larger society and strongly stated demands for justice, fairness, and equal rights. The movement questioned the value of assimilation and sought to increase awareness of the continuing exploitation of Mexican Americans; it adapted many of the tactics and strategies (marches, rallies, voter registration drives, etc.) of the civil rights movement of the 1960s.

Chicanismo is similar in some ways to the Black Power ideology (see Chapter 7). It is partly a reaction to the failure of U.S. society to implement the promises of integration and equality. It rejected traditional stereotypes of Mexican Americans, proclaimed a powerful and positive group image and heritage, and analyzed the group's past and present situation in American society in terms of victimization, continuing exploitation, and institutional discrimination. The inequalities that separated Mexican Americans from the larger society were seen as the result of deep-rooted, continuing racism and the cumulative effects of decades of exclusion. According to Chicanismo, the solution to these problems lay in group empowerment, increased militancy, and group pride, not in assimilation to a culture that had rationalized and abetted the exploitation of Mexican Americans (Acuña, 1988, pp. 307–358; Grebler et al., 1970, p. 544; Moore, 1970, pp. 149–154).

Some of the central thrusts of the 1960s protest movement are captured in the widespread adoption of Chicanos, which had been a derogatory term, as a group name for Mexican Americans. Other minority groups underwent similar name changes at about the same time. For example, African Americans shifted from *Negro* to *black* as a group designation. These name changes were not merely cosmetic; they marked fundamental shifts in group goals and desired relationships with the larger society. The new names came from the minority groups themselves, not from the dominant group, and they expressed the pluralistic themes of group pride, self-determination, militancy, and increased resistance to exploitation and discrimination.

Organizations and Leaders

The Chicano movement saw the rise of many new groups and leaders, one of the most important of which was Reies López Tijerina, who formed the Alianza de Mercedes (Alliance of Land Grants) in 1963. The goal of this group was to correct what Tijerina saw as the unjust and illegal seizure of land from Mexicans during the 19th century. The Alianza was militant and confrontational, and to bring attention to their cause, members of the group seized and occupied federal lands. Tijerina spent several years in jail as a result of his activities, and the movement eventually lost its strength and faded from view in the 1970s.

Another prominent Chicano leader was Rodolfo Gonzalez, who founded the Crusade for Justice in 1965. The crusade focused on abuses of Mexican American civil and legal rights and worked against discrimination by police and the criminal courts. In a 1969 presentation at a symposium on Chicano liberation, Gonzalez expressed some of the nationalistic themes of Chicanismo and the importance of creating a power base within the group (as opposed to assimilating or integrating):

> Where [whites] have incorporated themselves to keep us from moving into their neighborhoods, we can also incorporate ourselves to keep them from controlling our neighborhoods. We . . . have to understand economic revolution. . . . We have to understand that liberation comes from self-determination, and to start to use the tools of nationalism to win over our barrio brothers. . . . We have to understand that we can take over the institutions within our community. We have to create the community of the Mexicano here in order to have any type of power. (Moquin & Van Doren, 1971, pp. 381–382)

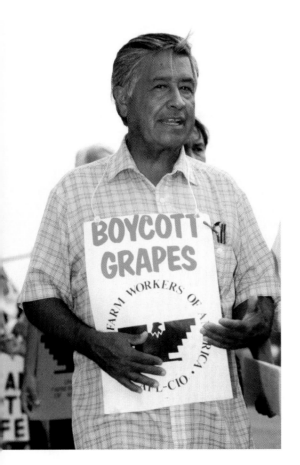

Photo 8.4

César Chávez organized the United Farm Workers and led a national grape boycott.

© Najlah Feanny/Corbis.

A third important leader was José Angel Gutiérrez, organizer of the party La Raza Unida (People United). La Raza Unida offered alternative candidates and ideas to those of Democrats and Republicans. Its most notable success was in Crystal City, Texas, where, in 1973, it succeeded in electing its entire slate of candidates to local office (Acuña, 1988, pp. 332–451).

Without a doubt, the best-known Chicano leader of the 1960s and 1970s was the late César Chávez, who organized the United Farm Workers, the first union to successfully represent migrant workers. Chávez was as much a labor leader as a leader of the Mexican American community, and he also organized African Americans, Filipinos, and Anglo-Americans. Migrant farmworkers have few economic or political resources, and the migratory nature of their work isolates them in rural areas and makes them difficult to contact. In the 1960s (and still today), many were undocumented immigrants who spoke little or no English and returned to the cities or to their countries of origin at the end of the season. As a group, farmworkers were nearly invisible in the social landscape of the United States in the 1960s, and organizing this group was a demanding task. Chávez's success in this endeavor is one of the more remarkable studies in group protest.

Like Dr. Martin Luther King Jr., Chávez was a disciple of Gandhi and a student of non-violent direct protest (see Chapter 7). His best-known tactic was the boycott; in 1965, he organized a grape-pickers' strike and a national boycott of grapes. The boycott lasted 5 years and ended when the growers recognized the United Farm Workers as the legitimate representative of farmworkers. Chávez and his organization achieved a major victory, and the agreement provided for significant improvements in the situation of the workers (for a biography of Chávez, see Levy, 1975).

Gender and the Chicano Protest Movement

Mexican American women were heavily involved in the Chicano protest movement. Jessie Lopez and Dolores Huerta were central figures in the movement to organize farmworkers and worked closely with César Chávez. However, as was the case for African American women, Chicano women encountered sexism and gender discrimination within the movement even as they worked for the benefit of the group as a whole. Their dilemmas are described by activist Sylvia Gonzales:

> Along with her male counterpart, she attended meetings, organized boycotts, did everything asked of her. . . . But, if she [tried to assume leadership roles], she was met with the same questioning of her femininity which the culture dictates when a woman is not self-sacrificing and seeks to fulfill her own needs. . . . The Chicano movement seemed to demand self-actualization for only the male members of the group. (Amott & Matthaei, 1991, p. 83)

Despite these difficulties, Chicano women contributed to the movement in a variety of areas. They helped organize poor communities and worked for welfare reform. Continuing issues include domestic violence, child care, the criminal victimization of women, and the racial and gender oppression that limits women of all minority groups (Amott & Matthaei, 1991, pp. 82–86; see also Mirandé & Enríquez, 1979, pp. 202–243).

Mexican Americans and Other Minority Groups

Like the Black Power and Red Power movements, Chicanismo began to fade from public view in the 1970s and 1980s. The movement could claim some successes, but perhaps the clearest victory was in raising the awareness of the larger society about the grievances and problems of Mexican Americans. Today, many Chicanos continue to face poverty and powerlessness and exploitation as a cheap agricultural labor force. The less-educated, urbanized segments of the group share the prospect of becoming a permanent urban underclass with other minority groups of color.

Over the course of the 20th century, the ability of Chicanos to pursue their self-interests has been limited by both internal and external forces. Like African Americans, the group has been systematically excluded from the institutions of the larger society. Continuing immigration from Mexico has increased the size of the group, but these immigrants bring few resources with them that could be directly or immediately translated into economic or political power in the United States.

Unlike immigrants from Europe, who settled in the urban centers of the industrializing East Coast, Mexican Americans tended to work and live in rural areas distant from and marginal to urban centers of industrialization and opportunities for education, skill development, and upward mobility. They were a vitally important source of labor in agriculture and other segments of the economy but only to the extent that they were exploitable and powerless. As Chicanos moved to the cities, they continued to serve as a colonized, exploited labor force concentrated at the lower end of the stratification system. Thus, the handicaps created by discrimination in the past were reinforced by continuing discrimination and exploitation in the present, perpetuating the cycles of poverty and powerlessness.

At the same time, however, the flow of immigration and the constant movement of people back and forth across the border kept Mexican culture and the Spanish language alive. Unlike African Americans under slavery, Chicanos were not cut off from their homeland and native culture. Mexican American culture was attacked and disparaged, but, unlike African culture, it was not destroyed.

Clearly, the traditional model of assimilation does not describe the experiences of Mexican Americans well. They have experienced less social mobility than European immigrant groups and have maintained their traditional culture and language more completely. Like African Americans, the group is split along lines of social class. Although many Mexican Americans (particularly of the third generation and later) have acculturated and integrated, a large segment of the group continues to fill the same economic role as did their ancestors: an unskilled labor force for the development of the Southwest, augmented with new immigrants at the convenience of U.S. employers. In 2004, more than 41% of employed Mexican Americans—nearly double the percentage for non-Hispanic whites—were in the construction, unskilled labor, and farm sectors of the labor force (U.S. Bureau of the Census, 2007a). For the less educated and for recent immigrants, cultural and racial differences combine to increase their social visibility, mark them for exploitation, and rationalize their continuing exclusion from the larger society.

PUERTO RICANS

Puerto Rico became a territory of the United States after the defeat of Spain in the Spanish-American War of 1898. The island was small and impoverished, and it was difficult for Puerto Ricans to avoid domination by the United States. Thus, the initial contact between Puerto Ricans and U.S. society was made in an atmosphere of war and conquest. By the time Puerto Ricans began to migrate to the mainland in large numbers, their relationship to U.S. society was largely that of a colonized minority group, and they generally retained that status on the mainland.

Migration (Push and Pull) and Employment

At the time of initial contact, the population of Puerto Rico was overwhelmingly rural and supported itself by subsistence farming and by exporting coffee and sugar. As the century wore on, U.S. firms began to invest in and develop the island economy, especially the sugarcane industry. These agricultural endeavors took more and more of the land. Opportunities for economic survival in the rural areas declined, and many peasants were forced to move into the cities (Portes, 1990, p. 163).

Movement to the mainland began gradually and increased slowly until the 1940s. In 1900, there were about 2,000 Puerto Ricans living on the mainland. By the eve of World War II, this number had grown to only 70,000, a tiny fraction of the total population. Then, during the 1940s, the number of Puerto Ricans on the mainland increased more than fourfold, to 300,000, and during the 1950s, it nearly tripled, to 887,000 (U.S. Commission on Civil Rights, 1976, p. 19).

This massive and sudden population growth was the result of a combination of circumstances. First, Puerto Ricans became citizens of the United States in 1917, so their movements were not impeded by international boundaries or immigration restrictions. Second, unemployment was a major problem on the island. The sugarcane industry continued to displace the rural population, urban unemployment was high, and the population continued to grow. By the 1940s, a considerable number of Puerto Ricans were available to seek work off the island and, like Chicanos, could serve as a cheap labor supply for U.S. employers.

Third, Puerto Ricans were pulled to the mainland by the same labor shortages that attracted Mexican immigrants during and after World War II. Whereas the latter responded to job opportunities in the West and Southwest, Puerto Ricans moved to the Northeast. The job profiles of these two groups were similar; both were concentrated in the low-wage, unskilled sector of the job market. However, the Puerto Rican migration began many decades after the Mexican migration, at a time when the United States was much more industrialized and urbanized. As a result, Puerto Ricans were more concentrated than Mexican immigrants in urban labor markets (Portes, 1990, p. 164).

Movement between the island and the mainland was facilitated by the commencement of affordable air travel between San Juan and New York City in the late 1940s. New York had been the major center of settlement for Puerto Ricans on the mainland even before annexation. A small Puerto Rican community had been established in the city, and as with many groups, organizations and networks were established to ease the transition and help newcomers with housing, jobs, and other issues. Although they eventually dispersed to other regions and cities, Puerto Ricans on the mainland remain centered in New York City. More than two thirds currently reside in the cities of the Northeast (U.S. Bureau of the Census, 2004).

Economics and jobs were at the heart of the move to the mainland. The rate of Puerto Rican migration has followed the cycle of boom and bust, just as it has for Mexican immigrants. The 1950s, the peak decade for Puerto Rican migration, was a period of rapid U.S. economic growth. Migration was encouraged, and job recruiters traveled to the island to attract workers. By the 1960s, however, the supply of jobs on the island had expanded appreciably, and the average number of migrants declined from the peak of 41,000 per year in the 1950s to about 20,000 per year. In the 1970s, the U.S. economy faltered, unemployment grew, and the flow of Puerto Rican migration actually reversed itself, with the number of returnees exceeding the number of migrants in various years (U.S. Commission on Civil Rights, 1976, p. 25). The migrations continued: Almost 4.3 million Puerto Ricans, or a little more than half of all Puerto Ricans, were living on the mainland in 2009 (U.S. Bureau of the Census, 2009a).

As the U.S. economy expanded and migration accelerated after World War II, Puerto Ricans moved into a broad range of jobs and locations in society, and the group grew more economically diversified and more regionally dispersed. Still, the bulk of the group remains concentrated in lower-status jobs in the larger cities of the Northeast. Puerto Rican men have often found work as unskilled laborers or in service occupations, particularly in areas where English language facility is not necessary (e.g., janitorial work). The women often have been employed as domestics or seamstresses for the garment industry in New York City (Portes, 1990, p. 164).

Transitions

Although Puerto Ricans are not "immigrants," the move to the mainland does involve a change in culture and language (Fitzpatrick, 1980, p. 858). Despite nearly a century of political affiliation, Puerto Rican and Anglo cultures differ along many dimensions. Puerto Ricans are overwhelmingly Catholic, but the religious practices and rituals on the mainland are quite different from those on the island. Mainland Catholic parishes often reflect the traditions and practices of other cultures and groups. On the island, "Religious observance reflects the spontaneous and expressive practices of the Spanish and the Italian and not the restrained and well-organized worship of the Irish and Germans" (p. 865). Also, there are few Puerto Rican priests or even Spanish-speaking clergy on the mainland; thus, members of the group often feel estranged from and poorly served by the church (Fitzpatrick, 1987, pp. 117–138).

A particularly unsettling cultural difference between the island and the mainland involves skin color and perceptions of race. Puerto Rico has a long history of racial intermarriage. Slavery was less monolithic and total, and the island had no periods of systematic, race-based segregation like the Jim Crow system. Thus, although skin color prejudice still exists in Puerto Rico, it never has been as categorical as on the mainland. On the island, race is perceived as a continuum of possibilities and combinations, not as a simple dichotomous split between white and black.

Furthermore, in Puerto Rico, other factors, such as social class, are considered to be more important than race as criteria for judging and classifying others. In fact, as we discussed in Chapter 6 ("Comparative Focus: Race in Another America"), social class can affect perceptions of skin color, and people of higher status might be seen as lighter skinned. Coming from this background, Puerto Ricans find the rigid racial thinking of U.S. culture disconcerting and even threatening.

The confusion and discomfort that can result was documented and illustrated by a study of Puerto Rican college students in New York City. Dramatic differences were found between the personal racial identification of the students and their perceptions of how Anglos viewed them. When asked for their racial identification, most of the students classified themselves as "tan," with one third labeling themselves "white" and only 7% considering themselves "black." When asked how they thought they were racially classified by Anglos, however, none of the students used the "tan" classification: 58% felt that they were seen as "white," and 41% felt that they were seen as "black" (Rodriguez, 1989, pp. 60–61; see also Rodriguez & Cordero-Guzman, 1992; Vargas-Ramos, 2005).

Another study documented dramatic differences in the terms used to express racial identity between women on the mainland and those in Puerto Rico. The latter identified their racial identities primarily in skin color terms: black, white, or *trigueña* (a "mixed-race" category with multiple skin tones), while mainland women identified themselves in nonracial terms, such as Hispanic, Latina, Hispanic American, or American. In the view of the researchers, these labels serve to deflect the stigma associated with black racial status in the United States (Landale & Oropesa, 2002). In the racially dichotomized U.S. culture, many Puerto Ricans feel they have no clear place. They are genuinely puzzled when they first encounter prejudice and discrimination based on skin color and are uncertain about their own identities and self-image. The racial perceptions of the dominant culture can be threatening to Puerto Ricans to the extent that they are victimized by the same web of discrimination and disadvantage that affects African Americans. There are still clear disadvantages to being classified as black in U.S. society. Institutionalized racial barriers can be extremely formidable, and in the case of Puerto Ricans, they may combine with cultural and linguistic differences to sharply limit opportunities and mobility.

Puerto Ricans and Other Minority Groups

Puerto Ricans arrived in the cities of the Northeast long after the great wave of European immigrants and several decades after African Americans began migrating from the South. They have often competed with other minority groups for housing, jobs, and other resources. A pattern of ethnic succession can be seen in some neighborhoods and occupational areas in which Puerto Ricans have replaced other groups that have moved out (and sometimes up).

Because of their more recent arrival, Puerto Ricans on the mainland were not subjected to the more repressive paternalistic or rigid competitive systems of race relations such as slavery or Jim Crow. Instead, the subordinate status of the group is manifested in their occupational, residential, and educational profiles and by the institutionalized barriers to upward mobility that they face. Puerto Ricans share many problems with other urban minority groups of color: poverty, failing educational systems, and crime. Like African Americans, Puerto Ricans find their fate to be dependent on the future of the American city, and a large segment of the group is in danger of becoming part of a permanent urban underclass.

Like Mexican Americans, Puerto Ricans on the mainland combine elements of both an immigrant and a colonized minority experience. The movement to the mainland is voluntary in some ways, but in others, it is strongly motivated by the transformations in the island economy that resulted from modernization and U.S. domination. Like Chicanos, Puerto Ricans tend to enter the labor force at the bottom of the occupational structure and face similar problems of inequality and marginalization. Also, Puerto Rican culture retains a strong vitality and is continually reinvigorated by the considerable movement back and forth between the island and the mainland.

Gender Images of Latinas

One part of the minority group experience is learning to deal with the stereotypes, images, and expectations of the larger society. Of course, everyone (even white males) has to respond to the assumptions of others, but given the realities of power and status, minority group members have fewer choices and a narrower range in which to maneuver: The images imposed by society are harder to escape and more difficult to deny.

In her analysis, Judith Ortiz Cofer (1995), a writer, poet, professor of English, and Puerto Rican, describes some of the images and stereotypes of Latinas with which she has had to struggle and some of the dynamics that have created and sustained those images. She writes from her own experiences, but the points she makes illustrate many of the sociological theories and concepts that guide this text.

THE ISLAND TRAVELS WITH YOU

JUDITH ORTIZ COFER

On a bus trip from London to Oxford University . . . a young man, obviously fresh from a pub, spotted me and as if struck by inspiration went down on his knees in the aisle. With both hands over his heart he broke into an Irish tenor's rendition of "María" from *West Side Story*. My politely amused fellow passengers gave his lovely voice the round of gentle applause that it deserved. Though I was not quite as amused, I managed my version of an English smile: no show of teeth, no extreme contortions of the facial muscles—I was at this time in my life practicing reserve and cool. . . . But Maria had followed me to London, reminding me of a prime fact of my life: You can leave the Island, master the English language, and travel as far as you can, but if you are a Latina, . . . the Island travels with you.

This is sometimes a very good thing—it may win you the extra minute of somebody's attention. But with some people, the same things can make *you* an island—not so much a tropical paradise as an Alcatraz, a place nobody wants to visit. As a Puerto Rican girl growing up in the United States and wanting like most children to "belong," I resented the stereotypes that my Hispanic appearance called forth from many people I met.

Our family lived in a large urban center in New Jersey during the '60s, where life was designed as a microcosm of my parents' casas on the island. We spoke Spanish, we ate Puerto Rican food bought at the bodega, and we practiced strict Catholicism. . . .

As a girl, I was kept under strict surveillance, since virtue and modesty were, by cultural equation, the same as family honor. As a teenager, I was instructed on how to behave as a proper señorita. But it was a conflicting message girls got, since the Puerto Rican mothers also encouraged their daughters to look and act like women and to dress in clothes our Anglo friends found too "mature" for our age. . . . At a Puerto Rican festival, neither the music nor the colors we wore could be too loud. I still experience a vague sense of letdown when I'm invited to a "party" and it turns out to be a marathon conversation in hushed tones rather than a fiesta with salsa, laughter, and dancing—the kind of celebration I remember from my childhood. . . .

Mixed cultural signals have perpetuated certain stereotypes—for example, that of the "Hot Tamale" or sexual firebrand. It is a . . . view that the media have found easy to promote. In their special vocabulary, advertisers have designated "sizzling" and "smoldering" as the adjectives of choice for describing not only the foods but the women of Latin America. . . .

It is custom, however, not chromosomes, that leads us to choose scarlet over pale pink. As young girls, we were influenced in our decisions about clothes and colors by the women . . . who had grown up on a tropical island where the natural environment was a riot of primary colors, where showing your skin was one way to keep cool as well as to look sexy. Most important of all, on the island, women perhaps felt freer to dress and move more provocatively, since . . . they were protected by the traditions, mores, and laws of a Spanish/Catholic system of morality and machismo whose main rule was: *You may look at my sister, but if you touch her I will kill you.* The extended family and church structure could provide a young woman with a circle of safety in her small pueblo on the island; if a man "wronged" a girl, everyone would close in to save her family honor. . . .

Because of my education and proficiency with the English language, I have acquired many mechanisms for dealing with the anger I experience. This was not true for my parents, nor is it true for the many Latin women working at menial jobs who must put up with stereotypes about our ethnic group such as: "They make good domestics." This is another facet of the myth of the Latin women in the United States. . . . The myth of the Hispanic menial has been maintained by the same media phenomenon that made "Mammy" from *Gone with the Wind* America's idea of a black woman for generations: María, the housemaid or counter girl, is now indelibly etched into the national psyche. The big and little screens have presented us with the picture of the funny Hispanic maid, mispronouncing words and cooking up a spicy storm in the kitchen. . . .

I am one of the lucky ones. My parents made it possible for me to acquire a stronger footing in the mainstream culture by giving me the chance at an education. . . . There are thousands of Latinas without the privilege of an education or the entrée into society that I have. For them, life is a struggle against the misconceptions perpetuated by the myth of the Latina as whore, domestic, or criminal. My personal goal in my public life is to try to replace the old pervasive stereotypes and myths about Latinas with a much more interesting set of realities. Every time I give a reading [of my poetry], I hope the stories I tell, the dreams and fears I examine in my work, can achieve some universal truth which will get my audience past the particulars of my skin color, my accent, or my clothes.

SOURCE: From the *Latin Deli: Prose & Poetry* by Judith Ortiz Cofer. Copyright 1993 by Judith Ortiz Cofer. Reprinted by permission of the University of Georgia Press.

CUBAN AMERICANS

The contact period for Cuban Americans, as for Puerto Ricans, dates back to the Spanish-American War. At that time, Cuba was a Spanish colony but became an independent nation as a result of the war. Despite Cuba's nominal independence, the United States remained heavily involved in Cuban politics and economics for decades, and U.S. troops actually occupied the island on two different occasions.

The development of a Cuban American minority group bears little resemblance to the experience of either Chicanos or Puerto Ricans. As recently as the 1950s, there had not been much immigration from Cuba to the United States, even during times of labor shortages, and Cuban Americans were a very small group, numbering no more than 50,000 (Perez, 1980, p. 256).

Immigration (Push and Pull)

The conditions for a mass immigration were created in the late 1950s, when a Marxist revolution brought Fidel Castro to power in Cuba. Castro's government was decidedly anti-American and began to restructure Cuban society along socialist lines. The middle and upper classes lost political and economic power, and the revolution made it impossible for Cuban capitalists to continue "business as usual." Thus, the first Cuban immigrants to the United States tended to come from the more elite classes and included affluent and powerful people who controlled many resources. They were perceived as refugees from Communist persecution (the immigration occurred at the height of the Cold War) and were warmly received by the government and the American public.

The United States was a logical destination for those displaced by the revolution. Cuba is only 90 miles from southern Florida, the climates are similar, and the U.S. government, which was as anti-Castro as Castro was anti-American, welcomed the new arrivals as political refugees fleeing from Communist tyranny. Prior social, cultural, and business ties also pulled the immigrants in the direction of the United States. Since gaining its independence in 1898, Cuba has been heavily influenced by its neighbor to the north, and U.S. companies helped develop the Cuban economy. At the time of Castro's revolution, the Cuban political leadership and the more affluent classes were profoundly Americanized in their attitudes and lifestyles (Portes, 1990, p. 165). Furthermore, many Cuban exiles viewed southern Florida as an ideal spot from which to launch a counterrevolution to oust Castro.

Immigration was considerable for several years. More than 215,000 Cubans arrived between the end of the revolution and 1962, when an escalation of hostile relations resulted in the cutoff of all direct contact between Cuba and the United States. In 1965, an air link was reestablished, and an additional 340,000 Cubans made the journey. When the air connection was terminated in 1973, immigration slowed to a trickle once more.

In 1980, the Cuban government permitted another period of open immigration. Using boats of every shape, size, and degree of seaworthiness, about 124,000 Cubans crossed to Florida. These immigrants are often referred to as the Marielitos, after the port of Mariel from which many of them departed. This wave of immigrants generated a great deal of controversy in the United States because the Cuban government used the opportunity to rid itself of a variety of convicted criminals and outcasts. The reception for this group was decidedly less favorable than for the original wave of Cuban immigrants. Even the established Cuban American community distanced itself from the Marielitos, who were largely products of the new Cuba, having been born after the revolution, and with whom they lacked kinship or friendship ties (Portes & Shafer, 2006, pp. 16–17).

Regional Concentrations

The overwhelming majority of Cuban immigrants settled in southern Florida, especially in Miami and the surrounding Dade County. Today, Cuban Americans remain one of the most spatially concentrated minority groups in the United States, with nearly 7 in 10 of all Cuban

Americans residing in Florida alone (Pew Hispanic Center, 2009). This dense concentration has led to a number of disputes and conflicts between the Hispanic, Anglo-, and African American communities in the area. Issues have centered on language, jobs, and discrimination by the police and other governmental agencies. The conflicts often have been intense, and on more than one occasion, they have erupted into violence and civil disorder.

Socioeconomic Characteristics

Compared with other streams of immigrants from Latin America, Cubans are, on the average, unusually affluent and well educated. Among the immigrants in the early 1960s were large numbers of professionals, landowners, and businesspeople. In later years, as Cuban society was transformed by the Castro regime, the stream included fewer elites—largely because there were fewer left in Cuba—and more political dissidents and working-class people. Today (as displayed in the exhibits presented later in this chapter), Cuban Americans rank higher than other Latino groups on a number of dimensions, a reflection of the educational and economic resources they brought with them from Cuba and the favorable reception they enjoyed from the United States (Portes, 1990, p. 169).

These assets gave Cubans an advantage over Chicanos and Puerto Ricans, but the differences between the three Latino groups run deeper and are more complex than a simple accounting of initial resources would suggest. Cubans adapted to U.S. society in a way that is fundamentally different from the experiences of the other two Latino groups.

The Ethnic Enclave

Most of the minority groups we have discussed to this point have been concentrated in the unskilled, low-wage segments of the economy in which jobs are not secure and not linked to opportunities for upward mobility. Many Cuban Americans have bypassed this sector of the economy and much of the discrimination and limitations associated with it. Like several other groups, such as Jewish Americans, Cuban Americans are an enclave minority (see Chapter 2). An ethnic enclave is a social, economic, and cultural subsociety controlled by the group itself. Located in a specific geographical area or neighborhood inhabited solely or largely by members of the group, the enclave encompasses sufficient economic enterprises and social institutions to permit the group to function as a self-contained entity, largely independent of the surrounding community.

The first wave of Cuban immigrants brought with them considerable human capital and business expertise. Although much of their energy was focused on ousting Castro and returning to Cuba, they generated enough economic activity to sustain restaurants, shops, and other small businesses that catered to the exile community.

As the years passed and the hope of a return to Cuba dimmed, the enclave economy grew. Between 1967 and 1976, the number of Cuban-owned firms in Dade County increased ninefold, from 919 to about 8,000. Six years later, the number had reached 12,000. Most of these enterprises are small, but some factories employ hundreds of workers (Portes & Rumbaut, 1996, pp. 20–21). By 2001, there were more than 125,000 Cuban-owned firms in the United States, and the rate of Cuban-owned firms per 100,00 population was 4 times greater than the rate for Mexican Americans and 14 times greater than the rate for African Americans (Portes & Shafer, 2006, p. 14).

In addition to businesses serving their own community, Cuban-owned firms are involved in construction, manufacturing, finance, insurance, real estate, and an array of other activities. Over the decades, Cuban-owned firms have become increasingly integrated into local economies and increasingly competitive with firms in the larger society. The growth of economic enterprises has been paralleled by a growth in the number of other types of groups and organizations and in the number and quality of services available (schools, law firms, medical care, funeral parlors, etc.). The enclave has become a largely autonomous community capable of providing for its members from cradle to grave (Logan, Alba, & McNulty, 1994; Peterson, 1995; Portes & Bach, 1985, p. 59).

Photo 8.5

This cigar factory is one of many small businesses in "Little Havana" in Miami.

© Morton Beebe/CORBIS.

The fact that the enclave economy is controlled by the group itself is crucial; it separates the ethnic enclave from "the ghetto," or neighborhoods that are impoverished and segregated. In ghettos, members of other groups typically control the local economy; the profits, rents, and other resources flow out of the neighborhood. In the enclave, profits are reinvested and kept in the neighborhood. Group members can avoid the discrimination and limitations imposed by the larger society and can apply their skills, education, and talents in an atmosphere free from language barriers and prejudice. Those who might wish to venture into business for themselves can use the networks of cooperation and mutual aid for advice, credit, and other forms of assistance. Thus, the ethnic enclave provides a platform from which Cuban Americans can pursue economic success independent of their degree of acculturation or English language ability.

The effectiveness of the ethnic enclave as a pathway for adaptation is illustrated by a study of Cuban and Mexican immigrants, all of whom entered the United States in 1973. At the time of entry, the groups were comparable in levels of skills, education, and English language ability. The groups were interviewed on several different occasions, and although they remained comparable on many variables, there were dramatic differences between the groups that reflected their different positions in the labor market. The majority of the Mexican immigrants were employed in the low-wage job sector. Less than 20% were self-employed or employed by another person of Mexican descent. Conversely, 57% of the Cuban immigrants were self-employed or employed by another Cuban (i.e., they were involved in the enclave economy). Among the subjects in the study, self-employed Cubans reported the highest monthly incomes ($1,495), and Cubans otherwise employed in the enclave earned the second-highest monthly incomes ($1,111). The lowest monthly incomes ($880) were earned by Mexican immigrants employed in small, non-enclave firms—many of whom worked as unskilled laborers in seasonal, temporary, or otherwise insecure jobs (Portes, 1990, p. 173; see also Portes & Bach, 1985).

A more recent study confirms the advantages that accrue from forming an enclave. Using 2000 Census data, Portes and Shafer (2006) compared the incomes of several groups in the Miami-Fort Lauderdale metropolitan area, including the original Cuban immigrants (who founded the enclave), their children (or the second generation), Cuban immigrants who arrived after 1980 (the *Marielitos* and others), and several other groups. Some of the results of the study for males are presented in Exhibit 8.9. The founders and primary beneficiaries of the Cuban enclave are identified as "self-employed, pre-1980 Cuban immigrant," the only group that approximates the income of non-Hispanic Whites (the difference in income is about $1,000, quite small and not statistically significant). The sons of the founding generation also enjoy a substantial benefit, both directly (through working in the enclave firms started by their fathers) and indirectly (by translating the resources of their families into human capital, including education, for themselves). Note that the incomes of post-1980 Cuban immigrants are comparable to non-Hispanic blacks and much lower than other groups, both self-employed and wage-salaried.

The ability of most Hispanic (and other) immigrants to rise in the class system and compete for place and position is constrained by discrimination and their own lack of economic and political power. Cuban immigrants in the enclave do not need to expose themselves to American prejudices or rely on the job market of the larger society. They constructed networks of mutual assistance and support and linked themselves to opportunities more consistent with their ambitions and their qualifications.

The link between the enclave and economic equality (an aspect of secondary structural integration) challenges the predictions of some traditional assimilation theories and the

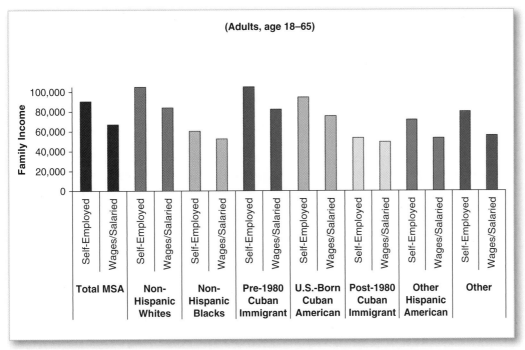

(Adults, age 18–65)

Exhibit 8.9 Family Incomes for Self-Employed and Wage/Salaried Males by Racial and Ethnic Group in Miami–Fort Lauderdale Metropolitan Area, 2000

SOURCE: Portes and Shafer (2006, p. 42).

NOTES: "MSA" is "Metropolitan Statistical Area".

"Others" were mostly first- and second-generation Asian Americans.

understandings of many Americans. The pattern long has been recognized by some leaders of other groups, however, and is voiced in many of the themes of Black Power, Red Power, and Chicanismo that emphasize self-help, self-determination, nationalism, and separation. However, ethnic enclaves cannot be a panacea for all immigrant or other minority groups. They develop only under certain limited conditions—namely, when business and financial expertise and reliable sources of capital are combined with a disciplined labor force willing to work for low wages in exchange for on-the-job training, future assistance and loans, or other delayed benefits. Enclave enterprises usually start on a small scale and cater only to other ethnics. Thus, the early economic returns are small, and prosperity follows only after years of hard work, if at all. Most important, eventual success and expansion beyond the boundaries of the enclave depend on the persistence of strong ties of loyalty, kinship, and solidarity. The pressure to assimilate might easily weaken these networks and the strength of group cohesion (Portes & Manning, 1986, pp. 61–66).

Cuban Americans and Other Minority Groups

The adaptation of Cuban Americans contrasts sharply with the experiences of colonized minority groups and with the common understanding of how immigrants are "supposed" to acculturate and integrate. Cuban Americans are neither the first nor the only group to develop an ethnic enclave, and their success has generated prejudice and resentment from the dominant group and from other minority groups. Whereas Puerto Ricans and Chicanos have been the victims of stereotypes labeling them "inferior," higher-status Cuban Americans have been stereotyped as "too successful," "too clannish," and "too ambitious." The former stereotype commonly emerges to rationalize exploitative relationships; the latter expresses disparagement and rejection of groups that are more successful in the struggle to acquire resources (see Chapter 3). Nonetheless, the stereotype of Cubans is an exaggeration and a misperception that obscures the fact that poverty and unemployment are major problems for many members of this group, especially for the post-1980 immigrants (see the exhibits at the end of this chapter).

Immigration in Europe Versus Immigration to the United States

The volume of immigration in the world today is at record levels. About 214 million people, a little more than 3% of the world's population, live outside their countries of birth, and there is hardly a nation or region that has not been affected (United Nations, 2010b). Exhibit 8.10 lists, in order of significance, the nations that are projected to be the major destinations and suppliers of immigrants for the next 40 years.

Exhibit 8.10 Major Sending and Receiving Nations for International Migration, in Order of Significance. (Projected for 2010–2050)

Destination Nations	Nations of Origin
United States	Mexico
Canada	China
United Kingdom	India
Spain	The Philippines
Italy	Pakistan
Germany	Indonesia
Australia	Bangladesh
France	

SOURCE: United Nations (2010b, p. 32).

The United States currently hosts 20% of all migrants and has by far the highest number of foreign-born citizens. However, the United States is only one of many destinations, and the issues of immigration and assimilation that are being debated so fervently here are echoed in many other nations.

In particular, the nations of Western Europe, with their highly developed, advanced industrial economies, are prime destinations for immigrants. Like the United States, these nations have high standards of living, and they offer myriad opportunities for economic survival, even though the price may be to live at the margins of the larger society or to take jobs scorned by the native-born. In addition, a powerful factor that "pulls" people to this region is that Western European nations have very low birthrates, and in some cases (e.g., Germany and Italy), their populations are projected to actually decline in coming decades (Population Reference Bureau, 2011). The labor force shortages thus created will continue to attract immigrants to Western Europe for decades to come.

The immigrant stream to Western Europe is varied and includes people from all walks of life, from highly educated professionals to peasant laborers. The most prominent flows include movements from Turkey to Germany, from Africa to Spain and Italy, and from many former British colonies (Jamaica, India, Nigeria, etc.) to the United Kingdom. This immigration is primarily an economic phenomenon motivated by the search for jobs and survival, but the stream also includes refugees and asylum seekers spurred by civil war, genocide, and political unrest.

In terms of numbers, the volume of immigration to Western Europe is smaller than the flow to the United States, but its proportional impact is comparable. About 13% of the U.S. population is foreign-born, and many Western European nations (including Belgium, Germany, and Sweden) have a similar profile (Dumont & LeMaitre, 2011). Thus, it is not surprising that in both cases, immigration has generated major concerns and debates about handling newcomers and managing a pluralistic society, including national language policy, the limits of religious freedom, and the criteria for citizenship.

To focus on one example, Germany has the largest immigrant community of any Western European nation and has been dealing with a large foreign-born population for decades. Germany began to allow large numbers of immigrants to enter as temporary workers or "guest workers" (*Gastarbeiter*) to help staff its expanding economy beginning in the 1960s. Most of these immigrants came from Turkey, and they were seen by Germans as temporary workers only, people who would return to their homeland when they were no longer needed. Thus, the host society saw no particular need to encourage immigrants to acculturate and integrate.

Contrary to this expectation, many immigrants stayed and settled permanently, and many of their millions of descendants today speak only German and have no knowledge of or experience with their "homeland." Although acculturated, they are not fully integrated, and, in fact—in contrast with the United States—they were denied the opportunity to become citizens until recently. A German law passed a century ago reserved citizenship for ethnic Germans, regardless of place of birth. Under this policy, a recent immigrant from, say, Ukraine was eligible for citizenship if he or she could prove German ancestry—even if this immigrant spoke no German and was not familiar with German culture or traditions. In contrast, Turks living in Germany were not eligible for citizenship regardless of how long they or their families had been residents. This law was changed in 2000 to permit greater flexibility in qualifying for citizenship, but still more recently, Germany has passed new laws that make it harder for foreigners to enter the country. To gain admission, immigrants from non-European Union nations may have to pass a language test, demonstrate that they earn a minimum of 66,000 euros a year (about $90,000), and have a guaranteed job. The immigrant community sees these new laws as a form of rejection, and there have been bitter (and sometimes violent) demonstrations in response ("Europe: The Integration Dilemma," 2007). Anti-immigrant attitudes seem to be hardening and, in the fall of 2010, German Chancellor Angela Merkel declared that German attempts to create a multicultural society have "utterly failed" (Westervelt, 2010).

Clashes of this sort have been common across Western Europe in recent years, especially with the growing Muslim communities. Many Europeans see Islamic immigrants as unassimilable, too foreign or exotic to ever fit into the mainstream of their society. These conflicts have been punctuated by violence and riots in France, Germany, the Netherlands, and other places.

Across Europe, just as in the United States (and Canada), nations are wrestling with issues of inclusion and diversity: What should it mean to be German, or French, or British, or Dutch? How much diversity can be tolerated before national cohesion is threatened? What are the limits of tolerance? What is the best balance between assimilation and pluralism? Struggles over the essential meaning of national identity are increasingly common throughout the developed world.

CONTEMPORARY HISPANIC–WHITE RELATIONS

As in previous chapters, we will use the central concepts of this text to review the status of Latinos in the United States. Where relevant, comparisons are made between the major Latino groups and the minority groups discussed in previous chapters.

Prejudice and Discrimination

The American tradition of prejudice against Latinos was born in the 19th-century conflicts that created minority group status for Mexican Americans. The themes of the original anti-Mexican stereotypes and attitudes were consistent with the nature of the contact situation: As Mexicans were conquered and subordinated, they were characterized as inferior, lazy, irresponsible, low in intelligence, and dangerously criminal (McWilliams, 1961, pp. 212–214). The prejudice and racism, supplemented with the echoes of the racist ideas and beliefs brought to the Southwest by many Anglos, helped justify and rationalize the colonized, exploited status of the Chicanos.

These prejudices were incorporated into the dominant culture and transferred to Puerto Ricans when they began to arrive on the mainland. As we have already mentioned, this stereotype does not fit Cuban Americans. Instead, their affluence has been exaggerated and perceived as undeserved or achieved by unfair or "un-American" means, a characterization similar to the traditional stereotype of Jews but just as prejudiced as the perception of Latino inferiority.

There is some evidence that the level of Latino prejudice has been affected by the decline of explicit American racism (discussed in Chapter 3). For example, social distance scale results show a decrease in the scores of Mexicans, although their group ranking tends to remain stable. On the other hand, anti-Latino prejudice and racism tend to increase during times of high immigration. In particular, there is considerable, though largely anecdotal, evidence of high levels of anti-Latino prejudice in the "borderlands" or the areas along the U.S.-Mexican border. Sparked by and deeply intermixed with concerns about undocumented immigration, the levels of prejudice and racism seem extreme, perhaps matching the levels of antiblack prejudice in the tumultuous days of the 1960s. Hate crimes and hate groups such as the Minutemen (see Chapter 1) seem to have increased, and the level of vitriol and racist rhetoric approach fever pitch along much of the borderlands. Many observers see racism in Arizona's widely publicized State Bill 1070 (which, if ever implemented, would allow police to check anyone for proof of citizenship) and its state-mandated ban on ethnic studies programs in public schools. At any rate, the level of immigrant-bashing and anti-Latino sentiments along the border demonstrate that American prejudice, although sometimes disguised as a subtle modern racism, is alive and well.

In Chapter 5, I mentioned that audit studies have documented the persistence of discrimination against blacks in the housing and job market: Many of the same studies also demonstrate anti-Hispanic biases (see Quillian, 2006, for a review). Discrimination of all kinds, institutional as well as individual, has been common against Latino groups, but it has not been as rigid or as total as the systems that controlled African American labor under slavery and segregation. However, discrimination against Latinos persists across the United States. Because of their longer tenure in the United States and their original status as a rural labor force, Mexican Americans probably have been more victimized by the institutionalized forms of discrimination than have other Latino groups.

Assimilation and Pluralism

Acculturation

Latinos are highly variable in their extent of acculturation but are often seen as "slow" to change, learn English, and adopt Anglo customs. Contrary to this perception, research shows that Hispanics are following many of the same patterns of assimilation as European groups. Their rates of acculturation increase with length of residence and are higher for the native-born (Espinosa & Massey, 1997; Goldstein & Suro, 2000; Valentine & Mosley, 2000).

The dominant trend for Hispanic groups, as for immigrants from Europe in the past (see Chapter 2) is that language acculturation increases over the generations, as the length of residence in the United States increases, and as education increases. One study, which combines six different surveys conducted since 2000 and is based on more than 14,000 respondents, illustrates these points. Results are displayed in Exhibits 8.11 and 8.12.

A different study showed that the values of Hispanics come to approximate the values of society as a whole as the generations pass. Exhibit 8.13 shows some results of a 2002 survey of Latinos and compares cultural values by English language proficiency, which increases with length of residence and by generation. For example, most Latinos (72%) who speak predominantly Spanish are first generation, while most (78%) who speak predominantly English are third generation. The second generation is most likely to be bilingual. The exhibit shows the results for four different survey items that measure values and opinions. The values of predominantly Spanish speakers are distinctly different from those of non-Latinos, especially on the item that measures support for the statement that "children should live with their parents until they are married." Virtually all the predominantly Spanish speakers supported the statement, but English-speaking Latinos approximate the more individualistic values of Anglos. For each of the other three items, a similar acculturation to American values occurs.

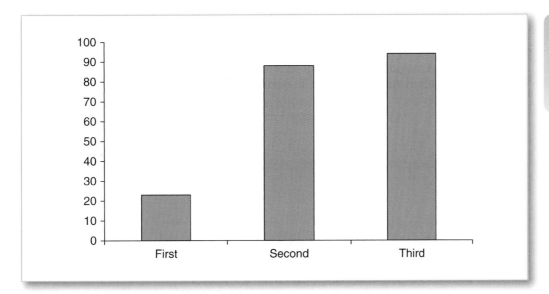

SOURCE: Hakimzadeh and Cohn (2007).

Exhibit 8.11 Percentage of Hispanic Americans Who Speak English "Very Well" by Generation

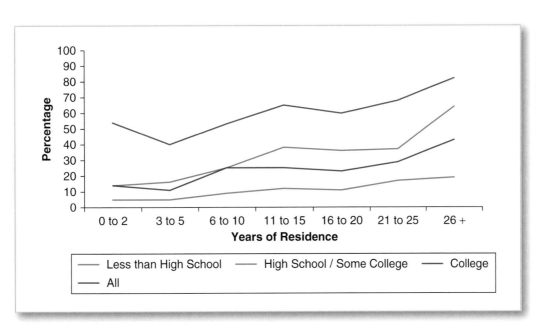

SOURCE: Hakimzadeh and Cohn (2007).

Exhibit 8.12 Percentage of Hispanic Americans Who Speak English "Very Well" by Years of Residence and Level of Education

Even while acculturation continues, however, Hispanic culture and the Spanish language are revitalized by immigration. By its nature, assimilation is a slow process that can require decades or generations to complete. In contrast, immigration can be fast, often accomplished in less than a day. Thus, even as Hispanic Americans acculturate and integrate, Hispanic culture and language are sustained and strengthened. What is perceived to be slow acculturation for these groups is mostly the result of fast and continuous immigration.

Furthermore, colonized minority groups such as Chicanos and Puerto Ricans were not encouraged to assimilate in the past. Valued primarily for the cheap labor they supplied, they were seen as otherwise inferior or undesirable and unfit for integration. For much of the 20th century, Latinos were excluded from the institutions and experiences (e.g., school) that could have led to greater equality and higher rates of acculturation. Prejudice, racism, and

Exhibit 8.13 Percentage of Hispanic Americans and Non-Latinos Agreeing by Primary Language

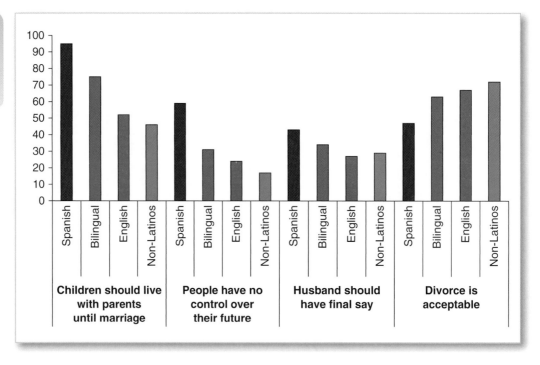

FULL TEXT OF SURVEY ITEMS:

"It is better for children to live in their parents' home until they are married."

"It doesn't do any good to plan for the future because you don't have any control over it."

"In general, the husband should have the final say in all family matters."

"Divorce is acceptable."

SOURCE: Pew Hispanic Center (2004).

discrimination combined to keep most Latino groups away from the centers of modernization and change and away from opportunities to improve their situation.

Finally, for Cubans, Dominicans, and other groups, cultural differences reflect the fact that they are largely recent immigrants. Their first generations are alive and well, and as is typical for immigrant groups, they keep the language and traditions alive.

Secondary Structural Assimilation

In this section, we survey the situation of Latinos in the public areas and institutions of American society, following the same format as the previous two chapters. We begin with where people live.

Residence. Exhibit 8.14 shows the regional concentrations of Latinos in 2008. The legacies of the varied patterns of entry and settlement for the largest groups are evident. The higher concentrations in the Southwest reflect the presence of Mexican Americans, those in Florida are the result of the Cuban immigration, and those in the Northeast display the settlement patterns of Puerto Ricans.

Exhibit 8.15 highlights the areas of the nation in which Latinos are growing fastest. A quick glance at the map will reveal that many of the high-growth areas are distant from the traditional points of entry for these groups. In particular, the Hispanic American population is growing rapidly in parts of New England, the South, the upper Midwest, the Northwest, and even Alaska. Among many other forces, this population movement is a response to the availability of jobs in factories, mills, chicken-processing plants and slaughterhouses, farms, construction, and other low-skilled areas of the economy.

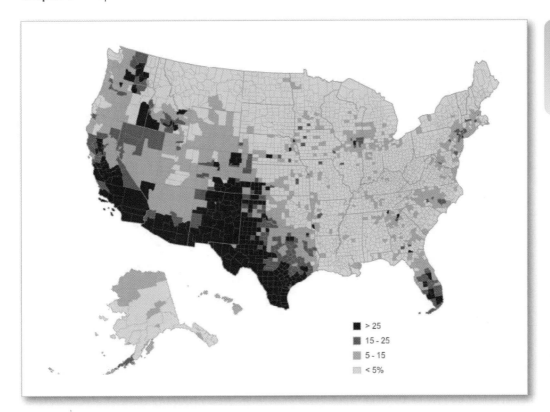

SOURCE: Pew Hispanic Center (2011a).

Exhibit 8.14 Geographic Distribution of Hispanic Americans by County, 2008. Percentage Share of County Population

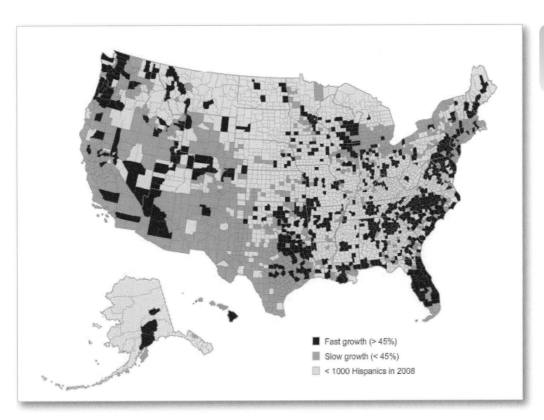

SOURCE: Pew Hispanic Center (2011b).

Exhibit 8.15 Growth of Hispanic Population by County, 2000 to 2008

Exhibit 8.16 Percentage of 10 Largest Hispanic American Groups and Non-Hispanic Whites Living in Urbanized Areas, 2000

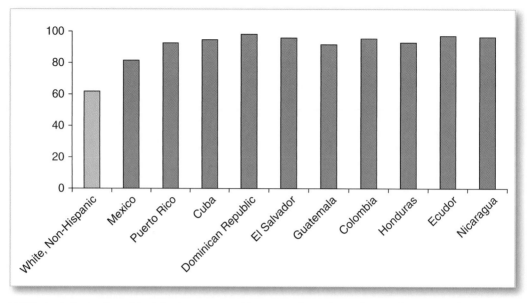

NOTE: An "urbanized area" is defined as an area with a minimal population density of 1,000 people per square mile and a minimum population of 50,000.

SOURCE: U.S. Bureau of the Census (2000d).

Within each of these regions, Latino groups are highly urbanized, as shown in Exhibit 8.16. With the exception of Mexican Americans, more than 90% of each of the 10 largest Hispanic American groups live in urban areas, and this percentage approaches 100% for some groups. Mexican Americans are more rural than the other groups, but in sharp contrast to their historical role as an agrarian workforce, the percentage of the group living in rural areas is tiny today.

The extent of residential segregation for Hispanic Americans is displayed in Exhibit 8.17, which shows the average dissimilarity index for 220 metropolitan areas grouped into four regions. Hispanic Americans are less residentially segregated than African Americans (see Exhibit 6.7), but in contrast to African Americans, their segregation has generally held steady or slightly increased over the 20-year period. Among other factors, this is a reflection of high rates of immigration and "chain" patterns of settlement, which concentrate newcomers in ethnic neighborhoods.

Exhibit 8.17 Residential Segregation in 220 Metropolitan Areas, Hispanic Americans

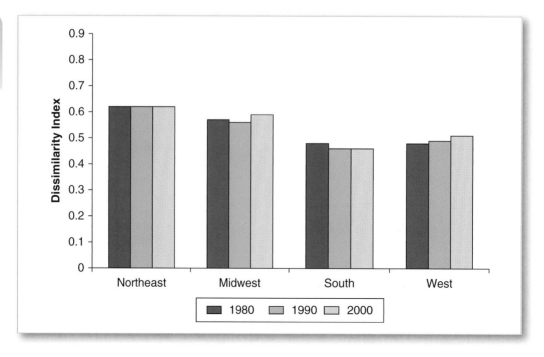

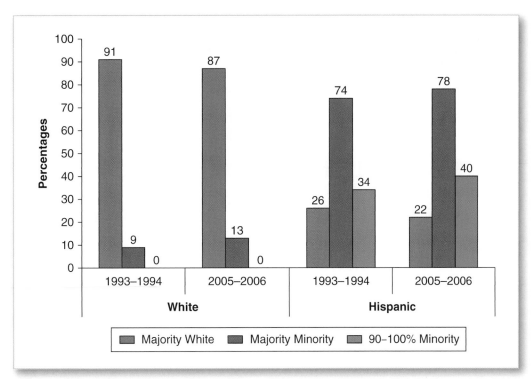

SOURCE: Fry (2007).

Exhibit 8.18 School Integration for Hispanic Americans, 1993–1994 and 2005–2006

Education. Exhibit 8.18, like Exhibit 6.9 for the black population, shows the extent of school segregation for Hispanic Americans for the 1993–1994 and the 2005–2006 school years. In both years, Hispanic American children were more segregated than either American Indian or African American children. Furthermore, the percentages of Hispanic children in both majority-minority and extremely segregated schools increased over the time period. These patterns reflect recent high rates of immigration and the tendency for newcomers to reside in the same neighborhoods as their co-ethnics (see the patterns of residential segregation in Exhibit 8.17).

Levels of education for Hispanic Americans have risen in recent years but still are far below national standards (see Exhibit 8.19). Hispanic Americans in general and all subgroups, except Colombian Americans, fall well below non-Hispanic whites for high school education. In particular, a little more than half of Mexican Americans and only 45% of Salvadorans and Guatemalans have high school degrees. At the college level, Colombian and Cuban Americans approximate national norms, but the other groups and Hispanic Americans as a whole are far below non-Hispanic whites. For all Hispanic groups, there is very little difference by gender: Males and females have about the same record of educational attainment.

The lower levels of education are the cumulative results of decades of systematic discrimination and exclusion for Mexican Americans and Puerto Ricans. These levels have been further reduced by the high percentage of recent immigrants from Mexico, the Dominican Republic, El Salvador, and other nations that have modest educational backgrounds.

Given the role that educational credentials have come to play in the job market, these figures are consistent with the idea that assimilation may be segmented for some Hispanic groups (see Chapters 2 and 10), who may contribute in large numbers, along with African Americans and Native Americans, to the growth of an urban underclass.

Political Power. The political resources available to Hispanic Americans have increased over the years, but the group is still proportionally underrepresented. The number of Hispanics of voting age has doubled in the past two decades, and Hispanics today constitute almost 14% of the voting-age population. Yet, because registration rates and actual turnout have been low, the Hispanic community

Exhibit 8.19 Educational Attainment for Non-Hispanic Whites, All Hispanic Americans, and 10 Largest Hispanic American Groups, 2009

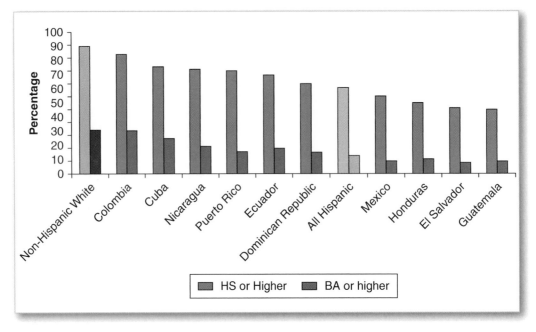

SOURCE: U.S. Bureau of the Census (2009a).

Photo 8.6

A polling station in New Mexico uses English and Spanish signs.

© Jerry McCrea/Star Ledger/ Corbis.

has not had an impact on the political structure proportionate to its size. For example, in the presidential elections between 1992 and 2004, actual voter turnout for Hispanic Americans was less than 30%, less than half the comparable rate for non-Hispanic whites (U.S. Bureau of the Census, 2010d). In the 2008 presidential election, turnout increased for Hispanic Americans (as well as African Americans and Asian Americans), and they accounted for about 9.5% of all voters, up from 8.2% in 2004 (Lopez & Taylor, 2009, p. 1). Clearly, the impact of the Hispanic American vote on national politics will increase as the group grows in size, but participation is likely to remain lower than other groups for some time because of the large percentage of recent, non-English speaking immigrants and noncitizens in the group.

At the national level, there are now 26 Hispanic Americans in the House of Representatives, more than double the number in 1990 and about 6% of the total. In addition, the 112th Congress includes two Hispanic American senators. Most of these representatives and senators are members of the Democratic Party, but, in a reflection of the diversity of the group, nearly 20% are Republicans. On the local and state level, the number of public officials identified as Hispanic increased by more than 65% between 1985 and 2008, from 3,147 to 5,240 (U.S. Bureau of the Census, 2011d, p. 259).

Although still underrepresented, these figures suggest that Hispanic Americans will become increasingly important in American political life as their numbers continue to grow and their rates of naturalization rise. A preview of their increasing power has been displayed in recent years as Hispanic communities across the nation have mobilized and engaged in massive demonstrations to express their opposition to restrictive immigration policies (e.g., see Aizenman, 2006).

Jobs and Income. The economic situation of Hispanic Americans is quite mixed. Many Latinos, especially those who have been in the United States for several generations, are doing "just fine. They have, in ever increasing numbers, accessed opportunities in education and employment and have carved out a niche of American prosperity for themselves and their children" (Camarillo & Bonilla, 2001, pp. 130–131). For others, however, the picture is not so promising. They face the possibility of becoming members of an impoverished, powerless, and economically marginalized urban underclass, like African Americans and other minority groups of color.

Occupationally, Hispanic Americans who are recent immigrants with modest levels of education and job skills are concentrated in the less-desirable, lower-paid service and unskilled segments of the job market. Those with higher levels of human capital and education compare more favorably with the dominant group.

Unemployment, low income, and poverty continue to be issues for all Hispanic groups. The official unemployment rates for Hispanic Americans run about twice the rate for non-Hispanic whites. Exhibit 8.20 compares median household incomes for white and all Hispanic Americans across four decades. The size of the income gap fluctuates but generally remains in the low to mid-70s and, in the most recent year, Hispanic American median household income was 73% of white median household income. As a group, Hispanic Americans historically have been intermediate between blacks and whites in the stratification system, and this is reflected by the fact that the Hispanic-white income gap is smaller than the black-white income gap (which was 63% in 2009. See Exhibit 6.12). This smaller gap also reflects the more favorable economic circumstances of Hispanics (especially those more "racially" similar to the dominant group) who have been in the United States for generations and are thoroughly integrated into the mainstream economy. Exhibit 8.21 shows that there is a good deal of income variability from group to group, but Hispanic Americans in general and all subgroups have, on the average, dramatically lower median household incomes than non-Hispanic whites, especially the groups with large numbers of recent immigrants who bring low levels of human capital.

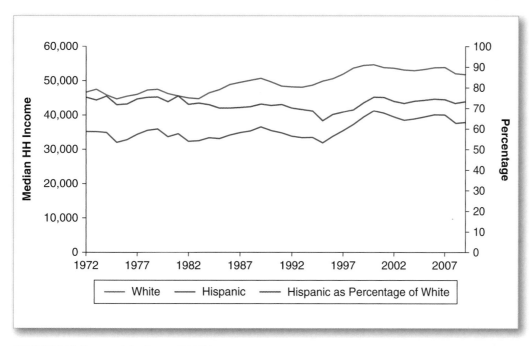

Exhibit 8.20 Median Household Income for White and Hispanic Americans, 1972 to 2009 (in 2009 Dollars)

SOURCE: U.S. Bureau of the Census (2011b).

NOTE: Read income on left-hand axis and percentage on right-hand axis.

Exhibit 8.21 Median Household Income for Non-Hispanic Whites, All Hispanic Americans, and 10 Largest Hispanic American Groups, 2009

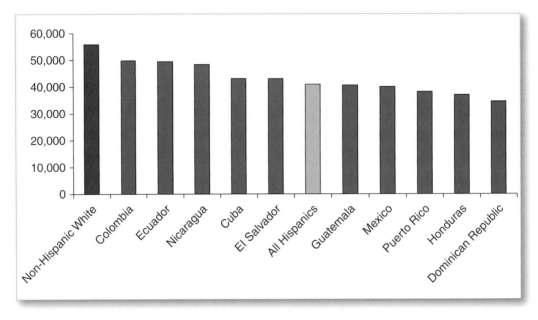

SOURCE: U.S. Bureau of the Census (2011a).

Exhibit 8.22 supplements the information on median income by displaying the overall distribution of income for Hispanic Americans and non-Hispanic whites for 2009. The figure shows a greater concentration (wider bars) of Hispanics in the lower-income categories and a lower concentration (narrower bars) in the income groups at the top of the figure. There is a noticeable concentration of both groups in the $50,000 to $124,000 categories, but whites outnumber Hispanics by about 40% to 34% in these income ranges. In the two highest income categories, whites outnumber Hispanic Americans by more than 2 to 1 (9.3–3.8%).

Recent detailed income information is not available for the separate subgroups, but we can assume that—although all groups have members in all income categories—Mexican

Exhibit 8.22 Distribution of Household Income for Non-Hispanic White and Hispanic Americans, 2009

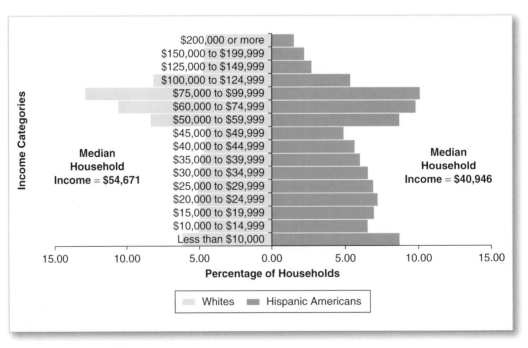

SOURCE: U.S. Bureau of the Census (2011a).

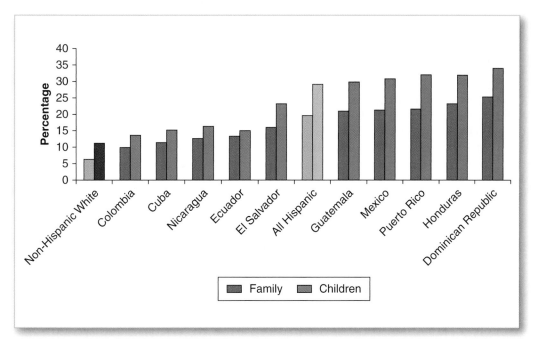

Exhibit 8.23 Poverty Rates for Non-Hispanic Whites, All Hispanic Americans, and 10 Largest Hispanic Groups, 2009

SOURCE: U.S. Bureau of the Census (2011a).

Americans, Dominican Americans, and Puerto Ricans would be disproportionately represented in the lowest income categories and Cuban Americans—especially, as we have seen, those that benefit from the enclave economy—in the higher groups.

Exhibit 8.23 finishes the socioeconomic profile by displaying the varying levels of poverty for Hispanic Americans, a pattern that is consistent with previous information on income and education. The poverty rate for all Hispanic families is almost 3 times the rate for non-Hispanic white families and slightly lower than that of African Americans (see Exhibit 6.14). However, there is considerable diversity across the subgroups, with Colombians and Cubans closest to non-Hispanic whites and Dominicans the most impoverished. For all groups, children have higher poverty rates than families.

These socioeconomic profiles reflect the economic diversity of Latinos. Some are "doing just fine," but others are concentrated in the low-wage sector of the economy. As a group, Cuban Americans rank higher than Mexican Americans and Puerto Ricans—the two other largest groups—on virtually all measures of wealth and prosperity. This relative prosperity would be even more pronounced for the earlier immigrants from Cuba and their children.

We should also note that the income gap and the picture of economic distress would be much greater if we focused on recent immigrants and, especially, undocumented immigrants, who are concentrated in the informal, irregular economy. These groups are sometimes paid "off the books" and less than minimum wage. As we have discussed, they tend to be focused on their families and villages back home and live as simply as possible—5 or even 10 to a room, for example—in order to maximize the money they can send home. Since they tend to live "below the radar," they are not likely to be included in the data-gathering efforts that supply the information for the exhibits in this chapter. If they were, the figures on average wages would be lower and rates of poverty higher for virtually all Latino groups in the United States.

Gender and Inequality. There is a split-labor market differentiated by gender within the dual market differentiated by race and ethnicity. Hispanic women—like minority group women in general—are among the lowest-paid, most-exploitable, and least-protected segments of the U.S. labor force. The impact of poverty is especially severe for Latino women because they often find themselves with the responsibility of caring for their children alone. In 2009, about 22% of all Hispanic American households were female-headed (vs. about 9% of non-Hispanic households), but this percentage ranged from a low of 13% for Cuban Americans to a high of about 35% for Dominicans (U.S. Bureau of the Census, 2009a). This pattern is the result of many factors, among them the status of Latino men in the labor force. The jobs available to Latino men often do not pay enough to support a family, and many jobs are seasonal, temporary, or otherwise insecure.

Female-headed Latino families face a triple economic handicap: They have only one wage earner, whose potential income is limited by discrimination against both women and Latinos. The result of these multiple disadvantages is an especially high rate of poverty. Whereas 22% of non-Hispanic, white, female-headed households fall below the poverty line, the percentage is about 38% for Hispanic households headed by females (U.S. Bureau of the Census, 2009a).

Summary. The socioeconomic situation of Latinos is complex and diversified. Many Latinos have successfully entered the mainstream economy, but others face poverty and exclusion. Highly concentrated in deteriorated urban areas (barrios), segments of these groups, like other minority groups of color, face the possibility of permanent poverty and economic marginality.

Primary Structural Assimilation

Overall, the extent of intimate contact between Hispanic Americans and the dominant group probably has been higher than for either African Americans or American Indians (e.g., see Quillian & Campbell, 2003; Rosenfield, 2002). This pattern may reflect the fact that Latinos are partly ethnic minority groups and partly racial minority groups. Some studies report that contact is greater for the more affluent social classes, in the cities, and for the younger generations (who are presumably more Americanized) (Fitzpatrick, 1976; Grebler et al., 1970, p. 397; Rodriguez, 1989, pp. 70–72). On the other hand, the rate of contact probably has been decreased by the rapid increase in immigration and the tendency of the first generation to socialize more with their co-ethnics.

Rates of intermarriage are higher for Latinos than for African Americans, but neither are a very high percentage of all marriages. Black and white interracial couples make up less than 1% of all marriages, and the comparable figure for Latinos is 4% of all marriages (U.S. Bureau of the Census, 2011d, p. 54).

Assimilation and Hispanic Americans

As test cases for what we have called the traditional view of American assimilation, Latinos fare poorly. Almost two centuries after the original contact period, Mexican Americans continue to be concentrated in the low-wage sector of the labor market, a source of cheap labor for the dominant group's economy. Puerto Ricans, who are more recent arrivals, occupy a similar profile and position.

The fundamental reality faced by both groups, in their histories and in their present situations, is their colonized status in U.S. society. Even while many Mexican Americans and Puerto Ricans have risen in the social class and occupational structure of the larger society, others share many problems with other urban minority groups of color.

The traditional views of the nature of assimilation likewise fail to describe the experiences of Cuban Americans. They are more prosperous, on the average, than either Mexican Americans or Puerto Ricans, but they became successful by remaining separate and developing the enclave in South Florida.

There is no single Hispanic American experience or pattern of adjustment to the larger society. We have focused mainly on three of the many Latino groups in the United States, and the diversity of their experiences suggests the variety and complexity of what it means to be a minority group in U.S. society. Their experiences also illustrate some of the fundamental forces that shape the experiences of minority groups: the split-labor market and the U.S. appetite for cheap labor, the impact of industrialization, the dangers of a permanent urban underclass, the relationships between competition and levels of prejudice and rejection, and the persistence of race as a primary dividing line between people and groups.

Is the United States Threatened by "Hispanization"?

As we have seen in this chapter, immigration from Latin America—and especially from Mexico—is voluminous and shows no sign of slowing. How will these new immigrants shape American culture? Will traditional American values such as individualism, the Protestant Ethic, democracy, and loyalty and patriotism be compromised? Are we developing into two nations, one Anglo and the other Hispanic?

Many people are deeply concerned that American culture cannot survive in its present form. For example, Samuel Huntington, a distinguished and prolific political scientist, argues in his influential book Who Are We? *(2004) that large-scale immigration (particularly from Mexico) is leading the United States away from its historical roots and its central values. Below, John O'Sullivan (2004) summarizes Huntington's arguments in a largely positive review of his book. In opposition to these alarms, Professor Francis Fukuyama (2004), a leading American academic, argues that the immigrants are the true carriers of the "Protestant Ethic" and that the United States is corrupting their stronger family and traditional values, not the other way around.*

WHO ARE WE?

JOHN O'SULLIVAN

Samuel Huntington's book was notorious . . . before [publication]. Rumors had circulated for at least a year that the author of [many] distinguished works of political theory was about to produce a book on immigration that was not wholly in favor of it. [But], in fact, [Huntington's] book . . . is about the wider and more important topic of national identity. . . .

Huntington argues that post-1965 immigration is very different from previous waves in two significant ways. First . . . , it consists of continuously high levels of immigration [which] . . . tends to retard assimilation . . . into the host community and to foster ethnic ghettoes . . . [especially] if the immigration occurs in conditions of official bilingualism and multiculturalism rather than of Americanization. Immigrants will then be less likely to assimilate and more likely to retain ethnic identities and links with home.

The second difference is that the new immigration . . . is much less diverse than [earlier] immigrants. . . . One half of new legal immigrants come from Latin America—and 25% of them from Mexico. Even in the absence of other factors, this would hinder assimilation. If immigrants speak several languages, they have a clear incentive to master the *lingua franca* that will help them to communicate both with each other and with the native-born. If they speak one language, however, they are more easily able to continue living in a linguistic enclave . . . , such as Miami, where it is the native-born who feel foreign.

That central difficulty in the case of Latinos in general is aggravated in the case of Mexicans. . . . They come from a nation contiguous to the U.S. with a long and porous border. They are regionally concentrated in the Southwest . . . so that they are more likely to concentrate themselves in linguistic enclaves. They seem likely to keep coming indefinitely . . . and, finally, Mexicans have a historical presence in the region—there are even some who cherish irredentist claims on what they call "Aztlan." . . . Huntington concluded that there was a real possibility that the American Southwest might become in time another Quebec—namely, a region of the U.S. where the dominant language and culture would be Hispanic—in a Nuevo United States that would be a bilingual and bicultural society. And as Quebec and Belgium demonstrate in different ways, bilingualism distorts and obstructs democratic governance. . . .

Three points emerge . . . from . . . criticisms [of Huntington's book]. First, almost all . . . ignored the vast wealth of social science, census, and polling data that the author laid out in support of his thesis. . . . Second, when his critics did seek to refute his array of evidence, they mostly got it wrong. . . . [For example], writing in *Time* magazine, Michael Elliot produced polling data that showed Mexicans expressing admiration for the U.S. and sharply criticized Huntington for not taking this into account. But Huntington had not denied that many Mexicans were grateful for the opportunities given to them by the U.S. . . . he had merely pointed out that such feelings were likely to be offset by a range of other influences over time—notably, that under multiculturalism they might assimilate not into Americanism but into a subordinate ethnic identity that was ambivalent at best towards the U.S. . . .

But the third point is more worrying. An alarming number of critics . . . denounced Huntington's arguments as "poisonous," "incendiary," "unabashed racism," . . . while misquoting and misunderstanding his actual arguments. . . .

Huntington's starting point is that the American nation . . . was built around certain core institutions, customs, and practices: . . . the English language, dissenting Protestant Christianity, individualism and work ethic, and the political culture of the Founding Fathers with its emphasis on individual rights. . . . Immigrants assimilated to the cultural core of "Anglo-Protestant Christianity" that evolved from these origins. . . . They added spicy cultural contributions of their own, of course, but these did not fundamentally alter the national character. And by the late 1950s, "Americans were one nation of individuals with equal political rights, who shared a primarily Anglo-Protestant core culture, and were dedicated to the liberal-democratic principles of the American creed." . . .

[In the 1960s, according to Huntington,] . . . some influential Americans set about systematically demolishing this [core culture]. Huntington lists the accomplishments of "the deconstructionists" in the following paragraph:

The deconstructionists promoted programs to enhance the status and influence of subnational, racial, ethnic, and cultural groups. They encouraged immigrants to maintain their birth country cultures . . . and denounced the idea of Americanization as un-American. They pushed the rewriting of history syllabi and textbooks so as to refer to the "peoples" of the United States in place of the single people of the Constitution. They urged supplementing or substituting for national history the history of subnational groups. They downgraded the centrality of English in American life and pushed bilingual education and linguistic diversity. They advocated legal recognition of group rights and racial preferences over the individual rights central to the American Creed. They justified their actions by theories of multiculturalism and the idea that diversity rather than unity or community should be America's overriding value. The combined effect of these efforts was to promote the deconstruction of the American identity that had been gradually created over three centuries.

So *Who Are We?* is worth 10 divisions in the new American culture war about patriotism. It demystifies every radical argument employed to deconstruct the American nation and the customs, habits, and traditions that sustain it. . . . Above all, perhaps, . . . Huntington's book has revealed that there is a substantial anti-American intelligentsia . . . within the American nation committed to a sort of "counter-tribalism." These are the patriots of an America that does not exist—the America of multiculturalism, bilingualism, and diversity. . . . They hate the America that does exist as an obstacle to their dreams. And they tend to sympathize with attacks upon it—and to react against anyone who defends it.

SOURCE: O'Sullivan (2004).

WHY WE SHOULDN'T WORRY ABOUT THE "HISPANIZATION" OF THE UNITED STATES

FRANCIS FUKUYAMA

It is not politically correct today to say that America is fundamentally a Protestant country, or that a specific form of religion is critical to its success as a democracy. Yet as historical facts, these statements are undoubtedly true, and they are the premise of *Who Are We?*, Samuel Huntington's new book. The United States, he argues, is a liberal democracy based on certain universal political principles regarding liberty and equality, summed up traditionally as the American Creed. But the country's success as a free and prosperous democratic society was not due simply to the goodness of these principles or the strength of America's formal institutions. There was a crucial supplement: cultural values that Huntington describes as "Anglo-Protestant." . . .

Huntington is following in the path of innumerable observers of the United States [who] have noted that the dissident, sectarian nature of the Protestantism transplanted to North America was critical to shaping American values like individualism, anti-statism, tolerance, moralism, the work ethic, the propensity for voluntary association, and a host of other informal habits and customs that augment our Constitution and legal system. *Who Are We?* is also perfectly consistent with Huntington's [work] in arguing that liberal democracy is less a universalistic system for organizing political life than an outgrowth of a certain northern European Christian culture, the appeal and feasibility of which will be limited in other cultural settings.

Huntington goes on to argue that . . . immigration [is a] threat to that traditional American identity. In his view, the American elite, from corporate executives to professors to journalists, sees itself as cosmopolitan, secular, and attached to the principle of diversity as an end in itself. That elite no longer feels emotionally attached to America and is increasingly out of touch with the vast majority of non-elite Americans who remain patriotic, morally conservative, and Christian. . . .

On no issue are elites and ordinary Americans further apart than on immigration, and Huntington takes the latter's concerns about the threat posed by Mexican immigration very seriously. This is because of the numbers involved, . . . the concentration of Mexican immigrants in a few Southwestern states and cities, and the proximity of their country of origin. The wave has occurred, moreover, at a time when American elites have lost confidence in their own cultural values and are no longer willing to use the public school system to assimilate these new immigrants to Anglo-Protestant culture. Huntington worries that unchecked immigration will sow the seeds of a later backlash, and may even lead one day to something new in the American experience, an ethnolinguistic minority with strong ties to a neighboring country that could potentially make territorial claims on much of the Southwest.

I am glad that a scholar like Huntington has raised these issues, since they deserve serious discussion. . . . Huntington poses some real questions about whether the large Mexican immigrant population will assimilate as other immigrant groups have done before them. . . . He is right that "culture matters," and he is right that the thoughtless promotion of multiculturalism and identity politics threatens important American values. But his book, ironically, offers grist for a rather different perspective on the problem: *Who Are We?* suggests that the more serious threat to American culture comes perhaps from its own internal contradictions than from foreigners.

Let's begin with the question of who the true bearers of "Anglo-Protestant" values are. . . . His chapter describing "core" Anglo-Protestant values ends up focusing almost entirely on the work ethic: "From the beginning," he writes, "America's religion has been the religion of work." But who in today's world works hard? Certainly not contemporary Europeans with their 6-week vacations. The real Protestants are those Korean grocery-store owners, or Indian entrepreneurs, or Taiwanese engineers, or Russian cab drivers working two or three jobs in America's free and relatively unregulated labor market. I lived in Los Angeles for nearly a decade, and remember passing groups of Chicanos gathered at certain intersections at 7 a.m. waiting for work as day laborers. No lack of a work ethic here: That's why Hispanics have pushed native-born African Americans out of low-skill jobs in virtually every city where they compete head-to-head. . . .

There are a number of grounds for thinking that the United States will assimilate Hispanic immigrants just as it has earlier ethnic groups. Most important is the fact that they are Christian—either Catholic or, to an increasing degree, Evangelical Protestant. When controlling for socioeconomic status, they have stronger traditional family values than their native-born counterparts. This means that culturally, today's Mexican immigrants are much less distant from mainstream "Anglos" than were, say, the southern Italian immigrants or Eastern European Jews from mainstream WASPs [white Anglo-Saxon Protestants] at the beginning of the 20th century. Their rates of second and third generation intermarriage are much closer to those of other European groups than for African Americans. And, from Gen. Ricardo Sanchez on down, they are serving honorably today in the U.S. armed forces in numbers disproportionate to their place in the overall population.

The problem . . . is not that Mexican and other Latino immigrants come with the wrong values but rather that they are corrupted by American practices. Many young Hispanics are absorbed into the underclass culture of American inner cities, which has then reexported gang violence back to Mexico and Central America; or else their middle-class leaders have absorbed the American post-civil-rights-era sense of victimization and entitlement. There is a sharp divide between elites—organizations like the National Council of La Raza, or the Mexican-American Legal Defense Fund—and the general population of Hispanic immigrants. The latter, overall, tend to be socially conservative, want to learn English and assimilate into the American mainstream, and were even supportive initially of California's Proposition 187 (denying benefits to illegal immigrants) and 227 (ending bilingualism in public education). . . .

If it is the case that high levels of immigration are inevitable for developed societies, then what we need to do is to shift the focus from immigration per se to the issue of assimilation. . . .

This will be a huge challenge for the United States, but I am more confident than Huntington that we can meet it. Indeed, Hispanic immigrants will help to reinforce certain cultural values like the emphasis on family and work, and the Christian character of American society.

SOURCE: Fukuyama (2004).

DEBATE QUESTIONS TO CONSIDER

1. Analyze these arguments in terms of assimilation and pluralism. Are these authors using Gordon's model of assimilation? Can these issues and concerns be expressed in terms of pluralism? How?

2. What issues do O'Sullivan and Huntington raise about the assimilation of Latinos and Mexicans? Does the information presented in this chapter tend to refute or confirm their concerns? How?

3. What points does Fukuyama make in response to the arguments presented by O'Sullivan and Huntington? What evidence does he present to back up his points? How convincing is the evidence?

4. Is it fair to say that Huntington is a pessimist and Fukuyama is an optimist about the future of American culture? Does immigration really threaten traditional American values?

MAIN POINTS

- Hispanic Americans are a diverse and growing part of U.S. society. There are many distinct groups, but the three largest are Mexican Americans, Puerto Ricans, and Cuban Americans. The various Hispanic groups tend not to think of themselves as a single entity.
- Hispanic Americans have some characteristics of colonized groups and some of immigrant groups. Similarly, these groups are racial minorities in some ways and ethnic minorities in others.
- Since the beginning of the 20th century, Mexico has served as a reserve labor force for the development of the U.S. economy. Immigrants from Mexico entered a social system in which the colonized status of the group was already established. Mexican Americans have been a colonized minority group despite the large numbers of immigrants in the group and have been systematically excluded from opportunities for upward mobility by institutional discrimination and segregation.
- A Mexican American protest movement has been continuously seeking to improve the status of the group. In the 1960s, a more intense and militant movement emerged, guided by the ideology of Chicanismo.
- Puerto Ricans began to move to the mainland in large numbers only in recent decades. The group is concentrated in the urban Northeast, in the low-wage sector of the job market.
- Cubans began immigrating after Castro's revolution in the late 1950s. They settled primarily in southern Florida, where they created an ethnic enclave.
- The overall levels of anti-Hispanic prejudice and discrimination seem to have declined, along with the general decline in explicit, overt racism in American society. Recent high levels of immigration seem to have increased anti-Hispanic prejudice and discrimination, however, especially in the borderlands and other areas with large numbers of immigrants.
- Levels of acculturation are highly variable from group to group and from generation to generation. Acculturation increases with length of residence, but the vitality of Latino cultures has been sustained by recent immigration.
- Secondary structural assimilation also varies from group to group. Poverty, unemployment, lower levels of educational attainment, and other forms of inequality continue to be major problems for Hispanic groups, even the relatively successful Cuban Americans.
- Primary structural assimilation with the dominant group is greater than for African Americans.

STUDY SITE ON THE WEB

For chapter-specific resources, such as self-quizzes, videos, and flashcards, go to **www.sagepub.com/ healeyregc6e.**

FOR FURTHER READING

Acosta-Belen, Edna, & Santiago, Carlos. 2006. *Puerto Ricans in the United States: A Contemporary Portrait*. Boulder Colorado: Lynne Reiner.

A good overview of the history and present situation of Puerto Ricans

Acuña, Rodolfo. 2010. *Occupied America* (7th ed.). New York: Prentice Hall.

Reviews Mexican American history and argues that the experiences of this group resemble those of colonized groups

Garcia, Maria Cristina. 1997. *Havana USA: Cuban Exiles and Cuban Americans in South Florida, 1959–1994*. Berkeley: University of California Press.

A comprehensive history of the Cuban community in southern Florida

Portes, Alejandro, & Bach, Robert L. 1985. *Latin Journey: Cuban and Mexican Immigrants in the United States*. Berkeley: University of California Press.

A landmark analysis of Latino immigration, ethnic enclaves, and the United States and assimilation

Smith, Robert C. 2006. *Mexican New York: Transnational Lives of New Immigrants*. Berkeley: University of California Press.

A ground-breaking study of globalization, transnationalism, and immigration focused on Mexicans in New York and Mexico

Telles, Edward, & Ortiz, Vilma. 2008. *Generations of Exclusion: Mexican Americans, Assimilation, and Race*. New York: Russell Sage.

An important look at assimilation among Mexicans Americans

QUESTIONS FOR REVIEW AND STUDY

1. At the beginning of this chapter, it is stated that Hispanic Americans "combine elements of the polar extremes [immigrant and colonized] of Blauner's typology of minority groups" and that they are "partly an ethnic minority group and partly a racial minority group." Explain these statements in terms of the rest of the material presented in the chapter.

2. What important cultural differences between Mexican Americans and the dominant society shaped the relationships between the two groups?

3. How does the history of Mexican immigration demonstrate the usefulness of Noel's concepts of differentials in power and competition?

4. Compare and contrast the protest movements of Mexican Americans, American Indians, and African Americans. What similarities and differences existed in Chicanismo, Red Power, and Black Power? How do the differences reflect the unique experiences of each group?

5. In what ways are the experiences of Puerto Ricans and Cuban Americans unique compared with those of other minority groups? How do these differences reflect other differences, such as differences in contact situation?

6. The Cuban American enclave has resulted in a variety of benefits for the group. Why don't other minority groups follow this strategy?

7. What images of Latinas are common in U.S. society? How do these images reflect the experiences of these groups?

8. Describe the situation of the major Hispanic American groups in terms of acculturation and integration. Which groups are closest to equality? What factors or experiences might account for the differences between groups? In what ways might the statement "Hispanic Americans are remaining pluralistic even while they assimilate" be true?

INTERNET RESEARCH PROJECT

In this exercise, you will use U.S. Census data to gather information about the total population of all Hispanic Americans and two subgroups of your choosing. This project adds to the information you gathered in Chapters 6 and 7 and adds some new variables. You can add the information for African Americans and American Indians and Alaska Natives (AIAN) from the previous exercise and add data for the new variables in this exercise. You will then use course concepts to assess and analyze this information and place it in the context of this text. *Visit the website for this text for instructions on finding the information needed to complete the table below.*

		Total Population	African Americans	AIAN	All Hispanic Americans	Hispanic American Groups	
						_____	_____
1	Number						
2	% of total population	—					
3	Median age						
4	Average household size						
5	% less than high school						
6	% speak English less than "very well"						
7	% unemployed						
8	Per capita income						
9	Median incomes for full-time, year-round workers						
	Males						
	Females						
10	Poverty rate, all families						
11							
12							

QUESTIONS

1. What stage of Gordon's model of assimilation (see Exhibit 2.1) do the variables in the table measure?

2. Using the Blauner hypothesis (see Chapter 4), we can say that both American Indians and African Americans are "colonized or conquered" minority groups. Hispanic Americans, on the other hand, are a mixture of colonized and immigrant origins, as well as a combination of ethnic and racial groups. What would the Blauner hypothesis predict about the relative status of these groups in American society? Does the evidence in the table support the prediction? How?

3. What important differences do you see between your two Hispanic American subgroups? Which is closer to national patterns? To African Americans and American Indians? What are some possible reasons for these patterns? For example, are the differences related to the timing of the group's immigration? What "human capital" does the group bring that might help account for the differences?

OPTIONAL GROUP DISCUSSION

Bring the information on your groups to class and compare with the information collected by others. Consider the issues raised in the questions above and in the chapter and develop some ideas about why the groups are where they are relative to one another and to the total population.

9

Asian Americans

"Model Minorities"?

*I . . . was riding a taxi to my hotel to attend a conference on multiculturalism.
My driver and I chatted about the weather and the tourists. . . . "How long have
you been in this country?" he asked. "All my life," I replied. . . .*

—Ronald Takaki, professor of Asian American studies[1]

These few seconds of conversation speak deeply about U.S. perceptions of Asian Americans (and other minority groups). The taxi driver certainly meant no insult, but his casual question revealed his view, shared with millions of others, that the United States is a white European society. At the time of this conversation, Takaki was a distinguished professor at a prestigious West Coast university, a highly respected teacher and internationally renowned expert in his field. His family had been in the United States for a hundred years—very possibly longer than the taxi driver's family. Yet, the driver automatically assumed he was an outsider.

Asian Americans, like other peoples of color, continually find themselves set apart, excluded, and stigmatized—whether during the 19th-century anti-Chinese campaign in California, after the 1922 Supreme Court decision (*Ozawa vs. U.S.*) that declared Asians ineligible for U.S. citizenship, or by a YouTube video that went viral on the Internet in 2011 in which a UCLA student complained bitterly about Asians in the library.[2] The stereotypes might be "positive"—as in the view that Asian Americans are "model minorities"—but the "othering" is real, painful, and consequential.

In this chapter, we begin with an overview of Asian American groups and then briefly examine the traditions and customs that they bring with them to America. For much of the chapter, we will focus on the two oldest groups, Chinese Americans and Japanese Americans. Throughout the chapter, we will be especially concerned with the perception that Asian Americans in general and Chinese and Japanese Americans in particular are "model minorities":

successful, affluent, highly educated people who do not suffer from the problems usually associated with minority group status. How accurate is this view? Have Asian Americans forged a pathway to upward mobility that could be followed by other groups? Do the concepts and theories that have guided this text (particularly the Blauner and Noel hypotheses) apply? Does the success of these groups mean that the United States is truly an open, fair, and just society? We explore these questions throughout the chapter.

Asian American groups vary in their languages, in their cultural and physical characteristics, and in their experiences in the United States. Some of these groups are truly newcomers to America, but others have roots in this country stretching back for more than 150 years. As was the case with American Indians and Hispanic Americans, "Asian American" is a convenient label imposed by the larger society (and by government agencies such as the Census Bureau) that deemphasizes the differences between the groups. Exhibit 9.1 lists all Asian Americans and the 10 largest Asian American groups, along with information about their size and growth rates.

Several features of this exhibit are worth noting. First, Asian Americans are a small fraction of the total U.S. population. Even when aggregated, they account for only 5% of all Americans. In contrast, African Americans are 13% and Hispanic Americans are 16%. Second, most Asian American groups have grown dramatically in recent decades, largely because of high rates of immigration since the 1965 changes in U.S. immigration policy. All the groups listed in Exhibit 9.1 grew faster than the total population between 1990 and 2009. The Japanese

Exhibit 9.1 Size and Growth of Asian American* Groups, 1990–2009

Group	1990	2000	2009	Growth (Number of Times Larger), 1990–2009	Percentage of Total Population, 2009
All Asian Americans	6,908,638	11,070,913	15,341,968	2.2	5.0
Chinese	1,645,472	2,879,636	3,651,336	2.2	1.2
Filipino	1,406,770	2,364,815	3,111,076	2.2	1.0
Asian Indian	815,447	1,899,599	2,800,612	3.4	< 1
Vietnamese	614,547	1,223,736	1,623,236	2.6	< 1
Korean	798,849	1,228,427	1,565,154	2.0	< 1
Japanese	847,562	1,148,932	1,260,351	1.5	< 1
Pakistani	N/A	204,309	311,798	—	< 1
Cambodian	147,411	206,052	255,202	1.7	< 1
Hmong	90,082	186,310	234,340	2.6	< 1
Laotian	149,014	198,203	228,121	1.6	< 1
Percentage of U.S. population	2.8	3.9	5.0		5.0
Total U.S. population	248,710,000	281,422,000	304,320,465	1.2	

*Asian Americans, alone and in combination with other groups

SOURCES: 1990—U.S. Bureau of the Census (1990); 2000—U.S. Bureau of the Census (2000d); 2007—U.S. Bureau of the Census (2007a).

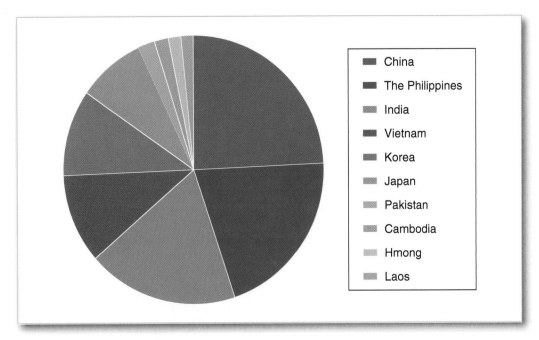

Exhibit 9.2 Ten Largest Asian American Groups by Nation of Origin, 2009

Legend:
- China
- The Philippines
- India
- Vietnam
- Korea
- Japan
- Pakistan
- Cambodia
- Hmong
- Laos

NOTE: The Hmong are from various Southeast Asian nations, including Laos and Vietnam.

SOURCE: U.S. Bureau of the Census (2009a).

American population grew at the slowest rate (largely because immigration from Japan has been low in recent decades), but the number of Asian Indians more than tripled, and most of the other groups doubled or more than doubled their populations. This rapid growth is projected to continue for decades to come, and the impact of Asian Americans on everyday life and American culture will increase accordingly. Today, 5 out of every 100 Americans are of Asian heritage, but this ratio will grow to nearly 1 out of every 10 by the year 2050 (see Exhibit 1.1). The relative sizes of the largest Asian American groups are presented in Exhibit 9.2, and their nations of origin are displayed in Exhibit 9.3.

Like Hispanic Americans, most Asian American groups have a high percentage of foreign-born members. The great majority of 4 of the 10 groups listed in Exhibit 9.4 are first generation, and even Japanese Americans, the lowest-ranked group, more than double the national norm for foreign-born members. Today, the vast majority of Asian Americans (86%) are either post-1965 immigrants or their second-generation children (Sakamoto, Goyette, & Kim, 2009, p. 269).

ORIGINS AND CULTURES

Asian Americans have brought a wealth of traditions to the United States. They speak many different languages and practice religions as diverse as Buddhism, Confucianism, Islam, Hinduism, and Christianity. Asian cultures predate the founding of the United States by centuries or even millennia. Although no two of these cultures are the same, some general similarities can be identified. These cultural traits have shaped the behavior of Asian Americans, as well as the perceptions of members of the dominant group, and compose part of the foundation on which Asian American experiences have been built.

Asian cultures tend to stress group membership over individual self-interest. For example, Confucianism, which was the dominant ethical and moral system in traditional China and

Exhibit 9.3 Map Showing Nations of Origin for 10 Largest Asian American Groups

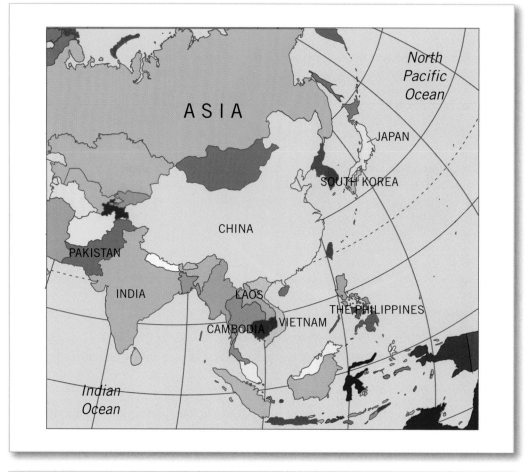

Exhibit 9.4 Percentage Foreign-Born by Nation of Origin, 2009

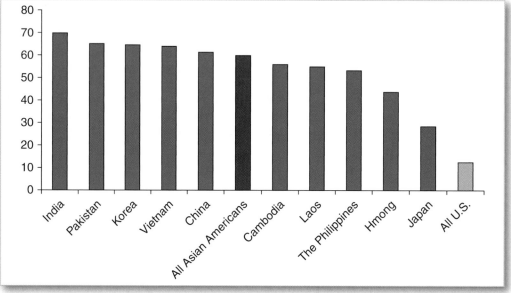

SOURCE: U.S. Bureau of the Census.

had a powerful influence on many other Asian cultures, counsels people to see themselves as elements in larger social systems and status hierarchies. Confucianism emphasizes loyalty to the group, conformity to societal expectations, and respect for one's superiors. In traditional China, as in other Asian societies, the business of everyday life was organized around kinship relations, and most interpersonal relations were with family members and other relatives (Lyman, 1974, p. 9). The family or the clan often owned the land on which all depended for survival, and kinship ties determined inheritance patterns. The clan also performed a number of crucial social functions, including arranging marriages, settling disputes between individuals, and organizing festivals and holidays.

Asian cultures stress sensitivity to the opinions and judgments of others and the importance of avoiding public embarrassment and not giving offense. Especially when discussing Japanese culture, these cultural tendencies are often contrasted with Western practices in terms of "guilt versus shame" and the nature of personal morality (Benedict, 1946). In Western cultures, individuals are encouraged to develop and abide by a conscience, or an inner moral voice, and behavior is guided by one's personal sense of guilt. In contrast, Asian cultures stress the importance of maintaining the respect and good opinion of others and avoiding shame and public humiliation. Group harmony, or *wa* in Japanese, is a central concern, and displays of individualism are discouraged. These characteristics are reflected in the Japanese proverb, "The nail that sticks up must be hammered down" (Whiting, 1990, p. 70). Asian cultures emphasize proper behavior, conformity to convention and the judgments of others, and avoiding embarrassment and personal confrontations ("saving face").

A possible manifestation of this tendency to seek harmony and avoid confrontation was documented by Chou and Feagin (2008) in interviews with Asian Americans from a variety of groups. They found that their subjects commonly used "compliant conformity" to cope with white racism, discrimination, and rejection (p. 222). Their respondents often expressed the idea that conformity and hard work would result in recognition and acceptance in the larger society. The parents of the respondents, even those who had experienced substantial discrimination, commonly pressured their children to conform to white expectations and Anglo values in the hope that their success (e.g., in school) would protect them from negative treatment and stereotyping. Chou and Feagin suggest that this strategy has had limited success (at best) and that, ultimately, it sustains white prejudicial values and the conventional racial hierarchy in U.S. society by complying with rather than challenging racism (p. 222).

Traditional Asian cultures were male dominated, and women were consigned to subordinate roles. A Chinese woman was expected to serve first her father, then her husband, and, if widowed, her eldest son. Confucianism also decreed that women should observe the Four Virtues: chastity and obedience, shyness, a pleasing demeanor, and skill in the performance of domestic duties (Amott & Matthaei, 1991, p. 200). Women of high status in traditional China symbolized their subordination by binding their feet. This painful, crippling practice began early in life and required women to wrap their feet tightly to keep them artificially small. The bones in the arch were broken so that the toes could be bent under the foot, further decreasing the size of the foot. Bound feet were considered beautiful, but they also immobilized women and were intended to prevent them from "wandering away" from domestic and household duties (Jackson, 2000; Takaki, 1993, pp. 209–210).

The experiences of Asian Americans in the United States modified these patriarchal values and traditional traits. For the groups with longer histories in U.S. society, such as Chinese Americans and Japanese Americans, the effects of these values on individual personality may be slight, but for more recently arrived groups, the effects may be more powerful. The cultural and religious differences among the Asian American groups also reflect the recent histories of each of the sending nations. For example, Vietnam was a colony of China for 1,000 years, but for much of the past century, it was a colony of France. Although Vietnamese culture has been heavily influenced by China, many Vietnamese are Catholic, a result of the efforts of the French to convert them. The Philippines and India were also colonized by Western nations—the former by Spain and then by the United States and the latter by Great Britain. As a result, many Filipinos are Catholic, and many Indian immigrants are familiar with English and with Anglo culture.

These examples are, of course, the merest suggestion of the diversity of these groups. In fact, Asian Americans, who share little more than a slight physical resemblance and some broad cultural similarities, are much more diverse than Hispanic Americans, who are overwhelmingly Catholic and share a common language and a historical connection with Spain (Min, 1995, p. 25).

CONTACT SITUATIONS AND THE DEVELOPMENT OF THE CHINESE AMERICAN AND JAPANESE AMERICAN COMMUNITIES

The earliest Asian groups to arrive in substantial numbers were from China and Japan. Their contact situations not only shaped their own histories but also affected the present situation of all Asian Americans in many ways. As we will see, the contact situations for both Chinese Americans and Japanese Americans featured massive rejection and discrimination. Both groups adapted to the racism of the larger society by forming enclaves, a strategy that eventually produced some major benefits for their descendants.

Chinese Americans

Early Immigration and the Anti-Chinese Campaign

Immigrants from China to the United States began to arrive in the early 1800s and were generally motivated by the same kinds of social and economic forces that have inspired immigration everywhere for the past two centuries. Chinese immigrants were "pushed" to leave their homeland by the disruption of traditional social relations, caused by the colonization of much of China by more industrialized European nations, and by rapid population growth (Chan, 1990; Lyman, 1974; Tsai, 1986). At the same time, these immigrants were "pulled" to the West Coast of the United States by the Gold Rush of 1849 and by other opportunities created by the development of the West.

The Noel hypothesis (see Chapter 4) provides a useful way to analyze the contact situation that developed between Chinese and Anglo-Americans in the mid-19th century. As you recall, Noel argues that racial or ethnic stratification will result when a contact situation is characterized by three conditions: ethnocentrism, competition, and a differential in power. Once all three conditions were met on the West Coast, a vigorous campaign against the Chinese began, and the group was pushed into a subordinate, disadvantaged position.

Ethnocentrism based on racial, cultural, and language differences was present from the beginning, but at first, competition for jobs between Chinese immigrants and native-born workers was muted by a robust, rapidly growing economy and an abundance of jobs. At first, politicians, newspaper editorial writers, and business leaders praised the Chinese for their industriousness and tirelessness (Tsai, 1986, p. 17). Before long, however, the economic boom slowed, and the supply of jobs began to dry up. The Gold Rush petered out, and the transcontinental railroad, which thousands of Chinese workers had helped build, was completed in 1869. The migration of Anglo-Americans from the East continued, and competition for jobs and other resources increased. An anti-Chinese campaign of harassment, discrimination, and violent attacks began. In 1871, in Los Angeles, a mob of "several hundred whites shot, hanged, and stabbed 19 Chinese to death" (Tsai, 1986, p. 67). Other attacks against the Chinese occurred in Denver; Seattle; Tacoma; and Rock Springs, Wyoming (Lyman, 1974, p. 77).

As the West Coast economy changed, the Chinese came to be seen as a threat, and elements of the dominant group tried to limit competition. The Chinese were a small group—there were only about 100,000 in the entire country in 1870—and by law, they were not permitted to become citizens. Hence, they controlled few power resources with which to withstand these attacks. During the 1870s, Chinese workers were forced out of most sectors of the mainstream economy, and in 1882, the anti-Chinese campaign experienced its ultimate triumph when the U.S. Congress passed the Chinese Exclusion Act, banning virtually all immigration from China. The act was one of the first restrictive immigration laws and was aimed solely at the Chinese. It established a "rigid competitive" relationship between the groups (see Chapter 5) and eliminated the threat presented by Chinese labor by excluding Chinese from American society.

Consistent with the predictions of split-labor market theory (see Chapter 3), the primary antagonists of Chinese immigrants were native-born workers and organized labor. White owners of small businesses, feeling threatened by Chinese-owned businesses, also supported passage of the Chinese Exclusion Act (Boswell, 1986). Other social classes, such as the capitalists who owned larger factories, might actually have benefited from the continued supply of cheaper labor created by immigration from China. Conflicts such as the anti-Chinese campaign can be especially intense because they can confound racial and ethnic antagonisms with disputes between different social classes.

The ban on immigration from China remained in effect until World War II, when China was awarded a yearly quota of 105 immigrants in recognition of its wartime alliance with the United States. However, large-scale immigration from China did not resume until federal policy was revised in the 1960s.

Population Trends and the "Delayed" Second Generation

Following the Chinese Exclusion Act, the number of Chinese in the United States actually declined (see Exhibit 9.5) as some immigrants passed away or returned to China and were not replaced by newcomers. The huge majority of Chinese immigrants in the 19th century had been young adult male sojourners who intended to work hard, save money, and return to their homes in China (Chan, 1990, p. 66). After 1882, it was difficult for anyone from China, male or female, to enter the United States, and the Chinese community in the United States remained overwhelmingly male for many decades. At the end of the 19th century, for example, males outnumbered females by more than 25 to 1, and the sex ratio did not approach parity for decades (Wong, 1995, p. 64; see also Ling, 2000). The scarcity of Chinese women in the United States delayed the second generation (the first born in the United States), and it wasn't until the 1920s, 80 years after immigration began, that as many as one third of all Chinese in the United States were native-born (Wong, 1995, p. 64).

The delayed second generation may have reinforced the exclusion of the Chinese American community, which began as a reaction to the overt discrimination of the dominant group (Chan, 1990, p. 66). The children of immigrants are usually much more acculturated, and their language facility and greater familiarity with the larger society often permits them

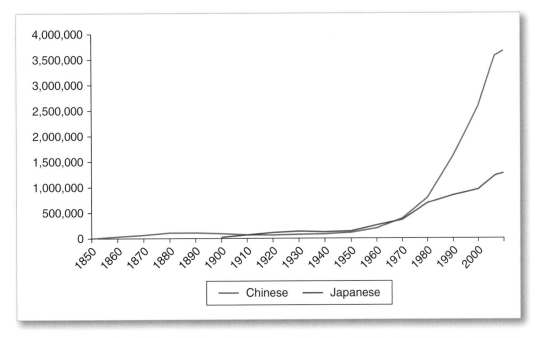

Exhibit 9.5 Population Growth for Chinese and Japanese Americans, 1850 to 2009

SOURCE: Kitano (1980, p. 562); Lee (1998, p. 15); U.S. Bureau of the Census (2007a, 2009a); Xie & Goyette (2004).

to represent the group and speak for it more effectively. In the case of Chinese Americans (and other Asian groups), members of the second generation were citizens of the United States by birth, a status from which the immigrants were barred, and they had legal and political rights not available to their parents. Thus, the decades-long absence of a more Americanized, English-speaking generation increased the isolation of Chinese Americans.

The Ethnic Enclave

The Chinese became increasingly urbanized as the anti-Chinese campaign and rising racism took their toll. Forced out of towns and smaller cities, they settled in larger urban areas, such as San Francisco, which offered the safety of urban anonymity and ethnic neighborhoods where the old ways could be practiced and contact with the hostile larger society minimized. Chinatowns had existed since the start of the immigration, and they now took on added significance as safe havens from the storm of anti-Chinese venom. The Chinese withdrew to these neighborhoods and became an "invisible minority" (Tsai, 1986, p. 67).

These early Chinatowns were ethnic enclaves like those founded by Jews on the East Coast and the more recently founded Cuban community in Miami, and a similar process formed them. The earliest urban Chinese included merchants and skilled artisans who, like the early wave of Cuban immigrants, were experienced in commerce (Chan, 1990, p. 44). They established businesses and retail stores that were typically small in scope and modest in profits. As the number of urban Chinese increased, the market for these enterprises became larger and more spatially concentrated. New services were required, the size of the cheap labor pool available to Chinese merchants and entrepreneurs increased, and the Chinatowns became the economic, cultural, and social centers of the community.

Within the Chinatowns, elaborate social structures developed that mirrored traditional China in many ways. The enforced segregation of the Chinese in America helped preserve much of the traditional food, dress, language, values, and religions of their homeland from the pressures of Americanization. The social structure was based on a variety of types of organizations, including family and clan groups and huiguan, or associations based on the region or district in China from which the immigrant had come. These organizations performed various, often overlapping, social and welfare services, including settling disputes, aiding new arrivals from their regions, and facilitating the development of mutual aid networks (Lai, 1980, p. 221; Lyman, 1974, pp. 32–37, 116–118). Life was not always peaceful in Chinatown, and there were numerous disputes over control of resources and the organizational infrastructure. In particular, secret societies called tongs contested the control and leadership of the merchant-led huiguan and the clan associations. These sometimes bloody conflicts were sensationalized in the American press as "Tong Wars," and they contributed to the popular stereotypes of Asians as exotic, mysterious, and dangerous (Lai, 1980, p. 222; Lyman, 1974, pp. 37–50).

Despite these internal conflicts, American Chinatowns evolved into highly organized, largely self-contained communities, complete with their own leadership and decision-making structures. The internal "city government" of Chinatown was the Chinese Consolidated Benevolent Association (CCBA). Dominated by the larger huiguan and clans, the CCBA coordinated and supplemented the activities of the various organizations and represented the interests of the community to the larger society.

The local CCBAs, along with other organizations, also attempted to combat the anti-Chinese campaign, speaking out against racial discrimination and filing numerous lawsuits to contest racist legislation (Lai, 1980, p. 223). The effectiveness of the protest efforts was handicapped by the lack of resources in the Chinese community and by the fact that Chinese immigrants could not become citizens. Attempts were made to mobilize international pressure to protest the treatment of the Chinese in the United States. At the time, however, China was itself colonized and dominated by other nations (including the United States). China was further weakened by internal turmoil and could mount no effective assistance for its citizens in the United States (Chan, 1990, p. 62).

Survival and Development

The Chinese American community survived despite the widespread poverty, discrimination, and pressures created by the unbalanced sex ratio. Members of the group began to seek opportunities in other regions, and Chinatowns appeared and grew in New York, Boston, Chicago, Philadelphia, and many other cities.

The patterns of exclusion and discrimination that began during the 19th-century anti-Chinese campaign were common throughout the nation and continued well into the 20th century. Chinese Americans responded by finding economic opportunity in areas where dominant group competition for jobs was weak, continuing their tendency to be an "invisible" minority group. Very often, they started small businesses that either served other members of their own group (e.g., restaurants) or relied on the patronage of the general public (e.g., laundries). The jobs provided by these small businesses were the economic lifeblood of the community but were limited in the amount of income and wealth they could generate. Until recent decades, for example, most restaurants served primarily other Chinese, especially single males. Since their primary clientele was poor, the profit potential of these businesses was sharply limited. Laundries served the more affluent dominant group, but the returns from this enterprise declined as washers and dryers became increasingly widespread in homes throughout the nation. The population of Chinatown was generally too small to sustain more than these two primary commercial enterprises (Zhou, 1992, pp. 92–94).

As the decades passed, the enclave economy and the complex subsociety of Chinatown evolved. However, discrimination, combined with defensive self-segregation, ensured the continuation of poverty, limited job opportunities, and substandard housing. Relatively hidden from general view, Chinatown became the world in which the second generation grew to adulthood. Some of this experience is captured in the next Narrative Portrait.

The Second Generation

Whereas the immigrant generation generally retained its native language and customs, the second generation was much more influenced by the larger culture. The institutional and organizational structures of Chinatown were created to serve the older, mostly male immigrant generation, but younger Chinese Americans tended to look beyond the enclave to fill their needs. They came in contact with the larger society through schools, churches, and voluntary organizations such as the YMCA and YWCA.

They abandoned many traditional customs and were less loyal to and interested in the clan and regional associations that the immigrant generation had constructed. They founded organizations of their own that were more compatible with their Americanized lifestyles (Lai, 1980, p. 225).

As with other minority groups, World War II was an important watershed for Chinese Americans. During the war, job opportunities outside the enclave increased, and after the war, many of the 8,000 Chinese Americans who served in the armed forces were able to take advantage of the GI Bill to further their education (Lai, 1980, p. 226). In the 1940s and 1950s, many second-generation Chinese Americans moved out of the enclave, away from the traditional neighborhoods, and pursued careers in the larger society. This group was mobile and Americanized, and with educational credentials comparable to the general population, they were prepared to seek success outside Chinatown.

In another departure from tradition, the women of the second generation also pursued education, and as early as 1960, median years of schooling for Chinese American women were slightly higher than for Chinese American men (Kitano & Daniels, 1995, p. 48). Chinese American women also became more diverse in their occupational profile as the century progressed. In 1900, three quarters of all employed Chinese American women worked in manufacturing (usually in garment industry sweatshops or in canning factories) or in domestic work. By 1960, less than 2% were in domestic work, 32% were in clerical occupations, and 18% held professional jobs, often as teachers (Amott & Matthaei, 1991, pp. 209–211).

Growing Up in Chinatown

Ben Fong-Torres grew up in the Chinatown enclave of Oakland, California, in the 1940s and 1950s. His seemingly Hispanic family name came from the fact that his father entered the United States illegally during the decades when America's doors were closed to the Chinese. Mr. Fong-Torres's father moved first to the Philippines, where he worked for several years, and then purchased Filipino identity papers on the black market and moved to the United States.

In this excerpt from his memoir, The Rice Room, *Fong-Torres recounts some of his experiences as a young boy and remembers the sometimes confusing challenges of negotiating the social and cultural spaces between his Chinese heritage and the larger society. Also note his descriptions of the institutions, organizations, networks, and customs that helped Chinatown function as a subsociety. How does his family begin to absorb the surrounding culture? How do they resist Americanization? Can you detect any gender dimensions in his account?*

Fong-Torres grew up to become an editor for Rolling Stone *magazine and a well-known journalist, DJ, television personality, and author.*

NEGOTIATING CHINESE AND AMERICAN CULTURES

BEN FONG-TORRES

Our parents had a mission in life: to instill Chinese culture in us. While Japanese Americans, stung by their experiences in internment camps during World War II, were more determined than ever to assimilate into the American mainstream, first-generation Chinese had no such goals. They were Chinese. That's how they thought, and that's what they read, wrote, and spoke.

Their children, they would grudgingly allow, were Americans as well as Chinese. Ideally, they would succeed—the boys as doctors, dentists, or lawyers; the girls as wives of doctors, dentists, or lawyers. Still, they'd be Chinese at the core.

And so, as each of us turned 8, Sarah, Barry, and I found our school days lengthened by several hours in Chinese school at the nearby Chinese Community Center, a modern, two-story building with a gymnasium and courtyard and a tiled pagoda facade. A perfect statement of Chinese American symbiosis.

Here, teachers taught language, calligraphy, culture, and history and, not incidentally, manners. We stood when the teacher entered the room and paid him more attention than any teacher at Lincoln [elementary school]. . . . Every afternoon, we'd go home, pick up our Chinese stuff—thin paperback lesson books, calligraphy books, pens, pencils, and ink—in a cigar box, and go off to Chinese school. . . .

We sat attentively through lectures about Sun Yat-sen, and we learned calligraphy by copying characters into books with pages of squares in vertical rows. We learned to hold a Chinese brush pen straight up, to dip it into black ink soaked in cotton balls in little bottles. We traced large characters onto tissue paper. . . .

American holidays came as a shock to my parents. Two months after her arrival in Oakland, my mother was home one evening when her doorbell rang. She pulled back the curtain on the front door window and found herself confronted by two children—one dressed as a ghost, the other a witch. Even though they were clearly children, they frightened Mom, and she hurried to the telephone to call Grace Fung.

"What is this?" she asked. "Children in make-believe-clothes at my front door!"

Grace told my mother about Halloween. For good measure, she also explained Thanksgiving and Christmas. . . .

But while we had tricks and treats and Thanksgiving and Christmas, we also had Chinese New Year every February. . . . The Chinese . . . make New Year a 2-week-long affair. . . . At some point, we knew that we'd receive *hoong bow*—little red envelopes containing a coin, given by adults to children to reward them for good manners and to wish them good luck.

I knew that, no matter how far from home, the children were expected to gather for dinner on those days in a show of family unity. Every year, our parents would put out their round, lacquered, wood platter—called by some a "tray of togetherness" and by others a "tray of prosperity"—with eight compartments for a variety of sweets—candied melon (for health), sugared coconut strips (togetherness), kumquat (prosperity), lichee nuts (strong family ties), melon seeds (dyed red to symbolize happiness), lotus seeds (many children), and longan (many good sons).

All over the house, there'd be bowls and platters piled high with oranges and tangerines, which meant good luck and wealth, and wherever Chinese visited during the 2 weeks of New Year celebration, they would bring gifts of fruit and go through an exercise of manners that befuddled us.

The hosts would chide the visitors for bringing oranges. "Oh, not necessary," they would say, knowing full well that the gift was almost mandatory in Chinese tradition.

The guests would insist; the hosts would relent. Then, at the end of the visit, the hosts would pile the guests up with oranges and tangerines.

"Oh, no, no," the departing guests would protest, fully prepared to accept the exchange of fruit, which they would bring to their next hosts.

At dinner, every course, as with every aspect of the New Year celebration, was laden with symbolism and purpose. We had to have chicken, simply steamed and presented whole, indicating completeness. The same reasoning applied to fish, roast suckling pig with thick, crunchy skin and an even thicker layer of fat, and, as a yin-yang balance, a vegetarian dish called "Buddha's monk stew," composed of Chinese vermicelli (noodles, uncut, symbolize long life), fermented bean curd, cloud ears, tiger lily flowers, and gingko nuts.

Before dinner, we'd set off firecrackers outside the house—to ward off evil spirits—and create an echo of what for most Chinese was the highlight of New Year's: the parade through Chinatown, San Francisco, with its block-long golden dragon. We rarely made it to *Dai Fow* [the "big city" of San Francisco], but contented ourselves with Oakland's street celebrations. On Webster and surrounding streets, teams of young lion dancers from judo and karate schools made the rounds of business establishments and family associations, which hired the lions to chase off bad influences with their supernatural powers. While neighbors and passersby gathered to watch, they performed amidst gongs, drums, and exploding firecrackers, and, at show's end, climbed high, ignoring lit fireworks at their feet, to snatch a string of *hoong bow*—red envelopes containing dollar bills—payment to the lions for warding off the demons.

I was fascinated by the lion's head, with the blinding primary colors, the bulging, bejeweled, fur-brewed eyes and the pom-poms springing out of its forehead. The lead dancer would hoist it over his head, thrust and jerk it up and about, and flap its extended tongue and white-whiskered lower jaw, dancing acrobatically with two other men who worked under a long, multicolored fabric train behind him, forming the body of the lion.

Back at the New Eastern [the family restaurant], I'd take a cardboard box that had held eggs and, with paper, water colors, crayons, string, and fabrics Mother had left over from her garment work, fashion my own lion's head, complete with a flapping lower lip. Barry and Shirley were happy to pound on garbage can lids or a Quaker Oats box while I pranced around the backyard. Our parents were delighted that we would embrace Chinese New Year with such enthusiasm.

SOURCE: Fong-Torres (1995, pp. 44–49).

An American Success Story?

The men and women of the second generation achieved considerable educational and occupational success and helped establish the idea that Chinese Americans are a "model minority." A closer examination reveals, however, that the old traditions of anti-Chinese discrimination and prejudice continued to limit the life chances of even the best-educated members of this generation. Second-generation Chinese Americans earned less, on the average, and had less-favorable occupational profiles than comparably educated white Americans, a gap between qualifications and rewards that reflects persistent discrimination. Kitano and Daniels (1995, p. 50) conclude, for example, that although well-educated Chinese Americans could find good jobs in the mainstream economy, the highest, most lucrative positions—and those that required direct supervision of whites—were still closed to them (see also Hirschman & Wong, 1984).

Furthermore, many Chinese Americans, including many of those who stayed in the Chinatowns to operate the enclave economy and the immigrants who began arriving after 1965, do not fit the image of success at all. A large percentage of these Chinese Americans face many of the same problems as do members of colonized, excluded, exploited minority groups of color. For survival, they rely on low-wage jobs in the garment industry, the service sector, and the small businesses of the enclave economy and are beset by poverty and powerlessness, much like the urban underclass segments of other groups.

Thus, Chinese Americans can be found at both ends of the spectrum of success and affluence, and the group is often said to be "bipolar" in its occupational structure (see Barringer, Takeuchi, & Levin, 1995; Min, 2006; Takaki, 1993, pp. 415–416; Wong, 1995, pp. 77–78; Zhou & Logan, 1989). Although a high percentage of Chinese Americans are found in more desirable occupations—sustaining the idea of Asian success—others, less visible, are concentrated at the lowest levels of society. Later in this chapter, we will again consider the socioeconomic status of Chinese Americans and the accuracy of the image of success and affluence.

Japanese Americans

Immigration from Japan began to increase shortly after the Chinese Exclusion Act of 1882 took effect, in part to fill the gap in the labor supply created by the restrictive legislation (Kitano, 1980). The 1880 Census counted only a few hundred Japanese in the United States, but the group increased rapidly over the next few decades. By 1910, the Japanese in the United States outnumbered the Chinese and remained the larger of the two groups until large-scale immigration resumed in the 1960s (see Exhibit 9.5).

The Anti-Japanese Campaign

The contact situation for Japanese immigrants resembled that of the Chinese. They immigrated to the same West Coast regions as the Chinese, entered the labor force in a similar position, and were a small group with few power resources. Predictably, the feelings and emotions generated by the anti-Chinese campaign transferred to them. By the early 1900s, an anti-Japanese campaign to limit competition was in full swing. Efforts were being made to establish a rigid competitive system of group relations and to exclude Japanese immigrants in the same way the Chinese had been barred (Kitano, 1980, p. 563; Kitano & Daniels, 1995, pp. 59–60; Petersen, 1971, pp. 30–55).

Japanese immigration was partly curtailed in 1907 when a "gentlemen's agreement" was signed between Japan and the United States limiting the number of laborers Japan would allow to emigrate (Kitano & Daniels, 1995, p. 59). This policy remained in effect until the United States changed its immigration policy in the 1920s and barred immigration from Japan completely. The end of Japanese immigration is largely responsible for the slow growth of the Japanese American population displayed in Exhibit 9.5.

Most Japanese immigrants, like the Chinese, were young male laborers who planned to eventually return to their homeland or bring their wives after they were established in their new country (Duleep, 1988, p. 24). The agreement of 1907 curtailed the immigration of men, but because of a loophole, females were able to continue immigrating until the 1920s. Japanese Americans were thus able to maintain a relatively balanced sex ratio, marry, and begin families, and a second generation of Japanese Americans began to appear without much delay. Native-born Japanese numbered about half the group by 1930 and were a majority of 63% on the eve of World War II (Kitano & Daniels, 1995, p. 59).

The anti-Japanese movement also attempted to dislodge the group from agriculture. Many Japanese immigrants were skilled agriculturists, and farming proved to be their most promising avenue for advancement (Kitano, 1980, p. 563). In 1910, between 30% and 40% of all Japanese in California were engaged in agriculture; from 1900 to 1909, the number of independent Japanese farmers increased from fewer than 50 to about 6,000 (Jibou, 1988, p. 358).

Most of these immigrant farmers owned small plots of land, and they made up only a minuscule percentage of West Coast farmers (Jibou, 1988, pp. 357–358). Nonetheless, their presence and relative success did not go unnoticed and eventually stimulated discriminatory legislation, most notably the Alien Land Act, passed by the California legislature in 1913 (Kitano, 1980, p. 563). This bill made aliens who were ineligible for citizenship (effectively meaning only immigrants from Asia) to be also ineligible to own land. The act did not achieve its goal of dislodging the Japanese from the rural economy. They were able to dodge the discriminatory legislation by various devices, mostly by putting titles of land in the names of their American-born children, who were citizens by law (Jibou, 1988, p. 359).

The Alien Land Act was one part of a sustained campaign against the Japanese in the United States. In the early decades of this century, the Japanese were politically disenfranchised and segregated from dominant group institutions in schools and residential areas. They were discriminated against in movie houses, swimming pools, and other public facilities (Kitano & Daniels, 1988, p. 56). The Japanese were excluded from the mainstream economy and confined to a limited range of poorly paid occupations (see Yamato, 1994). Thus, there were strong elements of systematic discrimination, exclusion, and colonization in their overall relationship with the larger society.

Photo 9.1

Japanese American farmer hauling cauliflower, 1942. Within weeks, he will be in an internment camp.

© Corbis.

The Ethnic Enclave

Spurned and disparaged by the larger society, the Japanese, like the Chinese, constructed a separate subsociety. The immigrant generation, called Issei (from the Japanese word *ichi*, meaning "one"), established an enclave in agriculture and related enterprises, a rural counterpart of the urban enclaves constructed by other groups we have examined.

By World War II, the Issei had come to dominate a narrow but important segment of agriculture on the West Coast, especially in California. Although the Issei were never more than 2% of the total population of California, Japanese-American-owned farms produced as much as 30% to 40% of various fruits and vegetables grown in that state. As late as 1940, more than 40% of the Japanese American population was involved directly in farming, and many more were dependent on the economic activity stimulated by agriculture, including the marketing of their produce (Jibou, 1988, pp. 359–360). Other Issei lived in urban areas, where they were concentrated in a narrow range of businesses and services, such as domestic service and gardening, some of which catered to other Issei and some of which served the dominant group (p. 362).

Japanese Americans in both the rural and urban sectors maximized their economic clout by doing business with other Japanese-owned firms as often as possible. Gardeners and farmers purchased supplies at Japanese-owned firms, farmers used other members of the group to haul their products to market, and businesspeople relied on one another and mutual credit associations, rather than dominant group banks, for financial services. These networks helped the enclave economy grow and also permitted the Japanese to avoid the hostility and racism of the larger society. However, these very same patterns helped sustain the stereotypes that depicted the Japanese as clannish and unassimilable. In the years before World War II, the Japanese American community was largely dependent for survival on their networks of cooperation and mutual assistance, not on Americanization and integration.

The Second Generation (Nisei)

In the 1920s and 1930s, anti-Asian feelings continued to run high, and Japanese Americans continued to be excluded and discriminated against despite (or perhaps because of) their relative success. Unable to find acceptance in Anglo society, the second generation, called Nisei, established clubs, athletic leagues, churches, and a multitude of other social and recreational organizations within their own communities (Kitano & Daniels, 1995, p. 63). These organizations reflected the high levels of Americanization of the Nisei and expressed values and interests quite compatible with those of the dominant culture. For example, the most influential Nisei organization was the Japanese American Citizens League, whose creed expressed an ardent patriotism that was to be sorely tested: "I am proud that I am an American citizen. . . . I believe in [American] institutions, ideas, and traditions; I glory in her heritage; I boast of her history, I trust in her future" (p. 64).

Although the Nisei enjoyed high levels of success in school, the intense discrimination and racism of the 1930s prevented most of them from translating their educational achievements into better jobs and higher salaries. Many occupations in the mainstream economy were closed to even the best-educated Japanese Americans, and anti-Asian prejudice and discrimination did not diminish during the hard times and high unemployment of the Great Depression in the 1930s. Many Nisei were forced to remain within the enclave, and in many cases, jobs in the produce stands and retail shops of their parents were all they could find. Their demoralization and anger over their exclusion were eventually swamped by the larger events of World War II.

The Relocation Camps

On December 7, 1941, Japan attacked Pearl Harbor, killing almost 2,500 Americans. President Franklin D. Roosevelt asked Congress for a declaration of war the next day. The preparations for war stirred up a wide range of fears and anxieties among the American public, including concerns about the loyalty of Japanese Americans. Decades of exclusion and anti-Japanese prejudice had conditioned the dominant society to see Japanese Americans as sinister, clannish, cruel, unalterably foreign, and racially inferior. Fueled by the ferocity of the war itself and fears about a Japanese invasion of the mainland, the tradition of anti-Japanese racism laid the groundwork for a massive violation of civil rights.

Two months after the attack on Pearl Harbor, President Roosevelt signed Executive Order 9066, which led to the relocation of Japanese Americans living on the West Coast. By the late summer of 1942, more than 110,000 Japanese Americans, young and old, male and female—virtually the entire West Coast population—had been transported to relocation camps, where they were imprisoned behind barbed-wire fences patrolled by armed guards. Many of these people were American citizens, yet no attempt was made to distinguish between citizen and alien. No trials were held, and no one was given the opportunity to refute the implicit charge of disloyalty.

The government gave families little notice to prepare for evacuation and secure their homes, businesses, and belongings. They were allowed to bring only what they could carry, and many possessions were simply abandoned. Businesspeople sold their establishments and farmers sold their land at panic sale prices. Others locked up their stores and houses and walked away, hoping that the evacuation would be short-lived and their possessions undisturbed.

The internment lasted for nearly the entire war. At first, Japanese Americans were not permitted to serve in the armed forces, but, eventually, more than 25,000 escaped the camps by volunteering for military service. Nearly all of them served in segregated units or in intelligence work with combat units in the Pacific Ocean. Two all-Japanese combat units served in Europe and became the most decorated units in American military history (Kitano, 1980, p. 567). Other Japanese Americans were able to get out of the camps by means other than the military. Some, for example, agreed to move to militarily nonsensitive areas far away from the West Coast (and their former homes). Still, when the camps closed at the end of the war, about half the original internees remained (Kitano & Daniels, 1988, p. 64).

The strain of living in the camps affected Japanese Americans in a variety of ways. Lack of activities and privacy, overcrowding, boredom, and monotony were all common complaints. The next Narrative Portrait summarizes the experiences of one Japanese American.

The Relocation

Joseph Kurihara was born in Hawaii in 1895. He moved to California at age 20 and served with the U.S. Army in World War I, completed a college education, and was a businessman working within the Japanese American enclave until World War II. He worked actively to promote acculturation and better relations with the larger society during the interwar years. He was sent to the relocation camp at Manzanar, California, in the spring of 1942 and continued to play an active role in the dislocated Japanese American community. Although he had never visited Japan and had no interest or connection with the country of his parents' birth, his experiences in the camp were so bitter that he renounced his American citizenship and expatriated to Japan following the war.

WE WERE JUST JAPS

JOSEPH KURIHARA

[The evacuation] . . . was really cruel and harsh. To pack and evacuate in 48 hours was an impossibility. Seeing mothers completely bewildered with children crying from want and peddlers taking advantage and offering prices next to robbery made me feel like murdering those responsible without the slightest compunction in my heart.

The parents may be aliens but the children are all American citizens. Did the government of the United States intend to ignore their rights regardless of their citizenship? Those beautiful furnitures [sic] which the parents bought to please their sons and daughters, costing hundreds of dollars were robbed of them at the single command, "Evacuate!" Here my first doubt of American Democracy crept into the far corners of my heart with the sting that I could not forget. Having had absolute confidence in Democracy, I could not believe my very eyes what I had seen that day. America, the standard bearer of Democracy had committed the most heinous crime in its history. . . .

[The camp was in an area that is largely desert.] The desert was bad enough. The . . . barracks made it worse. The constant cyclonic storms loaded with sand and dust made it worst. After living in well-furnished homes with every modern convenience and suddenly forced to live the life of a dog is something which one cannot so readily forget. Down in our hearts we cried and cursed this government every time when we were showered with sand.

We slept in the dust; we breathed the dust; and we ate the dust. Such abominable existence one could not forget, no matter how much we tried to be patient, understand the situation, and take it bravely. Why did not the government permit us to remain where we were? Was it because the government was unable to give us the protection? I have my doubt. The government could have easily declared Martial Law to protect us.

It was not the question of protection. It was because we were Japs! Yes, Japs!

After corralling us like a bunch of sheep in a hellish country, did the government treat us like citizens? No! We were treated like aliens regardless of our rights. Did the government think we were so without pride to work for $16.00 a month when people outside were paid $40.00 to $50.00 a week in the defense plants? Responsible government officials further told us to be loyal and that to enjoy our rights as American citizens we must be ready to die for the country. We must show our loyalty. If such is the case, why are the veterans corralled like the rest of us in the camps? Have they not proven their loyalty already? This matter of proving one's loyalty to enjoy the rights of an American citizen was nothing but a hocus-pocus.

My American friends . . . no doubt must have wondered why I renounced my citizenship. This decision was not that of today or yesterday. It dates back to the day when General DeWitt [the officer in charge of the evacuation] ordered evacuation. It was confirmed when he flatly refused to listen even to the voices of the former World War Veterans and it was doubly confirmed when I entered Manzanar. We who already had proven our loyalty by serving in the last World War should have been spared. The veterans asked for special consideration but their requests were denied. They too had to evacuate like the rest of the Japanese people, as if they were aliens.

I did not expect this of the Army. . . . I expected that at least the Nisei would be allowed to remain. But to General DeWitt, we were all alike. "A Jap's a Jap. Once a Jap, always a Jap." . . . I swore to become a Jap 100% and never to do another day's work to help this country fight this war. My decision to renounce my citizenship there and then was absolute.

[Just before he left for Japan (in 1946), Kurihara wrote:]

It is my sincere desire to get over there as soon as possible to help rebuild Japan politically and economically. The American Democracy with which I was infused in my childhood is still unshaken. My life is dedicated to Japan with Democracy my goal.

SOURCE: Swaine and Nishimoto (1946).

The camps disrupted the traditional forms of family life, as people had to adapt to barracks living and mess hall dining. Conflicts flared between those who counseled caution and temperate reactions to the incarceration and those who wanted to protest in more vigorous ways. Many of those who advised moderation were Nisei intent on proving their loyalty and cooperating with the camp administration.

Despite the injustice and dislocations of the incarceration, the camps did reduce the extent to which women were relegated to a subordinate role. Like Chinese women, Japanese women were expected to devote themselves to the care of the males of their family. In Japan, for example, education for females was not intended to challenge their intellect so much as to make them better wives and mothers. In the camps, however, pay for the few jobs available was the same for both men and women, and the mess halls and small living quarters freed women from some of the burden of housework. Many took advantage of the free time to take classes to learn more English and other skills. The younger women were able to meet young men on their own, weakening the tradition of family-controlled, arranged marriages (Amott & Matthaei, 1991, pp. 225–229).

Some Japanese Americans protested the incarceration from the start and brought lawsuits to end the relocation program. Finally, in 1944, the Supreme Court ruled that detention was unconstitutional. As the camps closed, some Japanese American individuals and organizations began to seek compensation and redress for the economic losses the group had suffered. In 1948, Congress passed legislation to authorize compensation to Japanese Americans. About 26,500 people filed claims under this act. These claims were eventually settled for a total of about $38 million—less than one tenth of the actual economic losses. Demand for meaningful redress and compensation continued, and in 1988, Congress passed a bill granting reparations of about $20,000 in cash to each of the 60,000 remaining survivors of the camps. The law also acknowledged that the relocation program had been a grave injustice to Japanese Americans (Biskupic, 1989, p. 2879).

The World War II relocation devastated the Japanese American community and left it with few material resources. The emotional and psychological damage inflicted by this experience is incalculable. The fact that today, only six decades later, Japanese Americans are equal or superior to national averages on measures of educational achievement, occupational prestige, and income is one of the more dramatic transformations in minority group history.

Japanese Americans After World War II

In 1945, Japanese Americans faced a world very different from the one they had left in 1942. To escape the camps, nearly half the group had scattered throughout the country and lived everywhere but on the West Coast. As Japanese Americans attempted to move back to their former homes, they found their fields untended, their stores vandalized, their possessions lost or stolen, and their lives shattered. In some cases, there was simply no Japanese neighborhood to return to; the Little Tokyo area of San Francisco, for example, was now occupied by African Americans who had moved to the West Coast to take jobs in the defense industry (Amott & Matthaei, 1991, p. 231).

Japanese Americans themselves had changed as well. In the camps, the Issei had lost power to the Nisei. The English-speaking second generation had dealt with the camp administrators and held the leadership positions. Many Nisei had left the camps to serve in the armed forces or to find work in other areas of the country. For virtually every American minority group, the war brought new experiences and a broader sense of themselves, the nation, and the world. A similar transformation occurred for the Nisei. When the war ended, they were unwilling to rebuild the Japanese community as it had been before.

Like second-generation Chinese Americans, the Nisei had a strong record of success in school, and they also took advantage of the GI Bill to further their education. When anti-Asian prejudice began to decline in the 1950s and the job market began to open, the Nisei were educationally prepared to take advantage of the resultant opportunities (Kitano, 1980, p. 567).

The Issei-dominated enclave economy did not reappear after the war. One indicator of the shift away from an enclave economy was the fact that the percentage of Japanese American women in

California who worked as unpaid family laborers (i.e., worked in family-run businesses for no salary) declined from 21% in 1940 to 7% in 1950 (Amott & Matthaei, 1991, p. 231). Also, between 1940 and 1990, the percentage of the group employed in agriculture declined from about 50% to 3%, and the percentage employed in personal services fell from 25% to 5% (Nishi, 1995, p. 116).

By 1960, Japanese Americans had an occupational profile very similar to that of whites except that they were actually overrepresented among professionals. Many were employed in the primary economy, not in the ethnic enclave, but there was a tendency to choose "safe" careers (e.g., in engineering, optometry, pharmacy, accounting) that did not require extensive contact with the public or supervision of whites (Kitano & Daniels, 1988, p. 70).

Within these limitations, the Nisei, their children (Sansei), and their grandchildren (Yonsei) have enjoyed relatively high status, and their upward mobility and prosperity have contributed to the perception that Asian Americans are a model minority group. An additional factor contributing to the high status of Japanese Americans (and to the disappearance of Little Tokyos) is that unlike Chinese Americans, immigrants from Japan have been few in number, and the community has not had to devote many resources to newcomers. Furthermore, recent immigrants from Japan tend to be highly educated professional people whose socioeconomic characteristics add to the perception of success and affluence.

The Sansei and Yonsei are highly integrated into the occupational structure of the larger society. Compared with their parents, their connections with their ethnic past are more tenuous, and in their values, beliefs, and personal goals, they resemble dominant group members of similar age and social class (Kitano & Daniels, 1995, pp. 79–81; see also Spickard, 1996).

COMPARING MINORITY GROUPS

What factors account for the differences in the development of Chinese Americans and Japanese Americans and other racial minority groups? First, unlike the situation of African Americans in the 1600s and Mexican Americans in the 1800s, the dominant group had no desire to control the labor of these groups. The contact situation featured economic competition (e.g., for jobs) during an era of rigid competition between groups (see Exhibit 5.6), and Chinese Americans and Japanese Americans were seen as a threat to security that needed to be eliminated, not as a labor pool that needed to be controlled.

Second, unlike American Indians, Chinese Americans and Japanese Americans in the early 20th century presented no military danger to the larger society, so there was little concern with their activities once the economic threat had been eliminated. Third, Chinese Americans and Japanese Americans had the ingredients and experiences necessary to form enclaves. The groups were allowed to "disappear," but unlike other racial minority groups, the urban location of their enclaves left them with opportunities for starting small businesses and providing an education for the second and later generations. As many scholars argue, the particular mode of incorporation developed by Chinese Americans and Japanese Americans is the key to understanding the present status of these groups.

CONTEMPORARY IMMIGRATION FROM ASIA

Immigration from Asia has been considerable since the 1960s, averaging close to 300,000 per year and running about 30% to 35% of all immigrants. Exhibit 9.6 shows that immigration is heaviest from China, India, and the Philippines but that there also have been sizeable contributions from Korea and Vietnam. As noted previously, immigration from Japan has been relatively low since their initial influx a century ago (see Exhibit 9.5).

Exhibit 9.6 Immigration From Asia by Group and Decade, 1950s to 2000s

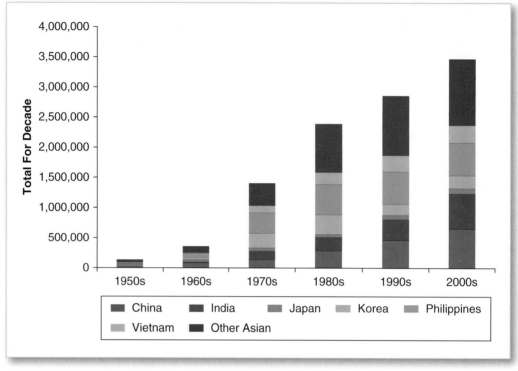

SOURCE: U.S. Bureau of the Census.

As was the case with Hispanic immigrants, the sending nations are considerably less developed than the United States, and the primary motivation for most of these immigrants is economic. However, unlike Hispanic immigration, the Asian immigrant stream also includes a large contingent of highly educated professionals seeking opportunities to practice their careers and expand their skills. While these more elite immigrants contribute to the image of "Asian success," many Asian immigrants are less skilled and less educated, and often undocumented. Thus, this stream of immigrants, like Chinese Americans, is "bipolar" and includes a healthy representation of people from both the top and the bottom of the occupational and educational hierarchies.

Of course, other factors besides mere economics attract these immigrants. The United States has maintained military bases throughout the region (including South Korea, Japan, and the Philippines) since the end of World War II, and many Asian immigrants are the spouses of American military personnel. Also, U.S. involvement in the war in Southeast Asia in the 1960s and 1970s created interpersonal ties and governmental programs that drew refugees from Vietnam, Cambodia, and Laos, many of whom lived in camps and relocation centers for years before immigrating to the United States. Because of the conditions of their escape from their homelands, they typically bring little in the way of human or material capital with them.

Among the refugee groups are the Hmong, hill people from Laos and other Southeast Asian nations, who fought with the American forces in the Vietnam War. They are relatively small in number and face some unique challenges in their adjustment to U.S. society. Their culture is very traditional and, in many ways, far removed from the modernized, Western world in which they find themselves. Prior to the Vietnam war, they were not much advanced past a hunter-gatherer subsistence technology and bring very little social and cultural capital with them. The scope of the challenges they face in making the transition to the United States is illustrated by anthropologist Anne Fadiman in her account of the fate of an epileptic Hmong girl. According to traditional Hmong cultural understandings, illness is caused by spirits and needs to be treated in the time-honored way, by shamans and traditional healers. The girl's parents found it difficult to accept and follow the instructions of the Western doctors that attempted to treat the girl's epileptic condition. The resultant tragedy underscores the distance between the Hmong and the

Western world and illustrates the challenges of acculturation for this group (Fadiman, 1998). Contrary to the image of Asian American success, the Hmong generally display a socioeconomic profile more consistent with America's colonized minority groups.

Another striking contrast is between immigrants from India, many of whom are highly educated and skilled, and Vietnamese Americans, who have a socioeconomic profile that in some ways resembles those of non-Asian racial minorities in the United States. Part of the difference between these two groups relates to their contact situations and can be illuminated by applying the Blauner hypothesis. Immigrants from India are at the "immigrant" end of Blauner's continuum. They bring strong educational credentials and are well equipped to compete for favorable positions in the occupational hierarchy. The Vietnamese, in contrast, began their American experience as a refugee group fleeing the turmoil of war. Although they do not fit Blauner's "conquered or colonized" category, most Vietnamese Americans had to adapt to American society with few resources and few contacts with an established immigrant community. The consequences of these vastly different contact situations are suggested by the data presented in the exhibits at the end of this chapter. We will address some of these groups in more detail in Chapter 10.

CONTEMPORARY RELATIONS

In this section, we once more use our guiding concepts to assess the situation of Chinese Americans and Japanese Americans and other Asian groups. This section is organized around the same concepts used in previous case study chapters.

Prejudice and Discrimination

American prejudice against Asians first became prominent during the anti-Chinese movement of the 19th century. The Chinese were believed to be racially inferior, docile, and subservient, but also cruel and crafty, despotic, and threatening (Lai, 1980, p. 220; Lyman, 1974, pp. 55–58). The Chinese Exclusion Act of 1882 was justified by the idea that the Chinese were unassimilable and could never be part of U.S. society. The Chinese were seen as a threat to the working class, to American democracy, and to other American institutions. Many of these stereotypes and fears transferred to the Japanese later in the 19th century and then to other groups as they, in turn, arrived in the United States. The social distance scores presented in Exhibit 3.6 provide the only long-term record of anti-Asian prejudice in society as a whole. In 1926, the five Asian groups included in the study were grouped in the bottom third of the scale, along with other racial and colonized minority groups. Twenty years later, in 1946, the Japanese had fallen to the bottom of the rankings and the Chinese had risen seven positions, changes that reflect America's World War II conflict with Japan and alliance with China. This suggests that anti-Chinese prejudice may have softened during the war as distinctions were made between "good" and "bad" Asians. For example, an item published in a 1941 issue of *Time* magazine, "How to Tell Your Friends From the Japs," provided some tips for identifying "good" Asians: "The Chinese expression is likely to be more placid, kindly, open; the Japanese more positive, dogmatic, arrogant. . . . Japanese are nervous in conversation, laugh loudly at the wrong time" (p. 33).

In more recent decades, the average social distance scores of Asian groups have fallen even though the ranking of the groups has remained relatively stable. The falling scores probably reflect the society-wide increase in tolerance and the shift from blatant prejudice to modern racism that we discussed in Chapter 3. However, the relative position of Asians in the American hierarchy of group preferences has remained remarkably consistent since the 1920s. This stability may reflect the cultural or traditional nature of much of American anti-Asian prejudice.

Although prejudice against Asian Americans may have weakened overall, there is considerable evidence that it remains a potent force in American life. The continuing force of anti-Asian prejudice is marked most dramatically, perhaps, by hate crimes against members of the group. Asian Americans of all types—citizens, immigrants, and tourists—have been attacked, beaten, and even murdered in recent years. According to official statistics on hate crimes, there were 147 attacks on Asian Americans and Pacific Islanders in 2009 (Federal Bureau of Investigation, 2010), about 4% of all racially motivated incidents. This percentage is roughly consistent with the relative size of the group in U.S. society (see Exhibit 9.1), but some of the most notorious hate crimes in recent history have been directed at Asian Americans, including the murder of Vincent Chin in 1982 by autoworkers in Detroit (see Chapter 3).

There are numerous reports of violent attacks and other forms of harassment on Asian Americans, especially on recent immigrants. High school and middle school students of Asian descent report that they are stereotyped as "high-achieving students who rarely fight back," making them excellent candidates for scapegoating by other groups (Associated Press, 2005). The level of harassment at one high school in New York rose to such severe levels that the U.S. Department of Justice intervened, at the request of school officials (Associated Press, 2005). Incidents such as these suggest that the tradition of anti-Asian prejudice is close to the surface and could be activated under the right combination of competition and threat.

Asian Americans also have been the victims of "positive" stereotypes. The perception of Asian Americans as a "model minority" is exaggerated and, for some Asian American groups, simply false. This label has been applied to these groups by the media, politicians, and others. It is not an image that the Asian American groups themselves developed or particularly advocate. As you might suspect, people who apply these labels to Asian Americans have a variety of hidden moral and political agendas, and we explore these dynamics later in this chapter.

Photo 9.2

Street sign in Chinatown, San Francisco.

© Ocean/Corbis.

Assimilation and Pluralism

Acculturation

The extent of acculturation of Asian Americans is highly variable from group to group. Japanese Americans represent one extreme. They have been a part of American society for more than a century, and the current generations are highly acculturated. Immigration from Japan has been low and has not revitalized the traditional culture or language. As a result, Japanese Americans are the most acculturated of the Asian American groups, as illustrated in Exhibit 9.7, and have the lowest percentage of members who speak English "less than very well."

Filipino and Indian Americans also have low percentages of members who are not competent English speakers, but for different reasons. The Philippines has had a strong American presence since the Spanish American War of 1898, while India is a former British colony in which English remains an important language for higher education and of the educated elite.

Chinese Americans, in contrast, are highly variable in their extent of acculturation. Many are members of families who have been American for generations and are highly acculturated. Others, including many recent undocumented immigrants, are newcomers who have little knowledge of English or of Anglo culture. In this dimension, as in occupations, Chinese Americans are "bipolar." This great variability within the group makes it difficult to characterize their overall degree of acculturation.

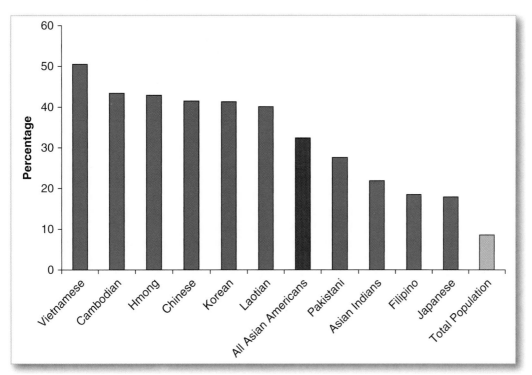

Exhibit 9.7 Percentage Speaking English "Less Than Very Well" for All Asian Americans and 10 Largest Asian American Groups, 2009

SOURCE: U.S. Bureau of the Census.

Gender and Physical Acculturation: The Anglo Ideal. Anglo-conformity can happen on levels other than the cultural. A number of studies document the feelings of inadequacy and negative self-images that often result when minority group members—especially women—compare themselves with the Anglo standards of attractiveness and beauty that dominate U.S. culture. Some of the studies in this tradition are classics of the social science literature, including the "doll studies" conducted by social psychologists Kenneth and Mamie Clark in the 1930s and 1940s. The Clarks showed pairs of white and black dolls to a sample of young African American children and asked them a series of questions, including, "Which doll is pretty?" "Which doll is nice?" "Which doll would you like to play with?" and "Which doll is ugly?" They documented a preference for the white doll, which they interpreted as evidence that the children had internalized white standards of beauty and had developed negative self-images as a consequence. Contemporary "replications" of the Clark doll study include a YouTube video titled "A Girl Like Me" by then-17-year old Kiri Davis[3] and a documentary by Chris Rock titled *Good Hair.*

Asian American women, like all women in this still paternalistic society, are pressured by the cultural message that physical beauty should be among their most important concerns. As racial minorities, they are also subjected to the additional message that they are inadequate by Anglo standards and that some of their most characteristic physical traits (e.g., their small, "slanted" eyes and flat noses) are devalued—indeed ridiculed—in the larger society (Kaw, 1997). These messages generate pressures for minority women to conform not only culturally but also physically. For example, African Americans have spent millions of dollars on hair straightening and skin bleachers. For Asian American women, the attempt to comply with Anglo standards of beauty may include cosmetic surgery on their noses or to "open" their eyes.

Eugenia Kaw (1997) studied these issues by conducting in-depth interviews with medical practitioners and with a small sample of Asian American women, most of whom had had surgery on their eyelids or noses. The women tended to see their surgeries as simply their personal choice, not unlike putting on make-up. However, Kaw found that they consistently described their presurgical features negatively. They uniformly said "that 'small, slanty' eyes and a 'flat' nose" suggest a person who is dull and passive and a mind that is "closed." For example, one subject said that she considered eyelid surgery while in high school to "avoid the stereotype of the Oriental bookworm who is dull and doesn't know how to have fun."

Kaw concludes that the decision of Asian American women to change the shape of their eyes and noses was greatly influenced by racist stereotypes and patriarchal norms: an attempt—common among all racial minority groups—to acculturate on a physical as well as a cultural level.

Secondary Structural Assimilation

We will cover this complex area in roughly the order followed in previous chapters.

Residence. Exhibit 9.8 shows the regional concentrations of all Asian Americans. The tendency to reside on either coast and around Los Angeles, San Francisco, and New York stands out clearly. Note also the sizable concentrations in a variety of metropolitan areas, including Chicago, Atlanta, Miami, Denver, and Houston.

Exhibit 9.9 shows that Asian Americans, like Hispanic Americans, are moving away from their "traditional" places of residence into new regions. Between 1990 and 2000, the Asian American population increased especially rapidly in North Carolina and other areas of the Southeast, in Nevada, and in some areas of the upper Midwest.

Preliminary results from the 2010 Census indicate that the tendency to disperse has continued over the past 10 years. About half the states increased their Asian populations by more than 50%, and Nevada, Arizona, and North Dakota doubled the size of their Asian populations. Other states that increased their Asian populations by more than 75% were Delaware, Arkansas, Georgia, and North Carolina, none of which has had large Asian populations in the past.

Asian Americans in general are highly urbanized, a reflection of the entry conditions of recent immigrants as well as the appeal of ethnic neighborhoods, such as Chinatowns, with

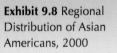

Exhibit 9.8 Regional Distribution of Asian Americans, 2000

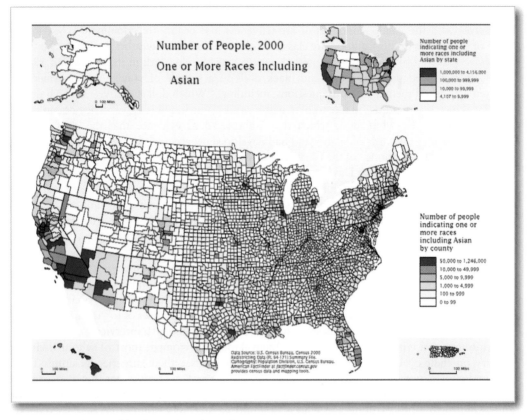

SOURCE: U.S. Bureau of the Census (2000b, p. 65).

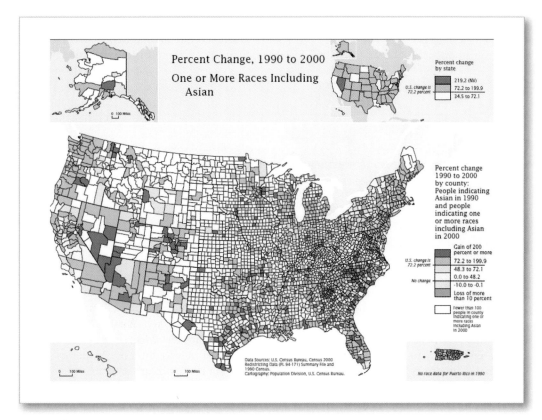

SOURCE: U.S. Bureau of the Census (2000b, p. 62).

Exhibit 9.9 Percentage Increase in Asian Population, 1990 to 2000

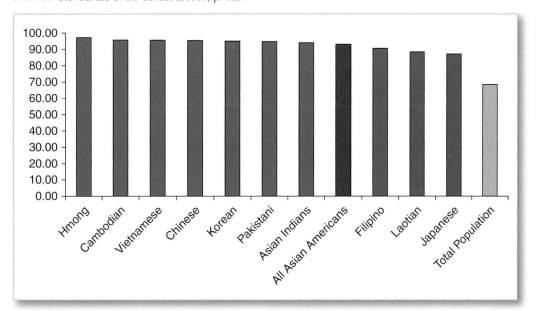

SOURCE: U.S. Bureau of the Census.

Exhibit 9.10 Urbanization of 10 Largest Asian American Groups, All Asian Americans, and Total Population, 2000

long histories and continuing vitality. As displayed in Exhibit 9.10, all but 2 of the 10 largest Asian American groups are more than 90% urbanized, and several approach the 100% mark.

Asian Americans are much less residentially segregated than either African Americans or Hispanic Americans in all four regions of the nation. Exhibit 9.11 shows the average dissimilarity index for 220 metropolitan areas using the same format as in the previous three

Multiple generations of Vietnamese in Clarendon, Arlington County, Virginia, a neighborhood with a high concentration of Vietnamese.

© Wally McNamee/ Corbis.

Exhibit 9.11 Residential Segregation for Asian and Pacific Islander Americans in 220 Metropolitan Areas, 1980 to 2000

chapters. Asian Americans are not "extremely" (dissimilarity scores greater than 0.6) segregated in any region, but the level of residential segregation is holding steady or slightly rising, a reflection of high rates of immigration and the tendency for newcomers to settle close to other members of their group.

Asian Americans are also moving away from their traditional neighborhoods and enclaves into the suburbs of metropolitan areas, most notably in the areas surrounding Los Angeles, San Francisco, New York, and other cities where the groups are highly concentrated. For example, Asian Americans have been moving in large numbers to the San Gabriel Valley, just east of downtown Los Angeles. Once a bastion of white, middle-class suburbanites, these areas have taken on a distinctly Asian flavor in recent years. Monterey Park, once virtually all white, is now majority Chinese American and is often referred to as "America's first suburban Chinatown" or the "Chinese Beverly Hills" (Fong, 2002, p. 49).

Education. The extent of school segregation for Asian Americans for the 1993–1994 and 2005–2006 school years is displayed in Exhibit 9.12, as was done in previous chapters. In the 2005–2006 school year, Asian American children were much less likely to attend "majority-minority" or extremely segregated schools than either Hispanic American or African American children. However, the extent of school segregation has increased over the time period, a reflection of the pattern of residential segregation in Exhibit 9.11.

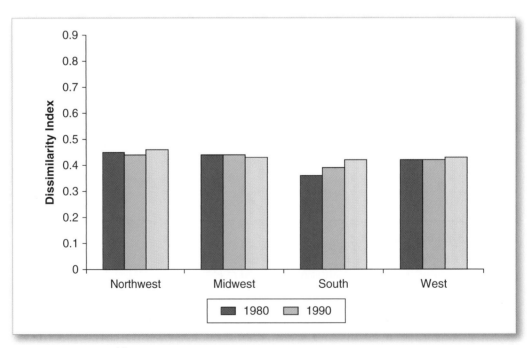

SOURCE: U.S. Bureau of the Census.

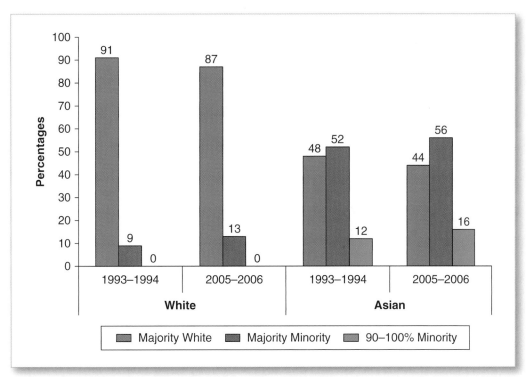

Exhibit 9.12 School Integration, 1993–1994 and 2005–2006

SOURCE: U.S. Bureau of the Census.

The extent of schooling for Asian Americans is very different from that for other U.S. racial minority groups. Considered as a whole, Asian Americans compare favorably with society-wide standards for educational achievement, and they are above those standards on many measures. Exhibit 9.13 shows that 3 of the 10 Asian American groups are higher than non-Hispanic whites in high school education and 6 of 10 are higher in college education, a pattern that has been reinforced by the high levels of education of many recent Asian immigrants. However, recall that many Asian Americans are first-generation immigrants. In these cases, their educational credentials may be from non-U.S. institutions and may not translate into higher-level jobs. Also note that four Asian American groups are far below non-Hispanic whites on both measures of educational attainment. These groups include a large percentage of refugees from the Vietnam War that ended in 1974.

Exhibit 9.13 partially reinforces the "model minority" image, but recall that Chinese Americans (and several other Asian American groups) are "bipolar" and have a sizable underclass group. This reality is captured in Exhibit 9.14, which compares the distribution of levels of education for non-Hispanic whites and Chinese Americans. More than 50% of Chinese Americans hold college and graduate degrees, far outnumbering whites (31%) at this level. Many of these highly educated Chinese Americans are recent immigrants seeking to pursue their careers in one of the world's most advanced economies.

Note, however, that Chinese Americans are also disproportionately concentrated at the lowest level of educational achievement. Some 18% of the group has less than a high school diploma, as opposed to just 10% of non-Hispanic whites. Many of these less educated

Photo 9.4

An Asian American family celebrates a graduation.

© Walter Hodges/ CORBIS.

Exhibit 9.13

Educational Attainment for All Asian Americans, Non-Hispanic Whites, and 10 Largest Asian American Groups

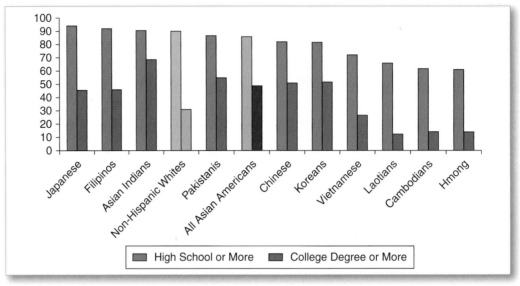

SOURCE: U.S. Bureau of the Census.

Exhibit 9.14

Education Levels for Non-Hispanic Whites and Chinese Americans, 2009

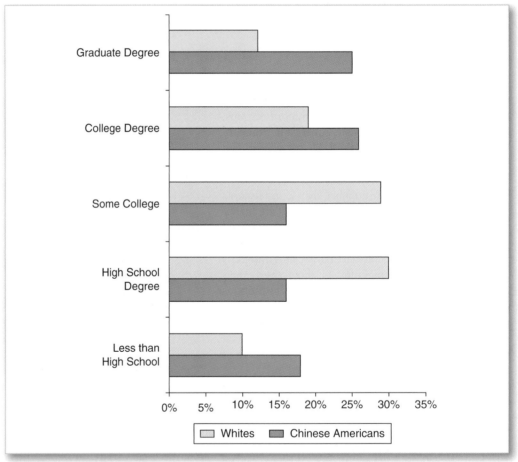

SOURCE: U.S. Bureau of the Census.

Chinese Americans are also recent immigrants (many of them undocumented), and they supply the unskilled labor force—in retail shops, restaurants, and garment industry "sweatshops"—that staffs the lowest levels of the Chinatown economy.

Assessments of Asian American success must also differentiate between the native-born and the foreign-born members of the groups. The native-born are generally better educated, and the foreign-born members of the same groups are split between highly educated professionals and those who bring lower levels of human capital. For example, according to the 2000 Census, almost all (96%) native-born Chinese Americans were high school graduates and 66% had college degrees. Comparable percentages among foreign-born Chinese Americans were 79% and 49% (Min, 2006, p. 82).

As illustrated by these examples, the image of achievement and success for Asian Americans needs to be balanced by the recognition that there is a full range of success and failure in the group and by the fact that average levels of achievement are "inflated" for some groups by recent immigrants who are highly educated, skilled professionals.

Political Power. The ability of Asian Americans to pursue their group interests has been sharply limited by a number of factors, including their relatively small size, institutionalized discrimination, and the same kinds of racist practices that have limited the power resources of other minority groups of color. However, and contrary to the perception that Asian Americans are a "quiet" minority, the group has a long history of political action, including a civil rights movement in the 1960s and 1970s (Fong, 2002, pp. 273–281).

The political power of Asian Americans today is also limited by their high percentages of foreign-born members and, for some groups, lack of facility in English. Rates of political participation for the group (e.g., voting in presidential elections) are considerably lower than national norms. For example, less than 37% of Asian Americans voted in the past three presidential elections (vs. about 64% of all Americans). However, participation has risen since the 2000 presidential election (when only 31% participated) and is much higher when considering only citizens. For example, in the 2008 presidential election, almost half of Asian Americans citizens (vs. 64% of all Americans) voted (U.S. Bureau of the Census, 2011d, p. 259). What this implies is that the participation of the group—and their relative political power—will increase as more members Americanize, learn English, and become citizens.

There are signs of the growing power of the group, especially in areas where they are most residentially concentrated. Of course, Asian Americans have been prominent in Hawaiian politics for decades, but they are increasingly involved in West Coast political life as well. For example, in 1996, the state of Washington elected Gary Locke as governor, the first Chinese American to hold this high office. Governor Locke was reelected in 2000. At present, there are eight Asian and Pacific Islanders in the U.S. House of Representatives (2% of the membership) and one in the Senate (Senator Daniel Inouye of Hawaii, a Japanese American and senator since 1963).

Jobs and Income. The economic situation of Asian Americans is mixed and complex, as is the case for Hispanic Americans. On some measures, Asian Americans as a whole exceed national norms, a reflection of the high levels of academic achievement combined with the impressive educational credentials of many new arrivals. However, overall comparisons can be misleading, and we must also recognize the economic diversity of Asian Americans.

Starting with occupation profiles, the image of success is again sustained. Both males and females are overrepresented in the highest occupational categories, a reflection of the high levels of educational attainment for the group. Asian American males are underrepresented among manual laborers, but otherwise, the occupational profiles of the groups are in rough proportion to society as a whole (U.S. Bureau of the Census, 2009a).

Exhibit 9.15 shows median household incomes for Asian Americans and whites for the past two decades and shows that Asian Americans have averaged *higher* median household incomes than whites, a picture of general affluence that is in dramatic contrast to the other racial minority groups we have examined in this text. The gap fluctuates, but Asian Americans' median household income is generally 120% of whites'.

This image of success, glittering at first glance, becomes more complicated and nuanced when we look at the separate subgroups within the Asian American community. Exhibit 9.16 displays median household incomes for all non-Hispanic Whites, all Asian Americans, and the 10 largest subgroups, and we can see immediately that economic success is not universally shared: Half of Asian American groups are below the average income for non-Hispanic whites.

A still more telling picture emerges when we consider income per capita (or per person) as opposed to median incomes for entire households. This is an important comparison because the apparent prosperity of so many Asian American families is linked to their ownership of small businesses in the enclave. These enterprises typically employ the entire family for many long hours each day, with

Exhibit 9.15 Median Household Incomes for White and Asian Americans, 1987 to 2009 (in 2009 dollars)

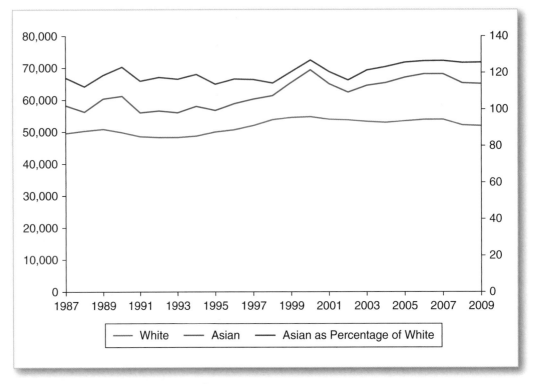

SOURCE: U.S. Bureau of the Census (2011b).

NOTE: Read income on left-hand axis and percentage on right-hand axis.

Exhibit 9.16 Median Household Income for All Asian Americans, 10 Largest Asian American Groups, and Non-Hispanic Whites, 2009

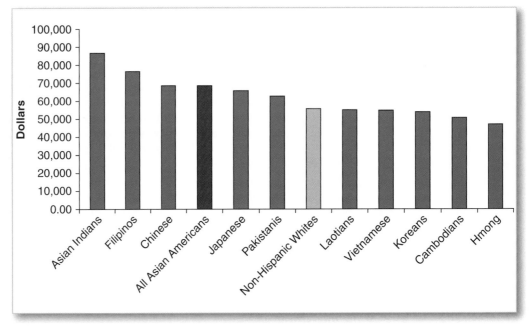

SOURCE: U.S. Bureau of the Census (2011a).

children adding their labor after school and on weekends and other relatives (many of them new immigrants, a percentage of which are undocumented) contributing as well. The household unit may post a high income as a result of these collective efforts, but, when spread across many family members, the glow of "success" is muted. Exhibit 9.17 shows that, on per capita income, only two Asian American groups exceed non-Hispanic whites. The other eight groups (including Chinese and Korean Americans, the groups most dependent on small-business ownership) enjoy much lower levels

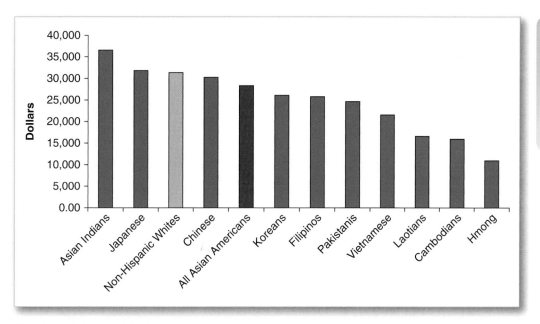

SOURCE: U.S. Bureau of the Census (2011a).

Exhibit 9.17 Per Capita Income for Non-Hispanic Whites, All Asian Americans, and 10 Largest Asian American Groups, 2009

of relative prosperity. In particular, the Southeast Asian groups with high percentages of refugees from the Vietnam War (especially the Hmong) are below national norms on this measure.

Exhibit 9.18 provides additional evidence that the image of a "model minority"—uniformly prosperous and successful—is greatly exaggerated. Asian Americans, unlike other racial minority groups, are overrepresented in the three highest income categories: 22% of all Asian Americans are in these categories versus only 14% of non-Hispanic whites. However, note that Asian Americans are also overrepresented in the lowest income category, a reflection of the "bipolar" distribution of Chinese Americans and some other groups.

Exhibit 9.18 Distribution of Household Income for White and Asian Americans, 2009

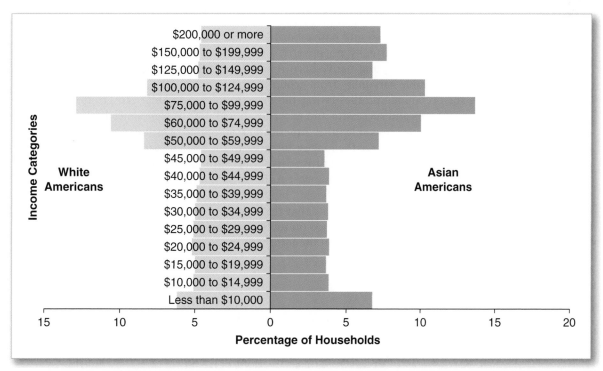

SOURCE: U.S. Bureau of the Census (2011a).

Exhibits 9.19 and 9.20 finish the economic portrait of Asian Americans and reinforce the picture of complexity and diversity. While the poverty levels of all Asian Americans, considered as a single group, are comparable to non-Hispanic whites, several of the groups have much higher rates of poverty, especially for children. As we have seen in other exhibits, Japanese Americans, Filipino Americans, and Asian Indians are "successful" on this indicator, but other groups have poverty levels comparable to colonized racial minority groups.

Exhibit 9.19

Percentage of Families and Children in Poverty for All Asian Americans, 10 Largest Asian American Groups, and Non-Hispanic Whites, 2009

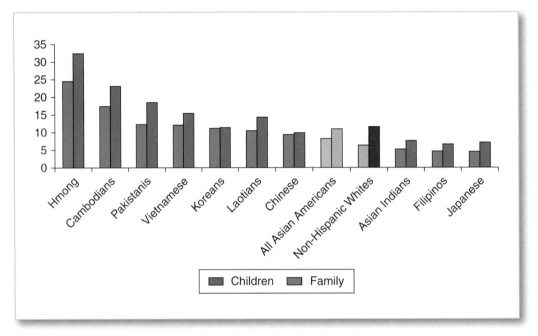

SOURCE: U.S. Bureau of the Census (2011a).

Exhibit 9.20 examines the situation of Asian Americans in terms of their nativity. Once again, we see the great diversity from group to group, with foreign-born Vietnamese Americans (largely refugees) exhibiting the highest level of poverty—almost 3 times higher than non-Hispanic whites—and native-born Japanese Americans (largely second generation and later) exhibiting virtually no poverty. Foreign-born Asian Americans generally have higher levels of poverty, and native-born Asian Americans generally have lower rates, but note the considerable variability from group to group.

These socioeconomic profiles reflect the diversity of Asian American groups. Some are, indeed, prosperous and successful and exceed national norms, sometimes by a considerable margin. Other groups resemble other American racial minority groups. Japanese Americans and Chinese Americans have the longest histories in the United States and generally rank at the top in measures of wealth and prosperity. Other groups—particularly those that include large numbers of refugees from Southeast Asia—have not fared as well and present pictures of poverty and economic distress. Some "bipolar" groups, such as Chinese Americans, fit in both categories. We should also note that the picture of economic distress for these groups would be much greater if we focused on undocumented immigrants, who are numerous in the community and concentrated in the informal, irregular economy.

Primary Structural Assimilation

Studies of integration at the primary level for Asian Americans generally find rates of interracial friendship and marriage that exceed those of other minority groups. A study

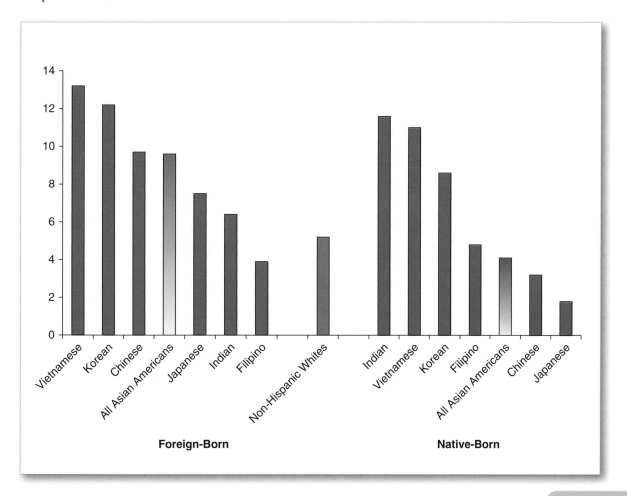

SOURCE: U.S. Bureau of the Census (2011a).

Exhibit 9.20 Percentage of Families in Poverty for Non-Hispanic Whites, All Asian Americans, and Selected Asian American Groups by Nativity, 2000

based on the 1980 Census, for example, found intermarriage rates from 15% to 34% for Asian Americans (depending on the specific group) versus rates of only 2% for African Americans and 13% for Hispanic Americans (Lee & Yamanaka, 1990). The same study also found that native-born Asian Americans were much more likely to marry outside their groups than were the foreign-born (see also Kitano & Daniels, 1995; Min, 1995; Sung, 1990).

More recent studies find that rates of primary integration remain relatively high but are declining as the number of Asian Americans grows and the percentage of foreign-born increases. One recent study (Passel, Wang, & Taylor, 2010) found almost exactly the same percentage of newlywed Asian Americans marrying outside the group in 1980 (32%) and 2008 (31%) but a declining percentage of all currently married Asian Americans with partners outside the group between 1980 and 2008 (see Exhibit 9.21). This pattern is a reflection of high rates of immigration and the stronger tendency of newcomers to marry within their group.

Intermarriage trends are highly dependent on gender and nativity. Exhibit 9.22 displays intermarriage trends for newly contracted marriages. Between 1980 and 2010, native-born females were the most likely to marry outside the group and immigrant males were the least.

Exhibit 9.21

Percentage of All Currently Married Asian Americans Married to Someone of a Different Race or Ethnicity

Year	Percentage
1980	21.0
1990	17.9
2000	16.2
2010	15.8

SOURCE: Passel, Wang, and Taylor (2010, p. 17).

Exhibit 9.22

Intermarriage Trends Among Newlyweds for All Asian Americans and by Gender and Nativity, 1980 to 2010

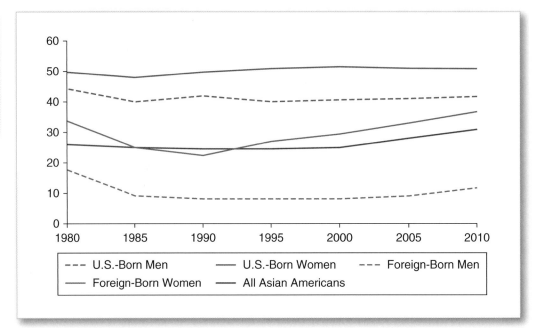

SOURCE: Passel, Wang, and Taylor (2010, p. 36).

Dr. C. N. Le, a sociologist who maintains the Asian Nation website (http://www.asian nation.org) has analyzed intermarriage patterns using the 2006 U.S. Census Bureau's American Community Survey. His data can be found at http://www.asian-nation.org/ interracial.shtml. He found that Japanese Americans, the most acculturated of the groups, are the most likely to marry outside their group. Also, many Japanese Americans are "war brides" who married American GIs stationed in Japan. The groups with the highest percentage of foreign-born—Asian Indians, Koreans, and Vietnamese—are also the most likely to marry within their groups.

COMPARING MINORITY GROUPS: EXPLAINING ASIAN AMERICAN SUCCESS

To conclude this chapter, let's return to a question raised in the opening pages: How can we explain the apparent success of Asian Americans? Relative affluence and high status are not characteristic of the other racial minority groups we have examined, and at least at first glance, there seems to be little in our theories and concepts to help us understand the situation of Asian Americans. Even after we recognize that the "success" label is simplistic and even misleading, the relatively high status of many Asian Americans begs a closer look.

The Current Debates section at the end of this chapter presents several different views on the nature and causes of Asian American success. In this section, we compare Asian Americans with European immigrant groups and with colonized minority groups. What crucial factors differentiate the experiences of these groups? Can we understand these differences in terms of the framework provided by the Blauner and Noel hypotheses and the other concepts developed in this text?

The debate over the causes of Asian American success often breaks down into two different viewpoints. One view offers a cultural explanation, which accepts the evidence of Asian American success at face value and attributes it to the "good values" of traditional Asian cultures that we briefly explored at the beginning of this chapter. These values—including respect for elders and for authority figures, hard work and thriftiness, and conformity and politeness—are highly compatible with U.S. middle-class Protestant value systems and presumably helped Asian Americans gain acceptance and opportunities. The cultural explanation is consistent with traditional assimilation theory and human capital theory, and an example of it can be found in the selection by Professor Harry Kitano in the Current Debates section.

The second point of view stresses the ways in which these groups entered American society and the reactions of Asian Americans to the barriers of racism and exclusion they faced. This approach could be called a "structural explanation," and it emphasizes contact situations, modes of incorporation, enclave economies, group cohesion, position in the labor market, and institutionalized discrimination rather than cultural values. Also, this approach questions the notion that Asian Americans are "successful" and stresses the realities of Asian American poverty and the continuing patterns of racism and exclusion. The structural approach is more compatible with the theories and concepts used throughout this text, and it identifies several of the important pieces needed to solve the puzzle of Asian "success" and put it in perspective. This is not to suggest that the cultural approach is wrong or irrelevant, however. The issues we raise are complex and will probably require many approaches and perspectives before they are fully resolved.

Asian Americans and White Ethnics

Chinese and Japanese immigrants arrived in America at about the same time as immigrants from Southern and Eastern Europe (see Chapter 2). Both groups consisted mainly of sojourning young men who were largely unskilled, from rural backgrounds, and not highly educated. European immigrants, like Asian immigrants, encountered massive discrimination and rejection and were also victims of restrictive legislation. Yet the barriers to upward mobility for European immigrants (or at least for their descendants) fell away more rapidly than the barriers for immigrants from Asia. Why?

Some important differences between the two immigrant experiences are clear, the most obvious being the greater racial visibility of Asian Americans. Whereas the cultural and linguistic markers that identified Eastern and Southern Europeans faded with each passing generation, the racial characteristics of the Asian groups continued to separate them from the larger society. Thus, Asian Americans are not "pure immigrant" groups (see Blauner, 1972, p. 55). For most of the 20th century, Chinese Americans and Japanese Americans remained in a less favorable position than European immigrants and their descendants, excluded by their physical appearance from the mainstream economy until the decades following World War II.

Another important difference relates to position in the labor market. Immigrants from Southern and Eastern Europe entered the industrializing East Coast economy, where they took industrial and manufacturing jobs. Although such jobs were poorly paid and insecure, this location in the labor force gave European immigrants and their descendants the potential for upward mobility in the mainstream economy. At the very least, these urban industrial and manufacturing jobs put the children and grandchildren of European immigrants in positions from which skilled, well-paid, unionized jobs were reachable, as were managerial and professional careers.

In contrast, Chinese and Japanese immigrants on the West Coast were forced into ethnic enclaves and came to rely on jobs in the small-business and service sector and, in the case of the Japanese, in the rural economy. By their nature, these jobs did not link Chinese and Japanese immigrants or their descendants to the industrial sector or to better-paid, more secure, unionized jobs. Furthermore, their exclusion from the mainstream economy was reinforced by overt, racially based discrimination from both employers and labor unions (see Fong & Markham, 1991).

Asian Americans and Colonized Racial Minority Groups

Comparisons between Asian Americans and African Americans, American Indians, and Hispanic Americans have generated a level of controversy and a degree of heat and passion that may be surprising at first. An examination of the issues and their implications, however, reveals that the debate involves some thinly disguised political and moral agendas and evokes sharply clashing views on the nature of U.S. society. What might appear on the surface to be merely an academic comparison of different minority groups turns out to be an argument about the quality of American justice and fairness and the very essence of the value system of U.S. society.

What is not in dispute in this debate is that some Asian groups (e.g., Japanese Americans) rank far above other racial minority groups on all the commonly used measures of secondary structural integration and equality. What is disputed is how to interpret these comparisons and assess their meanings. First, we need to recognize that gross comparisons between entire groups can be misleading. If we confine our attention to averages (mean levels of education or median income), the picture of Asian American success is sustained. However, if we also observe the full range of differences within each group (e.g., the "bipolar" nature of occupations among Chinese Americans), we see that the images of success have been exaggerated and need to be placed in a proper context (see the selection by Takaki in the Current Debates section). Even with these qualifications, however, discussion often slides onto more ideological ground, and political and moral issues begin to cloud the debate. Asian American success is often taken as proof that American society is truly the land of opportunity and that people who work hard and obey the rules will get ahead: In America, anyone can be anything they want as long as they work hard enough.

When we discussed modern racism in Chapter 3, I pointed out that a belief in the openness and fairness of the United States can be a way of blaming the victim and placing the responsibility for change on the minority groups rather than on the structure of society or on past-in-present or institutionalized discrimination. Asian success has become a "proof" of the validity of this ideology. The none-too-subtle implication is that other groups (African Americans, Hispanic Americans, American Indians) could achieve the same success Asian Americans have achieved but, for various reasons, choose not to. Thus, the relative success of Chinese Americans and Japanese Americans has become a device for scolding other minority groups.

A more structural approach to investigating Asian success begins with a comparison of the history of the various racial minority groups and their modes of incorporation into the larger society. When Chinese Americans and Japanese Americans were building their enclave economies in the early part of the 20th century, African Americans and Mexican Americans were concentrated in unskilled agricultural occupations. American Indians were isolated from the larger society on their reservations, and Puerto Ricans had not yet begun to arrive on the mainland. The social class differences between these groups today flow from their respective situations in the past.

Many of the occupational and financial advances made by Chinese Americans and Japanese Americans have been due to the high levels of education achieved by the second generations. Although education is traditionally valued in Asian cultures, the decision to invest limited resources in schooling is also quite consistent with the economic niche occupied by these immigrants. Education is one obvious, relatively low-cost strategy to upgrade the productivity and profit of a small-business economy and improve the economic status of the group as a whole. An educated, English-speaking second generation could bring expertise and business acumen to the family enterprises and lead them to higher levels of performance. Education might also be the means by which the second generation could enter professional careers. This strategy may have been especially attractive to an immigrant generation that was itself relatively uneducated and barred from citizenship (Hirschman & Wong, 1986, p. 23; see also Bonacich & Modell, 1980, p. 152; Sanchirico, 1991).

The efforts to educate the next generation were largely successful. Chinese Americans and Japanese Americans achieved educational parity with the larger society as early as the 1920s. One study found that for men and women born after 1915, the median years of schooling completed were actually higher for Chinese Americans and Japanese Americans than for whites (Hirschman & Wong, 1986, p. 11). Before World War II, both Asian groups were barred from the mainstream economy and from better jobs. When anti-Asian prejudice and discrimination declined in the 1950s, however, the Chinese and Japanese second generations had the educational background necessary to take advantage of the increased opportunities.

Thus, there was a crucial divergence in the development of Chinese Americans and Japanese Americans and the colonized minority groups. At the time that native-born Chinese Americans and Japanese Americans reached educational parity with whites, the vast majority of African Americans, American Indians, and Mexican Americans were still victimized by Jim Crow laws and legalized segregation and excluded from opportunities for anything but rudimentary education. The Supreme Court decision in *Brown v. Board of Education of Topeka* (1954) was decades in the future, and American Indian schoolchildren were still being subjected to intense Americanization in the guise of a curriculum. Today, these other racial minority groups have not completely escaped from the disadvantages imposed by centuries of institutionalized discrimination. African Americans have approached educational parity with white Americans only in recent years (see Chapter 6), and American Indians and Mexican Americans remain far below national averages (see Chapters 7 and 8).

The structural explanation argues that the recent upward mobility of Chinese Americans and Japanese Americans is the result of the methods by which they incorporated themselves into American society, not so much their values and traditions. The logic of their enclave economy led the immigrant generation to invest in the education of their children, who would be better prepared to develop their businesses and seek opportunity in the larger society.

As a final point, note that the structural explanation is not consistent with traditional views of the assimilation process. The immigrant generation of Chinese Americans and Japanese Americans responded to the massive discrimination they faced by withdrawing, developing ethnic enclaves, and becoming "invisible" to the larger society. Like Jewish and Cuban Americans, Chinese Americans and Japanese Americans used their traditional cultures and patterns of social life to create and build their own subcommunities, from which they launched the next generation. Contrary to traditional ideas about how assimilation is "supposed" to happen, we see again that integration can precede acculturation and that the smoothest route to integration may be the creation of a separate subsociety independent of the surrounding community.

Japan's "Invisible" Minority

One of the first things I did in this text was to list the five characteristics that, together, define a minority group. The first and most important of these characteristics is the disadvantage and inequality that minority groups face, and the second is visibility: Minority group members are easily identifiable, either culturally (e.g., language, accent, dress) or physically (e.g., skin color, stature). At the interpersonal level, these traits work in tandem. Members of the dominant group must be able to determine a person's group membership quickly and easily, preferably at a glance, so that the systematic discrimination that is the hallmark of minority group status can be practiced.

Cultural and racial visibility is such an obvious precondition for discrimination that it almost seems unnecessary to state it. However, every generalization about human beings seems to have an exception, and there is at least one minority group, the Burakumin of Japan, that has been victimized by discrimination and prejudice for hundreds of years but is virtually indistinguishable from the general population. That is, the Burakumin are a minority and fit all parts of the definition stated in Chapter 1—except that there is no physical, cultural, religious, or linguistic difference between them and other Japanese. How could such an "invisible" minority come into being? How could the disadvantaged status be maintained through time?

The Burakumin were created centuries ago, during feudal times in Japan. At that time, the society was organized into a caste system (see Chapter 4) based on occupation, and the ancestors of today's Burakumin did work that brought them into contact with death (e.g., as gravediggers, executioners) or required them to handle meat or meat products (e.g., as leather workers, butchers). These occupations were regarded as very low in status, and their practitioners were seen as being "unclean" or polluted. In fact, an alternative name for the group (*eta*) means "extreme filth." The Burakumin were required to live in separate, segregated villages and to wear leather patches for purposes of identification (thus raising their social visibility). They were forbidden to marry outside their caste, and any member of the general population who touched a Burakumin had to be ritually purified or cleansed of pollution (Lamont-Brown, 1993, p. 137).

The caste system was officially abolished in the 19th century, at about the time Japan began to industrialize. The Burakumin today, however, continue to suffer from discrimination and rejection, even though most observers agree that the levels of discrimination today are lower than in the past and that the overall situation of the Burakumin is improving (Ball, 2009). However, there is evidence that the Burakumin have lower levels of education and income than the general population (Neary, 2003, p. 288).

The Burakumin are a small group, about 2% or 3% of Japan's population. About 1 million still live in traditional Burakumin areas, and another 2 million or so live in non-Burakumin areas, mostly in larger cities. They continue to be seen as "filthy," "not very bright," and "untrustworthy"—stereotypical traits often associated with minority groups mired in subordinate and unequal positions (see Chapter 3). Also, as is the case for many American minority groups, the Burakumin have a protest organization—the Burakumin Liberation League (http://www.bll.gr.jp/eng.html)—that is dedicated to improving the conditions of the group.

The situation of the Burakumin might seem puzzling. If it is disadvantageous to be a member of the group and if the group is indistinguishable from the general population, why don't the Burakumin simply blend into the larger society and avoid the discrimination and prejudice? What keeps them attached to their group? In fact, it is relatively easy for those who choose to do so to disappear into the mainstream and to "pass," as attested by the fact that two thirds of the group no longer live in the traditional Burakumin areas. Why doesn't the entire group integrate into the larger society?

One answer to this question, at least for some Burakumin, is that they are committed to their group identity and are proud of their heritage. They refuse to surrender to the dominant culture, insist on being accepted for who they are, and have no intention of trading their identity for acceptance or opportunity. For others, even those attempting to pass, the tie to the group and a subtle form of social visibility are maintained by the ancient system of residential segregation. The identity of the traditional Burakumin villages and areas of residence are matters of public record, and it is this information—not race or culture—that establishes the boundaries of the group and forms the ultimate barrier to Burakumin assimilation.

There are reports that Japanese firms keep lists of local Burakumin addresses and use the lists to screen out potential employees. Also, the telltale information may be revealed when applying to rent an apartment (some landlords refuse to rent rooms to Burakumin because of their alleged "filthiness") or purchase a home (banks may be reluctant to make loans to members of a group that is widely regarded as "untrustworthy"). Another line of resistance to the complete integration of the Burakumin arises if they attempt to marry outside the group. It is common practice for Japanese parents to research the family history of a child's fiancé, and any secret Burakumin connections are very likely to be unearthed by this process. Thus, members of the Burakumin who pass undetected at work and in their neighborhood are likely to be "outed" if they attempt to marry into the dominant group.

This link to the traditional Burakumin residential areas means that this group is not really invisible. Although they are less visible than racial and ethnic minority groups, there is a way to determine group membership, a mark or sign of who belongs and who doesn't. Consistent with the definition presented in Chapter 1, this "birthmark" is the basis for a socially constructed boundary that differentiates "us" from "them" and for systematic discrimination, prejudice, inequality, and all the other disabilities and disadvantages associated with minority group status.

Asian American "Success": What Are the Dimensions, Causes, and Implications for Other Minority Groups?

The following selections continue the discussion of the causes of Asian American success. The first selection, from the writings of sociologist Harry Kitano (1980), is consistent with cultural explanations for the upward mobility of Asian groups. It argues that the success of the Japanese in America is due in part to their culture and in part to their strength of character, resilience, and flexibility.

In opposition to Kitano's views are two other selections. The first counterargument, by sociologists Alejandro Portes and Min Zhou (1992), presents a structural analysis that links the success of Chinese Americans to their enclave economy. Portes and Zhou also draw some provocative comparisons between Chinese Americans and African Americans, suggesting that the "thorough acculturation" of the African American community has weakened its economic vitality.

The second counterargument, by Professor Pyong Gap Min (2006), sharply questions the whole notion of the "model minority" and points out the limits and qualifications that need to be observed when comparing Asian Americans with other groups. Min also argues that the image of success is harmful, both to Asian Americans and to other racial minority groups.

THE SUCCESS OF JAPANESE AMERICANS IS CULTURAL

HARRY KITANO

Social interaction among Japanese Americans is governed by behavioral norms such as *enryo* and *amae.* These derive from Confucian ideas about human relationships and define the dimensions of interaction and exchange between superior and inferior members of a social group. Although these forms of behavior were brought over by Issei immigrants, they still survive in attenuated form among the Nisei and even the Sansei.

Enryo prescribes the way in which a social inferior must show deference and self-abnegation before a superior. Hesitancy to speak out at meetings, the automatic refusal of a second helping, and selecting a less desired object are all manifestations of *enryo.* . . .

Amae behavior softens a power relationship through the acting out of dependency and weakness, and expresses the need for attention, recognition, acceptance, and nurture. A child displays *amae* to gain the sympathy and indulgence of a parent. A young, anxious-to-please employee in a business firm will act with exaggerated meekness and confusion to give his superior an opportunity to provide paternal advice and treat him as a protégé. Through the ritual display of weakness and dependency, reciprocal bonds of loyalty, devotion, and trust are formed. In this way, *amae* creates strong emotional ties that strengthen cohesion within the family, business organization, and community.

Japanese Americans inherit an almost reverential attitude toward work. Their ancestors struggled for survival in a crowded island country with limited natural resources, and they placed great value on industry and self-discipline. Certain traditional attitudes encourage resilient behavior in the face of setbacks and complement the moral imperative to work hard. Many Japanese Americans are familiar with the common expressions *gaman* and *gambotte* which mean "don't let it bother you," "don't give up." These dicta, derived from Buddhist teachings, encourage Japanese people to conceal frustration or disappointment and to carry on. A tradition that places great value on work and persistence has helped many Japanese Americans to acquire good jobs and to get ahead.

The submerging of the individual to the interest of the group is another basic Japanese tradition, and one that produces strong social cohesion and an oblique style of behavior, one manifestation of which is the indirection or allusiveness of much communication between Japanese; another is the polite, consensual behavior expected in all social contacts. Both are common in Japan and visible among Japanese Americans. Today, even third- and fourth-generation Japanese Americans are apt to be seen by others as agreeable, unaggressive, willing to accept subordinate roles, and reluctant to put themselves forward. . . .

The history of the Japanese Americans in the United States is one of both resilience and adaptation. Suffering from discriminatory laws and racial hostility in the first half of the 20th century, Japanese Americans were nonetheless able to create stable ethnic communities and separate, but vital, social organizations. Since the end of World War II, with the disappearance of legal discrimination and the weakening of social restrictions, they have assimilated more readily into American society and shown rapid economic progress. Scholars have searched for the key to their remarkable record of adaptation. Some have pointed to the Japanese family, others to a strong group orientation, and still others to Japanese moral training; all of these theories often tend to overemphasize the degree to which Japanese traditions have been maintained. Japanese Americans have displayed a pragmatic attitude toward American life. [Rather] than rigidly maintaining their traditions, Japanese Americans have woven American values and behavior into the fabric of their culture and have seized new social, cultural, and economic avenues as they have become available, extending the limits of ethnicity by striking a workable balance between ethnic cohesion and accommodation.

SOURCE: Kitano (1980, pp. 570–571). Reprinted by permission of the publisher. Copyright © 1980 by the President and Fellows of Harvard College.

THE "SUCCESS" OF CHINESE AMERICANS IS STRUCTURAL

ALEJANDRO PORTES AND MIN ZHOU

[What lessons for ethnic poverty can we find in the experiences of Chinese Americans and other groups that have constructed ethnic enclaves?] A tempting option—and one to which many experts have not been averse—is to resort to culturalistic explanations. According to these interpretations, certain groups do better because they possess the "right" kind of values. This view is, of course, not too different from assimilation theory except that, instead of learning the proper values after arrival, immigrants bring them ready made. A moment's reflection suffices to demonstrate the untenability of this explanation. . . .

The very diversity of [the] groups [that have constructed enclave economies] conspires against explanations that find the roots of economic mobility in the unique values associated with a particular culture. If we had to invoke a particular "ethic" to account for the business achievements of Chinese and Jews, Koreans and Cubans, Lebanese and Dominicans, we would wind up with a very messy theory. In terms of professed religions alone, we would have to identify those unique values leading Confucianists and Buddhists, Greek Orthodox and Roman Catholics into successful business ventures. In addition, culturalistic explanations have little predictive power since they are invoked only after a particular group has demonstrated its economic prowess. . . .

There is no alternative but to search for the relevant causal process in the social structure of the ethnic community. [Several] common aspects in the economic experience of the immigrant communities [are] relevant. . . .

[First is] the "bounded solidarity" created among immigrants by virtue of their foreignness and being treated as [different]. As consumers, immigrants manifest a consistent preference for items associated with the country of origin, both for their intrinsic utility and as symbolic representations of a distinct identity. As workers, they often prefer to work among "their own," interacting in their native language even if this means sacrificing some material benefits. As investors, they commonly opt for firms in the country of origin or in the ethnic community rather than trusting their money to impersonal outside organizations.

Bounded solidarity [is accompanied by] "enforceable trust" against malfeasance among prospective ethnic entrepreneurs. Confidence that business associates will not resort to double-dealing is cemented in something more tangible than generalized cultural loyalty since it also relies on the ostracism of violators, cutting them off from sources of credit and opportunity. [Enforceable trust] is the key mechanism underlying the smooth operation of rotating credit associations among Asian immigrant communities.

Bounded solidarity and enforceable trust as sources of social capital do not inhere in the moral convictions of individuals or in the value orientations in which they were socialized. [These benefits] accrue by virtue of [the group's] minority [status] in the host country and as a result of being subjected to mainstream pressure to accept their low place in the ethnic hierarchy. Such pressures prompt the revalorization of the symbols of a common nationality and the privileging of the ethnic community as the place where the status of underprivileged menial labor can be avoided. . . .

Black Americans, Mexican Americans, and mainland Puerto Ricans today lag significantly behind the immigrant groups in their entrepreneurial orientation. [This] lack of entrepreneurial presence is even more remarkable because of the large size of these minorities and the significant consumer market that they represent. . . .

We believe that the dearth of entrepreneurship among these groups is related to the dissolution of the structural underpinnings of the social capital resources noted above: bounded solidarity and enforceable trust. A thorough process of acculturation among U.S.-born members of each of these groups has led to a gradual weakening of their sense of community and to a reorientation towards the values, expectations, and preferences of the cultural mainstream. [Complete] assimilation among domestic minorities leads to identification with the mainstream views, including a disparaging evaluation of their own group. . . .

[Even] groups with a modest level of human capital have managed to create an entrepreneurial presence when the necessary social capital, created by specific historical conditions, was present. This was certainly the case among turn-of-the-century Chinese. [It] was also true of segregated black communities during the same time period. The current desperate conditions in many inner-city neighborhoods have led some black leaders to recall wistfully the period of segregation. [As one black leader said]:

[T]he same kind of business enclave that exists in the Cuban community or in the Jewish community existed in the black community when the consumer base was contained [i.e., segregated from the larger society] and needed goods and services that had to be provided by someone in the neighborhood. Today, blacks will not buy within their neighborhood if they can help it; they want to go to the malls and blend with mainstream consumers.

Hence, thorough acculturation and the formal end of segregation led to the dissipation of the social capital formerly present in restricted black enclaves and the consequent weakening of minority entrepreneurship. As blacks attempted to join the mainstream, they found that lingering discrimination barred or slowed down their progress in the labor market, while consumption of outside goods and services undermined their own community business base.

SOURCE: Portes and Zhou (1992, pp. 513–518).

A CRITIQUE OF THE MODEL MINORITY THESIS

PYONG GAP MIN

Probably the most frequently cited thesis . . . in the Asian American social science literature over the past two decades is the model minority thesis. . . . Many Asian American community leaders might have felt appreciative of the success image, taking it as a positive acceptance of Asian Americans by U.S. society. Yet, Asian American scholars, teachers, social workers, and activists have never appreciated the success image. Instead, they have provided harsh criticisms of the so-called model minority thesis, examining its inadequacies and its political basis and negative consequences. . . .

Median Family Income Not a Good Measure of Asian Americans' Economic Well-Being

The success image of Asian Americans is partly based on the fact that the median household . . . income of Asian Americans is higher than that of white Americans. However, many . . . social scientists have . . . argued that the median family income is not a good measure of the economic success of Asian Americans because they have more workers per family and residentially concentrate in large cities, such as San Francisco, Los Angeles, New York, and Washington, DC, where living costs are very high.

The critics of the model minority thesis have also indicated that the thesis . . . distorts the . . . socioeconomic diversity [of Asian Americans]. While many college-educated Asian immigrants make high earnings . . . many others struggle for economic survival trapped in low-level, service-related jobs [and in] . . . the secondary labor market or the ethnic market. . . . [There is] a greater diversity in class among Asian Americans than among white Americans.

Issues of Lower Rewards to Human Capital Investment

The critics . . . do not consider Asian Americans successful mainly because Asian immigrants do not get rewards for their educational investments equal to white Americans. . . . Many college-educated Asian immigrants engage in low-status, low-paying occupations as taxi drivers, gas station attendants, or cleaners. Many Korean immigrants engage in labor-intensive small businesses to avoid low-paying service and blue-collar jobs. Some studies have indicated that even Asian immigrants who hold professional and government jobs are concentrated in periphery specialty areas or less influential positions. . . .

It is important to examine foreign-born Asian Americans separately from native-born, because the latter have a language barrier and other disadvantages for employment in the United States. [Some] studies . . . have found that native-born Asian American workers receive more or less equal rewards from their human capital investments to white Americans, while Asian immigrants get much lower returns. . . .

[Various studies] support the view that foreign-educated Asian immigrants' language barrier and their lack of job market information, along with the difference in quality of education between Asian countries and the United Sates, are mainly responsible for their lower returns for human capital investments. However, [the studies also show] that Asian immigrants do . . . experience discrimination, whether based on racism, nativism, or both, in the U.S. labor market. . . .

The Glass Ceiling Problem

Another important issue . . . is the underrepresentation [of Asian Americans] in upper-level administrative, executive, and managerial positions in corporate and public sectors. [Although they] are well represented in professional occupations . . . Asian Americans may be at a disadvantage for these upper-level administrative positions because they lack communication and leadership skills, a result of more authoritarian child socialization techniques practiced in many Asian immigrant families. But it is also true that some well-qualified Asian Americans are not given these desirable positions because Asians are stereotyped as lacking leadership skills. . . . However, as native-born Asian Americans have come of age, more and more of them have been able to move into high-ranking positions during recent years. . . . As more and more Asian Americans occupy upper-level managerial and administrative positions, the stereotype of Asian Americans as lacking leadership skills will change too.

Asian Americans' High Academic Achievement

The model minority image assumes that nearly all Asian American children are successful in school performance and that Asian cultural norms emphasizing children's education are mainly responsible for their educational success. The critics of the model minority thesis have challenged both of these assumptions. . . . Asian Americans outperform whites in the rate of college degree attainment almost 2 times [see Exhibit 9.13] and statistics [like these] may have led . . . reporters and some researchers to overgeneralize Asian Americans' educational success. But . . . Vietnamese Americans, especially foreign-born Vietnamese, [and some other groups] have a substantially lower level of education than white Americans. . . .

The model minority image includes the assumption that the Asian immigrant parents' cultural norms emphasizing their children's education are mainly responsible for the high academic achievement of Asian American students. This assumption is problematic, although it has some element of truth. . . . Contemporary Asian immigrants include a significant proportion of highly educated people who held professional and managerial occupations prior to immigration. Because of their parents' highly educated background, Asian American students have a huge advantage in school performance over other minority children and even white students. This background of Asian immigrants should be emphasized as the most significant determinant of Asian American students' academic success. Moreover, . . . immigrants . . . are self-selected in that those who are more . . . achievement oriented have taken the risk of immigrating to the United States. . . .

However, in addition to these class and selfselection effects, cultural factors contribute to Asian American students' academic success, and this is why I have indicated that the Asian cultural norms interpretation has some element of truth. People in other countries, especially Asian and Caribbean countries, tend to put more emphasis on education . . . than people in the United States and Western European countries. . . . I have seen many students from Asian and Caribbean countries . . . working exceptionally hard to advance to a graduate school despite their financial difficulty and language barrier, while many native-born white American students . . . were attending college simply to get a college degree. The high achievement orientation of Asian and Caribbean students in the United States reflects the values in their home countries. . . .

No doubt, Asian immigrant parents' emphasis on their children's success . . . and . . . the perception of Asian American children as model students have positively affected their academic performance. But they have also had negative effects on their psychological well-being by putting too much pressure on them. Although academically successful children are well rewarded in the family and the community, the students who perform at below-average or even average levels are not rewarded and are sometimes neglected by their parents. . . .

Negative Effects of the Success Image on Asian Americans' Welfare and Other Minority Groups

Asian American critics of the model minority thesis have argued that the success image . . . is not only invalid but also detrimental to the welfare of Asian Americans. . . . The critics point out that . . . Asian Americans have frequently been eliminated from affirmative action and other social service programs designed for disadvantaged minority groups. For example, the poverty rates of Chinese residents in New York Chinatown and Korean residents in Los Angeles Koreatown in 1990 were 25% and 26%, respectively. . . . Yet, those poor Chinese and Korean residents were not eligible for many welfare programs for which poor African Americans were eligible. The critics have also indicated that the success stories . . . stimulated anti-Asian sentiment and violence on college campuses and in communities. . . .

Asian American social work and mental health professionals in particular have been concerned about the negative implications of the success image for various social services to Asian Americans. . . . Policymakers and non-Asian social workers tend to assume that Asian Americans generally do not have serious juvenile, elderly, and other family problems. However, Asian American social workers have argued that Asian Americans' underuse of social services does not imply that they have fewer . . . problems . . . [but] rather . . . their help-seeking behavior patterns. . . . Moderately disturbed Asian Americans are reluctant to seek help from mental health services because of their cultural norms emphasizing shame and family integrity. Several studies reveal that Asian immigrants have a higher rate of stress and other mental health problems than white Americans. . . .

Finally, . . . the model minority thesis . . . negatively affects other minority groups as well. . . . By emphasizing the importance of cultural factors for the successful adjustment of Asian Americans, the success image in effect blames other less successful minority groups for their failure. It thus legitimates the openness of American society and leads people to fail to recognize social barriers encountered by other minority groups.

SOURCE: Min (2006, pp. 81–87).

DEBATE QUESTIONS TO CONSIDER

1. If Kitano's analysis is correct, what could other minority groups learn from the Japanese experience? If Portes and Zhou are correct, what could other minority groups learn from the Chinese experience? Do Portes and Zhou use cultural factors as part of their explanation? How? Are Portes and Zhou advocating segregation? Pluralism? Assimilation?

2. According to Min, what are the major limitations of the "model minority" image? What specific sociological concepts does Min use in his critique? What is the "glass ceiling" problem for Asian Americans, and how does it compare with similar problems faced by women (see Chapter 5)? What "self-selection" factors affect the academic performance of Asian Americans? What are some of the negative effects of the model minority image for Asian Americans and for other minority groups?

3. Which of these views are consistent with traditional assimilation theory? How? Which are consistent with human capital theory? How? Which views are consistent with the thinking of Noel and Blauner? How?

MAIN POINTS

-   Asian Americans and Pacific Islanders are diverse and have brought many different cultural and linguistic traditions to the United States. These groups are growing rapidly but are still only a tiny fraction of the total population.
-   Chinese immigrants were the victims of a massive campaign of discrimination and exclusion and responded by constructing enclaves. Chinatowns became highly organized communities, largely run by the local Chinese Consolidated Benevolent Associations and other associations. The second generation faced many barriers to employment in the dominant society, although opportunities increased after World War II.
-   Japanese immigration began in the 1890s and stimulated a campaign that attempted to oust the group from agriculture and curtail immigration from Japan. The Issei formed an enclave, but during World War II, Japanese Americans were forced into relocation camps, and this experience devastated the group economically and psychologically.
-   Recent immigration from Asia is diverse in terms of national origins, contact situations, levels of human capital, and mode of incorporation into U.S. society.
-   Overall levels of anti-Asian prejudice and discrimination have probably declined in recent years but remain widespread. Levels of acculturation and secondary structural assimilation are variable. Members of these groups whose families have been in the United States longer tend to be highly acculturated and integrated. Recent immigrants from China, however, are "bipolar." Many are highly educated and skilled, but a sizable number are "immigrant laborers" who bring modest educational credentials and are likely to be living in poverty.
-   The notion that Asian Americans are a "model minority" is exaggerated, but comparisons with European immigrants and colonized minority groups suggest some of the reasons for the relative "success" of these groups.

STUDY SITE ON THE WEB

For chapter-specific resources, such as self-quizzes, videos, and flashcards, go to **www.sagepub.com/ healeyregc6e.**

FOR FURTHER READING

Chou, Rosalind, & Feagin, Joe. 2008. *The Myth of the Model Minority: Asian Americans Facing Racism.* Boulder, CO: Paradigm.

Based on in-depth interviews and a comprehensive analysis of Asian Americans, including an analysis of the model minority image

Espiritu, Yen. 2007. *Asian American Women and Men: Labor, Laws, and Love (The Gender Lens)* (2nd ed.). Lanham, MD: Rowman & Littlefield.

Analyzes the intersections of race, class, and gender among Asian Americans

Kitano, Harry, & Daniels, Roger. 2001. *Asian Americans: Emerging Minorities* (3rd ed.). Englewood Cliffs, NJ: Prentice Hall.

Min, Pyong Gap (Ed.). 2006. *Asian Americans: Contemporary Trends and Issues* (2nd ed.). Thousand Oaks, CA: Sage.

Two good overviews of the Asian American groups covered in this chapter

Tuan, Mia. 2005. *Forever Foreigners or Honorary Whites?* New Brunswick, NJ: Rutgers University Press.

A penetrating account of the continuing anti-Asian racism and discrimination

Zhou, Min. 1992. *Chinatown.* Philadelphia: Temple University Press.

An excellent analysis of Chinatown, with a behind-the-scenes look at the realities often hidden from outsiders

QUESTIONS FOR REVIEW AND STUDY

1. Describe the cultural characteristics of Asian American groups. How did these characteristics shape relationships with the larger society? Did they contribute to the perception of Asian Americans as "successful"? How?

2. Compare and contrast the contact situations for Chinese Americans, Japanese Americans, and Cuban Americans. What common characteristics led to the construction of ethnic enclaves for all three groups? How and why did these enclaves vary from one another?

3. In what sense was the second generation of Chinese Americans "delayed"? How did this affect the relationship of the group with the larger society?

4. Compare and contrast the campaigns that arose in opposition to the immigration of Chinese and Japanese. Do the concepts of the Noel hypothesis help explain the differences? Do you see any similarities with the changing federal policy toward Mexican immigrants across the 20th century? Explain.

5. Compare and contrast the Japanese relocation camps with Indian reservations in terms of paternalism and coerced acculturation. What impact did this experience have on the Japanese Americans economically? How were Japanese Americans compensated for their losses? Does the compensation paid to Japanese Americans provide a precedent for similar payments (reparations) to African Americans for their losses under slavery? Why or why not?

6. How do the Burakumin in Japan illustrate "visibility" as a defining characteristic of minority group status? How is the minority status of this group maintained?

7. What gender differences characterize Asian American groups? What are some of the important ways in which the experiences of women and men vary?

8. Describe the situation of the Chinese and Japanese Americans in terms of prejudice and discrimination, acculturation, and integration. Are these groups truly "success stories"? How? What factors or experiences might account for this "success"? Are all Asian American groups equally successful? Describe the important variations from group to group. Compare the integration and level of equality of these groups with other American racial minorities. How would you explain the differences? Are the concepts of the Noel and Blauner hypotheses helpful? Why or why not?

INTERNET RESEARCH PROJECT

In this exercise, you will use U.S. Census data to gather information about the total population of all Asian Americans and two subgroups of your choosing. This project adds to the information you gathered in Chapters 6 through 8. You can add the information for African Americans, American Indians and Alaska Natives (AIAN), and Hispanic Americans from previous exercises, but you will need to add information for the new variable and for the variables you select for these groups. You will then use course concepts to assess and analyze this information and place it in the context of this text. *Visit the website for this text for instructions on finding the information needed to complete the table below.*

		Total Population	African Americans	AIAN	Hispanic Americans	All Asian Americans	Asian American Groups	
1	Number							
2	Percentage of total population*	——						
3	Median age							
4	Average household size							
5	% less than high school							
6	% of foreign-born who entered after 2000							
7	% speak English less than "very well"							
8	% unemployed							
9	Per capita income							
10	Median incomes for full-time, year-round workers							
	Males							
	Females							
11	Poverty rate, all families							
12								
13								

QUESTIONS

1. What stage of Gordon's model of assimilation (see Exhibit 2.1) do the variables in the table measure?

2. Using the Blauner hypothesis (see Chapter 4), we can say that both American Indians and African Americans are "colonized or conquered" minority groups and that Hispanic Americans are a mixture of colonized and immigrant origin groups. Are Asian Americans more "colonized" or more "immigrant"? What would the Blauner hypothesis predict about the relative status of these groups in American society? Does the evidence in the table support the prediction? How?

3. What important differences do you see between your two Asian American subgroups? Which is closer to national patterns? To African Americans and Hispanic Americans? What are some possible reasons for these patterns? For example, are the differences related to the timing of the group's immigration? What "human capital" does the group bring that might help account for the differences?

OPTIONAL GROUP DISCUSSION

Bring the information on your groups to class and compare with the information collected by others. Consider the issues raised in the questions above and in the chapter and develop some ideas about why the groups are where they are relative to one another and to the total population.

NOTES

1. Takaki (1993, p. 2).

2. http://www.youtube.com/watch?v=5f71JW2zJTU

3. http://www.youtube.com/watch?v=YWyI77Yh1Gg

PART IV

CHALLENGES FOR THE PRESENT AND THE FUTURE

Chapter 10 New Americans, Assimilation, and Old Challenges

Chapter 11 Minority Groups and U.S. Society: Themes, Patterns, and the Future

In this section, we analyze immigration since the 1960s, continuing issues of assimilation and equality, inclusion and racism. Many of these issues—what it means to be an American—have been discussed throughout this text, as they have been discussed and debated throughout the history of this society. In the final chapter, we summarize the major themes of this text, bring the analysis to a close, and speculate about the future of American race and ethnic relations.

PUBLIC SOCIOLOGY ASSIGNMENTS

LINDA M. WALDRON

ASSIGNMENT 1: SOCIAL CHANGE IN YOUR NEIGHBORHOOD

The preeminent leader of nonviolence, Mahatma Gandhi, once said, "Be the change you want to see in the world." As you learn about the challenges that many minority groups faced—and continue to confront—in terms of prejudice, discrimination, oppression, and inequality, do not forget about the enormous amount of change and success achieved in the situations of minority groups throughout history. Although change is often slow and can be an uphill battle, it is not an impossible feat. But change can occur only if you first envision that it is possible. This assignment requires you to take up this challenge.

Step 1

Pick a neighborhood that surrounds the area in which your school is located. Work in groups of two to three students, and research the area and the people who live in it. Although you can do some of this work on the Internet by searching census data or reading

IMAGE: Getty/William James Warren.

405

the local newspaper, the best way to do this is actually to go out into the neighborhood. Walk around, take photos, talk to people on the street, and visit local stores and restaurants. Really try to learn something about the community.

Step 2

Identify one problem you think should be addressed and the target population most affected by this issue. Make sure that your problem and/or population is somehow relevant to this text and this course. For example, is there a growing refugee population yet a lack of translators available at the local school to help these refugee parents talk to their children's teachers? Is there a significant population of elderly people and no free transportation to local health clinics? Is there a group of low-income high school students who could benefit from free homework help? Has a local gang sprayed graffiti in a local park where kids play? Does the local supermarket not sell any ethnic food for a growing immigrant population?

Step 3

Brainstorm possible ways to address the issue. Begin with some small-scale ideas (e.g., you will find three volunteers to agree to drive an elderly person to his or her weekly doctor's appointment for 1 year) and then build from there. Decide what the best *and* most feasible plan is.

Step 4

From your brainstorming session, develop a proposal that deals with the problem you see in the community. A good proposal generally contains the following sections:

- Background: What is the issue and why is it an important problem that needs to be addressed? Include research evidence showing that this is a problem.
- Target population: Who, specifically, will your social change plan impact?
- Description of the plan of action: What are the overall goals of the plan?
- Methods for implementation, or the "nuts and bolts": How will you accomplish this plan? Consider the time it would take and the cost, resources, and people you need to make this plan happen.
- Challenges: What problems do you think you might face and what are some possible methods for overcoming these obstacles?

Step 5

Consider sending a copy of your proposal to a local politician or presenting this proposal to local leaders at a public forum in your community.

Step 6

"Be the change you want to see in the world." Be ambitious! Actually follow through and create the change that you propose.

NOTE: This assignment was inspired by a lesson plan about social justice and urban planning developed by Kwanita Williams and posted on Cooper-Hewitt's Educator's Resource Center website: http://www .educatorresourcecenter.org/view_lesson.aspx?lesson_plan_id=716.

ASSIGNMENT 2: WORKING WITH REFUGEE COMMUNITIES

In 2010, the United Nations (UN) reported that more than 43 million people worldwide have been forcibly displaced from their homes due to conflict, persecution, and natural disaster. Of these, about 15.4 million are refugees. The United Nations distinguishes a refugee from other displaced persons because a refugee is someone who is forced out of his or her own country. The UN legally defines a refugee in the following way:

> A person who owing to a well-founded fear of being persecuted for reasons of race, religion, nationality, membership of a particular social group, or political opinion, is outside the country of his nationality and is unable or, owing to such fear, is unwilling to avail himself of the protection of that country; or who, not having a nationality and being outside the country of his former habitual residence as a result of such events, is unable or, owing to such fear, is unwilling to return to it.

Today, the majority of refugees are from Afghanistan, Iraq, and Somalia, although the UN notes that refugees have fled more than 100 countries. The United States currently hosts more than 260,000 refugees.

This is a service learning assignment that requires you to learn about the refugees living in your community and to volunteer to help them.

Step 1

Begin by learning something about refugees through a review of the *Yearbook of Immigration Statistics*, which is available to the public on the Department of Homeland Security website (www.dhs.gov). These statistics provide an overview of the country of origin for legal permanent immigrants, naturalized citizens, refugees, and asylum seekers. They also give you a sense of which states these immigrants are currently residing in. Another valuable resource for information on refugees is the United States Association for the United Nations High Commissioner for Refugees website (www.unrefugees.org).

Step 2

Write down some general information you learned about refugee populations in the United States. Also take note of any conflicts you didn't realize were happening in the world that may relate to these refugee groups and anything else that you discovered during the research process.

Step 3

Next, start investigating the refugee population in your community and organizations for which you might be able to work. This may take a little more digging. There are national and international organizations that might provide you with useful local information, such as the International Rescue Committee (www.rescue.org)—which works in 22 cities in the United States—or the UN Volunteers website (www.unv.org). Most local communities have refugee and immigration services, so a simple Internet search will usually yield some results, although you can also contact local officials in your city or town, ask a librarian, or even look in a phone book. The search engine Volunteer Match (www.volunteermatch.org) might help, since it allows you to search your city for volunteer opportunities. Many organizations have websites and e-mail contact information, but because of limited financial resources, you may find only an address or phone number; so be prepared to visit or call a potential volunteer site.

Step 4

Before contacting a local organization, research general types of volunteer services available in other communities. This will not only help you decide on the type of service you might want to partake in, but it will also provide you with some valuable information that you may want to share with your local organization. Such information might help the organization identify other ways to reach out to refugees in need. Some examples of different volunteer programs might include organizing something for World Refugee Day (June 20), advocating for refugees with your local politician, tutoring English to refugees with limited language proficiency, providing transportation for refugees to health clinics, or raising money for refugee programs. The opportunities are endless!

Step 5

Contact the local refugee organization that interests you the most and schedule a meeting with the director of volunteer services. (If the organization does not have a specific volunteer coordinator, just try to meet with a full-time staff member.) Keep in mind that many nonprofit organizations are vastly understaffed, so this may require several phone calls or e-mails on your part before someone has the time to respond to you. Don't give up!

Step 6

When you finally meet with a member of the organization, demonstrate your commitment to working with this population by sharing what you have learned about refugees and by asking specific questions about refugees in your community.

Then, ask about volunteer opportunities with the organization. Keep in mind that many nonprofit organizations require their volunteers to fill out an application or even undergo a criminal background check; so again, don't expect to start volunteering that day. Also, if the organization does not have an existing volunteer program, don't give up there. Suggest some service that you could provide that you learned about during your research and see if the organization thinks such a service could help local refugees.

Step 7

Commit to volunteering for at least 10 hours. Although it might be tempting to complete all this service in a weekend, try to spread it out over several weeks so you can really see how the organization functions over time. This will help you get to know the refugees in your community better and also the people who have dedicated their careers to helping those in need.

Step 8

If you are feeling ambitious, try to get at least one more person to volunteer with you. Remember that social change happens one person at a time! Your service, as well as your encouragement in getting others to serve, can be a transformative experience that helps solve real-world problems and enhance the lives of people living in your community.

10

New Americans, Assimilation, and Old Challenges

Police in Mexico's southern Chiapas state found 513 migrants on Tuesday inside two trailer trucks bound for the United States. . . . The migrants were [being charged] about $7,000 apiece . . . and were from Guatemala, El Salvador, Ecuador, India, Nepal, China, Japan, the Dominican Republic, and Honduras.

—Associated Press, May 18, 2011[1]

The world is on the move as never before, and migrant trails connect even the remotest villages of every continent in a global network of population ebb and flow. As we have seen, people are moving everywhere, but the United States remains the single most popular destination. As the opening news item suggests, migrants will pay huge amounts of money ($7,000 is a staggering amount of money in a world where half the population survives on less than $2.50 a day) and undergo enormous hardship (such as standing in the back of trailer truck for hundreds or even thousands of miles) to find work in the United States. What motivates this population movement? How does it differ from migrations of the past? What impact will the newcomers have on U.S. society? Will they absorb American culture? What parts? Will they integrate into American society? Which segments?

We have been asking questions like these throughout the text. In this chapter, we focus specifically on current immigrants and the myriad issues stimulated by their presence. We mentioned some groups of new Americans in Chapters 8 and 9. In this chapter, we begin by addressing recent immigration in general terms and then consider some additional groups of new Americans, including Hispanic, Caribbean, and Asian groups, Arab Americans and Middle Easterners, and immigrants from sub-Saharan Africa. A consideration of these groups will broaden your understanding of the wide cultural variations, motivations, and human capital of the current immigration stream to the United States.

We will then address the most important and controversial immigration issues facing U.S. society and conclude with a brief return to the "traditional" minority groups: African Americans, Native American, and other peoples of color that continue to face issues of equality and full integration and must now pursue their long-standing grievances in an atmosphere where public attention and political energy are focused on other groups and newer issues.

CURRENT IMMIGRATION

As you are aware, the United States has experienced two different waves of mass immigration. In Chapter 2, we discussed the first wave, which lasted from the 1820s to the 1920s. During this period, more than 37 million people immigrated to the United States, an average rate of a little less than 400,000 per year. This wave of newcomers, overwhelmingly from Europe, transformed American society on every level: its neighborhoods and parishes and cities, its popular culture, its accents and dialects, its religion, and its cuisine.

The second wave of mass immigration promises to be equally transformative. This wave began after the 1965 change in U.S. immigration policy and includes people from every corner of the globe. Since the mid-1960s, almost 30 million newcomers have arrived (not counting undocumented immigrants)—a rate of more than 600,000 per year, much higher than the earlier period (although the rate is lower as a percentage of the total population). Also, Exhibit 10.1 shows that the number of legal immigrants per year has been generally increasing. The official record for most immigrants in a year was set in 1907, when almost 1.3 million people arrived on these shores. That number was almost equaled in 2006, and if undocumented immigrants were included in the count, the 1907 record would have been eclipsed several times since the 1960s.

The more recent wave of immigration is much more global than the first. In 2009 alone, immigrants arrived from more than 200 separate nations—from Afghanistan and Albania to Zambia and Zimbabwe. Only about 9% of the newcomers were from Europe. A third were from North America (most from Mexico), and more than a third were from the nations of Asia, while South America supplied almost 10%. The top 20 sending nations for 2009 are

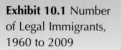

Exhibit 10.1 Number of Legal Immigrants, 1960 to 2009

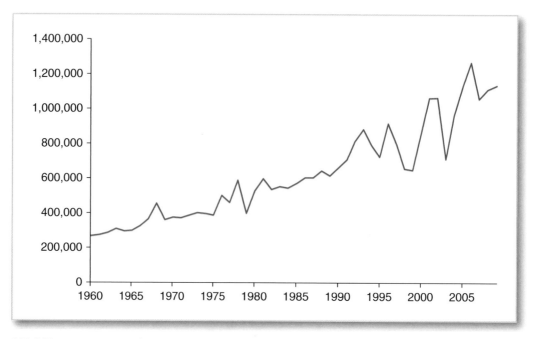

SOURCE: U.S. Department of Homeland Security (2010, p. 5).

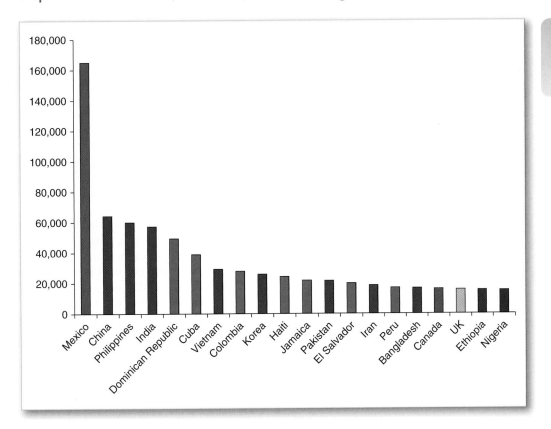

Exhibit 10.2 Number of Legal Immigrants for Top 20 Sending Nations, 2009

SOURCE: U.S. Department of Homeland Security (2010, pp. 27–30).

Key:

Blue = North America

Brown = Asia

Red = Central and South America and the Caribbean

Gray = Europe

Purple = Africa

listed in Exhibit 10.2. Note that the number of Mexican immigrants is more than double the number from the next-highest sending nation.

How will this new wave of immigration transform the United States? How will these new immigrants be transformed by the United States? What do they contribute? What do they cost? Will they assimilate and adopt the ways of the dominant society? What are the implications if assimilation fails? We begin by reviewing several case studies of new Americans, focusing on information and statistics comparable to those used in Chapters 6 through 9.

Each of the groups covered in this chapter has had some members in the United States for decades, some for more than a century. However, in all cases, the groups were quite small until the latter third of the 20th century. Although they are growing rapidly now, all remain relatively small, and none are larger than 1% of the population. Nonetheless, some will have a greater impact on American culture and society in the future, and some groups—Arab Americans, Muslims, and Middle Easterners—have already become a focus of concern and controversy because of the events of September 11 and the ensuing war on terrorism.

NEW HISPANIC GROUPS: IMMIGRANTS FROM THE DOMINICAN REPUBLIC, EL SALVADOR, AND COLOMBIA

Immigration from Latin America, the Caribbean, and South America has been considerable, even excluding Mexico. As with other sending nations, the volume of immigration from these regions increased after 1965 and has averaged more than 200,000 per year since the 1980s. Generally, Latino immigrants—not counting those from Mexico—have been about 25% of all immigrants since the 1960s (U.S. Department of Homeland Security, 2010, pp. 8–11).

The sending nations for these immigrants are economically less developed, and most have long-standing relations with the United States. In Chapter 8, we discussed the roles that Mexico and Puerto Rico have historically played as sources of cheap labor and the ties that led Cubans to immigrate to the United States. Each of the other sending nations has been similarly linked to the United States, the dominant economic and political power in the region.

Although the majority of these immigrants bring educational and occupational qualifications that are modest by U.S. standards, they tend to be more educated, more urbanized, and more skilled than the average citizens of the nations from which they come. Contrary to widely held beliefs, these immigrants do not represent the poorest of the poor, the "wretched refuse" of their homelands. They tend to be rather ambitious, as evidenced by their willingness to attempt to succeed in a society that has not been notably hospitable to Latinos or people of color in the past. Most of these immigrants are not only fleeing poverty or joblessness but also are attempting to pursue their ambitions and seek opportunities for advancement that are simply not available in their countries of origin (Portes & Rumbaut, 1996, pp. 10–11).

This characterization applies to legal and unauthorized immigrants alike. In fact, the latter may illustrate the point more dramatically because the cost of illegally entering the United States can be considerable, much higher than the cost of a legal entry. The venture may require years of saving or the combined resources of a large kinship group. Forged papers and other costs of being smuggled into the country can easily amount to many thousands of dollars, a considerable sum in nations in which the usual wage is a tiny fraction of the U.S. average. Also, the passage can be extremely dangerous and can require a level of courage (or desperation) not often associated with the undocumented and illegal.

Rather than attempting to cover all South and Central American groups, we will select three of the largest to serve as "case studies" and consider immigrants from the Dominican Republic, El Salvador, and Colombia (see Exhibit 10.3). Together, these three groups have made up 7% to 8% of all immigrants in recent years and about 30% of the immigrants from Central and South America and the Caribbean. These groups had few members in the United States before the 1960s, and all have had high rates of immigration over the past four decades. However, the motivation of the immigrants and the immigration experience has varied from group to group, as we shall see later.

Three Case Studies

Some basic information about these three groups is presented in Exhibit 10.4. Some of this information was also presented in Chapter 8 but is repeated here so as to provide a common frame of reference for all the groups covered in this chapter.

Each of these groups has a high percentage of foreign-born members, and, predictably with so many members in the first generation, proficiency in English is an important issue. Although Colombians approach national norms in education, the other two groups have relatively low levels of human capital (education), and all are well above national norms in terms of poverty.

Although these groups share some common characteristics, there are also important differences between them. They differ in their "racial" characteristics, with Dominicans being

Exhibit 10.3 Map of Central and South America and the Caribbean Showing the Dominican Republic, El Salvador, and Colombia

Group	Size	% High School Degree or More	% College Degree or More	% Foreign-Born	% That Speak English "Less Than Very Well"	% in Managerial and Professional Occupations	Median Household Income	% of Families in Poverty
NHW*	——	89.9	30.8	3.9	1.7	38.9	$55,763	6.3
Dominicans	1,295,746	63.5	15.1	57.9	24.8	17.6	$34,542	25.3
Salvadorans	1,595,385	45.4	7.8	64.1	29.7	10.4	$43,051	16.0
Colombians	854,109	84.3	30.4	67.3	31.7	28.8	$49,797	9.9

Exhibit 10.4 Characteristics of Three Hispanic Groups and Non-Hispanic Whites, 2009

*Non-Hispanic whites

SOURCE: U.S. Bureau of the Census.

more African in appearance, Colombians more European, and Salvadorans more Indian. The groups tend to settle in different places. Dominicans and Colombians are clustered along the East Coast, particularly in New York, New Jersey, and Florida, but Salvadorans are more concentrated on the West Coast (U.S. Department of Homeland Security, 2003). Finally, the groups differ in the conditions of their entry or their contact situations—a difference that, as we have seen, is quite consequential. Salvadorans are more likely to be political refugees who fled a brutal civil war and political repression, while Dominicans and Colombians are more likely to be motivated by economics and the employment possibilities offered in the United States. We will consider each of these groups briefly and explore some of these differences further.

Dominicans

The Dominican Republic shares the Caribbean island of Hispaniola with Haiti. The island economy is still largely agricultural, although the tourist industry has grown in recent years. Unemployment and poverty are major problems, and Dominicans average about 5 years of education ("Education Statistics," 2011). Dominican immigrants, like those from Mexico, are motivated largely by economics, and they compete for jobs with Puerto Ricans, other immigrant groups, and native-born workers with lower levels of education and job skills. Although Dominicans are limited in their job options by the language barrier, they are somewhat advantaged by their willingness to work for lower wages, and they are especially concentrated in the service sector, as day laborers (men) or domestics (women). Dominicans maintain strong ties with home and are a major source of income and support for the families left behind.

In terms of acculturation and integration, Dominicans are roughly similar to Mexican Americans and Puerto Ricans, although some studies suggest that they are possibly the most impoverished immigrant group (e.g., see Camarota, 2002). A high percentage of Dominicans are undocumented, and many spend a lot of money and take considerable risks to get to the United States. If these less visible members of the community were included in the official, government-generated statistics used in the exhibits presented later in this chapter, the portrait of poverty and low levels of education and job skills likely would be even more dramatic.

Salvadorans

El Salvador, like the Dominican Republic, is a relatively poor nation, with a high percentage of the population relying on subsistence agriculture for survival. It is estimated that about 50% of the population lives below the poverty level, and there are major problems with unemployment and underemployment. About 80% of the population is literate, and the average number of years of school completed is a little more than 5 ("Education Statistics," 2011).

El Salvador, like many sending nations, has a difficult time providing sufficient employment opportunities for its population, and much of the pressure to emigrate is economic. However, El Salvador also suffered through a brutal civil war in the 1980s, and many of the Salvadorans in the United States today are actually political refugees. The United States, under the administration of President Reagan, refused to grant political refugee status to Salvadorans, and many were returned to El Salvador. This federal policy resulted in high numbers of undocumented immigrants and also stimulated a sanctuary movement, led by American clergy, which helped Salvadoran immigrants, both undocumented and legal, stay in the United States. As is the case with Dominicans, if the undocumented immigrants from El Salvador were included in official government statistics, the picture of poverty would become even more extreme.

Colombians

Colombia is somewhat more developed than most other Central and South American nations but has suffered from more than 40 years of internal turmoil, civil war, and government corruption. The nation is a major center for the production and distribution of drugs to the world in general and the United States in particular, and the drug industry and profits are complexly intertwined with domestic strife. Colombian Americans are closer to U.S. norms of education and income than are other Latino groups, and recent immigrants are a mixture of less-skilled laborers and well-educated professionals seeking to further their careers. Colombians are residentially concentrated in urban areas, especially in Florida and the Northeast, and often settle in areas close to other Latino neighborhoods. Of course, the huge majority of Colombian Americans are law-abiding and not connected with the drug trade, but still they must deal with the pervasive stereotype that portrays Colombians as gangsters and drug smugglers (not unlike the Mafia stereotype encountered by Italian Americans).

NON-HISPANIC IMMIGRANTS FROM THE CARIBBEAN

Immigrants from the Western Hemisphere bring a variety of traditions to the United States other than Hispanic. Two of the largest non-Latino groups come from Haiti and Jamaica in the Caribbean. Both nations are much less developed than the United States, and this is reflected in the educational and occupational characteristics of their immigrants. A statistical profile of both groups is presented in Exhibit 10.5, along with that for non-Hispanic whites for purposes of comparison.

Group	Size	% High School Degree or More	% College Degree or More	% Foreign-Born	% That Speak English "Less Than Very Well"	% in Managerial and Professional Occupations	Median Household Income	% of Families in Poverty
NHW*	——	89.9	30.8	3.9	1.7	38.9	$55,763	6.3
Haitians	814,391	75.9	19.4	60.0	37.7	23.2	$44,091	15.2
Jamaicans	930,306	82.8	23.5	60.6	1.4	32.2	$48,013	11.6

Exhibit 10.5
Characteristics of Two Non-Hispanic Caribbean Groups and Non-Hispanic Whites, 2009

*Non-Hispanic whites

SOURCE: U.S. Bureau of the Census.

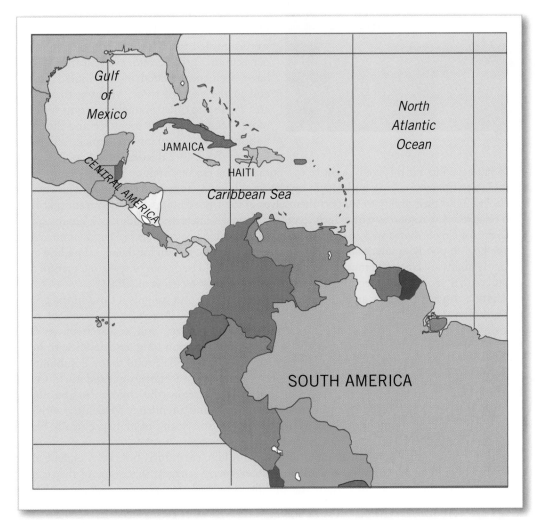

Exhibit 10.6 Map of Caribbean Showing Haiti and Jamaica

Two Case Studies

Haitians

Haiti is the poorest country in the Western Hemisphere, and most of the population relies on small-scale subsistence agriculture for survival. Estimates are that 80% of the population lives below the poverty line, and less than one third of adults hold formal jobs (Central Intelligence Agency, 2011a). Less than half the population is literate, and Haitians average less than 3 years of formal education ("Education Statistics," 2011). The already difficult conditions in Haiti were intensified by a massive earthquake in January 2010, and it will take years for the tiny nation to fully recover.

Haitian emigration was virtually nonexistent until the 1970s and 1980s, when thousands began to flee the brutal political repression of the Duvalier dictatorship, which—counting both father ("Papa Doc") and son ("Baby Doc")—lasted until the mid-1980s. In stark contrast to the treatment of Cuban immigrants (see Chapter 8), however, the United States government defined Haitians as economic refugees ineligible for asylum, and an intense campaign was commenced to keep Haitians out of the United States. Thousands were returned to Haiti, some to face political persecution, prison, and even death. Others have been incarcerated in the United States, and in the view of some, "During the 1970s and 1980s, no other immigrant group suffered more U.S. government prejudice and discrimination than Haitians" (Stepick, Stepick, Eugene, Teed, & Labissiere, 2001, p. 236).

Photo 10.1

Intercepted approximately six miles from the entrance of the Port of Miami, this boat carried over one hundred Haitians seeking asylum in the United States.

Getty.

What accounts for this cold, negative reception? Some reasons are not hard to identify. The first Haitian immigrants to come brought low levels of human capital and education. This created concerns about their ability to support themselves in the United States and also meant that they had relatively few resources with which to defend their self-interests. In addition, Haitians speak a version of Creole that is spoken only by Haitians, and a high percentage of Haitian immigrants spoke English poorly or not at all. Perhaps the most important reason for the rejection, however, is that Haitians are black and must cope with the centuries-old traditions of rejection, racism, and prejudice that are such an integral part of American culture (Stepick et al., 2001).

Haitian Americans today are still mostly first generation, and roughly a third of the group arrived after 1990. Overall, they are comparable to Hispanic Americans in terms of such measures of equality as level of education, income, and poverty. Still, research shows that some Haitians continue to face the exclusion and discrimination long associated with non-white ancestry. One important study of Haitians in South Florida found that a combination of factors—their hostile reception, their poverty and lack of education, and their racial background—combined to lead the Haitian second generation (the children of the immigrants) to a relatively low level of academic achievement and a tendency to identify with the African American community. "Haitians are becoming American but in a specifically black ethnic fashion" (Stepick et al., 2001, p. 261).

The ultimate path of Haitian assimilation will unfold in the future, but these tendencies—particularly Haitians' low levels of academic achievement—suggest that some of the second generation are unlikely to move into the middle class and that their assimilation will be segmented (Stepick et al., 2001, p. 261).

Jamaicans

The Jamaican economy is more developed than Haiti's, and this is reflected in the higher levels of education of Jamaican immigrants (see Exhibit 10.5). However, as is true throughout the less developed world, the Jamaican economy has faltered in recent decades, and the island nation has been unable to provide full employment opportunities to its population. Jamaica is a former British colony, and its immigrants have journeyed to the United Kingdom in addition to the United States. In both cases, the immigrant stream tends to be more skilled and educated and represents something of a "brain drain," a pattern we have seen with other groups, including Asian Indians. Needless to say, the loss of the more-educated Jamaicans to emigration exacerbates problems of development and growth on the island.

Jamaicans typically settle on the East Coast, particularly in the New York City area. Because they come from a former British colony, they have the advantage of speaking English as their native tongue. On the other hand, they are black, and like Haitians, they must face the barriers of discrimination and racism faced by all nonwhite groups in the United States. On the average, they are significantly higher than Haitians (and native-born African Americans) in socioeconomic standing, but poverty and institutionalized discrimination limit the mobility of a segment of the group. Like all other groups of color in the United States, they face a very real danger of segmented assimilation and permanent exclusion from the economic mainstream.

CONTEMPORARY IMMIGRATION FROM ASIA

Immigration from Asia has been considerable since the 1960s, averaging close to 300,000 people per year and running about 30% to 35% of all immigrants. As was the case with Hispanic immigrants, the sending nations are considerably less developed than the United States, and the primary motivation for most of these immigrants is economic. As I stated in Chapter 9, however, the Asian immigrant stream is "bipolar" and includes many highly educated professionals along with the less skilled and less educated. Also, many Asian immigrants are refugees from the war in Southeast Asia in the 1960s and 1970s, and others are spouses of U.S. military personnel who have been stationed throughout the region.

As before, rather than attempting to cover all Asian immigrant groups, we will concentrate on four case studies and consider immigrants from India, Vietnam, Korea, and the Philippines (see Exhibit 10.7). Together, these four groups make up about half of all immigrants from Asia.

Four Case Studies

The four groups considered here are small, and they all include a high percentage of foreign-born members. They are quite variable in their backgrounds, their occupational profiles, their levels of education, and their incomes. In contrast with Hispanic immigrants, however, they tend to have higher percentages of members who are fluent in English, members with higher levels of education, and relatively more members prepared to compete for good jobs in the American job market. A statistical profile of the groups is presented in Exhibit 10.8, along with that of non-Hispanic whites for purposes of comparison. The four groups vary in their settlement patterns. Most are concentrated along the West Coast, but Asian Indians are roughly equally distributed on both the East and West Coasts, and Vietnamese have a sizable presence in Texas, in part related to the fishing industry along the Gulf Coast.

Asian Indians

India is the second most populous nation in the world, and its huge population of more than a billion people incorporates a wide variety of different languages (India has 19 official languages,

Exhibit 10.7 Map of Asia Showing India, Republic of Korea (South Korea), the Philippines, and Vietnam

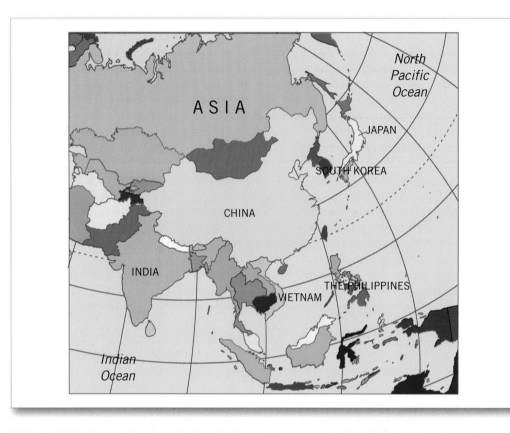

Exhibit 10.8 Characteristics of Four Asian Groups and Non-Hispanic Whites, 2009

Group	Size	% High School Degree or More	% College Degree or More	% Foreign-Born	% That Speak English "Less Than Very Well"	% in Managerial and Professional Occupations	Median Household Income	% of Families in Poverty
NHW*	——	89.9	30.8	3.9	1.7	38.9	$55,763	6.3
Asian Indians	2,800,612	90.5	68.5	69.8	21.9	63.7	$86,660	5.2
Koreans	1,565,154	81.5	51.6	64.6	41.3	45.5	$53,934	11.2
Filipinos	3,111,076	92.0	45.9	53.3	18.5	40.9	$76,455	4.6
Vietnamese	1,623,236	72.0	26.5	63.9	50.5	30.6	$54,799	12.1

*Non-Hispanic whites

SOURCE: U.S. Bureau of the Census.

including English), religions, and ethnic groups. Overall, the level of education is fairly low: The population averages about 5 years of formal schooling and is about 61% literate ("Education Statistics," 2011). However, about 10% of the population does reach the postsecondary level of education, which means that there are roughly 100 million (10% of a billion) well-educated Indians looking for careers commensurate with their credentials. Because of the relative lack of development in the Indian economy, many members of the educated elite must search for career opportunities abroad, and not just in the United States. It is also important to note that as a legacy of India's long colonization by the British, English is the language of the educated. Thus, Indian immigrants tend to be not only well educated but also English speaking.

Immigration from India to the United States was low until the mid-1960s, and the group was quite small at that time. The group more than quadrupled in size between 1980 and 2000, and Indians are now the third-largest Asian American group (behind Chinese and Filipinos).

Immigrants from India tend to be a select, highly educated, and skilled group. According to the 2000 Census, Indians are overrepresented in some of the most prestigious occupations, including computer engineering, medicine, and college teaching (U.S. Bureau of the Census, 2000d). Immigrants from India are part of a worldwide movement of educated peoples from less-developed countries to more-developed countries. One need not ponder the differences in career opportunities, technology, and compensation for long to get some insight into the reasons for this movement. Other immigrants from India are more oriented to commerce and small business, and there is a sizable Indian ethnic enclave in many cities (Kitano & Daniels, 1995, pp. 96–111; Sheth, 1995).

Koreans

Immigration from Korea to the United States began early in the 20th century, when laborers were recruited to help fill the void in the job market left by the 1882 Chinese Exclusion Act. This group was extremely small until the 1950s, when the rate of immigration rose because of refugees and "war brides" after the Korean War. Immigration did not become substantial, however, until the 1960s. The size of the group increased fivefold in the 1970s and tripled between 1980 and 2000 but is still only 0.5% of the total population.

Recent immigrants from Korea consist mostly of families and include many highly educated people. Although differences in culture, language, and race make Koreans visible targets of discrimination, the high percentage of Christians among them (about 26% of South Koreans are Christian, according to the Central Intelligence Agency, 2011b) may help them appear more "acceptable" to the dominant group. Certainly, Christian church parishes play a number of important roles for the Korean American community, offering assistance to newcomers and the less fortunate, serving as a focal point for networks of mutual assistance, and generally assisting in the completion of the myriad chores to which immigrant communities must attend (e.g., government paperwork, registering to vote, etc.) (Kitano & Daniels, 2001, p. 123).

Korean American immigrants have formed an enclave, and the group is heavily involved in small businesses and retail stores—particularly fruit and vegetable retail stores, or greengroceries. According to one study, Koreans had the second-highest percentage of self-employment among immigrant groups (Greeks were the highest), with about 23% of the group in this occupational category (Min, 2006, pp. 238–239). However, Korean Americans are typically more visible than many other entrepreneurial groups because of their size and their concentration in the largest metropolitan areas.

As is the case for other groups that have pursued this course, the enclave allows Korean Americans to avoid the discrimination and racism of the larger society and survive in an economic niche in which lack of English fluency is not a particular problem. However, the enclave has its perils and its costs. For one thing, the success of Korean enterprises depends heavily on the mutual assistance and financial support of other Koreans and the willingness of family members to work long hours for little or no pay (recall the story of Kim Park from Chapter 1). These resources would be weakened or destroyed by acculturation, integration, and the resultant decline in ethnic solidarity. Only by maintaining a distance from the dominant culture and its pervasive appeal can the infrastructure survive.

Furthermore, the economic niches in which Mom-and-Pop greengroceries and other small businesses can survive are often in deteriorated neighborhoods populated largely by other minority groups. There has been a good deal of hostility and resentment expressed against Korean shop owners by African Americans, Puerto Ricans, and other urbanized minority groups. For example, anti-Korean sentiments were widely expressed in the 1992 Los Angeles riots that followed the acquittal of the policemen charged in the beating of Rodney King. Korean-owned businesses were some of the first to be looted and burned, and when asked why, one participant in the looting said simply, "Because we hate 'em. Everybody hates them" (Cho, 1993, p. 199). Thus, part of the price of survival for many Korean merchants is to place themselves in positions in which antagonism and conflict with other minority groups is common (Kitano & Daniels, 1995, pp. 112–129; Light & Bonacich, 1988; Min, 2006; see also Hurh, 1998).

Filipino Americans

Ties between the United States and the Philippines were established in 1898 when Spain ceded the territory after its defeat in the Spanish-American War. The Philippines achieved independence following World War II, but the United States has maintained a strong military presence there for much of the past 60 years. The nation has been heavily influenced by American culture, and English remains one of two official languages. Thus, Filipino immigrants are often familiar with English, at least as a second language (see Exhibit 10.8).

Today, Filipinos are the second-largest Asian American group, but their numbers became sizable only in the past few decades. There were fewer than 1,000 Filipinos in the United States in 1910, and by 1960, the group still numbered fewer than 200,000. Most of the recent growth has come from increased post-1965 immigration. The group more than doubled in size over the past several decades (see Exhibit 9.1).

Many of the earliest immigrants were agricultural workers recruited for the sugar plantations of Hawaii and the fields of the West Coast. Because the Philippines was a U.S. territory, Filipinos could enter without regard to immigration quotas until 1935, when the nation became a self-governing commonwealth.

The most recent wave of immigrants is diversified, and like Chinese Americans, Filipino Americans are "bipolar" in their educational and occupational profiles. Many recent immigrants have entered under the family preference provisions of the U.S. immigration policy. These immigrants are often poor and compete for jobs in the low-wage secondary labor market (Kitano & Daniels, 1995, p. 94). More than half of all Filipino immigrants since 1965, however, have been professionals, many of them in the health and medical fields. Many female immigrants from the Philippines were nurses actively recruited by U.S. hospitals to fill gaps in the labor force. In fact, nurses have become something of an export commodity in the Philippines. Thousands of trained nurses leave the Philippines every year to work all over the world. About a third of the world's nurses are Filipino, and the United States currently employs more than 50,000 registered nurses from the Philippines (Kaye, 2010, pp. 30–34). Thus, the Filipino American community includes some members in the higher-wage primary labor market and others who are competing for work in the low-wage secondary sector (Agbayani-Siewert & Revilla, 1995; Espiritu, 1996; Kitano & Daniels, 1995, pp. 83–94; Min, 2006; Posadas, 1999).

Vietnamese

A flow of refugees from Vietnam began in the 1960s as a direct result of the war in Southeast Asia. The war began in Vietnam but expanded when the United States attacked communist forces in Cambodia and Laos. Social life was disrupted, and people were displaced throughout the region. In 1975, when Saigon (the South Vietnamese capital) fell and the U.S. military withdrew, many Vietnamese and other Southeast Asians who had collaborated with the United States and its allies fled in fear for their lives. This group included high-ranking officials and members of the region's educational and occupational elite. Later groups of refugees tended to be less well educated and more impoverished. Many Vietnamese waited in refugee camps for months or years before being admitted to the United States, and they often arrived with few resources or social networks to ease their transition to the new society (Kitano & Daniels, 1995, pp. 151–152). The Vietnamese are the largest of the Asian refugee groups, and contrary to Asian American success stories and notions of model minorities, they have incomes and educational levels that are somewhat comparable to colonized minority groups (see Exhibit 10.8). The story of one Vietnamese refugee family is recounted in the following Narrative Portrait.

Refugees

C. N. Le was a young boy when his family left Vietnam. They were in the first wave of refugees who left their homeland as the U.S.-supported South Vietnamese government collapsed. Although they had to leave all their possessions and their life savings behind, Le's family brought a number of resources, including the ability to speak English, and—unlike many refugee families—they made a successful adjustment to America. Notice the role played by ethnic networks and extended family in the adjustment process. Le became a sociologist and currently maintains the Asian Nation website at http://www.asian-nation.org/.

FROM SAIGON TO SUBURBIA

C. N. LE

Our "ticket" out of Viet Nam . . . was my mother's employment with the U.S. government. . . . Her superiors feared for her and her family's safety [and] they arranged for us to be evacuated. . . . We and other . . . Vietnamese workers for the U.S. military were taken to Phu Quoc island off the coast of Saigon. . . . Eventually, a cargo ship . . . was dispatched . . . to pick us up. At this point, my parents told me that the chaos became worse as everybody fought to get on the ship, which already had 2,000 refugees on board. . . . Then the . . . ship sailed to . . . Vung Tau to pick up several thousand more Vietnamese anxiously waiting to flee. . . . Among these were several close relatives of our family.

As the cargo ship approached, everyone tried to use whatever vessels they could find, steal, or rent to make their way to the ship. People were swimming in the sea and jumping from boat to boat in their efforts to board. . . . In this frantic confusion, my mother's mother and her brother and his family failed to get on board . . . and were . . . left behind. She would not see them again for almost 20 years. . . .

Conditions were very crowded [on the ship] and . . . it was hot, humid, and dirty. Because they had to leave all their possessions behind, my family literally had nothing . . . besides the clothes on their backs. My mother remembered that my sister was still nursing from a bottle and they had to leave her milk formula behind, so they struggled to make sure she was properly nourished. They also recalled that . . . the food . . . was terrible. As my mother put it, "We all got seasick and taking a bath or going to the bathroom was quite an unforgettable experience. But it was OK because we were able to escape Viet Nam." . . .

When I asked [them] how they felt [about being] relocated in the United States, . . . my mother said that she . . . was extremely upset that Viet Nam had lost the war and that . . . she was quite distraught, depressed, and in a state of shock worrying over what would become of her brother and mother. . . . As she put it, her sadness overshadowed any feelings of coming to the United States.

My father was also very sad at having to leave his home, his business, and our life savings back in Viet Nam, and at the thought that he probably would never see Viet Nam again. . . . He also mentioned that he was worried about the prospects for a good life in the United States. As he put it, "I was thinking about whether my skills could feed a family of five and could my children get along in school speaking a different language and having a different culture." . . . His pragmatism and vision fortunately compensated for my mother's feelings of distress. . . .

Because . . . my parents had extensive experience . . . interacting with . . . Americans . . . , they became familiar with many aspects of American society, culture, and values. . . . [My] family was extremely fortunate. We were not forced to resort to more dangerous measures in a desperate attempt to leave the country, like . . . trying to storm the American embassy in Saigon, or clinging to helicopters, or clutching airplane landing gear. . . . For that I am very thankful. It [also] gives me more reason to have compassion and admiration for those who were forced to resort to those more extreme measures and those who still do today.

Life in the United States Begins

We were flown to Fort Chaffee in Arkansas, one of the four major relocation centers that the U.S. government had set up to process the approximately 125,000 refugees who left Viet Nam in the first several months after the takeover. We arrived and began our life in the United States on May 15, 1975. . . .

[My] family moved to Camp Pendleton in California to take custody of my 2-year-old cousin, my mother's brother's daughter, who had become separated from her family. . . . We ended up adopting her as the fifth member of our family. . . . Our sponsor agency . . . eventually found us an apartment in Norwalk, California, located about 15 miles southeast of Los Angeles, on September 25, 1975. We were part of a group of 16 other families that were settled in the same apartment complex, the first group of refugees being settled into that area. The sponsor agency arranged for our first months' rent, along with a supply of groceries, to be paid for.

Since my mother knew enough English, she began working as a teacher's aide in an English class that all refugees were mandated to attend. . . . She went on to take vocational office-training classes [and obtained] her GED. . . . After my father's mother arrived to stay with us . . . and look after my sisters and me, she was able to . . . take nursing courses. . . . She became an LVN in 1979 and an RN in 1983. She now works as an auditor for the Los Angeles County hospital system.

My father also immediately went to find employment, riding the bus to the unemployment office and all around the greater metropolitan area. . . . After a month of searching, he found a position as a mechanical drafter. . . . Eventually, [he found work] as a mechanical and structural engineer.

We moved [again] in May 1978. When I asked each parent why we moved from Norwalk, . . . my mother said that we had saved up enough money and that they wanted something bigger and better than the small apartment we had. However, my father emphasized that the area and neighborhood were getting increasingly "bad," including more frequent incidents of graffiti, vandalism, and racial/ethnic tensions between . . . black and Latino residents and . . . Vietnamese refugees and that he did not want us to grow up in that environment.

The Road to Suburbia

My parents were able to borrow enough money from relatives so that, combined with their savings (which they regularly added to for just this occasion), we were eventually able to move to a . . . quiet, middle-class [neighborhood].

Everyone in our family is now a citizen of the United States, my parents having applied for citizenship in 1982, seven years after we came to the United States. When I asked each parent why they wanted to become citizens, . . . my father mentioned that there were benefits to be had as a citizen, as far as better employment and travel opportunities, and that we needed to take advantage of those. . . . My mother emphasized that she did not want to be a citizen of a communist country anymore. Rather, she wanted to be a citizen of a free country . . . with its better opportunities and benefits, which gave our family the chance to achieve the "American dream."

Since our arrival in the United States, we have sponsored two groups of Vietnamese immigrants. In 1981, we sponsored my father's niece and her husband [and] a year later . . . we sponsored my mother's cousin and her husband. To this day, both my parents are very active in the Vietnamese community, occasionally assisting recent immigrants and refugees, particularly if they're relatives, among their other activities.

SOURCE: Le (2005, pp. 348–351).

MIDDLE EASTERN AND ARAB AMERICANS

Immigration from the Middle East and the Arab world began in the 19th century but has never been particularly large. The earliest immigrants tended to be merchants and traders, and the Middle Eastern community in the United States has been constructed around an ethnic, small-business enclave. The number of Arab Americans and Middle Easterners has grown rapidly over the past several decades but still remains a tiny percentage of the total population. Exhibit 10.9 displays some statistical information on the group, broken down by ancestry group with which individuals identify, and Exhibit 10.10 shows the nations of origin.

Exhibit 10.9 shows that Middle Eastern and Arab Americans tend to rank relatively high in income and occupation. Most groups are at or above national norms in terms of percentage of high school graduates, and all groups have a higher percentage of college graduates than non-Hispanic whites, with some (Egyptians and Iranians) far more educated. Although

Group	Size	% High School Degree or More	% College Degree or More	% Foreign-Born	% That Speak English "Less Than Very Well"	% in Managerial and Professional Occupations	Median Household Income	% of Families in Poverty
NHW*	—	89.9	30.8	–3.9	–1.7	38.9	$55,763	–6.3
Arab	271,875	83.8	38.1	47.7	26.7	34.9	$47,753	20.3
Egyptian	189,297	96.0	65.9	60.1	24.9	49.3	$60,190	12.9
Lebanese	496,113	92.2	46.3	22.9	–8.3	48.2	$66,827	–7.0
Syrian	152,839	90.7	40.4	23.7	11.2	45.8	$63,527	–7.9
Iranian	438,132	92.7	59.0	64.1	28.1	54.7	$68,331	–8.8

Exhibit 10.9
Characteristics of Arab American and Middle Eastern Groups and Non-Hispanic Whites, 2009

*Non-Hispanic whites

SOURCE: U.S. Bureau of the Census.

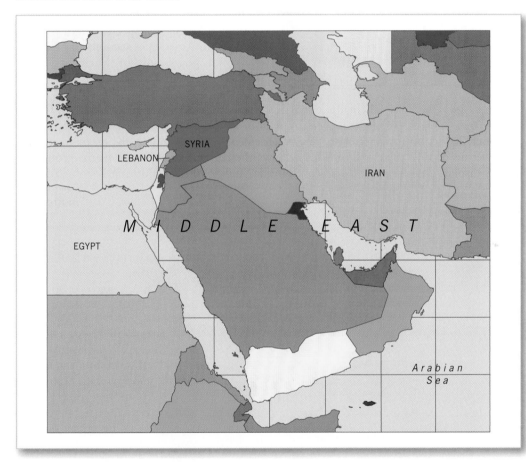

Exhibit 10.10 Map of the Middle East Showing Egypt, Iran, Lebanon, and Syria

poverty is a problem (especially for those who identify as Arab American), many of the groups compare quite favorably in terms of occupation and income.

Many recent Middle Eastern immigrants are, like Asian immigrants, highly educated people who take jobs in the highest levels of the American job structure. Also, consistent with the heritage of being an enclave minority, the groups are overrepresented in sales and underrepresented in occupations involving manual labor. One study, using 1990 Census data and a survey mailed to a national sample of Arab American women in 2000, found that immigrant Arab American women have a very low rate of employment, the lowest of any immigrant group. The author's analysis of this data strongly suggests that this pattern is due to traditional gender roles and family norms regarding the proper role of women (Read, 2004).

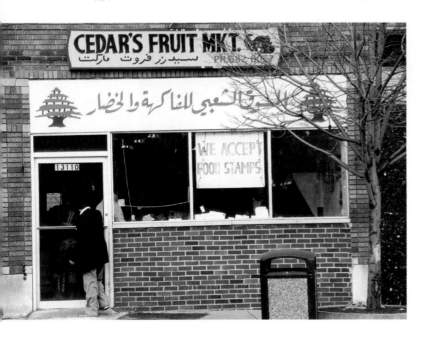

Arab Americans and Middle Easterners are diverse and vary along a number of dimensions. They bring different national traditions and cultures and also vary in religion. Most are Muslim, but many are Christian. Also, not all Middle Easterners are Arabic; Iranians, for example, are Persian. Also, about a third of all Muslims in the United States are native-born, and about 20% are African American.

Residentially, Arab Americans and Middle Easterners are highly urbanized, and almost 50% live in just five states (California, New Jersey, New York, Florida, and Michigan). This settlement pattern is not too different from that of other recent immigrant groups except for the heavy concentration in Michigan, especially in the Detroit area. Arab Americans account for 1.2% of the total population of Michigan, a far higher representation than in any other state. Arab Americans make up 30% of the population of Dearborn, Michigan, the highest percentage of any city in the nation. On the other hand, the greatest single concentration is in New York City, which has a population of about 70,000 Arab Americans. These settlement patterns reflect chains of migration, some set up decades ago. Exhibit 10.11 shows the regional distribution of the group and clearly displays the clusters in Michigan, Florida, and Southern California.

Exhibit 10.11 Regional Distribution of Arab Americans, 2000

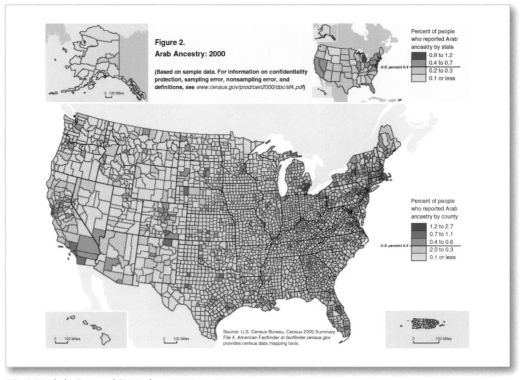

SOURCE: de la Cruz and Brittingham (2003, p. 6).

9/11 and Arab Americans

There always has been at least a faint strain of prejudice directed at Middle Easterners in American culture (e.g., see the low position of Turks in the 1926 social distance scales presented in Chapter 3; most Americans probably are not aware that Turks and Arabs are different groups). These vague feelings have intensified in recent decades as relations with various Middle Eastern nations and groups worsened. For example, in 1979, the U.S. Embassy in Tehran, Iran, was attacked and occupied, and more than 50 Americans were held hostage for more than a year. The attack stimulated a massive reaction in the United States, in which anti-Arab and anti-Muslim feelings figured prominently. Continuing anti-American activities across the Middle East in the 1980s and 1990s stimulated a backlash of resentment and growing intolerance in the United States.

These earlier events pale in comparison, of course, to the events of September 11, 2001. Americans responded to the attacks on the World Trade Center and the Pentagon by Arab terrorists with an array of emotions that included bewilderment, shock, anger, patriotism, deep sorrow for the victims and their families, and—perhaps predictably in the intensity of the moment—increased prejudicial rejection of Middle Easterners, Arabs, Muslims, and any group that seemed even vaguely associated with the perpetrators of the attacks. In the 9 weeks following September 11, more than 700 violent attacks were reported to the Arab American Anti-Discrimination Committee, followed by another 165 violent incidents in the first 9 months of 2002 (Arab American Anti-Discrimination Committee, 2002). In this same time period, there were more than 80 incidents in which Arab Americans were removed from aircraft after boarding because of their ethnicity, more than 800 cases of employment discrimination, and "numerous instances of denial of service, discriminatory service, and housing discrimination" (Ibish, 2003, p. 7).

Anti-Arab passions may have cooled somewhat since the multiple traumas of 9/11, but the Arab American community faces a number of issues and problems, including profiling at airport security checks and greater restrictions on entering the country. Also, the USA Patriot Act, passed in 2001 to enhance the tools available to law enforcement to combat terrorism, allows for long-term detention of suspects, a wider scope for searches and surveillance, and other policies that many (not just Arab Americans) are concerned will encourage violations of due process and suspension of basic civil liberties.

Thus, although the Arab American and Middle Eastern communities are small in size, they have assumed a prominent place in the attention of the nation. The huge majority of these groups denounce and reject terrorism and violence, but, like Colombians and Italians, they are victimized by a strong stereotype that is often applied uncritically and without qualification. A recent survey of Muslim Americans, a category that includes the huge majority of Arab Americans and Middle Easterners, finds them to be "middle class and mostly mainstream." They have a positive view of U.S. society and espouse distinctly American values. At the same time, they are very concerned about becoming scapegoats in the war on terror, and a majority (53%) say that it became more difficult to be a Muslim in the United States after 9/11 (Pew Research Center, 2007).

Relations between Arab Americans and the larger society are certainly among the most tense and problematic of any minority group, and given the continuing U.S. occupation of Iraq and Afghanistan and the threat of further terrorist attacks, they will not ease anytime soon. Some of the consequences of these relationships are discussed in the next Narrative Portrait.

The Arab American
Community in Detroit, Michigan

STEVE GOLD

The events of September 11, 2001, focused attention on Arab American communities. The Detroit area is home to more than 300,000 Arab Americans, one of the largest ethnic enclaves in the United States. Nineteenth-century immigrants from Syria and Lebanon were the first to arrive. With the increased demand for automobiles and the steel to make them at the beginning of the 20th century, more immigrants from the Middle East came to work in Detroit's many factories. By 1916, the Ford motor company counted 555 Arab men among its workforce. The first Islamic mosque in America was established in Highland Park in 1919. The relationship between Arab immigrants and auto manufacturing endures. Next to Ford's famous River Rouge plant is Dearborn's "Arab village."

Immigrants continue to arrive in Detroit, reuniting families that have been divided across borders and continents. Whether from Iraq, Yemen, or Palestine, they seek economic advancement and escape from the Middle East's chronic violence. In 1990, more than one third of Michigan's residents of Arab origin had been born outside the United States; about 40% had immigrated after 1980. Although all are Arab, their religious affiliations are diverse: Lebanese Christians; Sunni and Shiite Muslims; Palestinians and Jordanians who are Catholic, Protestant, Greek Orthodox, and Sunni Muslims; Eastern rite Catholic Chaldeans; and Yemenis of different Muslim sects.

The Arab community is also socioeconomically diverse, but the 1990 Census showed them to be generally well-off as a group. College graduation rates are high, and comparatively few are unemployed or struggling on below-poverty incomes. Besides careers in the auto industry, Arab Americans also become professionals, and many are self-employed.

With their new visibility since September 2001, Arab Americans have experienced renewed negative attention. But this, too, has deep roots. Metropolitan Detroit has a long history of racial and ethnic violence, and Arab American residents have become well acquainted with discrimination and stereotyping—from ethnic slurs like being called "camel jockeys" to the more pernicious dominance of European traditions and standards in schools. Neither is this the first conflict in the Middle East for which Arabs were demonized. With a rich community life, Arab Americans have developed a range of organizational supports that provide succor in the face of the episodic but persistent hostilities they face in America.

Recommended Resources

Abraham, Nabeel, & Shryock, Andrew (Eds.). 2000. *Arab Detroit: From Margins to Mainstream*. Detroit: Wayne State University Press.

Abraham, Sameer Y. 1983. Detroit's Arab-American Community. In Sameer Y. Abraham & Nabeel Abraham (Eds.), *Arabs in the New World* (pp. 84–108). Detroit: Wayne State University Center for Urban Studies.

Johnson, Nan E. 1995. *Health Profiles of Michigan Populations of Color*. Lansing: Michigan Department of Public Health.

SOURCE: Gold (2002). Reprinted with permission of the University of California Press.

Photos courtesy of Steven J. Gold.

9/11 and Middle Eastern Americans

Amir Marvasti and Karyn McKinney are sociologists who, between 2002 and 2004, conducted in-depth interviews with 20 Middle Eastern Americans. The interviews covered a variety of topics, but most centered on the reactions of the respondents to the attacks of 9/11, the ensuing public reaction, and their own rethinking of what it means to be an American. What follows are the personal reactions of the respondents, knit together by the narrative written by Marvasti and McKinney.

MIDDLE EASTERN AMERICANS AND THE AMERICAN DREAM

AMIR MARVASTI AND KARYN MCKINNEY

Difficulty with cultural assimilation is a common experience for most ethnic groups, but being designated public enemy number one is not. In the hours following the tragic attacks of September 11, 2001, being or just looking Middle Eastern became an instant offense. For members of this group, this was a turning point in terms of both the way they were viewed by others and the way they defined themselves. While the feeling of shock is similar to what everyone must have felt that day, in the case of Middle Eastern Americans, there was also a feeling of impending doom, the knowledge that their lives would never be exactly the same. Many of our respondents stated that after their sense of initial shock and sadness, the next thought they remember was that they hoped that the incident was perpetrated by domestic terrorists, as was the case with the Oklahoma City bombing. One Pakistani American stated,

> I was on my way to the gym listening to radio when it happened. And I thought it was a hoax. And then I got to the gym and it was on TV and I was like "Oh my God, please don't let it be Muslims." That was the first thing came to my mind, "God please don't let this be one of us."

As the day went by, a chasm began to form between Middle Eastern Americans and their fellow citizens. The perception that Middle Easterners were the aggressors and Americans the victims began to take hold, and out of this perception grew anger:

> I went to class that day and came back and from then on for two days, I was glued to CNN. . . . Wherever you went you always—that day even among my friends there was talk about anger and they looked really angry. . . . There was talk about "We should bomb Palestine." And "Who cares about these people now." In a way, I understood their anger because of what had just happened. I guess it was kind of lonely that day.

In the days following the attacks, Middle Eastern Americans had to accept the fact that they were seen by many as legitimate targets of anger. The news media were full of messages about hate being an acceptable emotion under the circumstances. In that atmosphere, it was indeed very "lonely" to be Middle Eastern American. What was most striking was the ordinary tone with which retaliatory violence was talked about. For example, in an introductory race and ethnicity course taught by [Marvasti], a young man passionately exclaimed, "I say we go bomb the Taj Mahal!" Although others in the class corrected his error in terms of his misplaced target, his general idea of bombing buildings where civilians would be the primary casualties was not disputed.

Some Middle Eastern Americans also felt a strong sense of impending doom related to this tragedy. . . . Perhaps the most significant realization for many Middle Eastern Americans was the awareness that their right to be part of the American Dream could be taken away for actions that they were not in any way responsible for. With this realization came the sense of not belonging and the real possibility of being physically separated from the rest of society and placed in an internment camp. One young Middle Eastern American remembered,

> I really thought I was going to be sent to like a camp. . . . It didn't—for those couple of days—it didn't feel like we were going to be back to normal again. Like I really didn't feel like—along with going to internment camp—I thought my life was never going to be the same. I no longer had a home here.

As this respondent puts it, realizing that one no longer has a home here was tantamount to realizing that the American Dream applied to some more than others. . . .

September 11 was an important turning point in the psyche of Middle Eastern Americans to the extent that it caused them to reevaluate their place in American society and its promises of freedom and equality. Consider, for example, how this Pakistani American woman (who was born in Pennsylvania) rethinks her status as an American in light of how she and her family have been treated since September 11:

My brother was assaulted three days after September 11th. It was part of the backlash. . . . I feel I'm even considered an outsider a lot of the times. I sound just as American as anyone else, and I was born and raised here. . . . [After September 11] I think a lot of people thought that if you're not going to consider me American, why am I going to consider myself an American. If you're not going to protect me like other Americans, if you are going to create laws that are going to undermine me, then I shouldn't be trying so hard to fit into a culture that consistently and perpetually rejects me.

According to this respondent, . . . it became particularly apparent that the ideals of equality in the American Dream did not apply to her and her family. Her ethnicity transcends her identity as an American and places her in the position of a second-class citizen. . . .

One of the most profound effects of September 11 on the lives of Middle Eastern Americans was the realization that their daily routines (i.e., the mundane tasks of going on a trip or even to a grocery store) would be subjected to scrutiny and potentially make them vulnerable to acts of violence. An Iranian American man describes how September 11 affected his life:

I actually canceled a trip. We usually take a trip on Thanksgiving with about 30–40 Iranian Americans. And that's when I realized there's a difference in this war [War on Terrorism]. There is a new order. . . . We can't go somewhere and not play our own music. We like our own music, we like our own dance, we like our own food and tradition so we couldn't do that therefore I canceled that trip. That's when it occurred to me there's a difference.

Interviewer: Did you put any other limitations on your life because of it? Did you restrict your life in any other way?

Respondent: I'm more alert these days about how I answer people. . . . In the past I wouldn't mind if they asked right off the bat where I'm from. . . . But now most of the time I say "God, please don't let them ask the question." . . . I don't volunteer information. . . . I'm more guarded about what I say. . . .

Collectively, these post-9/11 experiences have caused some Middle Eastern Americans to question the meaning of the American Dream and the extent to which its lofty promises apply to them. They have recognized that full assimilation into American culture will not provide protection against acts of ignorance and that their future in this country is uncertain. . . .

The very value of civility is that it should offer protection when things are the most tense. If it fails to do so, then it is in fact, just a "veneer." Similarly, laws . . . are of no value unless they defend those who are least able to protect themselves (e.g., the newest immigrants) at times when they are most vulnerable. . . . The fact that . . . constitutional rights (i.e., due process protections) are undermined with the passage of new laws, such as the Patriot Act, further reveals how thin this "veneer of civility" really is.

SOURCE: Marvasti and McKinney (2004, pp. 121–126).

IMMIGRANTS FROM AFRICA

Our final group of new Americans consists of immigrants from Africa. Immigration from Africa has been quite low over the past 50 years. However, there was the usual increase after the 1960s, and Africans have made up about 5% of all immigrants in the past few years.

Exhibit 10.12 shows the total number of sub-Saharan Africans in the United States in 2009, along with the two largest national groups. The number of native Africans in the United States has more than doubled since 1990, and this rapid growth suggests that these groups may have

Group	Size	% High School Degree or More	% College Degree or More	% Foreign-Born	% That Speak English "Less Than Very Well"	% in Managerial and Professional Occupations	Median Household Income	% of Families in Poverty
NHW*	——	89.9	30.8	−3.9	−1.7	38.9	$55,763	−6.3
Sub-Saharan African	2,815,592	85.4	29.3	38.2	12.3	32.7	$40,056	18.6
Ethiopian	168,839	84.2	28.3	73.1	36.6	25.1	$41,163	19.0
Nigerian	244,197	96.1	60.2	60.5	−9.9	50.5	$57,599	−9.3

Exhibit 10.12
Characteristics of Sub-Saharan African Groups and Non-Hispanic Whites, 2009

*Non-Hispanic whites

a greater impact on U.S. society in the future. The category "sub-Saharan African" is extremely broad and encompasses destitute black refugees from African civil wars and relatively affluent white South Africans. In the remainder of this section, we will focus on Nigerians and Ethiopians rather than on this very broad category (see Exhibit 10.13).

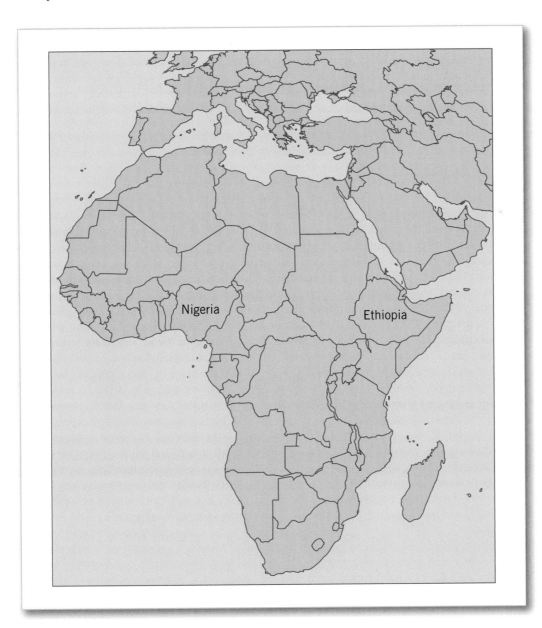

Exhibit 10.13 Map of Africa Showing Ethiopia and Nigeria

Clearly, although they may be growing, Nigerians and Ethiopians are tiny minorities: Neither group is as much as 0.1% of the total population. They are recent immigrants and have a high representation of first-generation members. They both compare favorably to national norms in education, an indication that this is another example of a "brain drain" from the countries of origin. Nigerian and Ethiopian immigrants tend to be highly skilled and educated, and they bring valuable abilities and advanced educational credentials to the United States. Like some other groups, many of the immigrants from Nigeria and Ethiopia are motivated by a search for work, and they compete for positions in the higher reaches of the job structure.

Nigeria is a former British colony, so the relatively high level of English fluency of the immigrants is not surprising. Exhibit 10.12 shows that, on the average, members of the group have been able to translate their relatively high levels of human capital and English fluency into a favorable position in the U.S. economy. They compare quite favorably with national norms in their occupational profiles and their income levels.

Compared with Nigerians, Ethiopians rank lower in their English fluency and are more mixed in their backgrounds. They include refugees from domestic unrest along with the educated elite. For example, almost 30% of Ethiopian immigrants in 2009 were admitted as "refugees and asylees" versus only 1% of Nigerian immigrants. Refugees, virtually by definition, bring fewer resources and lower levels of human capital and, thus, have a more difficult adjustment to their host nation. These facts are reflected in Exhibit 10.12. Although Ethiopians compare favorably with national norms in education, they have much higher rates of poverty and much lower levels of income. These contrasts suggest that Ethiopians are less able to translate their educational credentials into higher-ranked occupations.

SUMMARY: MODES OF INCORPORATION

As the case studies included in this chapter (as well as those in Chapters 8 and 9) demonstrate, recent immigrant groups occupy a wide array of different positions in U.S. society. One way to address this diversity is to look at the contact situation, especially the characteristics the groups bring with them (e.g., their race and religion, the human capital with which they arrive) and the reaction of the larger society. There are three main modes of incorporation for immigrants in the United States: entrance through the primary or secondary labor markets (see Chapter 5) or the ethnic enclave. We will consider each pathway separately and relate them to the groups discussed in this chapter.

Immigrants and the Primary Labor Market

The primary labor market consists of more desirable jobs with greater security, higher pay, and more benefits, and the immigrants entering this sector tend to be highly educated, skilled professionals and businesspeople. Members of this group are generally fluent in English, and many were educated at U.S. universities. They are highly integrated into the global urban-industrial economy, and in many cases, they are employees of multinational corporations transferred here by their companies. These immigrants are affluent, urbane, and dramatically different from the peasant laborers so common in the past (e.g., from Ireland and Italy) and in the present (e.g., from the Dominican Republic and from Mexico). The groups with high percentages of members entering the primary labor market include Indian, Egyptian, Iranian, and Nigerian immigrants.

Because they tend to be affluent and enter a growing sector of the labor force, immigrants with professional backgrounds tend to attract less notice and fewer racist reactions than their more unskilled counterparts. Although they come closer to Blauner's pure immigrant group than most other minority groups we have considered, racism can still complicate their assimilation. In addition, Arab American Islamic groups must confront discrimination and prejudice based on their religious affiliation.

Immigrants and the Secondary Labor Market

This mode of incorporation is more typical for immigrants with lower levels of education and fewer job skills. Jobs in this sector are less desirable and command lower pay, little security, and few benefits and are often seasonal or in the underground or informal economy. This labor market includes jobs in construction or the garment industry, in which workers are paid "off the books" and working conditions are unregulated by government authorities or labor unions; domestic work; and some forms of criminal or deviant activity, such as drug sales and prostitution. The employers who control these jobs often prefer to hire undocumented immigrants because they are easier to control and less likely to complain to the authorities about abuse and mistreatment. The groups with high percentages of members in the secondary labor market include Dominicans, Haitians, and the less-skilled and less-educated kinfolk of the higher-status immigrants.

Immigrants and Ethnic Enclaves

As we have seen, some immigrant groups—especially those that can bring financial capital and business experience—have established ethnic enclaves. Some members of these groups enter U.S. society as entrepreneurs and become owners of small retail shops and other businesses; their less-skilled and less-educated co-ethnics serve as a source of cheap labor to staff the ethnic enterprises. The enclave provides contacts, financial and other services, and social support for the new immigrants of all social classes. Korean Americans and Arab Americans, along with Cuban Americans and Jewish Americans in the past, have been particularly likely to follow this path.

This classification suggests some of the variety of relationships between the new Americans and the larger society. The contemporary stream of immigrants entering the United States is extremely diverse and includes people ranging from the most sophisticated and urbane to the most desperate and despairing. The variety is suggested by considering a list of occupations in which recent immigrants are overrepresented. For men, the list includes biologists and other natural scientists, taxi drivers, farm laborers, and waiters. For women, the list includes chemists, statisticians, produce packers, laundry workers, and domestics (Kritz & Girak, 2004).

The Roma: Europe's "True Minority"

ANDRIA D. TIMMER

Professor Timmer studies the Roma of Europe and, especially, of Hungary. She lived and worked in Roma communities in Hungary for several years while conducting research.

The European Union is known as a "diverse family of nations," but within this "family," the Roma—sometimes called "Gypsies"—stand out as Europe's "true minority." Collectively, the Roma are the most disadvantaged minority group in Europe and present the greatest challenge to integration. Their continued poverty, exclusion, and marginalization challenge the themes of multiculturalism and democracy that are purportedly valued throughout Europe. Furthermore, this is not a new situation and the Roma are by no means newcomers to Europe. According to many historical documents, they have been part of Central and Eastern European society since at least the 14th century. They now number about 10 million and are present in all European countries, although they are still more populous in the east. Despite the fact that they have lived in Europe for more than half a millennium, they are still treated as recent immigrants in many respects. Thus, the Roma illustrate the point made by Gordon (see Chapter 2) and many others that length of residence in a country is not necessarily related to the ability of a group to assimilate and gain acceptance.

Perhaps one of the biggest challenges to integration for the Roma is that they are not a single group or a homogeneous entity. Rather, there are several different ethnic enclaves, including, but by no means limited to, the Gitanos of Spain, the Sinti of Germany, the Travellers of England and Ireland, the Kalderash in Romania, and the Beás in Hungary. Members of these groups share little in common and are more similar to the majority members of the country in which they reside than to one another. However, from a pan-European perspective, they are often considered a single group. To understand how these different peoples get grouped together, it is necessary to return to the definition of *minority* provided in Chapter 1 of this text. We will use the first two elements of the definition to help us examine the situation of the Roma in Europe.

The first, and most important, defining characteristic of a minority group is disadvantage or inequality, and this is something that all Roma groups have in common. Violence and intolerance toward Roma is not only still very much present but is on the rise. According to a recent survey (European Union Agency for Fundamental Rights, 2009), 50% of Roma report being discriminated against in the past 12 months. Other recent surveys (European Commission, 2007, 2008) found that discrimination has decreased on all grounds except on the basis of ethnic origin and that Europeans are generally comfortable with ethnic diversity except in regard to the Roma. Discriminatory attitudes are especially on the rise in Central and Eastern Europe, where the European Roma Rights Center (www.errc.org) reports that, since 2008, there have been at least 48 violent attacks against the Roma in Hungary, 19 in the Czech Republic, and 10 in Slovakia resulting in at least 11 fatalities. These attacks involved the use of Molotov cocktails, hand grenades, guns, arson, and mob violence.

Even while violence against the Roma is on the rise, day-to-day discrimination and patterns of inequality continue everywhere. Roma neighborhoods are often lacking in basic amenities, such as running water and regular trash collection. During my field research with Roma groups in Hungary, I visited many segregated villages. In these locales, the Roma and the non-Roma stood in stark contrast to each other. In several cases, the sewage system stopped at the boundary of the village and the Roma had to contend with standing bodies of polluted water. Garbage dumps were often situated in or near Roma settlements, so flying debris was a constant problem. Roads were often poorly maintained and unpaved, so people had a difficult time traversing them. This often led to injury and, in some cases, prevented individuals from getting to the hospital because ambulances could not reach their homes (European Roma Rights Center, 2006).

Roma youth are frequently educated separately from their majority peers and, as a result, receive lower-quality education that leaves them unable to compete in the job market. In all European countries, the Roma have much lower school attendance and completion rates than do majority children. Throughout Hungary, it is common practice for non-Roma parents to transfer their children to other schools when the proportion of Roma children gets too high, largely because of the Roma's reputation for poor grades and behavior problems. The percentage of Roma children in a school is one of the main factors by which people judge the quality of the school.

The second defining characteristic of a minority is a visible trait or characteristic. Most researchers claim that the Roma migrated out of northern India sometime between the 10th and 12th centuries, and today they look more like contemporary Indians than they do Europeans, especially in terms of skin color. Apart from skin color, there is little that culturally ties them to India, and, as mentioned previously, there are few cultural characteristics that tie all Roma groups together. Very few— apart from Traveller groups of England and Ireland, who are not Indian descendants—still practice the stereotypical nomadic lifestyle. Many have lost the use of their native tongue or use it only in the privacy of their homes.

Because their lifestyles differ so dramatically, most European Roma today do not identify themselves as Indian descendants and they have little or no connection to their ancient homeland. In fact, the Roma today are often considered to be a nationless people. Cristian Tileag (2005) posits that the Roma constitute the "epitome of foreignness," because "they have no (national) place, no one wants them and they have no place to go. . . . Romanies are the eternal strangers in anybody's land" (pp. 604–605). In short, they are a classic "marginalized" group because they have no home country to return to and yet are still not considered European because they do not look European.

The deep divide between Roma and non-Roma in Europe is largely the result of a long history of isolation and segregated living. Government and civil-sector programs have done little to address the segregated living but rather, have, for the most part, endeavored to improve living conditions in Roma settlements. They have helped build new houses and sponsored environmental clean-up projects, but there are few programs to integrate Roma families into the larger national communities in which they reside. As long as residential segregation, prejudice, and discrimination persist, Europe will remain divided and the Roma will remain isolated and segregated.

IMMIGRATION: ISSUES AND CONTROVERSIES

The Attitudes of Americans

One factor that affects the fate of immigrant groups is the attitude of the larger society, particularly the groups that have the most influence with governmental policymakers. Overall, American public opinion is split on the issue of immigration, as demonstrated in Exhibit 10.14. Many Americans regard immigration as a positive force, but many others are vehemently opposed—and it is the latter whose voices seem to be more prominent in everyday discourse. The history of this nation is replete with anti-immigrant and nativist groups and activities, including those that opposed the immigration from Europe (Chapter 2), Mexico (Chapter 8), and China and Japan (Chapter 9). The present is no exception: As immigration has increased over the past several decades, so have the number and visibility of anti-immigrant groups, particularly in the states along the Mexican border.

The contemporary anti-immigrant movements have generated a number of state laws. The most controversial and widely publicized of these has been State Bill 1070, passed by the Arizona legislature in the spring of 2010. Among other provisions, the law required law enforcement officers to check the immigration status of anyone they stopped, detained, or arrested when they had a "reasonable" suspicion that the person might be in the country illegally. Supporters of the legislation argued that it would help control illegal immigrants, but opponents raised fears of racial profiling and legalized anti-Hispanic discrimination. There was also considerable concern that the legislation would deter Hispanic Americans from reporting crimes or otherwise cooperating with the police.

Public opinion polls showed that at least a slight majority of Americans supported S.B. 1070. For example, a Gallup poll conducted just days after the bill was passed found that 75% of all Americans had heard of the law and that 51% supported it while 39% opposed it (Jones, 2010). Although several other states, including Utah, Alabama, and Georgia, are considering similar legislation, S.B. 1070 has not been fully implemented because of a lawsuit brought by the federal

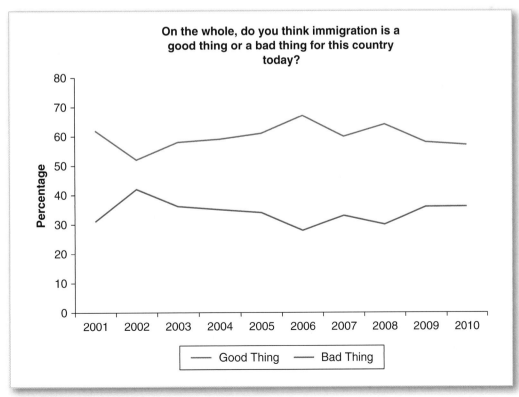

Exhibit 10.14 American Attitudes on Immigration, 2001 to 2010

SOURCE: Morales (2010).

government. The U.S. Justice Department argues that S.B. 1070 is unconstitutional because the right to make immigration policy is the exclusive province of the federal government.

What factors might account for people's views of immigration? One possibility is that negative views of immigrants are linked to fear of job loss and financial insecurity. To illustrate, one survey shows that white Americans who were dissatisfied with their financial situation were more likely to support a reduction in immigration. This relationship is displayed in Exhibit 10.15. The table shows that there is a lot of support for decreasing immigration regardless of people's satisfaction with their financial situations, but support is strongest for people who are most dissatisfied. This suggests a relationship between opposition to immigrants and prejudice, perhaps motivated by a sense of threat, that is consistent with the Noel hypothesis (see Chapter 4) and the outcome of the Robber's Cave experiment (see Chapter 3). This relationship should come as no surprise at this point in the text.

Exhibit 10.15 Position on Immigration by Satisfaction With Financial Situation, 2008 (Whites Only)

Do you think that the number of immigrants to America should be	So far as you and your family are concerned, would you say that you are pretty well satisfied with your present financial situation, more or less satisfied, or not satisfied at all?		
	Satisfied	More or Less Satisfied	Not at All Satisfied
Increased	12.1%	9.8%	9.4%
Remain the same	36.6%	37.8%	25.6%
Decreased	51.3%	52.4%	65.0%
	100% (224)	100% (286)	100% (203)

SOURCE: National Opinion Research Council (1972–2010).

What other factors might be associated with anti-immigrant attitudes? A recent study (Pettigrew, Wagner, & Christ, 2007) examined attitudes in Germany and compared these with other recent studies of European attitudes and anti-immigration feelings in Canada and the United States. The researchers found similar patterns in all locales and concluded that negative views of immigrants were highly correlated with other forms of prejudice. The same forces that produce prejudice—exposure to prejudiced norms and values during childhood, low levels of education—also produce anti-immigrant feelings. We discussed relationships of this sort in Chapter 3 when we noted that prejudice is partly cultural and is passed on from generation to generation.

However, remember that prejudice is also related to intergroup conflict. The researchers (Pettigrew et al., 2007, p. 35) found that a sense of collective threat was the single strongest predictor of antiforeigner attitudes, more so than the individual-level threat examined in Exhibit 10.15. That is, the most important cause of anti-immigrant attitudes was the sense that newcomers threatened the way of life, political freedoms, and cultural integrity of the nation as a whole, not just jobs or one's personal financial stability. As in so many other instances we have investigated, these forms of prejudice are defensive: They are reactions to the sense that the dominant status of one's group is at risk. As we have seen on numerous occasions (e.g., the Robber's Cave experiment discussed in Chapter 3, rigid competitive relations discussed in Chapter 5), competition between groups—or even the perception of competition—can stimulate powerful emotions and extreme forms of prejudice and discrimination.

Does this mean that everyone who has reservations and questions about immigration is a racist? Emphatically no. While anti-immigrant feelings, prejudice, and a sense of threat are linked, this does not mean that all who oppose immigration are bigots or that all proposals to decrease the flow of immigrants are racist. These are serious and complex issues, and it is not helpful simply to label people bigots or dismiss their concerns as prejudiced.

On the other hand, we need to clearly recognize that anti-immigrant feelings—particularly the most extreme—are linked to some of the worst, most negative strains of traditional American culture: the same racist and prejudicial views that helped justify slavery and the near-genocide of Native Americans. In popular culture, some talk radio and cable TV "news" shows, letters to the editor, and so forth, these views are regularly used to demonize immigrants, blame them for an array of social problems, and stoke irrational fears and rumors, such as the idea that Latino immigrants are aiming to return parts of the Southwest to Mexico. At any rate, when American traditions of prejudice and racism are linked to feelings of group threat and individual insecurity, the possibilities for extreme reactions, hate crimes, and poorly designed policy and law become formidable.

The Immigrants

One survey of immigration issues (National Public Radio, 2004) included a nationally representative sample of immigrant respondents. Not surprisingly, the researchers found that their attitudes and views differed sharply from those of native-born respondents on a number of dimensions. For example, immigrant respondents were more likely to see immigration as a positive force for the larger society and more likely to say that immigrants work hard and pay their fair share of taxes.

More relevant for the ultimate impact of the contemporary wave of immigration, the survey found that only about 30% were sojourners (i.e., ultimately planning to return to their homelands), a finding that suggests that issues of assimilation and immigration will remain at the forefront of U.S. concerns for many decades.

The survey also showed that immigrants are grateful for the economic opportunities available in the United States, with 84% agreeing that there are more opportunities to get ahead here than in their countries of origin. On the other hand, the immigrant respondents were ambivalent about U.S. culture and values. For example, nearly half (47%) said that the family was stronger in their homelands than in the United States, and only 28% saw U.S. society as having stronger moral values than their homelands.

We have seen that the immigrant stream is highly diversified, but it would be helpful to keep in mind the characteristics of the "typical immigrant." The modal or most common immigrant is from Mexico, China, or another Asian or Central American nation and has decided to cross the border largely out of desperation and the absence of viable opportunities at home. These immigrants would prefer to enter legally, but their desperation is such that they will enter illegally if necessary. Coming from less developed nations, they bring little human capital, education, or job skills. Some will come to the United States for a time and then return home, circulating between nations as has been done for decades. Others will stay in the United States, separated from their families and loved ones, because they fear that enhanced border security will prevent them from reentering the United States if they ever visit their homes.

As is typical of the first generation, they tend to be more oriented to their home villages than to the United States, and they are often less interested in acculturation or learning English. Frequently, they don't have the time, energy, or opportunity to absorb much of Anglo culture and are further hampered in their acquisition of English by the fact that they are not very literate in their native language. They are hardworking and frugal, often sharing living quarters with many others so as to save on rent. They send much of their earnings home to support their family and kin and spend little on themselves. They are generally determined to find a better way of life for their children, even if the cost is to live in poverty at the margins of society and in constant fear of being deported.

Costs and Benefits

Many Americans believe that immigration is a drain on the economic resources of the nation. Common concerns include the ideas that immigrants take jobs from native-born workers; strain societal institutions, including schools, housing markets, and medical facilities; and do not pay taxes. These issues are complex and hotly debated at all levels of U.S. society, so much so that passion and intensity of feeling on all sides often compromises the objective analysis of data. The debate is further complicated because conclusions about these economic issues can vary depending on the type of immigrants being discussed and the level of the analysis. For example, conclusions about costs and benefits can be very different depending on whether we focus on less-skilled or undocumented immigrants on one hand or on the highly educated professional immigrants entering the primary job market on the other. Also, conclusions might vary depending on the level of the analyses: National studies might lead to different conclusions than studies of local communities.

Contrary to the tenor of public opinion, many studies, especially those done at the national level, find that immigrants are not a particular burden. For example, a study conducted by the National Research Council (Smith & Edmonston, 1997) found that immigrants are a positive addition to the economy. They add to the labor supply in areas as disparate as the garment industry, agriculture, domestic work, and college faculty. Other researchers have found that low-skilled immigrants tend to find jobs in areas of the economy in which few U.S. citizens work or in the enclave economies of their own groups, taking jobs that would not have existed without the economic activity of their co-ethnics (Heer, 1996, pp. 190–194; Smith & Edmonston, 1997) and that they do not have a negative effect on the employment of native-born workers (Kochhar, 2006; Meissner, 2010). One important recent study of the economic impact of immigrants concluded that there is a relatively small effect on the wages and employment of native workers, although there may be negative consequences for earlier immigrants and for less-skilled African American workers (Bean & Stevens, 2003).

Another concern is the strain that immigrants place on taxes and services such as schools and welfare programs. Again, these issues are complex and far from settled, but research tends to show that immigrants generally cost less than they contribute. Taxes are automatically deducted from their paychecks (unless, of course, they are being paid "under the table"), and their use of such services as unemployment compensation, Medicare, food stamps, and Social Security is actually lower than their proportional contributions. This is particularly true for undocumented immigrants, whose use of services is sharply limited by their vulnerable legal status (Marcelli & Heer, 1998; Simon, 1989). Bean and Stevens (2003, pp. 66–93), in their recent study, found that immigrants are not overrepresented on the welfare rolls. Rather, the key determinant of welfare use is refugee status. Groups such as Haitians, Salvadorans, and Vietnamese—who arrive without resources and, by definition, are in need of assistance on all levels—are the most likely to be on the welfare rolls.

In general, immigrants—undocumented as well as legal—pay local, state, and federal taxes and make proportional contributions to Social Security and Medicare. The undocumented are the most likely to be paid "off the books" and receive their wages tax-free, but estimates are that the majority (at least 50%) and probably the huge majority (up to 75%) of them pay federal and state taxes through payroll deduction (White House, 2005). Also, all immigrants pay sales taxes and the other taxes (e.g., on gas, cigarettes, and alcohol) that are levied on consumers. (See the Current Debates section at the end of this chapter for a reprise of many of these issues.)

Also, there is evidence that immigrants play a crucial role in keeping the Social Security system solvent. This source of retirement income is being severely strained by the "baby boomers"—the large number of Americans born between 1945 and 1960 who are now retiring. This group is living longer than previous generations, and since the U.S. birthrate has stayed low over the past four decades, there are relatively fewer native-born workers to support them and replace the funds they withdraw as Social Security and Medicare benefits.

Immigrants may supply the much-needed workers to take up the slack in the system and keep it solvent. In particular, most undocumented immigrants pay into the system but (probably) will never draw any money out because of their illegal status. They thus provide a tidy surplus—perhaps as much as $7 billion a year or more—to help subsidize the retirements of the baby boomers and keep the system functioning (Porter, 2005).

Final conclusions about the impact and costs of immigration must await ongoing research, and many local communities are experiencing real distress as they try to deal with the influx of newcomers in their housing markets, schools, and health care facilities. Concerns about the economic impact of immigrants are not unfounded, but they may be confounded with and exaggerated by prejudice and racism directed at newcomers and strangers. The current opposition to immigration may be a reaction to "who" as much as to "how many" or "how expensive."

Photo 10.4

Becoming a U.S. citizen is an important step in the process of assimilation.

© O'Rourke, Skip/ZUMA Press/Corbis.

Finally, we can repeat the finding of many studies (e.g., Bean & Stevens, 2003) that immigration is generally a positive force in the economy and that, as has been true for decades, immigrants—legal and illegal—continue to find work and niches in American society in which they can survive. The highly skilled immigrants fill gaps in the primary labor market, in schools and universities, corporations, hospitals, and hundreds of other sectors of the economy. Less-skilled immigrants provide cheap labor for the low-wage secondary job market, and, frequently, the primary beneficiaries of this long-established system are not the immigrants (although they are often grateful for the opportunities) but employers, who benefit from a cheaper, more easily exploited workforce, and American consumers, who benefit from lower prices in the marketplace and reap the benefits virtually every time they go shopping, have a meal in a restaurant, pay for home repairs or maintenance, or place a loved one in a nursing home.

Undocumented Immigrants

Americans are particularly concerned with undocumented immigrants but, again, are split in their attitudes. A recent poll (Saad, 2010) asked about people's concerns regarding undocumented immigrants and found that 61% of respondents were concerned with the burden on schools, hospitals, and government services; 55% were concerned that "illegal immigrants might be encouraging others to move here illegally"; and 53% were concerned that undocumented immigrants lower wages for native-born workers. At the same time, 64% of respondents proclaimed themselves to be "very" or "somewhat" sympathetic toward undocumented immigrants. Only 17% said they were "very unsympathetic."

The high level of concern is certainly understandable because the volume of illegal immigration has been huge over the past few decades. As displayed in Exhibit 10.16, the estimated number of undocumented immigrants increased from 8.4 million in 2000 to a high of 12 million in 2007, an increase of more than 40%. The number has declined during the recession and is now about 11.2 million. On the average, about 55% of all unauthorized immigrants are from Mexico.

Some undocumented immigrants enter the country on tourist, temporary worker, or student visas and simply remain in the nation when their visas expire. In 2009 alone, more than 36 million tourists, business people, temporary workers, and foreign students entered the United States (U.S. Department of Homeland Security, 2010, p. 65), and these numbers suggest how difficult it is to keep tabs on this source of illegal immigrants. Others cross the border illegally in the hopes of evading the Border Patrol and finding their way into some niche in the American economy. The fact that people keep coming suggests that most succeed.

Exhibit 10.16 Estimated Number of Total and Mexican Undocumented Immigrants, 2000 to 2010

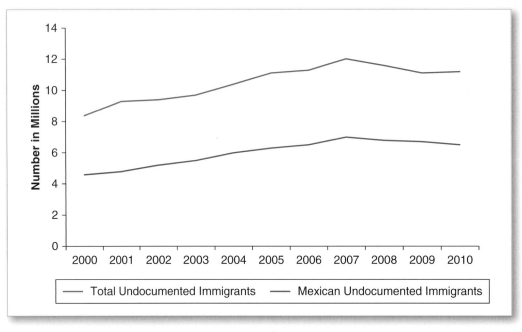

SOURCE: Passel and Cohn (2011).

One of the reasons that the supply of unauthorized immigrants is so high is because of the continuing demand for cheap labor in the U.S. economy. As we have noted on several occasions, the Global South—and Mexico in particular—has functioned as a reserve labor force for the U.S. economy for decades. Even in 2010, after several years of economic recession, undocumented immigrants provided a sizeable percentage of the workforce in many states and were as much as 10% of the workers in several (see Exhibit 10.17).

Exhibit 10.17 Unauthorized Immigrants as Share of Labor Force by State, 2010

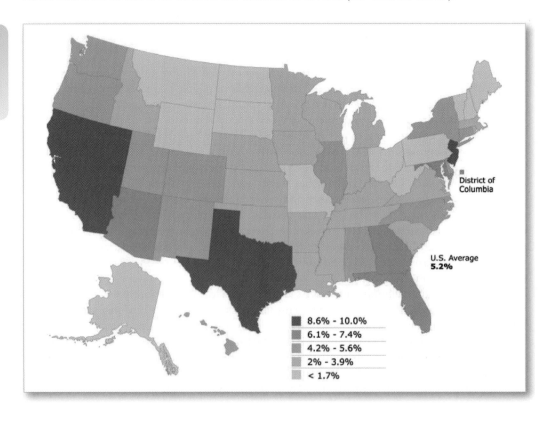

The United States is attempting to stem the flow of illegal immigration by reinforcing the border and building taller and bigger walls. These crosses commemorate those who lost their lives crossing the border.

© Christopher Morris/ Corbis.

The demand for cheap (undocumented) labor varies by the sector of the economy, and one of the biggest users has been the agricultural sector. Arturo Rodriguez (2011), the president of the United Farm Workers of America (the union founded by César Chávez and mentioned in Chapter 8), estimates that as much as 70% of the 2 million agricultural workers in the United States—the people who actually pick the crops and prepare them to be shipped to market—are undocumented immigrants. U.S. agriculture and the food supply would collapse without the contributions of undocumented workers.

A variety of efforts continue to be made to curtail and control the flow of illegal immigrants. Various states have attempted to lower the appeal of the United States by limiting benefits and opportunities. Other than the

aforementioned State Bill 1070 in Arizona, one of the best known of these attempts occurred in 1994, when California voters passed Proposition 187, which would have denied educational, health, and other services to illegal immigrants. The policy was declared unconstitutional, however, and was never implemented. Other efforts to decrease the flow of illegal immigration have included proposals to limit welfare benefits for immigrants, denying in-state college tuition to the children of illegal immigrants, increases in the size of the Border Patrol, and the construction of taller and wider walls along the border with Mexico. Over the past 8 years, a variety of proposals to reform the national immigration policy have been hotly debated at the highest levels of government, but none have been passed.

Although Americans will continue to be concerned about this problem, it seems unlikely that much can be done (within the framework of a democratic, humane society) to curtail the flow of people. The social networks that deliver immigrants—legal as well as illegal—are

Illegal immigration is a global phenomenon. These would-be immigrants from North Africa were apprehended in Spain and will be returned to their nations of origin.

© DARRIN ZAMMIT LUPI/ X01097/Reuters/Corbis.

too well established, and the demand for cheap labor in the United States is simply insatiable. In fact, denying services, as envisioned in Proposition 187, may make illegal immigrants more attractive as a source of labor by reducing their ability to resist exploitation. For example, if the children of illegal immigrants were not permitted to attend school, they would become more likely to join the army of cheap labor on which some employers depend. Who would benefit from closing public schools or denying in-state college tuition to the children of illegal immigrants?

IS CONTEMPORARY ASSIMILATION SEGMENTED?

In Chapter 2, we reviewed the patterns of acculturation and integration that typified the adjustment of Europeans who immigrated to the United States before the 1930s. Although their process of adjustment was anything but smooth or simple, these groups eventually acculturated and achieved levels of education and affluence comparable to national norms. Will contemporary immigrants experience similar success? Will their sons and daughters and grandsons and granddaughters rise in the occupational structure to a position of parity with the dominant group? Will the cultures and languages of these groups gradually fade and disappear?

Final answers to these questions must await future developments. In the meantime, there is considerable debate on these issues. Some analysts argue that the success story of the white ethnic groups will not be repeated and that assimilation for contemporary immigrants will be segmented: Some will enjoy success and rise to middle-class prosperity, but others will find themselves mired in the urban underclass, beset by crime, drugs, school failure, and marginal, low-paid menial jobs (Haller, Portes, & Lynch, 2011, p. 737). Other analysts find that the traditional perspective on assimilation—particularly the model of assimilation developed by Milton Gordon—continues to be a useful framework for understanding the experience of contemporary immigrants. We will review some of the most important and influential arguments from each side of this debate and, finally, attempt to come to some conclusions about the future of assimilation.

The Case for Segmented Assimilation

This thesis has attracted many advocates, including some of the most important researchers in this area of the social sciences. Here, we will focus on two of the most important works. The first presents an overview, and the second is based on an important, continuing research project on the second generation, the children of contemporary immigrants.

Assimilation Now Versus Assimilation Then

Sociologist Douglas Massey (1995) argued that there are three crucial differences between past (before the 1930s) and contemporary (after the mid-1960s) assimilation experiences, each of which calls the traditional perspective into question. First, the flow of immigrants from Europe to the United States slowed to a mere trickle after the 1920s because of restrictive legislation, the worldwide depression of the 1930s, and World War II. Immigration in the 1930s, for example, was less than 10% of the flow of the early 1920s. Thus, as the children and grandchildren of the European immigrants Americanized and grew to adulthood in the 1930s and 1940s, few new immigrants fresh from the old country replaced them in the ethnic neighborhoods. European cultural traditions and languages weakened rapidly with the passing of the first generation and the Americanization of their descendants.

It is unlikely, argues Massey, that a similar hiatus will interrupt contemporary immigration. As we saw in Exhibit 10.16, for example, the number of undocumented immigrants remains high in spite of the current recession. Immigration has become continuous, argues Massey, and as some contemporary immigrants (or their descendants) Americanize and rise to affluence and success, new arrivals will replace them and continuously revitalize the ethnic cultures and languages.

Second, the speed and ease of modern transportation and communication will maintain cultural and linguistic diversity. A century ago, immigrants from Europe could maintain contact with the old country only by mail, and many had no realistic expectation of ever returning. Modern immigrants, in contrast, can return to their homes in a day or less and can use telephones, television, e-mail, and the Internet to stay in intimate contact with the families and friends they left behind. Thus, the cultures of modern immigrants can be kept vital and whole in ways that were not available (and not even imagined) 100 years ago.

Third, and perhaps most important, contemporary immigrants face an economy and a labor market that are vastly different from those faced by European immigrants of the 19th and early 20th centuries. The latter group generally rose in the class system as the economy shifted from manufacturing to service (see Exhibit 5.5). Today, rates of upward mobility have decreased, and just when the importance of education has increased, schools available to the children of immigrants have fallen into neglect (Massey, 1995, pp. 645–646).

For the immigrants from Europe a century ago, assimilation meant a gradual rise to middle-class status and suburban comfort, a process often accomplished in three generations. Massey fears that assimilation today is segmented and that a large percentage of the descendants of contemporary immigrants—especially many of the Hispanic groups, Haitians, and other peoples of color—face permanent membership in a growing underclass population and continuing marginalization and powerlessness.

The Second Generation

An analysis of the second generation of recent immigrant groups (Haller et al., 2011) also found support for the segmented assimilation model. The researchers interviewed the children of immigrants in the Miami and San Diego areas at three different times—when they were average age 14 in the early 1990s, again 3 years later, and a final time 10 years later when the respondents were an average age 24. The sample was large (more than 5,000 respondents at the beginning) and representative of the second generation in the two metropolitan areas in which the study was conducted. This is an important study because its longitudinal design permits the researchers to track these children of immigrants in precise detail.

The researchers argue, consistent with Massey (1995) and with many of the points made previously in this text, that contemporary immigrants face a number of barriers to successful adaptation, including racial prejudice (since the huge majority are nonwhite), a labor market sharply split between a primary sector that requires high levels of education and a secondary sector that is low-paid and insecure, and a widespread criminal subculture based on gangs and drug sales that provides a sometimes attractive alternative to the conventional pursuit of success through education. Whether immigrants and their descendants are able to overcome these obstacles depends decisively on three factors, which are listed at the far left of Exhibit 10.18. The exhibit also depicts several different projected pathways of mobility across the generations. Immigrants who arrive with high levels of human capital enter the primary labor market, and their descendants generally enter the economic and social mainstream by the third generation (see the top row of the exhibit). The descendants of immigrants with lower levels of human capital can succeed if they benefit from strong families and strong co-ethnic communities that reinforce parental discipline. This pathway is depicted in the middle row of Exhibit 10.18 and also results in full acculturation and integration in the economic mainstream by the third generation.

Exhibit 10.18 Paths of Immigrant Mobility Across Generations

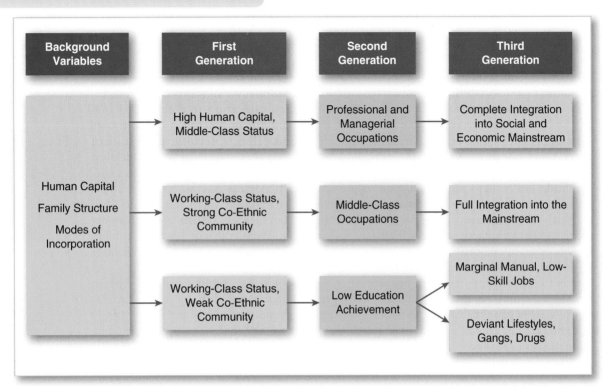

SOURCE: Based on Haller et al. (2011, p. 738).

The bottom row of the exhibit outlines a very different pathway for a large percentage of some contemporary immigrant groups. The mode of incorporation for these immigrants does not place them in a strong co-ethnic community, and they may also experience weaker family structures, sometimes because of their undocumented status or because the family is split between the United States and the home country. The result is lower educational achievement and economic marginalization or assimilation into gangs, the drug subculture, and other deviant lifestyles.

The researchers present a variety of evidence in support of segmented assimilation theory. For example, the second generations of different groups have very different experiences in school, very different income levels, and very different experiences with the criminal justice system. Some of the differences are presented in Exhibit 10.19, which displays large variations in the percentage of second-generation individuals who do not pursue education beyond high school, and Exhibit 10.20, which shows patterns of incarceration by group. As the researchers point out, these and the other patterns they examine are not random: They reflect large differences in the human capital of the immigrant generation and variations in modes of incorporation (especially in terms of legal status and racial prejudice). They show that large percentages of the second (and third and later) generations of some groups are destined for assimilation into low, marginalized, or deviant sectors of American society, in direct contradiction to the patterns predicted by some versions of traditional assimilation theory.

Another important recent study reinforces some of these points. Sociologists Telles and Ortiz (2008) studied a sample of Mexican Americans who were interviewed in 1965 and again in 2000. They found evidence of strong movements toward acculturation and integration on some dimensions (e.g., language) but not on others. Even fourth-generation members of their sample continued to live in "the barrio" and marry within the group, and did not reach economic parity with Anglos. The authors single out institutional discrimination (e.g., underfunding of schools that serve Mexican American neighborhoods) as a primary cause of the continuing separation, a point consistent with Massey's (1995) conclusion regarding the decreasing rates of upward mobility in American society.

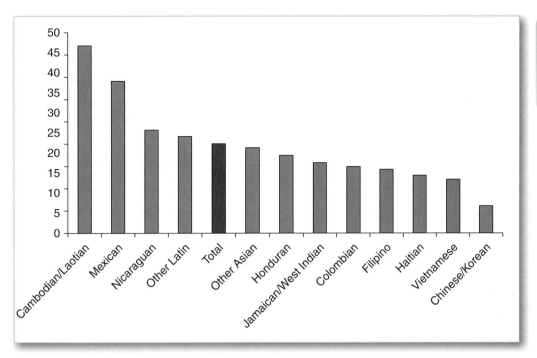

Exhibit 10.19
Percentage of Second
Generation Who Are
High School Graduates
or Less

NOTES:
Chinese and Korean Americans were combined, as were Cambodians and Laotians, because of similar patterns and
in order to create groups large enough for statistical analysis.
"Other Latin" is mostly Salvadoran and Guatemalan.
"Other Asian" is a diverse group of many nationalities.

SOURCE: Haller et al. (2011, p. 742).

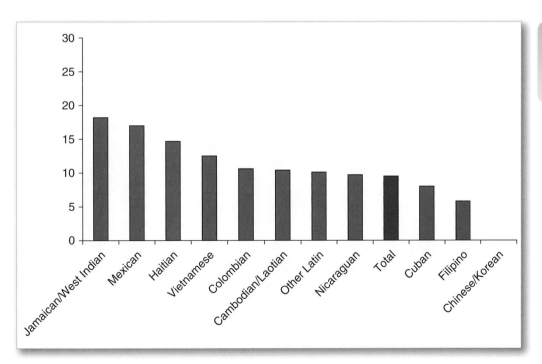

Exhibit 10.20
Percentage of Second-
Generation Males
Incarcerated

NOTES:
Chinese and Korean Americans were combined, as were Cambodians and Laotians, because of similar patterns and
in order to create groups large enough for statistical analysis.
"Other Latin" is mostly Salvadoran and Guatemalan.
"Other Asian" is a diverse group of many nationalities.

SOURCE: Haller et al. (2011, p. 742).

The Case for "Traditional" Assimilation Theory

Other recent studies come to a very different conclusion regarding the second generation: They are generally rising relative to their parents. This contradicts the segmented assimilation thesis and resurrects the somewhat tattered body of traditional assimilation theories. These studies (e.g., Alba & Nee, 2003; Bean & Stevens, 2003; Kasinitz, Mollenkopf, Waters, & Holdaway, 2008; White & Glick, 2009) argue that contemporary assimilation will ultimately follow the same course as that of European immigrant groups 100 years ago and as described in Gordon's theory (see Chapter 2). For example, two recent studies (Alba & Nee, 2003; Bean & Stevens, 2003) find that most contemporary immigrant groups are acculturating and integrating at the "normal" three-generation pace. Those groups (notably Mexicans) that appear to be lagging behind this pace may take as many as four to five generations, but their descendants will eventually find their way onto the primary job market and the cultural mainstream.

Studies of acculturation show that values Americanize and that English language proficiency grows with time of residence and generation (Bean & Stevens, 2003, p. 168). We discussed some of these patterns in Chapter 8 (see Exhibits 8.11 through 8.13).

In terms of structural integration, contemporary immigrant groups may be narrowing the income gap over time, although many groups (e.g., Dominicans, Mexicans, Haitians, and Vietnamese) are handicapped by very low levels of human capital at the start (Bean & Stevens, 2003, p. 142). Exhibits 10.21a and 10.21b illustrate this process with respect to wage differentials between Mexican and white non-Hispanic males and females of various generations and levels of education. In these exhibits, complete income equality with non-Hispanic whites would be indicated if the bar touched the 100% line at the top of the graph.

Looking first at males, recent Mexican immigrants earned a little less than half of what white males earned. The difference in income is lower for earlier immigrants, lower still for Mexican males of the second and third generations, and lowest for the most educated ("BA") members of those generations. In other words, income equality tends

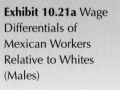

Exhibit 10.21a Wage Differentials of Mexican Workers Relative to Whites (Males)

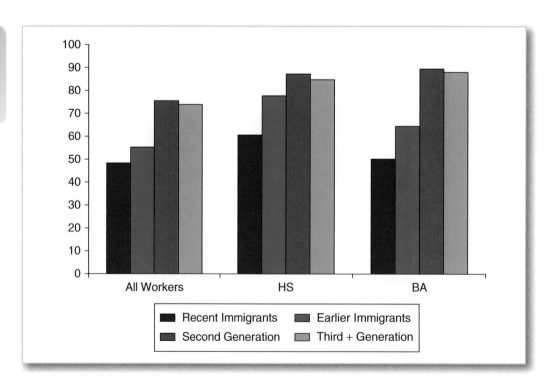

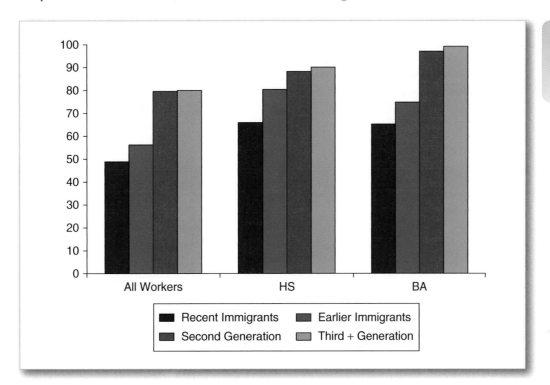

Exhibit 10.21b Wage Differentials of Mexican Workers Relative to Whites (Females)

to increase over the generations and as education increases. On the other hand, note that third-generation males do not rise relative to their parents' generation. This is contrary to the view that assimilation will proceed in a linear, stepwise fashion across the generations and is reminiscent of the findings of Telles and Ortiz (2008) cited earlier. For females, the wage differential also shrinks as the generations pass and as level of education increases. Note that for third-generation, college-educated females, the wage differential shrinks virtually to zero, indicating integration on this variable (at least compared with dominant-group females).

These patterns generally support the traditional perspective on assimilation. The wage gap shrinks by generation and level of education, and integration is substantial by the third generation (although complete only for one group). This pattern suggests that the movement of Mexican immigrants is toward the economic mainstream, even though they do not close the gap completely. Bean and Stevens (2003) conclude that this pattern is substantially consistent with the "three-generation model": The assimilation trajectory of Mexican Americans and other recent immigrant groups is not into the urban poor, the underclass, or the disenfranchised, disconnected, and marginalized. Assimilation is not segmented but is substantially repeating the experiences of the European groups on which Gordon (1964) based his theory.

Summary

How can we reconcile the direct contradictions between the segmented and traditional perspectives on assimilation? In large part, this debate concerns the nature of the evidence and judgments about how much weight to give to various facts and trends. On one hand, Massey's (1995) points about the importance of the postindustrial economy, declining opportunities for less-educated workers, and the neglect that seems typical of inner-city schools are well taken, as is the evidence supplied by other studies that generally support the segmented assimilation thesis. On the other hand, it seems that even the least-educated immigrant groups have been able to find economic niches in which they and their families can survive and eke out an existence long enough for their children and grandchildren to rise in the structure, a pattern that has been at the core of the American immigrant experience for almost two centuries.

Of course, this debate will continue, and new evidence and interpretations will appear. Ultimately, however, these disputes may continue until immigration stops (which is very unlikely to happen, as Massey points out) and the fate of the descendants of the last immigrant groups is measured.

RECENT IMMIGRATION IN HISTORICAL AND GLOBAL CONTEXT

The current wave of immigration to the United States is part of a centuries-old process that spans the globe. Underlying this immense and complex population movement is the powerful force of the continuing industrialization, economic development, and globalization. The United States and other advanced industrial nations are the centers of growth in the global economy, and immigrants flow to the areas of greater opportunity. In the 19th century, population moved largely from Europe to the Western Hemisphere. Over the past 50 years, the movement has been from the Global South to the Global North. This pattern reflects the simple geography of industrialization and opportunity and the fact that the more developed nations are in the Northern Hemisphere.

The United States has been the world's dominant economic, political, and cultural power for much of the century and the preferred destination of most immigrants. Newcomers from around the globe continue the collective, social nature of past population movements (see Chapter 2). The direction of their travels reflects contemporary global inequalities: Labor continues to flow from the less developed nations to the more developed nations. The direction of this flow is not accidental or coincidental. It is determined by the differential rates of industrialization and modernization across the globe. Immigration contributes to the wealth and affluence of the more developed societies and particularly to the dominant groups and elite classes of those societies.

The immigrant flow is also a response to the particular dynamics of globalization, particularly since the 1980s (Sen & Mamdouh, 2008). The current era of globalization has been guided by the doctrine of neoliberalism, or free trade, which urges nations to eliminate barriers to the free movement of goods and capital. The North American Free Trade Agreement (NAFTA), which we have mentioned on several occasions, is an example of a neoliberal policy. These policies open less-developed nations such as Mexico to consumer goods manufactured and controlled by large, transnational corporations. These corporations are often able to undersell indigenous goods, driving small-scale local farmers and manufacturers out of business. Finally, the international agencies that regulate the global economy pressure states to reduce the size of their governmental sector. This often means that the national budget for health and education is slashed and that services once controlled and subsidized by the government (e.g., water, electricity) are sold to private businesses. The combined result of these global forces is an increasingly vulnerable population in less-developed nations, unable to provide for themselves, educate their children, or afford the simplest of daily necessities.

Americans tend to see immigrants as individuals acting of their own free will and, often, illegally ("They chose to come to the United States and break the law"), but the picture changes when we see immigration as the result of these powerful, global economic and political forces. Globalization today allows for the free movement of capital and goods but not of people. While domestic economies and social systems crumble, the victims of neoliberal globalization are left with few choices: They cross borders not only to the United States but to other advanced industrial nations, illegally if they have to, because "it is the best choice to achieve a dignified life—if not for themselves, then for their children" (Sen & Mamdouh, 2008, p. 7). When viewed through the lens of globalization, it is clear that this population movement will continue because immigrants simply have no choice. It is unlikely that they can be stopped by further militarization of the border or by building bigger and taller walls. They come to the United States in their numbers, as immigrants did in the past, because the alternatives are unacceptable or nonexistent.

This perspective suggests that the tendency of many citizens of the more-developed world to reject, demonize, and criminalize immigrants is self-defeating. Punitive, militaristic policies will not stem the flow of people from the Global South to the Global North. Globalization, in its neoliberal form, is incomplete: It allows for the free movement of goods and capital but not of people. It benefits transnational corporations and the megabusinesses that produce consumer goods but victimizes the vulnerable citizens of the less-developed nations. As long as these forms of globalization hold, the population pressure from South to North will continue.

NEW IMMIGRANTS AND OLD ISSUES

In this chapter, we focused on some of the issues raised by high levels of immigration since the 1960s. As we discuss, debate, and consider these issues, we need to remember a fundamental fact about modern American society: The issues of the "traditional" minority groups—African Americans and American Indians, for example—have not been resolved. As we saw in earlier chapters, these groups have been a part of American society from the beginning, but they remain, in many ways, distant from achieving complete equality and integration.

Many of the current issues facing these groups relate to class as well as race. The urban underclass is disproportionately made up of peoples of color and remains marginal to the mainstream society in terms of access to education and job opportunities, decent housing, and good health care. While it is probably true that American society is more open and tolerant than ever before, we must not mistake a decline in blatant racism or a reduction in overt discrimination for its demise. In fact, as we have seen, there is abundant evidence that shows that racism and discrimination have not declined but have merely changed form, and that the patterns of exclusion and deprivation sustained in the past continue in the present.

Similarly, gender issues and sexism remain on the national agenda. As we have seen at various points throughout the text, blatant sexism and overt discrimination against women are probably at a historic low, but, again, we cannot mistake change for disappearance. Most importantly, minority women remain the victims of a double jeopardy and are among the most vulnerable and exploited segments of society. Many female members of the new immigrant groups find themselves in similarly vulnerable positions.

These problems of exclusion and continuing prejudice and sexism are exacerbated by a number of trends in the larger society. For example, the continuing shift in subsistence technology away from manufacturing to the service sector privileges groups that, in the past as well as today, have had access to education. The urban underclass consists disproportionately of groups that have been excluded from education in the past and have less access in the present.

The new immigrant groups have abundant problems of their own, of course, and need to find ways to pursue their self-interests in their new society. Some segments of these groups—the well-educated professionals seeking to advance their careers in the world's most advanced economy—will be much more likely to find ways to avoid the harshest forms of American rejection and exclusion. Similarly, the members of the "traditional" minority groups that have gained access to education and middle-class status will enjoy more opportunities than previous generations could have imagined (although, as we have seen, their middle-class position will be more precarious than that of their dominant-group counterparts).

Will we become a society in which ethnic and racial groups are permanently segmented by class, with the more favored members enjoying a higher, if partial, level of acceptance while other members of their groups languish in permanent exclusion and segmentation? What does it mean to be an American? What should it mean?

CURRENT DEBATES

Is Immigration Harmful or Helpful to the United States?

The continuing debate over U.S. immigration has generated plenty of controversy but little consensus. Following are two positions in the debate. The first argues against immigration on the grounds that it is harmful to native-born workers, especially those in the low-wage sector. Steven Camarota is director of research at the Center for Immigration Studies, a well-known "think tank" for immigration issues. The second excerpt was compiled by the Anti-Defamation League, one of the most important U.S. civil rights organizations, and attacks several common "myths" about immigration and argues, among other points, that immigrants contribute to the continuing health of the nation's economy.

IMMIGRATION IS HURTING THE U.S. WORKER

STEVEN A. CAMAROTA

The United States needs fewer immigrants, not more. . . . The growing number of undereducated people crossing our borders has hurt less-educated native-born workers. The U.S. needs to focus on reducing overall immigration levels. . . .

The number of immigrants—legal and illegal—living in the U.S. is growing at an unprecedented rate. U.S. Census Bureau data indicate that 1.6 million legal and illegal immigrants settle in the country each year. In 2006, the immigrant, or foreign-born population, reached about 38 million in the United States. . . . The U.S. has never confronted an immigrant population that has grown this much, this fast.

Low-paid American workers have borne the heaviest impact of immigration. This is largely because of the educational profile of the bulk of today's immigrants. Nine percent of adult native-born Americans (age 18 to 64) were high school dropouts in 2006, while 34 percent of recent adult immigrants had not completed high school. (The rate was 60 percent for illegal immigrants.)

Common sense, economic theory, and a fair reading of the research on this question indicate that allowing in so many immigrants (legal and illegal) with relatively little education reduces the wages and job prospects for Americans with little education. These are the Americans who are already the poorest workers. Between 2000 and 2005, the number of jobless natives (age 18 to 64) with no education beyond a high school degree increased by over 2 million, to 23 million, according to the Current Population Survey. During the same period, the number of less-educated immigrants (legal and illegal) holding a job grew 1.5 million.

Of greater concern, the percentage of employed native-born without a high school degree fell from 53 to 48 percent in the last 5 years. African Americans have particularly been affected. A September 2006 National Bureau of Economic Research paper found that immigration accounted for about a third of the decline in the employment rate of the least-educated African American men over the last few decades.

The disproportionate flow of undereducated immigrants to the U.S. has also depressed wages for native-born workers on the lower rungs of the economic ladder. In the last two-and-a-half decades, average hourly wages for male workers with less than a high school education declined more than 20 percent relative to inflation. For those with only a high school degree they are down almost 10 percent.

Typically, pro-immigration voices argue that immigration is essential because there are not enough Americans to fill all the low-wage jobs. But if this were so, then the wages and employment rates of such workers should be rising as employers try desperately to retain and attract workers. Yet quantitative evidence for such a phenomenon doesn't exist. The only evidence of a labor shortage comes from the employers.

In addition to harming the poorest and least educated American workers, our immigration system has created a large burden for taxpayers. The best predictor of poverty and welfare dependence in modern America is education level. Given the low educational levels of most recent immigrants, we would expect them to be a greater drain on public coffers than the immigrants who came before them. Indeed this is the case. In 1997, the National Academy of Sciences (NAS) estimated that immigrant households consumed $20 billion more in public services than they paid in taxes each year. Adjusted for inflation, with the current size of the immigrant population today, this figure would be over $40 billion.

Immigrants from Latin America place an especially heavy burden on American taxpayers. For example, 57 percent of households headed by Dominican immigrants in 2004 used at least one major welfare program; 43 percent of Mexicans took advantage of at least one welfare program; and about a third of the households headed by immigrants from Central America, Cuba and Colombia use the welfare system. In contrast only 18 percent of native households receive welfare assistance.

The biggest problem for taxpayers is not illegal aliens—though they are a drain. The biggest problem is less-educated legal immigrants, who represent the majority of the immigrants from Mexico and Central America. My own research indicates that the net costs (taxes paid minus services used) to the federal government alone would roughly triple if illegal aliens were legalized and began to use services and pay taxes like legal immigrants with the same level of education. . . .

SOURCE: Camarota (2007).

MYTHS AND FACTS ABOUT IMMIGRATION

THE ANTI-DEFAMATION LEAGUE

Myth #1: Immigrants are overrunning our country, and most are here illegally.

The Facts: It is true that there are more immigrants living in the U.S. than ever before. However, the percentage of immigrants in the overall population is not much different than during other large waves. Today immigrants make up about 12% of the total U.S. population. From 1900 to 1930, immigrants made up between 12% and 15% of the population, and similar spikes occurred in the 1850s and 1880s. The U.S. successfully absorbed immigrants during those periods, and there is no reason to believe that we are being "overrun" today.

Of the 36 million immigrants in the U.S. today, two thirds . . . are here legally, and half of those with legal status . . . are U.S. citizens. There are an estimated 12 million undocumented immigrants in the U.S. Half . . . of these people entered the country legally as tourists, students, or temporary workers and became "undocumented" when their papers expired and they didn't leave the country. Undocumented immigrants make up about 4% of the overall U.S. population.

Myth #2: Most immigrants aren't interested in fitting into our society. They don't want to learn English or become Americans.

The Facts: Most immigrants, if given the opportunity, work hard to adapt to their new countries. More than 80% of immigrants say they have tried to learn English. After 15 years in the U.S., for example, 75% of Spanish-speaking immigrants speak English regularly; and 91% of their children and 97% of their grandchildren can speak English well. For many immigrants, however, there are barriers to learning a new language. Many work two or three jobs and don't have enough time, money, or child care to allow for classes. English language programs in the U.S. are often underfunded and hard to get into. It is estimated that more than 90,000 immigrants across the nation are on waiting lists to learn English.

Similarly, many immigrants seek citizenship despite difficult requirements and long delays. In 2007, the Department of Homeland Security received 1.4 million citizenship applications, and in recent years the number of new citizens has risen to the highest level in 25 years. . . . Today's immigrants are adjusting and blending into U.S. society at the same rate as past generations of immigrants.

Myth #3: Immigrants bring crime and violence to our cities and towns.

The Facts: Study after study shows that immigrants are less likely than native-born citizens to commit crimes, even though immigrants are more likely to live in poverty and have less than a high school education. . . . Newly arrived immigrants are especially unlikely to be involved in crime, and teenage immigrants are less likely than native-born teens to be involved in delinquent behavior, such as violence and drug use.

Even as the U.S. experiences one of the largest spikes in immigration in many decades, crime rates across the country continue to go down. This is true even in cities with large immigrant populations, such as New York, Los Angeles, Chicago, and Miami, and border cities like San Diego and El Paso. Those who try to blame immigrants for a supposed rise in crime are twisting the facts to stir up stereotypes and bias against immigrants.

Myth #4: Immigrants hurt our country financially by taking jobs and services without paying taxes.

The Facts: Though many people fear that immigrants are taking job opportunities away from natives, immigrants actually help to create new jobs. States with large numbers of immigrants report lower unemployment for everyone. Immigrants are more likely to be self-employed and start new businesses. 18% of small businesses, which provide up to 80% of the new jobs in the U.S. each year, are started by immigrants. Though an increase in immigrant workers sometimes drives down wages for working class people, immigrants help to lift wages for workers as a whole in the U.S.

Immigrants pay between $90 and $140 billion each year in taxes. More than half of all undocumented immigrants are believed to be working "on the books," which means that they pay taxes on their salaries; and all people contribute by paying sales taxes on goods that they buy and property taxes on the homes they rent.

Studies show that immigrants pay $20 to $30 billion more in taxes each year than the amount of government services they use. While the cost of educating the children of immigrants may be high, many immigrants do not benefit . . . from food stamps and Social Security payments. In addition, immigrants are less likely to use services that may be open to them, such as health care. Overall, immigrants contribute more to the U.S. economy than they take.

Myth #5: Open borders and too many illegal immigrants make it more likely that the U.S. will suffer a terrorist attack.

The Facts: Since September 11, some people have tried to link the "War on Terror" to the recent wave of immigration. The U.S. government passed laws after 9–11 treating immigrants—especially Muslim and Arab people—in hostile ways. For example, a "Special Registration" program was set up that required immigrant boys and men from certain countries to be finger printed, photographed and interviewed by immigration officers. . . . Since 9–11, thousands of immigrants have been held without any proof that they were involved in terrorist activities. Many have been put on trial in secret courts without being allowed to talk to a lawyer or their family members.

These harsh actions . . . have led to the capture of almost no terrorists, and are unlikely to have made our country any more secure. Terrorist attacks are committed by people of all backgrounds, including U.S.-born citizens. . . . Many experts believe that unfairly targeting immigrants actually causes us to be less safe by making immigrants afraid to contact the police with information about crimes. The truth is that the vast majority of immigrants are . . . law-abiding people who come here to work hard and make a better life for their families.

Myth #6: We can solve the problem of illegal immigration by building walls and increasing security.

The Facts: In 2006 Congress passed the Secure Fence Act, which provided $3 billion for 700 miles of fencing stretching from California to Texas, designed to prevent illegal immigration from Mexico. The government also doubled the number of border patrol agents between 1995 and 2006, and increased the border security budget by over 10 times during that period. Even with all of the new walls and policing, though, the number of undocumented immigrants in the U.S. increased from about 8 million in 2000 to 12 million in 2009.

Rather than stopping immigration, the extra security has pushed it to more dangerous . . . places, leading to fewer arrests and triple the number of deaths at the border. These risky conditions also lead many immigrants—who might normally work in the U.S. only for a short time—to stay longer and bring their families with them.

As long as there is poverty and suffering in other parts of the world, people will continue to come to the U.S. to seek a better life, no matter how big a wall we build. While no country can take in unlimited numbers of immigrants, wealthy nations have a responsibility to help those who are less fortunate. This is especially true when their policies add to hardships elsewhere, such as U.S. trade laws that drive Mexican farmers out of business or the war in Iraq, which has created millions of refugees. The U.S. prides itself on being a "nation of immigrants," and on the values of fairness and equality. It is possible to create a process for managing immigration that treats immigrants with dignity instead of as criminals.

SOURCE: Anti-Defamation League (2009). © Anti-Defamation League, www.adl.org/education. Adapted with permission.

DEBATE QUESTIONS TO CONSIDER

1. Consider the nature of the arguments presented in these excerpts. To what extent do they appeal to emotion? To what extent do they base their arguments on evidence and logic? What specific disagreements over "facts" can you identify? What information would you need to resolve these disagreements? A good way to start answering these questions is by investigating the original documents: The URLs are given in the Reference section of this text. In particular, evaluate the sources of the information used by the authors.

2. Use the evidence presented in this chapter and in Chapters 8 and 9 to further evaluate these arguments. How persuasive is Camarota's argument that immigrants have a negative impact on low-wage American workers? What about the point made in response to "Myth #4" that immigrants contribute more than they take?

3. Similarly, evaluate these two points in terms of the evidence and arguments presented in Chapters 8 through 10: in response to "Myth #2" that contemporary immigrants are adjusting at the same rate as immigrants of the past and in response to "Myth #6" that immigration will continue as long as there is poverty and suffering in the world.

4. Many of the arguments in this debate are economic. What other dimensions should be added (cultural, linguistic, and so forth) to the debate? What arguments were raised in previous chapters that should be considered here?

5. What are the implications of this debate for the "traditional" minority groups? What gender and class dimensions can you identify in this debate?

MAIN POINTS

- Since the mid-1960s, immigrants have been coming to the United States at nearly record rates. Most of these immigrant groups have co-ethnics who have been in the United States for years, but others are "new Americans." How will this new wave of immigration transform America? Will they assimilate? How?
- Various groups of "New Americans" are considered, including Hispanic immigrants, non-Hispanic immigrants from the Caribbean, Asian immigrants, Arab and Middle Eastern immigrants, and African immigrants. Some are driven by economic needs; others are political refugees, and some are highly educated. All face multiple issues, including racism, institutionalized discrimination, and a changing U.S. economy. Arab Americans remain a special target for hate crimes and for security concerns.
- Contemporary immigrants experience three different modes of incorporation: the primary labor market, the secondary labor market, and the enclave. The pathway of each group is strongly influenced by the amount of human capital they bring, their race, the attitude of the larger society, and many other factors.
- Relations between immigrants and the larger society are animated by a number of issues, including the relative costs and benefits of immigration, concerns about undocumented immigrants, and the speed of assimilation. One important issue currently being debated by social scientists is whether assimilation for new Americans will be segmented or will ultimately follow the pathway established by immigrant groups from Europe in the 19th and 20th centuries.

STUDY SITE ON THE WEB

For chapter-specific resources, such as self-quizzes, videos, and flashcards, go to **www.sagepub.com/ healeyregc6e**.

FOR FURTHER READING

Alba, Richard, & Nee, Victor. 2003. *Remaking the American Mainstream: Assimilation and Contemporary Immigration*. Cambridge, MA: Harvard University Press.

Bean, Frank, & Stevens, Gillian. 2003. *America's Newcomers and the Dynamics of Diversity*. New York: Russell Sage Foundation.

Kasinitz, Philip, Mollenkopf, John H., Waters, Mary C., & Holdaway, Jennifer. 2008. *Inheriting the City: The Children of Immigrants Come of Age*. Cambridge, MA: Harvard University Press.

Three landmark studies of contemporary immigrants that find that assimilation is generally following a course consistent with the "traditional" model of assimilation

Portes, Alejandro, & Rumbaut, Rubén. 2001. *Ethnicities: Children of Immigrants in America*. New York: Russell Sage Foundation.

Portes, Alejandro, & Rumbaut, Rubén. 2001. *Legacies: The Story of the Immigrant Second Generation*. New York: Russell Sage Foundation.

Two landmark studies of new American groups whose findings are generally consistent with the segmented assimilation hypothesis

QUESTIONS FOR REVIEW AND STUDY

1. What differences exist between these new Americans in terms of their motivations for coming to the United States? What are the implications of these various "push" factors for their reception and adjustment to the United States?

2. Compare and contrast the Hispanic and Asian immigrant groups discussed in this chapter. What important differences and similarities can you identify in terms of modes of incorporation and human capital? What are the implications of the differences for the experiences of these groups?

3. Compare Arab and Middle Eastern immigrant groups with those from the Caribbean. Which group is more diverse? What differences exist in their patterns of adjustment and assimilation? Why do these patterns exist?

4. Compare and contrast African immigrants with the other groups. How do they differ? What are the implications of these differences for their adjustment to the larger society?

5. What, in your opinion, are the most important issues facing the United States in terms of immigration and assimilation? How are these issues playing out in your community? What are the implications of these issues for the future of the United States?

6. Will assimilation for contemporary immigrants be segmented? After examining the evidence and arguments presented by both sides and using information from this and previous chapters, which side of the debate seems more credible? Why? What are the implications of this debate? What will the United States look like in the future if assimilation is segmented? How will the future change if assimilation follows the "traditional" pathway? Which of these scenarios is more desirable for immigrant groups? For society as a whole? For various segments of U.S. society (e.g., employers, labor unions, African Americans, consumers, the college educated, the urban underclass, etc.)?

INTERNET RESEARCH PROJECT

In this exercise, you will use information gathered by the U.S. Bureau of the Census to learn more about two of the "New American" groups covered in this chapter. This project adds to the information you gathered in Chapters 6 through 9. You can add the information for African Americans, American Indians and Alaska Natives (AIAN), Hispanic Americans, and Asian Americans from previous exercises, but you will need to add information for the variables you select. You will then use course concepts to assess and analyze this information and place it in the context of this text. *Visit the website for this text for instructions on finding the information needed to complete the table below.*

		Total Population	African Americans	AIAN	Hispanic Americans	All Asian Americans	New American Groups	
1	Number							
3	Median age							
4	Average household size							
5	% less than high school							
6	% of the foreign-born who entered after 2000							
7	% speak English less than "very well"							
8	% unemployed							
9	Per capita income							
10	Median incomes for full-time, year-round workers							
	Males							
	Females							
11	Poverty rate, all families							
12								
13								

QUESTIONS

1. What stage of Gordon's model of assimilation (see Exhibit 2.1) do the variables in the table measure?

2. Describe your groups using the Blauner hypothesis (see Chapter 4). Are they closer to the "colonized" or the "immigrant" types? How much human capital do they bring? Are they targeted by racial prejudice?

Hate crimes? What stereotypes or perceptions dominate how they are perceived? Given this information, what would you predict about their relative status in American society?

3. Use the debate between the segmented assimilation thesis and the traditional (Gordon) assimilation model to compare and contrast your two groups. Are they adjusting successfully to U.S. society? Is there a strong ethnic community to assist new arrivals? Are a large percentage of your groups in danger of falling into the underclass? What are the crucial differences between groups that lead them to different fates?

OPTIONAL GROUP DISCUSSION

Bring the information on your groups to class and compare with the information collected by others. Consider the issues raised in the questions above and in the chapter, and develop some ideas about why the groups are where they are relative to one another and to the total population.

NOTES

1. Based on an Associated Press dispatch, May 18, 2011. Retrieved July 28, 2011, from http://www.msnbc.msn.com/id/43073023/ns/world_news-americas/t/x-rays-reveal-usbound-migrants-crammed-trucks/

11

Minority Groups and U.S. Society

Themes, Patterns, and the Future

Over the past 10 chapters, we have analyzed ideas and theories about dominant-minority relations, examined the historical and contemporary situations of minority groups in U.S. society, and surveyed a variety of dominant-minority situations around the globe. Now it is time to reexamine our major themes and concepts and determine what conclusions can be derived from our analysis.

SOME AMERICANS REVISITED

Let's begin with an exercise. Turn back to Chapter 1 and reread the biographies of the people at the beginning of the chapter. After reading this text, you should now see these people through different eyes.

You should recognize that Kim Park lives in an enclave economy and that Shirley Umphlett's life was profoundly affected by the migration of African Americans from the rural South to the urban North. Mary Ann O'Brien's family history exemplifies the slow rise to middle-class status characteristic of so many European American immigrants, whereas George Snyder seems trapped by the urban poverty and underclass marginality confronting so many racial minority groups today. Hector Gonzalez has a strong attachment to the culture of his Mexican ancestors even though he has been thoroughly integrated into the U.S.

job market. The busboy is one of millions of undocumented immigrants in the United States, most of them in marginal positions, still focused on their home villages. William Buford occupies an elite social and economic position but has no interest in his or anyone else's ethnic origin. He often argues that anyone, regardless of social class or race, could duplicate his success with sufficient diligence and hard work, conveniently forgetting that his wealth was inherited.

You might think that Buford's conclusions are not particularly insightful or informed. However, his superficial analysis is shared by millions of other Americans. Americans traditionally see success or failure as a matter of individual choice and personal effort. Blaming the victims of racism and discrimination for their situations can be comforting because it absolves the more fortunate of guilt or complicity in the perpetuation of minority group poverty and powerlessness. More accurate analyses and more compelling conclusions might be found in the thinking of people (like George Snyder) who are the victims of the system. Unlike the beneficiaries of the status quo, minority group members are sensitized to the dynamics of racism and discrimination by their efforts to avoid victimization. We should remember, however, that our understandings are always limited by who we are, where we come from, and what we have experienced. Our ability to imagine the realities faced by others is never perfect, and what we can see of the world depends very much on where we stand.

If we are to understand the forces that have created racial and ethnic minority groups in the United States and around the globe, we must find ways to surpass the limitations of our personal experiences and honestly confront the often ugly realities of the past and present. I believe that the information and the ideas developed in this text can help liberate our sociological imaginations from the narrow confines of our own experiences and perspectives.

In this final chapter, I restate the general themes of this text and draw conclusions from the material we have covered. I also raise speculative questions about the future. As we look backward to the past and forward to the future, it seems appropriate to paraphrase the words of the historian Oscar Handlin (1951): "Once I thought to write a history of the minority groups in America. Then, I discovered that the minority groups were American history" (p. 3).

THE IMPORTANCE OF SUBSISTENCE TECHNOLOGY

Perhaps the most important sociological idea we have developed is that dominant-minority relations are shaped by large social, political, and economic forces and change as these broad characteristics change. To understand the evolution of America's minority groups is to understand the history of the United States, from the earliest colonial settlement to the modern megalopolis. As we have seen throughout the text, these same broad forces have left their imprint on many societies around the globe.

Subsistence technology is the most basic force shaping a society and the relationships between dominant and minority groups in that society. In the colonial United States, minority relations were bent to the demands of a land-hungry, labor-intensive agrarian technology, and the early relationships between Africans, Europeans, and American Indians flowed from the colonists' desire to control both land and labor. By the mid-1800s, two centuries after Jamestown was founded, the same dynamics that had enslaved African Americans and nearly annihilated American Indians made a minority group out of Mexican Americans.

The agrarian era came to an end in the 19th century as the new technologies of the Industrial Revolution increased the productivity of the economy and eventually changed every aspect of life in the United States. The paternalistic, oppressive systems used to control the labor of minority groups in the agrarian system gave way to competitive systems of group relations. These newer systems evolved from more rigid forms to more fluid forms as industrialization and urbanization progressed.

As the United States grew and developed, new minority groups were created, and old minority groups were transformed. Rapid industrialization combined with the opportunities available on the frontier made the United States an attractive destination for immigrants from Europe, Asia, Latin America, and other parts of the world. Immigrants helped farm the Great Plains, mine the riches of the West, and above all, supply the armies of labor required by industrialization.

The descendants of the immigrants from Europe benefited from the continuing industrialization of the economy, rising slowly in the social class structure as the economy grew and matured. Immigrants from Asia and Latin America were not so fortunate. Chinese Americans and Japanese Americans survived in ethnic enclaves on the fringes of the mainstream society, and Mexican Americans and Puerto Ricans supplied low-paid manual labor for both the rural and the urban economy. For much of the 20th century, both Asian Americans and Hispanic Americans were barred from access to dominant-group institutions and higher-paid jobs.

The racial minority groups, particularly African Americans, Mexican Americans, and Puerto Ricans, began to enter the urban working class after European American ethnic groups had started to move up in the occupational structure, at a time when the supply of manual, unskilled jobs was starting to dwindle. Thus, the processes that allowed upward mobility for European Americans failed to work for the racial minority groups, who confronted urban poverty and bankrupt cities in addition to the continuing barriers of racial prejudice and institutional discrimination.

Immigration to the United States has been quite high for the past several decades and has delivered highly educated professionals to help staff the postindustrial economy, along with large numbers of undocumented immigrants to supply workers for the secondary labor market and the irregular economy. This stream has evoked the usual American nativism and racism along with very intense debates—in the social sciences as well as in the general public—about the cost and benefits of the immigrants and their ultimate fates in the social structure.

We can only speculate about what the future holds, but the emerging information-based, high-tech society is unlikely to offer many opportunities to people with lower levels of education and few occupational skills. It seems highly likely that, at least for the near future, a substantial percentage of racial and colonized minority groups and some recent immigrant groups will be participating in the mainstream economy of the future at lower levels than the dominant group, the descendants of the European immigrants, and the more advantaged recent immigrant groups. This outcome would be consistent with the segmented assimilation thesis, as discussed in Chapter 10. Upgraded urban educational systems, job training programs, and other community development programs might alter the grim scenario of continuing exclusion, but, as we discussed at the end of Chapter 3, current public opinion about matters of race and discrimination makes creation of such programs unlikely.

In a postindustrial society, education is a key pathway for upward mobility and an important venue in which members of different groups can encounter one another. In dormitories, classrooms, and cafeterias and across campus, the opportunities for meaningful, equal-status contact can enhance the education of all.

Inaction and perpetuation of the status quo will bar a large percentage of the population from the emerging mainstream economy. Those segments of the African American, Hispanic American, and Asian American communities currently mired in the urban underclass will continue to compete with some of the newer immigrants for jobs in the low-wage, secondary labor market or in alternative opportunity structures, including crime.

THE IMPORTANCE OF THE CONTACT SITUATION, GROUP COMPETITION, AND POWER

We have stressed the importance of the contact situation—the conditions under which the minority group and dominant group first come into contact with each other—throughout this text. Blauner's distinction between immigrant and colonized minority groups is fundamental, a distinction so basic that it helps clarify minority group situations centuries after the initial contact period. In Part III, we used Blauner's distinction as an organizing principle and covered American minority groups in approximate order from "most colonized" to "most immigrant." The groups covered first (African Americans and American Indians) are clearly at a greater disadvantage in contemporary society than the groups covered last (especially immigrants from Asia with high levels of human capital) and the white ethnic groups covered in Chapter 2.

For example, prejudice, racism, and discrimination against African Americans remain formidable forces in contemporary America even though they may have softened into more subtle forms. In contrast, prejudice and discrimination against European American groups such as the Irish, Italians, and Polish Americans have nearly disappeared today even though they were quite formidable just a few generations ago. In the same way, contemporary immigrant groups that are nonwhite and bring few resources and low levels of human capital (e.g., Haitians) may experience segmented assimilation and find themselves in situations resembling those of colonized minority groups. Contemporary immigrant groups that are at the opposite end of the continuum (e.g., Asian Indians) are more likely to approximate the experiences of white ethnics and find themselves in some version of middle-class suburbia. The Internet research exercises presented at the ends of Chapters 6 to 10 should have given you information to assess some of these patterns.

Noel's hypothesis states that if three conditions are present in the contact situation—ethnocentrism, competition, and the differential in power—ethnic or racial stratification will result. The relevance of ethnocentrism is largely limited to the actual contact situation, but the other two concepts help clarify the changes occurring after initial contact.

We have examined numerous instances in which group competition—or even the threat of competition—increased prejudice and led to greater discrimination and more repression. Recall, for example, the opposition of the labor movement (dominated by European American ethnic groups) to Chinese immigrants. The anti-Chinese campaign led to the Chinese Exclusion Act of 1882, the first significant restriction on immigration to the United States. There are parallels between campaigns for exclusion in the past and current ideas about ending or curtailing immigration. Clearly, some part of the current opposition to immigration is motivated by a sense of threat and the fear that immigrants are a danger not only to jobs and to the economy but also to the cultural integrity of U.S. society.

Noel's third variable, the differential in power, determines the outcome of the initial contact situation and which group becomes dominant and which becomes minority. Following the initial contact, the superior power of the dominant group helps it sustain the inferior position of the minority group. Minority groups, by definition, have fewer power resources, but they characteristically use what they have in an attempt to improve their situations. The improvements in the situations of American minority groups since the middle of the 20th century have been due in large part to the fact that they (especially African Americans, who typically led the way in protest and demands for change) finally acquired some power resources of their own. For example, one important source of power for the civil rights movement in the South during the 1950s and 1960s was the growth of African American voting strength in the North. After World War II, the African American electorate became too sizable to ignore, and its political power helped pressure the federal government to take action and pass the legislation that ended the Jim Crow era.

Minority status being what it is, however, each of the groups we have discussed (with the exception of the white ethnic groups) still controls relatively few power resources and is limited in its ability to pursue its own self-interests. Many of these limitations are economic and related to social class; many minority groups simply lack the resources to finance campaigns for reform or to exert significant pressure on political institutions. Other limitations include small group size (e.g., Asian American groups), language barriers (e.g., many Hispanic groups), and divided loyalties within the group (e.g., American Indians separated by tribal allegiances).

At any rate, the relative powerlessness of minority groups today is a legacy of the contact situations that created the groups in the first place. In general, colonized groups are at a greater power disadvantage than immigrant groups. Contact situations set agendas for group relations that have impacts centuries after the initial meeting.

Given all that we have examined in this text, it is obvious that competition and differences in power resources will continue to shape intergroup relations (including relations between minority groups themselves) well into the future. Because they are so basic and consequential, jobs will continue to be primary objects of competition, but there will be plenty of other issues to divide the nation. Included on this divisive list will be debates about crime and the criminal justice system, welfare reform, national health care policy, school busing, bilingual education, immigration policy, and multicultural curricula in schools.

These and other public issues will continue to separate us along ethnic and racial lines because those lines have become so deeply embedded in the economy, in politics, in our schools and neighborhoods, and in virtually every nook and cranny of U.S. society. These deep divisions reflect fundamental realities about who gets what in the United States, and they will continue to reflect the distribution of power and stimulate competition along group lines for generations to come.

DIVERSITY WITHIN MINORITY GROUPS

All too often, and this text is probably no exception, minority groups are seen as unitary and undifferentiated. Although overgeneralizations are sometimes difficult to avoid, I want to stress again the diversity within each of the groups we have examined. Minority group members vary from one another by age, sex, region of residence, level of education, urban versus rural residence, political ideology, and many other variables. The experience of one segment of the group (e.g., college-educated, fourth-generation, native-born Chinese American females) may bear little resemblance to the experience of another (e.g., illegal Chinese male immigrants with less than a high school education), and the problems of some members may not be the problems of others.

I have tried to highlight the importance of this diversity by exploring gender differentiation within each minority group. Study of minority groups by U.S. social scientists has focused predominantly on males, and the experiences of minority women have been described in much less depth. All the cultures examined in this text have strong patriarchal traditions. Women of the dominant group as well as minority women have had much less access to leadership roles and higher-status positions and have generally occupied a subordinate status, even in their own groups. The experiences of minority group women and the extent of their differences from minority group males and dominant group women are only now being fully explored.

One clear conclusion we can make about gender is that minority group females are doubly oppressed and disempowered. Limited by both their minority and their gender roles, they are among the most vulnerable and exploited segments of society. At one time or another, the women of every minority group have taken the least desirable, lowest-status positions available in the economy, often while trying to raise children and attend to other family needs. They have been expected to provide support for other members of their families, kinship groups, and communities, often sacrificing their own self-interests to the welfare of others. Jade Snow Wong (1993), a Chinese American daughter of immigrant parents, describes the subordinate role and circumscribed world of minority group females in a remembrance of her mother:

Photo 11.4

Jade Snow Wong (1922–2005) was an artist and writer. She was born to a poor, very traditional immigrant family and wrote two autobiographical volumes about her experiences.

AP Photo/Ernest K. Bennett.

My mother dutifully followed my father's leadership. She was extremely thrifty, but the thrifty need pennies to manage, and the old world had denied her those. Upon arrival in the new world of San Francisco, she accepted the elements her mate had selected to shape her new life: domestic duties, seamstress work in the factory-home, mothering each child in turn, church once a week, and occasional movies. (p. 50)

In their roles outside the family, minority women have encountered discrimination based on their minority group membership, compounded with discrimination based on their gender. The result is, predictably, an economic and social status that is often at the bottom of the social structure. For example, average incomes of African American females today are lower than those of white males, white females, and black males (see Exhibit 6.5). The same pattern holds for other groups, and the women of many minority groups are highly concentrated in the low-paid secondary labor market and employed in jobs that provide services to members of more privileged groups.

The inequality confronted by minority women extends beyond matters of economics and jobs: Women of color have higher rates of infant mortality and births out of wedlock and a host of other health-related, quality-of-life problems. In short, there is ample evidence to document a pervasive pattern of gender inequality within America's minority groups. Much of this gender inequality is complexly interconnected with rising rates of poverty and female-headed households, teenage pregnancy, and unemployment for minority males in the inner city.

Gender differentiation cuts through minority groups in a variety of ways. Specific issues might unite minority women with women of the dominant group (e.g., sexual harassment in schools and the workplace), and others might unite them with the men of their minority groups (e.g., the enforcement of civil rights legislation). The problems and issues of minority women are complexly tied to the patterns of inequality and discrimination in the larger society and within their own groups. Solving the problems faced by minority groups will not resolve the problems faced by minority women, and neither will resolving the problems of gender inequality alone. Women of color are embedded in structures of inequality and discrimination that limit them in two independent but simultaneous ways. Articulating and addressing these difficulties requires recognition of the complex interactions between gender and minority group status.

ASSIMILATION AND PLURALISM

It seems fair to conclude that the diversity and complexity of minority group experiences in the United States are not well characterized by some of the traditional, or "melting pot," views of assimilation. For example, the idea that assimilation is a linear, inevitable process has little support. Immigrants from Europe probably fit that model better than other groups, but as the ethnic revival of the 1960s demonstrated, assimilation and ethnic identity can take surprising turns.

Also without support is the notion that there is always a simple, ordered relationship between the various stages of assimilation: acculturation, integration into public institutions, integration into the private sector, and so forth. We have seen that some groups integrated before they acculturated, others have become more committed to their ethnic or racial identity over the generations, and still others have been acculturated for generations but are no closer to full integration. New expressions of ethnicity come and go, and minority groups emerge, combine, and recombine in unexpected and seemingly unpredictable ways. The 1960s saw a reassertion of ethnicity and loyalty to old identities among some groups, even as other groups developed new coalitions and invented new ethnic identities (e.g., pantribalism among American Indians). No simple or linear view of assimilation can begin to make sense of the array of minority group experiences.

Indeed, the very desirability of assimilation has been subject to debate. Since the 1960s, many minority spokespersons have questioned the wisdom of becoming a part of a sociocultural structure that was constructed by the systematic exploitation of minority groups. Pluralistic themes increased in prominence as the commitment of the larger society to racial equality faltered. Virtually every minority group proclaimed the authenticity of its own experiences, its own culture, and its own version of history, separate from but as valid as that of the dominant groups. From what might have seemed like a nation on the verge of integration in the 1950s (at least for white ethnic groups), America evolved into what might have seemed like a Tower of Babel in the 1960s. The consensus that assimilation was the best solution and the most sensible goal for all of America's minority groups was shattered (if it ever really existed at all).

Let's review the state of acculturation and integration in the United States on a group-by-group basis, following the order of the case studies in Part III. African Americans are highly acculturated. Despite the many unique cultural traits forged in America and those that survive from Africa, black Americans share language, values and beliefs, and most other aspects of culture with white Americans of similar class and educational background. In terms of integration, in contrast, African Americans present a mixed picture. For middle-class, more-educated members of the group, American society offers more opportunities for upward mobility and success than ever before. Without denying the prejudice, discrimination, and racism that remain, this segment of the group is in a favorable position to achieve higher levels of affluence and power for their children and grandchildren. At the same time, a large percentage of African Americans remain mired in urban poverty, and for them, affluence, security, and power are just as distant (perhaps more so) than they were a generation ago. Considering the group as a whole, African Americans are still highly segregated in their residential and school attendance patterns, and their political power, although rising, is not proportional to their size. Unemployment, lower average incomes, and poverty in general remain serious problems and may be more serious than they were a generation ago.

American Indians are less acculturated than African Americans, and some aspects of American Indian culture and language may be increasing in strength and vitality. On measures of integration, there is some indication of improvement, but many American Indians are among the most isolated and impoverished minority groups in the United States. One possible bright spot for some reservations lies in the further development of the gambling industry and the investment of profits in the tribal infrastructure to upgrade schools, health clinics, job training centers, and so forth.

Members of the largest Hispanic American groups are also generally less acculturated than African Americans. Hispanic traditions and the Spanish language have been sustained by the exclusion and isolation of these groups within the United States and have been continually renewed and revitalized by immigration. Cubans have moved closer to equality than Mexican Americans and Puerto Ricans but did so by resisting assimilation and building an ethnic enclave economy. Mexican Americans and Puerto Ricans share many of the problems of urban poverty that confront African Americans, and they are below national norms on measures of equality and integration.

The smaller Hispanic groups consist mostly of new immigrants who are just beginning the assimilation process. Many members of these groups, along with Mexican Americans and Puerto Ricans, are less educated and have few occupational skills, and they face the dangers of blending into a permanent urban underclass. Nonetheless, there is some evidence that these groups (or, more accurately, their descendants) may eventually find their way into the American mainstream (recall the debate over segmented assimilation in Chapter 10).

As with Hispanic Americans, the extent of assimilation among Asian Americans is highly variable. Some groups (e.g., third- and fourth-generation Japanese Americans and Chinese Americans) have virtually completed the assimilation process and are remarkably successful; others (the more elite immigrants from India and the Philippines) seem to be finding a place in the American mainstream. Other Asian American groups consist largely of newer immigrants with occupational and educational profiles that often resemble those of colonized minority groups, and these groups face the same dangers of permanent marginalization and exclusion. Still other Asian American groups (e.g., Korean Americans) have used their cohesiveness and solidarity to construct ethnic enclaves in which they have achieved relative economic equality by resisting acculturation.

Only European American ethnic groups, covered in Chapter 2, seem to approximate the traditional model of assimilation. The development even of these groups, however, has taken unexpected twists and turns, and the pluralism of the 1960s and 1970s suggests that ethnic traditions and ethnic identity, in some form, may withstand the pressures of assimilation for generations to come. Culturally and racially, these groups are the closest to the dominant group. If they still retain a sense of ethnicity, even if merely symbolic, after generations of acculturation and integration, what is the likelihood that the sense of group membership will fade in the racially stigmatized minority groups?

Assimilation is far from accomplished. The group divisions that remain are real and consequential; they cannot be willed away by pretending we are all "just American." Group membership continues to be important because it continues to be linked to fundamental patterns of exclusion

and inequality. The realities of pluralism, inequality, and ethnic and racial identity continue to persist to the extent that the American promise of a truly open opportunity structure continues to fail. The group divisions forged in the past and perpetuated over the decades by racism and discrimination will remain to the extent that racial and ethnic group membership continues to be correlated with inequality and position in the social class structure.

Along with economic and political pressures, other forces help sustain the pluralistic group divisions. Some argue that ethnicity is rooted in biology and can never be fully eradicated (see van den Berghe, 1981). Although this may be an extreme position, there is little doubt that many people find their own ancestries to be a matter of great interest. Some (perhaps most) of the impetus behind the preservation of ethnic and racial identity may be a result of the most vicious and destructive intergroup competition. In other ways, though, ethnicity can be a positive force that helps people locate themselves in time and space and understand their position in the contemporary world. Ethnicity remains an important aspect of self-identity and pride for many Americans from every group and tradition. It seems unlikely that this sense of a personal link to particular groups and heritages within U.S. society will soon fade.

Can we survive as a pluralistic, culturally and linguistically fragmented, racially and ethnically unequal society? What will save us from balkanization and fractionalization? Given our history of colonization and racism, can U.S. society move closer to the relatively harmonious models of race relations found in societies such as Hawaii? As we deal with these questions, we need to remember that in and of itself, diversity is no more "bad" than unity is "good." Our society has grown to a position of global preeminence despite, or perhaps because of, our diversity. In fact, many have argued that our diversity is a fundamental and essential characteristic of U.S. society and a great strength to be cherished and encouraged. Sociologist Ronald Takaki (1993) ended his history of multicultural America, *A Different Mirror*, with an eloquent endorsement of our diversity and pluralism:

> As Americans, we originally came from many different shores and our diversity has been at the center of the making of America. While our stories contain the memories of different communities, together they inscribe a larger narrative. Filled with what Walt Whitman celebrated as the "varied carols" of America, our history generously gives all of us our "mystic chords of memory."
>
> Throughout our past of oppressions and struggles for equality, Americans of different races and ethnicities have been "singing with open mouths their strong melodious songs" in the textile mills of Lowell, the cotton fields of Mississippi, on the Indian reservations of South Dakota, the railroad tracks high in the Sierras of California, in the garment factories of the Lower East Side, the cane fields of Hawaii, and a thousand other places across the country. Our denied history "bursts with telling." As we hear America singing, we find ourselves invited to bring our cultural diversity [into the open], to accept ourselves. (p. 428)

The question for our future might not be so much "Unity or diversity?" as "What blend of pluralistic and assimilationist policies will serve us best in the 21st century?" Are there ways in which society can prosper without repressing our diversity? How can we increase the degree of openness, fairness, and justice without threatening group loyalties? The one-way, Anglo-conformity mode of assimilation of the past is too narrow and destructive to be a blueprint for the future, but the more extreme forms of minority group pluralism and separatism might be equally dangerous.

How much unity do we need? How much diversity can we tolerate? These are questions you must answer for yourself, and they are questions you will face in a thousand different ways over the course of your life. Let me illustrate by citing some pertinent issues:

- Is it desirable to separate college dormitories by racial or ethnic group? Is this destructive self-segregation or a positive strategy for group empowerment? Will such practices increase prejudice (remember the contact hypothesis from Chapter 3), or will they work like ethnic enclaves and strengthen minority group cohesion and solidarity and permit the groups to deal with the larger society from a stronger position? For the campus as a whole, what good could come from residential separation? In what ways would minority students benefit? Is there a "correct" balance between separation and unity in this situation? Who gets to define what the balance is?

- How much attention should be devoted to minority group experiences in elementary and high school texts and curricula? Who should write and control these curricula? What should they say? How candid and critical should they be about America's often dismal past? How should such topics as slavery, genocide, and the racist exclusion of certain immigrant groups be presented in elementary school texts? In high school texts? Will educating children about the experiences of U.S. minority groups be an effective antidote to prejudice? Is it proper to use classrooms to build respect for the traditions of other groups and an appreciation of their experiences? If the realities of the experiences of minority groups are not addressed in school, what message will children hear? In the absence of minority group voices, what's left?

- What are the limits of free speech with respect to minority relations? When does an ethnic joke become offensive? When are racial and ethnic epithets protected by the First Amendment? As long as lines of ethnicity and race divide the nation and as long as people feel passionately about these lines, the language of dominant-minority relationships will continue to have harsh, crude, and intentionally insulting components. Under what conditions, if any, should a civil society tolerate disparagement of other groups? Should the racial and ethnic epithets uttered by minority group members be treated any differently than those uttered by dominant group members?

- What should the national policy on immigration be? How many immigrants should be admitted each year? How should immigrants be screened? What qualifications should be demanded? Should immigration policy continue to favor the family and close relatives of citizens and permanent residents? What should be done about illegal immigrants? Should they be given an opportunity to legalize their status? Should illegal immigrants or their children receive health care and schooling?

I do not pretend that the ideas presented in this text can fully resolve these issues or others that will arise in the future. As long as immigrants and minority groups are a part of the United States, as long as prejudice and discrimination persist, the debates will continue and new issues will arise as old ones are resolved.

As U.S. society attempts to deal with new immigrants and unresolved minority grievances, we should recognize that it is not diversity per se that threatens stability, but the realities of split labor markets, racial and ethnic stratification, urban poverty, and institutionalized discrimination. We need to focus on the issues that confront us with an honest recognition of the past and the economic, political, and social forces that have shaped us. As the United States continues to remake itself, an informed sense of where we have been will help us decide where we should go. Clearly, the simplistic, one-way, Anglo-conformity model of assimilation of the past does not provide a basis for dealing with these problems realistically and should not be the blueprint for the future of U.S. society.

MINORITY GROUP PROGRESS AND THE IDEOLOGY OF AMERICAN INDIVIDUALISM

There is so much sadness, misery, and unfairness in the history of minority groups that evidence of progress sometimes goes unnoticed. Lest we be guilty of ignoring the good news in favor of the bad, let us note some ways in which the situations of American minority groups are better today than they were in the past. Evidence of progress is easy to find for some groups; we need look only to the relative economic, educational, and income equality of European American ethnic groups and some Asian American groups, or recall the election of President Barack Obama. The United States has become more tolerant and open, and minority group members can be found at the highest levels of success, affluence, and prestige.

One of the most obvious changes is the decline of traditional racism and prejudice. As we discussed in Chapter 3, the strong racial and ethnic sentiments and stereotypes of the past are no longer the primary vocabulary for discussing race relations among dominant group members, at least not in public. Although the prejudices unquestionably still exist, Americans have become more circumspect and discreet in their public utterances.

The demise of blatant bigotry in polite company is, without doubt, a positive change. However, it seems that negative intergroup feelings and stereotypes have not so much disappeared as changed form. The old racist feelings are now being expressed in other guises, specifically in what has been called "modern" or "symbolic" racism: the view that holds that once Jim-Crow-type segregation ended in the 1960s, the opportunity channels and routes of upward mobility of American society were opened to all. This individualistic view of social mobility is consistent with the human capital perspective and the traditional, melting-pot view of assimilation. Taken together, these ideologies present a powerful and widely shared perspective on the nature of minority group problems in modern American society. Proponents of these views tend to be unsympathetic to the plight of minorities and to programs such as school busing and affirmative action, which are intended to ameliorate these problems. The overt bigotry of the past has been replaced by blandness and an indifference more difficult to define and harder to measure than "old-fashioned" racism, yet still unsympathetic to racial change.

This text has argued that the most serious problems facing contemporary minority groups, however, are structural and institutional, not individual or personal. For example, the paucity of jobs and high rates of unemployment in the inner cities are the result of economic and political forces beyond the control not only of the minority communities but also of local and state governments. The marginalization of the minority group labor force is a reflection of the essence of modern American capitalism. The mainstream, higher-paying, blue-collar jobs available to people with modest educational credentials are controlled by national and multinational corporations, which maximize profits by automating their production processes and moving the jobs that remain to areas, often outside the United States, with abundant supplies of cheaper labor.

We have also seen that some of the more effective strategies for pursuing equality require strong in-group cohesion and networks of cooperation, not heroic individual effort. Immigration to this country is (and always has been) a group process that involves extensive, long-lasting networks of communication and chains of population movement, usually built around family ties and larger kinship groups. Group networks continue to operate in America and assist individual immigrants with early adjustments and later opportunities for jobs and upward mobility. A variation on this theme is the ethnic enclave found among so many different groups.

Survival and success in America for all minority groups has had more to do with group processes than with individual will or motivation. The concerted, coordinated actions of the minority community provided support during hard times and, when possible, provided the means to climb higher in the social structure during good times. Far from being a hymn to individualism, the story of U.S. minority groups is profoundly sociological.

A FINAL WORD

U.S. society and its minority groups are linked in fractious unity. They are part of the same structures but are separated by lines of color and culture and by long histories (and clear memories) of exploitation and unfairness. This society owes its prosperity and position of prominence in the world no less to the labor of minority groups than to that of the dominant group. By harnessing the labor and energy of these minority groups, the nation has grown prosperous and powerful, but the benefits have flowed disproportionately to the dominant group.

Since the middle of the 20th century, minority groups have demanded greater openness, fairness, equality, respect for their traditions, and justice. Increasingly, the demands have been made on the terms of the minority groups, not on those of the dominant group. Some of these demands have been met, at least verbally, and the society as a whole has rejected the oppressive racism of the past. Minority group progress has stalled well short of equality, however, and the patterns of poverty, discrimination, marginality, hopelessness, and despair continue to limit the lives of millions.

As we face the 21st century, the dilemmas of America's minority groups remain perhaps the primary unresolved domestic issue facing the nation. The answers of the past—the simple faith in assimilation and the belief that success in America is open to all who simply try hard enough—have proved inadequate, even destructive and dangerous, because they help sustain the belief that the barriers to equality no longer exist and that any remaining inequalities are the problems of the minority groups, not the larger society.

These problems of equality and access will not solve themselves or simply fade away. They will continue to manifest themselves in myriad ways; through protest activities, rancorous debates, diffused rage, and pervasive violence. The solutions and policies that will carry us through these coming travails are not clear. Only by asking the proper questions, realistically and honestly, can we hope to find the answers that will help our society fulfill its promises to the millions who are currently excluded from achieving the American Dream.

The United States is one of many ethnically and racially diverse nations in the world today. As the globe continues to shrink and networks of communication, immigration, trade, and transportation continue to link all peoples into a single global entity, the problems of diversity will become more international in their scope and implications. Ties will grow between African Americans and the nations of Africa, agreements between the United States and the nations of Latin America will have direct impact on immigration patterns, Asian Americans will be affected by international developments on the Pacific Rim, and so forth. Domestic and international group relations will blend into a single reality. In many ways, the patterns of dominant-minority relations discussed in this text already have been reproduced on the global stage. The mostly Anglo industrialized nations of the Northern Hemisphere have continuously exploited the labor and resources of the mostly nonwhite, undeveloped nations of the Southern Hemisphere. Thus, the tensions and resentments we have observed in U.S. society are mirrored in the global system of societies.

The United States is neither the most nor the least diverse country in the world. Likewise, our nation is neither the most nor the least successful in confronting the problems of prejudice, discrimination, and racism. However, the multigroup nature of our society, along with the present influx of immigrants from around the globe, do present an opportunity to improve on our record and make a lasting contribution. A society that finds a way to deal fairly and humanely with the problems of diversity and difference, prejudice and inequality, and racism and discrimination can provide a sorely needed model for other nations and, indeed, for the world.

GLOSSARY

abolitionism: The movement to abolish slavery in the South

acculturation: The process by which one group (generally a minority or immigrant group) learns the culture of another group (generally the dominant group); also called cultural assimilation

affective prejudice: The emotional or "feeling" dimension of individual prejudice. The prejudiced individual attaches negative emotions to other groups.

affirmative action: Affirmative action programs are designed to counter the effects of institutional discrimination and the legacy of minority group inequality

Alien Land Act: Bill passed by the California legislature in 1913 that declared aliens who were ineligible for citizenship (effectively meaning only immigrants from Asia) were also ineligible to own land

Americanization: The one-sided process of assimilation that occurred with many immigrant groups in the United States

Anglo-conformity: The model of assimilation by which minority groups conform to Anglo-American culture

anti-Semitism: Prejudice or ideological racism directed specifically at Jews

apartheid: The policy of extreme racial segregation formerly followed in South Africa

ascribed status: A position in society that is assigned to the individual, usually at birth. Examples of ascribed status include positions based on ethnicity, race, and gender.

assimilation: The process by which formerly distinct and separate groups merge and become one group

Black Power movement: A coalition of African American groups that rose to prominence in the 1960s. Some central themes of the movement were black nationalism, autonomy for African American communities, and pride in race and African heritage.

Blauner hypothesis: Minority groups created by colonization will experience more intense prejudice, racism, and discrimination than those created by immigration. The disadvantaged status of colonized groups will persist longer and be more difficult to overcome than the disadvantaged status faced by groups created by immigration.

bourgeoisie: Marxist term for the elite or ruling class in an industrial society that owns or controls the means of production

Bureau of Indian Affairs (BIA): The agency of the U.S. government that has primary responsibility for the administration of American Indian reservations

capital-intensive: Capital-intensive technology replaces hand labor with machine labor. Large amounts of capital are required to develop, purchase, and maintain the machines.

caste system: A closed system of stratification with no mobility between positions. A person's class at birth is permanent and unchangeable.

chattel: An item of personal property. In a system of chattel slavery, slaves were defined by law not as persons but as the personal property of their owners.

Chicanismo: A militant ideology of the Mexican American protest movement that appeared in the 1960s. The ideology took a critical view of U.S. society, made strong demands for justice and an end to racism, expressed a positive image for the group, and incorporated other pluralistic themes.

Chicanos: A group name for Mexican Americans; associated with the ideology of Chicanismo, which emerged in the 1960s

civil rights movement: The effort of African Americans in the 1950s and 1960s to win the rights they were entitled to under the U.S. Constitution

cognitive prejudice: The "thinking" dimension of individual prejudice. The prejudiced individual thinks about other groups in terms of stereotypes.

colonized minority groups: Groups whose initial contact with the dominant group was through conquest or colonization

competition: A situation in which two or more parties struggle for control of some scarce resource

core group: The group that benefits from and, typically, tries to sustain minority group subordination (also called the dominant group)

cultural pluralism: A situation in which groups have not acculturated and each maintains a distinct identity

culture: All aspects of the way of life associated with a group of people. Culture includes language, beliefs, norms, values, customs, technology, and many other components.

culture of poverty theory: A theory asserting that poverty causes certain personality traits—such as the need for instant gratification—which, in turn, perpetuate poverty

de facto segregation: A system of racial separation and inequality that appears to result from voluntary choices about where to live, work, and so forth. Often, this form of segregation is really de jure segregation in thin disguise.

de jure segregation: The system of rigid competitive race relations that followed Reconstruction in the South. The system lasted from the 1880s until the 1960s and was characterized by laws mandating racial separation and inequality. Also called the Jim Crow system.

deindustrialization: The shift from a manufacturing economy to a service-oriented, information-processing economy

differential in power: Any difference between two or more groups in their ability to achieve their goals

discrimination: The unequal or unfair treatment of a person or persons based on their group membership

dominant group: The group that benefits from and, typically, tries to sustain minority group subordination (also called the core group)

enclave minority group: A group that establishes its own neighborhood and relies on a set of interconnected businesses for economic survival

equal status contact hypothesis: A theory of prejudice reduction asserting that equal status and cooperative contacts between groups will tend to reduce prejudice

ethclass: The group formed by the intersection of social class and racial or ethnic groups

ethnic minority groups: Minority groups identified primarily by cultural characteristics, such as language or religion

ethnic revival: The movement toward increased salience for ethnic identity, which began for European Americans in the 1960s

ethnic succession: The process by which European ethnic groups affected each other's position in the social class structure

ethnocentrism: Judging other groups, societies, or cultures by the standards of one's own

extractive (primary) occupations: Those that produce raw materials, such as food and agricultural products, minerals, and lumber; often involve unskilled manual labor, require little formal education, and are generally low paying

fatalism: The view that one's fate is beyond one's control

fluid competitive system: A system of group relations in which minority group members are freer to compete for jobs and other scarce resources; associated with advanced industrialization

gender roles: Expectations about the proper behavior, attitudes, and personality traits for males and females

genocide: The deliberate attempt to exterminate an entire group of people

glass ceiling: Discriminatory practices that limit opportunities for women to rise to higher levels in their careers, qualify for promotions, and earn higher salaries

huiguan: An association in Chinese American society based on the region of China from which an individual or his or her family came. The huiguan performed a number of social, welfare, and business functions.

human capital theory: Consistent with the traditional view of assimilation, this theory considers success in the United States to be a direct result of individual efforts, personal values and skills, and education.

ideological racism: A belief system asserting that a particular group is inferior. Although individuals may subscribe to racist beliefs, the ideology itself is incorporated into the culture of the society and passed on from generation to generation.

immigrant minority groups: Groups whose initial contact with the dominant group was through immigration

indentured servant: A contract laborer who is obligated to serve a particular master for a specified length of time

Indian Reorganization Act (IRA): Federal legislation passed in 1934 that was intended to give Native American tribes more autonomy

Industrial Revolution: The shift in subsistence technology from labor-intensive agriculture to capital-intensive manufacturing

institutional discrimination: A pattern of unequal treatment based on group membership that is built into the daily operations of society

integration: The process by which a minority group enters the social structure of the dominant society; also called structural assimilation

Issei: First-generation immigrants from Japan

jigsaw method: A learning technique that requires cooperation among students

Jim Crow system: The system of rigid competitive race relations that followed Reconstruction in the South. The system lasted from the 1880s until the 1960s and was characterized by laws mandating racial separation and inequality. Also called de jure segregation.

labor-intensive work: A form of work in which the bulk of the effort is provided by human beings working by hand. Machines and other labor-saving devices are rare or absent.

level of development: The stage of evolution of society. The stages discussed in this text relate to agrarian, industrial, and postindustrial subsistence technology.

machismo: A cultural value stressing male dominance, virility, and honor

manufacturing (secondary) occupations: Occupations involving the transformation of raw materials into finished products ready for the marketplace. An example is an assembly line worker in an automobile plant.

Marielitos: Refugees from Cuba who arrived in the United States in 1980

marital assimilation: Intermarriage between members of different groups

means of production: A Marxist term that refers to the materials, tools, resources, and organizations by which the society produces and distributes goods and services

melting pot: A type of assimilation in which all groups contribute in roughly equal amounts to the creation of a new culture and society

mestizo: A person of mixed white and Native American ancestry

middleman minority groups: Groups that rely on small businesses, dispersed throughout a community, for economic survival

minority group: A group that experiences a pattern of disadvantage or inequality, has a visible identifying trait, and is a self-conscious social unit. Membership is usually determined at birth, and group members have a strong tendency to marry within the group.

miscegenation: marriage between members of different racial groups

model minority groups: A description often applied to Asian Americans. It exaggerates the relative affluence of these groups and is sometimes used as a rhetorical device for criticizing other minority groups, especially African Americans.

modern institutional discrimination: A more subtle and covert form of institutional discrimination that is often unintentional and unconscious

modern racism: A subtle form of prejudice that incorporates negative feelings about minority groups but not the traditional stereotypes. Modern racism assumes that (a) discrimination no longer exists, (b) minority groups are responsible for their own disadvantages, and (c) special programs addressing ethnic and racial inequality are unjustified and unnecessary.

multiculturalism: A general term for some versions of pluralism in the United States in the 1990s. Generally, multiculturalism stresses mutual respect for all groups and celebrates the multiplicity of heritages that have contributed to the development of the United States.

New Immigration: Immigration from Europe to the United States between the 1880s and the 1920s

Nisei: Second-generation Japanese Americans

Noel hypothesis: A theory about the creation of minority groups that asserts that if two or more groups come together in a contact situation characterized by ethnocentrism, competition, and a differential in power, some form of racial or ethnic stratification will result

nonviolent direct action: An important tactic used during the civil rights movement in the South to defeat de jure segregation

Old Immigration: Immigration from Europe to the United States between the 1820s and the 1880s

Operation Wetback: A government program developed in the 1950s to deport illegal immigrants from Mexico

past-in-present institutional discrimination: Patterns of inequality or unequal treatment in the present that are caused by some pattern of discrimination in the past

paternalism: A form of dominant-minority relations often associated with plantation-based, labor-intensive, agrarian technology. In paternalistic relations, minority groups are extremely unequal and highly controlled. Rates of overt conflict are low.

patriarchy: Male dominance. In a patriarchal society, men have more power than women do.

plantation system: A labor-intensive form of agriculture that requires large tracts of land and a large, cheap labor force. This was a dominant form of agricultural production in the American South before the Civil War.

pluralism: A situation in which groups have separate identities, cultures, and organizational structures

power: The ability to achieve goals even in the face of opposition from others

prejudice: The tendency of individuals to think and feel negatively toward others

prestige: The amount of honor or respect accorded a particular person or group

primary labor market: The segment of the labor market that encompasses better-paying, higher-status, more-secure jobs, usually in large bureaucracies

primary sector: Relationships and groups that are intimate and personal. Groups in the primary sector are small.

principle of third-generation interest: The notion that the grandchildren of immigrants will stress their ethnicity much more than the second generation will

proletariat: In Marxist theory, the workers in an industrial society

pull: Factors that cause population movement out of an area

push: Factors that cause population movement into an area

race: Biologically, an isolated, inbreeding population with a distinctive genetic heritage. Socially, the term is used loosely and reflects patterns of inequality and power.

race relations cycle: A concept associated with Robert Park, who believed that relations between different groups would go through predictable cycles, from conflict to eventual assimilation

racial minority groups: Minority groups identified primarily by physical characteristics such as skin color (e.g., Asian Americans)

racism: A belief system that asserts the inferiority of a group

Reconstruction: The period of southern race relations following the Civil War. Reconstruction lasted from 1865 until the 1880s and witnessed many racial reforms, all of which were reversed during de jure segregation, or the Jim Crow era.

relocation camps: The camps in which Japanese Americans were held during World War II

repatriation: A government campaign begun during the Great Depression of the 1930s to deport illegal immigrants back to Mexico. The campaign also caused legal immigrants and native-born Mexican Americans to leave the United States.

revolution: A minority group goal. A revolutionary group wishes to change places with the dominant group or create a new social order, perhaps in alliance with other groups.

rigid competitive group system: A system of group relations in which the dominant group seeks to exclude minority groups or limit their ability to compete for scarce resources such as jobs

Sansei: Third-generation Japanese Americans

scapegoat hypothesis: A theory of prejudice that posits that under certain conditions, people will express their aggressions against substitute targets. When other groups are chosen as substitute targets, prejudice increases.

secondary labor market: The segment of the labor market that includes low-paying, low-skilled, insecure jobs

secondary sector: Relationships and organizations that are public, task oriented, and impersonal. Organizations in the secondary sector can be large.

segmented assimilation: The idea that assimilation in the United States is now fragmented and can have a number of outcomes in addition to eventual entry into mainstream society

selective perception: The tendency to see only what one expects to see. Associated with stereotyping in individual prejudice.

separatism: A minority group goal. A separatist group wishes to sever all ties with the dominant group.

service (tertiary) occupations: Jobs that involve providing services. Examples include retail clerk, janitor, and schoolteacher.

sharecropping: A system of farming often used in the South during de jure segregation. The sharecropper (often black), or tenant, worked the land, which was actually owned by someone else (usually white), in return for a share of the profits at harvest time. The landowner supplied a place to live and credit for food and clothing.

social class: A group of people who command similar amounts of valued goods and services, such as income, property, and education

social construction: A perception shared by members of a society or group that reflects habitual routines or institutionalized social processes. Social constructions (such as race or stereotypes) become real to the people who share them.

social distance: The degree of intimacy to which a person is willing to admit members of other groups

social mobility: Movement from one social class to another

social structure: The networks of social relationships, groups, organizations, communities, and institutions that organize the work of a society and connect individuals to each other and to the larger society

socialization: The process of physical, psychological, and social development by which a person learns his or her culture

sojourners: Immigrants who intend to return to their countries of origin split labor market theory: When the labor force is divided into a higher-paid segment composed of members of the dominant group and a lower-paid segment composed of minority group members, higher-paid labor uses prejudice and racism to limit the ability of cheaper labor to compete for jobs.

stereotypes: Overgeneralizations that are thought to apply to all members of a group

stratification: The unequal distribution of valued goods and services (e.g., income, job opportunities, prestige and fame, education, healthcare) in society; the social class system

structural mobility: Rising occupational and social class standing that is the result of changes in the overall structure of the economy and labor market, as opposed to individual efforts

structural pluralism: A situation in which a group has acculturated but is not integrated

subsistence technology: The means by which a society satisfies basic needs. An agrarian society relies on labor-intensive agriculture, whereas an industrial society relies on machines and inanimate fuel supplies.

symbolic ethnicity: A sense of ethnicity that is more superficial, voluntary, and changeable

termination: A policy by which all special relationships between the federal government and American Indians would be abolished

tongs: Secret societies in Chinatowns that sometimes fought with other Chinese American groups over control of resources

triple melting pot: The idea that structural assimilation for European immigrants took place within the context of the three major American religions

urban underclass: The urban lower classes, consisting largely of African Americans and other minority groups of color, which have been more or less permanently barred from the mainstream economy and the primary labor market

vicious cycle of prejudice: A process in which a condition is assumed to be true and forces are then set in motion to create and perpetuate that condition

Yonsei: Fourth-generation Japanese Americans

REFERENCES

Aberson, Christopher, Shoemaker, Carl, & Tomolillo, Christina. 2004. Implicit Bias and Contact: The Role of Interethnic Friendships. *Journal of Social Psychology* 144:335–347.

Abrahamson, Harold. 1980. Assimilation and Pluralism. In Stephan Thernstrom, Ann Orlov, & Oscar Handlin (Eds.), *Harvard Encyclopedia of American Ethnic Groups* (pp. 150–160). Cambridge, MA: Harvard University Press.

Acuña, Rodolfo. 1988. *Occupied America* (3rd ed.). New York: Harper & Row.

———. 1999. *Occupied America* (4th ed.). New York: Harper & Row.

Adarand Constructors Inc. v. Pena, 515 U.S. 200 (1995).

Adorno, T. W., Frenkel-Brunswick, E., Levinson, D., & Sanford, N. 1950. *The Authoritarian Personality*. New York: Harper & Row.

"The African Diaspora." n.d. *Slave Trade and African American Ancestry*. Retrieved December 4, 2007, from http://www.homestead.com/wysinger/mapofafricadiaspora.html

Agbayani-Siewert, Pauline, & Revilla, Linda. 1995. Filipino Americans. In Pyong Gap Min (Ed.), *Asian Americans: Contemporary Issues and Trends* (pp. 134–168). Thousand Oaks, CA: Sage.

Aizenman, N. C. 2006. Immigration Debate Wakes a "Sleeping Latino Giant." *Washington Post,* April 6, p. A1.

Alba, Richard. 1985. *Italian Americans: Into the Twilight of Ethnicity*. Englewood Cliffs, NJ: Prentice Hall.

———. 1990. *Ethnic Identity: The Transformation of White America*. New Haven, CT: Yale University Press.

———. 1995. Assimilation's Quiet Tide. *The Public Interest* 119:3–19.

Alba, Richard, & Nee, Victor. 1997. Rethinking Assimilation Theory for a New Era of Immigration. *International Migration Review* 31:826–875.

———. 2003. *Remaking the American Mainstream: Assimilation and Contemporary Immigration*. Cambridge, MA: Harvard University Press.

Aleiss, Angela. 2005. *Making the White Man's Indian: Native Americans and Hollywood Movies*. Westport, CT: Praeger.

Allen, Ernest, & Chrisman, Robert. 2001. Ten Reasons: A Response to David Horowitz. *The Black Scholar* 31(2): 49–55.

Almquist, Elizabeth M. 1979. Black Women and the Pursuit of Equality. In Jo Freeman (Ed.), *Women: A Feminist Perspective* (pp. 430–450). Palo Alto, CA: Mayfield.

Alvarez, Rodolfo. 1973. The Psychohistorical and Socioeconomic Development of the Chicano Community in the United States. *Social Science Quarterly* 53:920–942.

American Indian Higher Education Consortium. 2008. *Sustaining Tribal Colleges and Universities: The Tribal College Movement; Highlights and Profiles*. Retrieved March 23, 2011, from http://www.aihec.org/resources/documents/AIHEC-AIMS2006report_highlights.pdf

American Sociological Association. 2003. The Importance of Collecting Data and Doing Scientific Research on Race. Retrieved June 19, 2007, from http://www2.asanet.org/media/asa_race_statement.pdf

Amott, Teresa, & Matthaei, Julie. 1991. *Race, Gender, and Work: A Multicultural History of Women in the United States*. Boston: South End.

Andersen, Margaret L. 1993. *Thinking about Women: Sociological Perspectives on Sex and Gender* (3rd ed.). New York: Macmillan.

Anti-Defamation League. 2000. *Anti-Semitism in the United States*. Retrieved July 12, 2002, from http://www.adl.org/backgrounders/Anti_Semitism_us.html

———. 2009. Myths and Facts about Immigrants and Immigration. In *Challenging Anti-Immigrant Bias in the U.S.* Retrieved June 3, 2011, from http://www.adl.org/education/curriculum_connections/spring_2009/supplements/Myths_and_Facts.pdf

Antin, Mary. 1969. *The Promised Land*. Princeton, NJ: Princeton University Press.

Arab American Anti-Discrimination Committee. 2002. *ADC Fact Sheet: The Condition of Arab Americans Post 9/11.* Retrieved June 22, 2002, from http://www.adc.org/terror_attack/9–11aftermath.pdf

Aronson, E., & Patnoe, S. 1997. *The Jigsaw Classroom: Building Cooperation in the Classroom* (2nd ed.). New York: Addison Wesley Longman.

Aronson, Eliot, & Gonzalez, Alex. 1988. Desegregation, Jigsaw, and the Mexican-American Experience. In Phyllis Katz & Dalmas Taylor (Eds.), *Eliminating Racism: Profiles in Controversy* (pp. 301–314). New York: Plenum.

Ashmore, Richard, & DelBoca, Frances. 1976. Psychological Approaches to Understanding Group Conflict. In Phyllis Katz (Ed.), *Towards the Elimination of Racism* (pp. 73–123). New York: Pergamon.

Asia: Original Sin, Australia's Aborigines. 2007. *Economist,* June 2, p. 67.

Associated Press. 2005. "Asian Youth Persistently Harassed by U.S. Peers." Retrieved April 22, 2011, from http://www.usatoday.com/news/nation/2005–11–13-asian-teens-bullied_x.htm

Austin, Algernon. 2010. *Different Race, Different Recession: American Indian Unemployment in 2010* (issue brief 289). Washington, DC: Economic Policy Institute. Retrieved March 21, 2011, from http://epi.3cdn.net/94a339472e6481485e_hgm6bxpz4.pdf

Australian Bureau of Statistics. 2002. "Australian Social Trends 2002, Population, National Summary Tables." Retrieved July 5, 2002, from http://www.abs.gov.au

———. 2009. "National Summary Tables." Accessed July 28, 2011, from www.abs.gov.au

Australian Human Rights and Equal Opportunity Commission. 1997. *Bringing Them Home: Report of the National Inquiry Into the Separation of Aboriginal and Torres Strait Islander Children from Their Families.* Retrieved July 5, 2002, from http://www.austlii.edu.au/au/special/rsjproject/rsjlibrary/hreoc/stolen/

Avery, Robert, & Rendall, Michael. 2002. Lifetime Inheritances of Three Generations of Whites and Blacks. *American Journal of Sociology* 107:1300–1346.

Baca Zinn, Maxine, & Thornton Dill, Bonnie (Eds.). 1994. *Women of Color in U.S. Society.* Philadelphia: Temple University Press.

Baca Zinn, Maxine, & Eitzen, D. Stanley. 1990. *Diversity in Families.* New York: HarperCollins.

Ball, Richard. 2009. Social Distance in Japan: An Exploratory Study. *Michigan Sociological Review* 23:105–113.

Bames, Robert. 2007. Divided Court Limits Use of Race by School Districts. *Washington Post,* June 29, p. A1.

Barreto, Manuela, & Ellemers, Naomi. 2005. The Perils of Political Correctness: Men's and Women's Responses to Old-Fashioned and Modern Sexist Views. *Social Psychology Quarterly* 68:75–88.

Barringer, Herbert, Takeuchi, David, & Levin, Michael. 1995. *Asians and Pacific Islanders in the United States.* New York: Russell Sage Foundation.

Bean, Frank, & Stevens, Gillian. 2003. *America's Newcomers and the Dynamics of Diversity.* New York: Russell Sage Foundation.

Beaton, Anne, Tougas, Francine, & Joly, Stephane. 1996. Neosexism Among Male Managers: Is It a Matter of Numbers? *Journal of Applied Social Psychology* 26:2189–2204.

Becerra, Rosina. 1988. The Mexican American Family. In Charles H. Mindel, Robert W. Habenstein, & Roosevelt Wright Jr. (Eds.), *Ethnic Families in America: Patterns and Variations* (3rd ed., pp. 141–172). New York: Elsevier.

Beck, E. M., & Clark, Timothy. 2002. Strangers, Community Miscreants, or Locals: Who Were the Black Victims of Mob Violence? *Historical Methods* 35(2): 77–84.

Beck, E. M., & Tolnay, Stewart. 1990. The Killing Fields of the Deep South: The Market for Cotton and the Lynching of Blacks, 1882–1930. *American Sociological Review* 55:526–539.

Bell, Daniel. 1973. *The Coming of Post-Industrial Society.* New York: Basic Books.

Bell, Derrick. 1992. *Race, Racism, and American Law* (3rd ed.). Boston: Little, Brown.

Benedict, Ruth. 1946. *The Chrysanthemum and the Sword: Patterns of Japanese Culture.* Boston: Houghton Mifflin.

Benjamin, Lois. 2005. *The Black Elite.* Lanham, MD: Rowman & Littlefield.

Berkowitz, Leonard. 1978. Whatever Happened to the Frustration-Aggression Hypothesis? *American Behavioral Scientist* 21:691–708.

Bertrand, Marianne, & Mullainathan, Sendhil. 2004. Are Emily and Greg More Employable than Lakisha and Jamal? A Field Experiment on Labor Market Discrimination. *American Economic Review* 94:991–1013.

Bird, Elizabeth. 1999. Gendered Construction of the American Indian in Popular Media. *Journal of Communication* 49:60–83.

Biskupic, Joan. 1989. House Approves Entitlement for Japanese-Americans. *Congressional Quarterly Weekly Report,* October 28, p. 2879.

Black-Gutman, D., & Hickson, F. 1996. The Relationship Between Racial Attitudes and Social-Cognitive Development in Children: An Australian Study. *Developmental Psychology* 32:448–457.

Blassingame, John W. 1972. *The Slave Community: Plantation Life in the Antebellum South.* New York: Oxford University Press.

Blau, Peter M., & Duncan, Otis Dudley. 1967. *The American Occupational Structure.* New York: Wiley.

Blauner, Robert. 1972. *Racial Oppression in America.* New York: Harper & Row.

Blessing, Patrick. 1980. Irish. In Stephan Thernstrom, Ann Orlov, & Oscar Handlin (Eds.), *Harvard Encyclopedia of American Ethnic Groups* (pp. 524–545). Cambridge, MA: Harvard University Press.

Blumer, Herbert. 1958. Race Prejudice as a Sense of Group Position. *Pacific Sociological Review* 1:3–7.

———. 1965. Industrialization and Race Relations. In Guy Hunter (Ed.), *Industrialization and Race Relations: A Symposium* (pp. 200–253). London: Oxford University Press.

Bobo, Lawrence. 1988. Group Conflict, Prejudice, and the Paradox of Contemporary Racial Attitudes. In Phyllis Katz & Dalmar Taylor (Eds.), *Eliminating Racism: Profiles in Controversy* (pp. 85–114). New York: Plenum.

———. 2001. Racial Attitudes and Relations at the Close of the Twentieth Century. In N. Smelser, W. Wilson, & F. Mitchell (Eds.), *America Becoming: Racial Trends and Their Consequences* (Vol. 1, pp. 264–301). Washington, DC: National Academy Press.

Bobo, Lawrence, & Kluegal, James. 1997. Status, Ideology, and Dimensions of Whites' Racial Beliefs and Attitudes: Progress and Stagnation. In Steven Tuck & Jack Martin (Eds.), *Racial Attitudes in the 1990s: Continuity and Change* (p. 101). Westport, CT: Praeger.

Bobo, Lawrence, & Tuan, Mia. 2006. *Prejudice in Politics: Group Position, Public Opinion, and the Wisconsin Treaty Rights Dispute*. Cambridge, MA: Harvard University Press.

Bodnar, John. 1985. *The Transplanted*. Bloomington: Indiana University Press.

Bogardus, Emory. 1933. A Social Distance Scale. *Sociology and Social Research* 17:265–271.

Bonacich, Edna. 1972. A Theory of Ethnic Antagonism: The Split Labor Market. *American Sociological Review* 37:547–559.

Bonacich, Edna, & Modell, John. 1980. *The Economic Basis of Ethnic Solidarity: Small Business in the Japanese American Community*. Berkeley: University of California Press.

Bonilla-Silva, Eduardo. 2001. *White Supremacy and Racism in the Post–Civil Rights Era*. Boulder, CO: Lynne Riener.

———. 2006. *Racism without Racists* (2nd ed.). Lanham, MD: Rowman & Littlefield.

Booth, Alan, Granger, Douglas, Mazur, Alan, & Kivligham, Katie. 2006. Testosterone and Social Behavior. *Social Forces* 86:167–191.

Bordewich, Fergus. 1996. *Killing the White Man's Indian*. New York: Doubleday.

Boswell, Terry. 1986. A Split Labor Market Analysis of Discrimination Against Chinese Immigrants, 1850–1882. *American Sociological Review* 51:352–371.

Bouvier, Leon F., & Gardner, Robert W. 1986. Immigration to the U.S.: The Unfinished Story. *Population Bulletin* 41 (November): 1–50.

Brace, Matthew. 2001. A Nation Divided. *Geographical* 73:14–20.

Brittingham, Angela, & de la Cruz, C. Patricia. 2004. *Ancestry: 2000*. Washington, DC: U.S. Census Bureau. Retrieved June 29, 2007, from http://www.census.gov/prod/2004pubs/c2kbr-35.pdf

Brody, David. 1980. Labor. In Stephan Thernstrom, Ann Orlov, & Oscar Handlin (Eds.), *Harvard Encyclopedia of American Ethnic Groups* (pp. 609–618). Cambridge, MA: Harvard University Press.

Bronson, Po, & Merryman, Ashley. 2009. See Baby Discriminate. *Newsweek,* September 14. Retrieved October 13, 2010, from http://www.newsweek.com/2009/09/04/see-baby-discriminate.html

Brown, Dee. 1970. *Bury My Heart at Wounded Knee*. New York: Holt, Rinehart, & Winston.

Brown, Kendrick T., Brown, Tony N., Jackson, James S., Sellers, Robert M., & Manuel, Warde J. 2003. Teammates On and Off the Field? Contact with Black Teammates and the Racial Attitudes of White Student Athletes. *Journal of Applied Social Psychology* 33:1379–1404.

Brown, Rupert. 1995. *Prejudice: Its Social Psychology*. Cambridge, MA: Blackwell.

Brown v. Board of Education of Topeka, 247 U.S. 483 (1954).

Brunsma, David. 2005. Interracial Families and the Racial Identification of Mixed-Race Children: Evidence from the Early Childhood Longitudinal Study. *Social Forces* 84:1131–1157.

Buriel, Raymond. 1993. Acculturation, Respect for Cultural Differences, and Biculturalism Among Three Generations of Mexican American and Euro-American School Children. *Journal of Genetic Psychology* 154:531–544.

Burns, Peter, & Gimpel, James. 2000. Economic Insecurity, Prejudicial Stereotypes, and Public Opinion on Immigration Policy. *Political Science Quarterly* 115:201–205.

Camarillo, Albert, & Bonilla, Frank. 2001. Hispanics in a Multicultural Society: A New American Dilemma? In N. Smelser, W. Wilson, & F. Mitchell (Eds.), *America Becoming: Racial Trends and Their Consequences* (Vol. 2, pp. 103–134). Washington, DC: National Academy Press.

Camarota, Steven. 2002. *Immigrants in the United States, 2002: A Snapshot of America's Foreign-Born Population*. Washington, DC: Center for Immigration Studies. Retrieved February 15, 2005, from http://www.cis.org/articles/2002/back1302.html

———. 2007. Immigration Is Hurting the U.S. Worker. *Americas Quarterly*. Retrieved March 15, 2008, from http://www.cis.org/articles/2007/sacoped071107.html

Cameron, James. 2001. Social Identity, Modern Sexism, and Perceptions of Personal and Group Discrimination by Women and Men. *Sex Roles* 45:743–766.

Carroll, Joseph. 2007. "Hispanics Support Requiring English Proficiency for Immigrants." Gallup. Retrieved on October 13, 2010, from http://www.gallup.com/poll/28048/Hispanics-Support-Requiring-English-Proficiency-Immigrants.aspx

Carter, Nancy M., & Silva, Christine. 2010. *Pipeline's Broken Promise*. New York: Catalyst. Retrieved July 24, 2011, from http://www.catalyst.org/publication/372/pipelines-broken-promise

Central Intelligence Agency. 2011a. Central American and Caribbean: Haiti. *World Factbook*. Retrieved May 2011 from https://www.cia.gov/library/publications/the-world-factbook/geos/ha.html

———. 2011b. East and Southeast Asia: Korea, South. *World Factbook*. Retrieved July 28, 2011, from https://www
.cia.gov/library/publications/the-world-factbook/geos/ks.html

Central Statistics Office, Ireland. 2006. *Population Classified by Religion and Nationality, 2006*. Retrieved October
15, 2010, from http://www.cso.ie/statistics/popnclassbyreligionandnationality2006.htm

———. 2010. *Population and Migration Estimates*. Retrieved July 20, 2011, from http://www.cso.ie/releasespublica
tions/documents/population/current/popmig.pdf

Chan, Sucheng. 1990. European and Asian Immigrants into the United States in Comparative Perspective, 1820s to
1920s. In Virginia Yans-McLaughlin (Ed.), *Immigration Reconsidered: History, Sociology, and Politics* (pp. 37–75).
New York: Oxford University Press.

Charles-Toussaint, G., & Crowson, H. 2010. Prejudice against International Students: The Role of Threat Perceptions
and Authoritarian Dispositions in U.S. Students. *Journal of Psychology* 144:413–428.

Chirot, Daniel. 1994. *How Societies Change*. Thousand Oaks, CA: Sage.

Cho, Sumi. 1993. Korean Americans vs. African Americans: Conflict and Construction. In Robert Gooding-Williams
(Ed.), *Reading Rodney King, Reading Urban Uprising* (pp. 196–211). New York: Routledge & Kegan Paul.

Chou, Rosalind, & Feagin, Joe. 2008. *The Myth of the Model Minority: Asian Americans Facing Racism*. Boulder,
CO: Paradigm.

Churchill, Ward. 1985. Resisting Relocation: Dine and Hopis Fight to Keep Their Land. *Dollars and Sense*, December,
pp. 112–115.

Civil Rights Act of 1964, Pub. L. 88-352, § 42 U.S.C. 2000 (1964).

Clark, M. L., & Person, Willie. 1982. Racial Stereotypes Revisited. *International Journal of Intercultural Relations*
6:381–392.

Cofer, Judith Ortiz. 1995. The Myth of the Latin Woman: I Just Met a Girl Named Maria. In *The Latin Deli: Prose
and Poetry* (pp. 148–154). Athens: University of Georgia Press.

Cohen, Adam, & Taylor, Elizabeth. 2000. *American Pharaoh, Mayor Richard J. Daley: His Battle for Chicago and
the Nation*. New York: Little, Brown.

Cohen, Steven M. 1985. *The 1984 National Survey of American Jews: Political and Social Outlooks*. New York:
American Jewish Committee.

Conot, Robert. 1967. *Rivers of Blood, Years of Darkness*. New York: Bantam.

Conzen, Kathleen N. 1980. Germans. In Stephan Thernstrom, Ann Orlov, & Oscar Handlin (Eds.), *Harvard
Encyclopedia of American Ethnic Groups* (pp. 405–425). Cambridge, MA: Harvard University Press.

Cornell, Stephen. 1987. American Indians, American Dreams, and the Meaning of Success. *American Indian Culture
and Research Journal* 11:59–71.

———. 1988. *The Return of the Native: American Indian Political Resurgence*. New York: Oxford University Press.

———. 1990. Land, Labor, and Group Formation: Blacks and Indians in the United States. *Ethnic and Racial Studies*
13:368–388.

———. 2006. *What Makes First Nations Enterprises Successful? Lessons from the Harvard Project*. Tucson, AZ:
Native Nations Institute for Leadership, Management, and Policy.

Cornell, Stephen, & Kalt, Joseph. 1998. *Sovereignty and Nation-Building: The Development Challenge in Indian
Country Today*. Cambridge, MA: Harvard Project on American Indian Economic Development. Retrieved August
22, 2007, from http://sparky.harvard.edu/hpaied/docs/CornellKalt%20Sov-NB.pdf

Cornell, Stephen, Kalt, Joseph, Krepps, Matthew, & Taylor, Johnathan. 1998. *American Indian Gaming Policy and
Its Socioeconomic Effects: A Report to the National Impact Gambling Study Commission*. Cambridge, MA:
Economics Resource Group.

Cortes, Carlos. 1980. Mexicans. In Stephan Thernstrom, Ann Orlov, & Oscar Handlin (Eds.), *Harvard Encyclopedia
of American Ethnic Groups* (pp. 697–719). Cambridge, MA: Harvard University Press.

Cose, Ellis. 1993. *The Rage of a Privileged Class*. New York: HarperCollins.

Cowan, Gloria. 2005. Interracial Interactions at Racially Diverse University Campuses. *Journal of Social Psychology*
145:49–63.

Cox, Oliver. 1948. *Caste, Class, and Race: A Study in Social Dynamics*. Garden City, NY: Doubleday.

Crawford, James. 2008. *Frequently Asked Questions About Official English*. Retrieved on October 11, 2010, from
http://www.elladvocates.org/documents/englishonly/OfficialEnglishFAQ.pdf

Crow Dog, Mary. 1990. *Lakota Woman*. New York: HarperCollins.

Cuddy, A., Fiske, S., Kwan, V., Glick, P., Demoulin, S., Leyens, J.-C., et al. 2009. Stereotype Content Model across
Cultures: Towards Universal Similarities and Some Differences. *British Journal of Social Psychology* 48:1–33.

Curtin, Philip. 1990. *The Rise and Fall of the Plantation Complex*. New York: Cambridge University Press.

D'Alessio, Stewart, Stolzenberg, Lisa, & Eitle, David. 2002. The Effect of Racial Threat on Interracial and Intraracial
Crimes. *Social Science Research* 31:392–408.

Damico, Sandra, & Sparks, Christopher. 1986. Cross-Group Contact Opportunities: Impact on Interpersonal
Relationships in Desegregated Middle Schools. *Sociology of Education* 59:113–123.

D'Angelo, Raymond. 2001. *The American Civil Rights Movement: Readings and Interpretations*. New York: McGraw-Hill.

Debo, Angie. 1970. *A History of the Indians of the United States*. Norman: University of Oklahoma Press.

de la Cruz, Patricia, & Brittingham, Angela. 2003. *The Arab Population: 2000*. Retrieved March 19, 2008, from http://www.census.gov/prod/2003pubs/c2kbr-23.pdf

Deloria, Vine. 1969. *Custer Died for Your Sins*. New York: Macmillan.

Deutsch, Morton, & Collins, Mary Ann. 1951. *Interracial Housing: A Psychological Evaluation of a Social Experiment*. Minneapolis: University of Minnesota Press.

Devine, Patricia, & Elliot, Andrew. 1995. Are Racial Stereotypes Really Fading? The Princeton Trilogy Revisited. *Personality and Social Psychology Bulletin* 21:1139–1150.

Dinnerstein, Leonard. 1977. The East European Jewish Immigration. In Leonard Dinnerstein & Frederic C. Jaher (Eds.), *Uncertain Americans* (pp. 216–231). New York: Oxford University Press.

Dixon, Jeffrey. 2006. The Ties That Don't Bind: Towards Reconciling Group Threat and Contact Theories of Prejudice. *Social Forces* 84:2179–2204.

Dixon, Jeffrey, & Rosenbaum, Michael. 2004. Nice to Know You? Testing Contact, Cultural, and Group Threat Theories of Anti-Black and Anti-Hispanic Stereotypes. *Social Science Quarterly* 85:257–280.

Dollard, John, Miller, Neal E., Doob, Leonard W., Mowrer, O. H., & Sears, Robert R. (with Ford, Clellan S., Hovland, Carl Iver, & Sollenberger, Richard T.). 1939. *Frustration and Aggression*. New Haven, CT: Yale University Press.

D'Orso, Michael. 1996. *Like Judgment Day: The Ruin and Redemption of a Town Called Rosewood*. New York: Putnam.

Doyle, Anna Beth, & Aboud, Frances E. 1995. A Longitudinal Study of White Children's Racial Prejudice as a Sociocognitive Development. *Merrill-Palmer Quarterly* 41:209–228.

Drake, Richard. 1860. *Revelations of a Slave Smuggler*. New York: Robert M. Dewitt.

Du Bois, W. E. B. 1961. *The Souls of Black Folk*. Greenwich, CT: Fawcett.

Duleep, Harriet O. 1988. *Economic Status of Americans of Asian Descent*. Washington, DC: U.S. Commission on Civil Rights.

Dumont, Jean-Christophe, & LeMaitre, Georges. 2011. *Counting Immigrants and Ex-Patriots in OECD Countries: A New Perspective*. Retrieved April 3, 2011, from http://www.oecd.org/dataoecd/27/5/33868740.pdf

Dwyer, R. 2010. Poverty, Prosperity, and Place: The Shape of Class Segregation in the Age of Extremes. *Social Problems* 57:114–137.

Editor and Publisher. 2007. "Gallup: Americans Overwhelmingly Favor Interracial Dating." Retrieved December 5, 2007, from http://www.amren.com/mtnews/archives/2005/10/gallup_american.php

"Education Statistics: Average Years of Schooling of Adults (Most Recent) by Country." 2011. Retrieved April 1, 2011, from http://www.nationmaster.com/graph/edu_ave_yea_of_sch_of_adu-education-average-years-schooling-adults

Ehrenreich, Barbara, & Hochschild, Arlie. 2004. *Global Women: Nannies, Maids, and Sex Workers in the New Economy*. New York: Holt Paperbacks.

Eichenwald, Kurt. 1996. Texaco to Make Record Payment in Bias Lawsuit. *New York Times*, November 16, p. 1.

Elkins, Stanley. 1959. *Slavery: A Problem in American Institutional and Intellectual Life*. New York: Universal Library.

Ellison, Christopher, & Powers, Daniel. 1994. The Contact Hypothesis and Racial Attitudes Among Black Americans. *Social Science Quarterly* 75:385–400.

Ellsworth, Scott. 1982. *Death in a Promised Land: The Tulsa Race Riot of 1921*. Baton Rouge: Louisiana State University Press.

Espinosa, Kristin, & Massey, Douglas. 1997. Determinants of English Proficiency Among Mexican Migrants to the United States. *International Migration Review* 31:28–51.

Espiritu, Yen. 1996. Colonial Oppression, Labour Importation, and Group Formation: Filipinos in the United States. *Ethnic and Racial Studies* 19:29–49.

———. 1997. *Asian American Women and Men*. Thousand Oaks, CA: Sage.

Essien-Udom, E. U. 1962. *Black Nationalism*. Chicago: University of Chicago Press.

Europe: The Integration Dilemma: Minorities in Germany. 2007. *Economist* (July 19): 39.

European Commission. 2007. *Special Eurobarometer 263: Discrimination in the European Union*. Brussels: Commission of the European Communities.

———. 2008. *Special Eurobarometer 296: Discrimination in the European Union: Perceptions, Experiences, and Attitudes*. Brussels: Commission of the European Communities.

European Roma Rights Center. 2006. *Ambulance Not on the Way*. Budapest: Author.

European Union Agency for Fundamental Rights. 2009. *European Union Minorities and Discrimination Survey: Data in Focus Report: The Roma*. Retrieved May 30, 2011, from http://fra.europa.eu/fraWebsite/attachments/EU-MIDIS_ROMA_EN.pdf

Evans, Sara M. 1979. *Personal Politics*. New York: Knopf.

———. 1989. *Born for Liberty: A History of Women in America*. New York: Free Press.

Fadiman, Anne. 1998. *The Spirit Catches You and You Fall Down*. New York: Farrar, Straus, & Giroux.

Fanning, Bryan. 2003. *Racism and Social Change in the Republic of Ireland*. Manchester, UK: Manchester University Press.

Farley, John. 2000. *Majority-Minority Relations* (4th ed.). Englewood Cliffs, NJ: Prentice Hall.

Farley, Reynolds. 1996. *The New American Reality*. New York: Russell Sage Foundation.

Faux, Jeff. 2004. NAFTA at 10: Where Do We Go From Here? *Nation*, February 2: 11–14.

Feagin, Joe. 2001. *Racist America: Roots, Current Realities, and Future Reparations*. New York: Routledge.

Feagin, Joe R., & Feagin, Clairece Booher. 1986. *Discrimination American Style: Institutional Racism and Sexism*. Malabar, FL: Robert E. Krieger.

Feagin, Joe R., & O'Brien, Eileen. 1999. The Long-Overdue Reparations for African Americans: Necessary for Societal Survival? In Roy L. Brooks (Ed.), *When Sorry Isn't Enough: The Controversy Over Apologies and Reparations for Human Injustice* (pp. 417–421). New York: New York University Press.

Fears, Darryl. 2007. Hate Crime Reporting Uneven. *Washington Post*, November 20, p. A3.

Federal Bureau of Investigation. 2010. Table 1: Incidents, Offenses, Victims, and Know Offenders by Bias Motivation, 2009. *Hate Crime Statistics*. Retrieved April 22, 2011, from http://www2.fbi.gov/ucr/hc2009/data/table_01.html

Federal Glass Ceiling Commission. 1995. "Good For Business: Making Full Use of the Nations Human Capital." Retrieved February 15, 2011, from http://digitalcommons.ilr.cornell.edu/cgi/viewcontent.cgi?article=1117&context=key_workplace

Federation for American Immigration Reform. 2010. Anchor Babies Are too Costly. Retrieved on October 1, 2010, from http://www.fairus.org/site/News2?page=NewsArticle&id=16535&security=1601&news_iv_ctrl=1007&s_oo=87VNsd5j2aWWTdhPQi1k1g

Firefighters Local Union No. 1784 v. Stotts, 467 U.S. 561 (1984).

Fisher, Mary. 2008. Does Campus Diversity Promote Friendship Diversity? A Look at Interracial Friendships in College. *Social Science Quarterly* 89:623–655.

Fiske, S., Bergsieker, H., Russell, A., & Williams, L. 2009. Images of Black Americans: Then, "Them," and Now, "Obama!" *Du Bois Review* 6:83–101.

Fitzpatrick, Joseph P. 1976. The Puerto Rican Family. In Charles H. Mindel & Robert W. Habenstein (Eds.), *Ethnic Families in America* (pp. 173–195). New York: Elsevier.

———. 1980. Puerto Ricans. In Stephan Thernstrom, Ann Orlov, & Oscar Handlin (Eds.), *Harvard Encyclopedia of American Ethnic Groups* (pp. 858–867). Cambridge, MA: Harvard University Press.

———. 1987. *Puerto Rican Americans: The Meaning of Migration to the Mainland* (2nd ed.). Englewood Cliffs, NJ: Prentice Hall.

Fong, Eric, & Markham, William. 1991. Immigration, Ethnicity, and Conflict: The California Chinese, 1849–1882. *Sociological Inquiry* 61:471–490.

Fong, Timothy. 2002. *The Contemporary Asian American Experience* (2nd ed.). Upper Saddle River, NJ: Prentice Hall.

Fong-Torres, Ben. 1995. *The Rice Room: Growing Up Chinese; From Number Two Son to Rock N Roll*. Plume: New York.

Forbes, H. D. 1997. *Ethnic Conflict: Commerce, Culture, and the Contact Hypothesis*. New Haven, CT: Yale University Press.

Forner, Philip S. 1980. *Women and the American Labor Movement: From World War I to the Present*. New York: Free Press.

Franklin, John Hope. 1967. *From Slavery to Freedom* (3rd ed.). New York: Knopf.

Franklin, John Hope, & Moss, Alfred. 1994. *From Slavery to Freedom* (7th ed.). New York: McGraw-Hill.

Frazier, E. Franklin. 1957. *Black Bourgeoisie: The Rise of a New Middle Class*. New York: Free Press.

Fry, Richard. 2007. *The Changing Racial and Ethnic Composition of U.S. Public Schools*. Washington, DC: Pew Hispanic Center. Retrieved October 18, 2007, from http://pewhispanic.org/files/reports/79.pdf

Fukuyama, Francis. 2004. *Identity Crisis: Why We Shouldn't Worry About Mexican Immigration*. Retrieved April 2, 2005, from http://slate.msn.com/id/2101756/#continuearticle

Gallagher, Charles. 2001. *Playing the Ethnic Card: How Ethnic Narratives Maintain Racial Privilege*. Paper presented at the Annual Meetings of the Southern Sociological Society, April 4–7, Atlanta, GA.

Gallup. 2008. "Race Relations." Retrieved March 2, 2011, from http://www.gallup.com/poll/1687/Race-Relations.aspx#3

———. 2010. "Race Relations." Retrieved September 3, 2010, from http://www.gallup.com/poll/1687/Race Relations.aspx

Gans, Herbert. 1979. Symbolic Ethnicity: The Future of Ethnic Groups and Cultures in America. *Ethnic and Racial Studies* 2:1–20.

Garvey, Marcus. 1969. *Philosophy and Opinions of Marcus Garvey* (Vols. 1–2, Amy Jacques Garvey, Ed.). New York: Atheneum.

———. 1977. *Philosophy and Opinions of Marcus Garvey* (Vol. 3, Amy Jacques Garvey & E. U. Essien-Udom, Eds.). London: Frank Cass.

"Gender Development (Most Recent) by Country." 2011. Retrieved July 16, 2011, from http://www.nationmaster .com/red/graph/peo_gen_dev-people-gender-development&b_map=1

Genovese, Eugene D. 1974. *Roll, Jordan, Roll: The World the Slaves Made.* New York: Pantheon.

Gerstenfeld, Phyllis. 2004. *Hate Crime: Causes, Controls, and Controversies.* Thousand Oaks, CA: Sage.

Gerth, Hans, & Mills, C. Wright (Eds.). 1946. *From Max Weber: Essays in Sociology.* New York: Oxford University Press.

Geschwender, James A. 1978. *Racial Stratification in America.* Dubuque, IA: William C. Brown.

Glaeser, Edward, & Vigdor, Jacob. 2001. *Racial Segregation in the 2000 Census: Promising News.* Washington, DC: Brookings Institution.

Glazer, Nathan, & Moynihan, Daniel. 1970. *Beyond the Melting Pot* (2nd ed.). Cambridge: MIT Press.

Gleason, Philip. 1980. American Identity and Americanization. In Stephan Thernstrom, Ann Orlov, & Oscar Handlin (Eds.), *Harvard Encyclopedia of American Ethnic Groups* (pp. 31–57). Cambridge, MA: Harvard University Press.

Gold, Steven J. 2002. The Arab American Community in Detroit, Michigan. *Contexts* 1(2): 48–55.

Goldstein, Amy, & Suro, Robert. 2000. A Journey on Stages: Assimilation's Pull Is Still Strong but Its Pace Varies. *Washington Post,* January 16, p. A1.

Gooding-Williams, Robert. 1993. *Reading Rodney King, Reading Urban Uprising.* New York: Routledge & Kegan Paul.

Gordon, M. M. (1964). *Assimilation in American Life: The Role of Race, Religion, and National Origins.* New York: Oxford University Press.

Goren, Arthur. 1980. Jews. In Stephan Thernstrom, Ann Orlov, & Oscar Handlin (Eds.), *Harvard Encyclopedia of American Ethnic Groups* (pp. 571–598). Cambridge, MA: Harvard University Press.

Gratz v. Bollinger, 539 U.S. 244 (2003).

Gray, David J. 1991. Shadow of the Past: The Rise and Fall of Prejudice in an American City. *American Journal of Economics and Sociology* 50:33–39.

Grebler, Leo, Moore, Joan W., & Guzman, Ralph C. 1970. *The Mexican American People.* New York: Free Press.

Greeley, Andrew M. 1974. *Ethnicity in the United States: A Preliminary Reconnaissance.* New York: Wiley.

Green, Donald. 1999. Native Americans. In Antony Dworkin & Rosalind Dworkin (Eds.), *The Minority Report* (pp. 255–277). Orlando, FL: Harcourt-Brace.

Greenwald, A. G., & Banaji, M. R. 1995. Implicit Social Cognition: Attitudes, Self-Esteem, and Stereotypes. *Psychological Review* 102:4–27.

Greenwald, A. G., Banaji, M. R., Rudman, L. A., Farnham, S. D., Nosek, B. A., & Mellott, D. S. 2002. A Unified Theory of Implicit Attitudes, Stereotypes, Self-Esteem, and Self-concept. *Psychological Review* 109:3–25.

Grutter v. Bollinger, 539 U.S. 306 (2003).

Guilbault, Rose Del Castillo. 1993. Americanization Is Tough on "Macho." In Dolores La Guardia & Hans Guth (Eds.), *American Voices* (pp. 163–165). Mountain View, CA: Mayfield. (First published in "This World," *San Francisco Chronicle*, August 20, 1989.)

Gutman, Herbert. 1976. *The Black Family in Slavery and Freedom, 1750–1925.* New York: Vintage.

Hacker, Andrew. 1992. *Two Nations: Black and White, Separate, Hostile, Unequal.* New York: Scribner's.

Hakimzadeh, Shirin, & Cohn, D'Vera. 2007. *English Language Usage among Hispanics in the United States.* Washington, DC: Pew Hispanic Center. Retrieved April 4, 2011, from http://pewhispanic.org/files/reports/82.pdf

Haley, Alex. 1976. *Roots: The Saga of an American Family.* New York: Doubleday.

Haller, William, Portes, Alejandro, & Lynch, Scott. 2011. Dreams Fulfilled, Dreams Shattered: Determinants of Segmented Assimilation in the Second Generation. *Social Forces* 89:733–762.

Hamer, Fannie Lou. 1967. *To Praise Our Bridges: An Autobiography of Fannie Lou Hamer.* Jackson, MS: KIPCO.

Handlin, Oscar. 1951. *The Uprooted.* New York: Grosset & Dunlap.

Hansen, Marcus Lee. 1952. The Third Generation in America. *Commentary* 14:493–500.

Hanson, Jeffery, & Rouse, Linda. 1987. Dimensions of Native American Stereotyping. *American Indian Culture and Research Journal* 11:33–58.

Harjo, Suzan. 1996. Now and Then: Native Peoples in the United States. *Dissent* 43:58–60.

Hartley, E. L. 1946. *Problems in Prejudice.* New York: Kings Crown.

Hawkins, Hugh. 1962. *Booker T. Washington and His Critics: The Problem of Negro Leadership.* Boston: D. C. Heath.

Heaton, Tim, Chadwick, Bruce, & Jacobson, Cardell. 2000. *Statistical Handbook on Racial Groups in the United States.* Phoenix, AZ: Oryx.

Heer, David M. 1996. *Immigration in America's Future.* Boulder, CO: Westview.

Herberg, Will. 1960. *Protestant-Catholic-Jew: An Essay in American Religious Sociology.* New York: Anchor.

Higham, John. 1963. *Strangers in the Land: Patterns of American Nativism, 1860–1925.* New York: Atheneum.

Hill-Collins, Patricia. 1991. *Black Feminist Thought.* New York: Routledge.

Hirschman, Charles. 1983. America's Melting Pot Reconsidered. *Annual Review of Sociology* 9:397–423.

Hirschman, Charles, & Wong, Morrison. 1984. Socioeconomic Gains of Asian Americans, Blacks, and Hispanics: 1960–1976. *American Journal of Sociology* 90:584–607.

———. 1986. The Extraordinary Educational Attainment of Asian-Americans: A Search for Historical Evidence and Explanations. *Social Forces* 65:1–27.

hooks, bell. 1996. *Bone Black.* New York: Henry Holt.

Hopcroft, Rosemary. 2009. Gender Inequality in Interaction: An Evolutionary Account. *Social Forces* 87:1845–1872.

Horowitz, David. 2001. Ten Reasons Why Reparations for Blacks Is a Bad Idea for Blacks—and Racist Too. *FrontPageMag.com.* Retrieved February 22, 2011, from http://archive.frontpagemag.com/readArticle .aspx?ARTID=24317

Hostetler, John. 1980. *Amish Society.* Baltimore: Johns Hopkins University Press.

Hovland, Carl I., & Sears, Robert R. 1940. Minor Studies of Aggression: Correlation of Lynchings and Economic Indices. *Journal of Psychology* 9:301–310.

How to Tell Your Friends From the Japs. 1941. *Time,* October–December, p. 33.

Hoxie, Frederick. 1984. *A Final Promise: The Campaign to Assimilate the Indian, 1880–1920.* Lincoln: University of Nebraska Press.

Hraba, Joseph. 1994. *American Ethnicity* (2nd ed.). Itasca, IL: F. E. Peacock.

Huber, Joan. 2007. *On the Origins of Gender Inequality.* Colorado Springs, CO: Paradigm.

Hughes, Michael, & Thomas, Melvin. 1998. The Continuing Significance of Race Revisited: A Study of Race, Class, and Quality of Life in America, 1972 to 1996. *American Sociological Review* 63:785–803.

Human Rights Watch. 2009. *Decades of Disparity: Drug Arrests and Race in the United States.* Retrieved March 2, 2011, from http://www.hrw.org/en/reports/2009/03/02/decades-disparity-0

Huntington, Samuel. 2004. *Who Are We? The Challenges to America's National Identity.* New York: Simon & Schuster.

Hurh, Won Moo. 1998. *The Korean Americans.* Westport, CT: Greenwood.

Hyman, Herbert, & Sheatsley, Paul. 1964. Attitudes Toward Desegregation. *Scientific American* 211:16–23.

Ibish, Hussein (Ed.). 2003. *Report on Hate Crimes and Discrimination against Arab Americans: The Post–September 11 Backlash.* Washington, DC: American-Arab Anti-Discrimination Committee. Retrieved February 14, 2005, from http://www.adc.org/hatecrimes/pdf/2003_report_web.pdf

Iceland, John, Weinberg, Donald, & Steinmetz, Erika. 2002. *Racial and Ethnic Residential Segregation in the United States: 1980–2000* (U.S. Census Bureau, Series CENSR-3). Washington, DC: U.S. Government Printing Office. Retrieved August 17, 2006, from http://www.census.gov/prod/2002pubs/censr-3.pdf

Jackman, Mary. 1978. General and Applied Tolerance: Does Education Increase Commitment to Racial Integration? *American Journal of Political Science* 22:302–324.

———. 1981. Education and Policy Commitment to Racial Integration. *American Journal of Political Science* 25: 256–259.

Jackman, Mary, & Muha, M. 1984. Education and Intergroup Attitudes: Moral Enlightenment, Superficial Democratic Commitment, or Ideological Refinement? *American Sociological Review* 49:751–769.

Jackson, Beverly. 2000. *Splendid Slippers: A Thousand Years of an Erotic Tradition.* Berkeley, CA: Ten Speed.

Jacobs, David, & Wood, Katherine. 1999. Interracial Conflict and Interracial Homicide: Do Political and Economic Rivalries Explain White Killings of Blacks or Black Killings of Whites? *American Journal of Sociology* 105: 157–180.

Jacobs, Harriet. 1987. *Incidents in the Life of a Slave Girl, Written by Herself* (Jean Yellin, Ed.). Cambridge, MA: Harvard University Press.

Jibou, Robert M. 1988. Ethnic Hegemony and the Japanese of California. *American Sociological Review* 53:353–367.

Joe, Jennie, & Miller, Dorothy. 1994. Cultural Survival and Contemporary American Indian Women in the City. In Maxine Zinn & Bonnie T. Dill (Eds.), *Women of Color in U.S. Society* (pp. 185–202). Philadelphia: Temple University Press.

Jones, James. 1997. *Prejudice and Racism* (2nd ed.). New York: McGraw-Hill.

Jones, Jeffrey. 2001. *Racial or Ethnic Labels Make Little Difference to Blacks, Hispanics.* Retrieved July 5, 2002, from http://www.gallup.com/poll/releases/pr010911.asp

———. 2010. "More Americans Favor Than Oppose Arizona Immigration Law." Gallup. Retrieved May 26, 2011, from http://www.gallup.com/poll/127598/Americans-Favor-Oppose-Arizona-Immigration-Law.aspx

Jordan, Winthrop. 1968. *White Over Black: American Attitudes Towards the Negro: 1550–1812.* Chapel Hill: University of North Carolina Press.

Josephy, Alvin M. 1968. *The Indian Heritage of America.* New York: Knopf.

Kallen, Horace M. 1915a. Democracy Versus the Melting Pot. *Nation* 100 (February 18): 190–194.

———. 1915b. Democracy Versus the Melting Pot. *Nation* 100 (February 25): 217–222.

Karlins, Marvin, Coffman, Thomas, & Walters, Gary. 1969. On the Fading of Social Stereotypes: Studies in Three Generations of College Students. *Journal of Personality and Social Psychology* 13:1–16.

Kasarda, John D. 1989. Urban Industrial Transition and the Underclass. *Annals of the American Academy* 501:26–47.

Kasinitz, Philip, Mollenkopf, John H., Waters, Mary C., & Holdaway, Jennifer. 2008. *Inheriting the City: The Children of Immigrants Come of Age.* Cambridge, MA: Harvard University Press.

Katz, Michael B., & Stern, Mark J. 2008. *One Nation Divisible: What America Was and What It Is Becoming.* New York: Russell Sage Foundation.

Katz, Phyllis. 1976. The Acquisition of Racial Attitudes in Children. In Phyllis Katz (Ed.), *Towards the Elimination of Racism* (pp. 125–154). New York: Pergamon.

———. 2003. Racists or Tolerant Multiculturalists? How Do They Begin? *American Psychologist* 58:897–909.

Katz, Phyllis, & Taylor, Dalmas (Eds.). 1988. *Eliminating Racism: Profiles in Controversy.* New York: Plenum.

Katznelson, Ira. 2005. *When Affirmative Action Was White: An Untold History of Racial Inequality in Twentieth-Century America.* New York: Norton.

Kaw, Eugenia. 1997. Opening Faces: The Politics of Cosmetic Surgery and Asian-American Women. In M. Crawford & R. Under (Eds.), *In Our Own Words: Readings on the Psychology of Women and Gender* (pp. 55–73). New York: McGraw-Hill.

Kaye, Jeffrey. 2010. *Moving Millions: How Coyote Capitalism Fuels Global Immigration.* Hoboken, NJ: Wiley.

Kennedy, Randall. 2001. Racial Trends in the Administration of Criminal Justice. In N. Smelser, W. Wilson, & F. Mitchell (Eds.), *America Becoming: Racial Trends and Their Consequences* (Vol. 2, pp. 1–20). Washington, DC: National Academy Press.

Kennedy, Ruby Jo. 1944. Single or Triple Melting Pot? Intermarriage Trends in New Haven, 1870–1940. *American Journal of Sociology* 49:331–339.

———. 1952. Single or Triple Melting Pot? Intermarriage Trends in New Haven, 1870–1950. *American Journal of Sociology* 58:56–59.

Kephart, William, & Zellner, William. 1994. *Extraordinary Groups.* New York: St. Martin's.

Killian, Lewis. 1975. *The Impossible Revolution, Phase 2: Black Power and the American Dream.* New York: Random House.

Kinder, Donald R., & Sears, David O. 1981. Prejudice and Politics: Symbolic Racism Versus Racial Threats to the Good Life. *Journal of Personality and Social Psychology* 40:414–431.

King, C. Richard, Staurowsky, Ellen J., Baca, Lawrence, Davis, Laurel R., & Pewewardy, Cornel. 2002. Of Polls and Race Prejudice: *Sports Illustrated*'s Errant "Indian Wars." *Journal of Sport and Social Issues* 26:381–403.

King, Martin Luther, Jr. 1958. *Stride Toward Freedom: The Montgomery Story.* New York: Harper & Row.

———. 1963. *Why We Can't Wait.* New York: Mentor.

———. 1968. *Where Do We Go From Here: Chaos or Community?* New York: Harper & Row.

Kitano, Harry H. L. 1980. Japanese. In Stephan Thernstrom, Ann Orlov, & Oscar Handlin (Eds.), *Harvard Encyclopedia of American Ethnic Groups* (pp. 561–571). Cambridge, MA: Harvard University Press.

Kitano, Harry, & Daniels, Roger. 1988. *Asian Americans: Emerging Minorities.* Englewood Cliffs, NJ: Prentice Hall.

———. 1995. *Asian Americans: Emerging Minorities* (2nd ed.). Englewood Cliffs, NJ: Prentice Hall.

———. 2001. *Asian Americans: Emerging Minorities* (3rd ed.). Upper Saddle River, NJ: Prentice Hall.

Kleg, M., & Yamamoto, K. 1998. As the World Turns: Ethnoracial Distances After 70 Years. *Social Science Journal* 35:183–191.

Kluegel, James R., & Smith, Eliot R. 1982. Whites' Beliefs About Blacks' Opportunities. *American Sociological Review* 47:518–532.

Kochhar, Rakesh. 2004. *The Wealth of Hispanic Households: 1996 to 2002.* Washington, DC: Pew Hispanic Center. Retrieved February 15, 2004, from http://pewhispanic.org/files/reports/34.pdf

———. 2006. *Growth in the Foreign-Born Workforce and Employment of the Native Born.* Washington, DC: Pew Hispanic Center. Retrieved May 27, 2011, from http://pewhispanic.org/files/reports/69.pdf

Krauss, Michael. 1996. Status of Native American Language Endangerment. In G. Cantoni (Ed.), *Stabilizing Indigenous Languages.* Flagstaff, AZ: Center for Excellence in Education, Northern Arizona University.

Kraybill, Donald B., & Bowman, Carl F. 2001. *On the Backroad to Heaven: Old Order Hutterites, Mennonites, Amish, and Brethren.* Baltimore: Johns Hopkins University Press.

Kristof, Nicholas, & WuDunn, Sheryl. 2010. *Half the Sky: Turning Oppression into Opportunity for Women Worldwide.* New York: Vintage.

Kritz, Mary, & Girak, Douglas. 2004. *The American People: Immigration and a Changing America.* New York: Russell Sage Foundation.

Krysan, Maria, & Farley, Reynolds. 2002. The Residential Preferences of Blacks: Do They Explain Persistent Segregation? *Social Forces* 80:937–981.

Kuperman, Diane. 2001. Stuck at the Gates of Paradise. *UNESCO Courier,* September, pp. 24–26.

Lacy, Dan. 1972. *The White Use of Blacks in America.* New York: McGraw-Hill.

Lai, H. M. 1980. Chinese. In Stephan Thernstrom, Ann Orlov, & Oscar Handlin (Eds.), *Harvard Encyclopedia of American Ethnic Groups* (pp. 217–234). Cambridge, MA: Harvard University Press.

Lame Deer, John (Fire), & Erdoes, Richard. 1972. Listening to the Air. In *Lame Deer, Seeker of Visions* (pp. 119–121). New York: Simon & Schuster.

Lamont-Brown, Raymond. 1993. The Burakumin: Japan's Underclass. *Contemporary Review* 263:136–140.

Landale, Nancy, & Oropesa, R. S. 2002. White, Black, or Puerto Rican? Racial Self-Identification Among Mainland and Island Puerto Ricans. *Social Forces* 81:231–254.

LaPiere, Robert. 1934. Attitudes vs. Actions. *Social Forces* 13:230–237.

Le, C. N. 2005. Fleeing Dragon: The Refugee Experience of a Vietnamese Immigrant Family. In John Myers (Ed.), *Minority Voices: Linking Personal Ethnic History and the Sociological Imagination* (pp. 340–362). Boston: Pearson.

Lee, Sharon. 1998. Asian Americans: Diverse and Growing. *Population Bulletin* 53(2): 1–40. Washington, DC: Population Reference Bureau.

Lee, Sharon, & Edmonston, Barry. 2005. *New Marriages, New Families: U.S. Racial and Hispanic Intermarriage.* Washington, DC: Population Reference Bureau. Retrieved March 13, 2008, from http://www.prb.org/pdf05/60.2NewMarriages.pdf

Lee, Sharon M., & Yamanaka, Keiko. 1990. Patterns of Asian American Intermarriage and Marital Assimilation. *Journal of Comparative Family Studies* 21:287–305.

Lenski, Gerhard, Nolan, Patrick, & Lenski, Jean. 1995. *Human Societies: An Introduction to Macrosociology* (7th ed.). New York: McGraw-Hill.

Levin, Jack, & McDevitt, Jack. 1993. *Hate Crimes: The Rising Tide of Bigotry and Bloodshed.* New York: Plenum.

Levine, Lawrence. 1977. *Black Culture and Black Consciousness.* New York: Oxford University Press.

Levy, Jacques. 1975. *César Chávez: Autobiography of La Causa.* New York: Norton.

Lewis Mumford Center. 2001. *Ethnic Diversity Grows, Neighborhood Integration Lags Behind.* Retrieved July 2, 2002, from http://mumford1.dyndns.org/cen2000/report.html

Lewis, Oscar. 1959. *Five Families: Mexican Case Studies in the Culture of Poverty.* New York: Basic Books.

———. 1965. *La Vida: A Puerto Rican Family in the Culture of Poverty.* New York: Random House.

———. 1966. The Culture of Poverty. *Scientific American,* October, pp. 19–25.

Lieberman, Robert. 1998. *Shifting the Color Line: Race and the American Welfare System.* Cambridge, MA: Harvard University Press.

Lieberson, Stanley. 1980. *A Piece of the Pie: Blacks and White Immigrants Since 1880.* Berkeley: University of California Press.

Lieberson, Stanley, & Waters, Mary C. 1988. *From Many Strands.* New York: Russell Sage Foundation.

Light, Ivan, & Bonacich, Edna. 1988. *Immigrant Entrepreneurs: Koreans in Los Angeles, 1965–1982.* Berkeley: University of California Press.

Lincoln, C. Eric. 1961. *The Black Muslims in America.* Boston: Beacon.

Ling, Huping. 2000. Family and Marriage of Late-Nineteenth and Early-Twentieth Century Chinese Immigrant Women. *Journal of American Ethnic History* 9:43–65.

Livingstone, David. 1874. *The Last Journals of David Livingstone, in Central Africa, from 1865 to His Death* (Horace Waller, Ed.). London: John Murray.

Locust, Carol. 1990. Wounding the Spirit: Discrimination and Traditional American Indian Belief Systems. In Gail Thomas (Ed.), *U.S. Race Relations in the 1980s and 1990s: Challenges and Alternatives* (pp. 219–232). New York: Hemisphere.

Logan, John, Alba, Richard, & McNulty, Thomas. 1994. Ethnic Economies in Metropolitan Regions: Miami and Beyond. *Social Forces* 72:691–724.

Lopata, Helena Znaniecki. 1976. *Polish Americans.* Englewood Cliffs, NJ: Prentice Hall.

Lopez, Ian F. Haney. 2006a. Colorblind to the Reality of Race in America. *Chronicle of Higher Education* 53(11): B6.

———. 2006b. *White by Law: The Legal Construction of Race.* New York: NYU Press.

Lopez, Mark, & Taylor, Paul. 2009. *Dissecting the 2008 Electorate: Most Diverse in U.S. History.* Washington, DC: Pew Hispanic Center. Retrieved August 1, 2011, from http://pewhispanic.org/reports/report.php?ReportID=108

Lurie, Nancy Oestrich. 1982. The American Indian: Historical Background. In Norman Yetman & C. Hoy Steele (Eds.), *Majority and Minority* (3rd ed., pp. 131–144). Boston: Allyn & Bacon.

Lyman, Stanford. 1974. *Chinese Americans.* New York: Random House.

Malcolm X. 1964. *The Autobiography of Malcolm X.* New York: Grove.

Mannix, Daniel P. 1962. *Black Cargoes: A History of the Atlantic Slave Trade.* New York: Viking.

Marcelli, Enrico, & Heer, David. 1998. The Unauthorized Mexican Immigrant Population and Welfare in Los Angeles County: A Comparative Statistical Analysis. *Sociological Perspectives* 41:279–303.

Martin, Philip, & Midgley, Elizabeth. 1999. Immigration to the United States. *Population Bulletin*, 54(2): 1–44. Washington, DC: Population Reference Bureau.

Martinez, Gebe, Garcia, Ann, and Arons, Jessica. 2010. The Birthright Citizenship Debate Is a Thinly Veiled Attack on Immigrant Mothers. Retrieved October 1, 2010, from http://www.americanprogress.org/issues/2010/08/citizenship_debate.html

Marvasti, Amir, & McKinney, Karyn. 2004. *Middle Eastern Lives in America*. Lanham, MD: Rowman & Littlefield.

Marx, Karl, & Engels, Friedrich. 1967. *The Communist Manifesto*. Baltimore: Penguin. (Original work published 1848)

Massarik, Fred, & Chenkin, Alvin. 1973. United States National Jewish Population Study: A First Report. In *American Jewish Committee, American Jewish Year Book, 1973* (pp. 264–306). New York: American Jewish Committee.

Massey, Douglas. 1995. The New Immigration and Ethnicity in the United States. *Population and Development Review* 21:631–652.

———. 2000. Housing Discrimination 101. *Population Today* 28:1, 4.

———. 2007. *Categorically Unequal: The American Stratification System*. New York: Russell Sage Foundation.

Massey, Douglas, & Denton, Nancy. 1993. *American Apartheid*. Cambridge, MA: Harvard University Press.

Mauer, Marc, & Huling, Tracy. 2000. Young Black Americans and the Criminal Justice System. In Jerome Skolnick & Elliot Currie (Eds.), *Crisis in American Institutions* (11th ed., pp. 417–424). New York: Allyn & Bacon.

McConahy, John B. 1986. Modern Racism, Ambivalence, and the Modern Racism Scale. In John F. Dovidio & Samuel Gartner (Eds.), *Prejudice, Discrimination, and Racism* (pp. 91–125). Orlando, FL: Academic.

McDowell, Amber. 2004. Cracker Barrel Settles Lawsuit; Black Customers, Workers Reported Discrimination. *Washington Post*, September 10, p. E1.

McLaren, Lauren. 2003. Anti-immigrant Prejudice in Europe: Contact, Threat Perception, and Preferences for the Exclusion of Migrants. *Social Forces* 81:909–936.

McLemore, S. Dale. 1973. The Origins of Mexican American Subordination in Texas. *Social Science Quarterly* 53:656–679.

McNickle, D'Arcy. 1973. *Native American Tribalism: Indian Survivals and Renewals*. New York: Oxford University Press.

McPherson, Miller, Smith-Lovin, Lynn, & Brashears, Matthew. 2006. Social Isolation in America: Changes in Core Discussion Networks Over Two Decades. *Social Forces* 71:353–375.

McWhorter, John. 2008. The End of Racism? *Commentary*. Retrieved on October 13, 2010, from http://www.forbes.com/2008/11/05/obama-racism-president-oped-cx_jm_1105mcwhorter.html

McWilliams, Carey. 1961. *North from Mexico: The Spanish-Speaking People of the United States*. New York: Monthly Review.

Medoff, Marshall. 1999. Allocation of Time and Hateful Behavior: A Theoretical and Positive Analysis of Hate and Hate Crimes. *American Journal of Economics and Sociology* 58:959–973.

Meek, Barbara. 2006. And the Indian goes "How!": Representations of American Indian English in White Public Space. *Language in Society* 35:93–128.

Meissner, Doris. 2010. 5 Myths About Immigration. *Washington Post*, May 2, p. B2.

Meredith v. Jefferson County (Ky.) Board of Education, 551 U.S. (2007).

Merton, Robert. 1968. *Social Theory and Social Structure*. New York: Free Press.

Miller, Neal, & Bugleski, R. 1948. Minor Studies of Aggression: The Influence of Frustrations Imposed by the Ingroup on Attitudes Expressed Towards Outgroups. *Journal of Psychology* 25:437–442.

Miller, Norman, & Brewer, Marilyn (Eds.). 1984. *Groups in Contact: The Psychology of Desegregation*. Orlando, FL: Academic.

Min, Pyong Gap (Ed.). 1995. *Asian Americans: Contemporary Trends and Issues*. Thousand Oaks, CA: Sage.

Min, Pyong Gap (Ed.). 2006. *Asian Americans: Contemporary Trends and Issues* (2nd ed.). Thousand Oaks, CA: Sage.

Mirandé, Alfredo. 1985. *The Chicano Experience: An Alternative Perspective*. Notre Dame, IN: University of Notre Dame Press.

Mirandé, Alfredo, & Enríquez, Evangelina. 1979. *La Chicana: The Mexican-American Women*. Chicago: University of Chicago Press.

Moore, Joan W. 1970. *Mexican Americans*. Englewood Cliffs, NJ: Prentice Hall.

Moore, Joan W., & Pachon, Harry. 1985. *Hispanics in the United States*. Englewood Cliffs, NJ: Prentice Hall.

Moore, Joan, & Pinderhughes, Raquel. 1993. *In the Barrios: Latinos and the Underclass Debate*. New York: Russell Sage Foundation.

Moquin, Wayne, & Van Doren, Charles (Eds.). 1971. *A Documentary History of Mexican Americans*. New York: Bantam.

Morales, Lyman. 2010. "Amid Immigration Debate, Americans' Views Ease Slightly." Gallup. Retrieved April 4, 2011, from http://www.gallup.com/poll/141560/Amid-Immigration-Debate-Americans-Views-Ease-Slightly.aspx

Morawska, Ewa. 1990. The Sociology and Historiography of Immigration. In Virginia Yans-McLaughlin (Ed.), *Immigration Reconsidered: History, Sociology, and Politics* (pp. 187–238). New York: Oxford University Press.

Morgan, Edmund. 1975. *American Slavery, American Freedom.* New York: Norton.

Morin, Richard, & Cottman, Michael. 2001. Discrimination's Lingering Sting. *Washington Post,* June 22, p. A1.

Morris, Aldon D. 1984. *The Origins of the Civil Rights Movement.* New York: Free Press.

Morris, Edward. 2005. "Tuck in That Shirt!" Race, Class, Gender, and Discipline in an Urban School. *Sociological Perspectives* 48:25–48.

Moynihan, Daniel. 1965. *The Negro Family: The Case for National Action.* Washington, DC: U.S. Department of Labor.

Mujica, Mauro. 2003. Official English Legislation: Myths and Realities. *Human Events* 59:24.

Myrdal, Gunnar. 1962. *An American Dilemma: The Negro Problem and Modern Democracy.* New York: Harper & Row. (Original work published 1944)

Nabakov, Peter (Ed.). 1999. *Native American Testimony* (Rev. ed.). New York: Penguin.

National Advisory Commission. 1968. *Report of the National Advisory Commission on Civil Disorders.* New York: Bantam Books.

National Center for Health Statistics. 2010. *Health, United States, 2010: With Special Feature on Death and Dying.* Hyattsville, MD: Author. Retrieved March 15, 2011, from http://www.cdc.gov/nchs/data/hus/hus10.pdf#061

National Council on Crime and Delinquency. 2007. *And Justice for Some: Differential Treatment of Youth of Color in the Justice System.* Retrieved March 12, 2008, from http://www.nccd-crc.org/nccd/pubs/2007jan_justice_for_some.pdf

National Indian Gaming Commission. 2011. "NIGC Tribal Gaming Revenues." Retrieved March 21, 2011, from http://www.nigc.gov/LinkClick.aspx?fileticket=1k4B6r6dr-U%3d&tabid=67

———. n.d. *Gaming Revenue Reports.* Retrieved August 29, 2007, from http://www.nigc.gov/Default .aspx?tabid=67/

National Opinion Research Council. 1972–2010. *General Social Survey.* Chicago: Author.

National Origins Act, Pub. L. 139, Chapter 190, § 43 Stat. 153 (1924).

National Public Radio. 2004. "Immigration in America: Survey Overview." Retrieved February 15, 2005, from http://www.npr.org/templates/story/story.php?storyId=4062605

Neary, Ian. 2003. Burakumin at the End of History. *Social Research* 70:269–294.

Neissen, Jan, Schibel, Yongmi, & Thompson, Cressida. (Eds.). 2005. *Current Immigration Debates in Europe: Ireland.* Brussels, Belgium: Migration Policy Group. Retrieved March 8, 2008, from http://www.migpolgroup.com/multiattachments/3006/DocumentName/EMD_Ireland_2005.pdf

Nelli, Humbert S. 1980. Italians. In Stephan Thernstrom, Ann Orlov, & Oscar Handlin (Eds.), *Harvard Encyclopedia of American Ethnic Groups* (pp. 545–560). Cambridge, MA: Harvard University Press.

Nishi, Setsuko. 1995. Japanese Americans. In Pyong Gap Min (Ed.), *Asian Americans: Contemporary Trends and Issues* (pp. 95–133). Thousand Oaks, CA: Sage.

Noel, Donald. 1968. A Theory of the Origin of Ethnic Stratification. *Social Problems* 16:157–172.

Nolan, Patrick, & Lenski, Gerhard. 2004. *Human Societies.* Boulder, CO: Paradigm.

Novak, Michael. 1973. *The Rise of the Unmeltable Ethnics: Politics and Culture in the 1970s.* New York: Collier.

Ogunwole, Stella. 2002. *The American Indian and Alaska Native Population, 2000.* Retrieved March 13, 2008, from http://www.census.gov/prod/2002pubs/c2kbr01-15.pdf

O'Hare, William, Pollard, Kelvin, Mann, Taynia, & Kent, Mary. 1991. *African Americans in the 1990s.* Washington, DC: Population Reference Bureau.

Oliver, Melvin, & Shapiro, Thomas. 2001. Wealth and Racial Stratification. In N. Smelser, W. Wilson, & F. Mitchell (Eds.), *America Becoming: Racial Trends and Their Consequences* (Vol. 1, pp. 222–251). Washington, DC: National Academy Press.

———. 2006. *Black Wealth, White Wealth* (2nd ed.). New York: Taylor & Francis.

———. 2008. Sub-Prime as a Black Catastrophe. *American Prospect,* (October): A9–A11.

Olson, James, & Wilson, R. 1984. *Native Americans in the Twentieth Century.* Provo, UT: Brigham Young University Press.

Omi, Michael, & Winant, Howard. 1986. *Racial Formation in the United States from the 1960s to the 1980s.* New York: Routledge & Kegan Paul.

Orfield, Gary, & Lee, Chungmei. 2006. *Racial Transformation and the Changing Nature of Segregation.* Cambridge, MA: Civil Rights Project, Harvard University. Retrieved March 12, 2008, from http://www.civilrightsproject.ucla .edu/research/deseg/Racial_Transformation.pdf

———. 2007. *Historic Reversals, Accelerating Resegregation, and the Need for New Integration Strategies.* Los Angeles: Civil Rights Project, UCLA. Retrieved February 5, 2011, from http://www.eric.ed.gov/PDFS/ED500611.pdf

Osofsky, Gilbert. 1969. *Puttin' On Ole Massa.* New York: Harper & Row.

O'Sullivan, John. 2004. Who Are We? Samuel Huntington's New Book Forces a Debate on Immigration and American Destiny. *The American Conservative* (July 19). Retrieved April 19, 2011, from http://www.amconmag.com/article/2004/jul/19/00007/

Oswalt, Wendell, & Neely, Sharlotte. 1996. *This Land Was Theirs.* Mountain View, CA: Mayfield.

Parents Involved in Community Schools v. Seattle School District No. 1, 551 U.S. (2007).

Parish, Peter J. 1989. *Slavery: History and Historians.* New York: Harper & Row.

Park, Robert E., & Burgess, Ernest W. 1924. *Introduction to the Science of Society.* Chicago: University of Chicago Press.

Parke, Ross, & Buriel, Raymond. 2002. Socialization Concerns in African American, American Indian, Asian American, and Latino Families. In Nijole Benokraitis (Ed.), *Contemporary Ethnic Families in the United States* (pp. 211–218). Upper Saddle Brook, NJ: Prentice Hall.

Parrillo, Vincent. 2003. *Strangers to These Shores* (7th ed.). Boston: Allyn & Bacon.

Passel, Jeffrey, & Cohn, D'Vera. 2009. *Mexican Immigrants: How Many Come? How Many Leave?* Washington, DC: Pew Hispanic Center. Retrieved August 1, 2011, from http://pewhispanic.org/files/reports/112.pdf

Passel, Jeffrey, & Cohn, D'Vera. 2011. *Unauthorized Immigrant Population: National and State Trends, 2010.* Washington, DC: Pew Hispanic Center. Retrieved April 1, 2011, from http://pewhispanic.org/files/reports/133.pdf

Passel, Jeffrey, Cohn, D'Vera, & Lopez, Mark. 2011. *Census 2010: 50 Million Latinos. Hispanics Account for More Than Half of the Nation's Growth in the Past Decade.* Washington, DC: Pew Hispanic Center. Retrieved April 21, 2011, from http://pewhispanic.org/files/reports/140.pdf

Passel, Jeffrey, Wang, Wendy, & Taylor, Paul. 2010. *Marrying Out: One-in-Seven New U.S. Marriages is Interracial or Interethnic.* Pew Research Center. Retrieved May 12, 2011, from http://pewsocialtrends.org/files/2010/10/755 marrying-out.pdf

Pego, David. 1998. To Educate a Nation: Native American Tribe Hopes to Bring Higher Education to an Arizona Reservation. *Black Issues in Higher Education* 15:60–63.

Perez, Lisandro. 1980. Cubans. In Stephan Thernstrom, Ann Orlov, & Oscar Handlin (Eds.), *Harvard Encyclopedia of American Ethnic Groups* (pp. 256–261). Cambridge, MA: Harvard University Press.

Petersen, Williams. 1971. *Japanese Americans.* New York: Random House.

Peterson, B., & Zurbriggen, E. 2010. Gender, Sexuality, and the Authoritarian Personality. *Journal of Personality* 78:1801–1826.

Peterson, Bill, & Pang, Joyce. 2006. Beyond Politics: Authoritarianism and the Pursuit of Leisure. *Journal of Social Psychology* 146:442–461.

Peterson, Mark. 1995. Leading Cuban-American Entrepreneurs: The Process of Developing Motives, Abilities, and Resources. *Human Relations* 48:1193–1216.

Pettigrew, Thomas. 1958. Personality and Sociocultural Factors in Intergroup Attitudes: A Cross-National Comparison. *Journal of Conflict Resolution* 2:29–42.

———. 1971. *Racially Separate or Together?* New York: McGraw-Hill.

———. 1980. Prejudice. In Stephan Thernstrom, Ann Orlov, & Oscar Handlin (Eds.), *Harvard Encyclopedia of American Ethnic Groups* (pp. 820–829). Cambridge, MA: Harvard University Press.

———. 1998. Intergroup Contact Theory. *Annual Review of Psychology* 49:65–85.

Pettigrew, Thomas, & Tropp, Linda. 2006. A Meta-Analytic Test of Intergroup Contact Theory. *Journal of Personality and Social Psychology* 90:751–783.

Pettigrew, Thomas, Wagner, Ulrich, & Christ, Oliver. 2007. Who Opposes Immigration? Comparing German and North American Findings. *Du Bois Review* 4:19–39.

Pettit, Becky, & Western, Bruce. 2004. Mass Imprisonment and the Life Course: Race and Class Inequality in U.S. Incarceration. *American Sociological Review* 69:151–169.

Pew Charitable Trust. 2008. *One in 100: Behind Bars in America 2008.* Retrieved March 12, 2008, from http://www .pewtrusts.org/uploadedFiles/wwwpewtrustsorg/Reports/sentencing_and_corrections/one_in_100.pdf

Pew Hispanic Center. 2004. *Assimilation and Language.* Washington, DC: Author. Retrieved January 21, 2007, from http://pewhispanic .org/files/factsheets/11.pdf

———. 2005. *Hispanics: A People in Motion.* Washington, DC: Author. Retrieved March 16, 2008, from http:// pewhispanic.org/files/reports/40.pdf

———. 2009. *Hispanics of Cuban Origin in the United States, 2007.* Retrieved April 13, 2011, from http://pewhis panic.org/files/factsheets/50.pdf

———. 2011a. "Growth of Hispanic Population by County, 2000–2008." Retrieved April 2, 2011, from http:// pewhispanic.org/states/population/

———. 2011b. "Hispanic Share of Population by County." Retrieved April 4, 2011, from http://pewhispanic.org/ states/population/

Pew Research Center. 2007. *Muslim Americans: Middle Class and Mostly Mainstream.* Retrieved December 8, 2007, from http://pewresearch.org/assets/pdf/muslim-americans.pdf

Phillips, Ulrich B. 1918. *American Negro Slavery.* New York: Appleton.

Piersen, William D. 1996. *From Africa to America: African American History from the Colonial Era to the Early Republic, 1526–1790.* New York: Twayne.

Pilger, John. 2000. Australia Is the Only Developed Country Whose Government Has Been Condemned as Racist by the United Nations. *New Statesman* 129:17.

Pitt, Leonard. 1970. *The Decline of the Californios: A Social History of the Spanish-Speaking Californians, 1846–1890.* Berkeley: University of California Press.

Plessy v. Ferguson, 163 U.S. 537 (1896).

Pollard, Kelvin, & O'Hare, William. 1999. America's Racial and Ethnic Minorities. *Population Bulletin* 54(3): 29–39. Washington, DC: Population Reference Bureau.

Population Reference Bureau. 2011. *2011 World Population Data Sheet: The World at 7 Billion.* Retrieved August 1, 2011, from http://www.prb.org/pdf11/2011population-data-sheet_eng.pdf

Porter, Eduardo. 2005. Illegal Immigrants are Bolstering Social Security with Billions. *New York Times*, April 5, p. A1.

Portes, Alejandro. 1990. From South of the Border: Hispanic Minorities in the United States. In Virginia Yans-McLaughlin (Ed.), *Immigration Reconsidered* (pp. 160–184). New York: Oxford University Press.

Portes, Alejandro, & Bach, Robert L. 1985. *Latin Journey: Cuban and Mexican Immigrants in the United States.* Berkeley: University of California Press.

Portes, Alejandro, & Manning, Robert. 1986. The Immigrant Enclave: Theory and Empirical Examples. In Susan Olzak & Joanne Nagel (Eds.), *Competitive Ethnic Relations* (pp. 47–68). New York: Academic Press.

Portes, Alejandro, & Rumbaut, Rubén. 1996. *Immigrant America: A Portrait* (2nd ed.). Berkeley: University of California Press.

———. 2001. *Legacies: The Story of the Immigrant Second Generation.* New York: Russell Sage Foundation.

Portes, Alejandro, & Shafer, Steven. 2006. *Revisiting the Enclave Hypothesis: Miami Twenty-Five Years Later.* Princeton, New Jersey: Center for Migration and Development, Princeton University. Retrieved April 14, 2011, from http://ccddemocracy.org/Articulos/Revisiting-Enclave-Hypothesis.pdf

Portes, Alejandro, & Zhou, Min. 1992. Gaining the Upper Hand: Economic Mobility Among Immigrant and Domestic Minorities. *Ethnic and Racial Studies* 15:491–518.

Posadas, Barbara. 1999. *The Filipino Americans.* Westport, CT: Greenwood.

Potter, George. 1973. *To the Golden Door: The Story of the Irish in Ireland and America.* Westport, CT: Greenwood.

Poulan, Richard. 2003. Globalization and the Sex Trade: Trafficking and the Commodification of Women and Children. *Canadian Women Studies* 22:38–43.

Powers, Daniel, & Ellison, Christopher. 1995. Interracial Contact and Black Racial Attitudes: The Contact Hypothesis and Selectivity Bias. *Social Forces* 74:205–226.

Powlishta, K., Serbin, L., Doyle, A., & White, D. 1994. Gender, Ethnic, and Body-Type Biases: The Generality of Prejudice in Childhood. *Developmental Psychology* 30:526–537.

Price, S. L., & Woo, Andrea. 2002. The Indian Wars: The Campaign Against Indian Nicknames and Mascots Presumes That They Offend Native Americans—But Do They? We Took a Poll, and You Won't Believe the Results (Special report). *Sports Illustrated*, March 4, pp. 66–73.

Puzo, Mario. 1993. Choosing a Dream: Italians in Hell's Kitchen. In W. Brown & A. Ling (Eds.), *Visions of America* (pp. 56–57). New York: Persea.

Qian, Zhenchao, & Lichter, Daniel T. 2007. Social Boundaries and Marital Assimilation: Interpreting Trends in Racial and Ethnic Intermarriage. *American Sociological Review* 72:68–94.

Quillian, Lincoln. 2006. New Approaches to Understanding Racial Prejudice and Discrimination. *Annual Review of Sociology* 32:299–328.

Quillian, Lincoln, & Campbell, Mary. 2003. Beyond Black and White: The Present and Future of Multiracial Friendship Segregation. *American Sociological Review* 68:540–567.

Quinones, Sam. 2007. *Antonio's Gun and Delfino's Dream: True Tales of Mexican Migration.* Albuquerque: University of New Mexico Press.

Rader, Benjamin G. 1983. *American Sports: From the Age of Folk Games to the Age of Spectators.* Englewood Cliffs, NJ: Prentice Hall.

Raymer, Patricia. 1974. Wisconsin's Menominees: Indians on a Seesaw. *National Geographic*, August, pp. 228–251.

Read, Jen'nan Ghazal. 2004. Cultural Influences on Immigrant Women's Labor Force Participation: The Arab-American Case. *International Migration Review* 38:52–77.

Reich, Michael. 1986. The Political-Economic Effects of Racism. In Richard Edwards, Michael Reich, & Thomas Weisskopf (Eds.), *The Capitalist System: A Radical Analysis of American Society* (3rd ed., pp. 381–388). Englewood Cliffs, NJ: Prentice Hall.

Ricci v. DeStefano, 557 U.S. (2009).

Ridgeway, Cecilia. 2011. *Framed by Gender: How Gender Inequality Persists in the Modern World.* New York: Oxford University Press.

Rifkin, Jeremy. 1996. *The End of Work: The Decline of the Global Labor Force and the Dawn of the Post-Market Era.* New York: Putnam.

Robertson, Claire. 1996. Africa and the Americas? Slavery and Women, the Family, and the Gender Division of Labor. In David Gaspar & Darlene Hine (Eds.), *More Than Chattel: Black Women and Slavery in the Americas* (pp. 4–40). Bloomington: Indiana University Press.

Rockquemore, Kerry Ann, & Brunsma, David. 2008. *Beyond Black: Biracial Identity in America* (2nd ed.). Lanham, MD: Rowman & Littlefield.

Rodriguez, Arturo. 2011. "Testimony Before the Sub-Committee on Immigration Policy and Enforcement, U.S. House of Representatives, April 13, 2011." Retrieved May 31, 2011, from https://www.farmworkerjustice.org/files/immigration-labor/UFW_Statement_-_H2A_hearing_for_4_13_11_FINAL_w_edit.pdf

Rodriguez, C. 2010. Parent-Child Aggression: Association with Child Abuse Potential and Parenting Styles. *Violence and Victims* 25:728–741.

Rodriguez, Clara. 1989. *Puerto Ricans: Born in the USA*. Boston: Unwin-Hyman.

Rodriguez, Clara, & Cordero-Guzman, Hector. 1992. Placing Race in Context. *Ethnic and Racial Studies* 15:523–542.

Rodriguez, Luis. 1993. *Always Running: La Vida Loca*. New York: Touchstone Books.

Rosenblum, Karen E., & Travis, Toni-Michelle C. 2002. *The Meaning of Difference: American Constructions of Race, Sex and Social Class, and Sexual Orientation* (3rd ed.). New York: McGraw Hill.

Rosenfield, Michael. 2002. Measures of Assimilation in the Marriage Market: Mexican Americans 1970–1990. *Journal of Marriage and the Family* 64:152–163.

Rosich, Katherine. 2007. *Race, Ethnicity, and the Criminal Justice System*. Washington, DC: American Sociological Association. Retrieved June 10, 2010, from http://www.asanet.org/images/press/docs/pdf/ASARaceCrime.pdf

Rouse, Linda, & Hanson, Jeffery. 1991. American Indian Stereotyping, Resource Competition, and Status-Based Prejudice. *American Indian Culture and Research Journal* 15:1–17.

Royster, Deirdre. 2003. *Race and the Invisible Hand: How White Networks Exclude Black Men From Blue-Collar Jobs*. Berkeley: University of California Press.

Rumbaut, Rubén. 1991. Passage to America: Perspectives on the New Immigration. In Alan Wolfe (Ed.), *America at Century's End* (pp. 208–244). Berkeley: University of California Press.

Russell, James W. 1994. *After the Fifth Sun: Class and Race in North America*. Englewood Cliffs, NJ: Prentice Hall.

Saad, Lydia. 2010. "Americans Value Both Aspects of Immigration Reform." Gallup. Retrieved May 30, 2011, from http://www.gallup.com/poll/127649/Americans-Value-Aspects-Immigration-Reform.aspx

Saenz, Rogelio. 2005. *The Social and Economic Isolation of Urban African Americans*. Population Reference Bureau. Retrieved July 20, 2011, from http://www.prb.org/Articles/2005/TheSocialandEconomicIsolationofUrbanAfricanAmericans.aspx

Sakamoto, Arthur, Goyette, Kimberly, & Kim, ChangHwan. 2009. Socioeconomic Attainments of Asian Americans. *Annual Review of Sociology* 35:255–276.

Sanchirico, Andrew. 1991. The Importance of Small Business Ownership in Chinese American Educational Achievement. *Sociology of Education* 64:293–304.

Schafer, John, & Navarro, Joe. 2004. The Seven-Stage Hate Model: The Psychopathology of Hate Groups. *The FBI Law Enforcement Bulletin* 72:1–9.

Schlesinger, Arthur M., Jr. 1992. *The Disuniting of America: Reflections on a Multicultural Society*. New York: Norton.

Schmid, Carol. 2001. *The Politics of Language: Conflict, Identity, and Cultural Pluralism in Comparative Perspective*. New York: Oxford University Press.

Schoener, Allon. 1967. *Portal to America: The Lower East Side, 1870–1925*. New York: Holt, Rinehart, & Winston.

Sears, David. 1988. Symbolic Racism. In Phyllis Katz & Dalmas Taylor (Eds.), *Eliminating Racism: Profiles in Controversy* (pp. 53–84). New York: Plenum.

Sears, David, & Henry, P. J. 2003. The Origins of Modern Racism. *Journal of Personality and Social Psychology* 85:259–275.

See, Katherine O'Sullivan, & Wilson, William J. 1988. Race and Ethnicity. In Neil Smelser (Ed.), *Handbook of Sociology*, 223–242. Newbury Park, CA: Sage.

Selzer, Michael. 1972. *"Kike": Anti-Semitism in America*. New York: Meridian.

Sen, Rinku, & Mamdouh, Fekkak. 2008. *The Accidental American: Immigration and Citizenship in the Age of Globalization*. San Francisco: Berrt-Koehler.

Shannon, William V. 1964. *The American Irish*. New York: Macmillan.

Shapiro, Thomas. 2004. *The Hidden Cost of Being African American*. New York: Oxford University Press.

Sheet Metal Workers v. EEOC, 478 U.S. 421 (1986).

Shelton, B. A., & John, D. 1996. The Division of Household Labor. *Annual Review of Sociology* 22:299–322.

Sherif, Muzafer, Harvey, O. J., White, B. Jack, Hood, William, & Sherif, Carolyn. 1961. *Intergroup Conflict and Cooperation: The Robber's Cave Experiment*. Norman, OK: University Book Exchange.

Sheth, Manju. 1995. Asian Indian Americans. In Pyong Gap Min (Ed.), *Asian American: Contemporary Issues and Trends* (pp. 168–198). Thousand Oaks, CA: Sage.

Sigelman, Lee, & Welch, Susan. 1993. The Contact Hypothesis Revisited: Black-White Interaction and Positive Racial Attitudes. *Social Forces* 71:781–795.

Simon, Julian. 1989. *The Economic Consequences of Immigration*. Cambridge, MA: Blackwell.

Simpson, George, & Yinger, Milton. 1985. *Racial and Cultural Minorities: An Analysis of Prejudice and Discrimination*. New York: Plenum.

Sklare, Marshall. 1971. *America's Jews*. New York: Random House.

Small, Mario Luis, Harding, David J., & Lamont, Michèle. 2010. Reconsidering Culture and Poverty. *The Annals of the American Academy of Political and Social Science* 629: 6. Retrieved March 5, 2011, from http://ann.sagepub.com/content/629/1/6

Smedley, Audrey. 2007. *Race in North America: Origin and Evolution of a Worldview* (3rd ed.). Boulder, CO: Westview.

Smith, Christopher B. 1994. Back to the Future: The Intergroup Contact Hypothesis Revisited. *Sociological Inquiry* 64:438–455.

Smith, James, & Edmonston, Barry (Eds.). 1997. *The New Americans: Economic, Demographic, and Fiscal Effects of Immigration*. Washington, DC: National Academy Press.

Smith, Kevin, & Seelbach, Wayne. 1987. Education and Intergroup Attitudes: More on the Jackman and Muha Thesis. *Sociological Spectrum* 7:157–170.

Smith, Tom, & Dempsey, Glenn. 1983. The Polls: Ethnic Social Distance and Prejudice. *Public Opinion Quarterly* 47:584–600.

Snipp, C. Matthew. 1989. *American Indians: The First of This Land*. New York: Russell Sage Foundation.

———. 1992. Sociological Perspectives on American Indians. *Annual Review of Sociology* 18:351–371.

———. 1996. The First Americans: American Indians. In S. Pedraza & R. G. Rumbaut (Eds.), *Origins and Destinies: Immigration, Race, and Ethnicity in America* (pp. 390–403). Belmont, CA: Wadsworth.

Soares, Rachel, Combopiano, Jan, Regis, Allyson, Shur, Yelena, & Wong, Rosita. 2010. *2010 Catalyst Census: Fortune 500 Women Board Directors*. New York: Catalyst. Retrieved July 24, 2011, from http://catalyst.org/publication/460/2010-catalyst-census-fortune-500-women-board-directors

A Sorry Tale. 2000. *The Economist* 356:12.

Southern Poverty Law Center. 2010a. Ex-Skinhead Recalls Violent Past. *Intelligence Report*, Winter. Retrieved January 30, 2011, from http://www.splcenter.org/get-informed/intelligence-report/browse-all-issues/2010/winter/dark-angel

———. 2010b. *Hate Map*. Retrieved July 15, 2011, from http://www.splcenter.org/get-informed/hate-map

Spicer, Edward H. 1980. American Indians. In Stephan Thernstrom, Ann Orlov, & Oscar Handlin (Eds.), *Harvard Encyclopedia of American Ethnic Groups* (pp. 58–122). Cambridge, MA: Harvard University Press.

Spickard, Paul. 1996. *Japanese Americans: The Formation and Transformations of an Ethnic Group*. New York: Twayne.

Spilde, Kate. 2001. "The Economic Development Journey of Indian Nations." Retrieved July 5, 2002, from http://indiangaming.org/library/newsletters/index.html

Stampp, Kenneth. 1956. *The Peculiar Institution: Slavery in the Antebellum South*. New York: Random House.

Staples, Robert. 1988. The Black American Family. In Charles Mindel, Robert Habenstein, & Roosevelt Wright (Eds.), *Ethnic Families in America* (3rd ed., pp. 303–324). New York: Elsevier.

Statistics South Africa. 2008. *Income and Expenditures of Households, 2005–2006*. Retrieved February 2, 2011, from http://www.statssa.gov.za/publications/P0100/P01002005.pdf

Steinberg, Stephen. 1981. *The Ethnic Myth: Race, Ethnicity, and Class in America*. New York: Atheneum.

———. 2011. Poor Reason: Culture Still Doesn't Explain Poverty. *Boston Review*, January 13. Retrieved March 5, 2011, from http://www.bostonreview.net/BR36.1/steinberg.php

Stepick, Alex, Stepick, Carol Dutton, Eugene, Emmanuel, Teed, Deborah, & Labissiere, Yves. 2001. Shifting Identities and Intergenerational Conflict: Growing Up Haitian in Miami. In Rubén Rumbaut & Alejandro Portes (Eds.), *Ethnicities: Children of Immigrants in America* (pp. 229–266). Berkeley: University of California Press.

Stoddard, Ellwyn. 1973. *Mexican Americans*. New York: Random House.

Stoll, Michael. 2004. *African Americans and the Color Line*. New York: Russell Sage Foundation:

Stuckey, Sterling. 1987. *Slave Culture: Nationalist Theory and the Foundations of Black America*. New York: Harper & Row.

Sung, Betty Lee. 1990. Chinese American Intermarriage. *Journal of Comparative Family Studies* 21:337–352.

Swaine, Thomas, & Nishimoto, Richard S. 1946. *The Spoilage*. Berkeley: University of California Press. Retrieved February 11, 2005, from http://www.geocities.com/Athens/8420/kurihara.html

Swim, Janet, & Cohen, Laurie. 1997. Overt, Covert, and Subtle Sexism: A Comparison between the Attitudes toward Women and Modern Sexism Scales. *Psychology of Women Quarterly* 21:103–119.

Swim, Janet, Mallett, Robyn, & Stangor, Charles. 2004. Understanding Subtle Sexism: Detection and Use of Sexist Language. *Sex Roles* 51:117–128.

Takaki, Ronald. 1993. *A Different Mirror: A History of Multicultural America*. Boston: Little, Brown.

Taylor, Jonathan, & Kalt, Joseph. 2005. *American Indians on Reservations: A Databook of Socioeconomic Change Between the 1990 and 2000 Censuses*. Cambridge, MA: The Harvard Project on American Indian Economic Development. Retrieved March 13, 2008, from http://www.hks.harvard.edu/hpaied/pubs/documents/AmericanIndiansonReservationsADatabookofSocioeconomicChange.pdf

Telles, Edward. 2004. *Race in Another America: The Significance of Skin Color in Brazil*. Princeton, NJ: Princeton University Press.

Telles, Edward, & Ortiz, Vilma. 2008. *Generations of Exclusion: Mexican Americans, Assimilation, and Race*. New York: Russell Sage Foundation.

Thernstrom, Stephan, & Thernstrom, Abigail. 1997. *America in Black and White*. New York: Simon & Schuster.

Thornton, Russell. 2001. Trends Among American Indians in the United States. In N. Smelser, W. Wilson, & F. Mitchell (Eds.), *America Becoming: Racial Trends and Their Consequences* (Vol. 1, pp. 135–169). Washington, DC: National Academy Press.

Tileag, Cristian. 2005. Accounting for Extreme Prejudice and Legitimating Blame in Talk about the Romanies. *Discourse and Society* 16(5): 603–624.

Tilly, Charles. 1990. Transplanted Networks. In Virginia Yans-McLaughlin (Ed.), *Immigration Reconsidered: History, Sociology, and Politics* (pp. 79–95). New York: Oxford University Press.

Tougas, Francine, Rupert, Ann, & Joly, Stephane. 1995. Neosexism: Plus Ça Change, Plus C'est Pareil. *Personality & Social Psychology Bulletin* 21:842–850.

Trevanian. 2005. *The Crazy Ladies of Pearl Street*. New York: Crown Books.

Tsai, Shih-Shan Henry. 1986. *The Chinese Experience in America*. Bloomington: Indiana University Press.

Udry, Richard. 2000. Biological Limits of Gender Construction. *American Sociological Review* 65:443–457.

Unemployment Rate (Most Recent) by Country. n.d. Retrieved March 21, 2008, from http://www.nationmaster.com/red/graph/lab_une_rat-labor-unemployment-rate&ob=ws

United Nations. 2010a. *The Millennium Development Goals Report*. Retrieved February 11, 2011, from http://www.un.org/millenniumgoals/pdf/MDG%20Report%202010%20En%20r15%20-low%20res%2020100615%20-.pdf

———. 2010b. *World Population Policies 2009*. Retrieved April 3, 2011, from http://www.un.org/esa/population/publications/wpp2009/Publication_complete.pdf

———. 2011. "Social Indicators." Retrieved April 1, 2011, from http://unstats.un.org/unsd/demographic/products/socind/inc-eco.htm

United Steelworkers of America, AFL-CIO-CLC v. Weber, 443 U.S. 193 (1979).

U.S. Bureau of the Census. 1978. *Statistical Abstract of the United States, 1977*. Washington, DC: Government Printing Office.

———. 1990. "Summary File 3." Retrieved March 15, 2008, from http://factfinder.census.gov/servlet/DatasetMainPageServlet?_program=DEC&_submenuId=datasets_1&_lang=en

———. 1997. *Statistical Abstract of the United States, 1996*. Washington, DC: Government Printing Office.

———. 2000a. "American Indian and Alaska Native Summary File." Retrieved March 13, 2008, from http://factfinder.census.gov/servlet/DatasetMainPageServlet?_program=DEC&_submenuId=datasets_1&_lang=en

———. 2000b. Asian. *Mapping Census 2000: The Geography of U.S. Diversity* (pp. 62–71). Retrieved March 17, 2008, from http://www.census.gov/population/cen2000/atlas/censr01-108.pdf

———. 2000c. Black or African American. *Mapping Census 2000: The Geography of U.S. Diversity* (pp. 38–47). Retrieved March 13, 2008, from http://www.census.gov/population/cen2000/atlas/censr01-106.pdf

———. 2000d. "Summary File 4." Retrieved February 29, 2008, from http://factfinder.census.gov/servlet/DatasetMainPageServlet?_program=DEC&_submenuId=datasets_1&_lang=en

———. 2004. "Population by Region, Sex, and Hispanic Origin Type, With Percent Distribution by Hispanic Origin Type, 2004." Retrieved March 16, 2008, from http://www.census.gov/population/socdemo/hispanic/ASEC2004/2004CPS_tab19.2.pdf

———. 2005. *Statistical Abstract of the United States, 2005*. Washington, DC: Government Printing Office.

———. 2007a. *American Community Survey, 2006*. Retrieved March 11, 2008, from http://factfinder.census.gov/servlet/DatasetMainPageServlet?_program=ACS&_submenuId=datasets_2&_lang=en&_ts=

———. 2007b. *Statistical Abstract of the United States, 2007*. Washington, DC: Government Printing Office. Retrieved March 15, 2008, from http://www.census.gov/compendia/statab/past_years.html

———. 2008a. "1990 Summary Tape File 3." Retrieved March 7, 2008, from http://factfinder.census.gov/servlet/DatasetMainPageServlet?_program=DEC&_tabId=DEC2&_submenuId=datasets_1&_lang=en&_ts=222966429406

———. 2008b. *American Community Survey 3-Year Estimates, 2006–2008*. Retrieved February 18, 2011, from http://factfinder.census.gov/servlet/DatasetMainPageServlet?_program=ACS

———. 2008c. *National Population Projections*. Retrieved August 31, 2010, from http://www.census.gov/population/www/projections/downloadablefiles.html

————. 2009a. *American Community Survey 3-Year Estimates, 2007–2009.* Retrieved February 18, 2011, from http://factfinder.census.gov/servlet/DatasetMainPageServlet?_program=ACS

————. 2009b. "Regional Distribution of the Population by Sex, for Black Alone or in Combination and White Alone, Not Hispanic: 2009." *Current Population Survey, Annual Social and Economic Supplement, 2009.* Washington, DC: Government Printing Office. Retrieved February 4, 2011, from http://www.census.gov/population/www/ socdemo/race/ppl-bc09.html

————. 2010a. *Educational Attainment in the United States, 2009.* Retrieved March 2, 2011, from http://www.cen sus.gov/hhes/socdemo/education/data/cps/2009/tables.html

————. 2010b. Educational Attainment: People 25 Years and Over, by Total Money Earnings in 2009, Work Experience in 2009, Age, Race, Hispanic Origin, and Sex. *Current Population Survey, 2010 Annual Social and Economic Supplement.* Retrieved July 23, 2011, from http://www.census.gov/hhes/www/cpstables/032010/perinc/ new03_001.htm

————. 2010c. Occupation of Longest Job in 2009: People 15 Years Old and Over, by Total Money Earnings in 2009, Work Experience in 2009, Race, Hispanic Origin, and Sex. *Current Population Survey, 2010 Annual Social and Economic Supplement.* Retrieved July 23, 2011, from http://www.census.gov/hhes/www/cpstables/032010/perinc/ new06_001.htm

————. 2010d. *Statistical Abstract of the United States: 2010.* Washington, DC: Government Printing Office. Retrieved September 2, 2010, from http://www.census.gov/compendia/statab/2010/2010edition.html

————. 2010e. Table P-36: Full-Time, Year-Round Workers by Median Income and Sex. *2010 Census.* Washington, DC: Author. Retrieved from http://www.census.gov/hhes/www/income/data/historical/people/index.html

————. 2011a. *American Community Survey 5-Year Estimates, 2005–2009.* Retrieved July 24, 2011, from http:// www.census.gov/acs/www/

————. 2011b. Income: Households. *Current Population Survey, 2011.* Retrieved March 10, 2011, from http://www .census.gov/hhes/www/income/data/historical/household/index.html

————. 2011c. Poverty: Historical Poverty Tables. *Current Population Survey, 2011.* Retrieved March 11, 2011, from http://www.census.gov/hhes/www/poverty/data/historical/families.html

————. 2011d. *Statistical Abstract of the United States, 2011.* Washington, DC: Government Printing Office.

U.S. Bureau of the Census. 1990. *Statistical Abstract of the United States, 1990.* Washington, D.C. Government Printing Office.

U.S. Bureau of the Census. 2001. *Statistical Abstract of the United States, 2001.* Washington, D.C. Government Printing Office.

U.S. Bureau of Labor Statistics. 2011. "Unemployment by Race." *Current Population Survey.* Retrieved March 10, 2011, from http://data.bls.gov/cgi-bin/surveymost

U.S. Commission on Civil Rights. 1976. *Puerto Ricans in the Continental United States: An Uncertain Future.* Washington, DC: Government Printing Office.

————. 1992. *Civil Rights Issues Facing Asian Americans in the 1990s.* Washington, DC: Government Printing Office.

U.S. Department of Homeland Security. 2003. *Yearbook of Immigration Statistics, 2002.* Washington, DC: Government Printing Office.

————. 2009. *Yearbook of Immigration Statistics, 2009.* Washington, DC: Government Printing Office. Retrieved August 31, 2010, from http://www.dhs.gov/xlibrary/assets/statistics/yearbook/2009/ois_yb_2009.pdf

————. 2010. *Yearbook of Immigration Statistics, 2010.* Washington, DC: Government Printing Office.

U.S. Immigration and Naturalization Service. 1993. *Statistical Yearbook of the Immigration and Naturalization Service, 1992.* Washington, DC: Government Printing Office.

Utah Supreme Court Rules That Non-Indian Members of Native American Church Can Use Peyote in Church Ceremonies. 2004. *New York Times,* June 23, p. A20.

Valentine, Sean, & Mosley, Gordon. 2000. Acculturation and Sex-Role Attitudes Among Mexican Americans: A Longitudinal Analysis. *Hispanic Journal of Behavioral Sciences* 22:104–204.

Van Ausdale, Debra, & Feagin, Joe. 2001. *The First R: How Children Learn Race and Racism.* Lanham, MD: Rowman & Littlefield.

van den Berghe, Pierre L. 1967. *Race and Racism: A Comparative Perspective.* New York: Wiley.

————. 1981. *The Ethnic Phenomenon.* New York: Elsevier.

Van Hook, Jennifer. 2010. The Demographic Impacts of Repealing Birthright Citizenship. Retrieved October 1, 2010, from http://www.migrationpolicy.org/pubs/BirthrightInsight-2010.pdf

Vargas-Ramos, Carlos. 2005. Black, Trigueño, White . . . ? Shifting Racial Identification Among Puerto Ricans. *Du Bois Review* 2:267–285.

Vincent, Theodore G. 1976. *Black Power and the Garvey Movement.* San Francisco: Ramparts.

Vinje, David. 1996. Native American Economic Development on Selected Reservations: A Comparative Analysis. *American Journal of Economics and Sociology* 55:427–442.

Voting Rights Act, 42 U.S.C. § 1971 (1965).

Wagley, Charles, & Harris, Marvin. 1958. *Minorities in the New World: Six Case Studies*. New York: Columbia University Press.

Wall Street Journal. 2010. "A Changing Population." Retrieved September 9, 2010, from http://online.wsj.com/public/resources/documents/st_census0610b_20100610.html

Ward Connerly: Interview. 2003. *American Enterprise* 14 (April–May): 18–22.

Washington, Booker T. 1965. *Up From Slavery*. New York: Dell.

Waters, Mary. 1990. *Ethnic Options*. Berkeley: University of California Press.

Wax, Murray. 1971. *Indian Americans: Unity and Diversity*. Englewood Cliffs, NJ: Prentice Hall.

Weeks, Philip. 1988. *The American Indian Experience*. Arlington Heights, IL: Forum.

Weil, Frederick. 1985. The Variable Effects of Education on Liberal Attitudes: A Comparative-Historical Analysis of Anti-Semitism Using Public Opinion Survey Data. *American Sociological Review* 50:458–474.

Weitz, Rose, & Gordon, Leonard. 1993. Images of Black Women Among Anglo College Students. *Sex Roles* 28:19–34.

Weitzer, Ronald, & Tuch, Steven. 2005. Racially Biased Policing: Determinants of Citizen Perceptions. *Social Forces* 83:1009–1030.

Wellner, Alison. 2007. *U.S. Attitudes Toward Interracial Dating Are Liberalizing*. Population Reference Bureau. Retrieved December 5, 2007, from http://www.prb.org/Articles/2005/USAttitudesTowardInterracialDatingAreLiberalizing.aspx

Westervelt, Eric. 2010. "In Germany, Voices Against Immigration Grow Louder." National Public Radio. Retrieved April 3, 2011, from http://www.npr.org/templates/story/story.php?storyId=130649146

White, Deborah Gray. 1985. *Ar'n't I a Woman? Female Slaves in the Plantation South*. New York: Norton.

White House. 2005. *Economic Report of the President*. Washington, DC: Government Printing Office. Retrieved July 28, 2009, from http://www.gpoaccess.gov/eop/2005/2005_erp.pdf

White, Michael, & Glick, Jennifer. 2009. *Achieving Anew: How New Immigrants Do in American Schools, Jobs, and Neighborhoods*. New York: Russell Sage Foundation.

Whiting, Robert. 1990. *You Gotta Have Wa*. New York: Macmillan.

Wilkens, Roger. 1992. L.A.: Images in the Flames; Looking Back in Anger: 27 Years After Watts, Our Nation Remains Divided by Racism. *Washington Post*, May 3, p. C1.

Williams, Gregory. 1995. *Life on the Color Line*. New York: Dutton.

Wilson, William J. 1973. *Power, Racism, and Privilege: Race Relations in Theoretical and Sociohistorical Perspectives*. New York: Free Press.

———. 1987. *The Truly Disadvantaged: The Inner City, the Underclass, and Public Policy*. Chicago: University of Chicago Press.

———. 1996. *When Work Disappears*. New York: Knopf.

———. 2009. *More Than Just Race*. New York: W.W. Norton.

Wingfield, Adia, & Feagin, Joe. 2010. *Yes We Can? White Racial Framing and the 2008 Presidential Campaign*. New York: Routledge.

Wirth, Louis. 1945. The Problem of Minority Groups. In Ralph Linton (Ed.), *The Science of Man in the World* (pp. 347–372). New York: Columbia University Press.

Wittig, M., & Grant-Thompson, S. 1998. The Utility of Allport's Conditions of Intergroup Contact for Predicting Perceptions of Improved Racial Attitudes and Beliefs. *Journal of Social Issues* 54:795–812.

Wise, Tim. 2008. *White Like Me: Reflections on Race from a Privileged Son*. Brooklyn: Soft Skull Press.

Wolfenstein, Eugene V. 1993. *The Victims of Democracy: Malcolm X*. New York: Guilford.

Wong, Jade Snow. 1993. Fifth Chinese Daughter. In Dolores LaGuardia & Hans Guth (Eds.), *American Voices* (pp. 48–55). Palo Alto, CA: Mayfield.

Wong, Morrison. 1995. Chinese Americans. In Pyong Gap Min (Ed.), *Asian Americans: Contemporary Trends and Issues* (pp. 58–94). Thousand Oaks, CA: Sage.

Wood, Peter, & Chesser, Michele. 1994. Black Stereotyping in a University Population. *Sociological Focus* 27:17–34.

Woodward, C. Vann. 1974. *The Strange Career of Jim Crow* (3rd ed.). New York: Oxford University Press.

Worsnop, Richard. 1992. Native Americans. *CQ Researcher*, May 8, pp. 387–407.

Wright, Richard. 1940. *Native Son*. New York: Harper & Brothers.

———. 1945. *Black Boy: A Record of Childhood and Youth*. New York: Harper & Brothers.

———. 1988. *12 Million Black Voices*. New York: Thunder's Mouth.

Wyman, Mark. 1993. *Round Trip to America*. Ithaca, NY: Cornell University Press.

Xie, Yu, & Goyette, Kimberly. 2004. *A Demographic Portrait of Asian Americans*. New York: Russell Sage Foundation.

Yamato, Alexander. 1994. Racial Antagonism and the Formation of Segmented Labor Markets: Japanese Americans and Their Exclusion From the Work Force. *Humboldt Journal of Social Relations* 20:31–63.

Yancey, George. 1999. An Examination of the Effects of Residential and Church Integration on Racial Attitudes of Whites. *Sociological Perspectives* 42:279–294.

———. 2007. *Interracial Contact and Social Change.* Boulder, CO: Lynne Rienner.

Yinger, J. Milton. 1985. Ethnicity. *Annual Review of Sociology* 11:151–180.

Zhou, Min. 1992. *Chinatown.* Philadelphia: Temple University Press.

Zhou, Min, & Logan, John R. 1989. Returns on Human Capital in Ethnic Enclaves: New York City's Chinatown. *American Sociological Review* 54:809–820.

Chapter Opening Photo Credits

Chapter 1: a. © Peter Guttman/CORBIS; b. © Karen Kasmauski/Corbis; c. Taken by Rachel Walborn

Chapter 2: a. © Richard T. Nowitz/CORBIS; b. © Destinations/Corbis; c. © Jose Luis Pelaez, Inc./CORBIS

Chapter 3: a. © Daniel Lainé/CORBIS; b. Getty/Stephen Marks; c. Thinkstock/Creatas Images

Chapter 4: a. Getty/Colin Bootman; b. © Zave Smith/Corbis; c. Getty/After George Morland

Chapter 5: a. © Tim Wright/CORBIS; b. © Jon Hrusa/epa/Corbis; c. Getty/Doris De Witt

Chapter 6: a. © Dennis Van Tine/Retna Ltd./Corbis; b. © Daniel Lainé/CORBIS; c. © Peter Turnley/CORBIS

Chapter 7: a. © Raymond Gehman/CORBIS; b. Getty/Antonio RIBEIRO; c. © NewSport/Corbis

Chapter 8: a. © Najlah Feanny/Corbis; b. © Christopher Morris/Corbis; c. © Jerry McCrea/Star Ledger/Corbis

Chapter 9: a. © Walter Hodges/CORBIS; b. © Ocean/Corbis; c. Getty/Ronald Martinez

Chapter 10: a. © O'Rourke, Skip/ZUMA Press/Corbis; b. © Bettmann/CORBIS; c. © Christopher Morris/Corbis

Chapter 11: a. Getty/John Giustina; b. Getty/Jonathan Kim; c. Getty/Thomas Barwick

INDEX

Aberson, C., 119
Abolitionism, 157, 192
Aboud, F. E., 109
Abraham, N., 426
Abrahamson, H., 44, 51
Abraham, S. Y., 426
Acculturation
    African Americans, 257–258, 398–399, 462–463
    American Indians, 280–283, 288 (exhibit),
        294–296, 463
    Asian Americans, 380–381, 463
    black southern migrants, 191
    Chinese Americans, 380–381, 463
    coercive acculturation, 169, 280–283, 288 (exhibit)
    generational patterns, 65–67, 66 (exhibit)
    Gordon's stages of assimilation theory, 47 (exhibit),
        47–48, 52
    Hispanic Americans, 342–344, 343 (exhibit),
        344 (exhibit), 463
    historical perspective, 462–466
    Japanese Americans, 380–381, 463
    Mexican Americans, 169, 331–332, 442
    slavery, 160
Acosta-Belen, E., 357
Acuña, R., 168, 329, 330, 357
Adarand Constructors Inc. v. Pena (1995), 209
Adorno, T. W., 98
Affective prejudice, 28, 97–99, 103
Affirmative action, 209–211
African Americans
    acculturation, 257–258, 398–399, 462–463
    Anglo-conformity, 381
    assimilation, 257–266, 462–463
    Black Power movement, 237–239, 258
    business ownership, 257
    civil rights movement, 107, 233–240
    codes of conduct, 185
    competition with white ethnics, 187–188
    contact situations, 304
    criminal justice system, 244–247, 246 (exhibit)
    cultural influences, 172–174
    de facto segregation, 187, 237
    de jure segregation, 182–186, 190–191, 194–195,
        207, 232–242, 304
    descendants, 154
    discrimination, 256–257
    disenfranchisement, 185, 192
    dissimilarity index, 259 (exhibit)

education, 166 (exhibit)
educational attainment, 262 (exhibit), 395
elected political positions, 262–263
equal opportunities, 17 (exhibit)
European colonization, 171–172
fair employment rights, 233
family institution, 252–254, 253 (exhibit)
geographical distribution, 77, 77 (exhibit),
    258 (exhibit)
growth projections, 13
hate crimes, 127–128, 129 (exhibit), 131–133
homeownership, 208–209, 252
income data, 166 (exhibit), 263–265, 265 (exhibit),
    339 (exhibit)
industrialization impacts, 181–182, 184–185,
    196–197
institutional discrimination, 30, 208–211
intergroup cooperation, 120
interracial relationships, 265–266
job market, 263–264
labor supply, 151, 154–155, 155 (exhibit),
    170, 184, 304
median earnings, 254 (exhibit)
middle-class status, 247–250
minority group comparison studies,
    304, 394–395
minority status creation, 157–158, 158 (exhibit),
    160–161, 170
modern black-white relations, 231–270
modern institutional discrimination, 250–252,
    256–257
modern racism, 114, 115 (exhibit), 122–124,
    123 (exhibit), 124 (exhibit), 256–257, 267
net worth/financial assets, 248, 248 (exhibit)
physical beauty, 381
pluralism, 257–266, 462–463
political power, 262–263
population redistribution, 186 (exhibit), 186–188,
    187 (exhibit)
poverty, 166 (exhibit), 249–250, 253–254,
    265, 266 (exhibit)
prejudice, 256–257
protest movement, 189–191
racial identities, 255–256
racial progress, 267
racial status quo, 244
Reconstruction, 182
reparations debate, 211–215

residential patterns, 258 (exhibit),
	258–260, 259 (exhibit)
rigid competitive group systems, 181, 182
school integration, 260 (exhibit), 260–262,
	261 (exhibit)
separatism, 53
social change efforts, 211
social class inequality, 247–250, 260, 261
social distance, 110 (exhibit), 111
sports, 72
stereotypes, 101–104, 123 (exhibit),
	124 (exhibit), 304
structural assimilation, 258–266
unemployment rates, 251–252, 252 (exhibit)
urban poverty, 249–250, 253–254, 265,
	266 (exhibit)
urban underclass, 250, 257
urban unrest, 237, 244
voting rights, 232, 236
	see also Slavery
African diaspora, 150 (exhibit)
African National Congress (ANC), 195
Agbayani-Siewert, P., 420
Agrarian era, 171, 179, 181 (exhibit), 184–185,
	202 (exhibit)
Agrarian radicalism, 185
Agriculturalists, 372–373
Aizenman, N. C., 348
Alabama, 185
Alaska Natives, 276, 277 (exhibit),
	298 (exhibit), 302 (exhibit)
	see also American Indians
Alba, R., 48, 66 (exhibit), 71, 75,
	78, 82, 337, 444, 452
Alcatraz Island, 286
Aleiss, A., 293
Alianza de Mercedes (Alliance of Land Grants), 330
Alien Land Act (1913), 372–373
Allen, E., 211, 214–215
Allen, Richard, 215
Allport, G., 41, 138
All-weather bigot, 96, 96 (exhibit)
All-weather liberal, 96, 96 (exhibit)
Almquist, E. M., 192
Alvarez, R., 167, 168
Amae, 397
American Dream, 427–428
American GI Forum, 329
American Indian Higher Education
	Consortium, 299
American Indian Movement (AIM), 286–287
American Indians
	acculturation, 294–296
	assimilation, 43, 287, 294–296, 463
	Blauner hypothesis, 164, 275–276, 280
	broken treaties, 291
	coercive acculturation, 280–283, 288 (exhibit)
	colonization, 171–172
	contact situations, 162–164, 275, 304

contemporary American Indian–White relations,
	288–303
cultural diversity, 278–279
discrimination, 283–285, 293–294
economic development, 289–291, 305
educational attainment, 166 (exhibit), 290 (exhibit),
	293 (exhibit), 299 (exhibit), 299–300, 395
European colonization, 171–172
federal policies, 279–285, 287–288, 288 (exhibit)
fishing rights, 286
forced migration, 53
future directions, 304–305
gaming industry, 291–293, 292 (exhibit),
	293 (exhibit)
gender relations, 164
geographical distribution, 77, 77 (exhibit)
growth projections, 12 (exhibit), 13
income data, 166 (exhibit), 293 (exhibit), 300–302,
	301 (exhibit), 302 (exhibit)
Indian Reorganization Act (1934), 282,
	288 (exhibit)
intergroup cooperation, 120
interracial relationships, 302–303, 303 (exhibit)
job market, 300
labor supply, 151, 154, 155 (exhibit), 170, 304
land disputes, 163, 170
land ownership, 280
median household income, 290 (exhibit),
	301 (exhibit), 302 (exhibit)
minority group categories, 13, 14
minority group comparison studies, 304, 394–395
minority status creation, 162–164, 170
narrative portraits, 297
natural resources control, 288–289
Noel hypothesis, 163–164
paternalism, 279–280
pluralism, 43, 287, 463
political power, 300
population size, 276, 277 (exhibit)
poverty, 166 (exhibit), 289–291, 290 (exhibit),
	293 (exhibit), 302, 302 (exhibit), 303 (exhibit)
prejudice, 283–285, 293–294
protest movement, 285–288
religion, 295
relocation, 283–285, 288 (exhibit)
reservation life, 279–285, 288 (exhibit)
residential patterns, 298 (exhibit), 298–299
school integration, 299–300, 300 (exhibit)
self-determination, 285, 288 (exhibit), 289
separatism, 53
social distance, 110 (exhibit), 111, 294
sports team mascots, 275–276, 294, 307–309
stereotypes, 293–294, 304, 307–309
termination policy, 283, 285, 288 (exhibit)
traditional cultures, 293–295, 295 (exhibit)
tribal groups, 277 (exhibit)
tribal languages, 294–295, 295 (exhibit)
unemployment rates, 284, 293 (exhibit), 300
urbanization, 283–285, 284 (exhibit), 288 (exhibit)

Americanization
  American Indians, 280–283, 285,
      288 (exhibit), 291, 294, 395
  basic concepts, 45
  Chinese Americans, 368, 371–372
  generational patterns, 65–67, 440
  human capital theory, 49
  immigrant commitment, 76
  Japanese Americans, 373–374
  Mexican Americans, 329, 353–354
American Sociological Association, 24
Amish community, 51–52
Amott, T., 60, 70, 71, 161, 164, 192, 240,
      279, 311, 324, 328, 331, 365, 369, 376, 377
Anchor babies, 37–39
Andersen, M. L., 29, 161, 239
Anderson, E. R., 144, 146
Anderson, J., 214
Anger, 141–142
Anglo-conformity, 45, 381, 465
Anglo-Texans, 167–168
Antiblack racism, 158, 186
  see also De jure segregation
Anti-Catholicism, 63
Anti-Defamation League, 64, 449–450
Anti-immigration campaigns
  American public opinion, 433–434
  Asian Americans, 361, 379
  Chinese Americans, 366–369, 379, 460
  economic conditions, 107
  Europe, 341
  European immigrants, 62–65, 121, 121 (exhibit)
  France, 85–86
  Hispanic Americans, 342, 433–434, 439–440
  Japanese Americans, 372–374
  Middle Eastern Americans, 425
  threat levels, 434–435
Anti-Indian racism, 293–294
Antin, Mary, 61
Anti-Semitism, 63–64
Apartheid, 29, 193–195
Arab American Anti-Discrimination Committee, 425
Arab Americans
  characteristics, 422–424, 423 (exhibit)
  geographic locations, 423 (exhibit)
  hate crimes, 131
  immigration, 422–424
  Michigan communities, 426
  minority group categories, 13
  regional concentrations, 424, 424 (exhibit)
  social distance, 110 (exhibit)
  stereotypes, 425
Arizona, 168
Arizona State Bill 1070, 342, 433–434, 439
Arons, J., 37, 39
Aronson, E., 120
Aryan Nations, 127
Ascribed status, 18
Ashmore, R., 109

Asian Americans
  acculturation, 380–382, 381 (exhibit), 463
  Anglo-conformity, 381
  assimilation, 380–392, 463
  characteristics, 361–363
  colonized minority groups, 394–395
  contact situations, 366–369, 460
  contemporary immigrants, 377–379,
      417–420, 418 (exhibit)
  cultural success, 397–398
  cultural traits, 363–365
  discrimination, 379–380
  dissimilarity index, 383–384
  educational attainment, 385–387,
      400, 443 (exhibit)
  foreign-born population, 364 (exhibit)
  gender inequality, 365, 381
  globalization effects, 201
  growth projections, 12 (exhibit), 13
  hate crimes, 131, 380
  human capital theory, 399
  immigration, 411 (exhibit), 417–420
  incarcerated males, 443 (exhibit)
  income data, 387–389, 389 (exhibit)
  intergroup cooperation, 120
  interracial relationships, 390–392, 392 (exhibit)
  invisible minorities, 396
  job market, 387
  largest population groups, 363 (exhibit)
  median household income, 387–388,
      388 (exhibit), 399
  minority group categories, 13, 14
  minority group comparison studies, 392–395
  model minority thesis, 377, 380, 385, 399–400
  nations of origin, 364 (exhibit)
  per capita income, 387–388, 389 (exhibit)
  physical beauty, 381–382
  pluralism, 380–392, 463
  political power, 387
  population growth, 362 (exhibit), 362–363,
      367 (exhibit), 383 (exhibit)
  poverty, 390, 390 (exhibit), 391 (exhibit)
  prejudice, 379–380
  residential patterns, 382 (exhibit), 382–383,
      384 (exhibit)
  school integration, 384–385, 385 (exhibit)
  second generations, 443 (exhibit)
  socioeconomic status, 390
  stereotypes, 361, 379–382
  urbanization, 382–383, 383 (exhibit)
  White ethnics, 393–394
Asian Indians
  acculturation, 380, 463
  characteristics, 418 (exhibit)
  contact situations, 379
  educational attainment, 386 (exhibit)
  foreign-born population, 364 (exhibit), 391 (exhibit)
  immigration, 378 (exhibit), 379, 411 (exhibit),
      417–420, 418 (exhibit)

median household income, 388 (exhibit)
per capita income, 389 (exhibit)
population growth, 362 (exhibit), 363 (exhibit)
poverty, 390, 390 (exhibit), 391 (exhibit)
social distance, 110 (exhibit), 111
urbanization, 383 (exhibit)
"Asia: Original Sin" (*The Economist*), 306
"A Sorry Tale" (*The Economist*), 306
Assignments
  educational testing gaps, 224–226
  endangered languages, 228–230
  graffiti, 5–7
  hometown diversity, 2–3
  literacy volunteers, 226–228
  local diners, 144–146
  race and gender, 143–144
  refugee communities, 407–408
  school cafeterias, 222–224
  social change, 405–406
  televised family portrayals, 4–5
Assimilation
  African Americans, 257–266, 462–463
  American Indians, 43, 287, 294–296, 463
  Asian Americans, 380–392, 463
  assimilation patterns, 58, 65–72, 66 (exhibit), 84
  characteristics, 44–45
  Chinese Americans, 380–381, 463
  civil rights movement, 236, 239
  contemporary immigrants, 82–83, 410 (exhibit),
    410–430, 411 (exhibit), 440–446, 442 (exhibit)
  definition, 43
  English only debate, 88–90
  ethnic preference hierarchy, 73–76
  ethnic succession, 67–72
  French linguistic diversity, 87
  gender, 75–76
  generational patterns, 65–67, 66 (exhibit)
  Gordon's stages of assimilation theory,
    46–48, 47 (exhibit)
  Haitian immigrants, 416
  Hawaiians, 165–166
  Hispanic Americans, 342–352, 463
  historical perspective, 462–466
  human capital theory, 48–49
  interracial relationships, 265–266
  Jamaican immigrants, 417
  Japanese Americans, 380–381, 463
  Mexican Americans, 331–332, 442
  narrative portraits, 84
  Northern and Western Protestant European
    immigrants, 58
  Park's race relation cycle theory, 46
  Red Power movement, 287
  religion, 73–74
  segmented assimilation, 83, 440–446, 442 (exhibit)
  slavery, 160
  social class, 74–75
  traditional perspective, 44, 46–49, 83, 444–446
  variations, 73–76

Associated Press, 380, 409
Austin, A., 284
Australian Aborigines, 306
Australian Bureau of Statistics, 306
Australian Human Rights and Equal
    Opportunity Commission, 306
Austria, 121 (exhibit)
Authoritarian personality theory, 98–99
Authority support, 118–119
Avery, R., 248
Aztec Empire, 171

Baca, L., 308–309
Baca Zinn, M., 26, 41, 328
Bach, R. L., 337, 338, 357
Ball, R., 396
Bames, R., 210
Banaji, M. R., 139
Bangladesh, 411 (exhibit)
Bankston, C., 92
Barreto, 125
Barringer, H., 372
Bean, F., 92, 436, 437, 444, 445
Beaton, A., 125
Becerra, R., 170
Beck, E. M., 98
Belgium, 121 (exhibit)
Bell, Daniel, 20
Bell, Derrick, 18
Benedict, R., 365
Benjamin, L., 248
Bergsieker, H., 100, 101
Berkowitz, L., 98
Berry, Halle, 255
Bertrand, M., 209
Bibb, Henry, 159
Bilingual education, 88–90
Bipolar structure, 372, 378, 380,
    385, 389, 390, 420
Biracialism, 255
Bird, E., 293
Birthright citizenship, 37–39, 86
Biskupic, J., 376
Black Codes, 184
Black-Gutman, D., 109
Black Like Me (Griffin), 31
Black Muslims, 53, 238
Black Nationalism, 238, 239, 267
Black-owned businesses, 257
Black Power movement, 237–239, 258, 267
Black protest movement, 189–191
Black southern migrants, 187–192
Blassingame, J. W., 157, 160, 161, 174
Blauner hypothesis, 153–154, 158, 164, 169, 202,
    275–276, 280, 379, 459
Blauner, R., 153–154, 154, 160, 275, 393
Blau, P. M., 49
Blessing, P., 62, 75
Blue-collar occupations, 197–199, 204, 249

Bluestone, B., 217
Blumer, H., 106–107
Boarding schools, 280, 281
Bobo, L., 101, 103, 107, 122, 123
Bodnar, J., 62, 68, 74
Bogardus, E., 109
Bonacich, E., 53, 106, 395, 419
Bonilla, F., 349
Bonilla-Silva, E., 122
Booth, A., 27
Border identities, 255
Border Patrol, 33
Bordewich, F., 288, 290, 292, 293, 311
Boswell, T., 367
Bounded solidarity, 398
Bourgeoisie, 19
Bouvier, L. F., 324
Bowman, C. F., 52
Boxing, 72
Boycotts, 234–235, 331
Brace, M., 306
Bracero program, 323–324
Brashears, M., 266
Brazil, 243
Brewer, M., 119
Brittingham, A., 57, 77 (exhibit), 424 (exhibit)
Brody, D., 68
Broken treaties, 291
Bronson, Charles, 320
Bronson, P., 109
Brooke, Edward, 263
Brotherhood of Sleeping Car Porters, 233
Brown, D., 176, 278, 311
Brown, K. T., 120
Brown, Linda, 233
Brown, R., 109
Brown, T. N., 120
Brown v. Board of Education of Topeka (1954), 233–234, 260
Brunsma, D., 255, 256
Bugleski, R., 98
Burakumin, 396
Bureaucracy, 197
Bureau of Indian Affairs (BIA), 279–280, 286–287
Burgess, E. W., 46
Buriel, R., 278, 319
Burns, P., 107
Burris, Roland, 263
Business ownership, 257
Butch's story, 15
Byrd, James, 127, 131

California, 167–168
California Proposition 187, 439–440
Californios, 167–168
Calvin, L., 5
Camarillo, A., 349
Camarota, S., 414, 448–449
Cambodians

acculturation, 381 (exhibit)
educational attainment, 386 (exhibit), 443 (exhibit)
foreign-born population, 364 (exhibit)
immigration, 378
incarcerated males, 443 (exhibit)
median household income, 388 (exhibit)
per capita income, 389 (exhibit)
population growth, 362 (exhibit), 363 (exhibit)
poverty, 390 (exhibit)
second generations, 443 (exhibit)
urbanization, 383 (exhibit)
Cameron, 125
Campbell, Ben Nighthorse, 300
Campbell, M., 352
Canada
French colonization, 171–172
immigration, 411 (exhibit)
social distance, 110 (exhibit)
Canadian First Nations, 289
Capital-intensive work, 55, 179, 181 (exhibit)
Capitalism, 106
Carey, Mariah, 255
Caribbean region, 415, 415 (exhibit), 443 (exhibit)
Carroll, J., 45
Carter, Jimmy, 263
Carter, N. M., 206
Casinos, 291–293, 292 (exhibit), 293 (exhibit)
Caste systems, 155, 201, 202 (exhibit), 396
Castro, Fidel, 336
Catholicism, 63, 69, 71, 319, 365
Center for American Progress, 37
Center for Immigration Studies, 448
Central America, 242–243
Central Intelligence Agency, 416, 419
Central Statistics Office (Ireland), 85, 86
Chadwick, B., 186 (exhibit)
Chain immigration, 62
Chan, S., 57, 366, 367, 368
Chaplin, G., 23
Charles-Toussaint, G., 99
Chattel, 155
Chávez, César, 330–331
Chenkin, A., 60
Chesser, M., 101
Chicanismo, 329–331
Chicano protest movement, 329–331
Children, 108–109
Children's books assignment, 143–144
Chinatowns, 52, 368, 369
Chinese Americans
acculturation, 380–382, 381 (exhibit), 463
Anglo-conformity, 381
assimilation, 380–381, 463
citizenship rights, 154
contact situations, 366–369, 377, 460
cultural success, 398–399
discrimination, 366–369, 371–372, 379–380
educational attainment, 385–387, 386 (exhibit), 395, 443 (exhibit)

enclave groups, 52, 368–369, 395
expulsion policies, 53
foreign-born population, 364 (exhibit), 391 (exhibit)
gender, 369, 461
hate crimes, 131
immigration, 366–367, 378 (exhibit), 411 (exhibit)
incarcerated males, 443 (exhibit)
median household income, 388 (exhibit)
minority group comparison studies, 377, 394–395
narrative portraits, 370–371
Noel hypothesis, 366–367
per capita income, 389 (exhibit)
pluralism, 380–381, 463
population growth, 362 (exhibit), 363 (exhibit),
    367 (exhibit), 367–368
poverty, 390 (exhibit), 391 (exhibit)
prejudice, 371–372, 379–380
second generations, 443 (exhibit)
social distance, 110 (exhibit)
socioeconomic status, 369, 371–372, 390
stereotypes, 368, 379
urbanization, 368, 383 (exhibit)
Chinese Consolidated Benevolent Association
    (CCBA), 368
Chinese Exclusion Act (1882), 53, 366–367,
    372, 379, 419, 460
Chin, Vincent, 131, 380
Chirot, D., 20
Choctaw Nation, 290 (exhibit), 290–291, 295
    (exhibit), 299 (exhibit), 301 (exhibit), 303 (exhibit)
Cho, S., 419
Chou, R., 365, 402
Chrisman, R., 211, 214–215
Christ, O., 434
Church bombings, 235
Churchill, W., 282
Civil Rights Act (1964), 235–236
Civil rights movement, 107, 233–240
Clark doll study, 381
Clark, Kenneth and Mamie, 381
Clark, M. L., 101
Clark, T., 98
Clinton, Bill, 39, 263
Closed networks, 251
Closed stratification systems, 155
Coercive acculturation, 169, 280–283, 288 (exhibit)
Cofer, J. O., 335
Coffman, T, 101
Cognitive prejudice, 28, 99–103,
    100 (exhibit), 102 (exhibit)
Cohen, A., 237
Cohen, L., 124, 126
Cohen, S. M., 60
Cohn, D., 315, 324, 326 (exhibit),
    343 (exhibit), 438 (exhibit)
Colbert, S., 9
Collier, John, 282
Collins, M. A., 119
Colombia

characteristics, 412–413, 413 (exhibit)
demographics, 316 (exhibit)
educational attainment, 348 (exhibit), 443 (exhibit)
foreign-born population, 317 (exhibit)
geographic location, 413 (exhibit)
immigration, 411 (exhibit), 412–413, 414
incarcerated males, 443 (exhibit)
median household income,
    350 (exhibit), 351 (exhibit)
school integration, 347
second generations, 443 (exhibit)
urbanization, 346 (exhibit)
Colonization, 148, 153, 158, 171–172
Colorblindness, 257, 268–270
Combopiano, J., 206
Common goal hypothesis, 118
Community Service Organization, 329
Comparative focus
    contact hypothesis, 121
    contact situations, 171–172, 306
    cultural and racial visibility, 396
    French linguistic diversity, 87
    Hawaiians, 165–166, 166 (exhibit)
    international immigration, 340–341
    Irish emigration–immigration patterns,
        85–86, 86 (exhibit)
    North American colonization, 171–172
    Roma, 432
    two-race model, 242–243
Competition
    contact situations, 152 (exhibit), 152–153,
        154, 155 (exhibit), 158 (exhibit)
    group competition, 104–107, 118–119, 434
    intergroup cooperation, 118, 119–120,
        199, 236, 434
    Noel hypothesis, 152 (exhibit), 152–153,
        154, 155 (exhibit), 158
Confucianism, 363–364, 365
Connerly, Ward, 268
Conot, R., 237
Contact hypothesis, 117–121, 151–154,
    152 (exhibit), 158 (exhibit), 459–460
Contemporary immigrants
    African groups, 429 (exhibit)
    American public opinion, 433 (exhibit), 433–435,
        434 (exhibit)
    Asian groups, 417–420, 418 (exhibit)
    characteristics, 410 (exhibit),
        410–411, 411 (exhibit)
    economic impact, 436–437
    educational attainment, 443 (exhibit)
    globalization effects, 446–447
    harmful effects, 448–449
    Hispanic groups, 412–414, 413 (exhibit)
    immigrant opinions, 435
    incarcerated males, 443 (exhibit)
    income data, 444 (exhibit), 445 (exhibit)
    modes of incorporation, 430–431, 442
    myths and facts, 449–450

non-Hispanic Caribbean immigrants, 415 (exhibit), 415–417
  ongoing issues, 447
  second generations, 441–446, 442 (exhibit), 443 (exhibit), 444 (exhibit), 445 (exhibit)
  segmented assimilation, 440–446, 442 (exhibit)
  Sub-Saharan African groups, 428–430
  traditional perspective, 82–83, 444–446
  undocumented immigrants, 437–440, 438 (exhibit)
Continued subjugation, 53
Contract laborers, 148–150, 151, 154–155, 155 (exhibit)
Conzen, K. N., 57, 58
Cordero-Guzman, H., 334
Core groups, 16
Cornell, S., 280, 286, 288 (exhibit), 289, 291, 295, 296
Cortes, C., 167, 168, 318, 323, 328, 329
Cose, E., 248
Cottman, M., 247
Coughlin, Charles, 64
Council of Energy Resource Tribes, 289
Cowan, G., 120
Cox, O., 106
Crack cocaine, 245–246, 246 (exhibit)
Crawford, James, 88, 89–90
Criminal activities, 71
Criminal justice system, 244–247, 246 (exhibit)
Crow Dog, Mary, 281
Crowson, H., 99
Crusade for Justice, 330
Cuban Americans
  assimilation, 463
  contact situations, 336
  demographics, 315–316, 316 (exhibit)
  educational attainment, 348 (exhibit)
  enclave groups, 52, 337–339
  foreign-born population, 317 (exhibit)
  geographical distribution, 336–337
  globalization effects, 201
  immigration, 336, 411 (exhibit)
  incarcerated males, 443 (exhibit)
  income data, 339 (exhibit)
  job sector, 337–339, 339 (exhibit)
  median household income, 350 (exhibit)
  minority group comparison studies, 339
  points of origin, 317 (exhibit)
  poverty, 351 (exhibit)
  regional concentrations, 336–337
  second generations, 443 (exhibit)
  socioeconomic characteristics, 337
  stereotypes, 339
  urbanization, 346 (exhibit)
Cuddy, A., 100
Cultural assimilation, 47
Cultural pluralism, 51–52
Culture, 46
Culture of poverty theory, 253–254
Curtin, P., 151

D'Alessio, S., 131
Damico, S., 119
Dances with Wolves (1990), 293
D'Angelo, R., 235
Daniels, B. T., 222–223
Daniels, R., 53, 369, 371, 372, 373, 374, 377, 391, 402, 419, 420
Davis, Kiri, 381
Davis, L. R., 308–309
Dawes Allotment Act (1887), 280, 282, 288 (exhibit)
Debo, A., 282
Declining prejudice
  attitude changes, 114–115, 115 (exhibit)
  contact hypothesis, 117–121
  education levels, 115–117, 116 (exhibit)
De facto segregation, 187, 237
Degree of similarity, 73
Deindustrialization, 180, 196, 198–199, 204
De jure segregation, 182–186, 190–191, 194–195, 207, 232–242
de Klerk, F. W., 195
de la Cruz, C. P., 57, 77 (exhibit), 424 (exhibit)
Delany, Martin, 215
DelBoca, F., 109
Deloria, V., 283, 311
Democratic Party, 232
Demoulin, S., 100
Dempsey, G., 110 (exhibit), 294
Denial, 142
Denny, Reginald, 244
Denton, N., 208, 237, 249, 250, 254, 272
Descendants, 76–82, 77 (exhibit), 153–154
Detroit, Michigan, 426
Deutsch, M., 119
Devine, P., 101
Differential in power, 152 (exhibit), 152–153, 154, 155 (exhibit), 158 (exhibit), 169, 202 (exhibit), 460
Dinnerstein, L., 60
Disappearing languages, 228–230
Discrimination
  African Americans, 256–257
  American Indians, 283–285, 293–294
  anti-immigration campaigns, 62–65
  Asian Americans, 379–380
  basic concepts, 29, 96
  Chinese Americans, 366–369, 371–372, 379–380, 460
  criminal justice system, 244–247, 246 (exhibit)
  de facto segregation, 187, 237
  defense-related industries, 233
  gender discrimination, 203–206
  Haitian immigrants, 416
  Hawaiian society, 165–166
  Hispanic Americans, 341–342
  institutional discrimination, 30, 157–158, 158 (exhibit)
  Jamaican immigrants, 417
  Japanese Americans, 372–374, 379–380

Mexican Americans, 168–169, 328, 331–332,
        341–342
    modern institutional discrimination, 180, 207–211,
        250–252, 256–257
    modern racism, 256–257
    past-in-present institutional discrimination,
        207–209, 249
    prejudice–discrimination relationship,
        96, 96 (exhibit)
    Roma, 432
    sexism, 124–126, 126 (exhibit)
    situational influences, 113
    social class inequality, 247–250, 260, 261
Disenfranchisement, 185, 192
Disparate impact, 210
Diversity
    American stories, 10–11
    connectivity, 9–10
    hometown diversity assignment, 2–3
    minority group categories, 13–14
    minority group growth, 11–13, 12 (exhibit)
    televised family portrayal assignment, 4–5
Dixon, J., 119
Dollard, J., 98
Doll study, 381
Dominant-minority group relations
    affirmative action, 209–211
    black southern migrants, 187–192
    definition, 16
    discrimination, 29
    educational opportunities, 199, 210
    ethnic preference hierarchy, 73–76
    European colonization, 171–172
    evolutionary development, 141–142, 147–157
    gender, 75–76, 461
    globalization effects, 200–201
    group relations, 202 (exhibit)
    Hawaiian society, 165–166, 166 (exhibit)
    ideological racism, 29–30, 158
    industrialization, 179–185, 181 (exhibit), 196–197
    institutional discrimination, 30, 157–158,
        158 (exhibit)
    intergroup cooperation, 119–120
    key concepts, 28 (exhibit), 28–30
    Mexican Americans, 167–169
    minority group policies, 53
    minority group status, 21–22, 157–158,
        158 (exhibit), 160–164, 167–170
    modern black-white relations, 231–270
    modern institutional discrimination, 180, 207–211,
        250–252, 256–257
    modern racism, 114, 115 (exhibit), 122–124,
        123 (exhibit), 124 (exhibit), 135–136
    moral issues, 141–142
    Myrdal's vicious cycle theory, 108, 108 (exhibit)
    Noel hypothesis, 165–166
    positive progress, 466–468
    prejudice, 28–29, 99–109
    religion, 73–74

scapegoat hypothesis, 98, 131
    social change efforts, 211
    social class, 74–75, 171–172
    stereotypes, 99–104, 100 (exhibit)
    structural mobility, 72
    urbanization, 196–197
    see also African Americans; American Indians; Asian
        Americans; Hispanic Americans; Slavery
Dominican Republic
    characteristics, 412–413, 413 (exhibit)
    demographics, 316 (exhibit)
    educational attainment, 348 (exhibit)
    foreign-born population, 317 (exhibit)
    geographic location, 413 (exhibit)
    immigration, 411 (exhibit), 412–413, 414
    median household income, 350 (exhibit),
        351 (exhibit)
    school integration, 347
    urbanization, 346 (exhibit)
Doob, L. W., 98
D'Orso, M., 237
Douglass, Frederick, 147, 157, 215
Doyle, A. B., 109
Drug arrest rates, 245–247, 246 (exhibit)
Dual labor market, 200
Du Bois, W. E. B., 190–191, 212
Dumont, J.-C., 340
Duncan, O. D., 49
Duvalier dictatorship, 416
Dwyer, R., 260
Dying languages, 228–230

Eastern European Jewish immigrants
    anti-Semitism, 63–64
    assimilation patterns, 67
    degree of similarity, 73
    enclave groups, 59–60, 67
    gender, 75–76
    religion, 73–74
    social class, 74–75
Economic production, 19
Ecuador
    demographics, 316 (exhibit)
    educational attainment, 348 (exhibit)
    foreign-born population, 317 (exhibit)
    median household income, 350 (exhibit),
        351 (exhibit)
    urbanization, 346 (exhibit)
Editor and Publisher, 266
Edmonston, B., 14, 303 (exhibit), 436
"Eduaction Statistics," 324, 414, 416, 418
Educational opportunities, 199, 210
Ehrenreich, B., 207
Eichenwald, K., 244
Eitle, D., 131
Eitzen, D. S., 328
Elkins, S., 155, 160, 172, 174
Ellemers, 125
Elliot, A., 101

Elliot, Michael, 353
Ellison, C., 119
Ellsworth, S., 237
El Salvador
    characteristics, 412–413, 413 (exhibit)
    demographics, 316 (exhibit)
    educational attainment, 348 (exhibit)
    foreign-born population, 317 (exhibit)
    geographic location, 413 (exhibit)
    immigration, 411 (exhibit), 412–413, 414
    median household income, 350 (exhibit),
        351 (exhibit)
    school integration, 347
    urbanization, 346 (exhibit)
Enclave minority groups
    Blauner hypothesis, 154
    characteristics, 52–53, 431
    Chinese Americans, 368–369, 395
    Cuban Americans, 337–339
    Japanese Americans, 373, 395
    Jewish communities, 60
    Korean Americans, 419
    Roma, 432
Endangered languages, 228–230
Enforceable trust, 398
Engels, F., 106
English Americans
    colonization, 171–172
    social distance, 110 (exhibit), 111
English only debate, 88–90
Enríquez, E., 331
Enryo, 397
Equal opportunities, 17 (exhibit)
Equal status contact hypothesis, 118, 121
Erdoes, R., 281, 297
Espinosa, K., 342
Espiritu, Y., 26, 402, 420
Essien-Udom, E. U., 191, 238
Ethclass, 74
Ethiopia, 411 (exhibit), 429 (exhibit), 429–430
Ethnic minority groups
    affirmative action, 209–211
    assimilation, 462–466
    black southern migrants, 187–192
    Blauner hypothesis, 153, 158, 160, 169
    colonized minority groups, 153, 158, 160, 164, 169
    definition, 16
    descendants, 76–82, 153–154
    educational opportunities, 199, 210
    ethnic preference hierarchy, 73–76
    evolutionary development, 147–157
    gender, 75–76, 461–462
    geographical distribution, 76–77, 77 (exhibit)
    globalization effects, 200–201
    group relations, 202 (exhibit)
    hate crimes, 126–133, 129 (exhibit)
    immigrant minority groups, 153, 158
    income data, 339 (exhibit)
    industrialization, 180, 196–197
    low-skilled occupations, 199, 200
    modern institutional discrimination, 180, 207–211,
        250–252, 256–257
    pluralism, 462–466
    positive progress, 466–468
    religion, 73–74
    rigid competitive group systems, 181, 182, 201–202,
        202 (exhibit)
    social change efforts, 211
    social class, 74–75, 171–172
    urbanization, 196–197
    see also African Americans; American Indians;
        Asian Americans; Hispanic Americans; Slavery
Ethnic revival, 80
Ethnic succession
    assimilation patterns, 67
    criminal activities, 71
    labor unions, 68, 70–71
    political machines, 68, 69
    religion, 71
    sports, 72
Ethnocentrism, 152 (exhibit), 152–153, 154,
    155 (exhibit), 158 (exhibit), 168, 202, 366
Eugene, E., 416
European Americans, 81–82
European Commission, 432
European immigration
    anti-immigration campaigns, 62–65, 121,
        121 (exhibit)
    anti-Semitism, 63–64
    assimilation patterns, 58, 65–72, 66 (exhibit), 463
    assimilation variations, 73–76
    Australia, 306
    chain immigration, 62
    conditions of entry, 56
    degree of similarity, 73
    descendants, 76–82, 153–154
    Eastern European Jewish immigrants,
        59–60, 63–64, 67, 73–76
    ethnic preference hierarchy, 73–76
    ethnic succession, 67–72
    gender, 75–76
    geographical distribution, 76–77, 77 (exhibit)
    immigrant laborers, 58–59
    Industrial Revolution, 55, 72
    Irish immigrants, 58–59
    legal immigration, 56 (exhibit)
    major migratory flows, 53–54, 54 (exhibit)
    Northern and Western Protestant European
        immigrants, 56–58
    quota system, 64–65
    religion, 73–74
    social class, 74–75
    sojourners, 76
    Southern and Eastern European
        immigrants, 58–59
    structural mobility, 72
    United States–European immigration
        comparisons, 340 (exhibit)

European Roma Rights Center, 432
European Union Agency for Fundamental Rights, 432
"Europe: The Integration Dilemma"
    (*The Economist*), 341
Evans, S. M., 76, 164, 192, 240, 282
Exclusion support, 121, 121 (exhibit)
Executive Order No. 8802, 233
Executive Order No. 9066, 374
Expulsion, 53, 121, 121 (exhibit)
Extermination, 53
Extractive occupations, 198, 199 (exhibit)

Fadiman, A., 378–379
Fair Employment Practices Commission, 233
Fair Housing Act (1968), 208
Fair-weather liberal, 96, 96 (exhibit)
Fanning, B., 86
Farley, R., 202 (exhibit), 204, 259
Farnham, S. D.
    see Greenwald, A. G.
Fatalism, 253
Feagin, C. B., 208
Feagin, J., 41, 109, 136, 208,
    211, 212, 249, 272, 365, 402
Fears, D., 128
Federal Bureau of Investigation (FBI), 128, 380
Federal Glass Ceiling Commission, 205
Federal Housing Administration (FHA), 208
Federation for American Immigration Reform (FAIR),
    37–38
Female-headed families, 253 (exhibit), 253–254,
    351–352
Female immigrants
    assimilation variations, 75–76
    gender inequality, 25–26, 26 (exhibit), 202–205,
        351–352, 461–462
    labor unions, 70–71
    see also Gender; Women
Female slaves, 161, 174
Fifteenth Amendment (U.S. Constitution), 182, 192
Filipinos
    acculturation, 380, 381 (exhibit), 463
    characteristics, 418 (exhibit)
    educational attainment, 386 (exhibit), 443 (exhibit)
    foreign-born population, 364 (exhibit), 391 (exhibit)
    immigration, 378 (exhibit), 411 (exhibit), 420
    incarcerated males, 443 (exhibit)
    median household income, 388 (exhibit)
    per capita income, 389 (exhibit)
    population growth, 362 (exhibit), 363 (exhibit)
    poverty, 390, 390 (exhibit), 391 (exhibit)
    second generations, 443 (exhibit)
    social distance, 110 (exhibit)
    urbanization, 383 (exhibit)
Finland, 121 (exhibit)
Firefighters Local Union No. 1784 v. Stotts
    (1984), 209
First generations, 65, 66, 66 (exhibit), 442 (exhibit)
Fisher, M., 266

Fiske, S., 100, 101
Fitzpatrick, J. P., 333, 352
Fluid competitive group systems, 201–202,
    202 (exhibit)
Foner, N., 92
Fong, E., 394
Fong, T., 384, 387
Fong-Torres, Ben, 370–371
Forbes, H. D., 119
Forced migration, 53
Ford, Henry, 64
Forner, P. S., 70
Fourteenth Amendment (U.S. Constitution), 38
Fourth generations, 442
Foxwoods Casino, Connecticut, 291–292
Fragmented assimilation, 83
France, 121 (exhibit), 171–172
Franklin, J. H., 149, 155, 157, 161, 185,
    190, 233, 234, 262
Frazier, E. F., 247
Freedman's Bureau, 182
Freedom Party, 240
French linguistic diversity, 87
Frenkel-Brunswick, E., 98
Fry, R., 261, 261 (exhibit), 300 (exhibit),
    347 (exhibit)
Fukuyama, F., 353, 354–355

Gabriel (slave), 215
Gadsden Purchase (1853), 167
Gallagher, C., 81, 82
Gallup, 17 (exhibit), 245, 266, 433
Gaming industry, 291–293, 292 (exhibit),
    293 (exhibit)
Gandhi, Mohandas K., 235, 331, 405
Gans, H., 81
Garcia, A., 37, 39
Garcia, M. C., 357
Gardner, R. W., 324
Garment industry, 60, 70
Garnet, Henry Highland, 215
Garvey, Marcus, 191, 238
Garza, Al, 39
Gender
    American Indians, 164
    American Indian society, 278–279, 282, 284
    Anglo-conformity, 381
    Asian Americans, 365, 381
    assimilation variations, 75–76
    black southern migrants, 191–192
    Chicano protest movement, 331
    children's books, 143–144
    Chinese Americans, 369
    civil rights movement, 239–240
    defining characteristics, 25–27
    educational attainment, 262 (exhibit)
    exploitation, 207
    gender inequality, 25–26, 26 (exhibit), 202–205,
        461–462

gender roles, 25
globalization effects, 202–207
Hispanic Americans, 351–352
income data, 126 (exhibit)
income gap, 204 (exhibit), 204–206, 254 (exhibit)
Japanese Americans, 376
median earnings, 204 (exhibit), 205 (exhibit), 254 (exhibit)
Mexican Americans, 169–170, 328, 331
postindustrial society, 202–205
public sociology assignment, 143–144
Puerto Ricans, 334, 335
sexism, 124–126, 126 (exhibit)
slavery, 160
social construction, 27
stereotypes, 103–104, 104 (exhibit)
workforce participation, 203 (exhibit), 203–206
Generational patterns, 65–67, 66 (exhibit)
Genocide, 22, 53
Genovese, E. D., 155, 157, 160
German immigrants
   assimilation patterns, 57–58
   degree of similarity, 73
   educational attainment, 78 (exhibit)
   household income, 79 (exhibit)
   integration, 78
   international immigration, 340–341
   social distance, 110 (exhibit), 111
Gerstenfeld, P., 131
Gerth, H., 197
Geschwender, J. A., 46, 184, 186 (exhibit), 187 (exhibit), 232, 233
Ghettos, 338
Gimpel, J., 107
Girak, D., 431
Glaeser, E., 259
Glass ceiling, 205, 399–400
Glazer, N., 80
Gleason, P., 51
Glick, J., 444
Glick, P., 100
Globalization
   economic impacts, 446
   gender inequality, 202–206
   global trends, 206–207
   immigration issues, 36, 200–201, 325, 446–447
   United States trends, 202–206
Gohmert, Louie, 39
Gold Rush (1849), 366
Gold, S., 426
Goldstein, A., 342
Gonzales, Sylvia, 331
Gonzalez, A., 120
Gonzalez, Rodolfo, 330
Gooding-Williams, R., 244
Gordon, L., 103
Gordon, M., 47, 73, 74, 119, 170, 445
Gordon, Milton, 46–48
Goren, A., 59, 64, 70

Goyette, K., 363, 367 (exhibit)
Graffiti, 5–7
Graham, Lindsey, 39
Granger, D., 27
Grant-Thompson, S., 119
Grape boycotts, 331
Gratz v. Bollinger (2003), 210
Gray, David, 69
Great Britain, 121 (exhibit), 171–172, 411 (exhibit)
Great Depression, 69, 208, 374
Great Migration, 186–187
Grebler, L., 324, 329, 352
Greek Americans, 62
Greeley, A. M., 48, 80
Green, D., 283
Greenwald, A. G., 139
Gross, Betty Ann, 307
Group competition, 104–107, 118–119, 434, 460
Grutter v. Bollinger (2003), 210
Guatemala
   demographics, 316 (exhibit)
   educational attainment, 348 (exhibit)
   foreign-born population, 317 (exhibit)
   median household income, 350 (exhibit), 351 (exhibit)
   school integration, 347
   urbanization, 346 (exhibit)
Guilbault, R., 320
Guilt, 141–142
Gutiérrez, José Angel, 330
Gutman, H., 157, 192
Guzman, R. C., 324, 329, 352
Gypsies, 432

Hacker, A., 155, 272
Haiti, 411 (exhibit), 415, 415 (exhibit), 416, 443 (exhibit)
Hakimzadeh, S., 343 (exhibit)
Haley, A., 160
Haller, W., 440, 441
Hamer, Fannie Lou, 240
Hamer, F. L., 240
Handlin, O., 456
Hansen, M., 79
Hanson, J., 293, 294
Harding, D. J., 253
Hard work ethic beliefs, 251
Hardworking–laziness measures, 102 (exhibit), 102–103, 124 (exhibit)
Harjo, S. S., 275, 276, 289, 308, 314
Harlem Renaissance, 187
Harley-Davidson, 290
Harris, M., 16
Harrison, B., 217
Hartley, E. L., 101
Harvard Project on American Indian Economic Development, 311
Harvey, O. J., 105

Hate crimes, 98, 126–133, 129 (exhibit),
    130 (exhibit), 342, 380
Hawaiians, 165–166, 166 (exhibit)
Hawkins, H., 190
Health care
    African Americans, 232, 251, 267
    American Indians, 282, 283
    dominant-minority group relations, 83
    Mexican Americans, 324
    new immigrants, 437, 447, 460
Heaton, T., 186 (exhibit)
Heer, D. M., 436
Henry, P. J., 122
Herberg, W., 63, 74
Herberg, Will, 74
Hickson, F., 109
Higham, J., 63
Higher education affirmative action programs, 210
High-prestige occupations, 199, 203 (exhibit)
Hill-Collins, P., 26
Hill-Collins, Patricia, 21
Hirschman, C., 46, 371, 395
Hispanic Americans
    Americanization, 45
    anti-immigration campaigns, 342, 433–434,
        439–440
    assimilation, 342–352, 463
    characteristics, 318
    demographics, 315–316, 316 (exhibit)
    discrimination, 341–342
    dissimilarity index, 346 (exhibit)
    educational attainment, 347, 348 (exhibit),
        395, 443 (exhibit)
    foreign-born population, 317 (exhibit)
    gender inequality, 351–352
    geographical distribution, 345 (exhibit)
    growth projections, 12 (exhibit), 13
    growth rates, 317–318
    hate crimes, 128
    Hispanic–white relations, 341–352
    immigration, 353–355, 411 (exhibit), 412–413
    incarcerated males, 443 (exhibit)
    income data, 339 (exhibit), 349–351, 350 (exhibit)
    intergroup cooperation, 120
    interracial relationships, 352
    job market, 349
    language, 342–343, 343 (exhibit), 344 (exhibit)
    median household income, 349 (exhibit),
        350 (exhibit)
    minority group categories, 13, 14
    minority group comparison studies, 394–395
    pluralism, 342–352, 463
    points of origin, 317 (exhibit)
    political power, 347–348
    population growth, 345 (exhibit)
    poverty, 349, 351, 351 (exhibit)
    prejudice, 341–342
    residential patterns, 344–346, 345 (exhibit),
        346 (exhibit)
    school integration, 347, 347 (exhibit)
    second generations, 443 (exhibit)
    segregation, 346, 346 (exhibit)
    sports, 72
    unemployment rates, 349
    urbanization, 346, 346 (exhibit)
Hispanization, 353–355
Hmong
    acculturation, 381 (exhibit)
    educational attainment, 386 (exhibit)
    foreign-born population, 364 (exhibit)
    immigration, 378–379
    median household income, 388, 388 (exhibit)
    per capita income, 389 (exhibit)
    population growth, 362 (exhibit), 363 (exhibit)
    poverty, 390 (exhibit)
    urbanization, 383 (exhibit)
Hochschild, A., 207
Holdaway, J., 444, 452
Homeownership, 208–209, 252
Hometown diversity assignment, 2–3
Honduras
    demographics, 316 (exhibit)
    educational attainment, 348 (exhibit),
        443 (exhibit)
    foreign-born population, 317 (exhibit)
    median household income, 350 (exhibit),
        351 (exhibit)
    second generations, 443 (exhibit)
    urbanization, 346 (exhibit)
Hood, W., 105
hooks, bell, 241–242
Hopcroft, R., 27
Hopi tribe, 282
Horowitz, D., 211, 213–214, 215
Hostetler, J., 52
Hovland, C. I., 98
Hraba, J., 287
Huber, J., 27
Huerta, Dolores, 331
Hughes, M., 248
Huiguan, 368
Huling, T., 245
Human capital theory, 48–49, 399,
    442, 442 (exhibit)
Human evolution, 22–23
Human Rights Watch, 246 (exhibit)
Hunting-and-gathering societies, 278
Huntington, S., 36, 353–355
Hurh, W. M., 419
Hyman, H., 115 (exhibit)

Ibish, H., 131, 425
Iceland, J., 259, 298 (exhibit)
Ideological racism, 29–30, 158
Illegal drugs, 245–247, 246 (exhibit)
Illegal immigration, 32–36, 33 (exhibit),
    324, 437–440, 438 (exhibit), 449–450
Illiteracy, 226–228

Immigration
    African groups, 429 (exhibit)
    American public opinion, 433 (exhibit),
        433–435, 434 (exhibit)
    anchor babies, 37–39
    anti-immigration campaigns, 62–65, 85–86, 107
    anti-Semitism, 63–64
    Arab Americans, 422–424
    Asian Americans, 366–367, 372–373, 377–379,
        378 (exhibit), 417–420
    assimilation patterns, 58, 65–72, 66 (exhibit)
    assimilation variations, 73–76
    birthright citizenship, 37–39
    Blauner hypothesis, 153, 158
    chain immigration, 62
    Chinese Americans, 366–367, 378 (exhibit)
    contemporary immigrants, 82–83, 410 (exhibit),
        410–430, 411 (exhibit)
    Cuban Americans, 336
    degree of similarity, 73
    descendants, 76–82, 153–154
    economic impact, 436–437
    English only debate, 88–90
    ethnic enclaves, 431
    ethnic preference hierarchy, 73–76
    ethnic succession, 67–72
    European immigration, 53–65, 54 (exhibit),
        56 (exhibit)
    gender, 75–76
    geographical distribution, 76–77, 77 (exhibit)
    globalization, 200–201, 446–447
    harmful effects, 448–449
    Hispanization, 353–355
    historical perspective, 456–457, 459
    immigrant opinions, 435
    income data, 444 (exhibit), 445 (exhibit)
    international immigration, 340–341
    Japanese Americans, 372–373, 378 (exhibit)
    legal immigration, 56 (exhibit), 410 (exhibit),
        411 (exhibit)
    Mexican Americans, 32–36, 33 (exhibit),
        321 (exhibit), 321–328, 323 (exhibit),
        326 (exhibit), 327 (exhibit)
    Middle Eastern Americans, 422–424
    modes of incorporation, 430–431, 442
    myths and facts, 449–450
    non-Hispanic Caribbean immigrants,
        415, 415 (exhibit)
    ongoing issues, 447
    primary labor market, 430–431
    quota system, 64–65
    religion, 73–74
    secondary labor market, 431
    segmented assimilation, 440–446, 442 (exhibit)
    social class, 74–75
    sojourners, 76
    Sub-Saharan African groups, 428–430
    theoretical perspectives, 35–36
    top-sending nations, 411 (exhibit)
    traditional perspective, 82–83, 444–446
    undocumented immigrants, 32–36, 33 (exhibit), 324,
        437–440, 438 (exhibit), 449–450
    United States–European immigration comparisons,
        340 (exhibit)
    see also Second generations
Immigration Reform and Control Act (1986), 324, 326
Implicit Association Test (IAT), 139
Income data, 126 (exhibit)
Indentured servants, 148–150, 151, 154–155,
    155 (exhibit)
India, 417–419
    see also Asian Indians
Indian casinos, 291–293, 292 (exhibit), 293 (exhibit)
Indian Claims Commission, 286
Indian Removal Act (1830), 163, 164, 298
Indian Reorganization Act (1934), 282, 288 (exhibit)
Indian Self-Determination and Education
    Assistance Act (1975), 285, 289
Indian–white relations
    see American Indians
Indifference, 142
Industrialization
    African Americans, 181–182, 184–185
    characteristics, 181 (exhibit)
    dominant-minority group relations, 179–185,
        181 (exhibit), 196–197
    European immigration, 54–55, 72
    fluid competitive group systems, 201–202, 202 (exhibit)
    group relations, 201–202, 202 (exhibit)
    historical perspective, 457
    Industrial Revolution, 55
    occupational specialization, 196–197
    rigid competitive group systems, 181, 182, 201–202,
        202 (exhibit)
    structural mobility, 72
    white-collar occupations, 197–199
    workforce distribution, 197–199, 199 (exhibit)
Industrial Revolution, 55, 72, 151
Inequality
    gender inequality, 25–26, 26 (exhibit), 202–205,
        461–462
    minority groups, 16, 18, 157–158, 158 (exhibit)
    theoretical perspectives, 18–21
    see also Discrimination; Prejudice
Inouye, Daniel, 387
Instant gratification, 253
Institutional discrimination
    basic concepts, 30
    minority groups, 157–158, 158 (exhibit)
    modern institutional discrimination, 180, 207–211,
        250–252, 256–257
Integration
    American Indians, 463
    black southern migrants, 191
    educational attainment, 78 (exhibit), 262 (exhibit)
    generational patterns, 65–67, 66 (exhibit)
    Gordon's stages of assimilation theory, 47 (exhibit),
        48, 52

historical perspective, 462–466
household income, 79 (exhibit), 264 (exhibit)
job market, 263–264
Mexican Americans, 442
primary structural assimilation, 265–266
school integration, 260 (exhibit), 260–262,
    261 (exhibit), 299–300, 300 (exhibit), 347,
    347 (exhibit)
secondary structural assimilation, 258–265, 296,
    298–302, 344–352
white ethnics, 78, 78 (exhibit), 79 (exhibit)
Intelligent–unintelligent measures, 102 (exhibit),
    102–103
Intergroup cooperation, 118, 119–120, 199, 236, 434
Intermarriage
    Asian Americans, 390–392, 392 (exhibit)
    changing attitudes, 266
    colonized minority groups, 171
    generational patterns, 74
    Gordon's stages of assimilation theory,
        47 (exhibit), 48
    Hawaiians, 165
    Hispanic Americans, 352
    interracial marriage, 18, 114–115, 115 (exhibit),
        116 (exhibit), 123 (exhibit), 302–303, 303 (exhibit)
    Italian immigrants, 67
    mixed-race heritage, 243
    White Anglo-Saxon Protestants (WASPs), 67
    white ethnics, 78
International immigration, 340–341
Internment camps, 374–376
Interracial relationships, 265–266, 302–303,
    303 (exhibit), 352, 390–392, 392 (exhibit)
Invisible minorities, 396
Iran, 411 (exhibit)
Ireland
    anti-immigration campaigns, 121 (exhibit)
    emigration–immigration patterns, 85–86, 86 (exhibit)
Irish immigrants
    anti-immigration campaigns, 62–63
    assimilation patterns, 84
    degree of similarity, 73
    educational attainment, 78 (exhibit)
    ethnic succession, 67–72
    gender, 75
    geographical distribution, 77, 77 (exhibit)
    household income, 79 (exhibit)
    immigrant laborers, 58–59, 67
    integration, 78
    labor unions, 68, 70–71
    political machines, 68, 69
    religion, 71, 73–74
    social distance, 110 (exhibit)
    sports, 72
Issei, 373
Italian immigrants
    anti-immigration campaigns, 63
    assimilation patterns, 84
    criminal activities, 71

educational attainment, 78 (exhibit)
gender, 75
generational patterns, 66 (exhibit), 66–67
geographical distribution, 77, 77 (exhibit)
household income, 79 (exhibit)
labor unions, 70
social distance, 110 (exhibit)
sojourners, 76
sports, 72

Jackman, M., 117
Jackson, 365
Jackson, J. S., 120
Jacobs, D., 131
Jacobs, Harriet, 159
Jacobson, C., 186 (exhibit)
Jamaica, 411 (exhibit), 415, 415 (exhibit),
    417, 443 (exhibit)
Jamestown, 148, 162
Japanese American Citizens League, 374
Japanese Americans
    acculturation, 380–382, 381 (exhibit), 463
    Anglo-conformity, 381
    assimilation, 380–381, 463
    citizenship rights, 372–373
    contact situations, 377
    cultural success, 397–398
    cultural traits, 365
    discrimination, 372–374, 379–380
    educational attainment, 386 (exhibit), 395
    enclave groups, 373, 395
    foreign-born population, 364 (exhibit),
        391 (exhibit)
    gender inequality, 376
    immigration, 372–373, 378 (exhibit)
    interracial relationships, 392
    job sector, 376–377
    median household income, 388 (exhibit)
    minority group comparison studies, 377, 394–395
    narrative portraits, 375
    per capita income, 389 (exhibit)
    pluralism, 380–381, 463
    population growth, 362 (exhibit), 363 (exhibit),
        367 (exhibit), 372
    post-World War II, 376–377
    poverty, 390, 390 (exhibit), 391 (exhibit)
    prejudice, 379–380
    relocation camps, 374–376
    social distance, 110 (exhibit), 111
    socioeconomic status, 376–377, 390
    stereotypes, 373–374, 379
    urbanization, 383 (exhibit)
Jeter, Derek, 255
Jewish community
    anti-Semitism, 63–64
    assimilation patterns, 67
    degree of similarity, 73
    Eastern European Jewish immigrants, 59–60, 63–64,
        67, 73–76

enclave groups, 59–60, 67
gender, 75–76
hate crimes, 128
labor unions, 70
religion, 73–74
social class, 74–75
social distance, 110 (exhibit), 111
Jibou, R. M., 372, 373
Jigsaw method, 120
Jim Crow system, 182–186, 190–191, 194–195, 207, 232–242, 304
Job market, 263–264
Joe, J., 284
John, D., 205
Johnson, Lyndon B., 235–236
Johnson, N. E., 426
Joly, S., 124, 125
Jones, James, 99
Jones, Jeffrey, 99, 318, 433
Jones, Mother, 70
Jones, Peter, 85
Jordan, W., 155, 158
Josephy, A. M., 278, 280

Kallen, H., 51
Kallen, Horace, 49, 51
Kalt, J., 285, 288 (exhibit), 289, 293 (exhibit)
Karlins, M., 101
Kasarda, J. D., 249, 250
Kasinitz, P., 444, 452
Katz, M. B., 209
Katznelson, I., 208
Katz, P., 109, 119
Kaw, E., 381–382
Kaye, J., 420
Kennedy, John F., 263
Kennedy, Randall, 246, 247
Kennedy, R. J., 74
Kennedy, Ruby Jo, 74
Kent, M., 263
Kephart, W., 52
Kilkelly (song), 85
Killian, L., 235
Kim, C. H., 363
Kinder, D. R., 122
King, C. R., 308–309
King, Martin Luther, Jr., 235, 331
King, M. L., Jr., 235
King, Rodney, 244, 419
Kitano, H., 53, 367 (exhibit), 369, 371, 372, 373, 374, 376, 377, 391, 393, 397–398, 402, 419, 420
Kitchenettes, 189
Kivligham, K., 27
Klamath tribe, 283
Kleg, M., 110 (exhibit)
Kluegal, J., 101, 103, 122
Kochhar, R., 247, 436
Korean Americans

acculturation, 381 (exhibit), 463
characteristics, 418 (exhibit)
educational attainment, 386 (exhibit), 443 (exhibit)
enclave groups, 52, 419
foreign-born population, 364 (exhibit), 391 (exhibit)
immigration, 378 (exhibit), 411 (exhibit), 419
incarcerated males, 443 (exhibit)
median household income, 388, 388 (exhibit)
per capita income, 389 (exhibit)
population growth, 362 (exhibit), 363 (exhibit)
poverty, 390 (exhibit), 391 (exhibit)
second generations, 443 (exhibit)
social distance, 110 (exhibit), 111
urbanization, 383 (exhibit)
Krauss, M., 295
Kraybill, D. B., 52
Krepps, M., 288 (exhibit)
Kristof, N., 207
Kritz, M., 431
Krysan, M., 259
Ku Klux Klan, 64, 127–128, 132, 234
Kuperman, D., 243
Kurihara, Joseph, 375
Kwan, V., 100

Labissiere, Y., 416
Labor force, 438 (exhibit)
Labor-intensive work, 55
Labor market, 200
Labor supply problem
African Americans, 151, 154, 155 (exhibit), 158, 170, 184, 304
American Indians, 170
Hawaiians, 165
Mexican Americans, 169, 170, 318–319, 322–328, 323 (exhibit), 331–332
Puerto Ricans, 332–333
Labor unions, 68, 70–71, 329
Lacy, D., 151
Lai, H. M., 368, 369, 379
Lame Deer, John, 297
Lamont-Brown, R., 396
Lamont, M., 253
Landale, N., 334
Language, 342, 381 (exhibit)
Language and Education Policy, 88
Laotians
acculturation, 381 (exhibit)
educational attainment, 386 (exhibit), 443 (exhibit)
foreign-born population, 364 (exhibit)
immigration, 378
incarcerated males, 443 (exhibit)
median household income, 388 (exhibit)
per capita income, 389 (exhibit)
population growth, 362 (exhibit), 363 (exhibit)
second generations, 443 (exhibit)
urbanization, 383 (exhibit)
LaPiere, R., 113
La Raza Unida (People United), 330

Latino Americans
    see Hispanic Americans
League of United Latin American Citizens
    (LULAC), 329
Le, C. N., 392, 421–422
Lee, C., 199, 260, 260 (exhibit), 261, 303 (exhibit)
Lee, S., 367 (exhibit), 391
Legal immigration, 56 (exhibit), 410 (exhibit),
    411 (exhibit)
Legal support, 118–119
LeMaitre, G., 340
Lenski, G., 20, 148, 199 (exhibit), 278
Lenski, Gerhard, 20
Lenski, J., 199 (exhibit)
Level of development, 20
Levine, L., 176, 258
Levin, J., 131
Levin, M., 372
Levinson, D., 98
Levy, J., 331
Lewis Mumford Center, 259
Lewis, O., 253, 319
Leyens, J.-C., 100
Lichter, D. T., 303
Lieberman, R., 208
Lieberson, S., 81, 188
Light, I., 419
Lincoln, C. E., 238
Lindbergh, Charles, 64
Ling, H., 367
Linguistic assimilation, 87
Literacy rates, 226–228
Literacy tests, 185
Little, Malcom
    see Malcolm X
Local diner assignment, 144–146
Locke, Gary, 387
Locust, C., 278
Logan, J., 337
Logan, J. R., 372
Lopata, H. Z., 71
Lopez, I. F. Haney, 268, 269–270
Lopez, Jessie, 331
Lopez, M., 315, 348
López Tijerina, Reies, 330
Louisiana, 185
L'Ouverture, Toussaint, 215
Low-skilled occupations, 199, 200
Low-skill immigrant groups, 58–59
Lurie, N. O., 154, 163, 280
Lyman, S., 366, 368, 379
Lynchings, 98, 167, 185, 366
Lynch, S., 440, 441

Machismo, 319, 320
Malcolm X, 238
Mallett, R., 124, 125
Mamdouh, F., 446
Mandela, Nelson, 195

Manning, R., 52, 60, 339
Mannix, D. P., 160
Mann, T., 263
Manuel, W. J., 120
Manufacturing occupations, 198, 199 (exhibit)
Manzanar, California, 375
Maquiladoras, 206–207, 325
Marcelli, E., 436
Marielitos, 336
Marital assimilation, 47 (exhibit), 48, 67
Markham, W., 394
Marshall, Thurgood, 233
Martinez, G., 37, 39
Martin, P., 54
Marvasti, Amir, 427–428
Marxist theory of social inequality, 19, 106
Marx, K., 106
Marx, Karl, 18, 19, 22
Mascots, 275–276, 294, 307–309
Massarik, P., 60
Massey, D., 179, 208, 209, 237, 249, 250, 254, 272,
    342, 440–441, 442, 445–446
Matthaei, J., 60, 70, 71, 161, 164, 192, 240, 279, 311,
    324, 328, 331, 365, 369, 376, 377
Mauer, M., 245
Mazur, A., 27
Mbeki, Thabo M., 195
McCain, John, 90, 263
McConahy, J. B., 122
McDevitt, J., 131
McDowell, A., 244
McKinney, Karyn, 427–428
McLaren, L., 121
McLemore, S. D., 168
McNickle, D., 162, 163, 280, 283
McNulty, T., 337
McPherson, M., 266
McWhorter, J., 135
McWilliams, C., 168, 341
Means of production, 19
Media literacy, 329–331
Median household income, 265 (exhibit), 290 (exhibit)
Medicare benefits, 436–437
Medoff, M., 131
Meek, B., 293
Meissner, D., 436
Melanin, 22–23
Mellott, D. S.
    see Greenwald, A. G.
Melting pot metaphor, 44–45, 462
Menominee tribe, 283
Meredith v. Jefferson County (Ky.) Board of Education
    (2007), 210
Merryman, A., 109
Merton, R., 96 (exhibit), 103
Mestizos, 171
Metis, 171
Mexican Americans
    assimilation, 169, 331–332, 442, 463

assimilation patterns, 84

Blauner hypothesis, 169

cultural patterns, 319

demographics, 315–316, 316 (exhibit)

discrimination, 328, 331–332

educational attainment, 348 (exhibit), 395, 443 (exhibit)

European colonization, 171–172, 318

foreign-born population, 317 (exhibit)

gender inequality, 328

gender relations, 169–170

geographical distribution, 77, 77 (exhibit)

globalization effects, 36, 325

growth rates, 317

illegal immigration, 32–36, 33 (exhibit), 324, 437–438, 438 (exhibit), 449–450

immigration, 321 (exhibit), 321–328, 323 (exhibit), 326 (exhibit), 327 (exhibit), 353, 411 (exhibit)

incarcerated males, 443 (exhibit)

income data, 339 (exhibit), 444 (exhibit), 444–445, 445 (exhibit)

job sector, 338, 339 (exhibit)

labor supply, 169, 318–319, 322–328, 323 (exhibit), 331–332

land disputes, 168, 169

median household income, 350 (exhibit)

minority group comparison studies, 331–332, 394–395

minority status creation, 167–170, 318–319

per capita income, 324

points of origin, 317 (exhibit)

poverty, 351 (exhibit)

power differential, 169

protest movements, 328–331

second generations, 443 (exhibit)

settlements, 167

social distance, 110 (exhibit)

union organization, 329

urbanization, 346 (exhibit)

Michigan, 426

Middle class, 247–250

Middle Eastern Americans

characteristics, 422–424, 423 (exhibit)

geographic locations, 423 (exhibit)

immigration, 422–424

Michigan communities, 426

narrative portraits, 427–428

9/11 terrorist attacks, 427–428

regional concentrations, 424, 424 (exhibit)

stereotypes, 425

Middleman minority groups, 52–53, 154

Midgley, E., 54

Migrant deaths, 33 (exhibit)

Migrants, 32–36

Migration Policy Institute, 37

Miller, D., 284

Miller, Neal, 98

Miller, Norman, 119

Mills, Billy, 308

Mills, C. Wright, 69, 197

Minority groups

affirmative action, 209–211

assimilation, 462–466

black southern migrants, 187–192

Blauner hypothesis, 153, 158, 160, 169

categories, 13–14

colonized minority groups, 153, 158, 160, 164, 169

defining characteristics, 16–18, 22–25

descendants, 76–82, 153–154

educational opportunities, 199, 210

English only debate, 88–90

ethnic succession, 67–72

evolutionary development, 147–157

geographical distribution, 76–77, 77 (exhibit)

globalization effects, 200–201

global perspective, 32–36

group relations, 202 (exhibit)

growth projections, 11–13, 12 (exhibit)

hate crimes, 126–133, 129 (exhibit)

Hawaiians, 165–166, 166 (exhibit)

immigrant minority groups, 153, 158

industrialization, 180, 196–197

inequality, 16, 18

intergroup cooperation, 119–120

low-skilled occupations, 199, 200

modern institutional discrimination, 180, 207–211, 250–252, 256–257

Myrdal's vicious cycle theory, 108, 108 (exhibit)

pluralism, 43–44, 49–53, 462–463

positive progress, 466–468

revolutionary activities, 53

rigid competitive group systems, 181, 182, 201–202, 202 (exhibit)

scapegoat hypothesis, 98, 131

separatism, 53

social change efforts, 211

status creation, 157–158, 158 (exhibit), 160–164, 167–170, 318–319

stereotypes, 99–104, 100 (exhibit)

stratification, 21–22

urbanization, 196–197

see also Assimilation; Slavery

Min, P. G., 365, 372, 386, 391, 397, 399–400, 402, 419, 420

Minutemen, 32–35, 35 (exhibit), 39, 127, 342

Mirandé, A., 168, 319, 324, 331

Miscegenation, 18

Mitchell, F., 272

Mixed-race populations

minority group categories, 13–14

narrative portraits, 15

racial identities, 255–256

two-race model, 242–243

Modell, J., 53, 106, 395

Model minority groups, 377, 380, 385, 399–400

Modern institutional discrimination, 180, 207–211, 250–252, 256–257

Modern racism, 114, 115 (exhibit), 122–124, 123 (exhibit), 124 (exhibit), 135–136, 256–257, 267
Mollenkopf, J. H., 444, 452
Montgomery Bus Boycott, 234–235
Moore, J. W., 168, 169, 319, 324, 329, 352
Moquin, W., 167, 330
Morales, L., 327 (exhibit), 433 (exhibit)
Moral issues, 141–142
Morawska, E., 60, 72, 74, 76
Morgan, E., 150, 151
Morin, R., 247
Morris, A. D., 235, 272
Morris, E., 104
Mosely-Braun, Carol, 263
Mosley, G., 319, 342
Moss, A., 149, 155, 157, 161, 185, 190, 233
Mother Jones, 70
Mowrer, O. H., 98
Moynihan, D., 80, 253
Muha, M., 117
Muhammad, Elijah, 238
Mujica, Mauro, 88–89
Mullainathan, S., 209
Multiculturalism, 51
Muslims
    Michigan communities, 426
    social distance, 110 (exhibit)
    stereotypes, 425
    see also Arab Americans;
        Middle Eastern Americans
Myrdal, G., 108, 114

Nabakov, P., 176, 286, 311
Narrative portraits
    American Indians, 297
    assimilation patterns, 84
    black southern migrants, 189
    Chinese Americans, 370–371
    culturally-based prejudice, 112
    gender images, 335
    hate crimes, 132–133
    Irish political machine, 69
    Japanese Americans, 375
    Jim Crow system, 241–242
    machismo, 320
    Mexican immigration, 322
    Middle Eastern Americans, 427–428
    mixed-race individuals, 15
    9/11 terrorist attacks, 427–428
    privilege and whiteness, 31
    refugee communities, 421–422
    Russian Jewish immigrants, 61
    slavery, 159
    Vietnamese immigrants, 421–422
National Academy of Sciences (NAS), 448
National Advisory Commission, 237, 244
National Assessment of Adult Literacy (NAAL), 227
National Association for the Advancement of Colored People (NAACP), 190, 233

National Center for Health Statistics, 246
National Congress of American Indians (NCAI), 286
National Council on Crime and Delinquency, 245
National Indian Gaming Commission, 291, 292 (exhibit)
National Opinion Research Council, 115 (exhibit), 116 (exhibit), 122, 211, 251, 434 (exhibit)
National Origins Act (1924), 64–65, 181, 324
National Public Radio, 435
National Research Council, 436
Nation of Islam, 129, 238, 239–240
Native American Church, 295
Native Americans
    acculturation, 294–296
    assimilation, 43, 287, 294–296, 463
    Blauner hypothesis, 164, 275–276, 280
    broken treaties, 291
    coercive acculturation, 280–283, 288 (exhibit)
    colonization, 171–172
    contact situations, 162–164, 275, 304
    contemporary American Indian–White relations, 288–303
    cultural diversity, 278–279
    discrimination, 293–294
    economic development, 289–291, 305
    educational attainment, 166 (exhibit), 290 (exhibit), 293 (exhibit), 299 (exhibit), 299–300, 395
    European colonization, 171–172
    federal policies, 279–285, 287–288, 288 (exhibit)
    fishing rights, 286
    forced migration, 53
    future directions, 304–305
    gaming industry, 291–293, 292 (exhibit), 293 (exhibit)
    gender relations, 164
    geographical distribution, 77, 77 (exhibit)
    growth projections, 12 (exhibit), 13
    income data, 166 (exhibit), 293 (exhibit), 300–302, 301 (exhibit), 302 (exhibit)
    Indian Reorganization Act (1934), 282, 288 (exhibit)
    intergroup cooperation, 120
    interracial relationships, 302–303, 303 (exhibit)
    job market, 300
    labor supply, 151, 154, 155 (exhibit), 170, 304
    land disputes, 163, 170
    land ownership, 280
    median household income, 290 (exhibit), 301 (exhibit), 302 (exhibit)
    minority group categories, 13, 14
    minority group comparison studies, 304, 394–395
    minority status creation, 162–164, 170
    narrative portraits, 297
    natural resources control, 288–289
    Noel hypothesis, 163–164
    paternalism, 279–280
    pluralism, 43, 287, 463
    political power, 300
    population size, 276, 277 (exhibit)

poverty, 166 (exhibit), 289–291, 290 (exhibit),
293 (exhibit), 302, 302 (exhibit), 303 (exhibit)
prejudice, 283–285, 293–294
protest movement, 285–288
religion, 295
relocation, 283–285, 288 (exhibit)
reservation life, 279–285, 288 (exhibit)
residential patterns, 298 (exhibit), 298–299
school integration, 299–300, 300 (exhibit)
self-determination, 285, 288 (exhibit), 289
separatism, 53
social distance, 110 (exhibit), 111, 294
sports team mascots, 275–276, 294, 307–309
stereotypes, 293–294, 304, 307–309
termination policy, 283, 285, 288 (exhibit)
traditional cultures, 293–295, 295 (exhibit)
tribal groups, 277 (exhibit)
tribal languages, 294–295, 295 (exhibit)
unemployment rates, 284, 293 (exhibit), 300
urbanization, 283–285, 284 (exhibit), 288 (exhibit)
Native Hawaiians, 165–166, 166 (exhibit)
Navajo tribe, 289–291, 290 (exhibit), 295,
295 (exhibit), 299 (exhibit), 301 (exhibit),
303 (exhibit)
Navarro, J., 131
Nazi Holocaust, 63, 98
Neary, I., 396
Neely, S., 163, 164, 289
Nee, V., 48, 444, 452
Neissen, J., 86
Nelli, H. S., 76
Netherlands, 121 (exhibit)
Net worth/financial assets, 248, 248 (exhibit)
New Deal programs, 208
New Immigration
degree of similarity, 73
globalization effects, 446–447
harmful effects, 448–449
legal immigration, 56 (exhibit)
myths and facts, 449–450
ongoing issues, 447
Southern and Eastern European immigrants, 55, 58
New Mexico, 167, 168
New York Times, 272
Nicaragua
demographics, 316 (exhibit)
educational attainment, 348 (exhibit), 443 (exhibit)
foreign-born population, 317 (exhibit)
incarcerated males, 443 (exhibit)
median household income, 350 (exhibit),
351 (exhibit)
second generations, 443 (exhibit)
urbanization, 346 (exhibit)
Nigeria, 411 (exhibit), 429 (exhibit), 429–430
Nighthorse Campbell, Ben, 300
9/11 terrorist attacks, 425, 427–428
Nineteenth Amendment (U.S. Constitution), 192
Nisei, 373–374, 376–377
Nishimoto, R. S., 375

Nishi, S., 377
Nixon, Richard M., 95, 96, 239, 285
No Child Left Behind Act (2001), 224–226
Noel, D., 152, 154
Noel hypothesis
American Indians, 163–166
basic concepts, 152 (exhibit), 152–153
Chinese Americans, 366–367
group relations, 201–202
historical perspective, 460
racial inequality, 158, 158 (exhibit)
slavery, 154, 155 (exhibit)
Nolan, P., 20, 199 (exhibit)
Non-Hispanic Caribbean immigrants, 415, 415 (exhibit)
Non-Hispanic whites
Anglo-conformity, 45
characteristics, 413 (exhibit), 415 (exhibit),
418 (exhibit), 423 (exhibit), 429 (exhibit)
educational attainment, 290 (exhibit), 347,
347 (exhibit), 348 (exhibit), 385, 386 (exhibit)
growth projections, 12 (exhibit), 13
homeownership, 208
household income, 265 (exhibit)
income data, 339 (exhibit), 389 (exhibit),
444 (exhibit), 445 (exhibit)
median household income, 290 (exhibit), 291, 302,
302 (exhibit), 349 (exhibit), 350, 350 (exhibit),
388 (exhibit), 388–389
per capita income, 389 (exhibit)
poverty, 290 (exhibit), 351, 351 (exhibit), 390
(exhibit), 391 (exhibit)
school integration, 385 (exhibit)
urbanization, 346 (exhibit)
Nonviolent direct action protests, 234–235, 331
North American colonization, 171–172
North American Free Trade Agreement (NAFTA),
36, 325, 446
Northern and Western Protestant European immigrants
assimilation patterns, 58, 67
degree of similarity, 73
descendants, 76–82, 153–154
gender, 75–76
geographical distribution, 76–77, 77 (exhibit)
immigrant characteristics, 56–58
religion, 73–74
social class, 74–75
social distance, 110 (exhibit), 111
Norwegian immigrants
characteristics, 57
educational attainment, 78 (exhibit)
household income, 79 (exhibit)
social distance, 110 (exhibit)
Nosek, B. A.
see Greenwald, A. G.
Novak, M., 80

Obama, Barack, 17, 95, 135–136, 243, 255, 262–263
O'Brien, E., 138, 211, 212
Occupational specialization, 196–197

O'Hare, W., 187 (exhibit), 248, 263, 300
Old Immigration
  degree of similarity, 73
  Irish immigrants, 58
  legal immigration, 56 (exhibit)
  Northern and Western European
    immigrants, 55
Oliver, M., 247, 248 (exhibit), 252, 257
Olson, J., 287
Omi, M., 25, 41
One-drop rule, 242, 255
Operation Wetback, 324
Orfield, G., 199, 260, 260 (exhibit), 261
Organized crime, 71
Oropesa, R. S., 334
Ortiz, V., 357, 442, 445
Osofsky, G., 159
O'Sullivan, J., 353–354
Oswalt, W., 163, 164, 289
Outsourcing, 198–199
Ozawa vs. U.S. (1922), 361

Pacific Islander Americans
  growth projections, 12 (exhibit), 13
  hate crimes, 380
  minority group categories, 13
  segregation, 384 (exhibit)
Pakistanis
  acculturation, 381 (exhibit)
  educational attainment, 386 (exhibit)
  foreign-born population, 364 (exhibit)
  immigration, 411 (exhibit)
  median household income, 388 (exhibit)
  per capita income, 389 (exhibit)
  population growth, 362 (exhibit), 363 (exhibit)
  poverty, 390 (exhibit)
  urbanization, 383 (exhibit)
Pang, J., 99
*Parents Involved in Community Schools v. Seattle
  School District No. 1* (2007), 210
Parish, P. J., 156, 157, 173
Parke, R., 278
Park, R. E, 46
Park, Robert, 46
Parks, Rosa, 234
Parrillo, V., 110 (exhibit)
Passamaquoddy tribe, 291
Passel, J., 315, 324, 326 (exhibit), 391,
  392 (exhibit), 438 (exhibit)
Past-in-present institutional discrimination,
  207–209, 249
Paternalism, 155–157, 181, 201–202,
  202 (exhibit), 279–280
Patnoe, S., 120
Patriarchy/patriarchal societies
  American Indians, 164, 279
  Asian Americans, 365, 382, 461
  definition, 26
  gender inequality, 75

  Mexican Americans, 169–170
  slavery, 161
Patriot Act (2001), 425
Patterson, Brian, 132–133
Pearce, Russell, 39
Pego, D., 299
Penobscot tribe, 291
Pequot tribe, 291–292
Perez, L., 336
Perlman, J., 92
Person, W., 101
Peru, 411 (exhibit)
Petersen, W., 372
Peterson, B., 99
Peterson, M., 337
Pettigrew, T., 99, 108, 118, 119, 434
Pettit, B., 246
Pew Charitable Trust, 246
Pewewardy, C., 308–309
Pew Hispanic Center, 318, 319, 325, 337,
  344 (exhibit), 345 (exhibit)
Pew Research Center, 425
Peyote, 295
Philippines, 207
  see also Filipinos
Phillips, U. B., 160
Physical beauty, 381–382
Piersen, W. D., 173–174
Pilger, J., 306
Pincus, F., 217
Pinderhughes, R., 319
Pitt, L., 168, 169
Plantation system, 151, 155–157, 160–161, 165, 184
Plessy v. Ferguson (1896), 185, 233
Pluralism
  African Americans, 257–266, 462–463
  Asian Americans, 380–392, 463
  Black Power movement, 237–239
  Chinese Americans, 380–381, 463
  classifications, 51–53
  definition, 43
  French linguistic diversity, 87
  Hispanic Americans, 342–352, 463
  historical perspective, 462–466
  Japanese Americans, 380–381, 463
  Kallen's theory, 49, 51
  multiculturalism, 51
  Red Power movement, 287
  traditional perspective, 44
Polish immigrants
  educational attainment, 78 (exhibit)
  household income, 79 (exhibit)
Political machines, 68, 69
Pollard, K., 187 (exhibit), 248, 263, 300
Poll tax, 185
Population Reference Bureau, 340
Populism, 185
Pornography, 207
Porter, 437

Portes, A., 52, 60, 83, 327, 332, 333, 336,
    337, 338, 339, 339 (exhibit), 357, 397,
    398–399, 412, 440, 441, 452
Portugal, 121 (exhibit)
Posadas, B., 420
Postindustrial America, 180, 181 (exhibit), 201–203,
    202 (exhibit)
Potter, G., 62
Poulan, R., 207
Poverty
    African Americans, 166 (exhibit), 249–250,
        252–254, 265, 266 (exhibit)
    American Indians, 166 (exhibit), 289–291,
        290 (exhibit), 293 (exhibit), 302, 302 (exhibit),
        303 (exhibit)
    Asian Americans, 390, 390 (exhibit), 391 (exhibit)
    Haiti, 416
    Hawaiians, 166 (exhibit)
    Hispanic Americans, 349, 351, 351 (exhibit)
    Mexican Americans, 319
    minority group comparison studies, 166 (exhibit)
Powderly, Terence, 68
Powell, Colin, 263
Power
    Blauner hypothesis, 153–154
    characteristics, 20
    group relations, 202 (exhibit)
    historical perspective, 460
    Mexican Americans, 169
    Noel hypothesis, 152 (exhibit), 152–153,
        155 (exhibit), 158 (exhibit)
    racial inequality, 157, 158 (exhibit)
Powers, D., 119
Powlishta, K., 109
Prejudice
    affective prejudice, 97–99, 103
    African Americans, 256–257
    American Indians, 283–285, 293–294
    antiblack racism, 158, 186
    anti-immigration campaigns, 62–65, 107
    Asian Americans, 379–380
    authoritarian personality theory, 98–99
    basic concepts, 28–29, 96
    Brazil, 243
    children, 108–109
    Chinese Americans, 371–372, 379–380
    cognitive prejudice, 99–103, 100 (exhibit),
        102 (exhibit)
    group competition, 104–107, 118–119, 434
    Haitian immigrants, 416
    hate crimes, 98, 126–133, 129 (exhibit), 130 (exhibit)
    Hawaiian society, 165–166
    Hispanic Americans, 341–342
    intergroup cooperation, 118, 119–120
    Japanese Americans, 379–380
    Marxist theory of social inequality, 106
    Mexican Americans, 168–169, 341–342
    modern racism, 114, 115 (exhibit), 122–124,
        123 (exhibit), 124 (exhibit), 135–136, 256–257

Myrdal's vicious cycle theory, 108, 108 (exhibit)
    narrative portraits, 112
    prejudice–discrimination relationship,
        96, 96 (exhibit)
    race-based privilege, 107
    Roma, 432
    scapegoat hypothesis, 98, 131
    sexism, 124–126, 126 (exhibit)
    situational influences, 113
    social distance, 109–111, 110 (exhibit)
    socialization effects, 111, 113–114
    sociological causes, 104–107, 134
    split labor market theory, 106
    stereotypes, 99–104
    traditional prejudice, 114–120, 115 (exhibit),
        135–136
Prestige, 19–20
Price, S. L., 307–308
Primary labor market, 200
Primary occupations, 198, 199 (exhibit)
Primary sector, 47, 48
Primary structural assimilation
    African Americans, 265–266
    American Indians, 302–303
    Asian Americans, 390–392
    Hispanic Americans, 352
Principle of third-generation interest, 79
Privilege, 31
Prohibition, 71
Proletariat, 19
Property ownership, 185
Proposition 187, 439–440
Prosser, Gabriel, 215
Prostitution, 207
Protean identities, 256
Protestant European immigrants, 56–58, 73
Public housing study, 119
Public sociology, 1, 142
Pueblo Indians, 295, 295 (exhibit),
        299 (exhibit), 301 (exhibit), 303 (exhibit)
Puerto Ricans
    assimilation, 463
    background information, 332
    characteristics, 318
    cultural diversity, 333–334
    demographics, 315–316, 316 (exhibit)
    gender inequality, 334, 335
    globalization effects, 201
    labor supply, 332–333
    median household income, 350 (exhibit),
        351 (exhibit)
    migration patterns, 332–333
    minority group comparison studies, 334
    points of origin, 317 (exhibit)
    population growth, 332–333
    stereotypes, 335
    urbanization, 346 (exhibit)
Push and pull concept
    Cuban Americans, 336

Mexican Americans, 321
    Puerto Ricans, 332–333
Puzo, Mario, 84

Qian, Z., 303
Quillian, L., 122, 123, 124, 342, 352
Quinones, S., 322

Race/racism
    antiblack racism, 158, 186
    anti-immigration campaigns, 62–65
    biological characteristics, 24–25
    birthright citizenship, 39
    Black Power movement, 237–239, 258
    black southern migrants, 191–192
    children's books, 143–144
    Chinese Americans, 366–368, 379
    hate crimes, 98, 126–133, 129 (exhibit),
        130 (exhibit)
    Hispanic Americans, 341–342
    human evolution, 22–23
    ideological racism, 29–30, 158
    income data, 339 (exhibit)
    Jamaican immigrants, 417
    Japanese Americans, 374, 379
    median earnings, 254 (exhibit)
    modern institutional discrimination, 180, 207–211,
        250–252, 256–257
    modern racism, 114, 115 (exhibit), 122–124,
        123 (exhibit), 124 (exhibit), 135–136,
        256–257, 267
    Myrdal's vicious cycle theory, 108, 108 (exhibit)
    public sociology assignment, 143–144
    Puerto Ricans, 333–334
    race-based privilege, 107
    racial status quo, 244
    racial stratification, 184, 207–209
    social construction, 25
    stereotypes, 103–104
    urban unrest, 237, 244, 419
    Western European traditions, 23–24
    see also Slavery
Race relations cycle theory, 46
Racial exclusion, 251
Racial identities, 255–256
Racial minority groups
    see Ethnic minority groups
Racial Privacy Initiative, 269
Racial profiling, 246–247
Racial stratification
    African Americans, 181–188
    Chinese Americans, 366, 460
    dominant-minority group relations, 142, 148,
        158, 179–180, 196
    minority group status, 152 (exhibit)
    modern institutional discrimination, 207
    Myrdal's vicious cycle theory, 108, 108 (exhibit)
    Noel hypothesis, 152–153, 366, 460
    past-in-present institutional discrimination, 207–209

Rader, B. G., 72
Randolph, A. Philip, 233
Rationality, 197
Rawick, G. P., 176
Raymer, 283
Read, J. G., 423
Reagan, Ronald, 414
Recession impacts, 251–252, 252 (exhibit)
Reconstruction, 182
Red Power movement, 286–287, 305
Refugee communities, 407–408, 420–422
Regis, A., 206
Reich, M., 106
Religion
    American Indians, 295
    assimilation variations, 73–74
    Catholicism, 71
    ethnic succession, 71
    hate crimes, 128, 129 (exhibit)
    Mexican Americans, 319
    Puerto Ricans, 333
Relocation camps, 374–376
Rendall, M., 248
Reparations debate, 211–215
Repatriation, 323
Residential patterns
    African Americans, 258 (exhibit), 258–260,
        259 (exhibit)
    American Indians, 298 (exhibit), 298–299
    Asian Americans, 382 (exhibit), 382–383,
        383 (exhibit)
    Hispanic Americans, 344–346, 345 (exhibit),
        346 (exhibit)
Reverse discrimination, 209–210
Revilla, L., 420
Revolution, 53
Ricci v. DeStefano (2009), 209–210
Rice, Condoleezza, 263
Ridgeway, 205
Rifkin, J., 199
Rigid competitive group systems, 181, 182,
    201–202, 202 (exhibit)
Robber's Cave experiment, 105,
    118–119, 434
Robertson, C., 161
Rock, Chris, 381
Rockquemore, K. A., 255, 256
Rodriguez, A., 439
Rodriguez, C., 99, 334, 352
Rodriguez, Luis, 84
Roma, 432
Roosevelt, Franklin D., 208, 233, 282, 374
Roosevelt, Theodore, 43, 45
Rosenbaum, M., 119
Rosenblum, K. E., 27
Rosenfield, M., 352
Rosich, K., 245
Rouse, L., 293, 294
Royster, D., 251

Rudman, L. A.
    see Greenwald, A. G.
Rumbaut, R., 83, 324, 337, 412, 452
Runaway slaves, 157
Rupert, A., 124
Russell, A., 100, 101, 171
Russian Americans
    educational attainment, 78 (exhibit)
    household income, 79 (exhibit)
    Jewish immigrants, 59, 60, 61
    social distance, 110 (exhibit), 111

Saad, L., 437
Saenz, R., 249–250
Sakamoto, A., 363
Samaritans on the Border, 32 (exhibit), 32–35
Sanchirico, 395
Sanford, N., 98
San Francisco Chronicle, 214
Sansei, 377
Santa Fe, New Mexico, 167
Santiago, C., 357
Scapegoat hypothesis, 98, 131
Schafer, J., 131
Schibel, Y., 86
Schlesinger, A. M., Jr., 45
Schmid, C., 295
Schoener, A., 70
School desegregation
    African Americans, 233–234, 260 (exhibit),
        260–262, 261 (exhibit)
    American Indians, 299–300, 300 (exhibit)
    Asian Americans, 384–385, 385 (exhibit)
    Hispanic Americans, 347, 347 (exhibit)
    Supreme Court decisions, 233–234
    White Americans, 260 (exhibit), 260–262,
        261 (exhibit)
Schwarzenegger, Arnold, 320
Sears, D. O., 122
Sears, R. R., 98
Secondary labor market, 200
Secondary occupations, 198, 199 (exhibit)
Secondary sector, 47, 48
Secondary structural assimilation
    African Americans, 258–265
    American Indians, 296, 298–302
    Asian Americans, 382–383
    Hispanic Americans, 344–352
Second generations
    assimilation patterns, 65–66, 66 (exhibit)
    Chinese Americans, 369, 371–372, 395
    contemporary immigrants, 441–446, 442 (exhibit),
        443 (exhibit), 444 (exhibit), 445 (exhibit)
    income data, 444 (exhibit), 445 (exhibit)
    Japanese Americans, 373–374, 376–377, 395
    Jewish immigrants, 60
    White ethnics, 79
Secure Fence Act (2006), 450
See, K. O., 29

Seelbach, W., 117
Segmented assimilation, 83, 440–446, 442 (exhibit)
Segregation
    American Indians, 298 (exhibit)
    Asian Americans, 383–384, 384 (exhibit)
    declining support, 114–115, 115 (exhibit)
    de facto segregation, 187, 237
    de jure segregation, 182–186, 190–191, 194–195,
        207, 232–242, 304
    discriminatory behaviors, 29
    equal status contact hypothesis, 118
    Hispanic Americans, 346, 346 (exhibit)
    residential patterns, 258 (exhibit), 258–260,
        259 (exhibit), 298 (exhibit)
    Roma, 432
    school integration, 260 (exhibit), 260–262,
        261 (exhibit)
    Supreme Court decisions, 233–234
Selective perception, 99
Self-conscious social units, 17
Self-determination, 285, 288 (exhibit), 289
Sellers, R. M., 120
Selzer, M., 64
Seniority privileges, 208
Sen, R., 446
Separate but equal doctrine, 185
Separatism, 53
September 11, 2001, terrorist attacks, 425, 427–428
Serbin, L., 109
Service occupations, 198–199, 199 (exhibit), 204, 249
Seven Degrees of Social Distance, 109–111,
    110 (exhibit)
Sexism, 124–126, 126 (exhibit)
Sex trade, 207
Sexual orientation, 128, 129 (exhibit)
Shafer, S., 336, 337, 338, 339 (exhibit)
Shannon, W. V., 62
Shapiro, T., 247, 248, 248 (exhibit), 252, 257
Sharecropping, 184
Sheatsley, P., 115 (exhibit)
Sheet Metal Workers v. EEOC (1986), 209
Shelton, B. A., 205
Shepard, Matthew, 127
Sherif, C., 105
Sherif, M., 105
Sheth, M., 419
Shoemaker, C., 119
Shryock, A., 426
Shur, Y., 206
Silva, C., 206
Simon, J., 436
Simpson, G., 100, 108
Singular identities, 255–256
Sit-in demonstrations, 235
Situational prejudice, 113
Skin color, 22–23, 23 (exhibit), 333–334
Skinheads, 64, 127, 128, 132–133
Sklare, M., 60
Slavery

African American culture, 172–174
assimilation, 160
behavioral codes, 155–157
Brazil, 243
contact situations, 151–154, 152 (exhibit),
    158 (exhibit)
equal status contact hypothesis, 118
European colonization, 171–172
female slaves, 161, 174
gender inequality, 26
gender relations, 160
labor supply, 151, 154, 155 (exhibit), 158, 184, 304
Marxist theory of social inequality, 106
narrative portraits, 159
origins, 148–150, 150 (exhibit), 154–155
paternalism, 155–157
rationalizations, 158, 160
reparations debate, 211–215
runaway slaves, 157
slave revolts, 157, 215
southern legacy, 182
United States origins, 154–155
Slovak Americans
    educational attainment, 78 (exhibit)
    household income, 79 (exhibit)
Small, M. L., 253
Smedley, A., 25, 41, 150, 158
Smelser, N., 272
Smith, C. B., 119
Smith, E. R., 122
Smith, J., 14, 436
Smith, K., 117
Smith-Lovin, L., 266
Smith, R. C., 357
Smith, T., 110 (exhibit), 294
Snipp, C. M., 163, 283, 285, 289, 294, 303, 311
Soares, R., 206
Social change, 211, 405–406
Social class
    African Americans, 247–250, 260, 261
    assimilation variations, 74–75
    caste systems, 155
    Chinese Americans, 367, 395
    definition, 18
    enclave groups, 431
    ethnic succession, 67
    European colonization, 171–172
    hate crimes, 131
    Hispanic Americans, 352
    industrialization effects, 457
    Irish immigrants, 68
    Japanese Americans, 377, 395
    Marxist theory of social inequality, 19, 106
    Mexican Americans, 319, 332
    minority group status, 21, 460, 464
    Puerto Ricans, 334
    Southern and Eastern European immigrants,
        59, 60
    stereotypes, 103–104, 104 (exhibit)

two-race model, 243
    Weber's theory, 19
    white ethnics, 188
Social constructions, 14
Social distance, 109–111, 110 (exhibit), 294, 379
Socialization, 111, 113–114
Social mobility
    definition, 21
    second generations, 66
Social Security system, 436–437
Social structure
    definition, 46–47
    European colonization, 171–172
Sojourners, 76
South Africa, 194 (exhibit)
South African apartheid, 29, 193–195
South America, 242–243
Southern and Eastern European immigrants
    degree of similarity, 73
    gender, 75–76
    immigrant laborers, 58–59, 67
    religion, 73–74
    social class, 74–75
    social distance, 110 (exhibit), 111
Southern Poverty Law Center (SPLC), 128–129,
    130 (exhibit), 133
Southern white women, 161
Spain, 121 (exhibit), 171–172
Sparks, C., 119
Spicer, E. H., 280
Spickard, P., 377
Spilde, K., 291, 292
Split labor market theory, 106
Sports, 72
Sports Illustrated (SI), 307–309
Sports team mascots, 275–276, 294, 307–309
Stallone, Sylvester, 320
Stampp, K., 155
Stangor, C., 124, 125
Staples, R., 192
Statistics South Africa, 195
Status attainment theory, 48–49
Staurowsky, E. J., 308–309
Steinback, Robert, 132
Steinberg, S., 54, 59, 60, 75, 192, 253, 263, 264
Steinmetz, E., 259, 298 (exhibit)
Stepick, A., 416
Stepick, C. D., 416
Stereotypes
    affective prejudice, 103
    African Americans, 101–104, 123 (exhibit),
        124 (exhibit), 304
    American Indians, 293–294, 304, 307–309
    American stereotype content, 101–103,
        102 (exhibit)
    Asian Americans, 361, 379–382
    basic concepts, 28–29, 99–101
    Chinese Americans, 368, 379
    cognitive prejudice, 103

Cuban Americans, 339
    gender, 103–104, 104 (exhibit)
    Japanese Americans, 373–374, 379
    Jewish immigrants, 63–64
    Middle Eastern Americans, 425
    Puerto Ricans, 335
    race, 103–104
    sexism, 124–126, 126 (exhibit)
    social class, 103–104, 104 (exhibit)
    stereotypical patterns, 100 (exhibit)
Stern, M. J., 209
Stevens, G., 92, 436, 437, 444, 445
Stoddard, E., 168
Stoll, M., 260
Stolzenberg, L., 131
Stratification
    caste systems, 155, 201
    definition, 18
    dominant-minority group relations, 30
    group relations, 202 (exhibit)
    hate crimes, 131
    Hawaiian society, 165–166
    Hispanic Americans, 349
    Lenski's theory, 20
    Mexican Americans, 331–332
    minority group status, 21–22
    theoretical perspectives, 18–21
    Weber's theory, 19–20, 107
    see also Noel hypothesis; Racial stratification
Structural assimilation, 46–48, 47 (exhibit),
    65–67, 66 (exhibit), 165, 258–266
Structural mobility, 72
Structural pluralism, 52
Stuckey, S., 176, 258
Student Nonviolent Coordinating Committee
    (SNCC), 239
Subordinate groups, 16
Subprime home loans, 252
Sub-Saharan African groups, 428–430,
    429 (exhibit)
Subsistence technology
    American Indians, 162, 278
    Asian Americans, 378
    basic concepts, 20
    contemporary immigrants, 447
    deindustrialization, 180
    dominant-minority group relations, 55, 72,
        148, 179, 201, 202 (exhibit), 232
    gender relations, 203
    group relations, 202 (exhibit)
    importance, 456–457, 459
    Industrial Revolution, 55, 181
    North American colonization, 171
Sung, B. L., 391
Supreme Court decisions, 209–210, 233, 361
Suro, R., 342
Swaine, T., 375
Swanson, Karl, 308
Swedish immigrants

    educational attainment, 78 (exhibit)
    household income, 79 (exhibit)
Swim, J., 124, 125, 126
Symbolic ethnicity, 81

Takaki, R., 41, 328, 361, 365, 372, 394, 464
Takeuchi, D., 372
Tammany Hall, 68
Taylor, D., 119
Taylor, E., 237
Taylor, J., 285, 288 (exhibit), 293 (exhibit)
Taylor, P., 348, 391, 392 (exhibit)
Teed, D., 416
Tejanos, 167
Televised family portrayal assignment, 4–5
Telles, E., 243, 357, 442, 445
Tenant farming, 184
Tertiary occupations, 198–199, 199 (exhibit)
Texaco, 244
Texas, 167
Thailand, 207
Theory of social inequality, 106
Thernstrom, A., 265
Thernstrom, S., 265
Third generations, 66, 66 (exhibit), 79, 442 (exhibit),
    444 (exhibit), 445, 445 (exhibit)
Thomas, M., 248
Thompson, C., 86
Thoreau, Henry David, 235
Thornton Dill, B., 26, 41
Thornton, R., 276, 277 (exhibit), 284 (exhibit)
Tijerina, Reies López, 330
Tileag, C., 432
Tilly, C., 62
Time magazine, 379
Timid bigot, 96, 96 (exhibit)
Timmer, A. D., 432
Tolnay, S., 98
Tomolillo, C., 119
Tongs, 368
Tougas, F., 124, 125
Traditional prejudice, 114–120, 115 (exhibit),
    135–136
"Trail of Broken Treaties" march, 287
Transcendent identities, 256
Travis, T. C., 27
Treaty of Guadalupe Hidalgo (1848), 167
Trevanian, 112
Triangle Shirtwaist Company, 70
Tribally controlled colleges, 299
Triple melting pot, 74
Tropp, L., 119
Truman, Harry, 232
Truth, Sojourner, 157, 215
Tsai, S.-S. H., 366, 368
Tuan, M., 107, 402
Tubman, Harriet, 157, 215
Tuch, S., 247
Turks, 110 (exhibit)

Turner, Nat, 157, 215
Tuskegee Institute, 190
Tweed, Boss, 68
Two-race model, 242–243

Udry, R., 27
Ukrainian Americans
    educational attainment, 78 (exhibit)
    household income, 79 (exhibit)
Unauthorized populations, 38–39
Underground Railroad, 157
Undocumented immigrants, 32–36, 33 (exhibit),
    324, 437–440, 438 (exhibit), 449–450
Unemployment rates
    African Americans, 192, 251–252, 252 (exhibit)
    American Indians, 284, 293 (exhibit), 300
    Hispanic Americans, 349
    Ireland, 86
    White Americans, 251–252, 252 (exhibit)
Unionization, 68, 70–71
United Farm Workers, 330–331
United Kingdom, 411 (exhibit)
United Nations, 206, 340 (exhibit)
United Nations Educational, Scientific,
    and Cultural Organization (UNESCO), 229
United States–European immigration
    comparisons, 340 (exhibit)
*United Steelworkers of America, AFL-CIO-CLC
    v. Weber* (1979), 209
Universal Negro Improvement Association, 191
University of Michigan, 210
Upward mobility, 72
Urbanization
    American Indians, 283–285, 284 (exhibit),
        288 (exhibit)
    Asian Americans, 382–383, 383 (exhibit)
    Chinese Americans, 368, 383 (exhibit)
    dominant-minority group relations, 196–197
    Hispanic Americans, 346, 346 (exhibit)
Urban poverty, 249–250, 253–254, 265,
    266 (exhibit)
Urban underclass, 250, 257
Urban unrest, 237, 244
USA Patriot Act (2001), 425
U.S. Bureau of Labor Statistics, 252 (exhibit)
U.S. Bureau of the Census
    African Americans, 186 (exhibit), 187 (exhibit),
        258 (exhibit)
    American Indians, 276, 277 (exhibit), 284 (exhibit),
        289, 290 (exhibit), 295 (exhibit), 299 (exhibit),
        300, 301 (exhibit), 303 (exhibit)
    Asian Americans, 362 (exhibit), 363 (exhibit),
        367 (exhibit), 382 (exhibit), 383 (exhibit), 387,
        388 (exhibit), 389 (exhibit), 390 (exhibit),
        391 (exhibit)
    Asian Indians, 419
    educational attainment, 116 (exhibit), 203,
        204 (exhibit), 262 (exhibit)
    female-headed households, 253 (exhibit)

    female occupations, 203 (exhibit)
    Hawaiians, 166 (exhibit)
    Hispanic Americans, 316 (exhibit), 317 (exhibit),
        332, 346 (exhibit), 348, 348 (exhibit),
        349 (exhibit), 350 (exhibit), 351 (exhibit), 352
    homeownership, 208
    household income, 264 (exhibit), 265 (exhibit)
    income data, 126 (exhibit), 205 (exhibit),
        254 (exhibit)
    interracial relationships, 266
    mixed-race heritage, 14
    political power, 262, 263
    population diversity, 12 (exhibit)
    poverty, 266 (exhibit)
    Puerto Ricans, 333
    white ethnics, 78, 78 (exhibit), 79 (exhibit)
    workforce changes, 199 (exhibit)
U.S. Commission on Civil Rights, 131, 332, 333
U.S. Department of Education, 227
U.S. Department of Homeland Security,
    12, 321 (exhibit), 412, 437
U.S. English, Inc., 88
U.S. Immigration and Naturalization Service, 324
Utah Supreme Court, 295

Valentine, S., 319, 342
Van Ausdale, D., 109
van den Berghe, P. L., 155, 181, 464
Van Doren, C., 167, 330
Van Hook, J., 37, 38–39
Vargas-Ramos, C., 334
Vesey, Denmark, 215
Vicious cycle of prejudice theory, 108, 108 (exhibit)
Vietnamese
    acculturation, 381 (exhibit)
    characteristics, 418 (exhibit)
    contact situations, 379
    educational attainment, 386 (exhibit), 443 (exhibit)
    foreign-born population, 364 (exhibit),
        391 (exhibit)
    immigration, 378 (exhibit), 378–379,
        411 (exhibit), 420
    incarcerated males, 443 (exhibit)
    median household income, 388 (exhibit)
    narrative portraits, 421–422
    per capita income, 389 (exhibit)
    population growth, 362 (exhibit), 363 (exhibit)
    poverty, 390 (exhibit), 391 (exhibit)
    second generations, 443 (exhibit)
    social distance, 110 (exhibit)
    urbanization, 383 (exhibit)
Vigdor, J., 259
Vincent, T. G., 191
Vinje, D., 289
Violent uprisings, 237, 244, 419
Visible distinguishable traits
    definition, 16–17
    gender, 25–27
    race, 22–25

Vitter, David, 107
Voting rights, 232, 236, 263
Voting Rights Act (1965), 236, 263

Wagley, C., 16
Wagner, U., 434
Walker, David, 215
Wall Street Journal, 13, 136
Walters, G., 101
Wang, W., 391, 392 (exhibit)
War on drugs, 246 (exhibit), 246–247
Washington, Booker T., 190–191
Waters, M. C., 81, 444, 452
Watts riots, 237, 244, 419
Wax, M., 162, 163, 280
Wealth
    African Americans, 236, 247–248, 252, 257
    American Indians, 282
    Asian Americans, 363, 369, 390
    dominant-minority group relations, 168
    gender relations, 164
    Gordon's theory, 52
    group relations, 201
    Hispanic Americans, 351
    homeownership, 208, 252
    immigration effects, 446
    intergroup competition, 199
    job market, 199
    Lenski's theory, 20
    Mexican Americans, 167
    middle class, 248 (exhibit)
    minority group status, 21–22
    slaveholders, 155, 160
    Weber's theory, 19–20
Weber, Max, 18, 19–20, 107
Weeks, P., 286
Weil, F., 117
Weinberg, D., 259, 298 (exhibit)
Weitzer, R., 247
Weitz, R., 103
Wellner, A., 266
Western, B., 246
Westervelt, E., 341
West Germany, 121 (exhibit)
White Americans
    characteristics, 413 (exhibit)
    contemporary American Indian–White relations, 288–303
    educational attainment, 262 (exhibit), 348 (exhibit), 386 (exhibit)
    equal opportunities, 17 (exhibit)
    foreign-born population, 391 (exhibit)
    Hispanic–white relations, 341–352
    household income, 263–265, 264 (exhibit), 265 (exhibit)
    income data, 339 (exhibit), 350 (exhibit), 389 (exhibit)
    indentured servants, 154, 155 (exhibit)
    intergroup cooperation, 120

    interracial relationships, 265–266
    median household income, 302, 302 (exhibit), 349 (exhibit), 350 (exhibit), 388 (exhibit)
    per capita income, 389 (exhibit)
    poverty, 265, 266 (exhibit), 351 (exhibit), 390, 390 (exhibit), 391 (exhibit)
    privilege and whiteness, 31
    school integration, 260 (exhibit), 260–262, 261 (exhibit), 300 (exhibit), 385 (exhibit)
    social distance, 110 (exhibit)
    stereotypes, 101–104
    unemployment rates, 251–252, 252 (exhibit)
    urbanization, 346 (exhibit)
White Anglo-Saxon Protestants (WASPs), 66 (exhibit), 66–67
White Aryan Resistance (WAR), 127
White, B. J., 105
White Citizens' Councils, 234
White-collar occupations, 197–199
White, D., 109
White, D. G., 161, 173, 174
White ethnics
    Asian Americans, 393–394
    competition with black southern migrants, 187–188
    ethnic revival, 80
    evolutionary development, 79–82
    geographical distribution, 76–77, 77 (exhibit)
    household income, 79 (exhibit)
    integration, 78, 78 (exhibit)
    principle of third-generation interest, 79
    stereotypes, 101–104
    symbolic ethnicity, 81
White House, 436
White, M., 444
White Mountain Apaches, 289
White, William, 127
Whiting, R., 365
Who Are We? (Huntington), 353–355
Wilder, Douglas, 263
Wilkens, R., 244
Williams, G., 255, 256
Williams, J., 272
Williams, K., 406
Williams, L., 100, 101
Wilson, R., 287
Wilson, W., 272
Wilson, W. J., 29, 155, 156, 158, 181, 184, 186, 188, 211, 232, 234, 250, 254, 272
Winant, H., 25, 41
Wingfield, A., 136, 272
Wise, T., 31
Wittig, M., 119
Wolfenstein, E. V., 238
Women
    American Indian society, 164, 278–279, 282, 284
    Asian Americans, 365
    assimilation variations, 75–76
    black southern migrants, 191–192
    Chinese Americans, 369, 461

civil rights movement, 239–240
educational attainment, 262 (exhibit)
exploitation, 207
gender inequality, 25–26, 26 (exhibit), 202–205,
       351–352, 461–462
globalization effects, 202–207
Hispanic Americans, 351–352
income data, 126 (exhibit)
income gap, 204 (exhibit), 204–206, 254 (exhibit)
Japanese Americans, 376
labor unions, 70–71
median earnings, 204 (exhibit), 205 (exhibit),
       254 (exhibit)
Mexican Americans, 169–170, 329, 331
postindustrial society, 202–205
Puerto Ricans, 334, 335
sexism, 124–126, 126 (exhibit)
slavery, 161, 174
southern white women, 161
stereotypes, 103–104, 104 (exhibit)
workforce participation, 203 (exhibit), 203–206
Wong, J. S., 461
Wong, M., 367, 371, 372, 395
Wong, R., 206
Woo, A., 307–308
Wood, K. ., 131
Wood, P., 101
Woods, Tiger, 255
Woodward, C. V., 183, 185, 217
Working-class immigrants, 74–75, 80
World War I
    immigrant laborers, 54
    job opportunities, 201
    scapegoat hypothesis, 98
World War II
    American Indian protest movement, 286

anti-Asian prejudice, 379, 395
anti-Semitism, 64
Bracero program, 323 (exhibit),
       323–324
Chinese Americans, 367, 369
graffiti, 5
immigration quotas, 60, 367
industrialization, 198
Japanese Americans, 372, 373, 374–376
job opportunities, 201, 283
Mexican Americans, 323 (exhibit),
       323–324, 329, 333
Puerto Ricans, 332–333
social change, 111
veterans' benefits, 72
Worsnop, R., 291
Wounded Knee, South Dakota, 287
Wright, Richard, 189
WuDunn, S., 207
Wyman, M., 76

X, Malcolm, 238
Xerox, 290
Xie, Y., 367 (exhibit)

Yamamoto, K., 110 (exhibit)
Yamanaka, K., 391
Yamato, A., 373
Yancey, G., 119
Yinger, M., 48, 100, 108
Yonsei, 377

Zellner, W., 52
Zhou, M., 92, 369, 372, 397, 398–399, 402
Zuma, Jacob, 195
Zurbriggen, E., 99

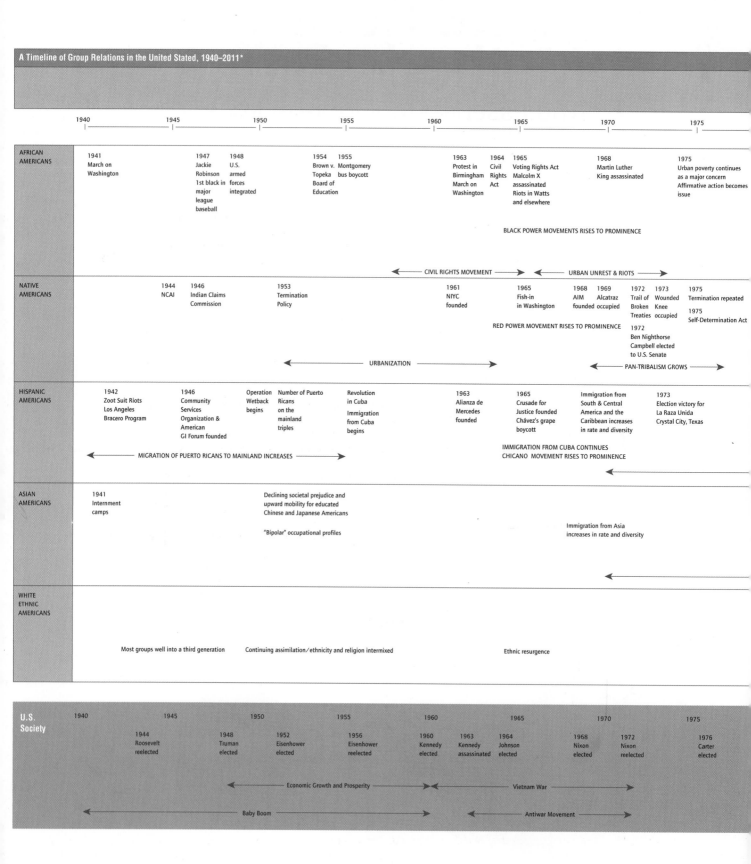

A Timeline of Group Relations in the United Stated, 1940–2011*

	1940	1945	1950	1955	1960	1965	1970	1975

AFRICAN AMERICANS

1941
March on Washington

1947
Jackie Robinson 1st black in major league baseball

1948
U.S. armed forces integrated

1954
Brown v. Topeka Board of Education

1955
Montgomery bus boycott

1963
Protest in Birmingham March on Washington

1964
Civil Rights Act

1965
Voting Rights Act Malcolm X assassinated Riots in Watts and elsewhere

1968
Martin Luther King assassinated

1975
Urban poverty continues as a major concern Affirmative action becomes issue

BLACK POWER MOVEMENTS RISES TO PROMINENCE

←——— CIVIL RIGHTS MOVEMENT ———→ ←——— URBAN UNREST & RIOTS ———→

NATIVE AMERICANS

1944
NCAI

1946
Indian Claims Commission

1953
Termination Policy

1961
NIYC founded

1965
Fish-in in Washington

1968
AIM founded

1969
Alcatraz occupied

1972
Trail of Broken Treaties

1973
Wounded Knee occupied

1975
Termination repeated

1975
Self-Determination Act

1972
Ben Nighthorse Campbell elected to U.S. Senate

RED POWER MOVEMENT RISES TO PROMINENCE

←——— URBANIZATION ———→   ←——— PAN-TRIBALISM GROWS ———→

HISPANIC AMERICANS

1942
Zoot Suit Riots Los Angeles Bracero Program

1946
Community Services Organization & American GI Forum founded

Operation Wetback begins

Number of Puerto Ricans on the mainland triples

Revolution in Cuba Immigration from Cuba begins

1963
Alianza de Mercedes founded

1965
Crusade for Justice founded Chávez's grape boycott

Immigration from South & Central America and the Caribbean increases in rate and diversity

1973
Election victory for La Raza Unida Crystal City, Texas

←——— MIGRATION OF PUERTO RICANS TO MAINLAND INCREASES ———→

IMMIGRATION FROM CUBA CONTINUES
CHICANO MOVEMENT RISES TO PROMINENCE

←———

ASIAN AMERICANS

1941
Internment camps

Declining societal prejudice and upward mobility for educated Chinese and Japanese Americans

"Bipolar" occupational profiles

Immigration from Asia increases in rate and diversity

←———

WHITE ETHNIC AMERICANS

Most groups well into a third generation

Continuing assimilation/ethnicity and religion intermixed

Ethnic resurgence

U.S. Society

1940	1945	1950	1955	1960	1965	1970	1975

1944
Roosevelt reelected

1948
Truman elected

1952
Eisenhower elected

1956
Eisenhower reelected

1960
Kennedy elected

1963
Kennedy assassinated

1964
Johnson elected

1968
Nixon elected

1972
Nixon reelected

1976
Carter elected

←——— Economic Growth and Prosperity ———→ ←——— Vietnam War ———→

←——— Baby Boom ———→ ←——— Antiwar Movement ———→